God and the Goddesses

THE MIDDLE AGES SERIES

Ruth Mazo Karras, Series Editor
Edward Peters, Founding Editor

A complete list of books in the series
is available from the publisher.

God and the Goddesses

Vision, Poetry, and Belief
in the Middle Ages

Barbara Newman

PENN

University of Pennsylvania Press

Philadelphia

Published by
University of Pennsylvania Press
Philadelphia, Pennsylvania 19104-4011

Library of Congress Cataloging-in-Publication Data

Newman, Barbara, 1953—
    God and the goddesses : vision, poetry, and belief in the Middle
Ages/Barbara Newman.
        p. cm.—(Middle Ages series)
    Includes bibliographical references and index.
    ISBN 0-8122-3691-2 (cloth : alk. paper); ISBN 0-8122-1911-2 (pbk. : alk paper)
    1. Poetry, Medieval—History and criticism. 2. Goddesses in literature.
3. God in literature. I. Title. II. Series.

PN688.G65 N49 2002
809.1′9382′0902—dc21
                                                        2002028504

For Peter Dronke

Contents

List of Illustrations   ix

Preface   xi

1. God and the Goddesses   1
   St. Francis and Lady Poverty   3
   The Soul and Lady Love   10
   The Servant and Eternal Wisdom   12
   Will and Lady Holy Church   14
   Christine and the Female Trinity   19
   Vision, Imagination, and Belief   24
   Why Goddesses?   35

2. Natura (I): Nature and Nature's God   51
   The Birth of Nature: Bernard Silvestris's *Cosmographia*   55
   Nature's Fall and Lament: *De planctu Naturae*   66
   Nature as Redeemed Redeemer: *Anticlaudianus*   73
   A Hildegardian Coda: Nature or Nature's God?   86

3. Natura (II): Goddess of the Normative   90
   "Ganymede and Helen" and Nature's Grammar   91
   In Nature's Forge: From Alan of Lille to Jean de Meun   97
   Nature at the Court of King Richard: Chaucer's
      Parlement of Fowles   111
   Nature and Culture: Christine's Revisionist Myths   115
   Testing the Norms: Nature, Nurture, *Silence*   122
   The Realm of the Natural   134

4. Love Divine, All Loves Excelling   138
   Caritas and *Amor*: The Twelfth Century   140

Love's Violence: The Thirteenth Century   151
The Beguine as Knight of Love: Hadewijch's *Stanzaic Poems*   169
Dante, Beatrice, and *l'amor che move il sole*   181

5. Sapientia: The Goddess Incarnate   190
Liturgical Wisdom: Poised Between Christ and Mary   194
Devotional Wisdom: Henry Suso and His Legacy   206
Contemplative Wisdom: Julian of Norwich   222
Esoteric Wisdom: The Alchemical Virgin   234

6. Maria: Holy Trinity as Holy Family   245
The Trinity as a Family   247
Divinizing the Virgin: The Marian Trinity in Art   254
Enacting the Virgin: The Lability of Female Roles   273
Domesticating the Virgin: The Invention of the
Holy Family   283

7. Goddesses and the One God   291
Imaginative Theology   294
The Gender of God and the Limits of Intolerance   304
Medieval Christianity as an Inclusive Monotheism   317

List of Abbreviations   329

Notes   331

Works Cited   409

Index   437

Illustrations

1.1. St. Francis marries Lady Poverty   5
1.2. Poverty excluded from the Garden of Love   7
1.3. Ecclesia nursing her children   16
1.4. Christine with Lady Reason, Lady Right, and Lady Justice   21
1.5. Christine and the Sibyl before the heavenly ladder   28
1.6. Lady Philosophy   32
1.7. Ecclesia with her children in her bosom   42
1.8. Annunciation with the four daughters of God   46
2.1. Neoplatonic cosmology   57
2.2. Liberal arts as handmaids of Philosophia   74
2.3. Natura receives the soul of the *novus homo*   77
2.4. Prudentia's heavenly journey   80
2.5. Christological reading of the *Anticlaudianus*   85
3.1. Nature at her forge making birds and beasts   102
3.2. Nature at her forge making a baby   103
3.3. Nature at her forge (two lovers in bed)   104
3.4. Art kneels before Nature   104
3.5. Genius gives Nature absolution   106
4.1. Christ crucified by the Virtues, Bonmont Psalter   161
4.2. Christ crucified by the Virtues, Lectionary   162
4.3. Christ crucified by the Virtues, Missal   163
4.4. Caritas stabbing the crucified Christ   164
4.5. Bride and Bridegroom: the wound of love   166
4.6. *Christus und die minnende Seele*   168
4.7. Ulrich von Liechtenstein as Lady Venus   170
4.8. Caritas with arrow and flaming heart   189
5.1. Sapientia with prophets of the Incarnation   201
5.2. Virgin of the Sign   202
5.3. Sapientia Regina, Bible of Saint-Martial   204
5.4. *Majestas Sapientiae*   213

5.5. Sapientia *magistra* at the school of theology   215
5.6. The Disciple falls in love with Eternal Wisdom   216
5.7. Sapientia and her three daughters   217
5.8. Sapientia and the Disciple watch Christ carrying his cross   219
5.9. Spiritual marriage with Sapientia   221
5.10. Sapientia nursing two philosophers   238
5.11. Alchemical hermaphrodite as black bride   239
6.1. Enthronement of Christ and Mary   257
6.2. Coronation of the Virgin by the Trinity, *Buch der heiligen Dreifaltigkeit*   258
6.3. Coronation of the Virgin by the Trinity, Master of the Rohrdorf Altar   259
6.4. Coronation of the Virgin by the Trinity, Book of Hours   260
6.5. Coronation of the soul by Christ and the Virgin   262
6.6. Double Intercession, Master of the Lower Rhine   263
6.7. Double Intercession, school of Konrad Witz   264
6.8. Intercession of Christ and the Virgin   265
6.9. Pietà with God the Father   267
6.10. Pietà of the Father   268
6.11. Shrine Madonna   270
6.12. The soul as bride of the Trinity   281

Preface

The epigraph of this book is taken from Ennodius, a Gallo-Roman poet and bishop of Pavia in the early sixth century. A kinsman of Boethius, he must have impressed his fellows as sufficiently pious to earn a place in the calendar of saints. Though betrothed as a young man, Ennodius followed in Augustine's footsteps and chose the priesthood instead of marriage; his fiancée became a nun. Yet in one of his occasional poems, written to celebrate a wedding, the good bishop allows the God of Love to complain to Venus about the triumph of Christian asceticism. Because of these Christians, Cupid laments, cold virginity now rules the world. Undaunted, Venus replies, "let the people learn that a goddess grows stronger while she lies neglected."[1]

Now Ennodius is not exactly a household name, even in my arcane household, so I am happy to credit C. S. Lewis with calling my attention to this forgotten poet. As Lewis long ago noted, "it is as if some mischievous spirit of prophecy took the pen out of his hand and wrote for us the history both of allegory and of courtly love."[2] If the present book is not quite the history that Lewis had in mind, it has much to say about both, and still more about goddesses who lie neglected.

God and the Goddesses casts a wide net, but let me be the first to note that it could have been cast wider still. In a book of this scope, the problem lies not in finding suitable material, but in deciding regretfully what to exclude. The limitations of space, not to mention those of my own knowledge and taste, must be blamed for the absence of many estimable authors, among them Jean de Hauteville, Brunetto Latini, Guillaume de Deguileville, and the English poet of the *Court of Sapience*. Marguerite Porete gets all too little space here, as does Hildegard of Bingen, who first taught me the importance of this subject. Frauenlob, the great minnesinger and a devotee of more than one goddess, deserves a much richer treatment than I have been able to give him. Nor have I even tried to account for the reams of medieval poetry and mythography that revolve around pagan goddesses and gods, for my concern is with those goddesses who function within overtly Christian schemes of representation. That Christian schemes did in fact make a place for such goddesses is the broadest and most important of this book's many theses. Its individual chapters attempt to parse the many ways that medieval writers found goddesses "good to think with," to adapt Lévi-Strauss's famous dictum.

A few portions of this book have been published as essays, in abridged and altered form. A part of Chapter 1 appeared in *Poetry and Philosophy in the Middle Ages: A Festschrift for Peter Dronke*, ed. John Marenbon (Leiden: Brill, 2001). The first half of Chapter 6 was printed as "Intimate Pieties: Holy Trinity and Holy Family in the Late Middle Ages," *Religion and Literature* 31, 1 (Spring 1999): 77–101. An excerpt from Chapter 5 appeared under the title, "Henry Suso and the Medieval Devotion to Christ the Goddess," *Spiritus* 2, 1 (Spring 2002): 1–14.

A word about translations is in order. Since this book deals with literature in multiple languages, I have provided both original texts and translations for all passages cited. As a general rule, poetry in the original language will be found in the body of the text, and prose passages in the notes. But I have made certain exceptions for the reader's convenience: for example, Julian of Norwich's Middle English prose remains in the text for all to see, while Hadewijch's Dutch verse has been relegated to the notes. Unless otherwise noted, translations are my own.

I would like to thank the institutions that provided financial support for my research on this project over many years: the American Council of Learned Societies, the Alice Berline Kaplan Center for the Humanities at Northwestern University, and most recently the John Simon Guggenheim Memorial Foundation. My thanks are also due to all the libraries and museums that have graciously supplied me with photographs, to Northwestern University for a research grant that helped pay for them, and to the Guggenheim Foundation for a generous publishing subvention. Portions of my work in progress have been presented at Fordham University, Yale Divinity School, the University of Nebraska, Nebraska Wesleyan, Notre Dame, the University of Pittsburgh, Princeton, and Stanford. I am grateful to my audiences at all these schools for their patience, generosity, and valuable feedback. Many friends, colleagues, and former students have offered advice on specific points: I would like to thank Elizabeth Archibald, Craig Berry, Diana Black, Maeve Callan, Burton Van Name Edwards, Monica Green, Jeffrey Hamburger, Robert Lerner, Pamela Sheingorn, Benjamin Sommer, Anne Sullivan, Stanton Thomas, and Claire Waters. Renate

Blumenfeld-Kosinski helpfully reviewed Chapter 3, and Rachel Fulton generously allowed me to cite her new book before its publication. Nicholas Watson and E. Ann Matter, as readers for the University of Pennsylvania Press, scrutinized both the prospectus and the completed manuscript of *God and the Goddesses* with exceptional care. Without their advice and suggestions, this book would be a more paltry thing than it is. Richard Kieckhefer has both read and heard (and occasionally debated) my arguments more times than either of us cares to remember, and has in addition provided invaluable help with photography. I owe debts of a different order to Felicitas, who obligingly sat in my lap and purred her way through many an antique text. Infelicities, as the saying goes, are my own.

It is with great pleasure and gratitude that I dedicate this book to one of my teachers, who recently retired from the Chair of Medieval Latin Literature at Cambridge. Admirers of Professor Peter Dronke will, I hope, be able to recognize his influence at many points in this volume, not least in a shared affection for "all things counter, original, spare, strange" in the capacious universe of medieval poetry.

Discant populi tunc crescere divam
Cum neglecta iacet—
        —Ennodius, *Carmina* I.4.84

I

God and the Goddesses

MEDIEVAL CATHOLICISM PRESENTS THE extraordinary spectacle of a religion, ostensibly monotheistic, that proclaimed one God in three persons and surrounded that God with three pantheons. First came the saints, a polymorphous group, with the Mother of God at their pinnacle. Their cultural presence was ubiquitous, their shrines beyond counting. Second were the old pagan gods, "disinfected of belief" but still immensely useful for literary and astrological purposes.[1] Poets and intellectuals could not imagine the cosmos without them. Their names survived as planets and days of the week; fragments of their cult lived on in Christian festivals, while every schoolboy learned their myths. Textually, however, these two pantheons never mixed: saints belonged to the realm of belief, pagan gods to that of make-believe. Mythography had no use for St. Catherine, nor did hagiography require Apollo, unless a virgin was denouncing him on the way to her martyrdom.

But the third pantheon, the allegorical goddesses, mingled freely with both of the others. The God of medieval Christendom was father of one Son but many daughters: Sapientia, Philosophia, Ecclesia, Frau Minne, Dame Nature, Lady Reason, and the list goes on. These goddesses have been something of an embarrassment to medievalists. Literary scholars treat them as personifications or ideological constructs; art historians sometimes glance at their iconography; historical theologians study them not at all. Yet the goddesses occupy a more spacious domain in medieval religious thought than scholarship has yet allowed. They freely cross the boundaries of language and genre, as well as that more delicate boundary where high seriousness meets serious play and imagination shades into belief. Goddesses abound not only in the creations of poets, but also in the theological writings of clerics and the revelations of holy women.

Alan of Lille was a distinguished schoolman, the author of a noted manual on preaching, who ended his life as a Cistercian monk (d. 1202/3). But when he wished to write an epic poem on the creation of a Divine Man, he turned his back on the Gospels and gave the task to a gynaeceum of goddesses.[2] Robert Grosseteste (d. 1253), a saintly bishop eulogized by Roger Bacon as the most learned philosopher of his age, produced an array of Latin works on subjects ranging from optics to sacraments. But he also wrote a poem in his Anglo-Norman vernacular, *Le Château d'Amour*, which has been described as a theological treatise in the form of a chivalric romance.[3] Ostensibly composed for the education of the laity, *Le Château* lifts the "four daughters of God" from the Talmud, makes them sisters of Christ without whom God could not govern his kingdom, and embroils them in debate over the redeemability of man. A century later, Dante rescued even that most disreputable of goddesses, Fortuna, from her opprobrium and set her rejoicing in heaven, "glad with the other primal creatures" (*con l'altre prime creature lieta*).[4] Of course Dante was not the only medieval pilgrim to visit heaven: many women also found the way, and they too met a galaxy of goddesses there, along with the Trinity and the Virgin, angels and saints.

These "primal creatures," as Dante called them, often bear the names of virtues, as do Grosseteste's Mercy, Truth, Justice, and Peace. But if we follow convention and refer to them as "personifications" or even "allegorical figures," we run the risk of blunting their emotional force and trivializing their religious import. The term "goddesses" may startle, yet it appears not infrequently in the texts under study, and such epithets as "daughter of God" are even more common. The mythic resonance of these terms is surely intended. If we neglect this dimension, we may take the goddesses' presence for granted and forget to ask *why* they should have proliferated in the high Middle Ages, appearing in such prominent roles in such a variety of contexts. A reader who knew of medieval religion only from Peter Lombard and Thomas Aquinas—or, for that matter, Alan of Lille's treatise *On the Art of Preaching* or Grosseteste's *On the Ten Commandments*—would never have suspected their existence.

Medieval goddesses are not one but many. Yet they share a certain family resemblance, for those examined in this book are all distinctive creations of the Christian imagination—neither "pagan survivals" nor versions of "the Great Goddess" constructed in speculative works on ancient religion and psychology.[5] Like other sacred symbols, goddesses could be taken with varying degrees of seriousness: at times they dwindled to the status of rhetorical tropes, and some writers used them parodically. But in the most imaginative and provocative texts, both Latin and vernacular, they add an irreducible fourth dimension to the spiritual universe. As emanations of the Divine, mediators between God and the cosmos, embodied universals, and not least, ravishing objects of identification and desire, the goddesses substantially transformed and deepened Christendom's concept of God, introducing religious possibilities beyond the ambit of scholastic theology and bringing them to vibrant imaginative life. How they did so will be the subject of this book.

My claim is an unorthodox one that raises a host of questions, not only about the roles of goddesses in general and the meanings that clustered around specific goddesses, but also about genre and hermeneutics. For example: how did medieval writers and readers understand the ontological status of their goddesses? Did they "believe in" them, and if so, in what manner? What philosophical convictions sustained their fascination with allegory? Is it possible to distinguish the personifications that appear in allegorical poems and visual art from those that appear in actual visions? How could medieval writers reconcile their statements about the daughters of God with orthodox devotion to the Son of God? For that matter, why did they have such an overwhelming preference for female personifications—for goddesses—in the first place? What religious functions did these goddesses serve? How deliberately and self-consciously did medieval authors, male and female, explore the possibilities of feminine God-language? Did their experiments encounter resistance?

For much of this book my emphasis will fall on the traits specific to individual goddesses, along with the multiple purposes they serve in texts. Readers hungry for generalizations will find some working hypotheses at the end of this chapter. Given the novelty of the subject, however, I have reserved my broader conclusions for Chapter 7, since their authority and conviction must rest on a detailed presentation of the evidence. I begin, then, *in medias res*. To establish a preliminary sense of the character, range, and variety of writings that feature goddess figures, I have chosen five texts representing authors of both sexes and diverse callings, religious and lay. They are derived from prose and verse writings in Latin, German, English, and French, written between the mid-thirteenth century and the early fifteenth. In each of the texts—which could be multiplied almost without number—a protagonist encounters a divine woman and enters into a life-changing dialogue with her. These five examples will provide a frame of reference for the theoretical discussion to follow.

St. Francis and Lady Poverty

As "God's troubadour," Francis of Assisi had a well-known penchant for lyric and romance, yet the hagiographic legend entitled *Sacrum commercium sancti*

Francisci cum domina Paupertate (*The Sacred Alliance of St. Francis with Lady Poverty*) is unique among early Franciscan texts.[6] Its authorship is unknown, its date contested, its genre difficult to define. Even the title poses difficulties; it might be translated as *The Sacred Bargain* or perhaps *Sacred Partnership,* for the *commercium* in question is both a romance and an alliance struck for mutual profit.[7] Just as devotional writers employed the idiom of erotic love to praise virginity, first-generation Franciscans coopted the language of the mercantile capitalism they rejected and used it to extol poverty.[8] In this brief allegorical text, Francis decides to woo Lady Poverty and, with his companions, scales the steep mountain where she dwells. There he delivers a panegyric on Poverty as queen of the virtues, to which she responds with a history of her life on earth from the Garden of Eden until the present day. Once she is persuaded that the Franciscans are sincere in their love for her, she exhorts them to persevere in the face of future temptations, then accepts Francis's invitation to join the friars for a "banquet" at their home. The meal consists of stale barley bread and cold water. Lady Poverty requests various items from her hosts—a towel to dry her hands, cooked dishes, a knife, and so forth—but they can provide none of these. When she asks for a grand tour of their "chapel, chapter-house, cloister, refectory, kitchen, dormitory, stable," and other fine buildings, they take her to a hilltop and point to the world, saying, "This, lady, is our cloister."[9] At last, overcome with joy at their meager lifestyle, she blesses the friars and tells them how all heaven rejoices in their apostolic life.

Several manuscripts of the *Sacrum commercium* include a colophon dating it to July 1227, which would place the text less than a year after Francis's death and exactly a year before his canonization.[10] If this date is accepted, the *Sacrum commercium* would reflect the self-understanding of the "primitive" Franciscans in their first blush of enthusiasm. But its most recent editor, Stefano Brufani, dates the work to the 1250s, seeing in its fully developed "teologia pauperistica" a response to anti-mendicant polemics launched by William of Saint-Amour in the Parisian schools. Brufani notes the conceptual distance between Francis's own *Testamentum,* which speaks concretely of his life among the poor, and the abstract, allegorical treatment of Poverty as a virtue in the *Sacrum commercium.*[11] Early or late, the text gestures toward the hagiographic legend of a "marriage" between Francis and Lady Poverty without actually presenting their pact in such terms (Figure 1.1).[12]

To create "domina Paupertas" the author drew in equal measure on the Song of Songs and the sapiential books, where he found a ready model in Solomon's romance with Lady Wisdom. Francis, aware of Poverty's infinite worth, goes forth to seek her:

Figure 1.1. St. Francis marries Lady Poverty. Pietro di Lorenzo ("Il Vecchietta"), fifteenth century. Munich, Alte Pinakothek, inv. nr. 650. Photo: Bayerische Staatsgemäldesammlungen.

Like a curious explorer, he began to go busily about the streets and lanes of the city, diligently seeking her whom his soul loved (Cant. 3.2). He questioned the bystanders and inquired of all comers, saying, "Have you seen her whom my soul loves?" But this word was hidden from them (Luke 18.34), as if in a foreign tongue. Not understanding, they said to him, "Man, we don't know what you're saying. Talk to us in our own language and we'll answer you."[13]

The challenge is an interesting one, assuming that these "bystanders" represent the ordinary layfolk addressed by Franciscan preaching. Not only is the text in Latin, but Francis is speaking of his still unnamed Lady Poverty in the elite, cloistered idiom of bridal mysticism, which seems foreign (*velut barbarum*) to the man in the street. Linguistic otherness thus becomes a metaphor for spiritual and social otherness. It was the Franciscans' choice of radical poverty ("the world is our cloister") that would soon enable them to translate their spirituality into the vernacular more effectively than any other religious movement.

First, however, Francis must "translate" Lady Poverty herself. The text offers no physical description of her, save that she is "reclining on the throne of her nakedness."[14] Much more vivid is a contemporary portrait from the *Roman de la Rose* by Guillaume de Lorris, who depicts Poverty—by no means a "lady," let alone a goddess—among those who are shut out of Love's rose garden (Figure 1.2):

Portraite fu au darrenier
Povreté, qui un seul denier
N'eüst pas, s'en la deüst pendre,
Tant seüst bien sa robe vendre,
Qu'ele ere nue comme vers.
Se le temps fust un poi divers,
Je croi qu'el acorast de froit,
Qu'el n'avoit qu'un viel sac estroit
Tout plain de mavés paletiaus:
S'estoit sa robe et ses mantiaus;
El n'avoit plus que afubler;
Grant loisir avoit de trambler.
Des autres fu un poi loignet;
Cum chiens honteus en un coignet
Se cropoit et se tapissoit.[15]

Painted last of all
Was Poverty, who had not a cent
To save herself from hanging.
She must have known how to sell her dress,

For now she was naked as a worm.
If the weather were a little treacherous,
I believe she would have died of cold,
For she had nothing but an old, tight sack,
All tattered, full of patches:
This served her for dress and cloak.
She had nothing better to wear
And ample cause to tremble.
She was a bit removed from the others:
There she crouched and cowered
Like a guilty dog in a corner.

This, presumably, is how Lady Poverty would have looked to the man in the street, who cannot understand Francis's desire for her. So he begins to translate her into a more exalted idiom, just as the marquis in the *Clerk's Tale* would "translate" the pauper Griselda, by clothing her nakedness in a magnificent robe of words:

Figure 1.2. Poverty excluded from the Garden of Love. *Roman de la Rose*. Oxford, Bodleian Douce 195, f. 4v. Photo: Bodleian Library.

We have come to you as our lady: we beg you, receive us in peace. We desire to become servants of the Lord of hosts (*virtutum*), for he is the King of glory (Ps. 23.10). We have heard that you are the Queen of virtues (*virtutum*), as indeed we have learned by experience. Therefore, prostrating ourselves at your feet, we humbly beseech that you will deign to be with us and be for us a way to reach the King of glory. . . . For we know that yours is the power, yours is the kingdom: you were enthroned by the King of kings as Queen and lady above all virtues. . . . For the King of kings, the Lord of lords (Rev. 19.16), the Creator of heaven and earth, himself desired your beauty and your loveliness. (Ps. 44.12)[16]

The biblical and courtly language becomes a patent of nobility, transforming the homeless *paupercula* into the queen that Francis insists she is. Like divine Wisdom, too, she is ageless—"ancient and full of days, knowing the order of the universe, the varieties of creatures, the changing times and seasons."[17] She says she was with Adam in paradise when both were blissfully nude, recalling the friars' motto, "naked to follow the naked Christ" (*nudus nudum Christum sequi*). And indeed, Lady Poverty is next cast in the role of Christ's bride: when all his disciples abandoned him at the cross, she alone remained, *fidelissima sponsa, amatrix dulcissima*.[18] The tenderness and familiarity of the language should not mask its deep irony, for Christ's traditional bride was the very Church that Francis was trying to reform. In her own discourse, Lady Poverty recounts the history of that institution, especially of the religious orders, as a never-ending cycle of corruption and renewal. Her sister Persecution has always been her faithful helper and counselor, while her enemy Avarice, disguised as Prudence, consistently betrays Christians into the treacherous hands of wealth. At the end of this speech Francis again praises Lady Poverty's wisdom, this time in terms borrowed from the love affair of Solomon and the queen of Sheba: "How true is the report that we heard in our land about your words and your wisdom; and indeed, your wisdom is much greater than the report that we heard. Blessed are your men and blessed are your servants, who are always in your presence and listen to your wisdom" (3 Kgs. 10.6–8).[19]

After this the friars, and the text, descend from their rhetorical heights into the vale of humor. Until now the allegory has consisted mainly of speeches, alternating between Francis's praise of Lady Poverty and her authoritative account of church history. The author could not have intended readers to visualize the scene: anyone literal-minded enough to try it would be compelled to observe that the friars had invited a naked, beautiful woman to be their guest.[20] Although the hospitality scene is no *déjeuner sur l'herbe*, Lady Poverty does leave the realms of abstraction long enough to remember that she has a body. Seeing that the friars have cooked no food, she asked that at least some raw aromatic herbs might be brought to her. But [the friars], having no gardener and knowing nothing of gardens, gathered wild herbs in the woods and set them before her. She said, "Bring me a little salt so that I can salt the herbs, for they are bitter."—"Wait, lady," they said, "until we can go into the city and bring you some, if there is anyone who will give us any."—"Give me a knife," she said, "to cut off the mold and slice the bread, for it is very hard and dry." They said to her, "Lady, we have no blacksmith to make swords for us; use your teeth for now instead of a knife, and we will provide for you later."—"Do you have a little bit of wine?" she said. They answered her, "Lady, we have no wine, for the beginning of human life is bread and water (Ecclus. 29.28)—and it is not good for you to drink wine, for the bride of Christ ought to flee wine as if it were poison."[21]

In this delicious scene we realize that the *sacrum commercium* has already occurred. St. Francis and his brothers have, as it were, *become* Lady Poverty, and she in exchange has become the fine lady we might expect to inhabit the rhetorical robes they have decked her in. As she requests more and more unavailable "luxuries," the friars are able to show themselves poorer than Poverty herself, until she finally ends the charade and blesses them, reverting to her original goddess persona. Her closing speech affirms the sacred partnership she has contracted with the friars: "Truly the Lord is with you, and I knew it not (Gen. 28.16). Behold! Now I see what I longed for, now I have what I desired—for I am united on earth with those who represent for me the image of him to whom I am married in heaven."[22] The language is careful: Lady Poverty calls Francis not her bridegroom but his image, an *alter Christus*. In her own roles as bride of Christ, queen of virtues, and teacher of wisdom, she remains in continuing ironic counterpoint with the Church, which implicitly deserves those titles only insofar as it lives up to the demanding standard of fidelity pledged by the Franciscans.

Although Francis himself had personified "Lady Holy Poverty" in his own writings,[23] the *Sacrum commercium* goes beyond those simple texts to create an enduring staple of the saint's legend, suitable for translation into the guilty bystander's native tongue. The text also stakes out a theological stand, one that either already was or soon would be sharply polemical. While the allegory is presented simply as a fable, not a vision, it claims supernatural sanction for the most extreme and radical interpretation of Franciscan poverty, later to become that of the order's Spiritual wing. In the presence of Lady Poverty, Francis and his companions make a solemn vow that would bind their successors forever: "We swear and establish by oath that we will uphold the judgments of your law even to eternity, world without end."[24] To create an indelible memory of that vow, the writer needed more than a principle. He needed a persona, and so devised the most paradoxical of goddesses, the empress whose sovereign glory is to have no clothes.

The Soul and Lady Love

From the 1250s—the same decade as the *Sacrum commercium*, if we accept Brufani's dating—comes the beguine Mechthild of Magdeburg's *Flowing Light of the Godhead*, a fluid compendium of visions, meditations, lyrics, and prophecies.[25] Mechthild's book begins with a prologue asserting its divine authorship, followed at once by a courtly dialogue between the Soul (called *Frouwe küneginne* or "Lady Queen") and a goddess-figure, Lady Love (*Frouwe Minne*). The Soul, we discover, has made a bargain with her goddess much like that of Francis with Lady Poverty.

The soul came to Love, greeted her with great deference (*mit tieffen sinnen*), and said:
"God greet you, Lady Love."
"May God reward you, Lady Queen."
"Lady Love, you are indeed perfect."
"Lady Queen, that is why I am above all things."
"Lady Love, you struggled many a year before you forced the exalted Trinity to pour itself utterly into the humble virginal womb of Mary."
"Lady Queen, that was to your honor and benefit."
"Lady Love, you have now come here to me and have taken from me everything I ever gained on earth."
"Lady Queen, you have made a happy exchange."
"Lady Love, you have taken from me my childhood."
"Lady Queen, in its place I have given you heavenly freedom."
"Lady Love, you have taken from me all my youth."
"Lady Queen, in its place I have given you many a holy virtue."
"Lady Love, you have taken from me possessions, friends, and relatives."
"Come now, Lady Queen, that is a petty complaint."
"Lady Love, you have taken from me the world, worldly honor, and all earthly riches."
"Lady Queen, I shall make that up to you in one hour with the Holy Spirit on earth, just as you wish it."
"Lady Love, you have brought me to such a pass that my body is racked by a strange weakness."
"Lady Queen, in exchange I have given you much sublime knowledge."
"Lady Love, you have devoured my flesh and my blood."
"Lady Queen, you have thereby been purified and drawn into God."
"Lady Love, you are a robber; for this as well shall you make reparation."
"Lady Queen, then take me."
"Lady Love, now you have recompensed me a hundredfold on earth."
"Lady Queen, in addition you may demand God and all his kingdom."[26]

Just as Francis in the *Sacrum commercium* takes the initiative to seek Lady Poverty, it is here the Soul who goes to greet Lady Love: the first steps are taken by the human partner. In each case, the goddess and the mystic celebrate a "happy exchange," what Mechthild terms *einen seligen wehsel*. But in her version of the pact, both partners seem considerably more aggressive, for a barely controlled fury animates their love. Minne plays the ruthless mistress, belying the deference with which she addresses the Soul as her superior, and the Soul, for her part, follows the initial exchange of compliments with sharp accusations. Her posture is that of the lyric lover, the poet who wills to give up everything for his lady's sake except the proud complaint that he has done so. As for Minne, who combines the courtly roles of the beloved lady and personified Love, her most salient trait is her absolute power.[27] Love's sway over the loving Soul knows no bounds; but so too her sway over God. As the Soul observes, Minne once "struggled" with the holy Trinity until she "forced" God to become incarnate, and now she has the power to bestow God and his kingdom at will on her votaries.

Thus paraphrased, the text may sound more theologically daring than it is. If one were to say in plain prose that God, in his infinite love, poured himself into the womb of Mary, and promised eternal life as a reward to those who renounce "houses or brothers or sisters or father or mother or children or lands" for the sake of his love (Matt. 19.27–29), the gospels themselves assert no less.[28] But in positing Minne as an independent force, a goddess who coexists with and indeed overpowers the Trinity, Mechthild makes God as vulnerable as the Soul is: he too is crazy-in-love. The goddess is a great leveler. Like Lady Poverty, Love demands absolute dispossession, yet those who possess her possess God and the world besides. Thus the Soul, at the end of her laments, can meet the infinite God on something like equal terms, because both have surrendered their all to the omnipotent goddess. The difference between the two goddesses is one of style. Lady Poverty is gentle, for she represents renunciation as freedom, not the fatedness of the born poor. Francis and his brothers *choose* her, just as Christ did before them, and on that common choice rests their sacred alliance. Lady Love, however, uses force. The Soul *struggles* with her, just as the Trinity had done before, so the Soul's union with God rests on their shared defeat.

Frau Minne did not come as a stranger into Mechthild's allegory: she brought with her a long and complex tradition, as we will see in Chapter 4. Most obviously, she hails from the realm of courtly lyric, with its ethos of erotic tyranny, but close behind her stands the personified Caritas of monastic theology, and in the distance, golden Aphrodite. A goddess with a past, Frau Minne would have a future too, for as medieval piety fixated increasingly on the passive and passionate Christ, the fortunes of the imperious goddess who subdued him (Figure 4.5) would continue to rise.

The Servant and Eternal Wisdom

In styling herself a *minnende Seele*, a "loving soul" with the passion of a mystic and the refined manners of a minnesinger, Mechthild was among the first German poets to broach a theme that would loom large in later medieval religious writing. But no figure in this tradition exercised a more powerful influence than Henry Suso, a Dominican mystic who called himself "the servant of Eternal Wisdom."

Suso's autohagiography, *The Life of the Servant*, is a unique case of a male saint's life authored with the help of a woman.[29] According to the prologue, it was Suso's protégée, the nun Elsbeth Stagel, who drew him out on the subject of his own spiritual life. But Stagel, in her teacher's absence, surreptitiously wrote down his confidences. When the friar discovered her project he reproached her and, it is said, started to burn the parchment, until a divine voice told him to desist. So instead of consigning Stagel's text to the flames, Suso revised and enlarged it after her death around 1360, placing the *Life* first in a collection of his German works entitled *The Exemplar*. This account, which we need not take literally, is meant to prove Suso's humility, while at the same time justifying the publication of his life as a model of devotional practice. It also witnesses to a genuine collaboration between Suso and Stagel, reversing the usual gender roles of the female mystic with her male confidant and scribe. The text as it comes down to us, however, represents Suso's final "authorized version," so that it is no longer possible to identify any of the language as Stagel's.

As Suso presents his own conversion, his soul was seduced for God by a text. Though he had worn the habit for several years as a lukewarm friar, he naturally "had a heart filled with love" that needed only to be set aflame. Fortunately a Galeotto was at hand. As the young man heard the wisdom books read in the refectory, the divine Sophia allured him from their pages. His "love-crazed spirit" began to pine for this exalted lady, for Solomon promised that Wisdom's love would make him noble, courtly, and esteemed. Although the youth feared that the pursuit of his high beloved might entail hardship, he recalled that according to the law of Minne, "no one can be a suitor unless he is a sufferer, nor can anyone be a lover unless he is a martyr."[30] Eternal Wisdom alone could offer him the pure sweetness of love with no bitterness in the end. As his infatuation deepened, he indulged in the time-honored reveries of a lover:

And he said to himself without hesitation, "Certainly it has to be the right thing. She must be my beloved, and I shall be her servant. O God, if I might just catch a glimpse of my dear one! If I could just once talk with her! What must my beloved look like if she has so many delightful things hidden within her! Is she divine or human, man or woman, art or knowledge or what?" And to the extent he was able to imagine her through the explanatory examples (*usgeleiten bischaften*) of scripture with his inner eyes, she presented herself to him thus: She was suspended high above him on a throne of clouds [see Figure 5.4]. She shone as the morning star and dazzled as the glittering sun. Her crown was eternity, her attire blessedness, her words sweetness, and her embrace the surcease of all desire. She was distant yet near, far above yet low, present yet hidden. . . . She spread herself out [from end to end mightily] and ordered all things sweetly. (Wisd. 8.1)[31]

Suso's act of imagination is not a vision, in the sense of an extraordinary spiritual experience. Rather, it is what he described in his earlier *Büchlein der ewigen Weisheit* (*Little Book of Eternal Wisdom*) as a "meditation in the light of Holy Scripture." Or, in the terms of courtly romance, it represents the charming first phase of love known as Sweet Thought. But Suso, unlike the typical romance lover, is not sure of his Beloved's gender:[32] "The minute he thought her to be a beautiful young lady, he immediately found a proud young man before him. Sometimes she acted like a wise teacher (*meisterin*), sometimes like a pert young thing (*minnerin*)."[33] This gender bending is a none-too-subtle hint of what the reader should already know: Eternal Wisdom, the "empress of [her Servant's] heart," is in fact Jesus and will shortly manifest herself on the cross. In the very next chapter the Servant, overcome with love, will take a stylus and inscribe the monogram of Jesus on his chest with his heart's blood.

Suso may well have seen his courtship of Eternal Wisdom as a devotion appropriate to beginners, male or female, who are traditionally enticed into God's service with "sweetness" and "consolations." For this reason he associated the feminine figure of Wisdom with the ardors of youth, and thus with an adolescent "theology of glory," whereas his mature theology of the cross focused on the human, masculine Jesus.[34] But wherever Sophia might belong in the continuum of piety, she was one goddess whom the Church absolutely had to accommodate, since she alone appears in the canonical Scriptures.[35] Lady Poverty could be represented as Christ's bride, Lady Love as God's mistress (or dominatrix). But Eternal Wisdom, ever since John's gospel transmuted her into the Logos and made her the heavenly subject of the Incarnation, had always been Christ's alter ego. In Suso's work she appears unmistakably as Christ the Goddess; and by the late fourteenth century, as we will see in Chapter 5, she would have her own paraliturgical cult.

Will and Lady Holy Church

About a decade after Henry Suso redacted his *Life*, a vagabond cleric in England began to revise and amplify the religious poem that would constitute his life's work. *The Vision of Piers Plowman* has always been an elusive text, and its author, William Langland, more elusive still.[36] In contrast to Suso, Mechthild, and the *Sacrum commercium* author, who were all deeply committed to various forms of religious life, Langland held profoundly conflicted views about the "religious life" as such, not to mention his own vocation.[37] Yet the depth and intensity of his Christian commitment are beyond doubt. *Piers Plowman*, no less than the *Sacrum commercium* or *Life of the Servant*, models a form of spiritual quest for its readers. But Langland does not adopt a persona who is already devoted to God under the auspices of poverty, love, or wisdom. His protagonist is a drifter and dreamer of a type familiar in allegorical poems, whose name—Will—bespeaks his salient traits of desire, self-assertion, rootless liberty, and wilfulness, as well as a partial and fitful identification with his author.[38] If the figures of the Servant and the loving Soul represent idealized versions of Suso and Mechthild, Will is more like a counter-idealized version of Langland, an image of questing humanity (and the poet's particular humanity) whose exaggerated naïveté asks of the reader not imitation but discernment.

Accordingly, the "marvelous dream" that befalls Will as the poem begins is in fact no marvel, but a vision of mundane reality—"a fair feeld ful of folk" who typify the winners and wasters, merchants and minstrels of the poet's London, all going about their business and blithely ignoring the symbolic representations of heaven and hell that frame their activities. After the lively events of the prologue, which include the coronation of a king, the dreamer encounters a divine woman of the sort that readers would expect at this point.

A lovely lady of leere in lynnen yclothed
Cam doun from the castel and called me faire,
And seide, "Sone, slepestow? Sestow this peple—
How bisie they ben aboute the maze?
The mooste partie of this peple that passeth on this erthe,

Have thei worship in this world, thei wilne no bettre;
Of oother hevene than here holde thei no tale."
 I was afered of hire face, theigh she faire weere,
And seide, "Mercy, madame, what may this be to mene?"³⁹ (B I.3–11)

A lady in linen clothes, lovely of face,
Came down from the castle and called me with courtesy,
And said, "Son, are you sleeping? Do you see these people—
How busy they are about the rat race?
Most of the people that pass through this earth
Wish nothing better than worldly esteem;
Of any heaven but here they will hear no talk."
I was afraid of her face, fair though she was,
And said, "Mercy, my lady, what might this mean?"

At this point neither Will nor the reader knows who the Lady is, but we have substantial clues. She is beautiful but scary, a moralist who disapproves of most earthly goings-on; she would like to awaken Will from his symbolic sleep; and she comes "doun from the castel," which she identifies in response to Will's question as the home of Truth. Before we learn the Lady's name she will say a great deal more, touching on mankind's obligations to Truth (now identified as the Creator); the evils of excessive drink; the unholy trinity of world, flesh, and devil; the proper use of money; and the "castel of care" inhabited by Truth's enemy, Wrong. In the course of sixty lines she also expounds two scriptural texts in Latin. By this time an alert reader should have formed a fair idea of the heavenly teacher's identity. But Will—who is not alert and does not realize he is a character in an allegory—"hadde . . . wonder in my wit what womman it weere."

"Holi Chirche I am," quod she, "thow oughtest me to knowe.
I underfeng thee first and the feith taughte.
Thow broughtest me borwes my biddyng to fulfille,
And to loven me leelly the while thi lif dureth." (B I.71, 75–79)

"I am Holy Church," she said, "you ought to know me.
I received you first and taught you the faith.
You brought me pledges to fulfill what I bid you,
And to love me loyally while your life endures."

 Lady Church (Figure 1.3) is one of the oldest personifications in the Christian pantheon. Already allegorized in the New Testament as the bride of Christ (Eph. 5.23–32, Rev. 21.2–3), she became a fully elaborated character as early as the second century, when the visionary prophet Hermas

Figure 1.3. Ecclesia nursing her children. Giovanni Pisano, pulpit of Pisa Duomo (1302–11). Photo: Richard Kieckhefer.

represented her in his *Shepherd* as an ageless teacher. In the main line of tradition, the woman Ecclesia was closely identified with the bride in the Song of Songs and both figures with Mary as queen of heaven. Langland, uninterested in this monastic and often triumphalist exegesis, makes his Holy Church not a queen but a teacher of economic and political justice. In reply to Will's burning question, "how I may save my soule," she cites a proverb that appears three times, at the beginning, middle, and end of her discourse: "Whan alle tresors arn tried, Treuthe is the beste" (B I.85, 135, 207).

"Truth" in the poem represents loyalty in word and deed, especially the integrity of honest labor, but is also one of Langland's two principal representations of God (the other being Kynde or Nature).[40] Lady Church illustrates the value of this "treasure" with pointed remarks on the judicial system, good and bad knights, the duties of the rich to the poor, and another proverb applied to hard-hearted clergy: "chastite withouten charite worth [will be] cheyned in helle" (B I.188, 194). Her teaching includes a celebrated lyrical passage on the nature of love, which points out that this "moost precious of vertues" is a decidedly political one.

Forthi is love ledere of the Lordes folk of hevene,
And a meene, as the mair is, inmiddes the kyng and the commune. (B I.159–60)

Therefore Love is leader of the Lord's folk in heaven,
And a mediator, as the mayor is, between the king and the commons.

The concrete sense of this teaching emerges through contrast when Lady Church presents Will with her opposite number, Lady Meed, in the next section. *Mede* is a broad term meaning "reward" in several senses, and the scarlet woman who goes by that name tries to pass herself off as the legitimate principle of just wages. But Holy Church and Conscience will have none of this, since the noun *mede* can also stand for bribery, kickbacks, and profiteering. As an allegorical composite, Lady Meed is a concrete universal whose embodiments include (among others) the Whore of Babylon, the king's mistress, mercenary lawyers, and the papal curia.[41] Her fiancé is Fals Fikel-tonge, and she has the seven deadly sins for her dowry. Lady Church turns out to be jealous of the upstart Meed, a devil's bastard:

"I oughte ben hyere than heo—I kam of a bettre.
My fader the grete God is and ground of alle graces,
Oo God withouten gynnyng, and I his goode doughter,
And hath yeven me Mercy to marie with myselve;
And what man be merciful and leelly me love

Shal be my lord and I his leef in the heighe hevene;
And what man taketh Mede, myn heed dar I legge
That he shal lese for hire love a lappe of *Caritatis*." (B II.28–35)

"I ought to be higher than she is—I came of better stock.
My father is the great God, ground of all graces,
One God without beginning, and I his good daughter.
He has given me Mercy to take in marriage,
And any man who is merciful and loyally loves me
Shall be my lord and I his beloved in the high heaven;
And any man who takes Meed, I dare wager my head,
Shall lose for her love a portion of charity."

The marriage metaphor that often hovers in the vicinity of medieval goddesses here takes an unexpected turn. Holy Church's lord and husband is not Christ but Mercy, that is, any and every man who will live by love without Meed. But clerics of the empirical church—Sire Symonie, Piers the Pardoner, and others—are lavishly represented in Meed's retinue, so God's daughter confronts the not-so-holy church of this world as its judge and rival, rather than a legitimizing projection of its authority. Her position resembles that of Lady Poverty in the *Sacrum commercium*, standing for the Church as it ought to be, while Meed prevails in the Church as it is.[42] Will, though still no more than an observer in his own dream, nonetheless confronts a clear choice. In a version of the classic male dilemma, the choice between Truth and Wrong has now revealed itself to him as a contest between two women. Lady Church and Lady Meed thus form one link in a long chain of allegorical dichotomies, stretching from Hercules's choice between Virtue and Pleasure to the medieval everyman's choices between Mary and Eve, Humility and Pride, or Philosophy and Fortune. The juxtaposition of these rival dames in the first two passus of *Piers Plowman* is all the more conspicuous because Langland, unlike most allegorical poets, tended to prefer male personifications.

As soon as she has raised the curtain on Meed's wedding, Lady Church disappears from the poem, never to return. Will goes on to meet and dispute with numerous other personifications in the course of his pilgrimage, whose object is variously described as Saint Truth, Dowel (doing-well), and the poem's Christlike hero, Piers Plowman. But Holy Church is virtually the only authoritative teacher in the poem whose doctrine is not in some way challenged by Will or subverted by context. Even though Lady Church does not remain onstage very long, her discourse establishes a framework of moral clarity and authority that functions almost nostalgically as a reference point for the reader, as the text amplifies her teachings about truth, love, and justice. To be sure, this clarity belongs to heaven, not earth. Will professes not to understand it, leading Holy Church after a particularly clueless question to call him a "doted daffe" (B I.140), and what seemed so lucid in the abstract is quickly muddied in the concrete. By the end of the poem, Will succeeds only in returning to his starting point, whether or not he knows the place for the first time. The Church now reappears in a new allegorical guise as "Unitee Holy Chirche," Piers Plowman's barn, where the faithful have assembled under the leadership of Conscience to resist the assaults of their enemies. But all is not well in Unitee. In the final pages, one Frere Flaterere insinuates his way into the barn and poisons Contricion with false physic, driving Conscience off yet again on his pilgrimage, as Will abruptly wakes from his dream.

Langland's two allegorical representations of the Church thus frame Will's dissatisfied quest for Dowel. Taught by Lady Holy Church at the outset to know the difference between Truth and Wrong and to save his soul through love, he travels through the confused world of his social, economic, and intellectual experience in search of a life that will embody that teaching until he finds himself at last in Piers's barn. The poem resists closure: Langland offers neither a mystical vision nor an apocalyptic finale to conclude— or occlude—the ongoing struggle of sin with grace. What he does provide is a symbolic frame. In the prologue, the "fair feeld ful of folk" lies midway between the castle of Truth and the dungeon of Wrong, caught in a moral force field whose polarities remain stable amid the instabilities of earthly workers and wanderers. This spatial symmetry is complemented by a temporal one. At its beginning and end, the pilgrimage of Will's life is bounded by the goddess and the crumbling barn, that is, by the divine and all-too-human Church. God's daughter disappears into heaven, yet still seeks embodiment on earth; while the barn, which becomes in turn a beleaguered fort and a hospital for wounded sinners, aspires to be the "tour on a toft" where Truth dwells. In this very earthy poem, then, the "lovely lady of leere" represents the absent but indispensable pole of an antinomy that could not exist—nor could the poem itself—without her.

Christine and the Female Trinity

The latest of the works in my quintet, Christine de Pizan's *Book of the City of Ladies* (1404–5), is the one most likely to seem out of place in a canon of

religious writings. Christine tends to be read as a purely secular author, a
"professional woman of letters," standing out from the crowd of female
mystics who were driven by divine command to take up their quills. She, it
is true, took up hers to support herself and her children, pushed into the
Field of Letters by what she called the "mutation of Fortune"—an early
widowhood—rather than a call from heaven. It is also true that Christine
did most of her prolific writing at court, retiring to a convent only late in life
under the stress of war.[43] She was certainly no mystic and may well have been
skeptical, as was her friend Jean Gerson, about the prevailing forms of female
spirituality.[44] Christine's religion, like that of her contemporary Chaucer,
bore a philosophical rather than a devotional stamp. Yet philosophical piety
is piety all the same, and Christine's works are suffused with Boethian Christianity—a high-minded, almost stoic resignation to Providence, coupled with
a reliance on God as guarantor of the moral and political order.

To the distress of some recent critics, the last third of *The City of
Ladies*—its rhetorical and argumentative climax—is devoted to the stories of
saints and martyrs. So perhaps it is time to reassess the religious basis of that
work, reading Part III as no mere strategic concession but the consummation of a theological project declared in the famous opening scene. When
three crowned goddesses visit Christine in her study, authorizing her bold
challenge to misogynist *auctores*, they do so by making a theological statement possible only to a writer who took the allegorical goddess tradition
with full seriousness. Maureen Quilligan observes that "what Christine does
is simply to take very seriously the metaphorically feminine gender of allegorical figures of authority—decreed by the grammar of romance languages
to be feminine—thereby literalizing them through a verbal play generic to
allegory and transforming them from female figures of authority into female
spokespersons for a vast range of pro-woman (anti-misogynist) positions."[45]
I would add that what Christine takes seriously is not only the goddesses'
gender but also the divine source of their authority.

The scene of writing sketched in Christine's opening pages is among the
most frequently analyzed set pieces in feminist criticism, no doubt because
readers today identify so easily with the persona she creates for herself.
Dispirited by her perusal of a third-rate misogynist satire, *The Lamentations
of Mathéolus*, Christine reflects on the ubiquity of antifeminist ideologies,
not just in trivial writers like Mathéolus but in the weightiest philosophers
and poets, until she herself starts to believe them and sinks into a profound
depression. But she also sinks into prayer, lamenting to God that she was
born a woman and begging him to forgive her weakness. This despondent

prayer is answered by what can only be called an epiphany. Sitting in darkness and the shadow of death, she suddenly perceives a ray of light falling into her lap:

And as I lifted my head to see where this light was coming from, I saw three crowned ladies standing before me, and the splendor of their bright faces shone on me and throughout the entire room [Figure 1.4]. Now no one would ask whether I was surprised, for my doors were shut and they had still entered. Fearing that some phantom had come to tempt me and filled with great fright, I made the Sign of the Cross on my forehead.[46]

The iconography is clearly modeled on the Annunciation.[47] Only supernatural visitors can enter through closed doors, so Christine, like Mary, is properly frightened. The first divine Lady, like Gabriel, tells her not to fear, for she has found favor with the heavenly ones—and there follows the annunciation of an everlasting realm, the City of Ladies, to be born of her consent to their message. In case anyone has missed the parallel, Christine ends the scene with an even more direct evocation of the Virgin. Fertilized by the "rain and dew" of the ladies' words, she now feels ready to "bear fruits of profitable virtue and sweet savor," knowing that "nothing is impossible for God" (Luke 1.37). And so she assents:

Figure 1.4. Christine de Pizan with Lady Reason, Lady Right, and Lady Justice. *Livre de la Cité des Dames.* London, BL Harley 4431, f. 290 (Paris, ca. 1410–15). Photo: British Library.

Thus, with all my strength, I praise God and you, my ladies, who have so honored me by assigning me such a noble commission, which I most happily accept. Behold your handmaiden ready to serve. Command and I will obey, and may it be unto me according to your words. (Luke 1.38)[48]

Having accepted the Virgin's role as handmaid, Christine is free to build the city that, in the end, the Virgin will enter as queen. With any luck, her project will put down the mighty from their thrones and exalt those of low degree.[49]

Christine's three visitors are not angels, however, but *deesses de gloire*— "goddesses of glory." She had good reason to lead off with Reason. Having criticized Jean de Meun's version of that venerable dame as irrational and lacking in decorum, Christine wished to show what a truly reasonable Lady Reason would teach.[50] It made sense too for Lady Right to eulogize political women and vindicate women falsely accused (*Droitture* implies both legal and moral rights),[51] and no one could be more fitting than Lady Justice to crown the souls of the just. But the three goddesses are not content to be mere personified virtues: they present themselves as daughters of God and, collectively, a feminine Trinity. Lady Reason speaks first:

Dear daughter, know that God's providence, which leaves nothing void or empty, has ordained that we, though celestial beings, remain and circulate among the people of the world here below, in order to bring order and maintain in balance those institutions we created according to the will of God in the fulfillment of various offices, that God whose daughters we three all are and from whom we were born.[52]

Lady Right continues, identifying herself (like the biblical Wisdom) as "the radiance and splendor of God and messenger of his goodness" (Wisd. 7.25–26): she visits the just, defends the rights of the innocent, resists evil, and rewards the virtuous. Lady Justice is the most explicit about their theological status:

My friend Christine, I am Justice, the most singular daughter of God, and my nature proceeds purely from his person. . . . I am in God and God is in me (John 14.11), and we are as one and the same. Who follows me cannot fail, and my way is sure. . . . And of the three noble ladies whom you see here, we are as one and the same, we could not exist without one another; and what the first disposes, the second orders and initiates, and then I, the third, finish and terminate it.[53]

A moralist like Christine could have named far more than three virtues, all with equal claim to be called "celestial beings" and "daughters of God." But the ones she does name are triple and coinherent (*comme une mesmes chose*), and their relationship parallels what theologians wrote of the Father, Son, and Holy Spirit: divine Reason wills and plans, Right executes, and Justice concludes. By Christine's day there was nothing especially novel or unorthodox about such a scheme. Robert Grosseteste, as we have seen, had made the four daughters of God instrumental to the redemption of mankind, in a widely popular allegory that Langland among others borrowed for the most dramatically potent section of *Piers Plowman*.[54] Christine is telling a different but parallel story: nothing less than the redemption of womankind, typified by a City of Ladies self-consciously modeled on Augustine's City of God.[55] So ambitious a project requires the inspiration of God's celestial daughters, not just as ornament but as serious theological claim. In presenting them as her high commissioners and collaborators, Christine asserts that her book derives not merely from her own reasoning, her own sense of what is right, her own cry for justice, but from the will of a God who can, when occasion demands, choose to be manifest in the form of a feminine Trinity.[56]

If the City of Ladies is meant to be a female City of God, "incomparably beautiful and everlasting in the world," it is at the same time a city of goddesses. I have said that the three pantheons of medieval Christendom never mingled in the same text, but *The City of Ladies* is a rare exception. By a humanist sleight of hand, Christine manages to include both pagan and Christian goddesses in her city, along with the female saints in the third book. Her euhemerism, learned from Boccaccio, explains the ancient deities as heroes and heroines of prehistory, allowing her to laud Minerva, Ceres, and Isis as outstanding women who were once mistakenly worshiped as goddesses for their contributions to culture.[57] The three celestial ladies, on the other hand, are "real" goddesses, which is to say, they are rooted as deeply in Christine's genuine theological beliefs as they are in the conventions of allegorical narrative. Bearing these convictions in mind, what would an appropriately serious reading of her allegory entail?

Minimally, I believe, she wanted readers to acknowledge the teaching of the three ladies as inspired and to recognize her as their handmaid, with a divinely appointed task to fulfill. It was not her authorship as such, but her mission of deconstructing and reconstructing the history of women, that she needed to authorize with this convention of visionary literature. Maximally, the authority of God's daughters, who "proceed purely from his person," would set a divine warrant on her daring analogy between the City of Ladies and the City of God. Though restricted to one gender, her city is otherwise remarkably inclusive, open alike to biblical women, amazons, Christian martyrs, transvestites, pagan goddesses, contemporary queens, and classical heroines, including a few notorious criminals, all under the queenship of Mary.[58] This universality makes a theological as well as a historical point: the female no less than the male could stand as a synecdoche for the human, *pars pro toto*. But the human is the image of the divine, so in order to represent genuine universality Christine's eternal city had to be buttressed by a female representation of its author and founder, God.

When Lady Justice assembles "all women" to welcome the Virgin as their queen, Mary graciously responds:

O Justice, greatly beloved by my Son, I will live and abide most happily among my sisters and friends, for Reason, [Right], and you, as well as Nature, urge me to do so. They serve, praise, and honor me unceasingly, for I am and will always be the head of the feminine sex. This arrangement was present in the mind of God the Father from the start, revealed and ordained previously in the council of the Trinity.[59]

The Virgin Queen invokes two distinct Trinities, one male and one female, whose divine wills coincide in her own coronation. This moment of convergent divinity is the veiled climax of Christine's theological project.

Vision, Imagination, and Belief

In many ways the five texts we have just examined are more different than they are alike. To summarize: the *Sacrum commercium* (probably 1250s) is a Franciscan hagiographic legend in Latin prose. Mechthild's courtly dialogue introduces a German mixed-genre work, *The Flowing Light of the Godhead* (also 1250s), that represents itself in toto as divine revelation. Suso's *Life* (1360s) is a vernacular autohagiography, incorporating materials from an earlier religious dialogue that exists in both German and Latin versions. *Piers Plowman* B (ca. 1377–79) is an allegorical dream vision in English alliterative verse, suffused with elements of satire and apocalyptic. Christine's *Book of the City of Ladies* (1405), in French, might best be described as a prose history, albeit with a sharp polemical edge. Yet these works, diverse as they are in language, genre, intention, and social context, reveal striking similarities in their use of the motif we are investigating: the encounter of a biographical or autobiographical persona with a goddess.

Of the seven goddesses who appear in the five texts, six are personified virtues (Lady Poverty, Lady Love, Eternal Wisdom, and Lady Reason with her sisters Right and Justice). The seventh, Lady Holy Church, represents the transcendent aspect of an institution that was seen as simultaneously divine and human, heavenly and earthly. All the goddesses stand in intimate relationship with God. Langland's Lady Church and Christine's three goddesses are represented as God's daughters; Lady Poverty is the bride of Christ; Suso's Eternal Wisdom, a biblical personage, *is* Christ in feminine guise; while Lady Love, who plays a variety of roles in Mechthild's text, is initially presented as a powerful goddess who overcomes the Trinity by force. As for the protagonists, two of them (Francis and Suso) are hagiographic figures, while another pair (Suso and Christine) are directly autobiographical. Mechthild's persona of the loving Soul ("Lady Queen") is an idealized and distanced representation of the author's own soul, whereas Langland's creation, Will, is a counter-idealized and universalized version of the poet's will. All five protagonists are engaged in some form of spiritual quest: for the most Christlike way of life (Francis), for a deeper union with God (Mechthild, Suso), for a *kynde knowing* or intuitive grasp of truth (Will), for liberation from oppressive lies (Christine).

It is in the context of these quests that the goddesses appear, forming intimate relationships with the protagonists or demanding acknowledgment of an intimate bond that already exists. Three of these relationships have a distinctly erotic cast (*Sacrum commercium*, *Flowing Light*, and *Life of the Servant*), while all except Mechthild's display an equally strong didactic element. The goddesses, in short, are lovers and teachers; they are also "ladies," indicating the pervasive influence of courtly discourse. The protagonists become their servants and handmaids, their suitors, disciples, and collaborators. Through his covenant with Lady Poverty, Francis becomes another Christ; through her assent to the female Trinity, Christine becomes another Mary. Yielding to the power of Lady Love, Mechthild imitates the triune God who has already yielded. Embracing Eternal Wisdom as his mistress, Suso embraces Christ as his master. At least three of the texts also have a significant sociopolitical dimension. Langland and the Franciscan writer use goddesses representing the heavenly Church to promote reform of the earthly Church, while Christine's goddesses help her build a City of Ladies to expose the androcentric City of God as the mere City of Men that it is.

These touchstones, gleaned from a small but diverse sampling of texts, begin to suggest the scope and pervasiveness of the goddess phenomenon in medieval writings. Bearing this diversity in mind, we are ready to approach two questions that must be confronted head on before we can take the goddesses seriously as elements of medieval religious culture. One is the question of genre: is there a line of demarcation between "authentic" and "fictional" visions, and if so, how porous is that boundary? The second, closely related question has to do with the degree of reality ascribed to the goddesses: how far are they to be understood as divine revelations, comparable to visions of Christ or the Virgin, and how far should they be seen as self-consciously fictional constructions?

Scholars have always maintained a rough-and-ready distinction between the genres of "authentic" visionary literature (such as revelations, spiritual diaries, and otherworld journeys) and "fictional" visions (such as allegories of love, dream poems, and tutelary dialogues). Many, perhaps most, texts fall clearly on one side or the other of the line. No one is likely to mistake the dream-vision prologue of Chaucer's *Legend of Good Women* for a record of the poet's inner experience, nor would anyone but an unremitting positivist take Julian of Norwich's *Revelation of Love* for a fiction. Yet, since few critics have undertaken the kind of comparative study attempted in this book, the boundary question has seldom been explored in depth. In fact, "in-between" cases are surprisingly numerous. Mechthild of Magdeburg and Henry Suso, for example, are classified as mystics, so until recently scholars have been much more interested in their religious experience and devotional practice than in their literary art. Yet, in the texts we have examined, Mechthild's courtly dialogue between the Soul and Lady Love does not advertise itself as a vision at all, while Suso's encounter with Eternal Wisdom is represented expressly as an act of imagination. Conversely, Langland and Christine de Pizan are always read as self-conscious literary artists. Yet the opening scenes of *Piers Plowman* and *The City of Ladies* not only use the conventions of visionary literature, but do so with a clear religious purpose.

As it happens, two of our authors—Suso and Christine, who are seldom mentioned in the same breath—both theorized helpfully about their own allegorical practice. In the prologue to his *Little Book of Eternal Wisdom*, Suso explains that his dialogues with Wisdom did not take place physically, but "only through meditation in the light of Holy Scripture." Some of the sayings he ascribed to Eternal Wisdom were spoken by her own mouth in the Gospel, that is, by Christ; others derive from "the loftiest teachers" and have "either the same words or the same meaning" as may be found in Scripture.[60] The text also records visions, but these too "did not happen in a bodily way; they are merely an illustrative parable" (*usgeleitú bischaft*). The dialogue form is justified as a pedagogical device: the author has taken on a variety of roles "as a teacher should," to explain his simple ideas in yet simpler words for the benefit of simple people.[61] Clearly Suso believed that by resorting to allegory, visions, and imaginary dialogues, he was making his thought more accessible than in his earlier speculative writing, which had led to accusations of heresy—and the lasting popularity of the later works proves he was right. Interestingly, his Latin reworking of the same material in the *Horologium Sapientiae* makes a slightly different but congruent distinction. Writing for a more sophisticated audience, he shifts his emphasis from the visionary event (corporeal versus spiritual) to the reader's interpretation of it (literal versus figurative): "Not all the visions contained in the following pages are to be taken at face value, although many could literally have occurred; rather, it is figurative language (*figurata locutio*)."[62] Suso here tells his readers that the genesis of the individual vision narratives is unimportant; any one of them may or may not have taken place *ad litteram*, but the reader should in every case interpret the language figuratively. Whether we read the German or the Latin text, it is clear that Suso's spiritual authority did not depend on his visions being accepted as "literally true."

Christine's vision in *The City of Ladies* is no more but also no less real than Suso's. It is hard to imagine a reader, then or now, naïve enough to think that the three goddesses appeared to her in bodily form and dictated her book. But it is easy to imagine Christine, like Suso, describing her dialogue with the ladies as a parable, a figurative way of speaking, or even a "meditation in the light of Scripture." We should not assume the alternative to an "authentic vision," in either his case or hers, to be a "fictional construct" in the sense that we now understand fiction. Whether the goddesses visibly appeared is irrelevant; the point is that they can and do appear to the mind's eye because they embody true revelations of God. When Christine reflected on her own habits as a writer, she expressed this conviction clearly. In her *Book of the Path of Long Study* (1402–3), the first homage to Dante in French, Christine has herself escorted around the world by a Beatrician figure, the Cumaean Sibyl (Figure 1.5). On Mount Parnassus the Sibyl points out two roads to heaven that are accessible only to the wise and learned. The straighter, narrower, and greener of the two is called the road of imagination, which "reveals the face of God to whoever follows it to the end."[63] But the Sibyl tells Christine to bypass this road because it is too difficult for her, and to follow instead the safer path of long study. This humility topos, more a tribute to the *Paradiso* than a disavowal of Christine's own powers, only amplifies her conviction that imaginative vision really does reveal the face of God.

A recent debate among German medievalists has illumined some of the difficulties involved in maintaining an either/or distinction between what Peter Dinzelbacher calls "erlebte Visionen" (experienced visions) and "literarische Visionen" (literary visions). Dinzelbacher, in an attempt to analyze

Figure 1.5. Christine and the Sibyl before the heavenly ladder. *Le Chemin de long estude*. London, BL Harley 4431, f. 188 (Paris, ca. 1410–15). Photo: British Library.

not just visionary texts, but the phenomenology of actual visions underlying such texts, has elaborated a set of criteria intended to distinguish the authentic visionary from the literary artist. His criteria themselves are inevitably literary: for example, a genuine seer is more likely to write prose, to describe ecstatic or waking visions, and to shun allegory, while an author of fictional visions is more inclined to write verse, to use the convention of dream visions, and to employ allegory extensively.[64] Once literary impostors have been eliminated from the field, the historian can trust real visionaries to tell the autobiographical truth about their experiences.[65] But Dinzelbacher's critics, Siegfried Ringler and Ursula Peters, rightly point out the naïveté of such an approach. No scholar, least of all one writing centuries after the fact, can reach "behind" a vision narrative to the experience on which it is ostensibly based, so we may as well acknowledge the force of literary convention in shaping such texts, particularly the covenant of genre that obligated writers to meet the expectations of readers.[66]

Ringler and Peters, however, are sometimes led by their oppositional logic to an extreme and unwarranted skepticism about the historicity of all visions. Positing a mutually exclusive relationship between conventionality and authenticity, they overlook the cyclical psychology by which texts not only beget other texts, but give rise to precisely the kinds of experience they represent. We might call this the Madame Bovary phenomenon. Fancying herself a *grande amoureuse*, Madame Bovary would have been indignant if someone had said her passion was unreal because it was too much like the passions she had read about in novels. On the contrary, the testimony of so many novelists authenticated her own feelings, just as hers in turn would have stimulated future *petites-bourgeoises* and future novels, had she not been so unlucky as to have Flaubert for her chronicler. Even so with medieval visionaries.

While most scholars today hold visions to be exceptional events, medieval visions were in some contexts not only encouraged but expected. We now know them to have been embedded in an elaborate nexus of religious practices, including the devotional use of images and the technique of visualization, that were by no means exceptional. A fuller list of these practices would include *lectio divina* with its complements of *oratio* and *meditatio*, or "rumination" on a sacred text; contemplation of the paintings in books and churches; frequent reading of visionary literature, including saints' lives; fasting; lengthy vigils and interrupted sleep; and guided meditations on such themes as Christ's Nativity and Passion and the life of the Virgin. The rosary, which combines an emotionally charged set of visualizations with recitation of a mantra, is the best known and most elaborate of such devotions. It would hardly be surprising if a nun or beguine, adept at spiritual exercises and gifted with a strong visual imagination, were to find the texts and images of her accustomed meditations "coming to life" from time to time in the form of visionary experience.[67] Such visions could and often did carry a powerful drive to immortalize the revelation in a text.

Conversely, however, the act of literary production might itself be the stimulus, and imaginative vision the response. The construction of allegory and the cultivation of visions could, in fact, serve as parallel modes of religious exploration, similarly free from the rigorous dogmatic and logical constraints of scholasticism. Unlike the disputations of the schools, both these forms of religious expression were open to laypeople, including women. In their non-Latinate forms, visionary and allegorical writings comprise a good part of what Bernard McGinn and Nicholas Watson have taught us to call vernacular theology.[68] Both involved distinctive and not dissimilar techniques, beginning with meditation on prior texts or images. Thus the *Sacrum commercium* author meditated on the life of St. Francis, Suso on the biblical wisdom books, Christine on the Annunciation, Mechthild on the figure of Frau Minne known to her from courtly lyrics. The next stage might be the evocation of a scene or personage, perhaps a snatch of dialogue. With skill and practice, such exercises could lead into a full-fledged, vividly experienced encounter between the visionary/persona and a divine or allegorical figure. Many of these time-honored techniques for inducing visionary experience have been revived in the New Age spirituality movement and are once again being assiduously cultivated.[69]

Novelists often testify that after a certain point in the creative process, their characters take on lives of their own and begin to do things their authors never expected, as if they were genuinely independent beings. One contemporary fiction writer has even confessed to picking up the telephone in order to call her own characters, only to recall with disappointment that they did not exist outside her mind.[70] If such is the case even with a genre as secular as the novel, would it not have been true a fortiori of medieval allegorical poets? Most of them were, after all, Christian Platonists who believed that their "characters," as universals, really did possess a prior and independent reality. Owen Barfield pointed out long ago that medieval allegory—not always and everywhere, but more often than not—had its grounding in philosophical realism. "For us, the characters in an allegory are 'personified abstractions,' but for [medieval readers] Grammar or Rhetoric, Mercy or 'Daunger,' were real to begin with, simply *because* they were 'names.' And names could be representations, in much the same solid-feeling way as things were."[71] It is small wonder that the allegorical vision as a genre underwent its great resurgence in the twelfth century, at the height of the Platonic revival. Carolynn Van Dyke has defined "pure allegory" as "Realistic narrative, or narrative whose agents are universals." By embodying these universals in personifications, giving them voice, and allowing them to interact with each other and with the visionary persona, the genre "envisions human life as a continual interchange between temporal event and eternal pattern."[72] Paul Piehler observes that medieval allegory tended toward psychological realism as well: its practitioners not only ascribed more reality to universals than we now do, but had a consequently greater ability to enter into direct psychic communication with them.[73]

The assumptions underlying Platonic or Realistic allegory are clarified once again by Christine de Pizan. In *Christine's Vision* (1405), an autobiographical work completed in the same year as *The City of Ladies*, she pays homage to another of her favorite authors, Boethius, by telling her life story to Lady Philosophy (Figure 1.6). At the end of a long complaint against Fortune, she attests her veracity with a remarkable assertion: "And that I speak the truth about these things, God and you know—God, who is properly you, and you, who are properly God."[74]

What can Christine possibly mean by this? Lady Philosophy (*lexcellent deesse*) goes on to refute her *planctus* in sound Boethian fashion, proving that all fortune is good fortune and leading into a discourse on true felicity. She concludes with a quotation from the master himself: "just as those who have justice are just and those who have wisdom are wise, so those who possess divinity are gods and one who has felicity is a god. Thus all the blessed are gods: although by nature there is only one God, by participation there are many."[75] With this passage in the *Consolation*, Boethius summed up his argument that all partial goods, such as glory, power, and pleasure, necessarily coincide when found in their perfection, that is, in God, since God alone is the highest good and the true beatitude. The ancient writer, keeping his argument distinct from his *fabula*, had never claimed that Lady Philosophy herself was God. But the logic of his Christian Platonism, with its doctrine of participated deity, allows Christine—and not only Christine—to present Philosophy or any other virtue as "you, who are properly God." That she does in fact mean this, and means it in a fully Christian sense, becomes yet clearer from her closing praise of Lady Philosophy, whom she has now transmuted into Christian theology: "I declare that you, Holy Theology and divinity, are a rich nourishment that contains within it all delights, just like

Figure 1.6. Lady Philosophy, from a Latin poem honoring Robert of Anjou. London, BL Royal 6 E IX, f. 27 (French, fifteenth century). Photo: British Library.

the manna that rained from heaven for the Jews and that tasted in everyone's mouth according to his desires" (Exod. 16, Ps. 77.24, Wisd. 16.20).[76] No medieval reader could have failed to recognize the manna as a type of the eucharist (John 6.58–59), and thus to see that with this analogy Christine assimilated the teaching of Lady Philosophy to the body of Christ.[77]

Given these convictions, it seems likely that another of Christine's goddesses, Lady Justice, was just as "real" to her as she was to Hildegard of Bingen, for both women claimed to have seen that crowned lady in their visions and both recorded her discourse at length.[78] The comparison is useful because it illustrates the limits of what might be, in other circumstances, a necessary distinction between two kinds of authors. Hildegard, who insisted as strenuously as any writer in history on the genuineness of her visions, relied on their authority so far as to claim verbal inerrancy for her writings. Christine did nothing of the sort—and may have had little sympathy with those who did. But from the standpoint of literary content, it hardly matters if Hildegard "really" had a vision of Lady Justice while Christine only imagined or pretended she did. And if, without derogating Hildegard's *bona fides*, we may suspect her of some literary artifice in phrasing Justitia's lament, we can just as reasonably suspect Christine of believing that her words were indeed those Justice in person might have uttered. In short, "authentic" visions, no matter how real the experience they record, necessarily become constructed visions when they come down to us as texts, while "fictional" visions, whether they originate in a religious meditation like Suso's or a poetic act like Christine's, may convey impassioned and articulate belief by means of allegorical personae. We should not be surprised, then, to find the same goddesses populating texts on both sides of the boundary, as well as some straddling the fence.

Nevertheless, it would be foolish to pretend that all personifications should be granted the same ontological status or the same degree of authorial conviction. One of the most delicate tasks facing the interpreter of visionary and allegorical texts is to decide how seriously to take the goddesses and other personifications that appear in them—or, in other words, to distinguish between substantive beings and mere rhetorical tropes. Often it is not easy to tell. C. S. Lewis, describing an early medieval otherworld vision, once complained that "all the actors and all the scenery are on the same plane of reality" because its monastic author, indifferent to theological nuance, "seems to have lost all power of distinguishing between his allegory and his pneumatology. The Virtues and Vices become as real as the angels and the fiends."[79] James Paxson observes in the same vein that "the

distinctions among gods, ghosts, genii, fantastic creatures, and personification characters were not always clear even to the principal theorists of classical, medieval, or Renaissance rhetoric."[80] In visual art we find the same
phenomenon. For instance, when a manuscript page depicts Christ wounded
in the heart by a woman identified as *Caritas* or *Sponsa* (Figures 4.1, 4.2),
there may be no visual clue that one figure is any less "real" than the other.[81]
Yet many works do make a distinction, using rhetorical cues that are often
quite subtle. Peter Dronke, discussing one of the most important and original twelfth-century allegories, poses the question: "What kind of reality do
the principal allegorical personages in the *Cosmographia* of Bernard Silvestris
have? In particular, the figure whom scholars call 'the goddess Natura': how
far is she a believable, and believed in, being, rather than a rhetorically personified abstraction?"[82] Dronke concludes that, even though "many questions
of the degree of reality remain unclear, and may never be decidable with certainty," Nature was indeed a goddess for Bernard, not just because she is
vividly personified, but because her activity seems so integral to his view of
the world that she can hardly be depersonified or imagined away.[83] But that
does not mean the same transcendental reality should be ascribed to every
personification who appears in the text.

　　To choose a different example, Mechthild of Magdeburg's rhetoric gives
the impression that Lady Love exists for her on the same plane as the divine
Bridegroom and the Virgin Mary, but when she later introduces Lady Trust,
Lady Estrangement, and Lady Pain[84] these figures seem indeed to be no
more than "rhetorically personified abstractions." In *Piers Plowman* very few
of the personifications enjoy the same transcendental status as Lady Church.
Certainly Piers himself does, as a figure of Christ's universal humanity, and
perhaps also the four daughters of God. But the many personifications of
Will's mental processes, and the elusive trio of Dowel, Dobet and Dobest,
subsist on a different level entirely; they do not command the same reverence,
and their authority can be challenged.[85] We might account for our perception
of different ontological planes by distinguishing Platonic personifications
from Aristotelian ones, reading the former as epiphanies or emanations of
a superior reality, the latter as "accidents existing in a substance," personified
only for the sake of analytical clarity.[86] While it is no easier to posit foolproof
criteria for these categories than it is to discern the authenticity of visions,
we can propose a few key guidelines for detecting a Platonic personification,
such as the figure's centrality to the conceptual scheme of the text; expressions of awe, love, and reverence on the part of the narrator; the appropriation of biblical and liturgical language to give the figure a numinous aura;

the predominantly serious, rather than ironic or parodic, character of the figure's discourse; and perhaps most important, the presumption of an intimate relationship between the figure and God. In the majority of cases, personifications that meet these criteria are described either as goddesses or as brides or daughters of God.

The subject of our study, then, will be goddess figures who meet most or all of the criteria for Realistic or Platonic personification. To be sure, a few exceptions will creep in. The goddess Natura, for example, became so well established in the pantheon that neither Jean de Meun's parody nor Chaucer's playfulness could dethrone her—and even in their hands the goddess retains some of her aura. It would seem churlish to omit texts so influential as the *Roman de la Rose* and the *Parlement of Fowles* because of their satiric edge. On the other hand, the criteria I have outlined will exclude at least one favorite personification who is often designated a goddess, namely Fortuna.[87] Originally a pagan deity, Fortuna gained new currency in the Middle Ages through Boethius's *Consolation*, where she is personified by another personification, Lady Philosophy, in the course of her lecture on divine providence. But Philosophia creates this rival goddess, and even ventriloquizes her words, only to prove in the end that Fortuna is not a real cosmic power, but an illusion of misguided human perception.[88] The elevation and dethronement of Lady Fortune was a formative scene in the history of allegory—and one often replayed, as in *Christine's Vision*. Boethius's arguments assured that, while Fortuna might become a useful and familiar personification, she could never be a Platonic one. Already deconstructed in the very text that constructed her, Fortune is rarely invested with a numinous character, seldom makes edifying speeches, is not addressed with love or reverence by the narrators who complain to her, and is hardly said to be on intimate terms with God.[89] In fact, the characters who invoke her most frequently—one thinks of Chaucer's Palamon, Arcite, and Troilus—are marked by this very preoccupation with Fortune as emotionally and intellectually immature.

Why Goddesses?

One of the phenomena that should be most puzzling and intriguing to the student of allegory has received surprisingly little attention. That fact is the overwhelming predominance of goddesses, of *female* personifications created to fill the niche of the divine mediator. Thirty years ago, Paul Piehler went so far as to assert that "the manifestation of goddesses in transcendent land-scapes . . . constitutes the central psychic experience in medieval allegory."[90] But while many scholars have commented in passing on this preponderance of goddesses, few have tried to explain it. The oldest and still most frequently cited hypothesis dates back to 1721, when Joseph Addison first noted the phenomenon and ascribed it to a grammatical fact. Abstract nouns in Latin (and most Romance languages) take the feminine gender, so when artists and poets wished to personify virtues they necessarily represented them "in petticoats."[91] Addison attributed the fairly late appearance of male personifi-cations to the decay of grammatical inflection in the European vernaculars. In support of his observation, one might add that in the native English tradi-tion, when it is uninfluenced by French, male personifications are much more common. Alfred the Great's translation of Boethius, for example, replaced Lady Philosophy with a masculine figure called Wisdom. Langland, whose alliterative verse developed out of Old English poetics, used far more male personifications than did the more Frenchified Chaucer, and John Bunyan used almost exclusively male figures in *Pilgrim's Progress*. It is striking, how-ever, that male personifications are virtually never of the type I have called Platonic or Realistic. One could hardly imagine referring to them as gods, with the exception of the *dieu d'Amors*—but he turns out to be none other than the pagan deity Cupid. With female personifications, however, goddess language is used with abandon.

While there is clearly some truth in the grammatical theory, it is far from being a full and adequate explanation. As Paxson observes, the theory "begs the philological question regarding the relationship between gender and grammar," allowing an unduly deterministic force to the latter.[92] Empirical evidence also demonstrates the comparative lack of interest in personifying masculine nouns. In classical Latin, for example, the semantic fields of *anima* (f.) and *animus* (m.) overlap, but *animus* is more commonly linked with the "higher" mental faculties—mind, spirit, purpose, imagination, courage, will—while *anima* is linked with the vital breath and the "lower" faculty of quickening the body. One might have expected medieval writers, with their well-known preference for the mental over the corporeal, to personify and valorize the *animus* rather than the *anima*, but they almost never did.[93] Instead, the *anima* or feminine Soul came to be personified as a bride of God, to the extent that even the disembodied soul after death was rendered exclusively by *anima*. The masculine noun *spiritus* likewise remained an ab-straction, rarely personified—even in the case of the Holy Spirit, third Person of the Trinity. When Bernard Silvestris decided to give the supreme goddess in his *Cosmographia* the Greek name of *Noys*, or "mind," he made her female even though *nous* is a masculine noun.[94] My point is not that knowledge of Greek was deficient in twelfth-century France (although it was), but that the logic of representation virtually demanded feminine figures.

Still more examples could be cited. One of the favorite school-texts of twelfth-century Platonists was Calcidius's commentary on the *Timaeus*. At one point the commentator describes three personifications, Natura, Fortuna, and Casus (Chance), as subordinate powers ministering to the triune God.[95] Why is it that the feminine Natura and Fortuna were continually personified, while the masculine Casus never was? When Bernard Silvestris sought analogues for the Trinity among the pagan deities, why did he choose Jove for God the Father (power), but Pallas Athene for the Son (wisdom) and Juno for the Holy Spirit (will)?[96] Apollo might have seemed a more suitable Christ-figure, and the jealous and vengeful Juno seems an unlikely choice for the Spirit, traditionally identified with *caritas*. Yet Bernard clearly felt that, beneath the remote masculine Godhead, the mediating figures had to be female. Even when Alan of Lille surrounded his Natura with significant male personifications, Genius and Hymen (linked with procreation and marriage respectively), these figures never won the same popularity or prestige as Natura herself. In a different sphere, female personifications of Love (Caritas, Dame Amour, Minne) were often employed to represent the Godhead itself, whereas male personifications (*li dieu d'Amors*, Italian *Amore*) seldom filled this role—with the rare exception of Dante in the *Commedia*. Clearly we have to do with something more than grammar, something tantamount to a cultural demand for goddesses.

More recent explanations of this demand have focused on the female as dichotomized Other. Joan Ferrante, the first critic to approach the subject from a systematic feminist perspective, observed that the allegorical tradition's tendency to idealize female figures balances the exegetical tradition's tendency to demonize them: in neither case are women represented as fully human. Like the lady of courtly lyric, the allegorical woman finally remains an abstraction rather than a person.[97] Others have connected the penchant for female personifications with the feminizing of rhetoric itself. Because rhetorical ornament was denigrated from antiquity throughout the Middle Ages as "cosmetic" and "seductive," thus effeminate, it made a kind of sense to give female bodies to the figures representing the very act of figuration.[98] Despite the general truth of this proposition, however, it tells us little about specific goddesses and their functions in texts. In *Allegory and Violence*, Gordon Teskey notes a counter-intuitive feature of medieval personifications. Allegorical poets presupposed a gendered cosmology in which feminine matter longs for the imposition of masculine form (as does Silva, the personification of matter, in Bernard Silvestris's *Cosmographia*), so it may seem peculiar that not only matter but also mind and many other ordering principles such as Sapientia and Philosophia likewise receive the feminine gender. In Teskey's view, this gendering is a mystification. By means of it, allegory attempts to disguise the "violent pleasure of thought," that is, the forceful and usually patriarchal imposition of meaning on a resistant material reality.[99] Unfortunately, such an extended notion of "violence" itself does violence to resistant medieval texts, whose authors viewed "meaning" as divinely given and humanly discovered rather than forcibly imposed.

I would like to suggest a new interpretation of medieval goddesses by reading them precisely *as* goddesses: *female* but not necessarily *women*. Thus my starting point is not "representations of woman" but "modes of religious imagination." An inquiry framed in these terms might begin with H. Richard Niebuhr's observation that what he called "radical monotheism" has been a rarity in the history of religions. Not only do most religious systems in the world admit a plurality of divine beings, but even within the Western religions of the book, pure monotheistic faith seems to be a difficult position for the religious psyche. Because human trust is more easily placed in goods and persons closer to home than in the transcendent, immutable One, a heaven and earth swept clean of rival deities tend to be quickly repopulated with angels, saints, and other mediating spirits. As Niebuhr wrote in 1943, "It is very questionable, despite many protestations to the contrary, . . . that anyone has ever yearned for radical faith in the One God."[100] In the case of medieval Catholicism, no sooner had the pagan gods been vanquished and aestheticized than the new faith began to generate its own pantheons: first the saints and then the goddesses.

To Niebuhr's perception about the difficulties of pure monotheism, I would add that *male* monotheism—evidently the only kind in existence—poses a further problem. Human beings come in two sexes, and once they have admitted the concept of personal deity they tend to imagine deities also in both sexes. To conceive of goddesses—or, within Christianity, to posit feminine "aspects" or "emanations" or "daughters" of God—is not to evince any particular attitude toward women. It is simply to exercise the religious imagination. On the one hand, medieval culture posed a formidable barrier to this exercise through the dogma of the Trinity, which pointedly excludes the feminine.[101] On the other, it supplied a valuable set of resources for it, including the biblical wisdom literature; the traditions of classical myth and mythography; late antique pedagogical texts, especially those of Boethius, Prudentius, and Martianus Capella; the habit of philosophical realism, which made it easy to divinize abstract ideas; and, not least, the figure of the Virgin Mary. From the perspective adopted here, what is surprising is not that medieval poets and visionaries should have imagined goddesses, but that their *absence* was seen for so long as natural and normative that their *presence* needed to be explained away or ignored. For the student of comparative religion, goddesses are not exceptional but normal. But for the medievalist, their presence may appear inexplicable because it seems to conflict so radically with the orthodox doctrine of God.

In the final section of this chapter, I argue four propositions about the religious functions of medieval goddesses. First, and most paradoxically, goddesses flourished because it was so much safer to theologize about them than about the Trinity. Second, goddesses were able to mediate various types of religious experience, or access to the Divine, that could not easily be accommodated within the framework of scholastic or pastoral doctrine. Third, the deployment of goddess figures allowed writers to probe the divine mind and analyze God's inner conflicts, so to speak, in much the same way that allegory enabled them to dramatize human conflicts. Finally, both male and female authors used goddesses to meet gender-specific psychological and cultural needs, which varied considerably from case to case.

To begin with the most counter-intuitive point, in an era preoccupied with extirpating heresy, texts about goddesses offered writers with or without credentials a safe space to say virtually anything they wished about God, under cover of *fabula*, without fear of prosecution. Writing about the Trinity, on the other hand, was risky even for professionals. Several innovative philosophical theologians—Peter Abelard, William of Conches, Gilbert Porreta—were tarred with the brush of Trinitarian heresy in the mid-twelfth century, at the very time that Bernard Silvestris was ascribing the creation of the world to goddesses in his *Cosmographia*. Unscathed and fearing no taint of heresy, he even tossed a compliment to the reigning pope, Eugene III, from the heart of his cosmological epic. Alan of Lille, who followed in Bernard's footsteps with two more goddess epics, was not only orthodox himself but a vehement foe of heresy, and the same may be said of Hildegard of Bingen, whose writings teem with goddess figures. It is a fascinating and seldom noted truth that the proliferation of goddesses in a medieval text did *not* render it heretical, nor did the ascription of goddess-like traits to the Virgin. To my knowledge, no medieval Christian was ever prosecuted for heresy on the charge of worshiping the feminine Divine except for the thirteenth-century Guglielmites, who also elected a female pope and claimed that the Holy Spirit had become incarnate in a woman.[102] This sect provides a useful but extreme limit case for the medieval tolerance of feminine deity: the Guglielmites were exterminated not because they regendered the Trinity, but because they posed a direct challenge to the Church's institutional authority.

By doctrinal decree, God could have only one Son, whose person and natures had been precisely defined by a series of ecumenical councils. To deify a male personification within a Christian frame of reference would have been to fall afoul of the Nicene Creed by introducing a rival god. Only by creating a carefully bounded alternate universe, the enclosed garden of *fin' amors*, could the God of Love be allowed his delimited yet dangerous sway.[103] But the daughters of God allowed more space to maneuver precisely because they did not compete with the Trinity. In other words, male God-language was taken more literally and therefore carefully regulated, while female God-language was accepted as figurative and granted some latitude. To take one example, the Old Testament already offered one goddess—Wisdom or Sapientia—who had been interpreted by the earliest Christians as a *figura* of Christ. One influential literary refraction of Wisdom appears at the end of Prudentius's *Psychomachia*, an epic poem of battle between Virtues and Vices. After the triumph of the good, Sapientia is enthroned in her temple, not only as queen of the Virtues, but as a direct figuration of the Son of God. The same theological status was readily extended to other goddess figures. As Carolynn Van Dyke remarks, "the representation of Christ as a personified abstraction is disturbing and even blasphemous unless we assume Christ to be the higher reality. And if *sapientia* is a name for Christ, perhaps all the virtues are ultimately versions of him."[104] Their relation may be one of identity, as with Suso's Eternal Wisdom, but it may also be one of sisterhood (the four daughters of God), filiation (Lady Reason), or marriage (Lady Poverty).

The relational terms "daughter" and "bride" proved useful because they implied not only a likeness to God and a nearness to him, but also a hierarchical subordination and thus a mediating role between God and humans. What allegory preferred to express through the filial relationship could also be asserted in the abstract philosophical language of participation. In identifying Lady Philosophy as "properly God," Christine de Pizan quoted Boethius's Platonic maxim that, "although by nature there is only one God, by participation there are many." Thus the just participate in justice, the wise in wisdom, the blessed in beatitude—but all these virtues are names for the deity, and if personified they become goddesses "by participation." Each goddess therefore represents a distinct way to approach and experience the Divine. To assert that Lady Reason is the daughter of God is to say that, by the diligent exercise of our reasoning powers, we participate in the divine nature; to assert that Lady Poverty is Christ's bride is to say that (only) those who embrace voluntary poverty are truly united with him. More audaciously, if Nature is a daughter of God then her chief responsibility, procreation, is indirectly a divine work in which humans partake through sexual activity. In these and many other possible ways, mortals may participate in the Godhead by way of the goddesses, who thus function as mediators in a Platonic hierarchy of being. Unlike Christ, technically "the only mediator between God and humans" (1 Tim. 2.5), goddesses could mediate a variety of relationships to the Divine that did not fall easily within the terms of atonement theology or the eschatological framework of Scripture.

The somewhat unfamiliar idea of goddesses as participated beings may be clarified by a look at their iconography. For instance, the beloved late medieval icon of the Virgin as *mater misericordiae*, sheltering a crowd of believers beneath her cloak (Figures 6.8, 6.11), represents her under a particular aspect as the embodiment of Mercy, a divine attribute. Those who participate in her mercy are visually incorporated into her image. The motif is illustrated just as vividly in the case of Mater Ecclesia, or Mother Church. Hildegard of Bingen's famous *Scivias* illuminations depict Ecclesia's children occupying the maternal spaces of her breast and womb, visibly participating in her body (Figure 1.7).[105] In traditional symbolism the Church not only represents the mystical body of Christ, but as a corporate person she is also the bride of Christ, and so is each of her individual members. Langland atypically reverses the allegorical figure of one god with many brides by presenting one goddess with many bridegrooms: his Lady Holy Church is married to Mercy, which is to say, "any man who is merciful" (B II.31–33). But his figure of the Church is, no less than Hildegard's, a participated goddess — even if the remainder of *Piers Plowman* demonstrates how imperfectly her members participate in her transcendent essence.

From a philosophical standpoint, the majority of allegorical goddesses personify the attributes of God, which may be defined according to one's particular brand of Platonism as divine names, ideas, primordial causes, theophanies, or energies (*virtutes*), and as universals in which believers participate to the degree that they are virtuous.[106] Every virtue, wrote Hildegard, is in essence "a luminous sphere from God gleaming in human action."[107] But to personify these virtues, to give the divine attributes body and voice,

Figure 1.7. Ecclesia with her children in her bosom. Hildegard of Bingen, *Scivias* II.5. Lost Rupertsberg ms., ca. 1165; facsimile 1927. Eibingen, Abtei St. Hildegard. Photo: Brepols.

is to make them accessible as mediators not only for the intellect but also for the imagination. One may "envision" them, enter into dialogue with them, take them as mothers or lovers, teachers or partners, mistresses or friends—and by means of these relationships encounter God. Such an encounter is not immediate or apophatic, but mediated, whether it occurs in an ecstatic vision or in the course of reading, contemplating an image, or composing a text. Even those goddesses that do not personify divine attributes still serve as mediators and enable the believer to participate in divinity. The most important of these exceptional "goddesses" are the Virgin and the Church. If Lady Wisdom is a feminine double for the Logos (Christ's divine nature), the personified Church is a feminine double for his mystical body (the extension of his human nature). To participate in God through this ubiquitous personification is to approach him in the most ordinary and accessible of ways, through the mediation of the Church's doctrine and sacraments. The Virgin Mary is very much a special case, but, as I will show in Chapter 6, the aim of late medieval devotion was not simply to honor her. Here, too, the goal was to participate, through the contemplation of texts and images, in Mary's own highly privileged familial relationship with God.

Mediation or participation in the Divine was certainly the main function of medieval goddesses, but by no means the only one. Among their secondary roles was one that seems indigenous to the medium of allegory: dramatizing internal conflict. As many scholars have observed, it is a rare psychological theory that can dispense with personification figures. Medieval writers personified Love and Reason, Conscience and Will, Virtues and Vices, but Freud had his id, ego, and superego and Jung his persona, shadow, and anima—all personifications that tend to assume quasi-independent lives. The "inner child" has emerged as a favorite character in contemporary pop psychology, while patients with multiple personality disorder act out the allegorizing impulse by turning their inner personifications into full-fledged characters. Psychologists of the most diverse schools, from Prudentius onward, have attempted to clarify inner conflicts by representing them as struggles for dominance among competing forces within the psyche. The medieval *locus classicus* for this type of allegory is Guillaume de Lorris's *Roman de la Rose*, where the Lady's vacillating moods of attraction and resistance to her lover are dramatized through the actions of Fair Welcome, Fear, Shame, Pity, Candor, and other personifications. In one of the more intriguing religious uses of allegory, the *Rose* strategy is applied to the mind of God: an inner conflict confronting the deity is exposed and resolved through a debate among goddesses.

Let us return to Robert Grosseteste's *Château d'Amour* and the four daughters of God. While Grosseteste's version of this allegory was not the first, it was by far the most influential.[108] In his version, a powerful king has one son and four daughters. The king does nothing without the help of his son, who knows all his counsel and shares in his rule, while each of the daughters has "diversely" received her own share of his wisdom, wealth, and power. Their names are Mercy, Truth, Justice, and Peace, and without them "the king could not govern his realm in peace or judge it righteously."[109] Trouble arises when a serf who has committed a grave offense against his lord is thrown into prison and tortured by his enemies, who will accept no ransom. Mercy pleads for the wretched captive's release, but Truth points out that, if he is freed, the king's power will no longer be respected and no transgressor will be deterred from crime. Justice seconds Truth, arguing that the prisoner fully deserves his fate. But Peace, offended that no one has sought her counsel, threatens to flee the realm if her sisters do not cease quarreling. Each sister appeals to the king by her own birthright—Mercy reminding him that he is king of humility and pity, Truth that he never swerves from the truth, Justice that he is righteous in all his judgments, and Peace that he is prince of peace. The king himself does not respond to these pleas, but his son does, promising to satisfy each sister's claim:

Misericorde merci crie,
Primerement serra oïe.
Trestut sun voleir ferai,
A Verité l'acorderai.
Del serf prendrai la vesteüre
En verité e en dreiture;
Sustendrai le jugement
E kant ke a Justise apent,
E Pès en terre frai crïer,
E Justice e Pès baiser.
E ensi finerai la guerre
E sauverai ta gent en terre. (445–56)

Mercy cries out for mercy:
she will be heard first of all.
I will do all her will
And reconcile it with Truth.
I will put on the serf's clothing
In truth and righteousness;
I will endure the judgment
And all that belongs to Justice,

And I will proclaim Peace on earth
And cause Justice and Peace to kiss.
And thus I will end the war
And save your people on earth.

In this way the poet-theologian works out the dynamics of Anselmian atonement theology and allows God to preserve all his attributes intact, giving truth and justice their due even as he shows mercy to fallen man and restores peace between heaven and earth. "Mercy and Truth have met together; Justice and Peace have kissed each other" (Psalm 84.11). The poem does not end here, but continues with Christ's incarnation in the Virgin's body, the "castle of love." Well into the sixteenth century, artists would continue to depict the four daughters of God in connection with the Annunciation (Figure 1.8) and even the Crucifixion (Figure 4.3). It is striking, though, that Grosseteste concludes his allegory of the four daughters with a cautionary gloss on the Trinity:

Cil ki cest ensample entent
Poet bien veer apertement,
Ke iceste signifiance
Est en Deu une puissance.
De Deu le pere est tute riens,
Par Deu le fiz sunt fet tuz biens,
E en Deu le Seint Espiriz
Est tute rien acompliz,
Un Deu sanz devision
Une sustance e plus non. (457–66)

Anyone who attends to this *exemplum*
Can see well and plainly
That its significance
Refers to one power in God.
From God the Father come all things,
Through God the Son all goods are made,
And in God the Holy Spirit
All things are accomplished:
One God without division,
One substance and not more.

The *signifiance* Grosseteste assigns to his allegory seems rather to contradict it, for the fable posits not a three-personed God but one who is father of five children; it tells of division among them rather than unity; and, although it gives a starring role to God the Son, it has none for the Holy

Figure 1.8. Annunciation with the four daughters of God. Book of Hours, Touraine, ca. 1473–80. New York, Pierpont Morgan Library, M. 73, f. 7. By permission, the Pierpont Morgan Library. Photo: David A. Loggie.

Spirit. Thus the gloss carefully closes the tantalizing prospect that the fable of goddesses had opened: namely, that man's fall posed a genuine conundrum for God, which he resolved by personifying and dramatizing the rival claims just as a mortal might have done. If Grosseteste was so concerned to promote belief in the Trinity, one might ask why he didn't simply imagine a conversation among the three Persons instead of introducing the fictional four daughters. But to have done so might have seemed blasphemous; even Milton achieved dubious results with that strategy. In this case, goddess allegory made it possible for the writer not just to express, but even to think theological thoughts of a kind the scholastic framework rendered unthinkable. Such liberties could be justified by an appeal to the text's lay audience, for in a Latin prologue to his work Grosseteste writes:

although the romance language has no savor of sweetness for clerics, yet this little work is appropriate for laypeople who understand less, because the prudent person who knows how to press honey from the rock and oil from the hardest stone (Deut. 32.13) will find a text full of heavenly sweetness containing all the articles of the faith, concerning both Christ's divinity and his humanity.[110]

The apologia may remind us of those bystanders in the *Sacrum commercium* who ask Francis to tell of his love for Lady Poverty in their own language. Grosseteste, a great admirer of the Franciscans, testifies to a pastoral concern for the laity that led (or at any rate permitted) him to follow the vernacular tongue and a vernacular literary form down fresh theological paths. A generation later, Jeun de Meun would go much further, allowing two of God's most prestigious daughters—Lady Nature and Lady Reason— not only to disagree, but to reach an embarrassing deadlock. That story, however, belongs to Chapter 3.

Finally, we must inquire about the gendered relationships between allegorical goddesses and their authors. When a goddess figure appears in the work of a female writer, we assume, usually with justice, that one of her roles is to legitimize the writer's authority. This is most obviously the case with Christine de Pizan, but it also holds true for Hildegard, Mechthild of Magdeburg, Marguerite Porete, and others.[111] Yet the same goddesses, appearing in the work of male writers, may lead the postmodern reader to suspect precisely what Gordon Teskey has theorized—an attempt to mask patriarchal authority in a beneficent female guise. Certainly that phenomenon occurs: when Alan of Lille's beguiling Natura veers from her praise of procreative sex toward an endorsement of celibacy, it is hardly a woman's voice we hear. In other cases men may construct goddess figures in the interest of erotic spirituality, as with Suso's marriage to Eternal Wisdom, so as to pursue the same kind of heterosexual relationship with the Divine that bridal mysticism made available to women. No single explanation covers the multitude of possibilities that we find in the broad range of allegorical and visionary texts.

It is irresistible to ask, though almost impossible to tell, whether goddesses were used by writers of either sex in resistance to the androcentric idiom of official theology. Bluntly expressed, the question sounds and surely is anachronistic. No medieval writer explicitly made the argument (now current among feminist theologians) that a God who transcends sex and gender must be represented in both male and female guise.[112] Yet some theologians reflected quite thoughtfully on the gender of their God-language. Anselm of Canterbury, for instance, asks in the *Monologium* "whether it is more fitting to call [the divine Persons] Father and Son, or Mother and Daughter, considering that there is no distinction of sex in them."[113] Indeed, both divine persons are *spiritus* (a masculine noun), but both are also *veritas* and *sapientia* (feminine nouns). Although rejecting biological notions of God in principle, Anselm finally resolves the question solely on the basis of Aristotle's claim that the father is always the first principle of generation—and the offspring, in order to resemble the parent most closely, must be of the same gender. Thierry of Chartres, a friend and teacher of Bernard Silvestris, maintained in his commentary on Boethius's *De Trinitate* that one must use masculine language for God because (a) the masculine sex is worthier than the feminine; (b) the Trinity is an odd number, and according to Pythagoras all odd numbers are masculine; and (c) the male acts and does not suffer, while the female suffers but does not act.[114] But Thierry may eventually have changed his mind, for in a later gloss on the same text he remarks like Anselm that the divine Persons could just as well have been designated by the names of Mother, Daughter, and Gift (f. *donatio*), since the attributes they represent (power, wisdom, and goodness) are feminine nouns.[115] Perhaps the philosopher had been swayed by the compelling goddess language his student Bernard Silvestris deployed in the *Cosmographia*.

The question of God's gender also arose in the context of Jewish-Christian debate. Spanish Jews arguing with Martin of León (d. 1221) asked him why Christ is called "son" and not "daughter," given that Scripture represents the Wisdom of God as female. The name of "son," Martin replied lamely, is "more honorable."[116] Yet some schoolmen conceded that Christ could indeed have been born a woman, if God had so pleased.[117] Such comments, which could be multiplied, indicate that at least some medieval theologians thought expressly about the gender of their God-language and were able to entertain alternatives, even if they did not endorse them. In such a climate, it seems likely that religious writers who gave extensive play to the four daughters of God, or Frau Minne, or Dame Nature, were no less deliberate about their gendered images of the Divine than those who rejected such options.

To sum up, then, the medieval goddesses open, and thrive within, a comparatively safe space for the imaginative exploration of Christian faith. They express and permit a certain degree of self-awareness about the gendering of God-talk, and they mediate in diverse ways between God and mortals—as also between vision and doctrine, between clerical Latin and the vernaculars, between classical humanism and "modern" devotionalism, between the needs of the institutional Church and the liberty of its mystics and artists. In the case studies that follow, I will aim to demonstrate and nuance these propositions by looking in depth at three of the most interesting and versatile goddesses—Natura (Chapters 2–3), Lady Love in her many guises (Chapter 4), and Eternal Wisdom or Sapientia (Chapter 5)—as these figures appear in a variety of poems, visionary texts, artworks, and allegories. Chapter 6 examines the cult of the Virgin, the one purely human figure among so many personified abstractions yet the most potent goddess of them all. This chapter does not pretend to explore the whole of Marian piety, but investigates that little-studied aspect of it which most resembles the mediation of allegorical goddesses: Mary's familial relationship to the Trinity and the path of *imitatio Mariae* by which her devotees hoped to participate in the intimate life of God.

Whereas other goddesses might have served our purpose equally well, the choice of these four is not altogether arbitrary. The chapters are arranged in rough chronological order insofar as their material permits. Thus Chapter 2 discusses twelfth-century texts, Chapters 3 and 4 center on the thirteenth century, and Chapter 5 on the fourteenth, while Chapter 6 examines the goddess-like exaltation of the Virgin through the eve of the Reformation. Readers will also notice a theological progression of sorts, from the periphery toward the very center of Catholic belief. For our subject is not simply "goddesses" but "God and the goddesses," with an emphasis on the links between medieval Christendom's "real" God and the figures of female sacrality that surrounded his throne. With this agenda, it makes sense to begin with the clearly extra-biblical daughter of God, Natura, and proceed by slow degrees to the divinized woman who is not only God's daughter, but also his mother, sister, and bride. In tracing the literary and iconographic careers of these goddesses, we bring to light a current of piety that was unofficial, but by no means marginal; undogmatic, but hardly unorthodox. For, under cover of *fabula*, the goddesses severally and collectively altered the face of Christendom's God.

Natura (I): Nature and Nature's God

Not in entire forgetfulness,
  And not in utter nakedness,
But trailing clouds of glory do we come
  From God, who is our home:
Heaven lies about us in our infancy! . . .
The Youth, who daily farther from the east
  Must travel, still is Nature's Priest . . .

— WILLIAM WORDSWORTH, "ODE: INTIMATIONS
    OF IMMORTALITY" (1807)

Man . . . trusted God was love indeed,
  And love Creation's final law—
  Though Nature, red in tooth and claw
With ravine, shrieked against his creed—

— ALFRED, LORD TENNYSON,
    "IN MEMORIAM" LVI (1850)

And for all this, Nature is never spent;
  There lives the dearest freshness deep down things;
And though the last lights off the black West went
  Oh, morning, at the brown brink eastward, springs—
Because the Holy Ghost over the bent
  World broods with warm breast and with ah! bright wings.

— GERARD MANLEY HOPKINS,
    "GOD'S GRANDEUR" (1895)

DIVINIZED, DEMONIZED, FEMINIZED, NEUTRALIZED, Nature is with us still. Despite frequent rumors of her death, despite even the frontal assaults of postmodernism, it is safe to say that the idea of Nature is unlikely to disappear any time soon, even if she no longer confronts us as the spell-binding enchantress or the faith-sucking vampire of the nineteenth century. Whatever we might mean by that slippery concept, "nature," behind it lurks the almost equally protean personage "Nature." In fact, one might argue that the personification of Nature—the invention of the goddess—was in part responsible for "nature's" emergence as one of the foundational categories of Western thought.[1] At the very least, the two reached maturity together: poems and myths about Nature, artistic representations of her, and even hymns to her deity sprang up side by side with scholastic ideas about human nature, natural law, and natural sexuality.[2]

The birth of Natura, the most enduring of all medieval goddesses, can be precisely dated. She first appears on the literary scene full-grown in the *Cosmographia*, a Latin epic composed by Bernard Silvestris of Tours in the 1140s. Bernard dedicated the work to his teacher, Thierry of Chartres, who, with his fellow philosophers William of Conches and Peter Abelard, had recently come under attack for identifying the Platonic world soul, Natura's close relative, with the Holy Spirit. The more conservative theologians of the 1130s held the Platonic and Christian terms to be incommensurable, but these twelfth-century Platonists' conception of Nature was not far from what Gerard Manley Hopkins, a Jesuit priest, would suggest in his sonnet on "God's Grandeur." In fact, poets of the nineteenth century—the last great age of Nature's literary career—not infrequently echoed the ideas of their precursors in the twelfth century, the goddess's first great epoch. "Nature's Priest" was a poetic self-concept dear to Wordsworth's heart, but a character by that name first appears in Alan of Lille's *De planctu Naturae* (*The Complaint of Nature*), written in the 1160s as part sequel, part rebuttal to the *Cosmographia*. Had Wordsworth been able to read Alan's text, he would have been delighted to discover that Nature's priest is there called Genius and represented as a poet and artist. While none of these twelfth-century thinkers could have imagined Tennyson's "Nature, red in tooth and claw"—an anguished response to the discovery of fossils and the extinction of species—they did use goddess mythology to explore the conflict, even then, between biblical literalism and cutting-edge scientific thought.

In this and the following chapter, I will analyze some of the most influential and provocative medieval texts to feature the goddess Natura. These include the epic of Bernard Silvestris; Alan of Lille's *Complaint of Nature* and its sequel, the *Anticlaudianus*; a twelfth-century debate poem known as "The Dispute Between Ganymede and Helen"; Jean de Meun's portion of *Le Roman de la Rose*; the thirteenth-century romance of *Silence*, ascribed to Heldris of Cornwall; Chaucer's *Parlement of Fowles*; and two allegories by Christine de Pizan, *Le Livre de la mutacion de Fortune* (*Book of the Mutation of Fortune*) and *Lavision-Christine* (*Christine's Vision*). This list is by no means exhaustive, and with the exception of Chaucer it includes only works composed in northern France, Natura's heartland, although the goddess's fame spread much further afield. I do not aim at a comprehensive reading of these rich, often lengthy texts, nor do I intend to produce a new study of sources and influences—although I will make use of the excellent ones that already exist. My goal is rather to chart the shifting uses and affiliations of the goddess, the company she keeps, the positions she adopts and opposes. For, although constancy is among the values Nature most frequently champions, her own meaning is anything but constant.

Tempting as it is to let these meanings emerge "naturally" in the course of analysis, a short précis will clarify the thread of my argument. We will see that Natura first emerges as a mediatrix between God and the world, or, in more strictly Platonic terms, between formless Matter and eternal Mind. Her intervention sets the cosmogony in motion, and her perpetual labor assures the orderly process of *creatio continua* through procreation. Although Natura's domain embraces the whole of the cosmos, her activity is often restricted to what medievals called the sublunary world, what we now call the biosphere. As the goddess of biological life, and specifically of sexuality and reproduction, Nature bestows a certain autonomy on this realm, representing ethical values geared toward the continuation of life rather than ascetic discipline. By extension, she authorizes the scientific and philosophical study of "nature": *physici* under her aegis may investigate the regular, if still mysterious and awesome, workings of a cosmos freed from arbitrary divine interventions. Yet Natura remains God's daughter, though medieval authors disagreed as to how fully she is initiated into her Father's secrets. Moreover, she is a modest divinity who like Diana cannot bear profane eyes to see her naked. Her fondness for veils and coverings extends from the mysteries of physical reality to those of language: the trope of her modesty would animate numerous defenses of myth, metaphor, and figurative speech in the pursuit of truth.[3]

Because her chief concern is the production of bodies, Natura is linked from the start with sexual behavior. "Natural" sexuality, as one would expect, turns out to be heterosexual and fertile—yet problems emerge almost immediately in the definition of Nature's way. Since she is goddess of the birds and the bees as well as humans, is natural sexuality to be modeled on animal behavior in all its observable variety? Or, conversely, do men and women behave more "naturally" when they do what is distinctively human, since human nature is superior to that of beasts? If homosexuality is "unnatural," as Alan of Lille's Natura proclaims in no uncertain terms, then what about celibacy? What about blithe promiscuity, or gender-bending, or the artful refinements of *fin' amors*? Each of these issues is addressed by or through Natura: one of her favorite habitats turns out to be ethical discourse about sex and gender, and in text after text she stakes out her position as goddess of the normative. Just what *is* normative, however, depends on what is currently being defined as non-normative, for Nature stands over against a variety of Others. Her opposite numbers in medieval literature, diverse as they are, can be reduced to three broad categories: the Supernatural, the Unnatural, and the Cultural.

In this chapter I consider the questions opened by Natura in twelfth-century texts, especially the delimitation of her creativity and dominion vis-à-vis God's and the consequent negotiation between two emerging discourses that later generations would call "natural theology" and "revealed theology." In the Latin epics of Bernard Silvestris and Alan of Lille, Nature as an instrument of God's creative power is set primarily over against the Super-natural, although Alan also opposes her to the Unnatural (homosexuality) and the Cultural (the arts and sciences, with the technologies they support). Together, these three works can be read as a mythical and theological trilogy featuring the *Cosmographia* as an epic of creation, *De planctu Naturae* as a diatribe on the fall, and its sequel, the *Anticlaudianus*, as an epic of redemption. But Natura is not the only goddess to appear in these texts, and her meaning cannot be understood apart from her place within the whole mythic cosmology elaborated by twelfth-century Platonists.[4] This problematic will lead us to explore the reasons Bernard Silvestris and Alan of Lille turned to goddess-language in the first place, as either an alternative or a complement to the rising tide of scholasticism.

Nature's roles as creatrix and *vicaria Dei* would set the stage for her part in constructing what is now stigmatized as "normative heterosexuality," the topic of Chapter 3. The *dramatis personae* surrounding Nature in debates over sexuality include Venus, Cupid, Hymen, the "priest" Genius, and Lady Reason, who is sometimes Nature's ally and sometimes her enemy. Insepa-rable from sex is the question of gender, so in Chapter 3 I will also examine texts that set the Natural over against the Cultural, thereby questioning the malleability of gender roles and social conventions. Heldris of Cornwall in *Silence* establishes a running debate between two goddesses, Nature and Nur-ture, who disagree vehemently about the hero/ine's cross-dressing. Christine de Pizan opposes Nature to Fortune in a comparable debate over her own situation, when after widowhood she finds herself metaphorically changed into a man in order to assume the male roles of writer and royal counselor. Finally, Chaucer in *The Parlement of Fowles* sets Nature in a typically ambigu-ous situation: on the one hand the goddess must personify the cheerful, amorous, and unproblematic fertility of "nature" over against the barrenness and hyper-sophistication of courtly love, while on the other she seeks to naturalize the refinements of aristocratic courtship in the face of earthy, common-sensical protests from the hoi polloi.

The Birth of Nature: Bernard Silvestris's *Cosmographia*

Natura's first recorded literary act is to complain. Through much of her history, in fact, she will be a complaining goddess, discontent with the status quo of things and determined to change it. Among the classical poets who personified Nature, foreshadowing the more robust goddess of the Middle Ages, the one who most nearly anticipated her later role was Claudian. In his epic *De raptu Proserpinae* (*The Abduction of Persephone*), the Roman poet brought Natura onstage as humanity's advocate before the gods. The Golden Age of Saturn has ended, yet savage men still wander in the woods like beasts until Natura comes to Jove, lamenting:

Nunc mihi cum magnis instat Natura querellis
humanum relevare genus, durumque tyrannum
inmitemque vocat regnataque saecula patri
commemorat parcumque Iovem se divite clamat . . .
"Quid mentem traxisse polo, quid profuit altum
erexisse caput, pecudum si more pererrant
avia, si frangunt communia pabula glandes?
Haecine vita iuvat silvestribus abdita lustris,
indiscreta feris?"[5]

Now Nature pesters me with great complaints
to lift up the human race: she calls me a harsh
and pitiless tyrant, recalls the world my father ruled,
cries out that Jove is stingy while she is rich . . .
"What use for men to have minds drawn from heaven,
to have lifted their heads on high, if they roam aimlessly
as sheep, and crack acorns for their common food?
Is this a pleasing life, hidden in forest lairs,
indistinct from beasts?"

Unimpressed by such rustic simplicity, Natura demands that humans be taught to live in accord with *human* nature—and Jove complies.

When Bernard Silvestris set out to compose his own, more ambitious celebration of cosmic order (and its discontents), he took not only part of his theme but also his distinctive sobriquet from Claudian's poem. *Silva* means wilderness or woodland—like the Arthurian forest of Broceliande, bristling with perils and errant knights—so that "Bernard Silvestris" in French would become "Bernardin li Sauvages."[6] But *silva* also means "primal matter," a technical term translating the Greek *hyle*, and Silva in this sense is the ambiguous heroine of the *Cosmographia*. Divided into two parts, the *Megacosmus* and *Microcosmus*, Bernard's prosimetrum[7] takes on the daunting task of making poetry from the cosmology of Plato's *Timaeus*.

Plato had posited three eternal principles: the changeless, immaterial Forms or Ideas; ever-changing and formless Matter (*hyle*); and a Demiurge who, being divine and thus free of envy, fashions the universe by creating a replica of the transcendent Forms from the crude material at hand. What Bernard Silvestris and his fellow twelfth-century Platonists inherited was a modified version of this system, for the Neoplatonists of antiquity, among them Plato's Latin translator Calcidius, had firmly anchored his free-floating Ideas within the divine mind (masculine *nous* in Greek but feminine *Noys* in Bernard's Latin).[8] No longer were these Ideas to be conceived as immaterial circles and triangles drifting through cosmic cyberspace; they had become the exemplars of all created beings living eternally in the Mind of God, which Christians identified with the second Person of the Trinity. This Neoplatonic cosmology was further refined by the great Carolingian philosopher, John Scotus Eriugena, in his *Periphyseon*, a difficult but seminal work that inspired a twelfth-century popularization by Honorius Augustodunesis, called the *Clavis physicae* or *Key to Science*. An early manuscript of the *Clavis* tidily illustrates the place of Aristotle's four types of causation within Eriugena's Neoplatonic cosmos (Figure 2.1). Above, the divine Ideas or primordial causes (Essentia, Vita, Sapientia, and so forth) cluster around Bonitas, that is, God as the efficient cause of the universe, identified with Plato's "Form of the Good." These Ideas are the formal causes of creation, whose feminine features show how easily they could be assimilated to the Virtues of moral allegory. In the second register, figures of masculine Time and feminine Space frame a many-eyed blob designated as "formless matter" (*hyle* or *silva*)—the material cause of creation. The four elements with their inhabitants (angels in the empyrean, birds in the air, fish in the water, humans and beasts on earth) fill the third register, which is an epitome of the created world ("Natura creata, non creans"). Finally, God as the final cause undergirds the whole creation, holding a pair of draperies as if he might, at any moment, ring down the curtain on the cosmic scene. A similar cosmology is found in Thierry of Chartres, who explained that the world has four causes: its efficient cause is God (the Father), its formal cause God's wisdom (the Son), its final cause his goodness (the Holy Spirit), and its material cause the four elements.[9]

Figure 2.1. Neoplatonic cosmology. Honorius Augustodunensis, *Clavis physicae*, twelfth century. Paris, Bibl. nat. lat. 6734, f. 3v. Photo: Bibliothèque Nationale de France, Paris.

The supreme deity in Bernard Silvestris's cosmology is called Tugaton (from Greek neuter *tagathon*, the Good), corresponding to Bonitas in Figure 2.1. But this "superessential" Godhead, like the Neoplatonic "One," is so transcendent as to have no interest in the project of creation. Mentioned only once, Tugaton dwells in inaccessible light beyond the cosmos, with a threefold radiance suggesting the Trinity. The highest God who speaks and acts in the poem—the Creator, in fact—is a goddess, whom Bernard designates interchangeably as Noys, Minerva, and Providentia. She plays the combined roles Plato had assigned to the Demiurge and the Forms, or the multiple roles Christian theology ascribed to Divine Wisdom. As Theodore Silverstein has shown, the figure of Noys is largely a coalescence of the biblical Sapientia, whom Christian exegetes had long since identified with Christ the Logos, and Minerva, the pagan goddess of wisdom, whom mythographers in their turn conflated with Sapientia.[10]

Silva, on the other hand, is both an authentically Platonic concept and an unforgettable character. Teeming and chaotic in her ceaseless flux, she is marked by an ominous "malignity" that no shaping hand can ever fully expunge—the Platonic equivalent of original sin[11]—and her shapeless visage is such as to frighten even her maker. Yet she is at the same time the inexhaustible womb of being, the mother of all, without whom the ideas of Noys would remain forever unmanifest. In this Timaean cosmogony there is no creation ex nihilo; there is only creation from Silva, pure possibility, who preexists the cosmos "in the spirit of eternal vivacity." As the *Megacosmus* begins, Silva appears filled with longing, for she is both superabundance and personified Lack:

Silva rigens, informe chaos, concretio pugnax,
Discolor Usie vultus, sibi dissona massa,
Turbida temperiem, formam rudis, hispida cultum
Optat, et a veteri cupiens exire tumultu,
Artifices numeros et musica vincla requirit. (*Meg.* I.18–22)[12]

Silva, stiff-limbed agglomeration of chaos,
iridescent face of being, inharmonious mass,
troubled, desires balance—she who is rough,
dishevelled, longs for beauty, longs to free
herself from the primeval tumult, longs
for shaping numbers and for music's chains.

Silva, however, is in no position to voice her own yearning, so for this purpose Bernard introduces Natura. Just as Claudian's Nature had complained to Jove about the bestial crudity of human life, Bernard's goddess complains to Noys about Silva's chaotic state:

Congeries informis adhuc, cum Silva teneret
Sub veteri confusa globo primordia rerum,
Visa deo Natura queri, mentemque profundam
Compellase Noym: "Vite viventis ymago,
Prima, Noys—deus—orta deo, substantia veri,
Consilii tenor eterni, michi vera Minerva:
Si sensu fortasse meo maiora capesso—
Mollius excudi Silvam, positoque veterno,
Posse superduci melioris imagine forme—
Huic operi nisi consentis, concepta relinquo. . . .
Quid prodest quod cuncta suo precesserit ortu
Silva parens, si lucis eget, si noctis habundat,
Perfecto descisa suo, si denique possit
Auctorem terrere suo male condita vultu? . . .
Pace tua, Nois alma, loquar: Pulcherrima cum sis,
Informi nudaque tibi regnatur in aula
Regnum, Silva, tuum; vetus et gravis ipsa videris—
Ut quid ab eterno comitata Carentia Silvam?
Ornatu specieque superveniente recedat!" (*Meg.* I.1–10, 28–31, 55–59)

While Silva, still a shapeless bulk, was keeping
primordial elements mazed in the age-old mire,
Nature was seen lamenting before God: she summoned
the profound Mind: "Image of living life,
divine Mind, God's first-born, ground of all truth,
substance of the eternal plan, my true Minerva—
tell me, do I grasp at things beyond my sense:
can Silva not be wrought more gracefully,
cast off her torpor, win a fairer shape?
Do you approve this task? If not, I am silent. . . .
What good to fecund Silva that she rose
before all other things, if she lacks light,
if she abounds only in night, cut off
from her perfection, if she terrifies
even her creator by her ugliness? . . .
Forgive me, gentle Mind, but I must speak:
though you are most fair, your kingdom, Silva, is ruled
by a misshapen, naked court; you look
ancient and grave—why is Want Silva's lasting friend?
Let her draw back, as grace and beauty come!"

Bernard here asks us to imagine a metaphysical impossibility: pure Matter confronts pure Mind, the stuff of the still-uncreated world petitions its would-be Creator. Rarefied though it is, the scene is psychologically compelling because it envisions creation from the bottom up, inverting the familiar perspective of Genesis and the *Timaeus* itself. Not omniscient Mind but refractory Matter, the archetypal raw beginner, demands our identification and sympathy. Nature, strictly speaking, ought not to exist yet, and initially she is no more than the voice of Silva's desire. But we will soon learn that Silva herself is "Nature's most ancient countenance," while Nature in turn is hailed by Noys as "the blessed fruitfulness of my womb . . . the daughter of Providence."[13] In short, the three goddesses are intimately linked: "Just as Noys is God, but not all of God that there is, so Nature is Noys, but not all of Noys that there is; and finally, Silva is Nature, but not all of Nature that there is."[14] Philosophically, Natura bridges the absolute gap between form and matter; psychologically, she voices the deep need that drives each ineluctably toward the other.[15]

Yet Nature has no further role in the *Megacosmus* except to stand by in wonder as Noys fulfills her wishes. The goddess separates and purifies the four elements; purges Silva's "malignity" as best she can; produces the world-soul, Endelichia, and marries her to the infant cosmos; fashions the heavens with their angelic spirits and all-foretelling stars; and finally molds the landscapes of earth and populates them with herbs, beasts, fishes, and birds, catalogued in lyrical detail. At the end of the *Megacosmus*, when all but humankind has been fashioned, we learn that "Nature is the artisan who compounds bodies, the dwelling places of souls, out of the qualities and materials of the elements."[16] Yet we do not actually see her doing this.

In the *Microcosmus*, Noys decrees the creation of Man as the sequel to her cosmic labor, asking Natura to assist in the grand task by seeking out her sister goddesses, Urania and Physis. Urania, queen of the heavens, is to fashion man's celestial soul; Physis (Greek for *Natura*) is to form his body from the four elements; and Natura will bind the two together. Once again, we hear of this task but do not observe it. Much of the book recounts Nature's epic journey, which gives Urania an opportunity to instruct her in astrology as the two goddesses traverse the heavens and descend through the planetary spheres to earth, where at last they find Physis, the goddess of biology and medicine, deep in her studies in the Eden-like garden of "Gramision." Here the creation of man takes place as Urania's disquisition on the celestial realms is balanced by an elaborate account of the body and its organs, for it is only Physis whose creative work we are allowed to watch. Her construction of the first man culminates with the penis and testicles, which Bernard hymns in some extraordinary double-coded lines to which we shall return. After this climax, however, the text ends abruptly, leaving the animation of the newly created man to the reader's imagination.

Oddly, though Natura remains "onstage" from the beginning of the text to its end, she plays little role in the cosmogony that we actually witness, beyond the act of setting it in motion. It is true that she undertakes a heroic quest and performs labors indispensable to the work of Noys—but these are summarized rather than dramatized. Nor does Bernard report any of her speeches after her initial complaint. Through most of the text, then, Natura's role is to watch, listen, and marvel as she is instructed—first by Noys, then by Urania, finally by Physis. In short, she is the perfect student, a *diligens speculatrix* or "attentive observer" of the universe (*Micr.* 3.1). As Brian Stock observes, Natura's education guides the reader's own initiation into the secrets of heaven and earth; she represents "not only the regulatory forces in the universe but the spirit of rational inquiry into them."[17] Her role as a stand-in for the scientific inquirer is especially marked at two points in Urania's discourse. As the two goddesses embark on their descent from the highest point of the firmament to the "dank impurity" of earth, Urania prophesies man's high destiny:

"Corpore iam posito congnata redibit ad astra,
    Additus in numero superum deus.
Sic erit, adde fidem: mea vox plenissima veri,
    Sidera mentiri nec enim licet.
I, Natura—sequar, nec enim vagus incidet error,
    Si directa tuis via ductibus." (*Micr.* 4.49–54)

"Once he has cast off the body, he will return to the stars
    as a native, a god among gods.
So shall it be, believe it! My voice is filled with truth,
    for stars are not allowed to lie.
Go, Nature! I will follow. For none can fall into error
    if your guidance directs the way."

The exhortation is at once spiritually consoling and intellectually bracing. On the one hand, Nature descends as all souls must, compelled to leave their bright natal stars awhile for dimmer climes, yet she (and we) need not fear. In the great cosmological process—Platonic rather than biblical—emanation will be crowned by triumphant return. On the other hand, wherever Natura goes, all may safely follow: it is Urania herself who pioneers the fearless researcher's mandate to "follow in Nature's footsteps."

The second key passage concludes Urania's long address. Her final poem begins with an exhortation to observe ("Perspice, mente sagax"), goes on to summarize her ambitious curriculum, and ends with the heights of philosophic wisdom:

"Quid morti licitum, que mortis causa, quis auctor,
    Alcius evolvens philosophando vide— . . .
Quid placeat per se, que sint aliunde petenda,
    Quid deceat, quid non, philosophando vide.
Iniustum iusto, falso discernere verum
    Sedula pervideas et ratione probes." (*Micr.* 8.37–38, 47–50)

"Rising higher in your philosophical quest, see
    what is allowed to death, what is its cause and who its author . . .
Learn by philosophy what is pleasing in itself, what should be sought
    from elsewhere, what is fitting and what not,
how to discern just from unjust, false from true:
    scrutinize all with care and let reason be the judge."

By this point Nature is indistinct from her fellow student, the reader, who has traversed the entire cosmos at her side, *philosophando* all the way.

Critics have often remarked on the tension between philosophical optimism and pessimism in the *Cosmographia*.[18] Such a tension is of course endemic to Platonism. Urania may declare with ringing confidence that the spirit will return to its native star, "a god among gods," yet as Natura roams the skies she comes upon a troupe of unborn souls weeping bitterly because they must descend "from splendor into darkness, from heaven to the realm of Dis, from eternity into bodies."[19] Not surprisingly, then, Bernard's description of the human body itself is rife with ambivalence. Physis, Natura's sister and alter ego, recoils with anger as she realizes the difficulty of her task. When Noys gives her the blueprint for her work, the Book of Memory, Physis must scan the whole array of plant and animal species before she can at last make out "the image of man, faintly inscribed at the very end of the final page."[20] Moreover, she has to work with mere scraps and dregs of the elements left over from Noys's prior creation, and Silva's intractable evil undermines her labors time and again. Although the body is the workmanship of a skilled artisan and an image of the cosmos, it proves to be a much cruder copy of that masterpiece, prone to constant decay. Unlike the great world, the microcosm is the creature of an hour:

Influit ipsa sibi mundi natura, superstes,
    Permanet et fluxu pascitur usque suo:

Scilicet ad summam rerum iactura recurrit,
  Nec semel—ut possit sepe perire—perit.
Longe disparibus causis mutandus in horas,
  Effluit occiduo corpore totus homo.
Sic sibi deficiens, peregrinis indiget escis,
  Sudat in hoc vitam denichilatque dies. (*Micr.* 14.171–78)

The nature of the world flows back upon itself:
  it abides, a survivor, fed by its very flux.
What is lost returns again into the whole:
  That it may often perish, it never perishes wholly.
By far different causes man must be changed in time:
  The whole man flows forth when the body fails.
Insufficient to himself, he requires food from without:
  [This is the way he toils, and a day brings his life to nought.]
  [In this he exudes his life and annihilates the days.]

Like the flux of the cosmos, Bernard's language "whirls dizzingly about itself."[21] Only a double translation can do justice to the last line, with its ambiguous grammar; for this quatrain may be primarily about death but it is also, as Peter Dronke notes, about sex.[22] *Effluit* and *sudat* are both double entendres, for if a brief time annihilates human life, it is through generation that mortals achieve immortality and annihilate time. For this reason the creation of man culminates with those members that enable the microcosm, lacking the cyclic perfection of the cosmos, to renew itself:

Cum morte invicti pugnant, genialibus armis:
  Naturam reparant, perpetuantque genus.
Non mortale mori, non quod cadit esse caducum,
  Non a stirpe hominem deperiisse sinunt.
Militat adversus Lachesim sollersque renodat
  Mentula Parcarum fila resecta manu. . . .
Format et effingit sollers Natura liquorem,
  Ut simili genesis ore reducat avos. (*Micr.* 14.161–66, 169–70)

[The testicles] battle death, unvanquished, with genial arms:
  They restore Nature and perpetuate the race.
What is mortal does not die, what is fleeting cannot fail utterly
  Because of them: they will not let mankind wither at the root.
The clever phallus fights against Lachesis, and reties
  The threads cut short by the hand of Fate. . . .
Clever Nature forms and shapes the fluid, so that birth
  May bring the likeness of ancestors back.

Here at the end of the *Cosmographia*, Natura assumes her lasting role as goddess of sexuality. It will not quite do to claim, as E. R. Curtius did in 1948, that Bernard's is a wholly pagan work "bathed in the atmosphere of a fertility cult,"[23] yet Curtius's insight was truer than many recent critics have acknowledged. For, as in a fertility cult, true immortality belongs to the goddesses—Noys, Natura, Silva—with their boundlessly fecund wombs, while mortal man plays the role of dying and rising god. In the absence of any Eve, the poet's Adam seems almost to be Natura's own partner in generation. Bernard cements the bond by using the same adjective, *sollers*, for Nature and the penis. But nowhere in the text does he depict either a masculine god or a mortal woman.

At one point we do glimpse a Godhead beyond Noys: Urania and Natura pray briefly to Tugaton before beginning their descent. But, as Jean Jolivet has noted, Bernard scrupulously avoids personifying the supreme divinity by using epithets in all three grammatical genders: neuter Tugaton, but also masculine Father and feminine *Usia prima* (Primal Being). "Bernard presents us then with an absolute First Principle that transcends all distinction of sex, and a series of original figures that are exclusively feminine."[24] We might well ask what prompted our poet to this remarkable feminization of deity—a question that can be answered on many levels. Considering one goddess at a time, we may note that Silva is already female in the *Timaeus*, which speaks of primal matter as the "nurse of generation," and Natura, as we have seen, appears in Claudian and other classical poets.[25] Noys experienced a sex change at Bernard's hands under the influence of biblical wisdom literature and patristic exegesis, which had made Sapientia interchangeable with Christ. From a different perspective, Bernard's goddesses flesh out an analogy latent in all Neoplatonic systems: the metaphoric equivalence between Mind and Womb. If Noys represents the divine mind/womb as stable *container* of the Ideas, Natura is the womb that gives birth by releasing them into matter, which is in turn feminine as the mother (*mater/materia*) of all existent beings. Ultimately, as Claire Fanger observes, Bernard's theophanies must be feminine simply because they *are* theophanies. In Neoplatonic gender symbology, the feminine is the principle of visibility itself, as also of plurality and movement, while the masculine denotes the invisible and stable One who eludes representation.[26]

The *Cosmographia* stands at best at an oblique angle to Christianity. To be sure, it includes a few biblical allusions, but chiefly as historical asides. Among the many events foretold by the stars, Christ's birth can be read there, while the catalogue of creatures includes the fig Adam ate, the frankincense brought by the Magi, and so forth. But these allusions seem little more than decorative, and more tellingly the epic nowhere suggests any connection between Christ and Noys. Though several apologists have tried to defend Bernard's orthodoxy, his text expounds such problematic doctrines as strict astral determinism, the preexistence of the soul, and the possible eternity of matter.[27] Even more damaging may be the status of man, who is created in the image of the cosmos, not of God, and seems to be a distinctly inferior product. While the macrocosm is produced directly by Noys, the human being is the work of her deputies and thus presumably further from the divine. In a word, twelfth-century heresy hunters might have had a field day with the *Cosmographia*—yet they did not.

In the decade prior to 1147, when Bernard's epic was recited before Pope Eugene III, events had not gone well for ambitious philosopher-theologians with a Platonic bent. At the Council of Sens, Peter Abelard had been branded a heretic for the second time; the Cistercian William of St.-Thierry had launched a serious attack on William of Conches, compelled him to recant his views on the world soul, and forced him into early retirement; and the pope even then was en route to the heresy trial of Gilbert Porreta, who would in turn be condemned. Yet Bernard had the audacity to compliment Eugene by name in his opus, and, if we can believe the gloss in an early thirteenth-century manuscript, "this book was recited in France and captured his good-will."[28] Was the pope soft on heresy, then? Hardly. Rather, it was Bernard's goddess-language that saved him, for the goddesses stamped his work un-mistakably as *fabula*—"literature," we would now say—and "what philosophy could not do, poetry might."[29] Had Bernard Silvestris been teaching theology instead of grammar and rhetoric, or had he been rash enough to express his views in a prose treatise entitled *Theologia christiana* or *De sex dierum operi-bus*, his fate might have been less kind. But poets, through much of the Middle Ages, had license to proclaim with impunity ideas, however radical, that if voiced as formal theology could have provoked a swift, hostile response. Because of its unofficial status, mere literature might well be denounced (as Ovid so often was), but it was hardly worth the trouble of repressing.

Yet Bernard Silvestris was a most influential writer. The *Cosmographia* survives in about fifty manuscripts and was well known to Latin and ver-nacular writers, not only in France (Peter of Blois, Alan of Lille, Vincent of Beauvais, Richard de Fournival, Jean de Meun), but also in Spain (Peter of Compostela), Italy (Boccaccio), and Britain (Gerald of Wales, Alexander Nequam, Chaucer).[30] It was through Alan, however, that Natura found her most definitive way into Western consciousness.

Nature's Fall and Lament: *De planctu Naturae*

Bernard Silvestris had been famed as a rhetorician and poet as well as a Platonist, but Alan of Lille had an even greater intellectual range. Acclaimed by his admiring contemporaries as *doctor universalis*, Alan was both a distinguished master of the arts and a theologian profoundly concerned with the relationship between the "queen of sciences" and her handmaids.[31] He was also concerned with orthodoxy: aside from poems and sermons, his works include a number of practical preaching aids and a four-part polemical treatise against Cathars, Waldensians, Jews, and Muslims. In retirement he would become a monk at Cîteaux.[32] When the youthful Alan read the *Cosmographia*, he found in it a compelling myth, but a theological system that from his perspective left much to be desired. For Bernard's is an exclusively natural theology: he mentions Christ in passing as "exemplar speciemque dei" (*Meg*. 3.53), but never as Savior, and even if his mythic cosmogony can (with difficulty) be squared with Genesis, the *Cosmographia* leaves no room for the specifically Christian doctrines of free will, sin, grace, and redemption. "Silva's malignity" is a physical and metaphysical evil, not a moral one; insofar as the human microcosm is at odds with the cosmos, it is because of man's mortality, not his sin. These are some of the theological defects Alan sought to remedy when he wrote not one but two sequels to the great Platonist's oeuvre, adapting Bernard's "fabulous cosmogony" to more self-consciously Christian ends. Despite his greater concern with orthodoxy, however, Alan did not stray from Bernard's mythopoeic method: he too tells his story with goddesses, and Natura figures largely in both works.

For his dream vision *De planctu Naturae*, Alan adopted the same prosimetrum genre Bernard Silvestris had used. The narrator, a typically obtuse dreamer-poet, falls asleep in high dudgeon while brooding on human sexual perversity. Although he has been lamenting Natura's absence, he does not recognize the goddess when she appears to him. At first blush Alan's Nature seems even more majestic and powerful than Bernard's. She has absorbed the functions of Physis, Urania, and Endelichia, who no longer appear as separate figures, while the feminine Noys has given way to the masculine Creator. The goddess thus enjoys even greater prominence than in the *Cosmographia*, though Alan has replaced Bernard's female pantheon with a more predictably male-dominated one. Nature has God for her father and Genius for her son, lover, and priest, in a quasi-incestuous relationship that mimics the bond of Christ and Mary (see Chapter 6). Although she is God's hand-picked deputy (*vicaria*) in the work of procreation, she herself has a *subvicaria*, none other than Venus, who in turn has a husband (Hymen), a legitimate son (Cupid), an illicit lover (Antigamus), and a bastard son (Jocus). As this list of *dramatis personae* suggests, the argument of *De planctu* will revolve entirely around "correct" and "incorrect" uses of sexuality. Yet the abuse of sexuality is correlated throughout the text with the abuse of language and the arts, which in their decadent state can no longer lead fallen man back to harmony with Nature and Nature's God. This predicament is dramatized in the tissue of self-contradictions that have made *De planctu* into a tar baby for generations of critics. For Alan's text, with its baroque and fiendishly difficult style, exemplifies all the "unnatural" perversions of language it denounces, even as Natura implicates herself in man's sexual plight by first condemning, then inventing and recounting, myths of divine immorality.

Unlike Bernard Silvestris, who avoids physical description of his goddesses, Alan revels in it. His Natura is less "female" but more "feminine" than Bernard's: Alan rejects the womb imagery that permeates the *Cosmographia* and even represents his goddess of sexuality as a virgin—one of the many paradoxes in which *De planctu* abounds. Moreover, she is not only a *virgo* and a *puella* but a titillating one: "her lips, rising in gentle swell, challenged the recruits in Venus' army to kiss them," while her arms "seemed to call for embraces."[33] The narrator even remarks pornographically, at the end of his *descriptio*, that he judged the hidden parts of Natura's body to be still lovelier than those on display. What veils this desirable body is the universe itself, for, instead of traveling through the cosmos on an epic journey, Alan's Natura wears it on her robes. She herself is an epiphany of the created world, crowned with the stars (again like the Virgin Mary) and clothed in birds, fish, and beasts. Flowers and foliage, Alan speculates, are hidden from view on her underwear. Here, for the first time, we see the representation of "Nature" (the goddess) as a metonym of "nature" (the whole natural universe), which takes on a feminine body. But the goddess's tunic is rent at precisely the point where man is depicted, since he alone among all her creatures has dared to disobey her laws (*nature naturalia denaturare*).[34] This detail is borrowed from Boethius: Lady Philosophy's robe had been torn by squabbling philosophical sects, each vying for one piece of her garment and claiming to possess the whole truth, whereas Natura's robe has been dishonored by sexual heretics. Implicitly, male homosexuality is represented as not merely a rejection of human females, but a symbolic rape of the divine feminine: unnatural men "lay violent hands" on their own mother and compel her "to go like a harlot to a brothel."[35]

I shall return to the subject of homosexuality in Chapter 3, since in his polemic on this theme Alan was responding to a poet very different from Bernard Silvestris. Natura's ultimate decision to excommunicate sodomites cannot, in any case, be understood apart from her claim to preside over a "church" in the first place. It is here that Alan apparently goes furthest toward Christianizing the goddess of the *Cosmographia*. While his Natura is much more active and vocal than Bernard's, she is also more explicitly subordinate to God. One of her self-revelatory speeches corrects the older poet's reliance on the *Timaeus* with Genesis: God made the world by a decision of his sovereign will alone, "not by the help of pre-existing matter, not at the insistent urgings of any need."[36] Once he had done so, he designated Natura as his deputy to produce like from like in the unending labor of procreation. But let there be no confusion about their respective roles, Natura says in a prose manifesto:

With certainty I profess myself to be the humble disciple of the Supreme Master. . . . For his activity is simple, mine is manifold; his work is sufficient, mine deficient; his work is wonderful, mine mutable. . . . He is the Creator, I was created. . . . . He creates from nothing, I beg what I need from another. . . . You may know indeed that, with respect to divine power, my power is impotence, my effects defective, and my vigor but vileness.[37]

After comparing her own *creatio continua* unfavorably with divine *creatio ex nihilo*, Natura confesses another of her limitations. She bears children for death, but God grants them new birth to eternal life—and "I, Nature, am ignorant of the nature of this birth."[38] Because Nature understands nothing of grace, she must refer the spiritual seeker to a goddess far greater than she—Theology: "I walk around the earth like a brute beast, she marches in the hidden places of heaven."[39] With this demurral Alan posits a gulf between earth and heaven, nature and grace, natural science and revealed theology: fallen, lamenting Natura will now be like Eve, and sublime Theologia like Mary. Urania's bold challenge to researchers ("Go, Nature, I will follow!") can no longer stand, as it cannot be fitting for a celestial goddess to follow an earthly one. Instead, to leave absolutely no doubt about the proper hierarchy, Alan has Natura declare: "Consult the authority of the theological faculty, as you should give assent to their faithfulness rather than to the firmness of my arguments."[40] Who should know better than Nature herself if the project of natural theology is bankrupt? This teaching is consistent with what Alan professed in theological writings throughout his career. In his early summa *Quoniam homines*, he had described *naturalis philosophia* as the lowest branch of study, inferior to "subcelestial" and "supercelestial" theology, and in his late sermon "De clericis ad theologiam non accedentibus" ("On clerics who do not advance to the study of theology"), he would once again underline the obligation of the liberal arts and natural sciences to remember their humble rank as "handmaids of celestial philosophy."[41]

Throughout *De planctu*, Alan confers authority on Nature with one hand and withdraws it with the other. After the majesty of her initial appearance, for example, he mentions an unnamed man who guides her chariot, "inpotentiam sexus supplendo feminei" ("assisting the weakness of the female sex"), as if even a goddess could not function without masculine help.[42] Natura's exaggerated femininity seems to be a corollary of her subordination to God. But when the long-awaited Genius finally arrives in the last chapter, his relationship with her only deepens the puzzle of her status. Genius is certainly not God or a direct representative of God.[43] When she writes an epistle to summon him, Nature places her own name first, suggesting superiority; but she goes on address him as her "other self" (*sibi alteri*), suggesting equality.[44] We learn almost incidentally that he is both her lover and her son, since they have a daughter, Veritas, who "was not born of Aphrodite's promiscuous itch but . . . of the generative kiss of Nature and her son at the time when the eternal Idea greeted Hyle."[45] This surprising information, supplied near the end of the text, belatedly encodes much of the Neoplatonic metaphysics which Bernard Silvestris had elaborated at leisure in his *Megacosmus*.

Nature and Genius are linked by their ceaseless scribal activity. Natura, we are told near the beginning of *De planctu*, constantly "called up various images by drawing on slate tablets," but these images, unlike the creatures depicted on her clothes, quickly fade and vanish.[46] The permanent designs on her robe seem to represent species, while the ephemeral ones on her tablet are individuals: as in the *Cosmographia*, Nature continually "fights against Lachesis" and renews herself through procreation. Genius, conversely, has on his iridescent robes the "images of objects, lasting but a moment," while the figures he inscribes with his pen are more enduring.[47] These include both noble characters drawn with his right hand (Helen, Hercules, Ulysses, Plato) and disgraceful ones drawn with the left (Thersites, Paris, Sinon). The drawings of Genius suggest that, while he is partnered with Nature to impress the divine ideas upon matter, he also serves as a figure of Art. Alan signals the relationship between the two deities through a subtle distinction: Natura writes on slate tablets with a stylus, appropriate for rough drafts, while Genius uses a more expensive reed-pen and parchment whose preparation is meticulously described ("the skin of a dead animal, shorn of its hair by the razor's bite").[48] With these tools he immortalizes only characters made famous by their own or others' writing. Thus, when Genius acts at the behest of Nature to "separate the sons of abomination from the sacramental communion of our church,"[49] it is apparently the power of Art—not God—that excommunicates "everyone who veers from the legitimate approach to Venus." The anathema of Genius declares sodomites and all other sinners to be "degraded from Nature's grace," a paradoxical formula indeed, since Nature herself has previously confessed that she cannot understand divine grace.[50]

Alan's booby-trapped text offers yet more conundrums for the unwary reader. When Genius sketches immoral and scurrilous characters with his left hand, after his right has grown weary, the narrator says that he "strays from the path of orthography into limping pseudography," or false writing.[51] Earlier in *De planctu*, however, the same figure of speech is used to denounce homosexuals. Natura had instructed Venus that, in her sexual inscriptions, she was never to let the masculine "pen" deviate from the norm of her true orthography "into the byways of pseudography," that is, sexual irregularity.[52] Genius, then, is at least metaphorically guilty of the very sin he anathematizes.[53] Indeed, he appears to be much like those lying poets Natura had previously condemned for their immoral fictions. Even the goddess's own moral authority is not beyond question. One of Alan's most obvious contradictions lies in the fact that, immediately after Natura denounces poets who "rave about a plurality of gods" and their sinful liaisons, she tells her own myth of divine adultery.[54] Humanity has arrived at its present unhappy state, she claims, because her deputy Venus grew bored with arranging the same old sexual unions in the same old way. So, leaving her husband Hymen (the god of marriage), she began to wanton with Antigamus ("anti-marriage")[55] and produced a son, Jocus, who stands for all forms of barren and frivolous sexuality—including the courtly *joi* of the troubadours.[56] Yet how does it happen that Venus was deputized to control procreation in the first place? This was not God's doing: rather, Natura herself got bored and opted for a semi-monastic withdrawal to her serene palace in the heavens. On her own telling, even Nature could not keep her writing-pen on course if it were not continually guided by the finger of God, so how does she expect Venus to do so?[57]

In short, neither Genius nor Nature has an impeccable claim to the authority required to play church. Nor do they have the power to do anything more than ratify the status quo, for they can hold out neither eternal sanctions nor the possibility of redemption for sinners.[58] Although several Virtues follow in Natura's train (Chastity, Temperance, Generosity, and Humility, along with the spurned Hymen), she must acknowledge that they are helpless to resist the onslaughts of vice and on the verge of abandoning earth for heaven, just as Natura had done when she passed her tools down to the irresponsible Venus. None of these contradictions imply that Alan's Nature is ill-meaning or consciously deceptive, but they do suggest that the reader should not take her words at face value. Even though her "personality" is far more vividly delineated than that of her counterpart in the *Cosmographia*, her limits are also more clearly marked. Nature can recognize sin but not redeem it, and she is at least humble enough to acknowledge that her authority is inferior to that of God and the theologians.

One clue to Natura's status in *De planctu* can be drawn from Alan's theological dictionary, the *Distinctiones*, in which he lists eleven philosophical definitions for "nature." The last of these is most relevant: nature is "the power imparted to natural things of procreating like from like."[59] But in the tenth definition, Alan equates *natura* with *ratio naturalis* or natural law, citing Romans 2.14: the righteous Gentiles, though living without the law, naturally do what the law requires because it is written on their hearts. Earlier in his argument, however, Paul had notoriously denounced those who disobey natural law: because the pagans refused to recognize and glorify God as the author of nature, he "gave them up" to sexual relations *contra naturam* (Rom. 1.26–27). Homosexuality in this context is not so much a sin to be punished as a punishment for prior sin. Similarly, when Natura in *De planctu* excommunicates all sinners against natural law, her punishment only assures the continuation of the sin she is protesting. At the end of the text she and Genius are, in effect, no more than stand-ins for the cherubim of Genesis 3.24, barring the gates of Eden with their flaming swords.

Perhaps the clearest sign of Natura's "fallenness" lies in her language. Throughout *De planctu*, both Nature and the narrator purport to uphold the severest standards of classical rhetoric: all figures of speech are held suspect because they can so easily slip into *vitium* or stylistic vice, a symbol of sexual vice.[60] Thus Natura—figuratively speaking, of course—forbids Venus to use strong metaphors that might "alienate a predicate from its resisting subject," lest "cleverness be turned into crime, urbanity into crudeness, figures into flaws, and colorful speech turn off-color."[61] An austere, unadorned plain style is Nature's supposed ideal in matters rhetorical and sexual alike, since "the corruption of language by irresponsible poets makes it impossible to conceive of the proper place of sexuality within the divinely ordered cosmos."[62]

Yet, as this very example proclaims, *De planctu Naturae* may well boast the most pyrotechnic Latin composed by any rhetor of its pyrotechnic age. C. S. Lewis, who was no fan of Alan's "bizarre luxury," wrote of him that "there is nothing so cold, so disinterested, as the heart of a stylist."[63] Yet Alan could hardly have been unaware that, with every word Natura uttered, she virtually shouted to readers to "do as I say, not as I do." At one point she herself, with maddening inconsistency, refuses to couch her narrative in plain style, but says she must "gild shameful things with the golden trappings of shamefast words, and invest them with the varied colors of charming diction (*uenustorum dictorum*)"—punning conspicuously on *Venus*.[64] But if Natura resorts to euphemism, how will Venus be content with candor? Nothing in this labyrinthine lament is what it seems: "we have no mirror . . . but rather a *trompe l'oeil* tapestry, behind which there is something or someone hidden."[65]

Some critics have not implausibly guessed Alan's hidden agenda to be a critique of the Cathars.[66] These twelfth-century dualists not only rejected any connection between the natural and the moral order, but denounced the whole natural world and especially the human body as the works of an evil god, created to trap spirits that had fallen from heaven. Cathar perfects, like Catholic priests, took vows of celibacy, but, unlike Catholics, the heretics abhorred marriage and believed procreation to be the most heinous form of sexual activity, since it produced new bodies in which more souls would be imprisoned. In representing Natura as a benign goddess working under God's direction, then giving her speeches in praise of fertility and marriage, Alan might well have been aiming barbs at Cathar theology. Moreover, sodomy had already become a trope for heresy, while accusations of sexual irregularity were a staple of anti-heretical propaganda. Several Cathars had been burned at Cologne in the summer of 1163, probably around the time Alan began work on *De planctu*, so if he had intended such a polemic it might not have escaped his contemporaries' notice. We know from his later work that Alan was deeply troubled by the spread of heresy; he would write expressly against the Cathars near the end of the twelfth century.[67]

The trouble with this view is that there would have been no need for a *veiled* polemic against Cathar beliefs, nor would the web of contradictions enmeshing Alan's goddess have served the cause of anti-heretical argument. Rather than opposing heretics who gave Nature *less* than her due, Alan was more likely proposing a tactful corrective to Platonists who gave her more—including such masters as Bernard Silvestris, Thierry of Chartres, and William of Conches. Mark Jordan has persuasively argued that the inconsistencies of *De planctu* are not the result of authorial bungling:

Alan intends for these gaps in the cloth of his *integumentum* to show.[68] He intends that they suggest the limits of Nature as a guide in morals. Nature cannot provide a compelling argument against a vice that directly affects what most concerns her, the reproduction of bodies. She is too various and variable to yield or to enact convincing regulations. . . . The *Plaint of Nature* is not only a complaint against sexual sins, it is a complaint against Nature's failure to speak satisfactorily about those sins.[69]

In short, Nature is well-meaning, but morally helpless without "the authority of the theological faculty." On this reading, *De planctu* is a deliberately esoteric text that could be read with profit on two levels. The "simple"— assuming that any of them could navigate the sea of Alan's clotted prose— might take Natura's preaching against sexual and other sins at face value, while initiates would catch the deeper message of caution: one must look beyond Nature to Theology, beyond Ovidian and Platonic mythography to Scripture, to heal Nature's own fallenness.

Nikolaus Häring, Alan's most recent editor, identified 133 manuscripts of *De planctu Naturae* from every part of Europe. But the great majority of these are late; only a handful date from the twelfth and thirteenth centuries, and there are few early allusions to the text.[70] It seems that *De planctu* did not reach a wide audience until after Jean de Meun introduced Alan's Natura, together with her celebrated oxymoronic speech on love, into his *Roman de la Rose*.[71] Contemporary chronicles and epitaphs for Alan are much more likely to mention the *Anticlaudianus*, a second poetic allegory written circa 1182–83, which gained immediate popularity. This epic, though composed in hexameters rather than prosimetrum, is much closer to the spirit and theme of Bernard's *Cosmographia*. In it Alan retreats from the conservative mood of *De planctu* and asks some radical questions: Can Nature and Theology make common cause after all? Can Natura, the fallen creator, make amends for her misdeeds? Can she indeed create a *perfect* man, one who can vanquish the vices so prominent in *De planctu* and restore the lost Golden Age?

Nature as Redeemed Redeemer: *Anticlaudianus*

Alan's epic takes its full title, *Anticlaudianus de Antirufino*, from the same Claudian who had invented the figure of *Natura plangens*. The ancient poet had written a satire against one Rufinus, a hated politician, by presenting him as the epitome of all vices, so Alan declares that he will compose "against Claudian" by making his own hero a paragon of all virtues. His epic trumpets other prestigious debts as well, since our poet was not one to wear his erudition lightly. In the *Anticlaudianus* he meant to update Martianus Capella's *Marriage of Philology and Mercury*, a late antique textbook of the liberal arts framed by the allegory of a divine wedding and a celestial quest. Martianus had supplied the twelfth century with one of its cherished human- ist commonplaces, the notion of the seven arts as handmaids of Wisdom (Figure 2.2), and this topos provided Alan with the allegorical machinery

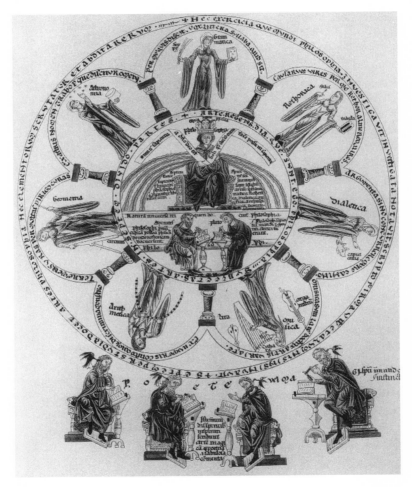

Figure 2.2. The seven liberal arts as handmaids of Philosophia. Herrad of Hohenbourg, *Hortus deliciarum*, ca. 1170 (reconstructed), f. 32r. By permission, the Warburg Institute. Photo: Richard Kieckhefer.

he needed to frame hundreds of lines of technical instruction, doubtless intended for classroom use. His interest in the myth of the Golden Age, which his hero is destined to restore, justified echoes of Virgil's Fourth Eclogue. And since the Perfect Man's flawless virtues could only be proven in conflict with the Vices, it was necessary to end the poem with a resumé of Prudentius's *Psychomachia*, an allegory of moral combat. More significant for our purpose, however, is Alan's return engagement with Bernard Silvestris. In *De planctu* he had "corrected" the earlier epic by highlighting Natura's limitations; in the *Anticlaudianus* he allows the goddess to make a fresh start and atone for her previous errors. Thus his new poem both recapitulates the action of the *Cosmographia* and, in another sense, takes up where Bernard left off. Bernard, as we have seen, had depicted the making of man's body but not his animation, which was supposed to be Natura's work. Alan shows us what might have been—or, presumably, what might yet be.

The plot of the poem, if not its diction, is fairly straightforward. Natura, still disgusted with human vice, has now repented her own share of responsibility for man's fallen estate, so she summons a council of the Virtues and announces her ambitious plan of amendment. Meeting in Nature's palace, a *locus amenus* modeled on Bernard's Gramision, the sisters enthusiastically support her proposal. Nature and the Virtues, pooling their resources, will create one perfect work, a divine man (*divinus homo*), who will be "human on the earth and divine among the stars."[72] Possessing all virtues, he will crush the vices and renew the lost harmonies of earth. All seems well until Wisdom—who is variously named Prudentia, Fronesis, and Sophia—points out that the proposed labor is beyond their power, since only God can make a soul. So the sisters designate Wisdom herself as their ambassador: she will ascend to heaven and ask God in person for the desired boon. After some modest demurrals, she assents. Her handmaids the seven arts construct a chariot for her, with Reason for charioteer and the five senses for horses. Rising through the celestial spheres, as Natura had done in the *Cosmographia*, Sophia marvels platonically at the planets and their influences, though not forgetting to add a Christian meditation on the "airy spirits," or demons, whose habitation she must also traverse.

Beyond the sphere of the fixed stars, Wisdom encounters trouble, for her charioteer can no longer control the horses: she has exceeded the scope of *philosophia naturalis*. But a radiant goddess comes to her rescue. Alan never names this "queen of heaven," but he gives numerous clues. Like Lady Philosophy, the queen holds a book in her right hand and a sceptre in her left. Her robe is woven by "the hand of God and the cunning right hand of Minerva,"

and she continually scrutinizes the *archana Dei*. Overawed, Prudentia prays
to her:

O regina poli, celi dea, filia summi
Artificis, facies nec enim diuina caducam
Te docet, aut nostri generis defflere litturam,
Quam probat esse deam uultus sceptrumque fatetur
Reginam natamque Deo tua gloria monstrat,
Cui superum sedes, celi uia, limes Olimpi,
Extramundanus orbis regioque Tonantis
Tota patet, soliumque Dei fatumque quod ultra est . . . (V, 178–85)

O Queen of the heights, goddess of heaven, daughter
of the Artist supreme—for your divine face teaches
that you are no mortal, nor do you lament our race's taint—
your countenance proves you a goddess, your sceptre
proclaims you queen, and your glory shows you are born of God:
To you the abode of the gods lies open, and the way of heaven,
the bounds of Olympus, the world beyond our world, the realm
of the Thunderer—and the throne of God and the fate beyond . . .

It is no wonder that some medieval commentators took this goddess
for Noys, but most agree that she is Theologia—the sublime deity to whom
Nature herself had deferred in *De planctu*.[73] She agrees to guide Wisdom on
the last stage of her journey, provided that she leaves Reason's chariot and
horses behind—all except one, the sense of Hearing through which faith
comes (Rom. 10.17).[74] Together the two goddesses behold the angelic choirs,
the saints, the blessed Virgin, and Christ himself (a problem to which we
shall return). Reaching the very throne of God, Wisdom swoons in ecstasy,
but is revived by Theology's sister, Faith, who gives her a mirror to temper
the excessive brightness of heaven's light. The mysteries of the Trinity are
unveiled at length—in regrettable contrast with Bernard Silvestris, who
had allowed Natura and Urania to pray only briefly before the mysterious
Tugaton. Perhaps Dante, who subsumed much of the *Anticlaudianus* in the
Paradiso,[75] learned reticence from Alan's prolixity. In any case, Wisdom at last
presents her prayer in the name of Natura, and God graciously consents.
Noys supplies an exemplar from which God fashions the perfect soul: it will
possess the wisdom of Judith, the patience of Job, the faith of Abraham, and
so forth.[76] She also anoints the fledgling soul with celestial dew to protect it
from hostile planetary influences on the return journey, until Natura receives
heaven's gift with wonder from the hands of Wisdom (Figure 2.3, top).
Noys's action can be read sacramentally as a figure of baptism, though a

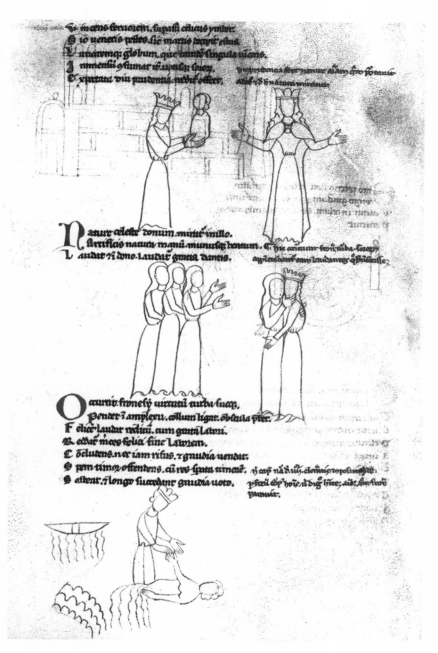

Figure 2.3. Natura receives the soul of the *novus homo* and fashions his body. Alan of Lille, *Anticlaudianus*. Verona, Biblioteca Capitolare ms. CCLI, f. 44v (mid-thirteenth century). By permission, Biblioteca Capitolare. Photo: Foto Roncaglia.

more humanistic reading is also possible in keeping with the maxim that "sapiens dominabitur astris" (the wise man dominates the stars). Alan thus corrects the astral determinism of the *Cosmographia*.

We next observe Nature fashioning the perfect body from the four elements, as Physis had done in the *Cosmographia* (Figure 2.3, bottom). It is once again beautiful and male ("another Adonis"), though Alan pays no special attention to its private parts. Next Concordia links body and soul with the bond of number, and the arts and virtues, like fairy godmothers, dower the newly created man with their gifts. The virtues Nature has assembled are conspicuously *courtois*: Fame, Favor, Youth, Laughter, Largesse, and *mesure* (Modestia) would seem more at home in a Garden of Love than an ethical summa.[77] In his panegyric on the New Man's gifts and accomplishments, Alan attempts something like the romance topos of the hero's glittering youth—with the difference that Tristan, for example, plays half a dozen instruments irresistibly, while the Perfect Man will have a flawless understanding of harmonic theory. The last of his benefactors is Nobility, the daughter of Fortune, whose lineage justifies one last digression—a description of Fortune's isle and the fickle goddess herself, who weeps with one eye while the other twinkles.

No sooner has the Divine Man sprung to life than the fury Allecto musters an army of vices to make war on the youth. These include the usual culprits (Discord, Envy, Violence, Perjury, Avarice), as well as a miscellaneous array of human miseries (Sickness, Sorrow, Old Age, Hunger, Labor, Ennui). In fact, the ensuing psychomachia has overtones of class warfare as our rich, well-born hero takes arms against Poverty and her proletarian cohort; Allecto even remarks that "Nature is not so plebeian as our assembly."[78] Poverty as a Vice figure anticipates Guillaume de Lorris (Figure 1.2) rather than St. Francis. But we are presumably to understand that the New Man is fighting a compassionate battle against the causes of suffering and need, rather than trampling a desperate pauper underfoot and grinding her face beneath his horse's hooves.[79] His victory is swift and total: among the last casualties is Venus, who has left Natura's employment to join the enemy camp. As the surviving Vices flee in disarray to Hades, a mere twenty lines suffice to establish the New Man's utopian rule, the Virtues' triumphant return to earth, and the restored Golden Age. In this messianic vision, Peace does more than beat swords into plowshares and spears into pruning-hooks: these tools are themselves superseded, for the earth spontaneously yields her increase while thornless roses bloom of their own accord.

Two related aspects of this audacious poem call for further attention. One is Natura's status vis-à-vis her allies and opposites; the other is the theological status of her masterpiece, the *divinus homo*. To begin with "Mother Nature," as Alan now calls her, we find that the *Anticlaudianus* is a much more optimistic work than *De planctu* or even the *Cosmographia*. In *De planctu* the goddess had wished irresponsibly to abandon the earth and make her home in the heavens, whereas in the epic she is, perhaps as a penance, unable to leave the sublunary realm. Prudentia must replace her as questing heroine, retracing the journey that had been Nature's in the *Cosmographia*. Alan also recapitulates some of his material on the goddess's inherent limitations. The paintings on her palace walls (*Anticlaudianus*, Book I), like the left- and right-handed sketches of Genius in *De planctu*, illustrate her moral and aesthetic failures as well as her successes. And Ratio, addressing the parliament of Virtues in Book II, echoes Natura's earlier distinction between her own flawed creativity and the flawless work of God. But where Natura in *De planctu* had been trapped in futile remorse and ambiguous attempts to justify herself, in the *Anticlaudianus* she is an active, energetic goddess whose repentance has issued in a brilliant and successful scheme of amendment. The Virtues are at her command, and she remains in their company from the beginning through the final victory of the Perfect Man. The moral ambivalence and linguistic playfulness that characterized her in *De planctu* have dissolved, making the tone relentlessly high-minded.

The position Alan assigned to Nature, vis-à-vis the Supernatural on one hand and the Cultural on the other, is beautifully summarized in a schematic illustration of the poem from circa 1420 (Figure 2.4). Below, Natura preaches to the Virtues (bottom right) while Prudentia lectures to the Liberal Arts (bottom left); above, Prudentia ascends through the planetary spheres in her chariot while Ratio drives the horses. A locked door in the inmost heaven marks the point beyond which reason, learning, and sense perception cannot go, yet Wisdom is able to press further with the guidance of Theologia and Fides until they arrive at the throne of God. While there is an obvious symmetry between the lower and upper registers, respectively depicting earth and heaven, a subtler symmetry divides the image vertically: on the left we see cultural and psychological powers (Wisdom, Reason, the senses, and the arts), while cosmic powers appear on the right. In fact, the throne of the goddess (*Natura naturata*) stands directly below that of God, who is designated *Natura naturans*.[80] The terms *naturata* and *naturans*, adapted from Eriugena, are roughly equivalent to *creata* and *creans*. God in this illustration, faithful to Alan's concept, is literally "super-natural" but he is also "Nature naturing"—the source of the uncreated creativity that is mediated and diffused through created nature. There is thus a clear demarcation of realms, but no fundamental rift such as we saw as in *De planctu*.

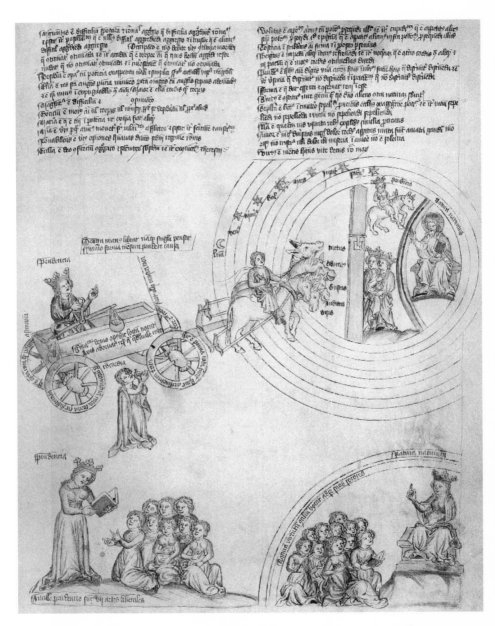

Figure 2.4. Prudentia's heavenly journey. *Anticlaudianus* illustration, southern Germany or Bohemia, ca. 1420. London, Wellcome Library, ms. 49, fol. 68r. Photo: Wellcome Library.

The harmony of God and Nature seems clearest from the remarkable fact that Nature, rather than God, engineers the scheme of salvation. Just as the idea of creation had been articulated by Natura in Bernard Silvestris, so here, addressing the Virtues, she articulates a plan of redemption.

Hoc in mente diu scriptum mihi sedit, ut omnes
Et simul instanter, caute, solerter ad unum
Desudemus opus, in quo tot munera fundat
Quelibet, ut post has dotes videatur egere,
Nostrorum crimen operum redimatur in uno,
Vnius probitas multorum crimina penset
Vnaque quamplures exterminet unda litturas.
Non terre fecem redolens, non materialis
Sed diuinus homo nostro molimine terras
Incolat et nostris donet solacia damnis,
Insideat celis animo, sed corpore terris:
In terris humanus erit, diuinus in astris.
Sic homo sicque deus fiet,[81] sic factus uterque
Quod neuter mediaque uia tutissimus ibit,
In quo nostra manus et munera nostra loquantur.
Sit speculum nobis, ut nos speculemur in illo
Que sit nostra fides, que nostra potencia . . . (I.228–44)

This plan has long been written in my mind:
Let us all labor together, urgently, with great care,
On a single work. Let each one lavish so many gifts
Upon it that she may afterward seem impoverished.
Let the reproach of our works be redeemed in one:
Let the integrity of one outweigh the crimes of many,
And a single flood cleanse a multitude of stains.
Let a divine man, not material, not reeking
Of earthly filth, dwell by our toil upon earth
And grant us consolation for our losses.
Let him live in the heavens in spirit, but on earth in the body;
On earth he will be human, among the stars divine.
Thus he will be a man in one way, a god in another,
And being both yet neither, he will go safely in the middle way.
Let our hand and our gifts speak plainly in him:
Let him be a mirror to us, that we may behold in him
What trust is ours, how far our power extends . . .

The echoes of atonement theology are unmistakable: one man's righteousness will purge the sins of many, one flood will wash away many stains, and a divine man will be the epitome and mirror of all virtues. But there are serious problems in regarding Natura's masterpiece as Christ, for Christ himself appears later in the poem, risen and glorified. At the culmination of Wisdom's celestial journey, she swoons upon seeing the Virgin Mary and her Son, but then, revived by the power of Faith, "marvels at the merit of that Virgin and adores the Child whom she bore" (VI.144–45). Alan has already narrated the Passion as a past event:

Hic est qui carnis intrans ergastula nostre,
Se pena uinxit ut uinctos solueret, eger
Factus ut egrotos sanaret, pauper ut ipsis
Pauperibus conferret opem, deffunctus ut ipse
Vita donaret deffunctos . . . (V.521–25)

This is he who broke into the prison of our flesh
And bound himself in pain to loose the bound:
He became sick to heal the sickly, poor
To make paupers rich, dead
To bring the dead to life . . .

It would be, at the very least, a serious lapse on Alan's part if Prudentia were to ask God for the soul of the still-unborn Christ when she has just seen him in glory. Moreover, it is difficult to understand the *novus homo* as Jesus, given the description of his gifts in Book VII: our hero is a wealthy nobleman, an accomplished scholar, and a courtly gentleman distinguished by moderation in all things—hardly the Christ of the Gospels. Nor does he win his victory through sickness, poverty, and death, as Alan says of Jesus, for the New Man's triumphant reign takes place here on this earth. In short, the *novus homo* is the Messiah Jesus failed to be—the Messiah of Virgil, perhaps, but certainly not of Matthew, Mark, Luke, and John.

What, then, did Alan, so jealous of Theology's prerogatives, intend in portraying his Perfect Man according to Nature? Probably not a panegyric for the young Philip Augustus, as some have argued.[82] Although a political subtext cannot be excluded, Alan was no John of Salisbury, and he never sought the ecclesiastical preferment a man of his gifts could surely have attained if he had wished to flatter. Yet his Perfect Man is indeed a kind of Philosopher-King, fulfilling the ideals of Platonic and Boethian humanism. He is "divine," not because he is God incarnate, but because he is fully and perfectly human, possessing every gift of Nature and Fortune—including free will and the determination to use it in the service of virtue. He is an embodiment of the universal *humanitas*, the Platonic idea of Man, as it might appear without original sin. Like the man of the *Cosmographia*, his soul is native to the stars, his body to the earth. Some critics have usefully compared him to the prelapsarian Adam, whose capacities were subject to lively debate among twelfth-century theologians. But unlike Adam, Alan's *novus homo* is born into an already fallen world to set it right. Perhaps the closest analogue medieval literature has to offer is a romance hero, Sir Galahad—the sinless savior-knight who achieves the Holy Grail, heals the languishing Fisher King, and makes the Waste Land fertile. Not coincidentally, *The Quest of the Holy Grail* was probably written by another Cistercian, about thirty years after the *Anticlaudianus,* as a belated fruit of twelfth-century humanism. Though Alan and the anonymous romancer did not inhabit the same stylistic universe, they set out with the same audacity to imagine a perfect man, Christlike but not Christ, who would combine the virtues of Christianity and secular *courtoisie* within an evocative semi-pagan setting, which is classical in the epic and Celtic in the *Quest.* "Theologically," writes G. R. Evans, "this is astonishing in its daring."[83] Indeed, Alan's daring did not go unappreciated by his contemporaries. But if his *Anticlaudianus* was destined to be widely read, glossed, and illustrated, it was also widely and swiftly misunderstood.

One of the most interesting recensions of the work is the *Ludus super Anticlaudianum* (ca. 1280), a kind of musical comedy version designed for performance. Its author, the canon Adam de la Bassée, reduced Alan's hexameters to simpler accentual verse and inserted 33 musical pieces.[84] In the *Ludus*, Alan's *novus homo* is interpreted as an *anima fidelis* whose victory over vices leads him to renounce the world and enter a monastery. Much more often, however, the epic was read in a christological sense. In fact, the earliest of Alan's many commentators, William of Auxerre (d. 1231), was the first to propose such a reading. According to William, the making of the *novus homo* by Nature and the Virtues is an allegory of the incarnation. An early manuscript from Prague suggests the same interpretation in its colophon: "Here ends the *Antirufinus* or *Anticlaudianus* of the venerable Alan, concerning the incarnation of Christ."[85] Such a reading is developed at greater length in the *Compendium Anticlaudiani*, a widely circulated Cistercian production of the thirteenth century. For this monastic author, Natura is no longer Alan's cosmic goddess, but "natura humana a deo naturata" (human nature as created by God). The celestial queen is not Theologia but Misericordia, for Wisdom's embassy implies that God has already had compassion on fallen humanity. Instead of commending the "most holy soul" of Christ into the hands of Prudentia—a procedure that may have seemed blasphemous to the writer—God promises to infuse it himself into the "most pure body" that Nature will prepare. In short, the critic explains, "if we wish to understand the formation of this new man, let the story be framed this way: all the Virtues entered the most blessed Virgin Mary and prepared her body and soul, with the cooperation of the Holy Spirit, for the conception of a new and most holy man."[86] The *Compendium* then concludes with a *historia Christi* that departs almost completely from Alan's text but touches on the Annunciation, Nativity, and miracles of Christ before proclaiming his victory over the hellish Furies, who have assembled to fight him "beneath the caps of Jews." The paraphrase achieves narrative consistency by omitting Prudentia's earlier vision of Mary and Jesus in heaven.

A Benedictine manuscript now at Schloss Pommersfelden (ca. 1322–58) illustrates the christological reading of Alan's epic in a remarkable pictorial cycle. The poem is illustrated in forty-eight scenes, arranged over four pages each containing twelve panels. On the last of these pages we see the following scenes, reading the columns from top to bottom beginning at the left (Figure 2.5):

1. Fronesis and Fides, with her mirror, appearing before the Trinity;
2. Fronesis making her prayer to God;
3. God summoning Noys to assist him in creating the perfect soul;
4. Noys fashioning the soul (*ydea*) on the model of biblical exemplars;
5. God exhorting Fronesis to return to earth with caution;
6. Fronesis and Ratio descending with their chariot;
7. Fronesis delivering the soul into the hands of Natura;
8. Natura, with Ratio, placing the *ydea* in the womb of the blessed Virgin;
9. Fronesis and Ratio kneeling before the Virgin and Child in a Nativity scene;
10. Megera inciting the Furies, shown as demons, against the adult Jesus;
11. Christ as a knight triumphing over Vices and Furies in armed combat;
12. Dedication: abbot Hermann of St. Peter's, Kastl, presents the book to St. Peter.

Interpretations such as those of the *Compendium* and the Pommersfelden artist are both more and less radical than the *Anticlaudianus* itself. They are more radical insofar as they transform Nature into the instigator and agent of what theologians, including Alan himself, had always seen as the most purely supernatural event in history. In fact, in his rhapsody on the incarnation, Alan remarks that here "Nature has no power, but all decrees are silent: her laws are stunned and take fright where the will of the supreme Architect alone prevails" (*Anticl.* VI.174–77).[87] Similarly, in the

Figure 2.5. Christological reading of the *Anticlaudianus*. Schloss Pommersfelden, Hs. 215, fol. 162v (ca. 1325–50). By permission, Kunstsammlungen Graf von Schönborn, Pommersfelden. Photo: Bildarchiv Foto Marburg.

poet's "Rithmus de incarnatione Domini," each of the seven liberal arts must in turn confess itself overthrown by the virgin birth: "In hac Verbi copula / Stupet omnis regula."[88] So to depict Natura impregnating Mary with the *ydea* of Christ (Fig. 2.5, panel 8) is, to say the least, a stunning reversal of normative Christian belief. On the other hand, the christological reading is less radical than Alan's poem insofar as it retreats from an unfamiliar concept to a familiar one, despite the problems entailed in such revision, in order to evade Alan's daring idea of a purely "natural" human perfection. The hero of the *Anticlaudianus* is a divine man but not an incarnate God; sinless but not miraculous; Nature's surpassing work, but not a work surpassing Nature. The poem's medieval reception indicates that, despite its popularity, this was an idea whose time had not yet come.

A Hildegardian Coda: Nature or Nature's God?

The three great monuments of twelfth-century Platonism, textually and philosophically linked as they are, present three distinct takes on a shared cosmology. These variations on a theme are most clearly seen in the poets' differing attitudes toward the relationship between Natura the goddess and *natura humana*. Bernard Silvestris, a purer Platonist than Alan of Lille, more nearly approaches the sublime: his *Cosmographia* conveys an electrifying sense of awe, first modelled by Natura herself as she contemplates the marvelous works of Noys. Nature observes herself in the making, so to speak, and we observe her observation. Thus she comes to personify not just the visible cosmos, but also the human quest to understand it, together with its causes—a quest that leads her from the throne of the superessential Good to the garden of making, Gramision. For Bernard Silvestris, natural theology *is* revealed theology: where Natura goes, Urania follows, and no place is off limits to her. But despite this intoxication with the joys of knowledge, there is also a tragic dimension to Bernard's cosmology. Just as the luminous serenity of the stars is offset by the maleficent pull of the planets, so man's celestial soul is weighed down by his mortality, which is the contagion of Silva inherent in his flesh. To combat this deathly force, however, Nature has provided the male body with "genial arms" so that her own fertile womb need never cease to bear. Thus the *Cosmographia* ultimately celebrates two divine elements in man, both of them closely linked to Natura: the mind's quest to know and the body's zest to beget. It is as if Bernard, knowing only Plato's *Timaeus*, had somehow managed to intuit the *Symposium* as well.

Alan of Lille was so taken with the *Cosmographia* that he responded to it not once but twice, teasing out the opposed possibilities inherent in his source and developing each separately in accord with his vision of orthodoxy. The Natura of *De planctu* is still a cosmic goddess, still responsible for generation, but hers is a fallen majesty. She has betrayed her God-given responsibility by placing sexuality in the hands of Venus—a figure for poetic license as well as moral licentiousness—and now, too late, she can only lament the tragic consequences of her lapse. For all its virtuosity, *De planctu Naturae* is in the end a work of profound pessimism. While Nature can expound natural law in her roundabout, tortuous way, she cannot understand divine grace, let alone bestow it, and her moral guidance is severely compromised by her own dereliction of duty. In the *Anticlaudianus*, on the other hand, Alan rehabilitated the goddess by ousting Venus and her retinue, restoring Nature to harmonious collaboration with God, and giving her the Virtues for inseparable companions. The joint masterpiece of Noys and Natura is a "divine man" perfect alike in learning, virtue, and courtliness—a specimen so dazzling that medieval commentators persisted, despite all evidence to the contrary, in reading him as Christ. Whether fallen or redeemed, however, Alan's Nature differs in significant ways from Bernard's. She is no longer a wisdom goddess (that role has fallen to Prudentia/Fronesis), and her dominion ends where that of Theology begins: a firm line separates the knowledge attainable through natural reason, sense perception, and the liberal arts from the revealed truth accessible only through faith. Moreover, no divine or heroic aura hovers around the work of procreation: Alan's metaphors link it rather with human craftsmanship, and border at best upon the comic.

Despite their differences, these three texts firmly established Natura's place in the medieval pantheon. As we will see in Chapter 3, she would soon become a flashpoint for the expression of assorted views on sexuality and gender. Even more fundamentally, however, the presence of "Nature" as a goddess secured the autonomy of "nature" as a realm of experience, whether sexual or scientific. That autonomy has now been so firmly established for so long that the goddess's career is almost played out. But in the twelfth century Natura did not serve so much to sacralize a realm of experience that would otherwise have been profane, as to displace that experience from the sphere of primary to what we might call secondary divinity. To see how radically the invention of Natura transformed "the symbolic cosmos of the twelfth century" (in Marie-Thérèse d'Alverny's words), we can do no better than to look at a text where we might reasonably expect to find her, but do not.

No twelfth-century thinker has been more widely celebrated for naturalism than Hildegard of Bingen—and rightly so. Yet in all her voluminous
works, rich though they are in goddess figures, Hildegard never once personified Natura. Her *Liber divinorum operum* (*Book of Divine Works*), a cosmological text contemporary with *De planctu Naturae*, opens instead with
this very "naturalistic" speech in the mouth of another goddess entirely:

I am the supreme and fiery force that kindled every living spark, and I breathed forth
no mortal thing—yet I discern them as they are. As I circled the whirling sphere with
my upper wings (that is, with wisdom), I ordered it rightly. And I am the fiery life of
the substance of God: I flame above the beauty of the fields; I shine in the waters; I
burn in the sun, the moon, and the stars. And, with the airy wind, I quicken all things
vitally by an unseen, all-sustaining life. For the air is alive in foliage and flowers; the
waters flow as if they lived; the sun too lives in its light; and when the moon wanes
it is rekindled by the light of the sun, as if it lived anew. The stars also glisten in their
light as if alive. . . . All these things are alive in their essence, nor are they found in
death; for I am Life. I also am Rationality. Mine is the blast of the resounding Word
through which all creatures came to be, and I breathed upon them all so that not one
of them is mortal in its kind; for I am Life. Indeed I am Life, whole and undivided—
not hewn from any stone, nor budded from branches, nor rooted in virile strength;
but all that is vital has its root in Me.[89]

The speaker of these words is Caritas, a dazzling winged figure whose
iconography associates her with the Trinity and more specifically with the
Holy Spirit. Hildegard in this passage is influenced less by Platonic than by
Stoic cosmology, mediated through Cicero's *De natura deorum*: the Stoic
intuition of God as all-pervading fiery force (*ignea vis*) or living fire (*ignis
vivens*) is central to the *Liber*. But her vision is also more biblical and "mystical" than that of Bernard Silvestris and Alan of Lille. For this living, fiery
force that courses through nature, that makes the four elements sparkle
with life and breathes divine spirit into all creation, is none other than God's
own being—not a "daughter of God" or subordinate power ordained by
God, and therefore not the goddess Natura. Caritas belongs instead to the
sphere of primary divinity: she is a direct and immediate manifestation of
God, for "Deus caritas est" (1 John 4.8). She is also a very precise representation of what Abelard and William of Conches had meant by identifying the
Holy Spirit as *anima mundi*—though Hildegard, writing in the 1160s, knew
better than to use a suspect term condemned in the 1130s.[90] As a good
Catholic, of course, she believed Caritas or the Holy Spirit, even under the
aspect of world soul, to be fully equal to God the Father and the Son, rather
than the third-ranking member (after "Tugaton" and Noys) in a Neoplatonic
hierarchy.

Even if the abbess of Bingen had known the *Cosmographia*, composed in distant France only twenty years earlier, it is unlikely that she would have adopted the figure of Natura. For her own cosmology, platonizing though it is in some respects, has no use for the supple theophanic gradations of Bernard Silvestris, much less for the sharp line that Alan would draw between the supercelestial realm of God and the sublunary world of Natura. Where Nature holds sway, God is by definition "the supernatural"; without her he is arch-natural, ubiquitous.[91] Hildegard, knowing nothing of the goddess Natura or of Nature as a separate sphere, is still innocent of supernaturalism. Her vision is one of radical immanence, even panentheism: all creatures exist in God, who is substantially present in them all. As we shall see in Chapters 4 and 5, other mystics who shared that perception would follow Hildegard in using Love or Wisdom, rather than Nature, as their goddess of choice.

In the meantime, however, Bernard and Alan succeeded remarkably well in establishing Natura's dominion within her own distinct realm. Once she had settled into cordial but rather distant relations with her heavenly Father, the goddess emerged as one of medieval literature's most fruitful and evocative means for exploring ethical questions related to sexuality and gender, and for articulating and testing ideas of the normative. After 1200, fine-tuning the relationship between Nature and Nature's God becomes a matter for the theologians; secular and vernacular poets who portray the goddess make a decisive turn away from cosmology toward the human world of gender, generation, and desire. They are interested less in Nature's metaphysical status than in the relationship of "natural" or instinctive behavior to the laws of reason on the one hand, and on the other, to the social norms that governed manhood, womanhood, and mating. It is to these secular texts that we turn our attention in Chapter 3.

3

Natura (II): Goddess of the Normative

SOME TIME IN THE LATTER HALF OF THE twelfth century an unknown poet, probably French, penned a naughty but delicious poem in sixty-seven rhyming quatrains. The "Altercatio Ganimedis et Helene" ("Dispute Between Ganymede and Helen") follows the then-popular conventions of both the dream vision and the debate poem.[1] One fine spring day, its narrator falls asleep beneath an olive tree and dreams of a meeting between Ganymede and Helen, each stunningly beautiful. After some small talk, the virginal but amorous Helen tries to seduce the boy. But Ganymede, not knowing the sexual role expected of him, presses against her "as if he wished to be passive." Disgusted, Helen pushes the "monster" away and "curses nature" on his account. The two enter into a heated argument and finally decide to present their case for the judgment of Nature and Reason. So they ride off to the palace of Jupiter, where they find Mother Nature "clothing Hyle with multifarious forms" as she weaves the pattern of life under Reason's guidance. Providence, "whom the Father of Nature bore from pure mind," announces the arrival of the young debaters. All the gods assemble, some on Helen's party and some on Ganymede's, barely able to restrain their desire as the gorgeous disputants take their places. "Jupiter shamelessly calls to Ganymede," but Nature takes the maiden's side. Helen opens the argument and the two debate for 33 stanzas, with more rancor than modesty, on the relative merits of gay love versus straight. In the end Ganymede falls silent when Helen asserts that sodomy is tantamount to child murder, for every "tear of Venus" shed between the legs of a boy represents "the loss of a human being." At this point Reason proclaims the boy conquered, Ganymede recants, and the converted Apollo declares that he has "come to [his] senses," while Jupiter is now aflame for his Juno. The gods join in banishing the "ancient heresy" as "Reason rejoices with the children of Nature." Ganymede asks for the hand of Helen in marriage. As the two are united in connubial bliss, the narrator awakens and declaims, "Let the Sodomites blush, let the Gomorrhans weep. Whoever is guilty of this deed, let him be converted. O God, should I ever do it, have mercy on me!" Or, according to another version of the line, "please look the other way."[2]

"Ganymede and Helen" and Nature's Grammar

"Ganymede and Helen" is one of the earliest texts to feature a personified Natura condemning homosexuality, whether or not the poet agreed with her. The poem had a wide if select clerical audience, circulating with the works of other twelfth-century Latin writers such as Hildebert of Lavardin, Serlo of Wilton, Matthew of Vendôme, Peter of Blois, Walter of Châtillon, and of course Alan of Lille.[3] "Ganymede's" relationship to *De planctu Naturae* is of particular interest, for the two poems share many verbal parallels and a few substantive arguments. Rolf Lenzen (the editor of "Ganymede") and earlier scholars thought the debate poem had been inspired by *De planctu*, but John Boswell saw Alan of Lille as the debtor, and Peter Dronke somewhat implausibly proposed Alan himself as author of the "Altercatio."[4] I will argue in favor of Boswell's position, proposing a date of composition for "Ganymede" in the 1150s. The poet's treatment of Natura, Hyle, and Providentia suggests a familiarity with Bernard's *Cosmographia*, as E. R. Curtius showed long ago,[5] while his off-handed use of grammatical metaphors to represent sexuality seems to have influenced Alan's much more serious, not to say labored, preoccupation with the same imagery.

Before the probably foregone conclusion of the debate, the disputants score some remarkable points. Helen's arguments are the more predictable. Ganymede's sport overturns the order of Nature, she claims; since he will never take a wife, he will not perpetuate his beauty—the same reasoning Shakespeare would adopt in his *Sonnets*. Moreover, sodomites are incapable of true love: beautiful boys only prostitute themselves for the money, and the old men who pay them are even worse. Only "natural" love is fruitful, as all animals know:

O quam felix amor est   in diverso sexu,
Cum mas fovet mutuo   feminam complexu!
Contrahuntur hic et hec   naturali flexu;
Aves, fere, pecora   gaudent isto nexu. (st. 33)

O how blessed is love   between the two sexes,
When male caresses female   in mutual embraces!
He and she are attracted   by their natural bent;
Birds, beasts, and livestock   take joy in this bond.

Ganymede is not at all fazed by Helen's argument, but responds:

> Non aves aut pecora   debet imitari
> Homo, cui datum est   ratiocinari;
> Rustici, qui pecudes   possunt appellari,
> Hii cum mulieribus   debent inquinari. (st. 34)

> Man need not imitate   birds or farm animals—
> For he has been given   the ability to reason.
> Let peasants, who   can be called brute beasts,
> Go defile themselves   with women!

Where Helen appeals to Nature, Ganymede appeals to class: the gods invented same-sex love, and the best and the brightest (*optimatibus*) enjoy it most (stanza 30). In fact, since the rulers and prelates are all enamored of boys, their Ganymedes have nothing to fear:

> Approbatis opus hoc   scimus approbatum:
> Nam, qui mundi regimen   tenent et primatum,
> Qui censores arguunt   mores et peccatum,
> Hii non spernunt pueri   femur levigatum. (st. 40)

> We know this act is approved   by men who deserve approval:
> For those who rule the world   and have the power
> To set themselves up as judges   of morality and sin—
> Such men do not resist   the smooth thighs of a boy.

The youth's taunt about clerical tastes is amply borne out by other twelfth-century evidence, ranging from moral denunciations to an epigram about a gay bishop who "out-ganymedes Ganymede," and is said to have banished married clergy from his diocese because he personally has no use for women.[6]

These excerpts from the "Altercatio" suggest the general tenor of debates about homosexuality in the later twelfth century. Appeals to animal behavior could backfire, as Helen discovers. Most animals are obviously not monogamous, but more to the point, there was no other ethical context in which clerics taught that rational humans should imitate irrational beasts. Boswell has shown that two contradictory ideas about "natural sexuality" seem to have taken hold among writers at about the same time: first, the notion that certain creatures—such as the hare, the hyena, and the weasel—were "innately" homosexual and therefore to be shunned, and second, the belief that homosexuality is "unnatural" because it does not occur at all among animals.[7] Alan of Lille alludes to both ideas in *De planctu*: although Natura protests indignantly that every species but man obeys her laws, her own robes display images of such sexually irregular beasts as the "hermaphrodite" bat, the polygamous ram, and the self-castrating beaver.[8] Helen's charge of male prostitution also bears on the disputed naturalness of homosexual relations: presumably, if the pleasure were mutual, money would not have to change hands. Ganymede does not deny Helen's accusation, but complacently acknowledges that sodomy can be a lucrative career path for boys like himself:

Odor lucri bonus est,   lucrum nemo vitat;
Nos, ut verum fatear,   precium invitat.
Hunc, qui vult ditescere,   ludum non dimittat!
Pueros hic evehit,   pueros hic ditat. (st. 42)

The smell of cash is good,   no one refuses it.
To tell the truth, the price   does tempt us.
Anyone who wants to earn money   should not forsake this sport!
This game advances boys,   it makes them rich.

Like Helen in the debate, Alan's Natura will also accuse pretty boys of prostituting themselves, "intoxicated with the thirst for money," and his narrator likewise denounces any man who "sells his sex for the love of gain."[9]

But the most interesting parallel between "Ganymede" and *De planctu* is a seemingly trivial yet far-reaching metaphor that favors the priority of "Ganymede." One of the boy's throwaway arguments on behalf of same-sex love is a grammatical analogy:

Impar omne dissidet,   recte par cum pari.
Eleganti copula   mas aptatur mari;
Si nescis: articulos   decet observari;
Hic et hic gramatice   debent copulari! (st. 36)

Odd couples never accord;   like should be paired with like.
Male is joined to male   in an elegant conjunction.
If you don't understand,   take note of their gender:
Grammatically speaking, "he"   ought to be joined to "him"!

Ganymede's point is a simple one, witty in part because it seems self-evident. In grammar, two masculines do agree, and a mixed pair creates a solecism. The satirists of the English Renaissance would play on the same conceit in their famous pamphlets against gender-bending, *Hic Mulier* and *Haec Vir*.[10] A similar grammatical trope occurs earlier in the "Altercatio," when Ganymede shows his ignorance of the male heterosexual role:

Sed ignorans Frigius   vicem predicati
Applicat se femine,   tanquam vellet pati. (st. 8)

But the Trojan youth,   not knowing the role of predicate,
Applies himself to the female   ' as if he wished to be passive.

The metaphor hinges on the suppressed term *subjectum*: the woman is tacitly
likened to a grammatical subject (*subjectum*) because her proper sexual position is to lie beneath (*subjecta*). Conversely, the man should play the role of
predicate or active verb; but Ganymede, the passive homosexual, is at best a
passive or deponent verb. As if to atone for this grammatical *vitium*, he later
produces his triumphant claim that a correct *copula* must link two articles of
the same gender.

A bit recherché, yet straightforward, these jests make sense in a humor-
ous debate written by and for clerics. Such grammatical jokes and figures, as
Jan Ziolkowski has shown, were not uncommon in twelfth-century Latin,
especially in satirical texts.[11] But when Alan of Lille took up his pen and
linked grammar to Nature, the intellectual and moral stakes of the argument
would rise considerably. *De planctu* opens with an anti-sodomy lament that
alludes to the "Altercatio," but parlays its simple witticisms into an elaborate
conceit:

In lacrimas risus, in luctus gaudia uerto . . .
Cum Venus in Venerem pugnans illos facit illas
Cumque sui magica deuirat arte uiros. . . .
Actiui generis sexus se turpiter horret
Sic in passiuum degenerare genus.
Femina uir factus sexus denigrat honorem,
Ars magice Veneris hermafroditat eum.
Predicat et subicit, fit duplex terminus idem.
Gramatice leges ampliat ille nimis.
Se negat esse uirum, Nature factus in arte[12]
Barbarus. Ars illi non placet, immo tropus.
Non tamen ista tropus poterit translatio dici.
In uicium melius ista figura cadit. (I.1, 5–6, 15–24)

I turn laughter into tears, joy into mourning . . .
When Venus, waging war on Venus, makes "hes" into "shes"
And unmans men with her magical art. . . .
The sex of the active gender is horrified at itself
So basely degenerating into the passive gender.
A man turned woman blackens the honor of his sex:
The witchcraft of Venus makes him a hermaphrodite.
He is both predicate and subject, a single ending becomes double:

He extends the laws of grammar too far!
He denies that he is a man, having become a barbarian
In Nature's art. He takes no pleasure in the art, only in a trope—
Yet this metaphor cannot even be called a trope.
Rather, such a figure falls into the category of vice.

In the "Altercatio," Nature had been present only as a silent judge of the debate; Ganymede's witticism about *hic et hic* did not directly concern her. But Alan will attempt throughout *De planctu* to counter the case for homosexuality by forging an alliance between grammar and Nature. At the outset, he makes a key move by identifying the *ars grammatica* as an *ars Nature*— not surprising since, as we have seen in the *Anticlaudianus*, he regarded all the liberal arts as protégées of Natura. Alan's sodomite has become a "barbarian," that is, hopelessly inept, in the wholesome, elementary art of sexual grammar. "Natural" usage no longer pleases him, for (much like the poet himself) he takes joy only in ornamental figures or metaphors so overwrought that they have become stylistic vices. Rejecting natural grammar, he delights instead in the unnatural art (*ars magica*) of Natura's nemesis, Venus. This gay sorceress alters genders at will, makes masculines into feminines, confuses actives with passives, and turns predicates into subjects.

So far, so good. But when our poet attempts to take this conceit further, he runs up against an uncomfortable fact of real grammar: just as Ganymede indicated, masculine nouns do require masculine adjectives, and the same holds for the feminine. To evade this difficulty, Alan lets Natura create a fantastic counterfactual grammar in which all nouns are feminine, all adjectives masculine, and all verbs active and transitive. Thus, woman is to be the substantive "modified" (impregnated) by the male adjective; or, alternatively, the passive subject acted upon by the male verb. Anomalies such as neuter nouns, deponent verbs, and reflexive constructions are not allowed to exist. In what seems like an elaborate joke, Natura presents this outlandish grammar as simple and normal; all deviations from it, symbolizing irregular sexual acts, constitute solecisms.

[Natura]: I taught [Venus], as if she were my pupil, which rules of grammar she should admit in the artful unions she constructs, and which she should exclude as anomalous, unredeemed by the excuse of any figure. Since Nature's scheme specifically recognizes two genders, to wit the masculine and the feminine, as grammar bears witness—although certain men deprived of their masculine endings could in my opinion be classified as neuter—I commanded Venus, with secret warnings and great thunderous threats, that in her conjunctions she should celebrate only the natural union of the masculine and the feminine gender, as reason demands. . . . For if the masculine gender should, for some irrational reason, demand a gender like itself, no decent figure of speech could justify such a faulty construction, but it would be disgraced as a monstrous, inexcusable solecism.

Moreover, my teaching instructed Venus that in her constructions, observing the ordinary rules for subjects and predicates, she should assign the role of subject to the marker of the feminine sex, and place the specified masculine part above it in the predicate position, in such a way that the predicate cannot decline into the subject position, nor the subject migrate into the place of the predicate. And since each requires the other, the predicate (with the quality of an adjective) is urgently attracted to the subject (which retains the quality of a noun).

Furthermore, I enjoined Venus that her conjugations should never admit intransitive constructions, reflexivity, or roundabout passives, but should be content with the directness of transitive verbs alone. . . . [13]

Most critics have been so preoccupied with untangling this snarl of technical terms (which I have simplified slightly) that they have overlooked the obvious point: language simply does not work this way.[14] In the terms of Alan's own metaphor, if heterosexuality is "natural" then grammar is not, and *vice versa*, as Gautier de Coincy would point out later in revisiting the trope:

La gramaire hic à hic acouple,
Mais nature maldit la couple.
La mort perpetuel engenre
Cil qui aimme masculin genre
Plus que le femenin ne face,
Et Diex de son livre l'efface:
Nature rit, si com moi sanble,
Quant hic et hec joignent ensanble;
Mais hic et hic chose est perdue,
Nature en est tot esperdue,
Ses poinz debat et tort ses mains.[15]

Grammar couples *hic* and *hic*,
But Nature curses this couple.
He who loves the masculine gender
More than he does the feminine
Engenders everlasting death,
And God erases him from his book.
Nature laughs, it seems to me,
When *hic* and *hec* join together;
But *hic* and *hic* are a lost cause.
Nature is utterly distraught by this:
She beats her fists and wrings her hands.

It is the vernacular poet, rather than the Latin scholar, who accords with the main line of medieval linguistic theory. Aristotle and Augustine had both taught that the rules of speech are conventional rather than natural, and this thesis remained current throughout the twelfth century.[16] In fact, Natura herself seems to acknowledge the violence she is doing to language when she tries (in vain) to extort compliance from Venus "with secret warnings and great thunderous threats." The spectacular failure of her whole metaphoric structure—which I believe the poet fully intended—parallels the discrepancy we noted earlier between Natura's austere rhetorical precepts and her aureate practice. So, unless Alan of Lille was of Ganymede's party without knowing it (which seems most unlikely), we must conclude once again that, in the very act of denouncing sexual sins, *De planctu* demonstrates Nature's unreliability as a moral guide. Or, to put it differently, Natura cannot be simultaneously the goddess of normative sexuality and normative language.

In Nature's Forge: From Alan of Lille to Jean de Meun

As we saw in Chapter 2, *De planctu Naturae* seems to have remained little known until the late thirteenth century, when the omnivorous Jean de Meun used it as a key source for his monumental *Roman de la Rose*. Jean adopted many of the goddess Natura's features from Alan while significantly altering her character and values. Before we turn to Nature's next metamorphosis, however, a brief summary of the famous poem is in order. Guillaume de Lorris, the shadowy poet who initiated the *Rose* circa 1230, conceived it as an allegorical dream vision in which a callow Lover (Amant) would receive instruction in the Ovidian art of love:

c'est li *Romans de la Rose*,
Ou l'art d'Amors est toute enclose. (ll. 37–38)

This is the *Romance of the Rose*
Where the art of Love is all enclosed.

Upon a May morn, a dreaming, nineteen-year-old Lover ambles into a Garden of Delight and there meets attractive courtly figures (such as Youth, Beauty, Gladness, Largesse) dancing a joyous carol. Idleness admits him to the garden, but uncourtly traits such as Old Age and Poverty (Figure 1.2) are depicted on its exterior wall, marking their exclusion from the realm of pleasure.[17] Presently the Lover reaches the perilous fountain of Narcissus.

Gazing at two bright crystals within its depth, he sees the reflected garden and swiftly homes in on one particular rosebud, which will represent his erotic goal throughout the poem. The Lover's incipient passion is activated by the God of Love (Cupid), whose arrows prompt the smitten youth to do homage and accept the god's commandments. He then proceeds with his courtship of the Rose, but this lady never appears in the poem in her own person. Instead, her receptiveness to his overtures is personified in the masculine figure of Fair Welcome (Bel Acuel). Other characters of both sexes—Jealousy, Fear, Shame, Gossip (Malebouche), and Resistance (Dangier)—oppose the Lover's suit. After an amorous setback, he encounters Lady Reason, who does her best to dissuade him from the follies of love, but he rejects her counsel and seeks the more practical aid of his Friend (Ami). With the Friend's help the Lover manages to steal a kiss. But this act arouses the fury of Jealousy, who builds and garrisons a castle where she imprisons Fair Welcome, posting a canny old woman (la Vieille) as jailer and chaperone. Shut out of the castle with little hope of success, the Lover despairs of his plight, and after a little more than four thousand lines, Guillaume abandons his poem.

Jean de Meun, taking up the unfinished romance circa 1270–75, made its delicate plot the foundation of a vast, sprawling edifice that both dwarfs and deconstructs the original. More than seventeen thousand lines later, Jean finally gets the Lover into bed with the Rose, but very little of the intervening text advances the plot. Instead, Jean introduces six lengthy discourses by persons who claim various sorts of authority and purport to instruct the Lover. Lady Reason returns first, attempting to wean Amant's affections away from the Rose by offering herself as a superior *amie*, but he rejects her even more emphatically than before, making himself a case study in the ways of irrational love. Supplanting Reason, the Friend plays the role of an Ovidian mentor, offering cynical advice on erotic strategy interlarded with misogynist slurs voiced by a character of his own invention, the Jealous Husband. False Seeming (Fausemblant) and his female companion, Constrained Abstinence, satirize clerical hypocrisy with special reference to the beguines and mendicant orders, which Jean detested. La Vieille—who would serve as a model for Chaucer's Wife of Bath—next advises Fair Welcome, providing him/her with the same kind of tactical counsel that the Friend had offered the Lover. At this point the plot intervenes as the Lover rallies his forces to make an assault on the castle. In the aftermath of their failed raid, the God of Love and his barons realize they will never succeed without the help of his mother, Venus, who is summoned forthwith. Jean's last two speakers,

Nature and Genius, make their orations just before the dénouement, aligning themselves with the forces of Love. With their assistance, Venus sets the castle on fire and the Lover gleefully claims his prize.

Controversial almost from the moment of its publication, the *Rose* has never ceased to stir debate, and there is still no canonical "received reading." From the *Querelle de la Rose* of 1400 to the critical disputes of the mid-twentieth century, much of the argument turned on the question of which speaker, if any, represents Jean de Meun's "own" point of view. It is probably truest to say that all of them sometimes do and none of them always do. But the two leading contenders are undoubtedly Reason and Nature, in conjunction with her sidekick Genius.[18] The problem is that these august dames take opposite sides: Lady Reason is an implacable foe of the God of Love, while Lady Nature supports him. This departure from Reason represents a novel and surprising turn in Natura's history. After all, Bernard Silvestris had introduced the goddess as a daughter of Noys and an exemplar of rational inquiry. In "Ganymede and Helen," Nature and Reason together decide the case in Helen's favor, while in the *Anticlaudianus*, it is Natura who sends Prudentia and Ratio on their celestial journey. Although Reason does not appear as a character in *De planctu*, Natura there allies herself with Hymen and Chastity; as a spokesman for the sexual morality of the Church, she would no more endorse Amant's brand of fornication than Ganymede's. What, then, prompted Jean de Meun to set Nature and Reason at odds?

To understand Nature's role in the *Rose*, it is helpful to have some idea of what the God of Love represents. Critics agree that in the original *Rose*, he stands for "courtly love" or *fin' amors*, the stylized form of desire and courtship that lyricists conventionally opposed to *fol amors*. For Jeun de Meun, however, this already clichéd distinction had no force: *fin' amors* is by definition *fol amors*, as we see from the Lover's decisive repudiations of Lady Reason.[19] Thus the God of Love in Jean's hands serves to debunk his own myth, for he now represents little more than male desire vis-à-vis the female brand personified by Venus.[20] More precisely, he stands for the sort of desire that self-serving and self-deluded lovers, such as Amant, pursue hypocritically under cover of *courtoisie*—just as False Seeming and Constrained Abstinence represent carnal desire hidden beneath the cloak of religion. Another complementary pair, the Friend and la Vieille, expose the realities masked by the God of Love's allegorical fictions when they expound the actual stratagems used by unscrupulous men and women to achieve their desires. Love's duplicity is further suggested by the ease with which he overcomes his initial scruples and welcomes False Seeming into his retinue.

In her unsuccessful preaching to Amant, Lady Reason tries to expose the Lover's own hypocrisy in a celebrated quarrel over language. While recounting the myth of Saturn's castration, Reason happens to use the colloquial words *viz* ("prick") and *coilles* ("balls")—a lapse at which the Lover professes shock and horror, protesting that such uncourtly language hardly belongs in the mouth of a lady. Reason retorts that if there is no obscenity in the members themselves, which were created by God, her father and the fount of all courtesy, then there is nothing obscene about their names. "Balls" by any other name—relics, for example—would serve as well, and moreover it is she, Lady Reason, who invented language and gave everything its proper name, just as her Father taught her. Obscenity lies not in the mention but in the abuse of these members, so it is foolish of the Lover to take umbrage at *verba* when he would not hesitate to employ the *res* for which they stand. Though the Lover more or less concedes the point, he remains unshaken in his own preference for euphemisms. At the end of the romance, when he finally speaks in his own voice, he proves Lady Reason's point by recounting his sexual conquest of the Rose in a hilarious but superficially pious fable about relics, pilgrimage, and shrines. Thus, without using a single word of obscenity, he performs one of the most outrageously explicit sexual monologues in all premodern literature.

This seeming digression leads us straight back to Alan of Lille's Natura, with her strangely distorted relationship to language. As we have seen, Natura in *De planctu* creates a bizarre fantasy version of Latin grammar in order to prove that sexual couplings should be simple and "natural," and she exhorts Venus to use the plainest possible speech, even though Venus herself is a product of Nature's wish to "gild shameful things with the golden trappings of shamefast words," that is, to teach morality by way of mythology. Such antics must have struck Jean de Meun as ironic and irrational, for he gives Natura's *teaching* on plain language to Lady Reason, while permitting the foolish Lover to imitate her self-contradictory *practice*. This paradigmatic case illustrates what I take to be Jean de Meun's response to Alan of Lille throughout the *Rose*. A keenly observant reader of *De planctu*, he discerned the subtle ways that Alan's Natura is divided against herself, reproduced some of them in his own characterization of the goddess, and accentuated others by dividing Alan's material between Lady Nature and Lady Reason.[21] It is Reason who undertakes the Lover's moral education, though it falls on deaf ears: she counsels him on virtuous love, friendship, and charity, while denouncing the kind of *amors* favored by the God of Love in a speech that Jean has translated verbatim from *De planctu*: "Love is amorous hatred, disloyal loyalty, confident fear, desperate hope," and so forth.[22] Jean's Nature, on the other hand, throws in her lot with Amant and the God of Love because her own interest in procreation happens to coincide with theirs in sexual pleasure.[23]

When Dame Nature first appears in the *Rose* she is hard at work in her forge, hammering out new individuals to replace those killed by Death. This is the heroic goddess we have met before, the tireless vanquisher of Fate, but her new character as blacksmith proves to be yet another borrowing from Alan. In *De planctu*, we recall, pen and parchment serve as metaphors for sexual organs, doubled by the transparent images of hammer and anvil.

[Natura]: To assure that faithful instruments would preclude the corruption of shoddy workmanship, I assigned [Venus] two prescription hammers with which to undo the snares of the Fates and prepare many kinds of things for existence. I also gave her noble workshops with anvils suited for this craft, instructing her to apply the same hammers to the anvils and devote herself faithfully to the formation of creatures. By no means should she let the hammers stray from the anvils in any deviation.[24]

The homosexual, of course, does let them stray; in Alan's mixed metaphor he "strikes on an anvil that coins no sparks" (*semina*) until "his very hammer shudders in horror of its anvil."[25]

Jean was less interested in sodomy, but he adapted Alan's metaphor of the smithy and made it a central feature of the goddess's iconography. Since Jean had other uses for Venus, he placed the hammer in Nature's own hand and thus created the phallic goddess who is so memorably pictured by illustrators of the *Rose*. Sometimes she is the cosmic artisan forging birds and animals in her smithy (Figure 3.1) against a backdrop that seems to belong in a Genesis illustration. The "sixth day of creation" image emphasizes Natura's role as the *vicaria Dei* without whom all life would perish.[26] More often, however, she appears to be forging a baby (Figure 3.2). This image, seen in countless miniatures and woodcuts,[27] has a faintly disturbing edge. Not only does Nature, with her lithe feminine body, engage in the historically and archetypally masculine labor of the smith, but hers is the very craft the Greeks assigned to Vulcan, the deformed and cuckolded husband of Venus.[28] Moreover, if the image is read "literally," the goddess's uplifted hammer can take on a more sinister meaning. A slight change of perspective transforms Dame Nature into a most unnatural mother, a veritable Medea poised to smash the vulnerable infant on her anvil, while the floor of her

Figure 3.1. Nature at her forge making birds and beasts. *Roman de la Rose*. Oxford, Bodleian Douce 195, f. 114v. Photo: Bodleian Library.

smithy is strewn with dismembered baby parts. This is not to say that any medieval viewer consciously read the image in such a light, but such grim reverberations may explain why some authors pointedly rejected the figure of Nature the Smith and, as we shall see, gave her a more traditionally feminine craft. One maverick *Rose* illustrator bypassed the signifiers of hammer and anvil entirely, moving straight to the signified. Where the standard iconographic program called for an image of Nature at her forge, he or she depicted two lovers in bed (Figure 3.3).

At first blush, Jean's Nature seems an attractive and authoritative goddess, not far removed from Alan's. Her relationship to God is described in familiar terms, and the narrator waxes eloquent in praise of Nature's beauty, which artists imitate in vain. Jean even introduces a vignette of Art on her knees before Nature, begging for instruction (Figure 3.4):

Figure 3.2. Nature at her forge making a baby. *Roman de la Rose*. London, BL Harley 4425, f. 140r (Netherlands, ca. 1490–1500). Photo: British Library.

Touz jors martele, touz jors forge,
Touz jors ses pieces renovele
Par generacion novele . . .
Qui lor donne formes veroies
En coins de diverses monnoies,
Dont Art fesoit ses exemplaires,
Qui ne fait pas choses si vaires;
Mes par mout ententive cure

Figure 3.3. Nature at her forge (two lovers in bed). *Roman de la Rose*. London, BL Add. 42133, f. 105v (France, early sixteenth century). Photo: British Library.

Figure 3.4. Art kneels before Nature. *Roman de la Rose*. Oxford, Bodleian Douce 195, f. 115v. Photo: Bodleian Library.

A genouz est devant Nature,
Si prie et requiert et demande,
Comme mendians et truande,
Povre de science et de force,
Qui de sivre la mout s'efforce,
Que Nature li veille aprendre
Comment elle puisse comprendre
Par son engin, en ses figures,
Proprement toutes creatures. (l 16,010–28)

[Nature] is always hammering and forging,
Always renewing her creation
By new acts of generation . . .
She gives her works true forms
In coins of different denominations
From which Art constructs her models—
Yet the things she makes are not as true.
But with the most attentive care
She kneels before Nature,
Begs and pleads and asks of her
Like a miserable beggar,
Poor in knowledge and strength,
Trying so hard to imitate her,
That Nature might deign to teach her
How to subsume all creatures properly
In her figures by her artistry.

Nature is capable of discoursing on a wide range of philosophical and scientific themes, including the heavenly bodies, elements, meteorology, mirrors, optical illusions, the reconciliation of divine foreknowledge with free will, destiny and contingency, true nobility, and the natural equality of human beings. Yet, in keeping with her subordinate status, she acknowledges her limitations and duly marvels at the Virgin Birth. There seems to be no direct irony in Nature's long philosophical speech. If she seems rambling and unfocused, as some critics have charged, she is no more so than Reason and other characters in the *Rose*, for the digressive style belongs to Jean de Meun himself.

Yet Nature's role is indeed ironic, and its irony arises from the dramatic context Jean creates for her discourse. In appropriating the character of Genius from *De planctu*, Jean retains his "priesthood" but carries it a step further. No longer does Nature merely summon Genius to excommunicate sinners; in the *Rose* she wishes to make a confession. This circumstance casts Genius and Nature in the roles of male priest/confessor and female penitent

(Figure 3.5), enabling Jean to extend the anticlerical satire he had begun
through the characters of False Seeming and Constrained Abstinence. In that
episode, Fausemblant in the guise of a friar, accompanied by Abstinence
dressed as a beguine, had murdered Malebouche by first preaching to him,
then persuading him to kneel and confess his sins, whereupon they strangle
him and cut out his tongue. This "confession" sets an ominous precedent.
Although Genius is no murderer, his priesthood is hardly more authentic
than Fausemblant's. No sooner is he called to Nature's side than he begins
preaching to her, delivering a vicious antifeminist rant addressed, with seeming irrelevance, to husbands. It culminates in the command to "flee, flee,
flee, flee, flee" from the dreadful beast called Woman.[29] Genius proves to be
just as hardened a misogynist as the Jealous Husband, and he even persuades
Nature to agree with his assertion that "nothing swears or lies more boldly
than a woman." Worse still, she calls him "courteous and wise" for making
such remarks.[30] After this preamble, Nature's authority is hardly enhanced
when she begins her denunciation of sin with the admission,

Figure 3.5. Genius gives Nature absolution. *Roman de la Rose*. London, BL Add.
42133, f. 127v (France, early sixteenth century). Photo: British Library.

Fame sui, si ne me puis taire,
Ains vuel des ja tout reveler,
Car fame ne puet rienz celer. (19,218–20)

I am a woman and cannot keep silent;
From now on I wish to reveal everything,
For a woman can keep nothing secret.

The scene of Nature's "confession" is not merely anticlerical and anti-feminist. It has a more precise target, for Jean's satire is aimed sharply and scathingly at beguine spirituality. Indeed, the situation has all the hallmarks of "abuse" that opponents of the beguine movement held up for ridicule.[31] A loquacious, high-minded woman with pretensions to learning summons "her" priest for confession; he jumps at her bidding, yet does not trouble to hide his contempt for her sex; and she in turn uses confession as a pretext to instruct the priest, rambling interminably about high theological matters and boasting of her intimate relationship with God.

Nul autre droit je n'i reclaime,
Ains l'en merci quant il tant m'aime
Que si tres povre damoisele
A si grant maison et si bele;
Icis granz sires tant me prise
Qu'il m'i a por chambriere prise.
Por sa chambriere? Certes vere,
Por connestable et por viquere,
Dont je ne fusse mie digne,
Fors par sa volenté benigne. (16,775–84)

I claim no other right from him,
But thank him that he loves me so much
That he has given me, such a poor damsel,
Such a great and beautiful mansion.
This great lord values me so much
That he has taken me to be his maid.
His chambermaid? Surely, in fact,
His vicar and his châtelaine—
A post which I by no means deserve
Except through his gracious will.

For a moment Nature sounds like nothing so much as a mystical beguine—Mechthild of Magdeburg, for example—exulting that so great a Sovereign has brought so lowly a maiden to his court.[32] But later in her "confession," when she is discussing dreams and hallucinations, Nature pauses to debunk religious visions. Some people, she says, through their "great devotion in excessive contemplation," imagine they see "spiritual substances" and even "hell and paradise" as if they were truly present—yet all this is but "trifling lies."[33] Nature's credibility on this point might be challenged, since if a vision were genuinely supernatural, she would by definition be incapable of grasping it. But the satirical technique Jean employs here is one characteristic of him (and his disciple Chaucer), in which a personage simultaneously embodies and exposes the object of satire. Just as Fausemblant (or Chaucer's Pardoner) explains his hypocritical wiles at the same time that he practices them, so Dame Nature plays the role of a deluded beguine even as she unmasks what Jean took to be the cause of such delusions.

A confession, of course, presupposes a sin. Like the false mystic she is satirizing, Nature takes much longer to parade her wisdom than she does to confess her supposed transgression—and when she finally does so, she reveals only the fallibility of her conscience. For the "sin" that Nature repents is nothing else than the creation of man. "Si m'aïst Diex li crucefis, / Mout me repent quant homme fis" ("So help me God who was crucified, I am terribly sorry that I made mankind!" 19,209–10). At a stroke, this misplaced contrition dismantles all the authority Nature has thus far achieved for herself. Ordinarily, of course, man would be seen as Nature's masterpiece—as indeed he is in the *Cosmographia* and the *Anticlaudianus*, works that Jean knew. If the goddess confesses any "sin" in *De planctu Naturae*, it would be her fateful mistake of deputizing Venus to be the arbiter of human sexuality. In the *Rose*, however, she shows her repentance by *committing* this very sin, for she commands Genius to go at once and bring her greetings to "my friend lady Venus" and her son, the God of Love, offering them her full support in the achievement of Amant's quest.[34] Just as the skeptics always warned, too much intimacy between a woman and her confessor can only end in carnality. Genius for his part absolves Nature and gives her a penance that is "good and pleasing" (*avenant*), just as excessively lax friars were often said to do.[35] To crown the irony, her penance consists in resuming her labors in the forge—the very activity she has just confessed as sinful.

Nature's parodic confession leads into Genius's still more parodic sermon. Leaving Nature's forge, he removes his priestly vestments and travels to Love's camp in secular garb, but on his arrival, the God of Love immediately revests him with the addition of ring, crozier, and mitre—signifying that Nature's priest has been elevated to the rank of Cupid's bishop, much to the delight of Venus who "could not stop laughing."[36] If we "translate" the allegory at this point, Jean seems to be saying that Genius and Nature—or male and female fertility—willingly place themselves at the service of Cupid and Venus, or masculine and feminine desire. Accordingly, Genius in his preaching to Love's barons tells them exactly what they wish to hear:

Arés, por Dieu, baron, arés,
Et vos linages reparés.
Se ne pensés forment d'arer,
N'est rienz qui les puist reparer.
Rescorciés vous bien par devant,
Aussi cum por coillir le vent,
Ou, s'il vous plaist, tuit nu soiés,
Mes trop froit ne trop chaut n'aiés. (19,701–8)

Ne vous lessiés pas desconfire,
Grefes avés, pensés d'escrire.
N'aiés pas les bras emmouflés:
Martelés, forgiés et souflés. (19,793–96)

Plow, for God's sake, barons, plow,
And renew your lineages!
If you don't think of plowing vigorously,
Nothing can restore them.
Tuck up your clothes in front,
As if to wanton with the wind,
Or if you wish, go completely naked,
But don't get chilled or overheated.

Don't let yourselves be vanquished!
You have a stylus; think of writing.
Don't let your arms be muffled:
Hammer away, use forge and bellows!

This is "normative heterosexuality" with a vengeance: Genius's aggressive sexual bravado will be echoed when Amant narrates his quasi-rape of the Rose. As in *De planctu*, the priest excommunicates sodomites, wishing them castration on earth and damnation hereafter. But the real point of interest is a novel one, for "by the authority of Nature" he also excommunicates virgins and celibates, reviving the old argument that, if all men vowed chastity, the human race would quickly die out. St. Jerome had long since refuted that objection with acid realism in his endlessly cited treatise *Against Jovinian*: "Be not afraid that all will become virgins: virginity is a hard matter, and therefore rare."[37] No one, he goes on to say, can maintain virginity without a special gift from God. But Genius in turn rebuts Jerome by appealing to a version of the categorical imperative. If God truly wills the good and loves all that he has made, he would desire the best path for everyone; but obviously not everyone is called to be a virgin; therefore virginity cannot be the right path for anyone; so "plow, barons, plow!"[38] In the eyes of Nature and Genius, procreation is the sovereign duty of man. Genius therefore ends his exhortation by promising heaven to all who toil zealously with their hammers and styluses. To the confusion of some readers and the dismay of others, his version of heaven—the Good Shepherd's Park—is explicitly and favorably contrasted with the Garden of Delight as described by Guillaume de Lorris. According to Genius, the *locus amenus* where Amant first encountered the God of Love cannot hold a candle to the true Christian paradise that he and Nature have in their power to bestow. To him, the ideological difference between the Lover's allies is an important one. Be that as it may, from the Lover's perspective all four deities—Genius and Nature, Venus and the God of Love—collaborate to the same end. Amant's desire for the Rose appears to be motivated neither by a reverence for ladies nor by zeal to propagate the race, but if he has gleaned anything at all from the ideological harangues he has heard, it is the supreme irrelevance of ideologies.

What of Jean de Meun, though? Since his *Rose* is satirical and didactic in equal measure, he is notoriously hard to pin down. But I would argue that, far from being a "naturalist," Jean's treatment of Nature shows that he has carried the supernaturalism of Alan of Lille even further. Alan had envisioned a Nature allied with Reason, but incapable of fathoming divine grace or the mysteries of theology. While Natura in *De planctu* is passionately committed to the natural law that decrees heterosexual union, we saw that her arguments for that law are fraught with contradiction. Jean's Nature, despite her impressive knowledge of philosophy and science, seems even more limited than Alan's in that she no longer holds any covenant with Reason. Their old alliance, dating back to the Stoics, has been broken: in the *Rose*, a life "according to Nature" is no longer a simple, rational, and virtuous life but one of promiscuous (though heterosexual) license. Thus the goddess degenerates into "a sort of arms-dealer supplying the wrong side in a war between body and soul."[39] Nature and Genius will have no truck with celibacy because, for them, there is no difference between the Unnatural and the Supernatural: if same-sex relations are unnatural then so, a fortiori, is lifelong virginity. Even marriage has disappeared from the picture, for Hymen, a member of Natura's retinue in *De planctu*, is nowhere in sight. The *Rose*, then, overtly fulfills Alan's covert agenda of disabling Nature as a guide to Christian sexual ethics. Henceforth any poet who wanted to argue the compatibility of "natural law" with the Church's teachings on sexuality would, one way or another, have to confront the *Rose*.

Nature at the Court of King Richard: Chaucer's *Parlement of Fowles*

A century after Jean de Meun completed his mammoth oeuvre, two court poets took up the challenge posed by Nature's quarrel with Reason, even as they opened up the momentous question of her relation to Culture. Geoffrey Chaucer, writing at the court of Richard II, used the boy-king's proposed marriage to Anne of Bohemia as occasion for a graceful but searching meditation on the rituals of mating.[40] In his dream-poem of circa 1380, *The Parlement of Fowles*, "the noble goddesse Nature" (303) presides over a clash between the contingencies of marital politics, which include the inconvenient fact of female consent, and a fantasy of blissful, instinctive sexual love.[41] About twenty-five years later, at a French court thrown into turmoil by the madness of Charles VI, Christine de Pizan would struggle mightily to re-enthrone Lady Reason, even if it meant challenging and redefining what virtually everyone took to be the order of Nature.

Chaucer's *Parlement* is, on the surface, a light and uncomplicated poem. Its narrator, one of those shy and bookish dreamers favored by the poet, begins with a review of his current reading, *The Dream of Scipio*. On retiring for the night, he himself dreams of Scipio Africanus. But the Roman, instead of guiding him through the heavenly spheres, shoves our timid dreamer through the gates of a garden, where he reads two contrasting inscriptions. One promises "that blysful place / Of hertes hele" (127–28), while the other threatens a lifetime of sterility and woe. Evidently both pertain to the Garden of Love, for either heaven or hell may await the lover there. The dreamer, like Amant in the *Rose*, finds himself in a paradisal park where "besyde a welle"— no doubt that of Narcissus—he sees the God of Love sharpening his arrows in the company of Plesaunce, Curteysie, and other less savory members of his troupe. But the dreamer himself is not Cupid's target. Wandering further, he comes upon a temple of brass, sacred to Venus and Priapus. In that luxurious but dismal place, the goddess reclines in *deshabille* in her darkened chamber, attended by her porter Richesse, while all around her the wall paintings tell grim tales of men and women who died for love. The dreamer

leaves this temple with relief and soon reaches a flowery hill where he finds
the empress Nature holding her annual court on Valentine's Day—an amorous festival that Chaucer himself invented.[42] A propos of the goddess, the
poet does not disguise his debts:

And right as Aleyn, in the *Pleynt of Kynde*,
Devyseth Nature of aray and face,
In swich aray men myghte hire there fynde. (316–18)

The purpose of Nature's court is to oversee the ceremonial mating
of birds, which in a well-established satirical tradition signify various social
classes—birds of prey for the nobility, waterfowl for the merchants, and so
forth. On her hand the goddess holds her own cherished pet, a beautiful
formel or female eagle. She announces only two rules for the ceremony: first,
mating will proceed down the social pecking order, beginning with the royal
tercel; and second, no match will be concluded without the desired female's
consent. Thereupon three eagles—Richard II with his French and German
rivals—proceed to sue all day for the hand of the formel, making long
courtly speeches to which she has no reply. The other birds finally grow
impatient, until Nature allows them to form a parliament or representative
assembly to resolve the disputed case. The falcon, speaking for the nobility,
sees no alternative to battle—unless the formel herself chooses the suitor
that is "worthieste / Of knyghthod, and lengest had used it, / Most of estat,
of blod the gentilleste" (548–50). As the formel continues to hold her peace,
a goose offers the commonsensical advice that the rejected suitors should
give up and look elsewhere. All the "gentil foules" laugh her to scorn, and
the faithful turtledove proposes as an alternative that they should serve the
lady until they die, even if she "everemore be straunge" (584). A duck agrees
with the goose; a cuckoo says that if the rivals can reach no accord they
should all remain single. Nature finally reminds the formel of her right to
choose, but adds the advice she would give "if I were Resoun" (632): namely,
do as the falcon urged and choose the royal bird. Opening her beak at last,
the formel declines all three suits, saying she "wol nat serve Venus ne Cupide,
/ Forsothe as yit, by no manere weye" (652–53). Undaunted, Nature grants
her a year's reprieve, exhorting the three tercels to continue their love-service
until she is ready to decide. Without further ado, the remaining birds mer-
rily pair off and fly away, first singing a roundel "to don Nature honour and
plesaunce" (676).

Several reasons for the anticlimactic ending can be offered, among them
Chaucer's well-known avoidance of narrative and intellectual closure; the

literary fashion for *demandes d'amour* that a live audience might continue to debate;[43] and not least the likelihood that Richard's actual marriage negotiations were still pending at the time of the poem. But if we were to take the *Parlement* more seriously than it takes itself, we could point to certain deep-seated contradictions that make it impossible for Nature to resolve the dispute she has set in motion. For, despite the festive occasion and the lightness of tone, the goddess turns out to be under no slight ideological pressure. Most obviously, she is supposed to provide a clear alternative to Venus in her oppressive "temple of bras" (231).[44] As in *De planctu*, Nature represents wholesome, fertile sexuality as opposed to the destructive and barren sort that Venus governs: the hot sighs, pale faces, and broken lives on display in the temple contrast vividly with the leafy, blossoming glade where Nature rules. Nature's matches appear to be marriages rather than adulterous liaisons; and since the formel in particular is being groomed for queenship, some critics have gone so far as to equate the goddess's political matchmaking with that service to the "commune profit" that Scipio commends to his grandson (75).[45] Yet this antinomy is complicated by the ambiguous position of "Cupide, oure lord" (212), whose persona comes straight from the *Rose*. Although Venus is interpreted *in malo*, her son seems to be at least morally neutral. The three tercels all speak the language of *fin' amors*, while the reluctant formel equates the marriage she begs to defer with the service of "Venus [and] Cupide." In short, it is not clear whether the God of Love is a guest in Nature's garden or she in his.

Jean de Meun's Nature willingly aligns herself with Venus and Cupid, although her real interest lies in procreation and not *fin' amors*, much less marriage. But Chaucer, much as he admired the *Rose*, could not take it at face value. In fact, in the prologue to his *Legend of Good Women*, the God of Love appears to the poet and denounces him as a mortal foe for translating the *Rose* into English:

> Thou maist yt nat denye,
> For in pleyn text, withouten nede of glose,
> Thou hast translated the *Romaunce of the Rose*,
> That is an heresye ayeins my lawe,
> And makest wise folk fro me withdrawe. (F prologue, vv. 327–31)

Chaucer's God of Love fears and despises the *Rose* because he understands that Jean was really on Reason's side and wrote the romance to dissuade potential lovers. Even though Chaucer protests as usual that he is just an innocent translator, Cupid presumably articulates the poet's own reading of the *Rose* as ironic. To represent Nature as a sympathetic figure and love as a politically useful force, then, Chaucer would have had to distance his goddess from Jean de Meun's. He does so by making his Nature more "rational," less obsessed with sex and more attuned to the social niceties, but this new concern with propriety causes her no end of trouble.

On the one hand, the poem encourages us to see Nature as the embodiment of all that is simple, joyful, instinctual, and fertile. Under her blithe dominion the pairing of all birds, except for the long-winded tercels, goes off without a hitch: no duck would dream of refusing her drake. On the other hand, Chaucer's Nature makes herself a champion of Culture in the form of social hierarchy: it seems utterly natural to her that the birds should choose their mates "by ordre" (400). But naturalizing class privilege also means naturalizing the rules of the social elite, which are in this case the rules of the God of Love. Very little about this courtly code could be described as instinctual, and the bemused or angry reactions of the more plebeian birds hint that Nature ought to be on their side. Who after all is more "natural"— the tercels, who feel compelled to cloak their political desire in the language of erotic desire, or the waterfowl, who see no point in making a masochistic cult of unrequited love? Again, who is more "natural"—the lower-class birds flying off in unproblematic pairs, or the aristocratic formel who can scarcely bear the thought of her matrimonial fate? Nature is in no position to resolve this dilemma because it is of her own making. Her two stated principles—social hierarchy and female choice—conflict first with the principle of instinct that she is supposed to embody, and secondly with each other (for the formel disregards her advice to marry the "gentilleste" suitor). In any case, the appealing fiction occludes the fact that in real life Anne of Bohemia had little say about her marital "choice," which was a decision reserved for her brother, the Holy Roman Emperor.

Within the framework of Chaucer's fable, it is interesting that Nature commends the royal suitor only by stating what she would say "if I were Resoun." This concession acknowledges that considerations of political self-interest cannot always be reconciled with the heart's desire—and the formel's heart may have reasons that Reason knows not of.[46] Elaine Tuttle Hansen has recently asked if she does not refuse the three males because she prefers her current status as the darling of a great goddess. "Nature hireself hadde blysse," after all, "To loke on hire, and ofte hire bek to kysse" (377–78). So "why should the formel desire, instead of this divine adoration by one of her own sex, any of the three egotistical, scrappy eagles who care only for themselves, for each other, and for the prestige of possessing her?"[47]

Whatever the formel might think, it is true that Nature—despite her well-known heterosexual tendencies—cherishes her more than she does any of the male birds. In this particular, the formel resembles many another romance heroine who is represented as Nature's special favorite, or the pride of her atelier. This connection of Nature's prowess with exemplary *female* beauty was not inevitable, for in both the *Cosmographia* and the *Anticlaudianus* we see the goddess laboring to produce a perfect *male* body. Far more common, however, are scenes such as the creation of the beauteous Virginia in *The Physician's Tale*:

> Nature hath with sovereyn diligence
> Yformed hire in so greet excellence,
> As though she wolde seyn, "Lo! I, Nature,
> Thus kan I forme and peynte a creature,
> Whan that me list; who kan me countrefete?" (9–13)

This topos usually functions, as it does in both the *Parlement* and the *Physician's Tale*, to depict a woman as a supreme object of masculine desire. The only way to outdo the topos would be to describe a woman as so beautiful that she must have been made not by Nature at all, but directly by the hand of God, like Chaucer's Criseyde.[48] But—to carry Hansen's question a step further—what might happen if such a masterpiece were to become Nature's *own* object of desire, or if the goddess took particular delight in creating women like herself? These are questions that perhaps only a female writer could have thought to broach.

Nature and Culture: Christine's Revisionist Myths

Early in his career, Chaucer served his literary apprenticeship by translating the *Romance of the Rose*. Early in hers, Christine de Pizan achieved celebrity by her relentless attack on that poem. Her famous critique of Jean de Meun in the *Querelle de la Rose* need not be rehearsed here, but we should note its obverse: the strategy of writing her own allegories to undo the damage she believed Jean to have done in his.[49] In particular, she took pains to reinvent Jean's allegorical figures so as to make them serve feminist ends. Thus, in her *Epistle of the God of Love* (1399), she turns the tables by making Cupid himself "excommunicate" misogynists such as Jean de Meun and seducers such as Amant, in response to a series of complaints from women. In *The City of Ladies* (1405) she rehabilitates Jean's Lady Reason, whom she found all too irrational in her defense of obscenity; and in two less familiar works, *The Book of the Mutation of Fortune* (1403) and *Christine's Vision* (1405), she takes up the cause of Lady Nature. Although the goddess occupies relatively little space in these texts, they mark a significant departure in her history. In them Christine articulates a new and strikingly feminized iconography for Dame Nature; reimagines her relationship to the divine; and repositions the goddess as a vehicle to discuss gender and culture rather than sexuality.

The Mutation of Fortune is an ambitious universal history prefaced by Christine's personal history, stressing the ambiguous role of Fortune in both narratives. The author represents her life as a tug of war between two goddesses: Lady Nature creates her to be a woman, but Lady Fortune has transformed her into a man. The autobiographical section begins with a eulogy for Christine's beloved father, "a noble and renowned man, who was known as a philosopher." Thomas de Pizan's legacy is symbolized by two priceless jewels, which stand for his twin professions of astrology and medicine. After a glowing account of her father's attainments, Christine launches into still more generous praise of her mother:

My mother who was great and grand and more valorous than Penthesilea (God had made her well!) surpassed my father in knowledge, power, and value, despite the fact that he had learned so much. She was a crowned queen from the moment that she was born. Everyone knows of her power and strength. It is clear that she is never idle, and, without being overbearing, she is always occupied with many, diverse tasks: her impressive works are found everywhere; every day she creates many beautiful ones. Whoever wanted to count all that she has done and continues to do would never finish. She is old without being aged, and her life cannot end before Judgment Day. God gave her the task of maintaining and increasing the world as He had made it, in order to sustain human life: she is called Lady Nature. She is the mother of every person: God thus calls us all brothers and sisters.[50]

Christine gives herself a sublime and mythic parentage. Like Aeneas, she is the child of a goddess and a mortal man, albeit one of nearly superhuman virtues. In this way she occludes her biological mother who, as she later reveals, did not encourage her daughter's intellectual ambitions, though otherwise treating her kindly enough. So, to endow herself with a female parent worthy of her esteemed father, Christine laid claim to a whole series of allegorical mothers and mentors: the Sibyl in *The Path of Long Study* (Figure 1.5), Lady Philosophy in *Christine's Vision* (Figure 1.6), Lady Reason in *The City of Ladies* (Figure 1.4), and here Lady Nature.[51] The goddess is depicted as an awesome virago, more valiant than the Amazon queen whom Christine would extol in *The City of Ladies* (I.19), while still playing her traditional role as God's partner in creation. In reaction against Jean de Meun, however, Christine desexualizes Nature's creative work, suppressing the blacksmith image. To invest the goddess's universal motherhood with a moral rather than merely biological character ("God calls us all brothers and sisters"), she even paradoxically invokes Mark 3.35. In its biblical context that verse serves, like Christine's allegory itself, to elevate the spiritual at the expense of the natural family: Jesus rejects the claims of his own biological mother with the assertion that "Whoever does the will of God is my brother and sister and mother."

Thomas de Pizan, writes his daughter, strongly desired a son who could inherit his wealth (that is, his learning), but it was not to be:

He failed in his intention, for my mother [Nature], who had much more power than he, wanted to have for herself a female child resembling her, thus I was in fact born a girl; but my mother did so much for him that I fully resembled my father in all things, only excepting my gender. . . . But because I was born a girl, it was not at all ordained that I should benefit in any way from my father's wealth, and I could not inherit, more because of custom than justice, the possessions that are found in the very worthy fountain [of the Muses].[52]

It is Nature who shapes Christine to be her father's daughter in mind and spirit, but Nature too who makes her a woman in her own image and likeness. Thus the writer carefully avoids blaming the goddess for her gender or hinting that femaleness is in any way a defect. Instead, she denounces the injustice that bars women from the learned professions.

While Christine clearly viewed sexism as unnatural, just what she considered to be "natural" is no easy question. Alan of Lille's Natura had acknowledged her ignorance of theology, while Jean de Meun's Nature not only opposed the counsel of Reason, but explained that rationality was a divine gift beyond her purview.[53] Christine seems at first to oppose Jean's position outright. She recounts that her mother Nature gave her a golden crown set with four precious jewels — not as precious as her father's, to be sure, yet more freely available. These gems are Discretion, Consideration, Recollection, and Memory, all endowments pertaining to reason. As if anticipating objections, however, Christine corrects herself with a more theologically precise explanation. Such qualities in fact belong to the soul, which is God's direct creation, for Nature fashions only bodies. Yet they are indeed her gifts insofar as the body's composition gives some people a greater receptiveness to intellectual gifts, while others have a diminished capacity for them. Thus, Christine concludes, "Nature allows or denies to us the opening of the body to the goods of the soul, according to the diverse capacities of the body to receive them, although God sends the soul into the body."[54] In this way she accounts for the natural inequality of human endowments while denying that gender is responsible for it, except insofar as "custom" or Culture distorts the intentions of Nature.

Yet Fortune giveth what Custom taketh away. When Christine reaches marriageable age, her "beautiful mother Nature" places her "in the service of a lady of high birth, who was slightly related to her, although they did not look at all like each other, and they were not cut from the same cloth."[55] This lady is Fortune, a goddess of dubious provenance. Christine's master Boethius had thoroughly discredited her, as had Alan of Lille in the *Anticlaudianus*, in a passage echoed by Jean de Meun's Reason and later by Christine herself. By pointing out the distant kinship and lack of affinity between the two queens, Christine could only be disparaging Lady Fortune. Nevertheless, Fortune at first favors her, giving her ten happy years at the court of Hymen. But after the death of her husband, allegorized as a disaster at sea, Christine feels her ship to be floundering and nearly throws herself overboard in grief. At this point Fortune intervenes once more. In the most celebrated passage of her poem, Christine recounts the "mutation of Fortune" that transformed her into a man. A physical sex change supplies the metaphor for a change of vocation and gender roles, as the vicissitudes of fate—emotional loss and financial need—give Christine what her sex had initially denied her: the right and obligation to chart the course of her own voyage.

Wearied by long crying, I remained, on one particular occasion, completely overcome; as if unconscious, I fell asleep early one evening. Then my mistress came to me, she who gives joy to many, and she touched me all over my body; she palpated and took in her hands each bodily part, I remember it well; then she departed . . . I awakened and things were such that, immediately and with certainty, I felt myself completely transformed. I felt my limbs to be stronger than before, and the great pain and lamentation which had earlier dominated me, I felt to be somewhat lessened. Then I touched myself all over my body, like one completely bewildered. Fortune had thus not hated me, she who had transformed me, for she had instantly changed the great fear and doubt in which I had been completely lost. Then I felt myself much lighter than usual and I felt that my flesh was changed and strengthened, and my voice much lowered, and my body harder and faster. However, the ring that Hymen had given me had fallen from my finger, which troubled me, as well it should have, for I loved it dearly.[56]

This startling sex change is framed and legitimized by Ovidian tales. Christine likens Fortune to Circe, noting that she can change men into beasts and beasts into "lords so great that everyone tries to please them."[57] From Ovid, too, come the metamorphoses of Tiresias and of Iphis, a girl raised as a boy to escape the wrath of a tyrannical king, then changed into an actual boy on the eve of his wedding.[58] In ascribing these mythic transformations to Lady Fortune, Christine opposes a powerful counterforce to Lady Nature: identity is shaped not only by birth, but just as much by random chance and political circumstance. In her own case, the trope of "becoming a man" means much the same as it did in early Christian hagiography: the martyr Perpetua dreamed that she had become a man on the eve of her battle with wild beasts in the arena, while the transvestite monks Marina and Euphrosyna (both commemorated in *The City of Ladies*) lived out their entire religious lives in male garb.[59] In this context the virile woman is one who possesses the intelligence, courage, and integrity that cultural norms denied to women as such. Yet why would Christine, with her insistence on the natural worth and equality of women, have felt the need to describe her transformation in such terms? The answer seems to be twofold.[60] First, she had represented her period of mourning as a near-suicidal depression, curable only by radical means: only by ceasing to be a woman at all could she cease to be a helpless widow and thus acquire control of her life. She needed to be released not from womanhood as such, but from what contemporary moralists stigmatized as "womanish grief." Second and more obviously, the new social roles she would undertake—as poet, scholar, political adviser, and primary wage-earner for her family—were in all eyes the roles proper to a man.

But Christine ends her account on a note of resignation and wistfulness:

As you have heard, I am still a man and I have been for a total of more than thirteen full years, but it would please me much more to be a woman, as I used to be when I used to talk with Hymen, but since Fortune has transformed me so that I shall never again be lodged in a woman's body, I shall remain a man, and with my Lady Fortune I shall stay.[61]

Does the lady protest too much? Even though she notes that the jewels in her mother Nature's crown, that is, her rational faculties, "grew much bigger" when she became a man, the protagonist Christine feels nostalgia for her original gender and still uses feminine adjectives (*estrangiee, logiee*) to modify her "virile" persona. Meanwhile, the author Christine is still casting about for a feminine—and feminist—poetics. In her two great works of 1405, *The City of Ladies* and *Christine's Vision*, she would find one.[62] So her metamorphosis, like that of Tiresias, proves to be transient after all: Lady Fortune will be cast out as Lady Nature returns triumphant.

Lavision-Christine deals primarily with French politics, but begins with an original and puzzling allegory of Nature. Midway through the pilgrimage of life, as Christine writes in homage to Dante, she has a marvelous dream, in which she beholds a Cosmic Man whose head pierces the clouds, while his feet span the abyss and his belly is wide as the earth. His eyes radiate brightness and his mighty breaths fill the world with freshness. With his insatiable mouth he takes in "material and corruptible bodies" as nourishment, and from his lower orifice he purges himself.[63] The Cosmic Man is dressed in a beautiful, subtly colored robe of silk, and on his forehead are stamped five letters spelling the name C*H*A*O*Z. Beside him stands "a great crowned shade in the form of a woman" who resembles a powerful queen.[64] Although this lady is never named, she is obviously Nature. Her duty is to attend to the continual feeding of Chaos, and for that purpose she is surrounded by cooking utensils, which Christine compares to the waffle irons one sees in Parisian shops. In her cosmic kitchen she compounds a "mortar" of bitter, sweet, heavy, and light ("fiel, miel, plomb, et plume") and pours it ceaselessly into her molds, which she then bakes in the enormous, furnace-like mouth of Chaos. As soon as she takes them out, little bodies spring from the molds, but immediately Chaos swallows them alive into his vast belly. Day and night the lady continues to feed him. As Christine's spirit draws nearer to witness the marvel, it falls into the hands of Nature, and she too is molded and baked like the others. At the lady's express wish "and not because of the mold," Christine is given a female body.[65] After she has been swallowed up by Chaos, the lady's chambermaid comes and gives her a sweet liqueur to drink. Nourished within the body of Chaos, she matures and begins to learn about "the diversity within the figure's belly," that is, the world.

Christine's original myth may have been distantly influenced by Plato's *Timaeus*, in which the world is called a living animal, but it stands self-consciously aside from the tradition of Bernard Silvestris, Alan of Lille, and Jean de Meun. The figure of Chaos is the first surprise, for male mythic figures of this type are much rarer than goddesses in medieval literature. The closest analogue to Christine's Chaos may be the Cosmic Man who dominates Hildegard of Bingen's *Liber vite meritorum* (*Book of Life's Merits*). But Hildegard's figure signifies God, while Christine's emphatically does not. In fact, the single reference to God in her myth occurs in the modesty preface, where she defends her vision on the ground that "the secrets of the Most High are not hidden from the most simple."[66] Apart from this covert claim to authority, Christine's revisionist myth makes no attempt to insert itself into a Christian world-picture. Her Chaos is an insistently material deity; his oven-like mouth represents the womb and his belly the world. The male, not the female, is thus made to signify corporeality, insatiable appetite, and in-exhaustible plenitude. In a delightful inversion of the scatology such a myth might lead us to expect, the "excrement" of Chaos is pure spirit, for only departing souls can leave the world-system in which all matter is endlessly recycled.

Strangely, however, Nature herself has become incorporeal. Christine calls her an *ombre* or shade (recalling Dante's disembodied spirits) and em-phasizes that she had "no visible or tangible body." The materiality of Chaos and the spirituality of Nature go some distance toward reversing traditional gender stereotypes. But in other respects, Nature seems more feminine than in the myth elaborated by Jean de Meun. No longer a hammer-wielding smith, she is now charged with the typically female tasks of cooking and feeding a man. As Sylvia Huot has perceptively observed, the use of this metaphor for Nature's creative work subordinates the act of sexual inter-course to the gestation of the fetus in the womb. "From the male perspec-tive, procreation is centered on the moment of sexual conquest . . . From the female perspective, however, procreation is a process of growth which begins with fertilization . . . and ends with fruition, itself a new beginning."[67] In the *Rose* a phallic Nature with her hammer and anvil had informed a poetics of male desire (Figure 3.2); in *Christine's Vision* Nature in her kitchen assimi-lates the work of reproduction to everyday female labor.

Once again Christine stresses the intentionality of Nature in assigning gender to bodies. As in *The Mutation of Fortune*, she is born female because Lady Nature wills it so, not because of any defect or irregularity in the "mold." Here Christine implicitly rejects the Aristotelian view of women as deficient males, an idea sanctioned by Thomas Aquinas and refuted by Reason in *The City of Ladies*.[68] The unnamed "chambermaid" of Nature, a "wise woman" who feeds the newborn babe with a "sweet and very mild liquid," must be Christine's biological mother, now given a modest role to complete the myth's validation of maternity above virile potency.[69]

Much later in the text, Nature makes one more brief but telling appear-ance. Christine is recounting the first stages of her career as a scholar and writer. As she begins to deepen her knowledge of poetry,

Nature rejoiced in me and said: "Daughter, be happy when you have fulfilled the desire I have given you, continue to apply yourself to study, understanding the writ-ings better and better." All this reading was not enough to satisfy my thoughts and intelligence; rather, Nature wanted that new books should be born from me, engen-dered by study and by the things I had seen. Then she said to me: "Take your tools and hammer on the anvil the matter I will give you, as durable as iron: neither fire nor anything else can destroy it; from this you should forge delightful things. When you carried your children in your womb, you felt great pain when giving birth. Now I desire that new books should be born from you, which you will give birth to from your memory in joy and delight; they will for all time to come keep your memory alive before the princes and the whole world. Just [as] a woman who has given birth forgets the pain and labor as soon as she hears her child cry (John 16.21), you will forget the hard work when you hear the voices of your books."[70]

This is Nature's first appearance as a literary muse. With remarkable economy Christine links a number of her central insights about vocation and gender. In the first place she stresses, as in *The Mutation of Fortune*, that it is Nature herself who endowed her with an aptitude for learning: thus the goddess's old covenant with Reason, broken by Jean de Meun, is back in force. By identifying her intellectual ability as Nature's gift, this time without qualifications, Christine defuses the objection that scholarship and writing are unnatural activities for a woman. No longer does she have to become a man in order to write: what need is there to "father" books when she can mother them? So, in the second place, she revises the ancient analogy between creation and procreation. Alan of Lille had used writing as a metaphor for sex; Christine reverses tenor and vehicle to make childbirth a metaphor for writing. Even as she adapts the hammer-and-anvil image from the *Rose*, she desexualizes it and strips away the salacious innuendoes with which Jean de Meun had invested the writing process. Unlike Jean's goddess Nature at her forge, forever toiling to produce ephemeral bodies, Christine as Nature's protégée will forge something indestructible and "durable as iron"—namely her books—to attain the same immortality sought by her male precursors. Finally, as she so often does at crucial junctures in her work, she invokes the Gospel and the long monastic tradition that contrasted the pain of carnal childbirth with the joy of spiritual motherhood. Her labor pangs as a writer are to issue in transcendence and eternal memory, in a sublimation of maternity that proceeds from the same feminine Nature who gave her a female body in the first place. Transcending the dichotomy of Nature and Culture, Christine now depicts the rehabilitated goddess prompting her to take the first steps on a path that will lead to the most sublime of her mentors, Lady Philosophy—and that goddess, as we saw in Chapter 1, "is properly God."

Testing the Norms: Nature, Nurture, *Silence*

All the antinomies we have seen within Nature's compass—heterosexual versus homosexual desire, biological versus social gender, reproduction versus abstinence, plain speech versus linguistic play, female achievement versus unjust laws—converge almost uncannily in *Silence*, a French romance from the second half of the thirteenth century.[71] By a fluke of literary history this poem, which survives in a single manuscript,[72] was lost until 1911, first published in an obscure serial in the 1960s, roundly ignored for twenty more years, then "discovered" by feminist and poststructuralist critics in the 1980s. But the romance's belated critical reception is not the only reason it seems fetchingly postmodern. Its transvestite hero/ine is called "Silence" and its authorship, fittingly enough, remains shrouded in mystery. "Master Heldris of Cornwall," the self-identified poet, is otherwise unknown. Linguistic features indicate that the text originated in Picardy, not Cornwall, and the poet's name is almost certainly a pseudonym, possibly that of a woman.[73] Since Heldris uses masculine pronouns for the biologically female Silence,[74] I will return the compliment by using feminine pronouns for the culturally male author, whose "true" identity eludes us. Whoever Heldris was, she knew *De planctu Naturae* and may have known the *Roman de la Rose*. Although we cannot be sure which poem is earlier, *Silence* can be read as an elaborate, ambivalent gloss on a speech Jean de Meun puts in the mouth of la Vieille:

Touz jors Nature retorra,
Ja por habit ne demorra.
Que vaut ce? Toute creature
Vuet retorner a sa nature,
Ja nou lera por violence
De force ne de convenance.
* * * * *
Trop est fors chose de Nature:
Nature passe norreture. (14,025–38)

Nature always comes running back:
No habit will ever chase her out.
What is that worth? Every creature
Wishes to return to its nature;
It will never forsake it through the violence
Of force, promise, or convenience.
* * * * *
Too mighty a force is Nature:
Nature surpasses Nurture.

The maxim that "Nature passe norreture" was proverbial,[75] but no text prior to *Silence* constructs "Norreture" as an allegorical character. In Heldris's romance, Nature and Nurture come onstage in person to argue about the protagonist's gender.

But first the plot. The tale begins when Ebain, King of England, ends a war by marrying the ironically named Norwegian princess Eufeme ("good wife" or "alas, woman!").[76] Soon afterward two counts are slain in a duel over the inheritance of their wives, and Ebain in his anger decrees that "no woman shall ever inherit again / in the kingdom of England" (RM 314–15). This rash law sets the stage for all that follows.[77] When the brave, handsome Sir Cador slays a dragon and nearly dies of its venom, he is healed by the beautiful, learned Eufemie ("good speech").[78] The two fall in love in proper courtly fashion and Ebain arranges their marriage, allowing Eufemie—an only child and now the bride of his heir apparent—to inherit Cornwall from her father. Cador and Eufemie also produce one child, a daughter, but they are determined to circumvent the king's decree and make her their heir. Hence they name the child "Silence" and disguise her from birth in boy's clothing.[79] Silence receives a chivalric education and soon demonstrates great skill in jousting and other knightly sports. Upon reaching puberty, s/he ponders the wisdom of remaining disguised, but quickly realizes that "a man's ways are worth more than a woman's" (2637–38). Nevertheless, Silence runs away with a pair of traveling minstrels in order to learn some gender-neutral skills that will stand him in good stead if he is ever unmasked. In minstrelsy he quickly surpasses his masters and, fleeing their murderous envy, strikes out on his own.

Silence eventually makes his way to the court of Ebain, where he has the misfortune to become the love-object of Queen Eufeme. Silence does not reciprocate her passion but pleads feudal honor, so the queen—unaware that she herself loves a woman—accuses Silence of being a homosexual and even a male prostitute.[80] Eufeme tries to avenge herself on the unwilling boy by staging a fictive rape and accusing him. When her "Potiphar's wife" scheme fails, she sends Silence to the king of France with a forged letter demanding the bearer's execution. But the canny French king, wiser than Ebain, defies the order and grants Silence knighthood instead. Summoned back to England, the new knight heroically saves the king's life in a battle against rebellious counts. Now in high favor with Ebain, Silence is victimized once again by the wrathful Eufeme. This time she tries to get rid of him by sending him on a quest to capture Merlin, knowing that only a woman can succeed in that task. Silence does catch the sly master of disguise, with Merlin's own help, but his success inevitably leads to his exposure. In the final scene, a laughing Merlin appears at court and unmasks not only Silence but also Eufeme—who turns out to have been keeping a male lover disguised as a nun for many years. Enraged, Ebain has his queen and her lover put to death, repeals the law against female inheritance, and marries the newly regendered heiress, Silence.

This tantalizing tale has been diversely interpreted. Some critics read the ending as a victory, others as a defeat for Silence, while Heldris has been variously hailed as a protofeminist, denounced as a misogynist, and post-modernized as a champion of ambiguity and indeterminacy.[81] The reading I will propose stands at an oblique angle to most others, for, rather than focusing on the central figure, I will read *Silence* as if its protagonist were Nature herself. From the vantage point of this study, it is Heldris who, more than any other medieval poet except Alan of Lille, most fully probes the dilemmas posed by Nature: How far does her power extend and what are its limits? How much that goes by the name of "nature" is actually due to nurture, or to human choice, custom, or chance? If it is possible to tamper with Nature's will, is it ever desirable? If indeed "Nature / Signorist desor Noreture" ("Nature has lordship over Nurture," 2423–24), is her sovereignty benign or despotic? The goddess's contested terrain in *Silence* turns out to involve not only gender, but also class, morality, and even species.

Heldris highlights the significance of Nature by using the word more than forty times in the prominent end-rhyme position. In at least eight of these occurrences, *Nature* is made to rhyme with *aventure*—the element of chance, high-stakes gambling, and open-ended questing central to romance.[82] For Nature in *Silence* is playing against the odds, like a famous but aging knight who must fend off all challengers to retain his title. The goddess stakes her all on her masterpiece, the lovely child in whom she means to show the full extent of her power, but she brooks a forceful challenge from her adversary, Nurture, and loses the first several rounds of the fight. Nature bides her time angrily and at length emerges triumphant, only to carry off a pyrrhic victory that would not have been possible without Merlin's clair-voyance and Ebain's heavy-handed authority—two forces that are not at all "natural."

The question at stake in Nurture's challenge is whether anyone can or should be "denatured," temporarily or permanently. The possibility first arises at the stereotypical moment when Cador falls in love and complains that he is no longer able to nurture (*norir*) his own flesh:

S'en moi peüst valoir *Nature*,
Ja voir si estrange *aventure*
A mon las cor n'en avenist . . .
Mais jo sui tols denaturés
Et si cuic estre enfaiturés. (1027–32)

If Nature could prevail in me,
Such a strange adventure
Would not be happening to my weary body . . . ,
But I am all denatured:
I think I have been bewitched.

Cador's "denaturing" is conventional and of short duration, yet Heldris implies that if love had not defeated nature in him, Silence would never have been begotten. The tale of the hero/ine's own, much less conventional, denaturing is introduced with the same rhyme pair when Heldris remarks, after Silence's christening,

Or vos ai jo dite la some,
L'oquison de ceste *aventure*,
Com cis ouevrent contre *Nature*,
Ki l'enfant on si desvoié . . . (2252–55)

Now I have told you the whole
Reason for this adventure:
How [Cador and Eufemie] worked against Nature
When they made the child deviate from Nature's path . . .

After eighteen years of this deviant life, the almost fully denatured Silence finds himself in combat, fighting to save his own and Ebain's life, and sends up a hasty prayer:

Silences dist: "Bials Dex, chaieles, . . .
Cho qu'afoiblie en moi *Nature*
Cho puist efforcier T'*aventure*." (5604–8)

Silence said, "Dear God, I beg you, . . .
What Nature has made weak in me
Your own *aventure* can make strong."

Here even God seems to be enjoying Silence's adventure and raising the stakes against Nature. Our virgin warrior is briefly aligned with all the female saints and martyrs who revealed God's "strength perfected in weakness" (2 Cor. 12.9), even if the weakness s/he claims at this juncture is purely rhetorical. Heldris remarks a few lines later, after the hero has happily lopped off a few more arms and legs of the enemy, that "God was on Silence's side, as you can plainly see, for he won the war" (RM 5646–47). If Nature is to prevail in this contest, her victory will be at least as hard won.

The goddess makes her first appearance in the scene of Silence's birth.

Heldris's Nature, like Christine de Pizan's, is a bakerwoman.[83] Proud of her art, Nature announces her intention to create a masterpiece (*ouvre forcible*): she is tired of crude, vulgar work and resolves to use only her finest white flour and her most exquisite mold. With her own hand she inscribes (*escrist*) the girl's delicate features and paints her face with lilies and roses, asserting that "once in a while I must show what I can do" (RM 1885). Having invested so much in Silence, Nature sees the child as her own little girl ("sa puciele," 1868; "ma mescine," 1873; "ma fille," 1927). Thus she is furious when Cador and Eufemie deface her art by "changing her daughter into a son" (RM 2263). What seems to irritate her most is that Silence's lovely complexion will be damaged, for as a boy he must be tanned by the sun and hardened by winds. This concern recurs throughout the text and surfaces once more at the end: after Silence is revealed to be a woman, Nature takes three days to "repolish" her entire body, removing every trace of suntan, before she can marry the king. This obsession with surfaces suggests that gender itself is a superficial matter: Silence's core identity cannot or does not change, but a new dress and a makeover suffice to restore her womanhood.

The scene set in Nature's bakery serves Heldris for an extended commentary not on gender but on class. The narrator explains that Nature has many grades of dough or flour: "She always makes quality folk from the refined clay, and riff-raff from the coarse" (RM 1833–34). Deviations from the expected norm—aristocrats aren't always noble, nor peasants base—are explained by defects in the baking process: if a little coarse matter is mixed in with the fine, it goes straight to the heart and sullies the whole creation. Conversely, some men of low birth possess a noble character because they have, by accident as it were, a bit of fine clay in their makeup. In Silence's case, for once, character and status are perfectly congruent, since she is made from only the purest material. After Nature has sifted her flour and kneaded her dough she proceeds to mold, inscribe, and paint it. Heldris seems here to be making a distinction analogous to the Aristotelian dichotomy of form and matter, though with antithetical meaning. Silence's matter—the fine white flour—represents her noble character, while her gender is signified by the inscription and coloring, or superficial form, stamped upon that matter. This unusual privileging of matter over form explains why gender is more mutable than character.

But Nature, a goddess scorned, does not like her work to be altered in either respect. After Silence's fateful baptism as a boy, she vows to prove that she is stronger than Nurture:

"Il ont en mon desdaing cho fait
Quanses que miols valt Noreture
Que face m'uevre!" dist Nature.
"Par Deu! par Deu! or monte bien!
Il n'a en tiere nule rien,
Ki par nature ait a durer,
Ki puist al loing desnaturer." (2266–72)

"They have done this to spite me,
As if the work of Nurture
Were worth more than mine!" said Nature.
"For God's sake! A fine state of affairs!
There is nothing on earth
Living in Nature's realm
That can be denatured for long."

Heldris quickly chimes in to second Nature's complaint: "Segnor, par Deu, Nature a droit!" ("Lords, by God, Nature is right!" RM 2295). But critics who charge her with essentialism fail to notice that these editorial comments have nothing to do with gender. They deal instead with morals — and here Heldris shows herself to be an essentialist of the most pessimistic stripe. Nurture, she says, can make a person of "vile nature" behave honorably for years, but nature will out at last and he will die a villain. Moreover, bad nurture can corrupt an inherently fine and generous nature, yet no amount of fancy education "can mend a heart intrinsically evil" (RM 2342). Nature will later use Adam as a case in point: God created him good but he was spoiled by Nurture, in the person of Satan (6035–84). The logic is not altogether consistent, however; as Silence is quick to observe, Nature speaks in sophistries (2540). In denying responsibility for Adam's fall, she claims that even the most hardened sinners, for whom evil seems to be second nature, are in reality corrupted by nurture. Here she skirts the question of original sin, as if to say that no one is "born bad": a high crime rate is due to unemployment, bad schools, and dysfunctional familes, not to some hereditary taint. But this "liberal" stance contradicts the narrator's earlier "conservative" explanation of evil, namely that the hearts of mortals are inherently good or bad because of the fine or coarse material used by Nature to fashion them. So, even though Nurture loses points with the exemplum of Adam, their debate must on logical grounds be judged a draw.

This unresolved argument about *human* nature further problematizes the utterances about *female* nature proclaimed by the misogynist narrator and various male characters, including Ebain and Cador. In the meantime, we are left to decide for ourselves whether Silence's masculine nurture qualifies as "good" or "bad." Nature of course thinks it bad because it is *contra naturam*, and even Silence, when he adopts a secondary disguise as a minstrel, takes the stage name of Malduit or "badly brought up."[84] But Silence's education in itself seems excellent. Like Tristan, on whom his character is partly based, he acquires a superb knowledge of the liberal arts, languages, and music as well as chivalry and sports. Indeed, this "nurture" is far superior to the training he would have received as a girl, so that—*pace* Nature—in his case an outstanding education seems to have improved upon an already splendid nature.

Like Alan of Lille, Heldris links offenses against Nature with the artful manipulation of grammar. In a witty and oft-quoted passage, Cador outlines his plan for the naming of Silence:

"Il iert nomé Scilenscius;
Et s'il avient par *aventure*
Al descovrir de sa *nature*
Nos muerons cest -us en -a,
S'avra a non Scilencia.
Se nos li tolons dont cest -us
Nos li donrons natural us,
Car cis -us est contre nature,
Mais l'altres seroit par nature." (2074–82)

"He will be named Silentius;
And if it happens by chance
That his nature is discovered,
We'll change this -*us* into -*a*:
She will be called Silentia.
If we take this -*us* from her,
We will give her natural usage,
For this -*us* is against Nature,
But the other would accord with Nature."

The Latin masculine ending -*us* coincides with the Old French noun *us*, meaning usage or custom (from Latin *usus*). Thus maleness, as in Christine's *Mutation of Fortune*, is linked with the hegemony of Nurture, femaleness with that of Nature. But as Erin Labbie reminds us, the hero/ine normally evades this dilemma by using a gender-neutral French name that can translate either of the Latin forms and thus "includes both feminine and masculine attributes as 'natural' to Silence's identity."[85] The Latin names recur only at the end of the romance and in the celebrated Nature-Nurture debate that takes place when Silence reaches puberty.

At this point Nature appears and visits the boy-girl with sharp reproaches. She is wasting her fabulous beauty and deceiving the "thousand women" who have allegedly fallen in love with her; she should abandon her free-wheeling forest life and "go to a chamber and learn to sew" (RM 2528) because, after all, she is not really "Scilentius"—it is all a fraud. Silence is puzzled by this charge: "Donques sui jo Scilentius, / Cho m'est avis, u jo sui *nus*" (2537–38). It is a brilliantly punning line: "Either I am Scilentius, so I think, or else I am no one / or else I am nude." Without his carefully nurtured masculine identity, Silence is either a social nobody or a naked female body—which may after all amount to the same thing.[86] This sober reflection enables Nurture to frame her counter-argument: she commands Nature to "leave [her] nursling alone" because Silence has been completely "denatured" and will always resist her. Both ladies have become fiercely possessive about the youth: as Nature had once called her "my daughter," Nurture now calls him "my foster-child" (*noreçon*, 2593). Punning in turn, Nurture boasts that she can succeed perfectly in turning a *noble enfant* into a *malvais home* (2602). The vaunt is both true and false: Silence may indeed be a "defective male" but s/he is hardly a "bad man."[87] Further slippage arises from the context. Nurture claims that she can make "a thousand people" work against Nature, just as Silence does, but since we do not know if the natures they were born with are good or bad, we cannot decide whether her power is beneficial or harmful. Nurture, like Nature, is a morally ambiguous force.

When the two adversaries have argued to a standstill, the debate is resolved by Reason, who—here as in the *Roman de la Rose*—sides against Nature. Heldris's Reason is no celestial daughter of God; she represents something more like shrewd pragmatism. Nevertheless, her victorious arguments should preclude any simplistic reading of Nature as the poet's mouthpiece. Reason's case reinforces Nurture's on three counts. First, Silence at twelve already understands that in his society a man's life is valued far more than a woman's: "miols valt li us d'ome / Que l'us de feme, c'est la some" (2637–38). Since he is now on top, why should he willingly step down? "Deseure sui, s'irai desos?" (2641). In addition, he remembers the law that initially prompted his disguise: he does not want to lose his inheritance or prove his father a liar. Finally, as a youth governed by Reason, Silence has no taste for the games of Cupid: his "mouth [is] too hard for kisses, / and arms too rough for embraces" (RM 2646–47). This declaration can be read as a rejection of female sexuality, for Silence insists that he is really a boy, not a girl ("vallés sui et nient mescine," 2650). Yet Nature's promptings never go so far as to awaken desire for *any* partner in the young hero. The opposite of Jean de Meun's Amant, he heeds Reason and resolves to renounce sexuality altogether: "C'onques ne fu tels abstinence" ("Never was there such abstinence," 2659). It might be objected that Silence is only twelve, after all; but s/he is eighteen by the end of the romance and still completely sexless. Heldris's Nature is so eminently resistible that, by the time Silence is knighted, he no longer has the least regret about his exceptional *usage* (5178).

The final Nature-Nurture debate concerns not Silence but Merlin, who has also challenged the "nature of man." Like the protagonist, the wizard is ambiguously gendered. Though male, he is neither a warrior nor a father, and in traditional Arthurian lore (adopted by Heldris from the *Estoire Merlin*), he is fated to be undone by the woman to whom he reveals his secrets. As Eufeme tells Ebain, the wizard can only be captured by a "woman's trick" (*engien de feme*, 5803). Yet since Merlin himself devises this trick and explains it to Silence, he must be at least dabbling in womanhood.[88] Even more fundamentally, he straddles the boundary between human and animal: "Ne sai s'il est u hom u bieste," says Silence ("I don't know whether he's man or beast," 5908).[89] The ruse by which he is captured turns on this double ambivalence. Since Nature has made Merlin a man (human and male), he has the same carnivorous instincts as any other man. But Nurture—that is, his own predilection—has taught him to live like a beast in the forest, subsisting on a vegetarian diet. Silence, tutored by Merlin in the guise of an old graybeard, lures Merlin the Wild Man with roast meat, which he cannot resist. But the salted meat induces a great thirst the wizard tries to assuage with the honey, milk, and wine that Silence has laid out in succession, until he collapses in a dyspeptic, drunken stupor. Seeing Merlin thus turn away from the *noreture* (food/training) to which he had long been accustomed, Nature gloats in triumph. But what we actually see in the episode is not so much a one-sided victory for Nature as a Lévi-Straussian synthesis. The foods that Silence uses to ensnare the wizard are coded both masculine and feminine: roast meat and wine evoke the warriors' banquet hall, milk and honey the female body. Likewise, cooked meat and wine are processed foods, raw honey and milk unprocessed, symbolizing the spheres of Culture and Nature respectively.[90] But to confound any simple resolution, Heldris has tied Merlin's human "nature" to culture—the world of the court, to which he must now return—and his "nurture" to the wilderness of a self-imposed exile. As a final paradox Merlin, captured with his own complicity, is on the one hand completely helpless, on the other in complete control. Though bound and threatened with death, he laughs heartily at all he sees, "for he knows already where the story is going" (6160).

In effect, Silence and Merlin trap one another (6457–58), so it would not be amiss to read Merlin's ending as a mirror image of Silence's. Nature humiliates both of them, seizing Merlin by the scruff of his neck to thrust him toward the meat, and compelling Silence to bear the shame of a public disrobing. But the goddess, though vindicated, does not have the final word, for by dint of their nurture and their wits, both Silence and Merlin manage to remain "on top" in spite of their apparent undoing. Just before the capture scene, the disguised Merlin tells the disguised Silence not to abandon hope:

Jo ai veü jadis enter
Sovent sor sur estoc dolce ente,
Par tel engien et tele entente
Que li estos et li surece
Escrut trestolt puis en haltece. (5916–20)

I have often seen
a young bud grafted onto a sterile stock
with such skill and purposefulness
that both stock and graft
soon grew and flourished. (trans. Roche-Mahdi)

Grafting is a classic image for the propensity of art, or nurture, to improve on nature. It is no coincidence that in *The Winter's Tale*, one of Shakespeare's masquerade plays, the disguised king of Bohemia tells the disguised Perdita:

You see, sweet maid, we marry
A gentler scion to the wildest stock,
And make conceive a bark of baser kind
By bud of nobler race. This is an art
Which does mend Nature, change it rather; but
The art itself is Nature.[91]

Heldris proclaims no such elegant synthesis, but in *Silence* the story itself is often wiser and more sophisticated than its narratorial voice.[92] Interpreting Merlin's metaphor, we might say that Silence is the sweet young bud and King Ebain the sterile stock, but we might also call the graft an image of female nature "changed and mended" by masculine nurture, in such a way that Nature is still allowed to take credit for it.

If, as many critics have noted, the romance retreats in the end from its radical premise, it does not retreat nearly as far as some have claimed. Much discussion of the text has been bedevilled by a confusion of the nature/nurture question with the problem of misogyny. It is true that *Silence* does not ultimately challenge the medieval gender hierarchy. Heldris and most of her characters, including the protagonist, remain convinced that men's lives, opportunities, and achievements are more valuable than women's. Within that framework, however, *Silence* does demonstrate that the best man for the job might be a woman, given sufficient scope—that is, nurture—to exercise her talents. As for the opaque ending, with the self-revelation and concomitant silencing of Silence, very few alternatives would have been available to the poet. Since Silence cannot escape discovery by becoming a monk, thus disabling himself as heir of Cornwall, s/he must eventually marry, and with marriage, some resolution of the sex/gender ambiguity is inevitable. In two fourteenth-century transvestite romances, the cross-dressed hero marries a woman and is magically transformed into a male, but that possibility either did not appeal or did not occur to Heldris, a writer who generally eschews the supernatural.[93] The only other possible outcome would have been exposure followed by punishment: life imprisonment or death for violating the king's decree. Yet neither Silence nor her parents are punished for the gender masquerade; she is in fact rewarded, in the only terms a thirteenth-century audience would have recognized.[94] If not for the ministrations of Nurture—for the eighteen years she lived as a male—Silence could never have become *either* Ebain's most valiant knight *or* his queen, nor could women have regained their inheritance.

In a problematic disclaimer at the end of the poem, Heldris praises the woman who "works well against Nature," adding formulaically that no "good woman" should be offended by the disgrace of bad women like Eufeme.

Maistre Heldris dist chi endroit
C'on doit plus bone feme amer
Que haïr malvaise u blasmer.
Si mosterroie bien raison:
Car feme a menor oquoison,
Por que ele ait le liu ne l'aise,
De l'estre bone que malvaise.
S'ele ouevre bien contre nature,
Bien mosterroie par droiture
C'on en doit faire gregnor plait
Que de celi qui le mal fait. (6684–94)

Master Heldris says right here
That one should love a good woman more
Than one hates or blames a bad one.
I will show you exactly why:
For a woman has less occasion

(If she has the opportunity at all)
To be good than to be wicked.
If she works well against Nature,
I will show as a matter of right
That one should take more account of her
Than of the one who does evil.

Freed from the confusion created by an early editorial mistake,[95] this oft-reviled passage actually softens and nuances the apparent triumph of Nature. Silence, Heldris suggests, qualifies as a "good woman" precisely *because* she "works well against Nature," that is, against the devalued *us de fème* ("women's ways") that Nurture and Reason had taught her to reject. This is necessary not because "female nature" is intrinsically evil, despite the mis-behavior of Eufeme and the misogynist generalizations it elicits from Ebain and the narrator. Rather, the problem is that female *nurture*—misinterpreted as nature—gives women like Eufeme so many occasions to do harm, and so few to perform acts of conspicuous valor and virtue. Thus Silence, like Christine de Pizan in *The Mutation of Fortune*, finds that "becoming male" allows her to reveal the sterling stuff of her *human* nature in the public sphere, the only space that counts. If in the end, like Christine in *Lavision*, she reverts to her "natural" womanhood, it is only after her gender mas-querade has deconstructed the forced reduction of a noble and aspiring nature (what Christine would call *la femme naturelle*) to a limited and con-stricting nurture (*us de fème*). So, even though Nature claims the victory in her *aventure* with Silence, mollifying any conservatives in the audience, the romance as a whole embodies a far more ambivalent version of the proverb it dramatizes: "Nature passe nourriture / Et nourriture survainc nature" ("Nature surpasses Nurture, and Nurture vanquishes Nature").[96]

The Realm of the Natural

At this point it may be useful to step back from the trees for a glance at the forest. Nature, we have noted, is a goddess of the normative, but the norms she embodies are not always the same. In "The Dispute between Ganymede and Helen," she aligns herself with Reason on Helen's side, representing heterosexual as opposed to same-sex desire, as she will continue to do in *The Complaint of Nature*. In the *Roman de la Rose* the goddess is still proudly heterosexual, but Jean de Meun alters the emphasis to make her stand for procreative sex, as opposed not only to sodomy but also to chastity—and the promptings of Reason. Jean's Nature is a divinely ordained, necessary, but irrational and therefore amoral force, easily manipulated by the unreliable God of Love. To rehabilitate this somewhat degraded goddess, Chaucer tries in *The Parlement of Fowles* (though with limited success) to reconcile her role as a proponent of instinctual sexuality with due respect for the class hierarchy, while Christine de Pizan brings Nature back into Reason's camp. In *Silence* and *The Mutation of Fortune*, the goddess signifies anatomical as opposed to socially constructed gender. More precisely, she signifies *female* anatomy: the term *natura* was routinely used in gynecological texts as a synonym for the vagina, and this usage may well have inflected the goddess's interest in assuring that women continue to dress and behave like women.[97] In defiance of Nature, Silence's masquerade and Christine's fictive sex change both prove that anatomy does not have to be destiny. By the time she wrote *Lavision*, however, Christine had changed her strategy and turned Nature into an all-purpose figure of female creativity, whether expressed through motherhood, domestic labor (Nature's kitchen), or intellectual work (her own writing).

One factor that remains constant through all these vagaries is an affirmation of Nature's "givenness." She is always prior and often superior to some force representing Culture, and is therefore associated with a poetics of simplicity. In "Ganymede and Helen," the sexuality favored by Nature is artless, linked with animals and peasants, whereas gay sexuality is artful, connected with playfulness or sport (*ludus*) as well as social prestige. Jean de Meun would continue to oppose Nature and Art, although he also introduced the topos of Art imitating Nature (Fig. 3.4), which in the thirteenth century was not yet a cliché. While the forces supporting Amant's quest eventually make common cause in the *Rose*, there remains a conceptual distinction between the raw sex advocated by Nature and her ally, Genius, and the artful, cunning, Ovidian desire personified by Cupid. Significantly, it is also Genius who extols the naturalism of the Golden Age, a time of bucolic simplicity when Saturn reigned and the corrupting arts of civilization had not yet been invented. Chaucer attempts a fusion of Nature and Culture, integrating the rituals of courtly and political mating into a green world of springtime innocence, though the result does not come off quite as Nature intends it.

As the goddess whose work precedes and surpasses the artifice of mortals, Nature stands in a particularly vexed relationship to grammar, the first and most purely conventional of the seven arts. For the "Ganymede" poet, what is grammatically natural (*hic et hic*) is sexually unnatural and vice versa.

In his difficult and often misunderstood tour de force, *De planctu Naturae*, Alan of Lille appears to argue the contrary, forcing an alliance between grammar and Nature, but he succeeds only in demonstrating the unnaturalness of poetic language and the unreliability of Nature as a guide to sexual ethics. His goddess Natura makes a speech in praise of plain style and simple, elementary syntax, yet the poem itself (like "unnatural" love) is characterized by rhetorical excess, aureate style, and complex figures of speech. In *Silence*, too, the parents' decision to "denature" their child involves them in complicated language games, linking the masculine ending *-us* with the social and behavioral norms that determine gender (*us*). Interestingly, though, the play on *Silentius* and *Silentia* depends on a bilingual pun, for the French name *Silence* conceals the hero/ine's gender just as effectively as his masculine garb. In this case, at least, the vernacular tolerates greater ambiguity than Latin.

Christine de Pizan modified the traditional dialectic of Nature and Culture. Although she still used Nature to represent what is given, or created at least indirectly by God rather than mortals, she did not set Nature against rhetoric, art, or learning. In *The Mutation of Fortune*, the rationality of Nature is opposed to the folly of Custom (the oppression of women) and later to the random if ethically neutral machinations of Fortune. Christine's sex change may be "unnatural," but it is not morally good or bad: it is a survival strategy necessitated by circumstance. Only in *Lavision* does all opposition between Nature and Culture cease. In this highly atypical work, Nature is a promoter of culture and specifically of women's cultural achievements—a role she shares with her old friend Reason in *The City of Ladies*, a book completed in the same year. This revisionist view of Nature was a vital plank in Christine's feminist platform. In fact, she may well have been the first thinker to understand how readily dichotomies between Nature and Culture tend to marginalize Nature's "own" sex.[98]

In tracing Natura's trajectory from the twelfth century through the early fifteenth, we have observed a progressive secularizing of the goddess and her concerns. The wide-eyed celestial voyager of Bernard Silvestris gives way to Alan's fallen goddess, Jean de Meun's apostle of free love, and Heldris of Cornwall's champion of anatomical destiny. By the time of Chaucer and Christine de Pizan, Dame Nature had become a seasoned habituée of court life, more at home with the politics of matchmaking than with the stars in their courses. Although she would always retain her theological niche as God's daughter, Natura's most enduring literary function proved to be removing sex and gender from the sphere of primary divinity—that is, from the dictates of biblical and ecclesiastical ethics—and setting them in a semi-autonomous realm of discourse where the interaction of biological with social determinants (Custom, Nurture, Fortune) could be frankly discussed. The goddess would hold her own within this realm of secondary divinity until the nineteenth century, when the Romantics tried once again to merge Nature with Nature's God, and the Victorians in anguish rediscovered their conflict.

4

Love Divine, All Loves Excelling

Fames enim anime desiderium est. Sic vere Deum amans anima
amore non satiatur quia Deus amor est, quem qui amat amorem
amat. Amare autem amorem circulum facit, ut nullus sit finis
amoris.[1]

Now the soul's hunger is desire. Hence a soul that truly loves
God is insatiable in love because God is love; whoever loves
God is in love with Love. To love Love completes a circle so that
love may never end.

— YVO, *Epistola ad Severinum de caritate*

ONE OF THE GODDESS NATURA'S EARLIEST functions, as we saw in Chapter
2, was to supersede the Platonic world soul as the presiding spirit or energiz-
ing force of the cosmos. After several Platonists of the early twelfth century,
including Peter Abelard and William of Conches, had incurred charges of
heresy for equating the *anima mundi* with the Holy Spirit, the platonizing
poets Bernard Silvestris and Alan of Lille avoided this critique by transferring
many of the world soul's attributes to Natura. In the process, they separated
God from the biosphere and the Holy Spirit from sexuality, allowing their
ambiguous new goddess to fill the gap. Over the course of time, Natura lost
some of her transcendent aura and came to be identified increasingly with
the sexual, gendered, earthly dimensions of human existence. In a word, she
became secular—a manifestation of secondary rather than primary divinity,
limited in power and knowledge and, at times, distinctly fallen. The exaltation of Nature, at least in the work of Alan of Lille and Jean de Meun, thus
furthered the theological agenda of supernaturalism: Natura might indeed
be the daughter of God, but she was in no sense equal to her Father.

Yet one prominent contemporary of Alan, Hildegard of Bingen, rejected
this solution to the cosmological problem. In Hildegard's books, the figure
designated as Caritas fills the roles of both the Holy Spirit *and* the world
soul, although the German abbess carefully avoided the suspect terminology
of the French Platonists. Unlike Alan of Lille and his followers, Hildegard
would hear of no buffer zone between Creator and creature, no intermediate

or subordinate deity. Both Natura and Caritas "quicken all things vitally by an unseen, all-sustaining life," in the words of the *Liber diuinorum operum*.[2] But while Alan's Natura is a goddess *under* God, Hildegard's Caritas is God *as* a goddess. The visionary thus stands as a pivotal figure between the Platonists of the early twelfth century and the mystics of the later twelfth and thirteenth, whose devotion centered on the same potent divinity. If Natura served ultimately to distance earth from heaven, and still more to divide eroticism from spirituality, the alternative goddess known as Caritas (or Frau Minne or Dame Amour) labored to unite them. And if Natura focused her attention on the instrumental aspects of sexuality—anatomy, procreation, gender roles—with the goal of preserving biological life, Lady Love zeroed in on its fiery core of desire, with the goal of attaining divine life.

Love or charity had been a central theological concept ever since the New Testament, but she had not always been a goddess. As of 1100, shortly before her emergence, no literate Christian would have mistaken *caritas*—divine love, the root of the tree of virtues—for anything other than the immortal foe of *cupiditas*, satanic vice and root of all evils. Yet by 1400—after the "age of Ovid" and the *Ovide moralisé*, after the beguine mystics and the flowering of *mystique courtoise*, after Beatrice and Dante—carnal and celestial loves had come to resemble each other so convincingly that erotic spirituality, and with it the "discernment of spirits," emerged as a compelling pastoral problem.[3] The story of how Caritas came to bear Cupid's arrows and Aphrodite's flaming torch, of how rival deities and competing discourses on love came so close to merging, will be the theme of this chapter.

Scholars used to argue vehemently as to whether priority in such transactions should be ascribed to courtly or monastic, Latin or vernacular culture. But these apparently distinct spheres were in fact porous and mutually permeable: the monks who anatomized charity and the virgins who swooned in mystical love were often literally brothers and sisters of the great lords who patronized minnesingers and trouvères. Indeed, a few prominent monks and clerics were themselves former love poets.[4] By the thirteenth century, the road of influence was traversed by a noisy two-way traffic, enabling "crossover" poets to flourish in both lay and religious life. As erotic love was progressively christianized—clothed in the garb of liturgical language, Marian piety, and Neoplatonic philosophy—divine love was simultaneously eroticized, made to speak the languages of *fin' amors* and pagan mythology.[5]

These lively exchanges between the religious and courtly discourses of love were facilitated by another kind of two-way traffic that has been much less noticed. I refer to the literary passage between exegesis and myth. If

Caritas rose above the ranks of her sisters, the allegorical virtues, to become a Christian goddess of might, her exaltation was due in large part to monastic exegesis. Already personified in some well-loved New Testament chapters, especially 1 Corinthians 13 and 1 John 4, charity was hypostasized and eulogized even more fervently by the great rhetoricians of the twelfth-century cloister, who conflated her now with Divine Wisdom, now with the Bride from the Song of Songs. Instead of demythologizing Scripture, these Cistercian and Victorine exegetes mythologized it further, elaborating its metaphors to create compelling mythic systems of their own. Once Caritas had emerged as a goddess in her own right, whether as a female manifestation of God or as his celestial bride, she readily made her way into vernacular theology, where she merged with the lyric poets' Frau Minne and, through her, with Lady Venus herself. But even as monastic writers midwifed the birth of Caritas from exegesis into myth, mythographers and grammarians were busy transforming pagan myth into Christian exegesis. The Carolingians, as we have seen, had long since identified the classical Minerva with the biblical Sapientia. It was only a matter of time before Cupid would become a figure of Christ, and the Incarnation itself furnish proof of the Virgilian maxim that *omnia vincit amor* ("love conquers all").[6]

Caritas and *Amor*: The Twelfth Century

It is hardly news that the twelfth century was a golden age of love, an age when the theory and practice of highly refined, stylized forms of erotic behavior flourished as never before. *Why* this should have been the case is one of history's great unanswerable questions. Among the religious, we can point to the rapid expansion of the clerical and monastic orders, the renaissance of Latin letters, and the growing tide of adult converts who brought a greater self-consciousness to the cloister than did child oblates. Among the laity, we should recall the gradual spread of literacy, the emergence of the vernaculars into writing, the new prominence of regional courts as cultural centers, and the burgeoning economic growth and political centralization that enabled the aristocracy to begin its slow transformation into a leisure class. But these convergent factors hardly "explain" the celebration of a new kind of interiority among those, both religious and lay, who had leisure to cultivate it. C. Stephen Jaeger has emphasized the roles of cathedral schools and episcopal courts in fostering the ideals of *urbanitas* and *curialitas*, in which love would come to play an essential part, while Gerald Bond conversely links the rise of "the loving subject" and its lyrical expressions to the cultivation of a "new secularity" in the courts of romanesque France.[7] More recently, Jaeger has pointed out that the real novelty of *fin' amors* lay not in the pursuit of love as a source of refinement, nobility and virtue, but in the insertion of women into a discourse that had hitherto been reserved for intense, highly public exchanges of friendship among elite males.[8]

Our subject here, the emergence of "Lady Love" as a Christian goddess, represents only one specialized aspect of a far-ranging revolution in sensibility. But the power vested by mystics in this new deity cannot be understood apart from the competing theoretical literatures on love that flourished simultaneously in several twelfth-century milieux. The rivalry among these medieval erotic theorists echoes that of their great classical teachers. As Bond has written, the whole tradition of medieval writing about love "can be conceived abstractly but usefully as a set of complex reactions to the fundamental disagreements between the positions represented by Ovid and Augustine—between what Richard Lanham once characterized as the referential mystics and the rhetorical stylists."[9] To Ovid and Augustine we can add Cicero, the apostle of pure disinterested friendship, as a lesser third. Now and then we come upon a thinker original enough to fuse elements of all three, as in the incandescent letters of Heloise.[10] For the most part, however, Ovidians and Augustinians in the twelfth century stood firmly opposed.

The clash between secular and monastic theorists of love can be summed up in three terms: *caritas, cupiditas, amor*. The broadest of the Latin words for love, *amor* is as radically ambiguous as its vernacular equivalents, with a semantic range that extends from the rapist's leer to Christ's death on the cross.[11] In the terminology of Christian Latin, there is no such ambivalence: *caritas* is by definition holy ("Deus caritas est," I John 4.8), while *cupiditas* is by definition evil ("radix omnium malorum est cupiditas," I Timothy 6.10). Augustine famously opposed the two loves in *De doctrina christiana*, defining *caritas* as the love of God, self, and neighbor only for God's sake, and *cupiditas* as the love of anything at all without reference to God.[12] In *De civitate Dei* he asserts that the earthly city is built on "self-love even to the point of contempt for God" (*cupiditas*) and the celestial city on "love of God even to the point of contempt for self" (*caritas*).[13] Yet both terms retain some elasticity. *Caritas* overlaps with *amicitia* or friendship and also with *dilectio*, another brand of love more spiritual than carnal (the word is a Christian coinage from *diligere*, a verb connoting choice, attentiveness, and care). In theological usage, "charity" can refer to mercy or almsgiving, love of one's neighbor, love of God, God's love of humanity, the divine nature or essence, and the Holy Spirit, characterized in Augustinian theology as the substantial bond of love between Father and Son.[14] *Cupiditas* too has many shades of meaning; it can denote any sort of greed, especially sexual or financial (the latter is intended in 1 Timothy), and can be used like *concupiscentia* to signify original sin.

Given the terminology available to them, Ovidians preferred to theorize about *amor* and its cognates, taking advantage of their ambiguity and avoiding the stark moral valence vested in the biblical terms. At times this ambiguity could be problematic: when lyric poets begged their ladies not to confuse their own worthy love with the identical-seeming but duplicitous love of their rivals, they had to resort to adjectives to distinguish the genuine article (*fin' amors, hohe Minne*) from its counterfeits (*fol amors, niedere Minne*). Wishing to disambiguate, Augustinians theorized about *caritas* and *cupiditas*, yet always within the overarching context of *amor*, which enabled them to investigate the psychology of love more broadly without losing sight of the moral opposition they wished to enforce. A generation ago, D. W. Robertson built a whole theory of medieval literature on the dichotomy of the two loves. That theory is now widely discredited, for a multitude of reasons that need not be rehearsed here.[15] Notwithstanding Robertson's critical faults, however, the differentiation of *caritas* and *cupiditas* looms undeniably large in monastic writings and remains essential to our theme. Curiously, Robertson himself paid little attention to the twelfth-century Cistercians and Victorines, who built variously on their Augustinian foundations to explore the psychology of *eros* with great subtlety. But even—or especially—when denouncing the folly of "carnal love," these theorists also betrayed their debt to secular love poets, a debt that mystical poets of the thirteenth century would owe in turn to them.[16]

When the abbot William of St.-Thierry published his treatise *De natura et dignitate amoris* (*On the Nature and Dignity of Love*) in the early 1120s, he cast himself explicitly as an anti-Ovid.[17] "Foul, carnal love," he remarks, "once had teachers of its foulness"—persons so skilled in the art of seduction that they managed to destroy the whole natural order in their unflagging pursuit of lust. One such teacher sank so low in this depravity that his own companions forced him to recant and write the *Remedia amoris*.[18] In opposition to Ovid's unnatural magisterium (perpetuated in the schools of the twelfth century), William asserts that true love originates with Nature and her author, and "teaches itself to those who are willing to be taught by God." Even William, however, believes with his worldly foes that "the art of arts is the art of love."[19] Fortunately for the abbot, he did not live long enough to read his century's most celebrated update of Ovid's *Ars amatoria*—the scandalous *De amore* of Andreas Capellanus. In 1277 the bishop of Paris, Etienne Tempier, would condemn the Chaplain's then century-old treatise as heretical, showing that he took the pseudo-Augustinian rejection of love in its final book as a gesture no more definitive than Ovid's *Remedia*.[20] William and Andreas were worlds apart in their convictions, not to mention their tone: the one was instructing in all seriousness, the other amusing himself with a *jeu d'esprit*. Yet abbot and courtier alike concerned themselves with the great theoretical problem of the age: delineating the nature of *amor* and the proper techniques for its cultivation and refinement.

A comparable moment of self-definition occurs in Aelred of Rievaulx's *Speculum caritatis* (*Mirror of Charity*), a treatise published in the early 1140s at the urging of his friend and fellow Cistercian, Bernard of Clairvaux. Aelred records his dialogue with a puzzled novice who claims that he used to love God more fervently when he was still in the world, weeping frequent tears of compunction and divine sweetness. Now, however, he is so worn out by the toil and austerity of Cistercian life that he cannot squeeze a single tear from his eyes. Aelred, wishing to convince the novice that genuine love is measured by action rather than tender feelings, appeals to the sympathy we feel for fictional characters. However moved we might be when we hear someone sing the sufferings of a tragic hero, Aelred says, we would not pay a cent to rescue the bloke "even if all these events were taking place before our very eyes."[21] Blushing, the novice admits that he too has been moved to tears by "the tales they tell of some chap called Arthur," and he realizes that the pious tears he once shed for Christ's passion were of the same genre.[22] Before, he was only responding to Jesus as a literary character, not exhibiting holiness. Now that he obeys God's commandments, his love must be judged stronger even if it gives less pleasure.

This is an Augustinian moment, indebted in theme and style to the *Confessions*. Just as the young Augustine learned to grieve his loss of God by remembering how he had once grieved Dido's loss of Aeneas, Aelred shows that he too had learned something about human feeling from his experience of literature.[23] We do not know exactly what literature he had in mind, but in the ten years he spent at the court of King David of Scotland, he must have heard many a minstrel.[24] To be sure, Aelred the monk, like Augustine the bishop, is inclined to belittle this experience: to be so moved by mere poetry (*uanis carminibus*) is nothing short of ridiculous (*perabsurdum*). Yet the transformation of human love has to begin somewhere. As Bernard of Clairvaux taught, all love starts out as the sheerest carnality: our self-love, or innate *cupiditas*, progresses by slow degrees into charity.[25] So if Aelred's novice learned from his love of King Arthur how to love a greater hero, Jesus, and the sweetness of that attraction led him at last into the cloister, then even his abbot cannot wholly reprehend the vain poets. Aelred's revealing treatment of literary emotion would later be echoed and expanded by Peter of Blois:

In tragedies and other lyric poetry, and in the songs of minstrels (*joculatorum*), we often hear described some man who is wise, good-looking, brave, lovable, and charming in every way. The sufferings and injuries cruelly inflicted on him are also recited, as when performers (*histriones*) tell fabulous tales about Arthur, Gawain, and Tristan. In hearing these things the hearts of the audience are moved with compassion and even pricked to the shedding of tears. So then, you who are moved to pity by storytelling, if you should hear something about the Lord so pitiful that it wrings tears from you, can you profess for that reason to love God? If you have compassion for God, you have the same compassion for Arthur. Hence you squander your tears for both alike if you do not truly love God, if you do not pour forth tears of devotion and penitence from the fountains of the Savior—that is, from hope, faith, and charity.[26]

What is this tender feeling so readily evoked by minstrels and preachers alike, so swift to wring tears from a twelfth-century eye? Augustinian to the core, Aelred asks God himself to define *amor*:

But what is love, my God? If I am not mistaken, it is a marvelous delight of the spirit. The more chaste it is, the sweeter it becomes; the purer it is, the more tender; the more ample, the more joyful. Love is the heart's palate which tastes that you are sweet, the eye which sees that you are good, and the place which is capable of holding you, the Supreme One. For anyone who loves you grasps you, and the more he loves the more he grasps, for you yourself are love (*amor*), because you are charity.[27]

Aelred goes on to identify love with the will, that faculty of the soul which chooses, pursues, and enjoys the object it takes as its good. Considered as the capacity for loving, *amor* like all human faculties is good in itself, but once embodied in a particular act of love, it may be either good or bad. *Caritas* then is "the right use of love," *cupiditas* its abuse. The same faculty is capable of both, but charity enlarges our capacity for loving while cupidity diminishes it: *amorem cupiditas coangustat*.[28] Because love wasted on too petty an object—indeed, on anything less than God—renders the soul less and less capable of happiness, even the hunger of charity gratifies more than the satisfaction of cupidity. But the fulfillment of charity will be the eternal Sabbath rest of God:

Charity alone is his changeless and eternal rest, his eternal and changeless tranquillity, his eternal and changeless Sabbath. Charity alone is the reason why he created what was to be created, guides what needs guidance, moves what needs moving, advances what needs to be advanced and perfects what needs perfection. . . . For his charity is his very will and also his very goodness, and all this is nothing but his being.[29]

The several modalities of charity—as the highest theological virtue, as will in action, as Holy Spirit, as God's substantial being—required theologians such as Aelred to make careful and subtle distinctions. But theology by itself did not demand the personification of Caritas. Only the catalyst of secular poetry, acting on a religious culture already fascinated with the dynamics of love, can account for the creation of this new goddess. When monastic theorists turned to allegory, they had no need to invent a figura for *cupiditas*, since the pagans had conveniently done so already. The patron deity of *cupiditas* was Cupid, alias Amor, whom we have met in his French guise as *li dieu d'Amors* in the *Roman de la Rose*. In secular lyric, prose fiction, and iconography from the mid-twelfth century onward, but especially in the thirteenth, this God of Love is ubiquitous to the point of becoming clichéd. He had his myths and rituals, his epiphanies and commandments, and indeed, his own fictive religion.[30] Seldom far from Cupid was his mother Venus, who sometimes represented plain sexual passion vis-à-vis her son's stylized religion of love.[31] Far more than other pagan divinities, these two stood in an unusually vexed relation to Christian theology, for in poetry Love is a god, while in Christianity God is love.[32] In this light, the twelfth- and thirteenth-century exaltation of Caritas to mythic stature can be seen as a way to fight fire with fire. It had more to do with the literary vogue for Cupid and Venus than it did with the standard iconography of virtues and vices, where *caritas* is usually opposed to avarice or envy rather than to *cupiditas*.[33]

Since personification is a figure of rhetoric, it is not surprising that Caritas the goddess first appears in highly rhetorical texts. St. Bernard's letters, which circulated so widely that almost four hundred manuscripts survive, undoubtedly helped to popularize her. Bernard used Lady Charity as a rhetorical shield: the more unwelcome his message, the more vigorously he invoked her to insist that love alone prompted it. Around 1120 he wrote reproachfully to Fulk, a young man who had dared to abandon the cloister, in the following terms:

Our good mother Charity loves all her children but shows herself differently to each, whether she is fostering the weak, training the proficient, or blaming the restless. When she blames you she is gentle; when she flatters she is sincere. It is her custom to rage kindly, to caress without guile; she knows how to be patiently angry and humbly indignant. It is she, the mother of men and angels, who has made peace not only on earth but also in heaven. It is she who has reconciled God to humanity and humankind to God. . . . This is the venerable mother who grieves that you have offended her, complains that you have wounded her. . . . But although she is wounded and offended, if you return to her she will meet you like an honored mother (Ecclus. 15.2). Forgetting her injury, she will fall into your embrace, rejoicing that the one she had lost is found, the one who was dead has come to life. (Luke 15.32)[34]

Interweaving the sublime with the intimate, Bernard exercises that peculiar "compound of charm and threat" so characteristic of his style.[35] In another instance, he invokes Lady Charity to stave off the pleas of an importunate friend who wrote letters faster than Bernard could answer them:

To tell the truth, my dear Oger, I am compelled to feel vexed for your sake that I have so much to do, even though, as my conscience bears witness, I desire to serve charity alone in all my cares. . . . What then? Does Charity refuse you what you ask out of charity? You have asked, you have sought, you have knocked, and Charity has thwarted you. Why do you blame me? If you wish, if you dare, be angry at Charity. . . . You see how unwillingly I am torn away from writing a longer letter, as, led on by the delight of conversing with you and the desire to satisfy you, I become irksome to Lady Charity, for she long ago commanded me to put an end to this, yet I am still not silent. How much material in your letter requires a reply! . . . But she who bids otherwise is my lady, or rather, my Lord. For God is Charity, and has such authority that I must obey her rather than myself or you.[36]

In this remarkable paragraph Bernard invests the smallest decisions of his daily life with the force of divine authority. What to do next—finish writing to his friend or greet the visiting dignitaries? conclude his letter or review the week's budget with the cellarer? By his own confession, he can have no motive for any act except charity, and the slipperiness of that concept lets him glide with such ease from vexation at his busy schedule to the divine nature that poor Oger must be content: God herself will not allow him to receive as full a response as he would like. Doubtless the panache of this rhetorical performance compensated Oger for its brevity.

A still more influential personification of Charity derived from the Cistercians' older contemporary, Hugh of St.-Victor (d. 1141), whose treatises on love were sometimes wrongly though understandably ascribed to Augustine. In *De substantia dilectionis* (*On the Essence of Love*) Hugh pursues a course similar to Aelred's, asserting that in the human heart there is but a single wellspring of love (*fons dilectionis*) that waters two streams: *cupiditas* or *amor mundi*, and *caritas* or *amor Dei*. Taking his lead from Cant. 2.4 ("ordinavit in me caritatem"), Hugh defines cupidity as inordinate love and charity as love well-ordered with respect to its movement and its object.[37] But in his more flamboyant encomium, *De laude charitatis* (*In Praise of Charity*), he personifies Caritas in a passage that would inscribe itself indelibly on the consciousness of mystics:

You are the fullness of justice, the perfection of the law, the consummation of virtue, the knowledge of truth. Therefore, Charity, you are the way. . . . You bring God to man and guide man to God. He descended when he came to us; we ascend when we go to him. For neither he nor we can cross over to one another without you. You are the mediatrix, reconciling enemies, uniting opposites, equalizing those who are far from equal—humbling God and exalting us, drawing him to the depths and raising us to the heights. Yet you do this in such a way that his descent is not abject but merciful, and our exaltation is not arrogant but glorious. O Charity, great is your power! You alone were able to draw God down from heaven to earth. How mighty is your chain by which even God could be bound, and man who had been bound broke the chains of iniquity! . . . O Charity! How much can you accomplish? If you were so strong against God, how much stronger will you be against men? If God suffered so much for man's sake, what will man refuse to endure for God's? But perhaps you conquer God more easily than man, and you can prevail against God more readily than you do against man, because the more blessed it is to be overcome by you, the more fitting it is to God. . . . We were still rebels when you compelled him, who obeyed you, to descend from the throne of his Father's majesty and take on the weakness of our mortality. You led him bound in your chains, you led him wounded by your arrows. How ashamed man should be to resist you when he sees that you have triumphed even over God! You have wounded the Impassible, bound the Invincible, dragged the Changeless One down, made the Eternal One mortal.[38]

In this tour de force Hugh oversteps the bounds of exegesis and enters the sphere of myth. By envisioning Caritas as a force independent of God and more potent than he, he has perhaps unwittingly created a goddess, giving her for attributes the chains of a victor leading captives in triumph and the remorseless arrows of Cupid. To be laid low by these arrows is the height of glory, so God's lovers pray to be similarly smitten: "Many now bear your arrows fixed in their inmost hearts and desire to have them pierce yet more deeply. For they are sweetly and delightfully wounded, and they neither grieve nor blush to have received your wounds. O Charity! How great is your victory!"[39] At this point readers would be expected to recall the wound of love inflicted by the Bride in the Song of Songs: "Vulnerasti cor meum, soror mea sponsa" (Cant. 4.9). As Gilbert of Hoyland would write a few decades later, in his continuation of Bernard's Sermons on the Song, "Would that he might multiply such wounds in me, from the sole of my foot to the crown of my head, that there might be no health in me! For health is evil without the wounds that Christ's gracious gaze inflicts."[40]

But Hugh, as if suddenly recalling that his portrait of Caritas the archer is more mythic than scriptural, returns in closing to St. John's oft-cited assertion:

> O Charity! . . . I know not whether it is greater to say that you *are* God or that you have conquered God. If it be greater, even this I will say of you gladly and confidently: "God is charity, and whoever abides in charity abides in God, and God in him" (1 John 4.16). Hear, O man, and lest you reckon it a small thing to have charity, hear that God himself is charity. Is it a small thing to have God dwelling in yourself? So great is it to possess charity, for God is charity. To charity alone this privilege is granted, that she may be called—and actually be—God, an honor that is accorded to no other virtue. For it is not said that "God is humility" or "God is patience," as it is said that "God is charity."[41]

With this double affirmation the die is cast. On the authority of Hugh (or "Augustine"), devotional writers through the end of the Middle Ages would use Lady Love on the one hand to represent God herself in female guise, and on the other, to depict Almighty God vanquished by the same omnipotent goddess who now subdues her devotees. Hildegard of Bingen's visions and Hadewijch of Brabant's poems realize the first of these possibilities more fully than any other medieval author.[42] Mechthild of Magdeburg's dialogue with Frau Minne, cited in Chapter 1, is a superb example of the second. In a more learned vein, the English Franciscan John Ridewall (fl. 1330) cites Hugh's passage on Love's chains and arrows to explain how the pagan god Pan, yielding to the seductions of a nymph, could allegorically signify the Incarnation.[43]

We cannot end this survey of twelfth-century erotic theory without a glance at Hugh's great successor, Richard of St.-Victor. In his astonishing treatise *De IV gradibus violentae caritatis* (*On the Four Degrees of Violent Charity*), Richard carries Hugh's thought several steps further, dwelling with particular force on the motifs of binding and wounding. "Vulnerata caritate ego sum," he begins (Cant. 2.5),[44] establishing his authority as a sufferer, and goes on to exult in the progressively disabling stages of love's malady: "charity wounds, charity binds, charity sickens (*languidum facit*), charity extinguishes the mind (*defectum adducit*)."[45] Richard uses *caritas*, *amor*, and *dilectio* interchangeably, but even though one of his chief purposes is to compare the worldly lover's progress with the mystic's, he says nothing of *cupiditas*. The absence of the old antinomy is telling. In contrast to the usual emphasis on ordinate love, all love for Richard is limitless by nature and tends to extremes. "Violent charity" is no oxymoron but the defining category of his thought. Without emphasizing Hugh's personification of Caritas, he presupposes the same conception of love as an irresistible, conquering force that takes possession of the lover's being and overpowers his faculties one by one. It is a conception at least as old as the Greek tragedies, more at home in Ovid's *Metamorphoses* than in the New Testament. Insuperable love wounds the soul's affections, inseparable love binds the power of thought, singular love destroys the capacity for action, and insatiable love "leads to the brink of death and makes one despair of recovery."[46] The only—but crucial—difference between divine and human attachments is that in the latter, only the first degree of charity is good; the further stages bring evil and misery. In spiritual desires, on the other hand, the more extreme and violent the love, the more precious it is.

De IV gradibus would become a virtual road map for the Netherlandish mystics of the thirteenth century. Hadewijch of Brabant and Beatrice of Nazareth, in particular, set out to "live love with Love" in all its glory and misery, ringing their own variants on what are still recognizably the stages described by Richard. But their writings lay more than a half century in the future at the time of Richard's treatise, composed circa 1170. No one, not even Bernard in his sermons on the Song, had ever described mystical love in quite this way before, with the same ferocity and violence.[47] The startling originality of Richard's treatise begins to make sense only when we set it in the context of contemporary secular writing, and then we can see in him a brilliant literary critic, keenly aware of the ways that lyric poets and romancers were representing love and able to schematize these varieties of passion with his formidable analytic powers. *De IV gradibus* was penned only a few years before Andreas's *De amore* and at the height of Chrétien de Troyes's poetic career.[48] Richard's text, like the works of Andreas and Chrétien, is saturated with Ovidian metaphors: the lover is a soldier wounded in battle, a prisoner of war borne off in chains, a patient languishing on his bed. In the first degree of love, the sufferer burns with desire and gasps with feverish affection, for "these are sure signs of a wounded soul—groans and sighs, a pale and emaciated face."[49] As the afflicted one passes into the second stage, love "occupies the whole mind with the constant memory of itself, entangles and binds the mind so completely that it cannot escape or think of anything else."[50] Or, as Andreas would put it, "every lover is wont to grow pale at the sight of his partner," and "a true lover is constantly and unremittingly obsessed by the image of his beloved."[51]

Richard cites lavish biblical exempla to illustrate the stages of divine love, drawing on the Song of Songs, the Psalter, and the letters of Paul. He gives no such examples for the degrees of earthly love, but any reader familiar with contemporary romances can supply them readily enough. Richard's wounded lover in the first degree feels himself "smitten to the heart" by a "fiery dart of love,"[52] not unlike Chrétien's Yvain:

> Love's pursuit's a gentle art:
> through the knight's eyes she strikes his heart.
> The wound that Love has dealt the lord 🖎
> won't heal like wounds from lance or sword,
> for any wound a sword has cut
> the doctors can cure quickly, but
> the wounds of Love, by definition,
> are worst when nearest their physician.[53]

In the second degree, the binding love that takes every thought captive until the lover becomes incapable of carrying out life's necessary duties, can we not see Chrétien's Erec, a knight so besotted by the love of his wife Énide that he no longer cares for joust or tourney?[54] Richard asserts that, while the first degree of love makes marriages happy, the second "is undoubtedly bad" because it destroys the prudence and foresight that worldly affairs demand. The third degree paralyzes action and, "like a sickness, makes the hands and feet go limp, so that henceforth the mind can do absolutely nothing by its own will."[55] Here surely is Sir Lancelot, who at one point is toppled ignominiously into a ford because, lost in reveries of Guenevere, he is completely oblivious to the challenge of a knight riding full tilt to unhorse him.[56] And what of the fourth degree, where insatiable love turns into hatred that paradoxically increases desire, causing lovers to manufacture pointless quarrels and burn like the damned in alternate fire and frost? Richard claims that one "often" sees such love-hate relationships in the world. But, unless he had been hearing some truly extraordinary confessions, one suspects the passion of Tristan and Yseult as a likelier source for this shrewd anatomy of obsessive love.[57]

Needless to say, Richard did not write this treatise in order to dissect the follies and tragedies of fictional lovers. Far more of the text is devoted to the sweetness of contemplation, the ecstatic love of God, and the soul's mystical death than to the distresses of earthly love. Nevertheless, it was only the idiom of amorous passion, as it had been refined and heightened over the course of a century by troubadours, trouvères, and romancers, that enabled the Victorine to interpret the contemplative soul's adventures precisely as he did. His all-consuming *caritas* has swallowed up not only *amor* but even *cupiditas,* making the love of God seem more obsessive, more incapacitating, and certainly more violent than ever before. Fifty years earlier, William of St.-Thierry had set out to counteract Ovid by competing with him. Richard of St.-Victor incorporates, or rather subsumes the old master, in a kind of Hegelian *Aufhebung*. His Caritas behaves exactly like Andreas Capellanus's Cupid or Chrétien's Amors (a female personage), with the sole difference that she uses her devastating might to pierce hearts on behalf of God as well as mortals. In the crucible of *De IV gradibus*, the sophistication of the court melts at white heat into the wisdom of the cloister, to produce an amalgam that would prove both mercurial and unexpectedly stable.

Love's Violence: The Thirteenth Century

Toward the end of the twentieth century, music industry executives began to tap a new market for "crossover" recordings—operatic tenors singing Irish folksongs, Gregorian chant yoked with jazz saxophone, electronic synthesizers pulsing over melodies by Hildegard of Bingen. Demographically diverse and artistically uneven, the crossover phenomenon spurred the creation of new art forms as well as new audiences for old ones, reinvigorating the staid world of classical music with infusions of the "popular" while repackaging time-honored "elite" genres to appeal to the masses. We can discern a similar phenomenon within thirteenth-century *mystique courtoise*, if for "elite" and "popular" we substitute monastic and courtly, with the beguines and their affiliates providing a buffer zone. Devotional texts and artworks that witness to this crossover phenomenon not only appropriate the language of romance and *fin' amors*, but do so in an idiom characteristic, then as now, of romance literature: they exploit the convergence of love and violence in deliberately provocative ways.

Around 1250 one Gérard of Liège, Cistercian abbot of Val-Saint-Lambert, wrote a tract entitled *Quinque incitamenta ad deum amandum ardenter*, or *Five Incitements to the Ardent Love of God*.[58] Gérard's abbey lay in the heart of beguine country, so he may well have composed this extraordinary treatise for an audience of beguines and their confessors as well as monks.[59] But he plainly assumed that his readers, male and female, would be as steeped as he was in the literature of *fin' amors*. The treatise is one half of a diptych: its companion tract, *Seven Useful Remedies Against Illicit Love*, is a wholly predictable text teaching contempt of the world and its corollary, contempt of women. In *Five Incitements*, however, Gérard takes a different tack. Following the lead of Richard of St.-Victor, he shows that divine and carnal love, though opposed in morality, are identical in psychology. But Gérard goes still further than Richard, for along with citations from Augustine, pseudo-Augustine, and

Bernard, he includes a generous sprinkling of French love songs among his *auctores*, producing a strange macaronic text that spans the gap between Latin devotional writing and vernacular lyric.[60] For instance, to reinforce his point that God asks nothing but our love in return for all his gifts to us, he quotes this song:

Quankes il fist entiere
il le fist pour mamour auoir,
et quankes ie ferai dorenavant
ie le ferai pour plaire a lui seulement
et pour samour auoir.[61]

Whatever he has done till now
he has done to win my love,
and whatever I do henceforth
I will do to please him alone
and to win his love.

Like his twelfth-century precursors, Gérard cites the maxim that "God is charity" (1 John 4.8), but he does so explicitly to identify the Creator of the world with the *fin' amors* sung by poets, and even the *dieu d'Amors* so memorably portrayed by Guillaume de Lorris in the *Rose*. "Deus enim caritas est, dicit Iohannes, idest *amours*."[62] Even though *caritas* and *amours* could have the same denotation, as we have seen, their connotations still differed radically because of the linguistic boundary that normally separated courtly from monastic discourse. In obliterating this boundary and equating the two, Gérard is performing a remarkable sleight-of-heart trick. To love God, he wants to say, is to practice what the poets call *fin' amors*, and he can even take St. Paul to witness (1 Cor. 13.1): If I speak in the tongues of men and of angels, but have not charity—"idest, *se ie naime par amours*"—it profits me nothing.[63] A lover aspiring to please the biblical God who is Love must have the same qualities as one who seeks favor from the old pagan god of love: "oportet esse gratiosum exterius et deuotum interius eum qui uult amare et *au diu damours* placere" ("One who wishes to love and to please the God of Love ought to be outwardly gracious and inwardly devoted").[64] Here, with surprisingly little ado, Gérard has transmogrified the capricious winged archer of Ovid, Andreas, and Guillaume de Lorris into Jesus Christ. We must recall that the abbot wrote this tract before Jean de Meun completed the *Rose*, so he probably envisioned the *diu damours* as a genteel and idealized figure, rather than the opportunistic, heavily ironized deity who finally secures the lover's Rose. Gérard's own rosy view of Cupid recalls that of a thirteenth-century abbot of St. Étienne in Caen, who had the words "Ecce mitto angelum meum" ("Behold, I send my angel") engraved around an antique image of the love-god, thereby transforming the winged Cupid into the angel of the Annunciation.[65]

Jesus Christ is not only the God of Love in Gérard's text; he is also likened to the Fair Unknown, the hero of an Arthurian romance by Renaut de Bâgé.[66] The motif of hidden identity in the quest of this knight, who turns out to be the son of Sir Gawain and a fairy, might have seemed appropriate to Gérard because of the mixed parentage of Jesus and the humble, mortal disguise adopted by the Son of God in the Incarnation. Thus Gérard laments that Jesus, for all his beauty and prowess, remains for many

li biaus descouneüs,
li sages pau creüs,
et li fors pau cremus,
et li boins pau ames.[67]

the Fair Unknown,
the wise man scarcely believed,
the strong man scarcely feared,
the good man scarcely loved.

Throughout his exhortation to divine love, Gérard appeals to lyric and romance paradigms, encouraging the reader to envision God as both a desirable lover and a jealous one. If even the most miserable boy ("uilissimus et miserrimus gartio") will not tolerate it when his girlfriend bestows her favors on someone else, how should we imagine that God feels?[68] When a young cleric or layman falls in love with a woman, he showers her with fancy jewels and expensive gifts from Paris. What could make him more jealous and angry than to learn that she has given these very gifts to some new lover? That is exactly how God feels when we give his tokens of affection—our beauty and strength, our knowledge, wealth, and honor—not only to his rivals but to his worst enemies (the world, the flesh, and the devil). *Fin' amors* demands fidelity as well as courage and patience. In a tournament, the winning knight is not the one who spends the most or wins the most ransom money, but the one who "keeps his helm on his head the longest and most continuously, endures the most, and remains the longest in combat. Such a man is praised and appreciated, and no matter how poor he may be, he should rightly have the prize and glory of the tournament."[69] Henry Suso in his *Exemplar* would apply the same analogy to himself as a knight of love, serving faithfully on behalf of his lady, Eternal Wisdom.[70]

In his discussion of "insuperable love," one of Richard's four degrees, Gérard claims that love is rightly compared to death because both are invincible: no one can taste either love or death without losing all the powers of body and soul. "Thus love or charity is undoubtedly the strongest passion, which no one can feel or experience without necessarily losing all his senses and bodily movements; and even the movements of the soul, that is, his knowledge, his power, and his will, are taken captive in love's service. Augustine, *li anguisseus damours,* was keenly aware of this when he said, 'Mighty and almighty is the passion of love! It is indeed powerful, because it renders the spirit possessed by it powerless over itself.'"[71] Typically, Gérard represents his hero Augustine (though the text is actually by Gilbert of Hoyland) as a lovesick knight of romance. It is precisely this brand of *mystique courtoise* that Marguerite Porete would echo, fifty years later, in her *Mirror of Simple Souls*. Like Gérard's *anguisseus damours*, her Free Soul has "lost the use of her senses": she knows nothing, wills nothing, and can do nothing, being completely powerless and wholly possessed by Love.[72]

Like a lyric husband, says Gérard, the biblical God is jealous, so his lovers will doubtless share the sentiments of the *mal-mariée* in the song:

Quant plus me bat et destraint li ialous,
tant ai ie mius en amours ma pensee.
Deus enim, ut dixit Moyses, est fortis zelotes, idest *ialous*.[73] (Exod. 20.5)

The more the jealous one beats and confines me,
the more I think of love.
For God, as Moses said, is powerfully jealous.

But Gérard is wilfully distorting the lyric situation, for the female speaker in this song intends to *contrast* her jealous, violent husband with the lover she refuses to abandon. Gérard, on the contrary, conflates the jealous husband with the desired lover: the female speaker in his scenario loves God all the more in spite of, or rather because of, his violence. This interpretation is confirmed by another passage in which Gérard presents God as the most desirable lover because he is not only the most beautiful and devoted, but also the most aggressive and threatening:

If our love requires violence, *cest con li face force*, no one will do greater violence to attain it than he. For he seeks it as if with an unsheathed sword: either you will love him or you will die an eternal death. Hence David says, "unless you are converted" from love of the world to the love of God, "he will brandish his sword" (Ps. 7.13). So here a certain popular song can be applied: *Tout a force maugre uostre uorsai uostre amour auoir* [By main force, in spite of you I will have your love].[74]

The divine violence allegorized by Hugh in *De laude caritatis*, and psychologized by Richard in *De IV gradibus*, is for Gérard no longer description but incitement. In this version of a divine pastourelle, violence becomes sexy, the threat of hell seductive. To be raped (or in more polite language, "ravished") by God at swordpoint is the height of bliss.[75]

Gérard's editor in the early 1930s, the distinguished Benedictine André Wilmart, was annoyed by his author's frequent resorts to the vernacular. Wilmart wondered if Gérard's fondness for French tags might be due to "an odd sort of quirk . . . , an instinctive and bizarre desire to distinguish himself . . . by means of this somewhat childish artifice."[76] But from a contemporary critical perspective, Gérard's "quirk" marks him as one of the most conscious forgers of *la mystique courtoise*. This new idiom of divine love blended not only two languages, but the diverse thought-worlds they represented: the Latinate realm of monastic bridal mysticism, known to Gérard primarily through Augustine and Bernard, and the vernacular realm of *courtoisie* represented by his French lyrics. Peter Dronke was closer to the mark when he observed "that if sacred and profane love are wholly divorced, as by Gérard, then, as nothing is found in the intellect which was not first found in the senses, their metaphorics will be identical, as much as if they were wholly united." Further, "the more deeply religious the language, the closer it is to the language of *courtoisie*."[77] The two languages—the Song of Songs and the tongue of the trouvères—have fused completely by the last page of Gérard's treatise, when the "holy soul" cries out, "*oi*, osculetur me, *mes tres dous amis*, osculo oris sui!" ("Ah, let him kiss me, my sweetest love, with the kiss of his mouth!")[78]

Five Incitements leads in a direct line of development to the all-vernacular *Règle des Fins Amans* (*Rule for Courtly Lovers*, ca. 1300), a didactic rule for beguines which I have analyzed elsewhere.[79] In the *Règle*, the beguinage is likened explicitly to a court of love, and Jesus Christ to "the abbot of courtly lovers" (*fins amans*). This figural equation of earthly with heavenly love pivoted on a point so fine that the balance could tilt in either direction. Thus in *The Council of Remiremont*, a twelfth-century satire, a female cardinal visits a community of nuns consecrated to the cult of Amor and the gospel according to Ovid. *Das Kloster der Minne* (*The Monastery of Love*), a fourteenth-century German allegory of love, presents a reversed mirror image of the *Règle des Fins Amans*. In the French text, religious life is the reality and *fin' amors* the metaphor, whereas in the German poem, monastic life is the metaphor and *hohe Minne* the reality.[80] Since every metaphor is an unlike likeness, the rhetorical effectiveness of such crossover texts depended both on a fundamental similarity—all erotic lovers experience comparable feelings, be the object of their longing man, woman, or God—and on a difference as absolute as any known to medieval society. Until the very end of the Middle Ages, "love celestial" remained the prerogative of the chaste: even the throngs of semi-religious who so troubled thirteenth-century churchmen (beguines, lay penitents, tertiaries, unattached hermits) were expected to be celibate or widowed. *Fin' amors*, on the other hand, was a pastime for laymen and women who were, or at any rate wished to be, sexually active. Beguines and monastics could luxuriate in the rhetoric of heightened eroticism only by virtue of their sexual renunciation; the rare noncelibate who embraced this mode of piety (Margery Kempe, for example), created massive social confusion. Likewise, the courtly knight and his lady could imagine themselves as members of an elite *ordo amantium* only because, in the eyes of canon law, they belonged to no estate higher than the *ordo laicorum*. Yet members of the lay and religious estates, so rigidly divided in law, crossed paths in myriad ways in the course of ordinary life. The knight and his lady were almost certain to have relatives in religious vows, just as the nun and her confessor had kinsfolk in what they disparagingly called "the world." Crossover texts won favor, in part, because they enabled men and women on either side of this great divide to imagine themselves on the other side; they titillated by representing, seriously or playfully, how the other half lived.

But this picture overstates the symmetry between secular and devotional facets of the crossover movement. In reality the religious, although never more than a numerical minority, produced vastly more texts, since they were more likely to be literate and to have the leisure and inclination for writing. More important, they had vastly more *need* of crossover as an imaginative mode. While secular love poets often borrowed the language of devotion with semi-playful or parodic intent, spiritual writers tended to use the idiom of *fin' amors* in high seriousness. Passionate lovers can express themselves in any number of ways without reference to religious themes, whereas lovers of God must perforce speak metaphorically. To be sure, devotional writers need not model their love for God on the analogy of sexual passion, and before the twelfth century they rarely did so.[81] By the mid-thirteenth, however, many seemed unable to represent or imagine divine love in any terms *other* than those of intense eroticism. The profusion and wide diffusion of twelfth-century sermons and commentaries on the Song of Songs was at once a cause and an effect of this profound shift in sensibility; but that story has been expertly told by others and need not detain us here.[82] More germane to our purpose is the ever-growing prestige of "love" as a vernacular literary theme, which drove spiritual writers to outright competition with secular poets for the souls of their audience. This competitive urge is sometimes admitted quite frankly, as in the lyric "Qui bien vuet amors descrivre" by the thirteenth-century poet Robert of Rheims. In his preface, Robert states his intention to compose

> rime novelle . . .
> plaisans asses et plus belle
> Et plus vraie bien dire lose
> Et plus honeste que nest celle
> Dou roumant con dist la rose.[83]

> a new poem . . .
> pleasant enough, and more beautiful
> and more true, I dare say,
> and more honorable than the one
> they call *The Romance of the Rose*.

The sheer ubiquity of love as a subject, endlessly iterated from the early Occitan troubadours to the late medieval romances, inevitably shaped the religious imagination, making passionate yearning and violent charity seem not only respectable, but the *sine qua non* of a serious spiritual life. Even St. Bonaventure, a philosophical theologian not known for bridal mysticism, bowed to the new conception of love we have seen so vividly delineated by Richard of Saint-Victor and Gérard of Liège. *Caritas*, he asserted, entails two complementary movements of the soul: *amicitia* or friendship, which wills to serve and please God, and *concupiscentia* or amorous desire, which longs to see and possess him.[84]

One of the most skillful crossover poets of the mid-thirteenth century was distant from Gérard of Liège geographically, but close kin to him in spirit. Mechthild of Magdeburg's visionary recital, *The Flowing Light of the Godhead*, begins with a dialogue between her soul and Frau Minne, the imperious goddess who initiates her into the joys of love, as we saw in Chapter 1. Mechthild's Minne, like Hugh's Caritas, has power even over Almighty God; and, like Richard's Caritas, she wounds and binds her devotees, sickens and slays them. As the love dialogue continues, the Soul complains to Frau Minne, "You have hunted me, trapped me, bound me, and wounded me so deeply that I shall never be healthy again. You have meted out to me many a cudgel blow. Tell me, am I ever going to recover from you?" Minne replies:

That I hunted you was my fancy.
That I captured you was my desire.
That I bound you made me happy.
When I wounded you, you were joined to me.
When I cudgel you, I take you into my power.
I drove God the almighty from heaven,
Took his human life,
And returned him to his Father in honor.
How do you, vile worm, expect to survive before me?[85]

Minne's violence is welcomed by the Soul, for all her laments. Mechthild's lyric speaker desires nothing more than to suffer the same fate as her divine Beloved, and she goes on to envision all creatures, herself included, bowing down before the sovereignty of Love. "One who dies of love," she exults, "shall be buried in God."[86]

The topos of violent love, as Hildegard Keller has recently observed, "turns literature into a sort of casualty ward [where] wounded minnesingers languish beside lovesick brides of Christ. A powerful maelstrom encompassing love, death, injury, aggression and illness thus comes together in the work of Lady Love."[87] One of Mechthild's contemporaries, the Franciscan priest Lamprecht of Regensburg, promulgated the cult of this fierce goddess among nuns in his allegorical poem, *Tochter Syon* (*Daughter of Zion*, ca. 1246–52). Lady Love, whom Lamprecht refers to interchangeably as "diu Minne" and "Vrouwe Karitas," is mistress over all the allegorical virgins dwelling in the castle of the heart; she is also the prime mover of the action. It is Lady Love who inspires the bridal soul with longing, travels at her behest to greet the divine Beloved in heaven, pierces him in the heart with her fateful arrows, and revives the lovesick soul with four drops of therapeutic blood from his wounds. When the bride at last arrives in heaven to consummate her nuptials, Minne stands by and "smiles mischievously with secret pride, for she has consciously contrived all."[88] Yet a revelation lies in store for the reader. Although Lady Love might appear to be God's enemy, hurling him right out of heaven into the Virgin's womb and thence onto the Cross, in reality

got und diu minne sint al ein,
dehein scheidunge ist an in zwein.
diu minne ist got, got ist diu minne,
einz ist in dem andern inne.
sie zwei hânt beide einen site:
swar sie in warf, dar viel si mite,

swâ er ist, dâ ist ouch sie.
ûf erde in himel und in helle
geliez si in und er sie nie,
sie was ie sin geselle
und immer ist dort unde hie.[89]

God and Minne are all one:
nothing separates these two.
Minne is God, God is Minne,
the one dwells in the other.
Both of them act the same way:
wherever she threw him, she fell too,
wherever he is, there she is also.
On earth, in heaven and in hell
she never left him, nor he her.
She was his companion forever
and always is, both there and here.

This emphatic coinherence of Minne with God seems, if not exactly to re-place the Trinity, at least to supplement it with a dyad of God and Goddess, a celestial/terrestrial couple whose eternal union facilitates the *unio mystica* between those other loving partners, God and the Soul:

die wîl ist ungescheiden
der wille in in beiden,
sô wehselt sich ir zweier gir,
sie ist in im und er in ir.
ei welh ein süeziu wehselunge
wirt von ir zweier gerunge!
er gert ir und sie gert sîn,
sus wirt ir lieb einander schîn.[90]

In both of them all the while
their will is undivided,
their desire is interchanged,
she is in him and he in her.
Ah, what a sweet exchange
comes of their mutual longing!
He wants her and she wants him;
thus their love becomes manifest.

Lady Love's archery, a motif that links her directly to Cupid, is also correlated with a startling iconography that first appeared in the Rhineland around 1250, at the same time that Mechthild and Lamprecht were writing, and remained current through the fourteenth century. The image of "Christ crucified by the Virtues" turns an allegory favored by mystics into a baffling and paradoxical emblem.[91] An example from the Upper Rhine, ca. 1275 (Figure 4.1), includes the traditional figures of Ecclesia collecting Christ's blood in a chalice and a blindfolded Synagoga turning away. More novel are the fierce maidenly Virtues: Humilitas hammers a nail into Christ's feet, while Obedientia and Misericordia pound away at his hands and Caritas stabs his heart with a spear. A lectionary from Regensburg (Figure 4.2) shows the *Sponsa* (a figure interchangeable with Caritas) piercing Christ's heart. The Virtues selected for the grisly office of executioner could vary. Sometimes, as in a late example from Salzburg (Figure 4.3), their roles were filled by Mercy, Truth, Justice, and Peace—the celebrated Four Daughters of God, whose conflict we witnessed in Robert Grosseteste's *Château d'Amour* (cf. Figure 1.8). Most startling of all may be a stained glass window from the Cistercian convent of Wienhausen in lower Saxony (ca. 1330). In this panel (Figure 4.4) the Four Daughters serve as adoring witnesses to the crucifixion, the act by which their ancient dispute has been resolved. Karitas, however, embraces the Crucified with one arm (a gesture he returns) even as she stabs him to the heart with a dagger.

The likeliest meaning of these icons emerges from abundant textual evidence. Christ was motivated to endure the cross by his own exemplary virtues—humility before sinful men, obedience to the will of God, and above all, the compassionate love that pierced his heart, just as Hugh had written in *De laude charitatis*. By extension Christ's lovers, insofar as they had acquired the virtues, were to be imitators of his Passion, crucifying their self-will with obedience, their pride with humility, and so forth.[92] Twelfth-century painters had sometimes depicted Virtues hovering around the cross, presumably to represent the gifts that flowed from Christ's redemptive act; and it might seem but a small step for thirteenth-century artists to assign these figures a more active role. To explain the iconography only thus far, however, is to explain it away—for this symbolic Crucifixion was surely meant to disturb. It is one of several late-medieval images whose power depends on a deliberate incongruity between their literal and symbolic meanings, with the cognitive dissonance such incongruity provokes in the beholder. Compare the image of "Nature at her forge" so popular in illuminated *Rose* manuscripts (Figure 3.2). In this subject, a symbolic representation of lovemaking is constructed to resemble a literal image of child abuse or infanticide. In the Crucifixion by the Virtues, similarly, a symbolic portrayal of Christ's charity suggests a literal depiction of the most perfidious treachery. What loving bride would stab her bridegroom in the heart while embracing him, or violate his corpse with a spear-thrust?

Figure 4.1. Christ crucified by the Virtues. Bonmont Psalter, Upper Rhine, ca. 1275. Besançon, Bibliothèque municipale, MS 54, f. 15v. Photo: Bibliothèque municipale de Besançon.

Figure 4.2. Christ crucified by the Virtues. Lectionary, Convent of the Holy Cross, Regensburg. Oxford, Keble College Library, ms. 49, f. 7r. By permission, Master and Wardens of Keble College. Photo: Keble College.

Figure 4.3. Christ crucified by the Virtues, "T" initial of "Te igitur." Missal painted by Berthold Furtmeyr, 1481. Munich, Bayerische Staatsbibliothek, Clm. 15709, f. 72r. Photo: Bayerische Staatsbibliothek.

An uninitiated—or willfully perverse—viewer might interpret this iconography in various ways. She might, for example, take the image to exonerate Christ's historical executioners. He did after all ask his Father to "forgive them, for they know not what they do" (Luke 23.34). So perhaps they committed their monstrous deed with the best intentions: they were only following orders (Obedientia), they dared not question authority (Humilitas), they genuinely believed in the righteousness of Roman law (Justitia), or they knew, with Caiaphas, that it was "expedient that one man should die for the people" (Fides; John 11.50–52). If our independent-minded viewer were

Figure 4.4. Caritas stabbing the crucified Christ. Stained glass window, Cistercian convent of Wienhausen. Lower Saxony, ca. 1315. By permission, Kloster Wienhausen. Photo: Neidersächsisches Landesamt für Denkmalpflege.

a proto-Calvinist, she might read the Crucifixion by the Virtues as a symbol of human depravity. Without the grace of God there is no health in us; all our righteousness is as filthy rags (Isa. 64.6); even our putative virtues, no less than our sins, torment the Savior and demand his death on the cross. Or, if our spectator were inclined toward prophetic critique of the Church (as Mechthild was), she might take the duplicitous action of Sponsa/Ecclesia as typifying the Church's sins: while embracing Christ with her amorous words she betrays him, Judas-like, and cuts him to the heart with her deeds. The image of Caritas as murderer might even pierce the devotee's own loving heart with an intimation of Oscar Wilde's sentiment: "Each man kills the thing he loves, By each let this be heard. . . . The coward does it with a kiss, the brave man with a sword."[93] None of these readings were necessarily intended by the medieval artists, but all are possible, for the meaning of the icon is far from self-evident. Like all esoteric images, it compels the beholder to think, and so to internalize the conception more deeply than a conventional image would require.

Found chiefly in German nunneries, the Crucifixion by the Virtues used the figure of the Sponsa/Caritas to transfer the bridal role from Ecclesia, who traditionally stands beneath the Cross, to the individual soul who yearns to pierce Christ's heart with her love. In mystical texts, as we have seen, Caritas or Minne is a liminal figure who may represent both the loving self and the divine beloved; she may also signify the force that joins them. In Augustinian theology, Caritas as the Holy Spirit—the love binding Father and Son—is a personal relationship which has itself been personified. Sometimes, as in Hugh's *De laude charitatis* and Mechthild's *Flowing Light*, Lady Love is imagined as an autonomous power who lords it over lovers, God included; sometimes she merely personifies the lover's own emotions. This lability makes it possible to slip easily between subjective and objective representations of Love: she might be an abstract potency at certain moments, an individual or collective person at other moments in the same text. In a visual image, these possibilities may coexist simultaneously. A unique illumination from the *Rothschild Canticles*, a deluxe mystical prayer book produced for an unknown nun around 1300, provides a case in point (Figure 4.5). In this diptych, which belongs to a cycle illustrating the Song of Songs, the Bride is a composite figure combining the traits of Ecclesia, Caritas, and the loving soul—in this case, the nun for whom the manuscript was created. She first embraces her Bridegroom and enters with him into an enclosed garden (upper left), then aims the spear of her love directly at his heart (lower left). On the facing page, Christ stands upright amid the instruments of his Passion, pointing to his wounded side, his nudity suggesting both the humiliation of the Cross and the consummation of love. The Bride's gesture of touching her eyes recalls a verse from the Song of Songs on the preceding folio: "You have wounded my heart, my sister, my bride, with one [glance] of your eyes" (Cant. 4.9). At the same time, this gesture links the mystical iconography to objective portrayals of the Crucifixion, where the Roman centurion Longinus pierces Christ's side with his spear (Mark 15.39; John 19.34).[94] According to legend, when blood from the wound touched the centurion's eyes, his blindness was healed and he proclaimed Jesus to be the Son of God. The Bride's gesture, then, suggests spiritual illumination as well as the wounding and binding charity with which she has captivated her Beloved.

Figure 4.5. Bride and Bridegroom: the wound of love. *Rothschild Canticles*, Franco-Flemish, ca. 1300. New Haven, Conn., Yale University, Beinecke Rare Book and Manuscript Library, ms. 404, ff. 18v-19r. Photo: Beinecke Library.

The texts and images that we have considered thus far are unusual, surviving in only a handful of manuscripts. But their assimilation of divine love to literary romance, though pioneered by a spiritual elite, proved to be a crossover move so successful that it assured the eventual diffusion of such mystical piety beyond the charmed circle that could afford opulent illuminated books. By the fourteenth century, the spread of vernacular literacy and the invention of less costly media enabled a much wider audience to participate in the romance of Christ and the loving soul. One such medium was the *Bilderbogen* or broadsheet, a single leaf of parchment or paper that displayed images in multiple panels, each accompanied by its own text or caption, rather like a comic strip. These sheets, mass-produced and eventually printed, could be tacked to the walls of religious cells or private homes; they could be used as inexpensive aids to meditation; they could be sent as letters between friends in token of spiritual affection.[95] The broadsheet of *Christus und die minnende Seele* (*Christ and the Loving Soul*) includes twenty panels, complete with rhyming couplets, that depict the love affair of God and the soul as a complete narrative loosely based on the Song of Songs, from betrothal to eventual consummation (Figure 4.6).[96] Two of the panels (second row from top, left) portray the soul taking on the role of Caritas or Minne: she shoots her beloved with an arrow, then binds him to her with the *vinculum amoris*. The accompanying text records a dialogue between the lovers:

Ich will mein lieb durch schiessen,
Ob ich sein mag geniessen.
Mich hat der meine schmertz
Geschossen durch mein hertz.

Ich han mein lieb funden,
Gefangen und gebunden.
Ir layd mich sehre zwinget,
Mein lieb mich darzu dringet.

I will shoot my love with an arrow
So that I may enjoy him.
This pain of mine
Has pierced me through my heart.

I have found my beloved,
Captured and bound him.
Your suffering compels me;
My love drives me to do this.

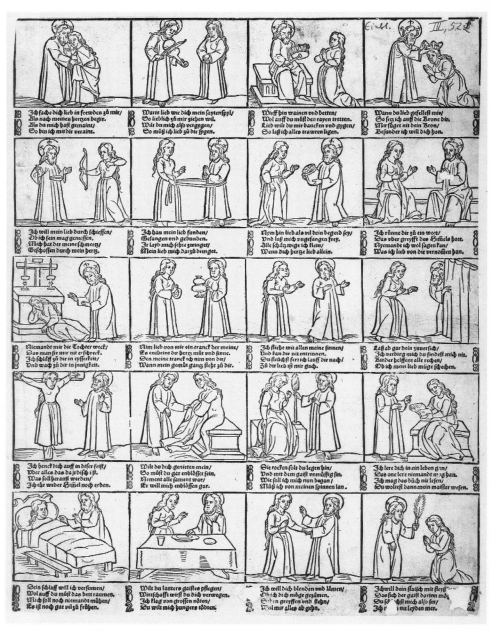

Figure 4.6. *Christus und die minnende Seele*. Woodcut, fifteenth century. Munich, Bayerische Staatsbibliothek, Einblatt III, 52f. Photo: Bayerische Staatsbibliothek.

Such folk mysticism represents a popularized, watered-down version of the *mystique courtoise* first created by such aristocratic souls as Mechthild and her contemporary, Hadewijch. As late as the fifteenth century a German poet named Conrad, who penned a *Little Book on Spiritual Marriage* for Viennese nuns, could evoke the same now-hackneyed gesture: before his Bride and Bridegroom can consummate their mystical union, Caritas must take her bow and ritually shoot the divine lover through his heart.[97] Thus, for more than three centuries, Lady Love maintained her firm hold on Cupid's quiver, deploying its Ovidian arrows to win ever more souls for Christ.

The Beguine as Knight of Love: Hadewijch's *Stanzaic Poems*

In secular iconography, no image of Minne (or Venus) is more celebrated than the one that adorns the portrait of Ulrich von Liechtenstein in the famous Manesse Codex (Figure 4.7). Smiling beneath her crown, with a torch in her left hand and an arrow in her right, the goddess towers above the *Minneritter*'s helm as he rides across the sea to a joust. Ulrich (ca. 1200–1275/6) was a politically prominent knight and minnesinger best known today for his mock-epic "autobiography" of 1255, entitled *Frauendienst (Service of Ladies)*, in which he claims to have performed a most unusual quest to win his lady's favor and honor all women.[98] The poet alleges that in May 1227 he rode all the way from northern Italy to Bohemia disguised as "the noble Queen Venus, Goddess of Love." Clad and armed entirely in white, accompanied by musicians and maidens in the same livery, "Lady Venus" began her journey by rising from the sea at Mestre—hence the waves beneath the horse's hooves—and proceeded for twenty-eight days to joust with all comers at pre-announced stations. Any knight willing to break a spear against the goddess would be rewarded with a golden ring which, bestowed upon his lady, would increase her beauty and assure her fidelity. But any knight unhorsed by Venus had to bow to the four corners of the earth in honor of a lady. Those who refused to joust with her would be placed "under the ban of love and of all good women."[99] By the end of his quest, Ulrich claimed to have broken 307 spears, donated 271 rings, and unhorsed four knights, without once being overthrown himself. Among his opponents were another knight dressed as a woman and one wearing monk's garb, making that particular joust into a graphic combat of *caritas* and *cupiditas*.

The Manesse portrait and the *Frauendienst* offer a flamboyant embodiment, which is at the same time a spoof, of the erotic idealism that animated

Figure 4.7. Ulrich von Liechtenstein as Lady Venus (Frau Minne). Codex Manesse. Heidelberg, Universitätsbibliothek, Cod. Pal. Germ. 848, f. 237 (Zürich, early 14th century). Photo: Ruprecht-Karls-Universität Heidelberg.

courtly poets. To please his capricious lady, Ulrich fights in endless tournaments and composes endless songs; hearing that she does not like his looks, he submits to cosmetic surgery (without anesthesia, of course); wounded in battle, he chops off his injured finger and sends it, van Gogh-like, to his beloved; in hope of her favor, he endures nights of abuse outside her castle walls in the company of lepers. Such adventures concretize the abstract *leit* and *nôt* endured by the lyric lover and, in the process, make his sufferings seem faintly ridiculous. On his Venus tour, Ulrich dramatizes another aspect of *hohe Minne*, the relationship between the beloved lady and Minne herself. While cross-dressed for this journey, he endeavors to *become* the Goddess of Love in order to serve his lady. Other knight-lovers are invited to engage Lady Love in battle: the terms of the challenge establish that it is no shame to be vanquished by the goddess, while it is profoundly shameful to refuse the fight.

Ulrich's extravagant tale is parodic and almost certainly fictional,[100] but the fifty-five lyrics sprinkled throughout the work are serious enough, and it is on them that the poet's contemporary reputation rested. In its own comic way, the *Frauendienst* testifies to the same narrativizing impulse that affected courtly lyric throughout Europe in the thirteenth century. Provençal literary critics constructed *vidas*, or pseudo-biographies, of the troubadours on the basis of their poems; Gottfried von Strassburg names specific lays sung by Tristan and Isolde at different points in their story; and Dante famously interprets his own lyrics within the prose frame of the *Vita Nuova*, an autobiography far more serious than Ulrich's. Such efforts reveal a desire, much like that of nineteenth-century critics, to anchor the sometimes maddeningly abstract and impersonal "I" of the courtly lyric within the biography of a specific historical person. In religious literature, the same impulse appears as early as the twelfth century in commentaries on the Song of Songs, inspiring such exegetes as Honorius Augustodunensis and Rupert of Deutz to construct a full-fledged dramatic plot (with the Virgin Mary as heroine) from a book that modern biblical scholars read as an anthology of Hebrew love songs.[101] This quest for narrative testifies to a dissatisfaction with the lyric idea of love as merely a shifting kaleidoscope of moods and feelings experienced by the lover. In narrative, such lyrical moments take their place within the context of a relationship with a definite beginning and end, and a process of development whose stages can be subjected to rational (or quizzical) scrutiny.

The narrative frame devised by Ulrich for his *Minnelieder* can provide us with an unexpected angle on the work of his contemporary Hadewijch—the greatest mystical poet of the thirteenth century. Next to nothing is known about this writer except that she lived in Brabant in the first half of the century and was sometime spiritual director to a small group of beguines.[102] One late manuscript identifies her as "Blessed Hadewijch of Antwerp," but there is no independent confirmation of this nor, indeed, any record of her life outside her works. Among these are a collection of forty-five *Stanzaic Poems* (so-called to distinguish them from her sixteen epistolary *Poems in Couplets*), thirty-one *Letters* in prose, and a sequence of fourteen *Visions*.[103] The *Stanzaic Poems* reveal Hadewijch to have been a spiritual minnesinger of rare gifts, while the *Visions* provide an autobiographical account of her *Minnedienst* from the outset of her quest to its triumphant consummation.[104] Preserved in the same few manuscripts as the lyrics, they serve to personalize the mystic/chivalric "I" who speaks in the poems. But my purpose in this discussion of Hadewijch is not to trace connections between her lyrics and her prose works. Much less is it to provide a précis of her mystical theology—a task that has been ably carried out by Bernard McGinn, Louis Bouyer, Kurt Ruh, and others.[105] I seek, rather, to delineate as precisely as possible what is "courtly" about Hadewijch's doctrine of love, and to elucidate the reasons she might have chosen Minnesang as a vehicle for mystical theology in the first place.[106]

Like Ulrich of Liechtenstein on his Venus tour, Hadewijch poetically cross-dresses, so to speak, exchanging the bridal self of her visions for the courtly self of the *Minneritter*, the knight of love. Yet gender remains malleable throughout her oeuvre: the courtly knight *is* the bride under a different aspect, just as Minne is an alternative form of the Bridegroom.[107] Hadewijch speaks often of conquering and being conquered by Minne, yet also of "becoming Minne": images of combat and union alternate and at times coincide. Most important, the determination to do battle with Minne—that is to say, with God—is for Hadewijch the first prerequisite of the mystical life. Without *orewoet* or "love's fierce fury," there can be no union; without violent conflict, no embrace.[108] "Aliens" who refuse to take up Minne's challenge, because they lack courage for the struggle, become objects of Hadewijch's withering scorn, while she has only sympathy for those whom Love has cast into pitiful abjection. Marieke van Baest, in her profound and lyrical introduction to Hadewijch's poems, points out that the author identifies most fully with three quite different biblical characters: the *amica* or bride of Solomon's Song; the patriarch Jacob, who in his nightlong wrestling match with God gained a blessing but also an incurable wound; and the suffering yet scarcely patient Job, who never ceased to accuse and indict his divine Enemy.[109] Minne herself is precisely this enemy, an invincible fighter and a ferocious victor, a fierce Lady who shows herself most fickle toward her most faithful vassals, but she is also the Lover who woos and the Beloved who is wooed, a "noble maiden and queen" and "mother of the virtues" (2.12, 20).

Hadewijch was well versed in the Vulgate and in Latin spiritual litera-ture, especially those writers we would most expect her to know and love: Augustine, Bernard, William of St.-Thierry (known to her as Bernard), and Hugh and Richard of St.-Victor. She must also have been familiar with Latin lyric, for one of her letters is a commentary on a hymn verse by Hildebert of Lavardin (which she probably knew as Abelard's);[110] and the first and last of her *Stanzaic Poems* are macaronic. Her vernacular debts are harder to trace, partly because the repertoire of themes and tropes in the courtly lyric was so universally shared, but partly too because a late thirteenth-century reaction against the genre resulted in the near total loss of what must once have been a substantial corpus of love lyrics in Middle Dutch. Only those of Hendrik van Veldeke (ca. 1145–ca. 1200) survive, and even those only in High Ger-man transcriptions. Hendrik's extant corpus is all secular, but, intriguingly, a German writer of the 1180s happens to mention a lost poem of his with the title *Van Salomon ende die Minne* (*Of Solomon and Lady Love*).[111] We do not know its contents, but the title at least suggests that Hendrik, a generation before Hadewijch, might already have attempted some kind of rapproche-ment between the Song of Songs tradition and the courtly lyric, à la Gérard of Liège.

Brabant in the thirteenth century was a linguistic crossroads, and Hadewijch's own poetry reveals both Germanic and Romance elements. She used Germanic stress rhythm, with marked alliteration, rather than the Romance syllabic line, and did not favor the more difficult rhyme schemes preferred by some troubadours. On the other hand, some of her poetic devices, such as the *tornada* or envoi, occur in troubadour lyrics but not in the extant repertoire of Minnesang. It is probable that she knew French, and perhaps even Provençal, as well as her native Dutch.[112] One strange but not impossible route for the transmission of troubadour poetry to the northern beguines might have been through Folc of Marseille, bishop of Toulouse and himself a former troubadour, who visited Liège in 1212 to meet with Jacques de Vitry, an influential supporter of the beguine movement.[113] But if the lin-guistic past of Hadewijch's writing is uncertain, its future trajectory is clear enough, for her work remained unknown in francophone lands but influenced Dutch spiritual authors from Ruusbroec through the Devotio Moderna, and portions of it were translated into German in at least three fourteenth-century manuscripts.[114] It is for this reason that I have contextualized her *Stanzaic Poems* within the world of Minnesang, rather than troubadour lyrics, from the late twelfth and early thirteenth centuries. Although we cannot demonstrate the influence of any specific poet, the minnesingers of Hadewijch's time do illumine the uses of Minne, as concept and personification, that she would have been likely to know.

We have seen what she learned of love from the apostles of Caritas; what would she have learned from the singers of Minne? Why, indeed, did Hadewijch decide to compose Minnesang in the first place? Although we can only speculate, the likeliest answer lies in her status as a beguine, an anomalous half-lay, half-religious vocation that positively demanded a crossover mentality. No matter how fluent Hadewijch was in Latin, it would have been pointless for her to create hymns and sequences, as Hildegard of Bingen had done in the twelfth century, for she had no convent to command and no authority to introduce liturgical innovations at the parish church where she would have worshiped.[115] But among her own circle of women—Sara, Emma, Margriet, and the rest—she might sing anything she liked. We know from Hadewijch's letters that she and her disciples spent much of their time caring for the poor and sick, a far cry from the court life to which she could probably have aspired "in the world."[116] But at night what was to keep her from holding her own mystical court of love? For

> they who serve Love with truth
> Shall in love walk with Love
> All round that kingdom where Love is Lady,
> And united with her receive all that splendor
> And taste to the full her noble fidelity.[117] (34, 36–40)

We do not know whether Hadewijch intended her poems to be sung, as no music is preserved in the manuscripts. But for medieval vernacular song in all languages, survival of melodies is the exception rather than the rule, and in any case new lyrics could often be sung to pre-existing tunes. Specialists in Dutch prosody have come to differing conclusions about the "singability" of Hadewijch's poems.[118] Yet the simplest, most plausible reason anyone would compose love songs is in order to sing them, or enable others to do so, and we have ample evidence that courtly poets in general wrote their lyrics to be sung. If Hadewijch was indeed a "performative mystic," as Mary Suydam has recently argued,[119] her performance of sacred Minnesang could, given the connotations of the genre, have converted the béguinage into a miniature court of love, creating the very ambience that is presupposed by later texts such as *Five Incitements* and *La Règle des Fins Amans*. More precisely, by performing the role of *Minneritter* Hadewijch would have fostered among her beguines a self-image quite different from the meek persona required of nuns, for the knight of love is proud, mettlesome, heroic, daring.[120] To serve Minne in this way was to serve God as the romance knight served his lady, by questing and jousting, with ardent submission and passionate rebellion, in exalted longing and bitter exile.

The word *minne/n*, noun and verb, appears 987 times in Hadewijch's *Stanzaic Poems*; it is her one and only theme.[121] No minnesinger was so obsessed or invoked Minne half so relentlessly, since Lady Love was for them a personification but for Hadewijch a real and infinite Being. Nonetheless, their representations of Minne as the goddess of love laid the groundwork for her pursuit of Minne as the Love that is God. Hendrik van Veldeke, Hadewijch's countryman, sang Minne's praise in typically idealized terms:

Sô wê der minnen is sô vrût
dat hê der minnen dînen kan,
ende hê dore minne pîne dût,
wale heme, dê is ein sâlech man.
van minnen komet allet gût,
dî minne maket reinen mût,
wat solde ich âne minne dan?[122]

Whoever is worthy of Love,
so that he can serve Love
and take pains for the sake of Love—
bless him, he is a happy man!
From Love comes all that is good,
Love purifies the mind.
What could I do without Love?

The same conviction of love's absolute value, its all-sufficiency, underlies every word Hadewijch wrote. Though she often rebels against Minne's baffling harshness, never does she question or ironize its worth. The "school of Minne" is a frequent motif: Hadewijch muses that "in the school of Love the highest lesson / Is how one can content Love" (14, 47–48), and dreams of the day when Minne will at last take pity and say to her, "I am what I was in times past; / Now fall into my arms, / And taste my rich teaching!" (20, 74–76).[123] This image of Minne as *magistra* was a staple in the repertoire of courtly poets. Reinmar von Zweter (ca. 1200–ca. 1260) illustrates the trope in his lyric "Alle schuole sint gar ein wint":

All schools are but empty wind
except the school where Love's disciples are:
she is so learned that one must bow to her mastery.
Her rod tames the wildest man and makes him able

to do what he never yet heard or saw he could.
Where has anyone ever heard or seen so high a school?[124]

Despite such extravagant praise, the minnesingers lament love's sorrows more often than they celebrate its joys, helplessly entreating the goddess to ease their pain. Walther von der Vogelweide (ca. 1170–ca. 1230) complains that the divine archer shoots only him, leaving his lady impervious to love:

ir habet mich geschozzen,
und si gât genozzen;
ir ist sanfte und ich bin aber ungesunt.
    * * *
Ich bin iuwer, frowe Minne;
schiezent dar dâ man iu widerstê.[125]

You have shot me
and she goes scot-free;
she has an easy life, while I am stricken.
    * * *
I am your own, Lady Love;
shoot where you are resisted.

In a mood of periodic rebellion against Minne, Gottfried von Neifen (fl. 1230–1255) laments that she is quick to make demands on her vassals but slow to reward them:

Love, I am your servant; you should
lovingly pay me my wages.
Great is your power over me: it is time!
If your help obtains [a reward] for me,
I will be forever obliged to you.
The pain that clings so close must depart from me.
Loving Love, I have been bound to you
Since childhood. If you wound me now,
What use then is loyal faith? Love, forbear.[126]

This kind of complaint recurs throughout Hadewijch's poems. She too knows the wound of Love's arrow (16, 37) and laments—or boasts—that in her long battle with Minne her "shield has warded off so many stabs / There's no room left on it for a new gash" (3, 26–27). Like Gottfried von Neifen, she complains bitterly that Love promises much but pays little:

Since I ought to love totally,
Why did she not give me total love?
* * * * *
I no longer know what to live on.

She knows well what I imply.
For I have so spent what is mine,
I have nothing to live on—or she must give it.[127] (6, 61–70)

Alas, Love, if you play the niggard with me,
I vow I will play the niggard with you!
I wonder how it comes to pass
That you stay a great distance off?
You are far from me, and I am near you;
Therefore I live continually in the sad season.[128] (44, 43–48)

In one poem Hadewijch goes so far as to "bid farewell to Love now and forever," comparing her to a scorpion that first charms and then cruelly stings (21, 46–53). Yet, unless she wants her song to be silenced, the poet must circle back in the end to her trust that "Love always rewards, even though she comes late" (9, 57; 15, 83). This stormy relationship, modeled on the ceaseless dialectic between fidelity and revolt that constitutes the minnesinger's devotion, may seem to compromise Hadewijch's integrity as a Christian poet. Given that Minne is God, or at least one potent aspect of God, how can the mystic maintain that her love for Love is unrequited? In theological terms, the *Sturm und Drang* of Hadewijch's love-service translates into a tension between faith and experience, or memory and desire: the knowledge of God that she has gained from past fulfillment (*ghebruken*) contrasts miserably with her sense of his present absence (*ghebreken*). The mystic must endure this condition of nonfulfillment just as the courtly lover must endure the periodic absence or indifference of his beloved. In her involuntary exile, Hadewijch most often sustains her fidelity by recourse to reason, patience, and practical charity. But more distinctive, if not unique to her teaching, is the unorthodox virtue she calls "unfaith" (*ontrouwe*). Like the tenacity of Jacob or the intransigence of Job, unfaith is an angry, no-holds-barred demand for reciprocity. In one of her visions Hadewijch sees in heaven souls who "called continually for fruition and did not believe in the love of their Beloved; it rather appeared to them that they alone were loving and that Love did not help them. Unfaith made them so deep that they wholly engulfed Love and dared to fight her with sweet and bitter."[129] *Ontrouwe* translates the rebellious phase of Minnesang into a spiritual belligerence which, in its very despair of Love, paradoxically gives the lover strength and courage for a final assault.

Fidelity must often be absent
So that unfaith can conquer;

Noble unfaith cannot rest
So long as it does not conquer to the hilt;
It wishes to conquer all that Love is.[130]

Absence and exile—classic themes of the love lyric—had inspired at least one minnesinger before Hadewijch to experiment with a christianized version of Minne. Hartmann von Aue (fl. 1180–1205) sang obliquely of a long voyage he was obliged to make:

No one need ask about my journey,
I will tell you truly why I go.
Love has seized me and released me on my bond.
Now she has commanded me by her love to leave.
It is irrevocable: I must go at last.
Never would I break my promise and my oath!

Many a man boasts of what he would do for Love.
Where are their deeds? Their words I hear indeed.
Yet I would gladly see her bid one of them
Serve her even as I must serve.
He is truly in love who goes for Love's sake into exile.
* * * * *
I can truly boast that I sing well of Love,
For Love possesses me, and I her.
That which I desire, you see, desires me just as much.[131]

The real subject of Hartmann's song is betrayed by a single reference to "Saladin and all his army" in the second stanza: the poet is going on crusade. For him too, Minne thus supplies a figure for divine love and the obligations it entails. Since Hartmann, unlike rival minnesingers who "often miss the mark," is willing to fulfill what he conceives as his Christian duty, he can boast of a true possession of Minne, while the others have only their "fantasy" (*wân*).

A later poet, Ulrich von Winterstetten (fl. 1240–80), also plays on the sacred connotations of Minne in his lyric "Sumer ouget sîne wunne." Although he sings the unrequited love of a lady, who is his "treasure" (*hort*), he deliberately evokes a different love by using a Gospel verse as his refrain:

Minne diu ist gewalteclîchen
allen dingen obe.
ir kan niht ûf erde entwîchen,
ez gevâhe ir klobe.
wîsheit hort diu beide nîgent ir.

Minne süeze, kumber büeze, nach der gir,
twinge mînen hort gelîche mir.
est ein alt gesprochen wort,
swâ dîn herze wont, dâ lît dîn hort.[132]

Love is powerful
above all things.
Nothing on earth can escape her;
her cleft stick catches every bird.
Wisdom and treasure both bow to her.
Sweet Love, ender of cares, as I desire,
compel my treasure as you have done me.
There is an old saying:
where your heart is, there lies your treasure.

The "old saying" cited by Ulrich in fact ironizes his love by recalling Christ's command in the Sermon on the Mount: "Do not lay up for yourselves treasures on earth, where moth and rust consume and where thieves break in and steal, but lay up for yourselves treasures in heaven, . . . for where your treasure is, there will your heart be also" (Matt. 6.19–21).

Hadewijch's treasure is, like Ulrich's, unattainable here below, but of such infinite worth as to make all other rewards insipid. Her sacred Minnesang therefore plays out a drama of perpetual quest, or knight-errantry, in the pathless forests of Love. This drama has four principal characters:[133] indomitable Minne, wildly unpredictable in giving and withholding her love; the valiant *Minneritter* (always "he") who represents the perfect lover of God and enjoys the "rich fief" Minne bestows on her faithful ones; a usually lamenting "I," whose experience of love is characterized by pain, bitterness, disappointment, intermittent revolt, and ever-renewed fidelity; and finally the "aliens"—uncourtly rubes who never studied at Love's school and know nothing of her value. Minne combines the roles of Lady Love and the beloved lady in secular Minnesang, while the aliens or worldlings stand in for all those outside the charmed circle of courtliness. But the recurrent and deliberate contrast of "I" and "he," which is not typical of Minnesang, reveals much about Hadewijch's conception of her audience. In light of her *Visions*, which are filled with bliss and triumph, it would be foolhardy to read the "I" but not the "he" of her lyrics as autobiographical. Rather, Hadewijch seems to have divided her experience of Minne between these two contrasting figures as a technique of erotic pedagogy. "He," like a conquering hero of romance, personifies a chivalric ideal for her young beguines and shows them what to strive for:

He must march far who presses on to Love—
Through her broad width, her loftiest height, her deepest abyss.
In all storms he must explore the ways;
Then her wondrous wonder is known to him:
    That is—to cross her desert plains,
    To journey onward and not stand still;
    To fly through and climb through the heights,
    And swim through the abyss,
    There from Love to receive love whole and entire.[134] (21, 19–27)

"I," on the other hand, can offer a role model for daily practice. Hadewijch expects her disciples to meet with frustration and disillusionment in their pursuit of Minne, so the aspect of her own experience that she holds up for imitation is not the joy of union, but a steadfast, even grim determination to continue the struggle.

Whereabouts is Love? I find her nowhere.
Love has denied me all love.
Had it ever happened to me by Love
That I lived for a moment
In her affection, supposing I did,
I would have sought amnesty in her fidelity.
Now I must keep silence, suffer, and face
Sharp judgments ever anew.
* * * * *
It is plain that Love has dealt with me deceitfully.
From whom shall I now seek remedy?
I shall seek it from Fidelity . . .[135] (35, 33–40, 65–67)

Hadewijch's unique quest as a knight of love was more complex than that of the secular poets, for she was obligated not only to do battle *for* Love (like a romance knight), but also *as* Love (like Ulrich von Liechtenstein in the guise of Venus), and most crucially *against* Love (like Ulrich's opponents). Despite the peculiarities of her role, Minnesang alone provided her with a model of heroic love that achieves greatness by suffering and submitting to the inscrutable will of the Beloved, while presenting that submission very much as an active—which is to say "masculine"—virtue. Though Hadewijch could revel in the transports of a celestial bride, she had no use for the "feminine" virtues as they were commonly preached—meekness, timidity, caution. Rather, pride or fierceness (*fierheid*) is for her a consummate virtue; without it, what lover could have the audacity to conquer God?[136] It is characteristic that, in one of her letters, Hadewijch warns her disciples against reason—not because of its pride, so feared by generations of monks, but because of its misplaced *humility*: "Reason well knows that God must be feared, and that God is great and man is small. But if reason fears God's greatness because of its littleness, and fails to stand up to his greatness, and begins to doubt that it can ever become God's dearest child, and thinks that such a great Being is out of its reach—the result is that many people fail to stand up to the great Being. Reason errs in this."[137] The attitude championed by Hadewijch—a fierce determination to "stand up to" infinite Being, demanding all of Love's love for all of one's own—is the ultimate *hohe Minne*, supremely embodied in the *Minneritter*. The knight of love is long-suffering, but never self-deprecating; patient perforce, but never passive. To the same measure that he is awed by Love's greatness, he is confident of his own worth as Love's image and likeness. No discourse that had yet been created by or for women upheld such a proud ideal; and that is why Hadewijch had to become a minnesinger. It was not enough for her to be a *mulier virilis*, for what she wanted to vanquish was not merely her "female nature," but God. In this she stood peerless.[138]

Dante, Beatrice, and *l'amor che move il sole*

Hadewijch ended one of her more joyful poems with a vision of fulfilled lovers, freed at last from the scorn of aliens and the disdain of Minne herself, "to cry: *I am all Love's, and Love is all mine! / What can now disturb them? / For under Love's power stand / The sun, moon and stars!*"[139] These lines cannot help but recall the close of Dante's *Paradiso*:

> ma già volgeva il mio disio e'l velle,
> sì come rota ch'igualmente è mossa,
> l'amor che move il sole e l'altre stelle.[140] (*Par.* XXXIII, 143–45)

> But already my desire and will were turned,
> like a wheel that spins with even motion,
> by the Love that moves the sun and the other stars.

This Love is, of course, God in his aspect as Prime Mover. Strictly speaking, no goddess of love appears in Dante's poetic oeuvre: *Amore*, whether as god of lyric poets in the *Vita Nuova* or Lord of the Universe in the *Commedia*, is masculine, while Beatrice is a mortal woman, the wife of Signor Portinari of Florence, canonized by no authority save Dante's own. Yet so indelible is the impression she makes on even the most casual reader that, if she did not figure in our narrative, her absence would be noticed. In these

few pages, there can be no question of venturing even a day's journey into
the savage wood of Dante criticism, much less offering a novel interpretation
of "the figure of Beatrice."[141] I wish only to explore the implications of one
crucial point: Dante, alone among medieval poets, makes the transit from
courtly to mystical love by heightening, not renouncing, his devotion to a
lady. To be sure, Beatrice must die first, and so must Amore: the "lord of terrible aspect" who haunts the young lover's dreams must be demythologized,
reduced to a mere "accident in a substance," before he can merge with the
supersubstantial Love that moves the heavens. Even so, it is only Beatrice
who enables the god of love to become the God of Love. She remains his
inseparable companion in both courtly and Christian paradigms, and it is
only through her mediation that Dante can gaze upon Love's face. For this
reason the Beatrice of the *Vita Nuova* and the *Paradiso* does what no abstract
or purely allegorical figure can do: she not only personifies but incarnates,
and thereby unites, Amor and Caritas.

Dante was not alone among the *stilnovisti* in ascribing near-divine status
to his lady, but he was unique in granting the language of poetic hyperbole
its full theological seriousness. Even the child Beatrice, when she first appears
in the *Vita Nuova*, seems "to be the daughter not of a mortal man, but of
God,"[142] and as a saint in paradise, the glorified Beatrice has all the honors
of a celestial bride. Dante hails her as such, speaking not just as her lover but
as a Christian pilgrim: "O amanza del primo amante, o diva" ("O beloved
of the First Lover, O goddess!" *Par.* IV, 118). The christological dimensions
of Beatrice are familiar enough to need only the barest summary: her mystic
name, signifying "she who makes blessed"; her crimson garments, the color
of blood and flame; her association with the number nine, marking her as a
miraculous being whose square root, so to speak, is the Blessed Trinity; her
friendship with the lady Giovanna, who precedes her on one momentous
occasion just as John the Baptist (Giovanni) preceded Christ, thus transforming an everyday street scene into a liturgical pageant; and the more elaborate
pageant that ends the *Purgatorio*, where Beatrice's epiphany is the culmination of a symbolic display representing the totality of divine revelation.[143]
The numinous power of her greeting (*salute*) not only floods her lover with
bliss or, withdrawn, plunges him into torment; it is also quite literally his
salvation (*salute*).[144] During Beatrice's lifetime, Dante imagines all the saints
and angels beseeching God to summon her, on the ground that heaven's
beauty has no defect but the lack of her, while her saving power (*vertute*)
on earth is such that no one who speaks with her can ever be lost.[145] To the
poet's chagrin, God soon grants his imaginary prayer:

For the pure light of her humility
shone through the heavens with such radiance,
it even made the Lord Eternal marvel;
and then a sweet desire
moved Him to summon up such blessedness (*salute*).[146]

In the *Paradiso*, just before he attains the beatific vision, Dante offers a final prayer to Beatrice as if she were indeed his savior, the one who harrowed hell to redeem his soul from bondage:

"O donna in cui la mia speranza vige,
  e che soffristi per la mia salute
  in inferno lasciar le tue vestige, . . .
La tua magnificenza in me custodi,
  sì che l'anima mia, che fatt'hai sana,
  piacente a te dal corpo si disnodi." (*Par*. XXXI, 79–81, 88–90)

"O Lady, in whom my hope flourishes,
  you who suffered for my salvation
  to leave your footprints even in hell, . . .
Preserve your magnificence in me,
  so that my soul, which you have healed,
  may depart the body well-pleasing to you."

More perplexing than Beatrice's apotheosis, and more central to our theme, is her complex relationship with Amore. While the God of Love is conventional enough, Dante's deployment of him is not. On the one hand, his Amore is a more solemn, awe-inspiring figure than the *dieu d'Amors* of the *Rose*, and he is never ironized. Within the vernacular prose of the *Vita Nuova*, the God of Love speaks portentous Latin, and is given to such oracular, quasi-theological pronouncements as "Ego dominus tuus" ("I am your lord") and the notoriously obscure maxim, "Ego tanquam centrum circuli, cui simili modo se habent circumferentie partes" ("I am like the center of a circle, equidistant from all points on the circumference").[147] With this utterance, Love evades a simple question asked by the poet and echoes a hermetic paradox about the divine nature, first introduced into Christian theological discourse by Alan of Lille.[148] It seems here as if Dante is already trying to affiliate the poetic god of love with the God of the Church. On the other hand, he goes to extraordinary lengths to show that Amore is a mere figure of speech—what I referred to in Chapter 1 as an Aristotelian rather than a Platonic personification. In *Vita Nuova* 25, Dante carefully explains that he has ascribed speech, laughter, and embodiment to Love only through poetic license, *as if* Love were a substantial being, even though "according to the truth this is false, since Love is not a substance existing in itself, but an accident within a substance."[149] Vernacular poets, like classical ones, may be permitted such license, but only if they are able to strip away the rhetorical dress on demand and explain their "true meaning" in paraphrase, as Dante tries to do throughout the *Vita Nuova*.

In fact, discerning readers will have noticed many earlier hints of Love's insubstantial status. Dante remarks in chapter 2 that Amore had governed his soul from the time of his first childhood vision of Beatrice, but only because "the power of [his] imagination" gave him such lordship. In chapter 9, when the poet is leaving Florence, he encounters Love in the guise of a tattered pilgrim, like "a once-great ruler since bereft of power." The bedraggled god suggests a stratagem that will in fact backfire, for it will earn Beatrice's contempt: Dante should conceal his love by paying hypocritical attentions to a "screen lady." Having proposed this scheme, Amore vanishes as it were into the poet: "Allora presi di lui sì gran parte, / ch'elli disparve, e non m'accorsi come" ("Then he began to fuse with me so strangely, / he disappeared before I knew he had").[150] Just before he is officially deconstructed, Amore appears once again, but this time he vanishes into the beloved. The god first explains the allegorical progress of the two ladies, Giovanna (also called Primavera) and Beatrice—Guido Cavalcanti's lady followed by Dante's, or John the Baptist by Christ, or the lyric spring by the celestial summer. "After this, Love seemed to speak again and say these words: 'Anyone of subtle discernment would call Beatrice Love, because she so greatly resembles me.'"[151] As many critics have noted, this is the last of the four times that Amore appears and speaks in the *Vita Nuova*, as if he had indeed been supplanted by Beatrice. In Aristotelian terms, one might say that the "accidental" passion of love inheres in the two "substances" (or persons) of Dante and Beatrice. As this truth has now been sufficiently demonstrated, the personification that has completed its work is allowed to retire from the scene.

But the matter is not so simple. For why, after all, should Beatrice be called Amore? If love is only an accident inhering in a substance, it seems that it should inhere in the lover, not the beloved. And Dante is never so bold in the *Vita Nuova* as to claim that Beatrice reciprocates his love. Being a virtuous matron, how could she? The only favor she had ever shown Dante was her public greeting, and even that for only a brief while. If it is proposed that she "resembles Love" because of her beauty—which Dante claims all Florentines admire—why should it require a person of "subtle discernment" to acknowledge this? To be sure, many troubadours known to Dante had already conflated the feminine Amors with the beloved lady; but, for a poet exacting enough to supply prose commentaries on his own sonnets, recourse to poetic convention seems an insufficient answer. The likeliest solution, it seems to me, is that by the time he wrote the *Vita Nuova* Dante had already come to believe that his love was *initiated* by Beatrice or, rather, by divine love acting through Beatrice. She becomes, then, not so much a "figure" of Caritas, as Caritas embodied for his own salvation, and acting vigorously to that end. When we first hear Beatrice's voice in the *Inferno*—for nowhere in the *Vita Nuova* does Dante put words in her mouth—she is speaking to Virgil by the agency of Love:

P' son Beatrice che ti faccio andare;
   vegno del loco ove tornar disio;
   amor mi mosse, che mi fa parlare. (*Inf.* II, 70–72)

I am Beatrice who bid thee go;
   I come from the place where I desire to return;
   Love moved me and makes me speak.

Dante, like most lyric poets, had an inveterate habit of making Love the subject of active verbs, despite his earlier demythologizing essay. Yet Beatrice's first speech does not in itself show how her relationship to Love might differ from that of the doomed Francesca in hell: "Love, which absolves no one beloved from loving, seized me" (*Inf.* V, 103–4). To understand Dante's mature conception of redeemed and redemptive love, we must turn to the *Paradiso*, where we will find him vindicating the words of Amore in the *Vita Nuova* and silently correcting the critical dictum he had used to usher the god offstage.

As the pilgrim-poet approaches the earthly Paradise where he will meet the transfigured Beatrice, he must go by the way of transfigured poetry. So, on the upper terraces of Purgatory, he will meet first the epic poet Statius, to whom (against all precedent) he grants conversion and salvation, and then some of his vernacular precursors, notably Guido Guinizelli and Arnaut Daniel. In perhaps the most famous of these meetings, Dante responds to a compliment from Bonagiunta da Lucca with what amounts to his poetic manifesto:

E io a lui: "P' mi son un che, quando
   Amor mi spira, noto, e a quel modo
   ch'e' ditta dentro vo significando." (*Purg.* XXIV, 52–54)

I said to him, "I am one who takes note
   when Love breathes in me, and whichever way
   he dictates within, I go and signify."

The older poet is satisfied with Dante's definition of the *dolce stil novo* (a term coined in this passage) and admits that his own verse fell short because his pen did not follow so closely behind Amor, the inner poet (*dittator*) who writes upon the heart. The famous credo may now remind us of the Romantics or perhaps of Sir Philip Sidney: "'Foole,' said my Muse to me, 'looke in thy heart and write.'"[152] But Dante's proud claim was not yet hoary with age and overuse. He himself seems to have been indebted to an obscure twelfth-century writer on love—the monk Yvo, who supplied us with the epigraph to this chapter.[153] Yvo had introduced his *Epistle on Charity* with the modest disclaimer,

How can a person speak of love if he is not himself in love, if he does not feel Love's power? On other subjects ample matter can be found in books; as for this, if it does not all come from within, it is nowhere. For Love does not transcribe the mysteries of his sweetness from the outside in, but from the inside out. Hence the only person who can speak of them fittingly is one who composes his words outwardly just as his heart dictates within. So do not marvel if I would rather hear someone else on this subject than speak myself. The one I would like to hear, I say, is one who has dipped the pen of his tongue in his heart's blood, for then his teaching would be true and worthy of reverence.[154]

So Dante aspired to do, and if he agreed with Yvo about the source of the sweetest style, he most assuredly agreed that "whoever loves God is in love with Love" and so revolves in Love's orbit, with the same endless, even motion as the sun and the other stars.

Fittingly, Dante's most original contribution to the metaphysics of love occurs in the third heaven, the one governed by Venus. There he encounters the spirit of yet another poet, Folc of Marseille—the same who perhaps introduced troubadour song to the beguines of the north. Addressing Folc, Dante unleashes three of those startling neologisms, unique to the *Paradiso*, that are meant to reveal the nature of love in heaven:

"Dio vede tutto, e tuo veder *s'inluia*,"
    diss' io, "beato spirto, sì che nulla
    voglia di sè a te puot'esser fuia.
Dunque la voce tua . . .
perchè non satisface a' miei disii?
    Già non attendere' io tua dimanda,
    s'io *m'intuasse*, come tu *t'inmii*." (*Par.* IX, 73–81)

"God sees all, and your sight in-hims itself,"
    I said, "blessed spirit, so that no wish
    can be hidden from you.

Why then does your voice . . .
not satisfy my desires?
  I would not wait for your question
  could I in-you myself as you in-me yourself."

This is the idiom of coinherence, and it wreaks havoc on the Aristotelian
ontology of *Vita Nuova* 25. For love here is not an accident inhering in a substance, but one substance inhering in another: each soul can indwell any
other because all dwell in the mind of God. "This is one of Dante's most
concise and most intense sayings, and one of the most significant. . . . It is
the very definition of all heaven, but especially of the heavens that are to
follow; it is their mode of life. Something of this is known, on occasion,
in the life of lovers; not, perhaps, in many; not, certainly, often. There is
some kind of experience which can only be expressed by saying, 'Love you?
I *am* you.'"[155] Dante sprinkles these celestial solecisms throughout the cantica. Each seraph "en-Gods itself" (*s'india*, *Par.* IV, 28); the wills of all the
blessed are "in-willed" in the divine will (*invoglia*, *Par.* III, 84); Beatrice
"imparadises" the poet's mind ("quella che 'mparadisa la mia mente," *Par.*
XXVIII, 3). Once, on the brink of the empyrean, the idiom serves to feminize the divine nature:

"Tu se' sì presso all' ultima salute"
  cominciò Beatrice, "che tu dei
  aver le luci tue chiare ed acute;
e però, prima che tu più *t'inlei*,
  rimira in giù . . ." (*Par.* XXII, 124–28)

"You are so near the final salvation,"
  Beatrice began, "that you must
  have your eyes clear and keen;
and so, before you in-her yourself more deeply,
  look down . . ."

The promise of being "in-hered" within the Godhead is especially telling in
conjunction with the feminine *salute*, the name for beatitude consistently
linked with Beatrice.

In sum, the metaphysics of divine love proferred in the *Paradiso* revises
the *Vita Nuova* in several ways, while preserving what is most essential to it.
First, Dante implies in the *Commedia* that Amore, the god of young love
and lyric poets, is no mere personification after all, but a partial and mythic
figura of true and substantial Love—*l'Amor che move il sole e l'altre stelle*.
This new vision of Love entails not merely his lordship over an individual

cor gentile, but the coinherence of all the blessed in God, and so in one another—an ontological discovery so radical that it demands a new poetics, transforming personal pronouns into verbs and tacitly overthrowing the Aristotelian theory that had reduced the personality of Love to a rhetorical figure. Second, while the unambiguously divine Amor continues to act as redemptive agent in and through Beatrice, her own co-agency is more fully asserted. The *donna angelicata* is no longer the passive object of Dante's gaze, as she was through much of the *Vita Nuova*. Rather, she is portrayed as the initiator and means of his salvation (*salute*) from beginning to end (*Purg.* XXX, 121–41). The theophany that is her own gaze grows in intensity as her brightening eyes propel the pilgrim from sphere to sphere, until she must remind him that "not only in my eyes is paradise" (*Par.* XVIII, 21). Finally, because of Beatrice's centrality, the divine Love she enacts and reveals can no longer be confined to one gender, but is programmatically represented throughout the *Paradiso* by paired feminine and masculine nouns, with their accompanying pronouns: *bontà* and *bene*, *luce* and *lume*, *fontana* and *fonte*.[156]

Thus, although the *Commedia* stands at some distance from the traditions of Caritas and Minne analyzed earlier, it can also be said to represent the culmination of a trend that began in the mid-twelfth century and lingered until the end of the Middle Ages: the convergence of lyrical and theological ideas of love, *amor* and *caritas*, under the sign of a feminized deity. So we can fittingly end this narrative with two footnotes to Dante: one showing his influence, the other illustrating the early modern retreat from "Beatrician love."

The great Sienese painter Ambrogio Lorenzetti created his altarpiece of the Maestà, or Madonna with Angels and Saints (Figure 4.8), around 1335, fourteen years after the death of Dante. Aside from artistic debts to Duccio and Simone Martini, the iconography of this Maestà also reveals the influence of *Paradiso* XXIV-XXVI. Before Dante arrives at the beatific vision, which he attains through the prayers of the Virgin Mary, he must pass *viva voce* exams on the virtues of faith, hope, and charity. Accordingly, Lorenzetti has depicted the allegorical figures of Fides, Spes, and Caritas on three ascending stairs of the Virgin's throne. Caritas, clad in a diaphanous classical tunic, resembles nothing so much as a female version of Amore. She is winged, like the God of Love but unlike traditional images of the virtue,[157] and her attributes are an arrow and a burning heart. "Among all Caritas figures," observes Robert Freyhan, "this is the one which comes nearest in type to the figure of Amor."[158] In the spirit of Dante, Lorenzetti has conflated the Christian theological virtue with the lyrical God of Love—or, we might say, the *Paradiso* with the *Vita Nuova*. For in the first dream vision of the *Vita* Amore also holds a flaming heart—Dante's own, which he feeds to the reluctant Beatrice.[159]

In sharp contrast to Lorenzetti's artistic appropriation of Dante stands the textual history of the *Vita Nuova* itself. Not until 1576 did the book appear in print, and when it did censors bowdlerized Dante's text in accord with the more rigid pieties of the post-Tridentine church. His audacious theologizing of Beatrice could no longer be tolerated, so *la gloriosa donna della mia mente* ("the glorious lady of my mind"), suggesting sainthood, was emended to *la graziosa donna*, suggesting no more than ordinary charm. *Beatitudine* gave way to the mildly secular *felicità*, while the highly charged *salute* became *dolcezza* or *quiete* (!). Dante's bold analogy comparing Giovanna and Beatrice to John the Baptist and Christ had to be deleted entirely.[160] In an age that still turned out Petrarchan sonnets by the hundreds, it was not the praise of ladies as such that offended, but the uniquely Dantesque notion that, by adoring a lady, one might be led to adore and praise God. The long-running medieval experiment in love was decidedly over.

Figure 4.8. Caritas with arrow and flaming heart. Ambrogio Lorenzetti altarpiece, Maestà (Madonna with Angels and Saints), ca. 1335. Palazzo Municipale, Massa Marittima. By permission, Ministero per i Beni e le Attività Culturali, Soprintendenza per il Patrimonio Storico e Artistico di Siena e Grosseto.

5

Sapientia: The Goddess Incarnate

I [Sophia] came forth from the mouth of the Most High, the firstborn before all creation.

— ECCLUS. 24.5

He [Christ] is the image of the invisible God, the firstborn of all creation.

— COL. 1.15

Although she is one, she can do all; in herself unchanging, she makes all things new.

— WISD. SOL. 7.27

And he who sat upon the throne said, "Behold, I make all things new."

— APOC. 21.5

From the beginning, before the ages I was created, and until the age to come I shall not cease to be; and in his holy habitation I ministered before him.

— ECCLUS. 24.14; LESSON FOR THE ASSUMPTION OF THE BLESSED VIRGIN MARY

THE MATRIARCH OF MEDIEVAL GODDESSES, casting a faint glow of canonicity over them all, was none other than the goddess of the Bible. Called Hagia Sophia in Byzantium, Sapientia and Philosophia in Latin Christendom, Dame Sapience or Lady Wisdom or die ewige Weisheit in the vernaculars, this figure was far better known to medieval clerics than she is today. Of the three scriptural books that portray her—Proverbs, Ecclesiasticus, and the Wisdom of Solomon—only the first is considered canonical by Jews and Protestants; but the Vulgate includes all three. A quick overview of the biblical texts depicting personified Wisdom, once so familiar to students of the sacred page, will convey a sense of this divine, feminine figure's variety and vitality.

The Wisdom of the sapiential books is a powerful, iridescent character: street preacher, prophet, Temple priestess, daughter and counselor of God, creatrix of the world, all-pervading spirit, celestial bride of sages and philosopher-kings.[1] If we trace her career from the earliest to the latest of the scriptural texts, we find that she becomes progressively more universal, ethereal, and goddess-like. In the late, post-exilic portion of Proverbs (chapters 1–9; probably fifth-century B.C.E.), where Sophia first appears, she personifies the ethical wisdom summed up in fear of the Lord, plain speech, honest work, and faithful marriage. Her voice has many registers. Sometimes she is an angry prophet threatening "scoffers" with calamity (1.20–33), sometimes a teacher of righteousness offering rich rewards (8.1–21), and sometimes the good Israelite woman providing a foil to the dreaded adulteress, foreigner, or "foolish woman" (6.24–35, 7.6–23). But she is also, most famously, the firstborn of all creation—older than the hills, more ancient than the ocean—the Creator's beloved companion and playmate (8.22–31). In the later books of Ecclesiasticus and Wisdom, Sophia is not merely present at the creation, but herself the creatrix who "came forth from the mouth of the Most High" and "encircled the vault of heaven alone" (Ecclus. 24.5, 8). Both these intertestamental books, though written by Jews, exercised a more formative influence on Christianity than they ever did on Judaism.

Ecclesiasticus (meaning "the church's book") is also known by its author's name as Sirach, or the Wisdom of Jesus ben Sirach. Written in Hebrew in the second century B.C.E. and translated into Greek by the author's grandson, it should not be confused with the canonical book of Ecclesiastes, traditionally ascribed to Solomon. The sage ben Sirach wrote Ecclesiasticus in part to stem the assimilation of Diaspora Jews, so he employed the erotic allure of Sophia to compete with the popular hellenistic cult of Isis.[2] Wisdom in Ecclesiasticus, like a Jewish fertility goddess, makes her appeal through the lush imagery of spices, fruitful vines, life-giving streams, and aromatic trees. "Come unto me, all you who desire me," she pleads, "and take your fill of my produce" (Ecclus. 24.26). In the Vulgate text, based on the Septuagint but amplified by early Christian scribes, she additionally names herself "the mother of fair love and of fear, of knowledge and of holy hope" (Ecclus. 24.24). Ben Sirach reinforced the superiority of Judaism over pagan worship by identifying this seductive yet maternal Wisdom with the most resonant symbols of Jewish identity—Jerusalem, the Temple cult, and the Torah.

The pseudonymous Wisdom of Solomon, composed in Greek by an Alexandrian Jew, is about a century later than Sirach and goes even further in its divinization of Sophia. Here she becomes the divine protagonist of Israel's providential history, doubling the role of the Lord. But the author, writing in a sophisticated multicultural milieu, is less concerned than ben Sirach to preserve Israel's cultural uniqueness, and much more concerned to demonstrate the universality of Jewish faith and attract potential converts. His Sophia is therefore more thoroughly hellenized and spiritualized, even defined in terms reminiscent of the Platonic world soul—and thus, more distantly, of the medieval goddess Natura. Wisdom "pervades all things on account of her purity, for she is a breath of the power of God, and a pure emanation of the glory of God almighty" (Wisd. 7.24–25). If Sophia is the world soul, then the narrator "Solomon" is a Platonic philosopher-king, eager to attest that he has gained all his vaunted knowledge, wealth, power, and glory through an intimate union with Divine Wisdom: "Her I have loved and searched out from my youth; I sought to take her as my bride, and fell in love with her beauty" (Wisd. 8.2). In this book, which for the first (and nearly the last) time in Jewish history lauds celibacy as a religious ideal, Sophia is not only God's partner but also the chosen bride of the sage, as epitomized by King Solomon.[3]

New Testament writers not only identified the divine Sophia with Jesus, as is well known. More important, they reflected on her creative activity and her relationship with God as scriptural guidelines to follow in developing their own christologies.[4] It is fair to say that Jesus would not so easily have been accepted as God's eternal Son if Sophia had not first been portrayed as his immortal Daughter. Paul was the first to identify Christ explicitly as "the power of God and the wisdom of God" (1 Cor. 1.24), thereby legitimizing the ascription of Sophia's attributes to him in the deutero-Pauline letters of Colossians (1.15–17) and Ephesians (1.9–10). The evangelist Luke understood Jesus as Sophia's child and prophet, while Matthew more radically identified him as Wisdom in person, "justified by her deeds" (Matt. 11.19; cf. Luke 7.35). John's revered prologue is a virtual Sophia-hymn in honor of Jesus, and would have been recognized as such by its original audience. The fourth evangelist followed the lead of Philo, the great first-century Jewish Platonist exegete of Alexandria, in assimilating the biblical Sophia to the masculine Logos of Stoic philosophy. The resulting change of gender made it easier for John to represent this eternal divine being as the One who became incarnate in Jesus.

Our concern in this chapter lies with the reception of these biblical texts in the Middle Ages. Perhaps surprisingly, the scriptural provenance of Lady Wisdom did not foster a more univocal tradition than we have seen with the goddesses Natura and Caritas, but a more variegated one. In the case of Natura, we were able to trace the gradual creation of a sphere of "secondary divinity," increasingly secular yet not profane, in which the earthiest of God's daughters presided over sexuality, gender, and reproduction. The deification of Caritas (Frau Minne), on the other hand, enabled a convergence between sacred and secular arts of love, until the metaphors, emotions, visual images, and psychological processes associated with the love of God became virtually indistinguishable from those of *fin' amors* or *hohe Minne*. With Sapientia, what we find is more like a prismatic refraction of the scriptural goddess, or—to change the metaphor—a number of streams deriving from one font. The oldest of these is a liturgical and exegetical tradition poised uneasily between Christ and Mary, affiliating Wisdom now with one and now with the other. Running parallel to and often converging with this stream is an ethical, didactic tradition fostered by such well-beloved school texts as *The Consolation of Philosophy*, *The Marriage of Philology and Mercury*, and the *Anticlaudianus*. In this tradition Sapientia (or Philosophia or Prudentia) is closely linked with the seven liberal arts on one side and the seven principal virtues on the other.[5] Elaborated in countless allegorical poems and iconographic programs, this tradition locates Wisdom on the boundary between divine and human. Occasionally she crosses that border, as when Christine de Pizan reveals at the end of *Lavision-Christine* that Lady Philosophy "is properly God."[6] Sapientia is thus the most protean of goddesses. Seen as a manifestation of Christ she belongs, like Caritas, to the sphere of primary divinity; considered as an allegorical figure she belongs, like Natura, to that of secondary godhead. When she is identified with Mary, she once again straddles the boundary.

If we attempted to survey all the innumerable wisdom-figures of medieval didactic poetry, this book (like some of the more tedious poems) would seem to have no end. I have chosen instead to concentrate on the more strictly theological and mystical appropriations of Lady Wisdom, which take the scriptural data as their point of departure and tend toward one of two logical endpoints: the feminization of Christ and the divinization of Mary. The first of these currents surfaces in the fourteenth century with two near-contemporary but strikingly different mystics, Henry Suso and Julian of Norwich. Suso, meditating deeply on the sapiential books and their liturgical derivations, cherished a devotion to Christ as Eternal Wisdom and contracted a spiritual marriage with this divine beloved. The Dominican promulgated his new devotion throughout Europe in his hugely popular *Horologium Sapientiae*, which was translated into nine languages, while its associated *Hours of Eternal Wisdom*, translated by Geert Grote, formed part of the standard prayerbook of the Modern Devout.[7] This paraliturgical cult of Eternal Wisdom, which swept Christendom in the fifteenth century, is today all but forgotten. Conversely, Julian of Norwich's contemplation of divine Wisdom as Jesus our Mother, now so widely celebrated, seems to have had almost no influence on anyone before the twentieth century. Nevertheless, Julian's *Revelation of Love* represents one of the most profound and original theological syntheses of the late Middle Ages, and her Wisdom theology stands in fascinating counterpoint with Suso's. Both mystics insist strongly upon the principle of incarnation: the eternal God assumes human flesh without ceasing to be divine, and at the same time, the eternal feminine assumes masculine gender without ceasing to be mother and bride.

An alternative theological current springs from the liturgical identification of Wisdom with Mary, alongside or instead of Christ. Sapiential Mariology thrives on the tension between official dogma, in which Mary is the Mother of God but not herself divine, and the rhetoric of praise, in which no epithet can do full justice to her glory. Whenever the balance tilts toward Mary's divinity, a doctrine that could never be openly proclaimed, sapiential piety takes an esoteric turn. If Christ *qua* Sapientia is androgynous, Mary qua Sapientia is amphibious, so to speak, with one foot in the official Church and the other on more dangerous ground. At the turn of the fifteenth century, chiefly in Germanic lands, we glimpse the beginnings of a genuinely esoteric tradition surrounding Sophia/Maria. In this tradition, Wisdom's yearning to be incarnate takes the form of fascination with the mystery of Matter itself, with the possibility of purifying and divinizing not only human flesh but the very elements of the universe. In the enigmatic and richly illustrated *Aurora consurgens*, once improbably ascribed to Thomas Aquinas, Wisdom is the goddess of alchemists, and devotion to her becomes a quest for the philosopher's stone. The *Book of the Holy Trinity*, a later alchemical text, draws on sapiential Mariology to make the Virgin, in effect, into a fourth member of the Trinity. Indeed, the sapiential liturgy of the Virgin came to inspire a kind of reverence for her that would have amazed and quite probably dismayed its anonymous framers. But all these late medieval developments, however long they took to ripen, are ultimately rooted in the early Church's exegetical and liturgical response to the Bible's goddess.

Liturgical Wisdom: Poised Between Christ and Mary

The ecclesiastical reception of the wisdom books, from the patristic era to about 1200, can be divided into three stages. In the first, Greek and Latin church fathers applied all that the Old Testament said of Wisdom to Christ alone, although they made careful efforts to distinguish between passages pertaining to his divinity and those describing his humanity. In the second period, the seventh and eighth centuries—an era when theological activity was sparse—observance of the four major Marian feasts of the Annunciation (Mar. 25), Nativity (Sept. 8), Purification (Feb. 2), and Assumption (Aug. 15) gradually spread from Rome through the Western church. Lessons for these feasts were drawn largely from the sapiential books. Finally, between the ninth and twelfth centuries, exegesis followed where liturgy had led, as theologians developed a high sapiential Mariology to explain and justify the lectionary. As so often, it was a case of *lex orandi, lex credendi*: the innovations in worship came first, while the theological rationale lagged behind.

During the Arian controversy of the fourth century, debate swirled about Proverbs 8.22–31, the text describing Wisdom's primal origins and her presence at creation. Sophia begins her great cosmological speech with a claim that "the Lord created me at the beginning of his work, the first of his acts of old" (8.22, according to the Revised Standard Version)—an admission that the heretical Arians seized as triumphant proof of their belief that the Son of God was a creature, however exalted, rather than a divine Person equal to the uncreated Father. Jerome solved this problem for readers of his Vulgate by translating the Hebrew verb *qanah* as *possedit* rather than *creavit*: the Lord could never have *created* his Son, divine Wisdom, but rather *possessed* him from eternity.[8] After much argument, however, the fathers made their peace with the verb, reaching a consensus that biblical texts alluding to Wisdom as created should be applied to the humanity (or human body) of Christ, while descriptions of Wisdom as uncreated pertained to his divine nature as the eternal Logos, second Person of the Trinity.[9] Even "created" Wisdom as the incarnate Christ might be declared prior to the whole universe, not in time but in the mind of God, who had foreordained his Son's incarnation as the purpose and consummation of all his works. Proverbs 9.1 goes on to proclaim that "Wisdom has built herself a house, she has hewn out her seven pillars"—a metaphor usually applied to the body of Christ, with the seven gifts of the Holy Spirit (Isa. 11.1–3) as its pillars.[10]

The prestige of "Wisdom" as a christological title was much enhanced by the magnificent cathedral of Hagia Sophia, or Holy Wisdom, in Constantinople. First built by the emperor Constantine in the fourth century, but rebuilt by Justinian in 532–37 on a scale of unprecedented grandeur, Hagia Sophia inspired many copycat dedications in eastern Christendom, though comparatively few in the west. Its original dedication was understood as referring to Christ, "the Only-Begotten Logos," and in particular to his incarnation: the consecration feast of the church was December 23, two days before Christmas. Only much later did some of the Russian Sophia churches transfer their dedication festivals to the Mother of God: in the late fifteenth century the anniversary of St. Sophia of Novgorod was moved to August 15, and in the seventeenth the feast of St. Sophia of Kiev was transferred to September 8, the Nativity of Mary.[11] Despite the overwhelmingly christological tenor of Orthodox devotion to Sophia, however, the biblical goddess-figure occasionally surfaces. The ninth-century *Life of Constantine*, for example, recounts an event very rare in eastern hagiography—the saint's mystical marriage to Sophia. This Constantine, also known as Cyril (d. 869), was with his brother Methodius a tireless evangelizer of the Slavs. His *vita*, probably written by Methodius, states that as a boy of seven Constantine dreamed he was betrothed to Sophia according to the ceremonial of the imperial court, in keeping with Proverbs 7.4: "Say to Wisdom, you are my sister, and call insight your intimate friend."[12] This betrothal shaped the subsequent course of his life: as the spouse of Wisdom Constantine became librarian at Hagia Sophia, learned Hebrew, engaged in theological debates with Muslims and Jews, and ultimately invented the glagolitic alphabet in order to translate the Bible and liturgy into Slavonic. Not coincidentally, he refused a promising marriage, since he was already united to Another.

The account of Constantine's dream is exceptional. For the most part, neither Byzantine nor Latin writers of the early centuries showed much interest in Sophia's gender. In fact, the controversies about created versus uncreated Wisdom seem nearly to have exhausted the church fathers' interest in the sapiential books. Very few early commentaries are known, perhaps because the texts contain primarily self-evident maxims on conduct that posed no great exegetical challenge. For Proverbs we know only of a lost work by Origen, a few Greek fragments, a commentary by Bede, and an anonymous Carolingian work;[13] for Ecclesiasticus there is no extant commentary before Rabanus Maurus, and for Wisdom none before Bonaventure. The very absence of authoritative exegesis devoted to these books might have encouraged original meditation on them as part of the *lectio divina*, at a time when liturgical devotion to Mary was increasing.[14]

In the late seventh century, the Byzantine Pope Sergius I (687–701) greatly amplified the splendor of Marian worship at Rome by adding solemn processions to all four major feasts of the Virgin. The procession on the Vigil of the Assumption was especially grand: the pope in person led a celebrated icon of Christ "not made with hands" from the basilica of St. John Lateran to meet an icon of the Virgin, ostensibly painted by St. Luke, at Santa Maria Maggiore. After the year 1000, when the Emperor Otto III attended this ceremony in Rome, it began to be replicated in cathedrals and monasteries throughout northern Europe, including Cluny.[15] Liturgies of course require lessons, and it seems to have been during the seventh and eighth centuries that readings from the sapiential books were deemed appropriate for the veneration of Christ's mother.[16] While the origins of the sapiential Marian liturgy are obscure, several of its lessons were first used either for the consecration of virgins or the commemoration of virgin martyrs, to which they seemed well-suited because of their feminine imagery, and only later extended to honor *the* Virgin.[17] The epistolaries of Corbie and Murbach (ca. 700) give Ecclus. 24.11–13, 15–20 as a lesson for both the Nativity of Mary and her Assumption.[18] It is Wisdom herself who speaks:

In my strength I have trodden down the hearts of all the proud and the humble,
and in all of these I sought rest,
and I will dwell in [the Lord's] inheritance.
Then the Creator of all things commanded and spoke to me,
and he who created me rested in my tabernacle
and said to me, "Dwell in Jacob
and make your inheritance in Israel,
and take root among my chosen ones." (Ecclus. 24.14 is omitted)
And so I was confirmed in Zion,
and in the holy city likewise I rested,
and in Jerusalem is my power.
And I took root among the honored people,
and in the portion of my God is his inheritance,
and in the fullness of the saints is my dwelling place.
I am exalted like a cedar in Lebanon,
like a cypress on Mount Zion,
like a palm tree I am exalted in Cades,
like a rose garden in Jericho.
I am like a lovely olive tree in the fields,
like a plane tree I am planted in well-watered streets.
Like cinnamon and aromatic balm I gave forth my fragrance,
like fine myrrh I gave forth a sweet odor.[19]

Aside from whatever theological meaning it may have, this text creates an overwhelming impression of lushness and fertility: Sophia/Maria is indeed "a tree of life to those who lay hold of her" (Prov. 3.18). But the most salient fact about this reading may be the verse that is pointedly omitted from it— Ecclus. 24.14: "From the beginning, before the ages I was created, and until the age to come I shall not cease to be; and in his holy habitation I ministered before him." Clearly the liturgists felt that this verse, with its assertion of eternal preexistence and high priesthood, was inappropriate to any creature, even the Virgin Mary. But once the floodgates had been opened the tide could not be turned back, and the verse that had once been censored would eventually appear as the *beginning* of the Marian lesson. The Norcia Missal (late tenth century) gives two epistle readings for the Vigil of the Assumption: one is Ecclus. 24.14–16 (*ab initio ante saecula creata sum*), and the other is Song of Songs 1.1–2.14 ("let him kiss me with the kiss of his mouth").[20] Even more striking, a supplement to Alcuin's sacramentary gives this passage from Ecclesiasticus as the epistle to be read every Saturday at the votive mass of the Virgin,[21] a celebration that grew in popularity along with the idea that each day of the week should have its own special commemoration, with the Sabbath belonging to Mary. By the later Middle Ages, every priest or religious community celebrating daily Mass could be expected to affirm once a week that Sophia/Maria was "created before the ages." The long-term theological impact of this proclamation cannot be overemphasized.

Other early missals and lectionaries supply alternative readings for Marian feasts, virtually all from the sapiential books. For the "festival of St. Mary," that is, the Assumption, Alcuin's lectionary gives three lessons: Prov. 31.10–31 ("Who shall find a valiant woman?"), Ecclus. 24.23–31 ("like a vine I bore sweet-smelling fruit"), and Wisd. 7.30–8.4:[22]

Evil does not conquer Wisdom:
she reaches from end to end mightily
and orders all things sweetly.
Her I have loved and searched out from my youth;
I sought to take her as my bride
and fell in love with her beauty.
Her intimate fellowship with God (*contubernium Dei*) glorifies her noble birth,
and the Lord of all has loved her,
for she is a teacher of the discipline of God
and chooses what his works shall be (*electrix operum illius*).

Interpreted as praise of Mary, this lesson seems to bestow enormous power on a human being, and it would take some time for devotional writers to catch up with it—but in the fullness of time, they did precisely that. By the eleventh century, even the classic christological text of Prov. 8.22–35 had been adopted as a Marian reading:[23]

The Lord possessed me as the beginning of his ways,
before he made anything at all, from the beginning;
I was ordained from eternity and from of old,

before the earth was made.
The abysses were not yet formed when I was conceived,
nor had the springs of waters gushed forth;
the mountains with their heavy mass did not yet exist.
I was born before the hills . . .
When he laid the foundations of the earth
I was with him, fashioning all things,
and it was my delight every day to play before him,
playing at all times over all the earth,
and delighting to be with the children of men. . . .
Whoever finds me will find life
and quaff salvation from the Lord.

Along with these sapiential texts, readings from the Song of Songs (ascribed to the same author, Solomon) were introduced into the Marian office. These lessons did not come to be read liturgically because of any prior Marian interpretation of the Song, for in the early Middle Ages, the Bride was normally taken to be the Church. But when the expanding liturgy came to require "canonical" accounts of events in Mary's life (such as the Assumption) for which there was otherwise no scriptural warrant, the Song of Songs was pressed into new service. As Rachel Fulton writes, "We must recognize liturgical use of a scriptural text as a form of exegesis, equally potent as formal commentary for unveiling the meaning latent in the words."[24] Only much later, in the twelfth century, did exegetes, beginning with Honorius Augustodunensis, try to explain the liturgy by constructing an erotic Mariology centered around the Song. The same process took place with the sapiential lessons, but considerably earlier.[25] A Carolingian exegete from Auxerre states that Ecclesiasticus 24.14, which pertains "to the praise of eternal Wisdom," has been applied "by learned and catholic fathers to the feast of the ever-virgin Mary, through whom the Wisdom of God took flesh," because "she was created by that very Wisdom of God in such a way that, through her, the Son of God might be created without human concupiscence to redeem human nature."[26] Remigius of Auxerre likewise identifies the house of Wisdom (Prov. 9.1) as "either the mother from whom [Christ] took flesh, or else his body in the Virgin."[27] By the mid-twelfth century, the liturgical link between Sophia and the Virgin had inspired a full-fledged sapiential Mariology: the eternal predestination of God's Mother was taught by numerous monastic authors, including Peter Damian, Rupert of Deutz, Bernard of Clairvaux, Godfrey of Admont, and Hildegard of Bingen.[28] The anonymous author of the *Speculum virginum* (*Mirror of Virgins*, ca. 1140) makes the point in a cascade of rhetorical questions:

The providence of God, in which the treasures of all wisdom and knowledge are hidden (Col. 2.3), comprehends all things simultaneously. . . . Therefore, since all things existed within the wisdom of the Word of God, waiting to be unfolded as and when God willed, according to their nature, manner, order, and species, how could the Mother not preexist with the Son . . . ? How could she be absent, in whom an eternal decree had laid the foundation of an eternal building, the celestial Jerusalem? . . . How could the Mother ordained from of old, from eternity, not preexist with her Son in a mysterious unity? Did not the primal origin of all divine works lie hidden in them invisibly, with the perfect fullness of the eternal will and the supreme goodness, to be unfolded at the foreordained time?[29]

This constellation of ideas informs a famous illumination from the Stammheim Missal (ca. 1160) in which Sapientia, representing the Incarnation as God's eternal purpose, supports a bust of Christ still-to-be-born (Figure 5.1). The inscription on her scapular, now effaced, once read "cum eo eram cuncta componens" (Prov. 8.30, "I was with him, fashioning all things"), thereby identifying Wisdom as the creatrix. Around her, prophets and patriarchs hold scrolls proclaiming the mystery of redemption about to unfold. The image echoes a medieval Byzantine iconic type called the Great Panagia ("All-Holy") or Virgin of the Sign, after Isaiah 7.14. In this icon it is Mary herself, hands uplifted in prayer, who appears with a similar medallion of the Christ to come (Figure 5.2).[30] The twelfth-century German painter probably did not intend his central figure to represent "Sophia incarnated in Mary," as one recent scholar has claimed,[31] yet such an interpretation does not strain credibility too far. Indeed, it would be hard to exaggerate the long-term effects of the sapiential liturgy in promoting not just devotion to Mary, but concepts of her as a quasi-divine being, a goddess in all but name. By the late Middle Ages, the lectionary prescribed the wisdom books for liturgical reading throughout the month of August, as if to showcase the chief Marian feast of the Assumption (Aug. 15) as the centerpiece of sapiential piety.

But the growing tendency to link Wisdom with the Virgin did not supersede the older christological meaning. Alcuin, our earliest witness to the Saturday votive Mass of the Virgin, also composed a votive Mass of the Holy Wisdom, which remained in use through 1570. Its prayers invoke Christ and the Holy Spirit rather than Mary:

Collect: O God, who through the Wisdom coeternal with Thee created man when he did not exist, and mercifully reformed him when he had fallen, grant, we beseech Thee, that by the inspiration of the same, we may love Thee with all our mind and follow Thee with all our heart.

Secret: O Lord, we beseech Thee, may the gift of this our offering be sanctified by the cooperation of Thy Wisdom, that it might please Thee unto praise and profit us unto salvation.

Figure 5.1. Sapientia with prophets of the Incarnation. Stammheim Missal, f. 11r, mid-twelfth century. Los Angeles, J. Paul Getty Museum. By permission, J. Paul Getty Museum.

Figure 5.2. Virgin of the Sign (Great Panagia). After a Russian icon, Kievan school, original early twelfth century. Moscow, Tretyakov Gallery. Photo: Richard Kieckhefer.

Postcommunion: Through these holy gifts which we have received, we beseech Thee, Lord God, pour the light of Thy Wisdom into our hearts, that we may truly know Thee and faithfully love Thee.

Prayer over the people: O God, who didst send Thy Son and revealed the Creator to the creature, look with favor upon us, Thy servants, and prepare within our hearts a dwelling place worthy of Holy Wisdom (*agie sophie*).[32]

Although the feminine Sophia is not overtly mentioned in these prayers, neither is she altogether absent—for the Mass is prescribed to be said on Wednesdays, and the litany of saints specified for that day invokes exclusively women, of whom more than eighty virgin martyrs and holy abbesses are named.[33] It may have been Alcuin's postcommunion prayer that inspired yet another invocation of the biblical goddess, this time by Paschasius Radbertus (d. 860). In a poem on the eucharist addressed to Charles the Bald, Paschasius invites the "Virgin Sophia" to descend from on high and expound to the king the mysteries of the "rose-red blood" which he has just received.[34]

Finally, we must note an additional layer of meaning that makes the Carolingian construction of Sapientia still more complex. Whatever else she may represent, Wisdom personifies, among other things, wisdom. In the biblical Wisdom of Solomon (ch. 7), the narrator describes her doctrine as encompassing the entire hellenistic curriculum, from chemistry to astronomy to zoology—not to mention the art of governing, of particular interest to King Solomon. Alcuin, himself a king's servant and a universal pedagogue who styled himself "the least slave of Holy Wisdom,"[35] made no hard-and-fast distinction between the power that created heaven and earth and the ideals of the educational system he strove to establish for Charlemagne.[36] From his perspective as a teacher, the seven pillars of Sophia's house (Prov. 9.1) could be interpreted as the seven liberal arts, not invented but discovered by the great philosophers of antiquity.[37] In the interest of their educational mission, Alcuin and other Carolingian humanists readily conflated the biblical Sapientia not only with Christ and Mary, but also with allegorical figures such as Lady Philosophy. Boethius, an author newly discovered and avidly glossed by the Carolingians, even supplied them with a sacred iconography for Sapientia.[38] In ninth-century Bibles, the "O" initial of Ecclesiasticus ("Omnis sapientia a Domino Deo est") is often illuminated with an image of Wisdom enthroned as queen, holding a scepter and an open book, just as Boethius had described her.[39] The later Bible of St.-Martial of Limoges shows her with seven books representing the seven arts (Figure 5.3). After the twelfth-century renascence of arts instruction, variations on this theme abounded: the liberal arts could be portrayed as maidens fed by the

Figure 5.3. Sapientia Regina. O initial of Ecclesiasticus, Bible of Saint-Martial de Limoges. Paris, Bibliothèque nationale, lat. 8, t. II, f. 74v. Photo: Bibliothèque nationale de France.

nurturing streams from Philosophia's breasts (Figure 2.2) or as eager students sitting at the feet of their mistress Prudentia (Figure 2.4).

The point to bear in mind is that these diverse appropriations of Wisdom—as Christ, as Mary, as Philosophia—did not necessarily clash; but much less did they remain chemically pure and distinct. As the streams of tradition intermingled, each altered the connotations of the others. Thus an anti-humanist monk of the eleventh century could admonish a colleague to forsake profane learning for the study of *ipsa philosophia Christus*—"Christ, who is Philosophy in person."[40] In the same vein, a twelfth-century English abbot exhorted his brethren to "philosophize in the name of Mary" if they wished to attain true wisdom.[41] Mary herself was increasingly portrayed as a great philosopher, not because the maid of Galilee had been renowned for erudition, nor even solely because of her intimate converse with Christ, but because the liturgy had long since conjoined the Queen of Heaven with the Mind of God. To Rupert of Deutz in the early twelfth century, Mary was already the *magistra magistrorum*, "mistress of masters."[42] At Chartres, the south tympanum of the west façade depicts the Virgin enthroned, surrounded by figures of the seven liberal arts. Around 1300 a boy named John, who lived and studied in the cathedral close, dreamed that he fled through this portal, pursued by a devil, into Mary's comforting embrace. Not long afterward, as the monk John of Morigny, he composed a magical *Book of Visions* purporting to grant the operator perfect knowledge of philosophy and all the arts, to be attained from the Virgin herself in a series of ritually induced apparitions.[43] Virtual omniscience was ascribed to Mary by the fifteenth-century preacher Bernardino of Siena: he claimed that the Virgin was not only the greatest theologian who ever lived, but "understood all things better than any philosopher in the world" and perfectly contemplated God while still a fetus in her mother's womb.[44]

The sapiential theology of the high Middle Ages, nurtured by the diverse streams of patristic christology, Marian liturgy, Carolingian humanism, and twelfth-century Platonism, attained its classical zenith in the writings of Hildegard of Bingen.[45] For Hildegard, Sapientia (along with her *alter ego*, Caritas) was a primary manifestation of the feminine Divine, active in creation, in the Incarnation, and in the ongoing work of sanctification through the *virtutes*, or divine energies. Through a complex play of metaphors Wisdom is closely linked with Mary and also with Ecclesia, the personified Church. But the strongly feminine God-language associated with Sapientia and the Virtues in Hildegard's theology is balanced by her traditionally masculine images for Father and Son, together with a conventional view of salvation history centered on male patriarchs, prophets, apostles, and teachers. Hildegard's concern for equilibrium in the gendering of God-talk—one of many such balancing acts typical of twelfth-century authors—temporarily resolved the ambivalence created by the Church's dual-gendered appropriation of Wisdom. In the long run, however, such equilibrium could not be sustained. The ambiguity of the biblical Sapientia, as manifested in the two-pronged liturgical tradition, tended to resolve itself in favor of either a feminized Christ or a divinized Virgin.

Scholars have been attuned to the womanly Christ of late medieval devotion ever since Caroline Bynum documented the intricate complex of ideas that linked the female body with suffering, sacrificial feeding, and the eucharist.[46] But this feminizing of Jesus had more than one intellectual source: It was nurtured from a very different quarter by the strains of sapiential piety and *hohe Minne*, above all in the case of Henry Suso.

Devotional Wisdom: Henry Suso and His Legacy

Two of Suso's German works, as we saw in Chapter 1, express his devotion to Christ as Eternal Wisdom. In the *Vita* or *Life of the Servant* (1360s), coauthored with his protégée Elsbeth Stagel, Suso presents his conversion and courtship of the divine Beloved in the form of an autobiographical narrative, enhanced with literary visions. His earlier *Büchlein der ewigen Weisheit* or *Little Book of Eternal Wisdom* (ca. 1330), written in dialogue form, is a protracted meditation on Christ's passion. Prompted by Eternal Wisdom, the Servant contemplates the sorrows of Christ and his Mother at the Crucifixion, then proceeds in Part II to give counsel on such standard devotional themes as the art of dying, recollection and detachment, adoration of the eucharist, and unceasing praise of God. Although the *Büchlein* begins by citing Wisdom 8.2 ("Hanc amavi et exquisivi"), the female figure of Wisdom is not prominent in this text, for *diu ewige Weisheit* is clearly the suffering Jesus. If anyone is feminized it is Suso himself, in the long tradition of male bridal mysticism popularized by St. Bernard. At one point the writer refers to his own soul as Wisdom's "poor servant girl" (*diner armen dirnen*), and Wisdom responds to Suso as "my daughter" (*min tohter*).[47]

Much of the Dominican's ministry was devoted to the spiritual direction of nuns and beguines, and it was largely for this audience that he wrote his German works, compiled under the title of *The Exemplar*. Because Suso was self-consciously fashioning his life as an example for imitation by his spiritual daughters, he may have felt the model of *Brautmystik* to be especially appropriate.[48] Nuptial or erotic mysticism had long been recommended as an appropriate form of devotion for women. Before Suso, however, it was highly unusual for a man to play the male role in a scenario of celestial love. If homoeroticism was to be avoided, as it usually was, either he had to take on the woman's role as *anima* or else God had to be recast as a goddess.[49] In the *Büchlein*, Suso represents himself as a traditionally feminine soul. But when he decided to expand and recast this popular book in Latin, so as to reach an international audience of monks, friars, and secular priests, he chose the other option. The revised and translated *Büchlein*, called the *Horologium Sapientiae* or *Clock of Wisdom* (translated by Edmund Colledge as *Wisdom's Watch upon the Hours*), was completed in 1334 and enjoyed a phenomenal success.[50] In it Suso programmatically oscillates between two versions of the divine love affair: sometimes the writer speaks as the female Soul pining for her divine Bridegroom, but more often as the male Disciple ravished by love of his heavenly Bride. As he himself explains in the prologue, he "changes his style in different ways according to what seems suited to the material. Now he presents the Son of God as bridegroom of the devout soul, and then he introduces the same as Eternal Wisdom betrothed to the just man."[51]

As an example of the alterations Suso made for his Latinate readers, he replaces chapter 7 of the *Büchlein*, "How Loving God Is," with chapter 6 of the *Horologium*: "What the Divine Bride, Eternal Wisdom, Is Like, and the Quality of Her Love." Suso here constructs a typical romance scene: a young man strolls through a blooming meadow on a spring morning, resolved to sing and dance with his fellows and gather rosebuds while he may. But alas, these "human flowers," so fresh and lovely, wither before his eyes in an instant, leaving their beholder stunned. As he meditates on the brevity of the world's bliss, another vision accosts his sight:

Suddenly, from the region of the highest and loftiest peaks, there appeared a stunning flower of the field (Cant. 2.1), delightful to see, and it seemed incomparably more beautiful than all the flowers I had seen before. As I hastened to gaze on it, behold! suddenly it changed and appeared no more. But one like the goddess [*dea*] of all beauty stood before me, blushing like a rose and gleaming with snowy brightness; and she shone more brightly than the sun and uttered words of beauty. This lady presented in herself the sum of all that could be desired, and with the sweetest fragrance, diffused far and wide in all directions like the scent of the panther, she drew all people to her love, and said in the most dulcet voice, "Come unto me, all you who desire me, and take your fill of my produce. I am the mother of fair love and of fear, of knowledge and of holy hope." (Ecclus. 24.26, 24)[52]

There ensues a lengthy and rhapsodic love-dialogue. The astonished seer muses that "abyss calls to abyss" (Ps. 41.8): in this vision the depth of love encounters the depth of all beauty. Suso's "goddess" identifies herself as Eternal Wisdom, declaiming the words of Solomon from Proverbs and the Song of Songs. She is the true sun of righteousness at whose beauty the sun and moon marvel; she dwells in light unapproachable, in the splendor of the holy ones, born of the womb before the morning star.[53] Her loveliness is so great that, if a man suffered a lifetime of tortures to gaze on her for a single instant, he would pronounce his reward far surpassing his labor. The vision of her "most simple essence" and "supersubstantial divinity" will be, as Boethius wrote, "the whole, simultaneous, and perfect possession of a life that cannot end."[54] Moreover, this supreme deity is the very embodiment of Minne. "See how skillful I am in love," she entices. "How eager I am to enjoy the embraces and deep kisses of a pure soul, how supremely delightful! O sweet and most precious kiss, bestowed with love by honey-flowing lips! O how blessed the soul to whom this is granted even once in a lifetime! And if for such a kiss one should happen to die, it would be no grave loss."[55]

The sources of Suso's devotion are not in doubt. As he explains in the first chapter of the *Horologium*, as well as the *Vita*, his youthful passion for Eternal Wisdom was inspired by hearing the sapiential books read during August, the month of Mary's Assumption. Thus the friar knew Proverbs, Ecclesiasticus, and the Wisdom of Solomon not "in their historical context," as we would now say, but in their liturgical context—as building blocks in the Saturday Mass of the Virgin and the great Marian feasts. Since the Marian liturgy accentuates the seductive allure of these texts by interweaving them with praises of the Bride, taken from the Song of Songs and Psalm 44 (Vg), it is easy to see why Suso, even in a christological interpretation, retained the eroticism of the biblical verses. Yet there is a distinct novelty in his fervent adoration of Sapientia as a goddess. As Edmund Colledge observes, "Suso seems to have been the first to do for Wisdom what Boethius did for Philosophy, Alan of Lille and Jean de Meun for Nature: to endow her with the character and attributes of a queen, a Queen of the Universe."[56] Colledge is undoubtedly right in pointing to the vogue for these goddesses as a factor in Suso's characterization of Sapientia, although I believe he was influenced still more by the courtly portrayals of Caritas and Frau Minne analyzed in Chapter 4.[57] He may also have known Mechthild of Magdeburg's *Flowing Light of the Godhead*, which was read in the same circles as his own book. Heinrich of Nördlingen, for example, sent copies of both the *Horologium* and the *Flowing Light* to his spiritual daughter, Margaretha Ebner.[58]

We must also bear in mind that Suso, a skilled rhetorician, wrote with an eye to the needs of specific audiences. Granted his personal devotion to Eternal Wisdom as a bride, he must have had a reason for suppressing her womanly character in the *Büchlein* and stressing it in the *Horologium*; and that reason surely has to do with the gender of his readers. For nuns and beguines—professional brides of Christ—there was no particular need to feminize Jesus. For monks and priests, however, Suso could offer something more attractive than either the rhetorical cross-dressing of a Bernard or the spiritual director's typical role as "friend of the bridegroom," which left clerics perennially suspicious or envious of the divine intimacies that only women, by virtue of their gender, could enjoy.[59] What he offered was, in fact, heterosexual marriage to God, without the psychological complications involved in the man's having to assume the female role. In the penultimate chapter of the *Horologium*, Suso imagines that marriage formally solemnized and consummated:

I come from the royal wedding, I am intoxicated with the heavenly wine I have drunk, I go forth rejoicing from the bridal chamber. Moreover I bring good news, I bear glad tidings for all! So I cannot contain myself for bliss, but, utterly filled with joy, I exult in the Lord. Do you ask whence such a rare and exceptional cause of mirth has arisen in our land? Truly, in this Easter joy, in these royal and spiritual nuptials, the supreme King and divine Emperor himself has given me his only beloved daughter, Eternal Wisdom, as a bride;[60] he has contracted a marriage and somehow made me his son-in-law. O who am I that I should be son-in-law to the King? (1 Sam. 18.18). Who would dare aspire to such honor? O what a wonder that someone so poor and insignificant, so vile and unworthy, with no antecedent merits, should be exalted to a dignity so high! . . . Yet the munificent king, not content with these gifts, has added even more. . . . For this lowly disciple of Wisdom, given the grace to behold her, received from her a new and mystical name, "Brother Amandus." While he sought a quiet, solitary place with his most divine bride in the marriage bed of his heart, and fell sweetly asleep in the arms of his love, yet remained perfectly awake in the fervent affection of his heart, he conversed with her about the salvation of others, and the Bride uttered these dulcet words, in an intellectual and supernatural fashion far beyond all mortal speech: "From you shall go forth that in which all nations shall be blessed." (Gen. 22.18)[61]

The messianic prophecy from Genesis here alludes to the *Horologium* itself and the devotion it will inspire. By imitating Suso's spiritual marriage, which as always he fashions into an example for others, "all nations" will be privileged to enjoy the same intimate union with God as "Brother Amandus." No longer is the divine marriage reserved only for consecrated women or the feminized souls of men. Nor is it a coincidence that Suso, a teaching and preaching friar, saw his own espousal to Holy Wisdom as a prelude to the salvation of others. Remembering the constant rivalry between the mendicant orders, we might see his marriage to Eternal Wisdom as a Dominican answer to St. Francis's union with Lady Poverty.[62]

At one point, however, Suso deliberately draws back from his intoxicating vision of Christ the Goddess. In the middle of the lover's breathless dialogue with the "goddess of all beauty," he raises an obvious difficulty posed by the representation of God as courtly Beloved. Quoting Ovid as an authority on love, the Disciple reminds Eternal Wisdom that "an intense love cannot bear a companion, it cannot stand being shared by many."[63] In his jealousy, he thinks it unfair that, although he has forsaken all others for "the one and only possessor of [his] heart," his divine Lover cherishes many besides himself. This bold complaint is not new in the literature of devotion. Already in Hugh of St.-Victor's early twelfth-century dialogue, *De arrha animae* (*On the Betrothal Gift of the Soul*), the new convert resents having to share God's bounties with "criminals and lechers," even "reptiles and the worms of the earth." But the soul's teacher instructs her with a telling bit of allegory from the book of Esther. She and her peers are like virgins in the harem of King Ahasuerus: in the gynaeceum which is the Church, they remain for a time to beautify themselves with bathing (baptism), delicacies from the King's table (the eucharist), and magnificent finery (good works), until they are ready to enter the bridal chamber of heaven.[64] This model, with all its asymmetry, is deeply rooted in medieval exegesis. Solomon too had "sixty queens and eighty concubines, and maidens without number" (Cant. 6.7), while the Lamb has 144,000 virgins to follow him wherever he goes (Apoc. 14.3–4). But the model is inescapably gendered: in a patriarchal society that insisted in real life on strict monogamy, God could be imagined as a king with an enormous harem, but hardly as a queen with innumerable lovers.[65] Hence in this part of his dialogue Suso quietly changes the gender of Eternal Wisdom. Masculine nouns ("unicus et singularis cordis mei possessor," "dilectus meus unicus," "amor meus," "domine mi") prevail as long as the topic of jealousy is discussed. As soon as this discourse ends, the delectable Bride returns: "Ecce tu pulchra es, amica mea" (Cant. 6.3).

Would Suso's original readers have been aware of his studied manipulations of gender in the *Horologium*? Artists painted Sapientia as both a man and a woman, and one late medieval scribe described the text as "truly a most devout book, extremely wholesome for devout minds and well-intentioned religious of both sexes."[66] But the eroticism that fascinates contemporary readers was not Suso's central message. His central message was suffering:

the passion of Christ Crucified, the compassion of Mary, the anguish of a sinner's death, the torments of hell, and, above all, "how a true disciple of Christ ought to conform himself to his sufferings."[67] Even the Virgin in the *Horologium* is *mater dolorosa* rather than Queen of Heaven.[68] In all this Suso was a man of his time, for in fourteenth-century art, sermons, and pious writings of every kind, devotion to the Cross far outweighs the gospel of the Resurrection. The Christ of late medieval piety shifts back and forth between suffering Savior and apocalyptic Judge, bypassing the radiant figure of the risen Lord who so dominates patristic and Byzantine spirituality.[69] But it is precisely here that Eternal Wisdom, as a goddess, enables Suso to recover balance. Where we might expect to find the glorified Lord, we see instead the glorious Lady, Eternal Wisdom. She is the alpha and omega of the *Horologium*, the Beloved who first ravishes the young Disciple's heart and the Bride he triumphantly weds in the end—but in between there is Jesus, carrying his cross. So the discerning reader of the *Horologium* gradually learns to see Eternal Wisdom with a theological double vision: s/he is at once the Creatrix of the Old Testament and the Redeemer of the New, at once glorified and crucified, divine and human, woman and man. In a famous analogy, Hildegard of Bingen once wrote that "man signifies the divinity of the Son of God and woman his humanity."[70] Suso reverses that formula: for him it is the woman Sapientia who signifies celestial glory, and the man Jesus who embodies suffering flesh. But the only way to attain the infinitely desirable Bride is to take up the cross she bore as the God-Man.

To judge from the number of surviving manuscripts, the *Horologium Sapientiae* was the most widely read devotional book of the Middle Ages, with the sole exception of *The Imitation of Christ*—written almost a century later and heavily indebted to it. Suso's editor, Pius Künzle, lists 233 extant manuscripts, 88 lost ones, and innumerable excerpts; the exemplars come from Germany, Switzerland, Austria, Bohemia, Poland, France, Spain, Italy, Belgium, Holland, England, Sweden, and Denmark (and one lost manuscript is known to have been in St. Petersburg). They were owned by Benedictines, Carthusians, Augustinians, Dominicans, Cistercians, Franciscans, and Birgittines (in descending order), as well as numerous secular clergy and laity.[71] No fewer than ten printed editions, published in Paris, Venice, and Cologne, appeared between 1480 and 1540. Ludolph of Saxony, whose *Vita Jesu Christi* nearly rivaled Suso's work in popularity, was also his debtor; he probably wrote his *Life of Christ* in the Charterhouse at Mainz, which at the time possessed nine copies of the *Horologium*. Other works indebted to Suso's devotional masterpiece include the Carthusian Hugh of Balma's *Theologia mystica*, the Dominican Jakob von Lilienstein's *De divina sapientia*, Nicholas of Cusa's *Idiota de sapientia*, Jean Gerson's *Trésor de sapience*, Nicholas Love's *Mirrour of the blessed Lyf of Jesu Christ,* and the English morality play *Wisdom*. Geert Grote, founder of the movement that came to be known as the Devotio Moderna, had great affection for the *Horologium*, so the book was one of several designated for professional copying in his scriptorium at Windesheim. As for translations, the French *Horloge de Sapience*, completed by a Franciscan in 1389, survives in 63 manuscripts, many of them lavishly illustrated. There are about 90 manuscripts of a Middle Dutch version, 25 of an Italian translation, and 14 of a Middle English adaptation, *Seuene poyntes of trewe loue and euerlastynge wisdame*, printed by Caxton ca. 1490.[72] Bohemian, Hungarian, and Polish translations have also been discovered, and by 1500, Birgittine nuns of Sweden and Denmark possessed the *Horologium* in their own languages for reading in the refectory. Although the text was never retranslated into German, the manuscripts of its precursor, the *Büchlein der ewigen Weisheit*, are themselves "legion."[73] This evidence should give pause to anyone who assumes such a text must have been marginal, much less heretical. Far from representing an offbeat or dissident religious option, Suso's *Horologium* stood in the mainstream of late medieval devotion.

Among the many translations, by far the most interesting is the *Horloge de Sapience*, a book owned by monastic houses of every order as well as nuns, canons, and noble ladies. More than half the extant manuscripts are illustrated, but one of these is of truly exceptional merit. The Brussels *Horloge de Sapience* (Bibl. Royale, Ms. IV 111), painted in the mid-fifteenth century by an artist known as the "Master of Jean Rolin," originally belonged to a French courtier. Its elaborate iconographic program includes thirty-six pictures but 108 distinct scenes, since many of the paintings are polyptychs. More exceptional still, Suso's illustrated text is prefaced by a *Déclaration des Hystoires de l'Orloge de Sapience*, which is an independent commentary on the paintings and, indirectly, on the work itself. Presumably written to educate the book's lay owner, the *Déclaration* together with the paintings offers an invaluable witness to the reception of Suso's text.[74]

Fittingly enough, the first illustration of the *Horloge* is a *Majestas Sapientiae* (Figure 5.4). Eternal Wisdom—transmuted to Dame Sapience, by analogy with Dame Nature and other French allegorical ladies—sits on a large Gothic throne within a mandorla of seraphim. Wearing a blue mantle over a crimson tunic, with her long hair unbound, she has a cruciform nimbus and holds the traditional attributes of Christ in majesty: an open book in her right hand, an orb in her left. As the commentator writes:

Figure 5.4. *Majestas Sapientiae. Horloge de Sapience*, mid-fifteenth century. Brussels, Bibliothèque royale ms. IV III, f. 13r. Photo: Bibliothèque royale de Belgique.

First of all, at the beginning of the book, is Lady Wisdom in the form and likeness of a woman, signifying Jesus our Savior, who is called the power and wisdom of God the Father (1 Cor. 1.24). She is seated on a throne of majesty as true God. And she holds a book in her right hand and in her left, the world, signifying that through her and from her have emanated all the knowledge and wisdom by which the world is governed and restored. At the right of this Lady Wisdom is the Disciple, author and composer of this book, who stands in a pulpit as if preaching to the different estates of the world, telling them to savor God in goodness and seek him in simplicity of heart.[75]

Clearly the artist, patron, and commentator understood the equivalence of Lady Wisdom and Christ, without feeling any need to suppress the *figure de femme* that Suso had given her.

Part II of the *Horloge* opens with a second *majestas* image (Figure 5.5). In the first chapter of this section Suso reminisces about his education, observing that the arts curriculum whets the appetite for wisdom but cannot satisfy it, then satirically denouncing ambitious, self-indulgent, and hypocritical masters of theology. The monumental painting is divided into two registers. Below is the school of arts, where seven ladies stand around a hexagonal reading-stand filled with books, each engaged in her characteristic activity: Grammar teaches boys, Music plays a psaltery, Astronomy holds an astrolabe up to the stars, and so forth (cf. Figure 2.2). The painting draws on traditional iconography—Suso had written of actual scholars, not allegorical maidens—and deliberately blunts the critique in his text. In the upper panel is a theological academy portrayed as a Dominican *studium generale*, with a French inscription that reads "the School of Theology, whose master (*maistre*) is Wisdom, whose doctrine is truth, and whose end is everlasting glory." At the center Lady Wisdom teaches from her professorial chair, appropriately dressed in doctoral robes, her virginal hair still unbound. Scholars of all ranks are studying here: some are tonsured, some not, and one in the center wears a bishop's miter. According to the text, these students are divided into three groups. At right are the scholars who desire only worldly honors; ape-like demons move among them. At left are others motivated by the sheer love of learning; in the center are contemplatives who study for the love of God and eternal life. These alone, according to the commentator, "sont dignes de presider en saincte Esglise."[76] Golden rays from the chair of Wisdom illumine the last two groups, but not the first.

Several paintings in the cycle illustrate the drama of the Disciple's conversion. In Figure 5.6, divided into four quadrants, the upper left panel shows Dame Sapience in a terebinth tree, literally illustrating Ecclus. 24.22: "like a terebinth I have stretched out my branches." This tree, in the commentator's words, "has great medicinal virtue and sweet-smelling flowers; and Lady Wisdom holds a box full of sweet-smelling ointment and a sprig of balsam in her right hand and a book in her left, signifying that her doctrine is gentle, fragrant, full of grace and honor."[77] At right, she leans down from her seraphic throne and solicits the Disciple's love: "My son, give me your heart" (Prov. 23.26). In the *Horologium* at this juncture, the Disciple prostrates himself at the feet of Eternal Wisdom, his heart "melted in the exceeding sweetness of love, as if in ecstasy, giving thanks and delighting magnificently in her presence."[78] In the lower left panel, the Disciple is ready to avow his love publicly: as he hears a lector in the refectory reading from the sapiential books, he is moved to pound on the table and cry, "Verum

Figure 5.5. Sapientia *magistra* at the school of theology. *Horloge de Sapience*, mid-fifteenth century. Brussels, Bibliothèque royale ms. IV III, f. 90v. Photo: Bibliothèque royale de Belgique.

Figure 5.6. The Disciple falls in love with Eternal Wisdom. *Horloge de Sapience*, mid-fifteenth century. Brussels, Bibliothèque royale ms. IV III, f. 20v. Photo: Bibliothèque royale de Belgique.

est, it is true!"—words that appear in Latin on his speech scroll. Finally, at the bottom right, we see the Disciple studying in his cell: he questions St. Paul about Wisdom's identity and gets the expected christological answer (1 Cor. 1.24).

The Disciple's quest continues in Figure 5.7, a triptych. At left, he again offers his heart—now engraved with the monogram of Christ—to Eternal Wisdom, who stands upon an altar in token of her divine nature. This scene is echoed in the next painting (not reproduced here) by an image of the Disciple offering his soul in the form of an infant to the Trinity enthroned. The strict parallelism of the iconography—heart for soul, altar for throne, Dame Sapience for the Trinity—reinforces Suso's theological point that Wisdom, although specially identified with Christ, is in reality an attribute of the undivided Godhead.[79] Returning to Figure 5.7, we see in the center panel a scene not included in Suso's text, but introduced by the artist or patron. Here Sapientia with her three daughters—Faith, Hope, and Charity—knocks at the door of the Disciple's cell and he gladly admits them. This allegory alludes to the old Roman legend of a matron named Sophia or Sapientia, who was supposed to have encouraged her three daughters in martyrdom. In the tenth century Hrotsvit had told their story in one of her plays, but their cult had faded by Suso's time and here functions as pure allegory.[80] Despite these spiritually promising scenes, at right we see a distracted Disciple closing his

Figure 5.7. Sapientia and her three daughters. *Horloge de Sapience*, mid-fifteenth century. Brussels, Bibliothèque royale ms. IV 111, f. 49v. Photo: Bibliothèque royale de Belgique.

window against the rays of divine light, while Dame Sapience departs in sorrow, "carrying her lantern hidden and sheltered between her hands." The painting as a whole demonstrates the inevitability of sin: no believer, however devout, can remain in a state of perpetual religious enthusiasm "because of the corruption of the body, which grieves and burdens the soul so that it can no longer think of what it loves, but sinks down to think about earthly things."[81]

The heart of the *Horologium* is represented by a small painting that illustrates its second chapter (Figure 5.8). Suso has just asked Eternal Wisdom to manifest herself "in that most loving form and disposition you took on in the bitter pain of your Passion." But when he actually sees the Crucified, he is appalled at his sordid appearance and protests, "How can you call him lovable, since the plain fact shows he is miserable?"[82] In the commentator's words, the Disciple objects that a naked and wounded man, bowed beneath a cross, is hardly a "forme ne figure amoureuse." So Wisdom instructs him with analogies. The true lover of the rose has no fear of its thorns; the wise man will choose precious jewels in a shabby box, rather than a gilded coffer full of filth; even so "the bride of your soul, Eternal Wisdom, may be judged outwardly of no account, abject and despicable, but inwardly she is adorned for a feast of living light."[83] The painter sets this complex scene in a rich interior with a tiled floor and an arcade of leaded windows. Sapientia stands at left, holding a rose branch full of thorns and blossoms. She points out two long, narrow wooden boxes to illustrate the second analogy: the one at her feet is worm-eaten but full of precious goblets, while the one behind her, along the wall, is draped with rich brocade beneath which a rotting corpse can be glimpsed. The Disciple stands with open hands, his body still turned toward Sapientia as he looks over his shoulder at Christ carrying the cross, tormented by three ill-wishers. This scene is clearly a symbolic one, for Jesus already bears the stigmata. Although he and his torturers stand in the same room with the Disciple and Sapientia, the interior opens onto a landscape that forms the backdrop for the "historical" half of the miniature.

This painting is as clear an instance as any of the *Horologium*'s characteristic double vision. Christ/Sapientia appears to the Disciple simultaneously in two forms: glorious and abject, female and male, eternal and historical, divine and human. The emblem of the rose with thorns indicates that he is to embrace both of these forms at once, for they are in truth inseparable. This duality is again signified by the paradox of the worm-eaten coffer ("he had no comeliness or beauty, that men should desire him") with its precious vessels within ("behold him on whose beauty the angels desire to gaze"). Christ's suffering is likewise doubled, for it is depicted as at once historical

Figure 5.8. Sapientia and the Disciple watch Christ carrying his cross. *Horloge de Sapience*, mid-fifteenth century. Brussels, Bibliothèque royale ms. IV III, f. 24r. Photo: Bibliothèque royale de Belgique.

and timeless. On the one hand, he is framed by an idealized landscape meant to represent the Holy Land, while on the other, his feet are grounded in the present reality of the Disciple's cell, and the cross he carries is the one on which he has already died. The friar's anxious backward glance evokes the necessity of *imitatio Christi*, yet he lifts his hands as if in prayer to his Beloved, longing for the rose that has ever signified the lover's reward.

The reward itself is depicted in the final miniature of the *Horloge* (Figure 5.9). Two distinct scenes illustrate the Disciple's spiritual marriage. At left is shown "God the Father as high priest, joining the loving Disciple in marriage to Divine Wisdom, who is the true Son of God."[84] The Father wears the triple tiara of the Papacy—an attribute often seen in fifteenth-century painting[85]—as he joins the lovers' hands and utters the Pauline marriage formula of 2 Cor. 11.2: "I betrothed you to a single husband as a chaste virgin." Although these words (typically applied to Christ and the Church) are quoted in Suso's text, they seem to belie his insistence that the divine Bride will be delighted to embrace any husband who desires her fellowship. Moreover, the postures of the happy couple seem more suited to *fin' amors* than to marriage. Lady Wisdom as the superior party stands at the Father's right, clad in the elegant white and gold robe she has worn throughout the cycle, while the Disciple kneels before her in his habit, and the Holy Spirit in the form of a dove hovers above their joined hands. The wedding of Mary and Joseph, a frequent subject in late medieval art, could have provided the painter with a model for this intimate scene. At right Dame Sapience is seated on a canopied bed, while her husband still kneels with his face buried amorously in her lap. He is asking, "Who am I that I should be son-in-law to the King?" (1 Sam. 18.18), and she replies, "Frater Amandus." The two-part miniature may well be unique as a representation of the male Christian joined in marriage to his feminine God.

Many manuscripts of the *Horologium* conclude with the *Cursus de Aeterna Sapientia* or *Hours of Eternal Wisdom*, a set of devotions Suso prepared for those who wished to imitate the Brother Amandus of his text. This little prayerbook also circulated independently.[86] "Whosoever desires to have Eternal Wisdom as his intimate bride," says the opening rubric, "should devoutly recite these hours for her every day."[87] The prayers and lessons that comprise the Hours are drawn from the sapiential books, the New Testament, and the psalms, as well as the breviary for August, the first O antiphon of Advent ("O Sapientia"), and Alcuin's votive Mass of Holy Wisdom. The hymn is a twelfth-century classic, "Jesu dulcis memoria." Suso's original prayers are well represented by the following sample:

Figure 5.9. Spiritual marriage with Sapientia. *Horloge de Sapience*, mid-fifteenth century. Brussels, Bibliothèque royale ms. IV 111, f. 127v. Photo: Bibliothèque royale de Belgique.

O Eternal Wisdom, splendor of the Father's glory and image of his substance (Hebr. 1.3), who created the universe from nothing and, in order to bring man back to the joys of paradise, descended into this vale of misery, showed him the way of return through your most gentle manner of life, and willed to be sacrificed to the Father on the Cross like an innocent lamb, to offer satisfaction for all sins! Open my heart through your precious death, that I may always behold you, the King of kings and Lord of lords (Apoc. 19.16), with the eyes of unclouded faith. Set my philosophy in your wounds and my wisdom in your stigmata, that henceforth my study may be in you, the sole book of charity, and in your death, and that I may so turn away from all changeable things that I—or rather not I, but you in me and I in you (Gal. 2.20)— may remain eternally united in an indissoluble bond of love.[88]

Like the text of the *Horologium*, the Hours combine a deep devotion to the suffering Christ with a courtship of the feminine Sapientia. In England they were printed by Wynkyn de Worde as "Hours of the Name of Jesus," misattributed to Richard Rolle (London, 1503).[89] But it was chiefly thanks to Geert Grote that Suso's new devotion achieved a popularity even more phenomenal than that of the *Horologium* itself. There still exist 354 manuscripts (plus 22 known to be lost) of Grote's Dutch recension, the *Getijden van de eeuwige Wijsheid*, which circulated as an independent text; and about 800 copies of Grote's complete Dutch book of hours, which includes the *Hours of Eternal Wisdom*.[90] It is interesting that these Dutch manuscripts, unlike those of the French *Horloge*, rarely depict Sapientia as a woman. The Hours of Eternal Wisdom are commonly introduced by such scenes as Christ with a hand raised in blessing, the boy Jesus disputing with the doctors, and in at least one manuscript, God the Father holding the dead and bleeding body of Christ (cf. Figures 6.9. 6.10).[91] It is hardly surprising that these more conventional images should outnumber such rarities as the Brussels *Horloge de Sapience*. Nevertheless, Grote's labor of popularization assured that, for generations, many of the same readers who practiced the imitation of Christ would also be praying daily to have him as their bride. "Wisdom cries out in the streets: If anyone loves Wisdom, let him turn to me and he will find her; and when he has found her, blessed will he be if he can keep her."[92]

Contemplative Wisdom: Julian of Norwich

Suso's younger contemporary Julian of Norwich (1342–after 1416) was the first known woman writer in English. A visionary and contemplative, she seems superficially to fit the familiar pattern of Continental women writers.

Yet she was neither prophet nor reformer nor bridal mystic, and there is no evidence that she was ever a nun. Unusually confident and therefore unusually self-effacing, Julian reveals only one central fact about her past. At the age of thirty she suffered a near-fatal illness, which she took to be a kind of dress rehearsal for death, granted in response to a childhood prayer. After receiving the last rites, as she gazed upon a crucifix and waited to die, she saw instead the body of Christ come to life before her eyes and bleed pro-fusely. Wishing to experience the devotional "wound" of compassion, Julian watched him die by stages until, quite suddenly, agony and blood gave way to "joy and blisse," making her "as glad and mery as it was possible" to be.[93] When she recovered—perhaps soon afterward, perhaps not—Julian wrote a book to disclose her "showings" of Christ's passion and the theological insights she had wrestled from them, focusing especially on God's inexplica-ble failure to prevent sin. If only he had done so, Julian protested, the world would have been spared great suffering and all would have been well. Christ, in response to this objection, famously replied that all should be well any-how: "Synne is behovabil [necessary], but al shal be wel, and al shal be wel, and al manner of thyng shal be wele."[94]

Most believers, granted such an assurance from the very mouth of God, would have been more than satisfied. But Julian, a stubborn intellec-tual, continued the dialogue. Decades later, after taking the strict vows of an anchoress, she completely rewrote her book, producing a text still grounded in her near-death experience but now venturing far into the realms of spec-ulative theology. The heart of this second version, known as the Long Text, is revelation fourteen, which we shall be considering here. It contains all Julian's teaching on the motherhood of God, along with her strikingly orig-inal solution to the problem of theodicy. The latter is grounded in a "show-ing" or parable about a lord and a servant, part of her original revelation which, as Julian candidly admits, she had suppressed in her earlier account because she did not know what it meant. In her relentless quest for fresh theological understanding, Julian differs sharply from mystical nuns on the Continent such as Elisabeth of Schönau, Gertrude of Helfta, Mechthild of Hackeborn, and Margaretha Ebner. Only the French beguine Marguerite Porete is comparable in her radically speculative approach to mystical theol-ogy, though hardly in her specific teachings. In particular, it is the absence of any liturgical or monastic dimension in the *Revelation of Love* that makes Sister Benedicta Ward's theory so plausible. At the time of her illness and visionary experience in 1373, Ward argues, Julian was most likely a young widow, perhaps with children, living in her own home. When she became a recluse she would, like many other English women, have entered the anchorhold as a laywoman, not a nun.[95]

From Margery Kempe's account of her visit to Norwich around 1413, we know that Julian had by then achieved the reputation of a gifted spiritual director.[96] But her fame did not extend to her book, which even Margery—always avid to hear devotional reading—seems not to have known. Although Julian devoted well over twenty years to the labor of love that is her *Revelation*, a book addressed with meticulous care to the spiritual needs of her contemporaries or "even-Christians," neither she nor they made any discernible effort to publish it, for no medieval manuscripts of the Long Text have survived.[97] Needing no amanuensis, Julian also had no clerical promoter, or at any rate, none before Dom Augustine Baker (d. 1641), the Benedictine who introduced her, Henry Suso, and other medieval writers to his community of recusant nuns at Cambrai. Were it not for his efforts and the scribal work of English nuns in Cambrai and Paris, the Long Text of the *Revelation of Love* would have been lost to us.[98]

The medieval obscurity of Julian's book is no freak of fate. She was not only a woman writing in a country that lacked any tradition of female visionary authors, but also had the bad luck to live at a particularly unpropitious moment for theological speculation in the vernacular. As Nicholas Watson has persuasively argued, Julian finished her Long Text not in 1393, as the received dating has it, but perhaps as late as the early fifteenth century, in an English Church alarmed by the spread of Lollardy and determined to crush even potentially heterodox thought.[99] John Wycliffe had been condemned in 1382; in 1401 Parliament passed the act *De heretico comburendo*, which for the first time legalized the burning of heretics in England; and in 1409 Thomas Arundel, archbishop of Canterbury, issued his notorious *Constitutions*, whose far-reaching provisions banned the authorship or ownership of any vernacular work treating scriptural material "set forth in the time of John Wickliff, or since, or hereafter."[100] Julian was no Lollard, and she hedged the most controversial claims of her book—its hints of universal salvation—with careful qualifications and explicit appeals to hold to "the feith of Holy Church." Nevertheless, a hostile reader could easily have plucked propositions from her book out of context to create a list as incriminating as the one that sent the more flamboyant and defiant Marguerite Porete to the stake in Paris a century earlier. One of the seventeenth-century manuscripts of the *Revelation of Love* has a scribal colophon that warns readers: "beware thou take not on[e] thing after thy affection and liking and leve another, for that is the condition of an heretique. But take everything with other, and trewly understonden all is according to holy scripture and growndid in the same."[101] Under these circumstances, it is easy to see why the book must have circulated, if at all, only among the author's most discreet and intimate friends.

Yet there are some tantalizing affinities between Suso, whom everyone read, and Julian, whom almost nobody read.[102] Most fundamentally, both the *Horologium* and the *Revelation of Love* are rooted in devotion to Christ's Passion. Julian, like the Disciple, admits that in youth she "desired a bodily sight wherein [she] might have more knowledge of the bodily peynes of our Saviour, and of the compassion [of] our Lady and of all His trew lovers" (ch. 2). It is with this "bodily sight" of the Crucified, recorded in graphic detail, that her revelations begin. Again like Suso, Julian introduced the feminine Christ to her book only in the course of revision. All her teaching about Jesus as Mother appears only in the Long Text, just as the female persona of Eternal Wisdom—mentioned only in passing in the *Büchlein*—is adored lovingly and at length in the *Horologium*. This similarity is perhaps coincidental, but it does suggest that, while such representations were hardly unknown or unprecedented, neither were they likely to provide points of departure for the novice theological writer. In these two cases, at any rate, only mature and sustained reflection on the nature of God's love, as manifested on the cross, led to the reemergence of feminine Wisdom. Finally, both the German friar and the English anchoress found highly individual (though very different) ways to combine themes from received sapiential theology with their distinctive formulations of the feminine Divine.

Suso's cult of Eternal Wisdom was grounded in the sapiential books and the Marian liturgy, and it was through the paraliturgical devotion of his *Hours* that he promulgated that cult. While Julian probably knew the Vulgate—though the evidence is inconclusive—her scriptural allusions tend to be distant and inexact, as was only prudent at a time when lay familiarity with the Bible aroused prima facie suspicion of heresy.[103] Thus her conviction that "the depe wisdam of the Trinite is our moder, in whom we arn al beclosid" (ch. 54) is only indirectly grounded in scriptural sources. But three other strands are inseparably braided in her theology of divine motherhood: her own experience of prayer and, I suspect, childbearing; her acquaintance with a sapiential theology grounded in Neoplatonism; and her awareness of the affective devotion to Mother Jesus, popularized in England by such writers as Anselm, Aelred of Rievaulx, and the Monk of Farne. Julian's uniqueness as a theologian lies partly in her conflation of the latter two themes. The idea of Christ, or the Second Person of the Trinity, as Sophia was a commonplace, rooted in Scripture and its platonizing early Christian interpreters. Common, too, was the incidental comparison of Jesus to a mother, suffering labor pangs on the cross and nursing her children with sacramental "milk." Only Julian, however, united a sapiential, Trinitarian theology of creation with the devotional theme of Christ's sacrificial maternity. In the process, she lifted the conception of Christ/Sapientia as Mother from the status of casual metaphor to the core of her theological program.

In much of the recent literature on Julian, as Watson dryly observes, "the general feeling appears to be that 'mother' Julian makes God into a mother in order to be able to make him do what she would do if she were God."[104] In other words, a maternal God is supposed to be more tender, more nurturing, and of course, more inclined to save all her children than a harsh, judgmental father would be. Caroline Bynum has shown that, for twelfth-century Cistercian abbots, the image of Jesus as mother functioned in precisely this way.[105] But Julian was no abbot needing to temper paternal authority with maternal affection, nor is her theology based on a principle of gender complementarity, for she associates not only God's motherhood, but also his fatherhood and lordship, with love, generosity, and protection. Structurally, in fact, Julian's long and difficult exposition of her fourteenth showing (ch. 41–63) pairs motherhood with lordship, not fatherhood: the divine mother is to her human child what the divine lord in her parable is to his human servant. These two parallel relationships are expounded in chapters 44–63, a complex unit which Julian may have written and interpolated after completing an earlier draft of the Long Text.[106] Just as the lord looks on with love and pity when his servant falls, planning to honor the poor, broken fellow for what the servant himself takes to be his inexcusable failure, so the mother "may suffre the child to fallen sumtyme, and be disesid in dyvers manners for the owen profitt, but she may never suffre that ony maner of peril cum to the child, for love" (ch. 61). In other words, she cherishes but does not coddle the child. Julian is not sentimental, although her view of motherhood is gentler than that of her contemporary William Flete, who compares God to a "loving mother" because he does not hesitate to thrash his children soundly when they offend.[107]

Although Julian notes that God is not only our mother but also our father, brother, and spouse, it is to the relationships of lord-servant and mother-child that she devotes the bulk of her analysis. Each of these relationships is explored with a view to the questions of theodicy that govern the whole *Revelation*. The parable of the lord and servant demonstrates how it can be that—despite the teaching of Holy Church—God does not blame and punish man for sin, but pities and ultimately rewards him. In her interpretation of this showing, Julian notes a doubleness in lord and servant alike: the lord at once grieves for his servant and honors him, for this servant is simultaneously the sinful Adam and the compassionate Christ. Among other things, the parable establishes the ontological unity of all humankind—or at any rate, "all that shall be saved"; for Julian discerns in the servant's plight that "when Adam fell, God's Son fell" (ch. 51), and she clarifies that by "Adam" we are to understand "all man." Her recognition of the servant as "the general man," fallen from a temporal perspective yet unfallen *sub specie aeternitatis*, leads Julian to perceive a further duality in human nature and to pose a further question: how can our "substance" (or "godly will"), which has never sinned, be conjoined with our "sensuality," which does nothing but sin? It is this question, among others, that the metaphor of God's motherhood addresses.

"Substance" and "sensuality" are key terms that have confused many readers, since their pairing is not standard and Julian herself never defines the terms.[108] Their context must be sought in an exemplarist ontology and anthropology derived ultimately from Augustine, though its proximate source may be impossible to determine. In the strictest sense, Julian's distinction parallels an Augustinian one between higher and lower parts of the soul: the higher part seeks wisdom and is oriented toward God through the intellect, whereas the lower part animates the body and is oriented toward the world through sense perception. Augustine and many of his medieval followers expressed the distinction of "higher" and "lower" through the gender hierarchy of marriage: the higher reason ought to govern the lower sensation or appetite as a husband rules his wife.[109] William of St.-Thierry likewise contrasts the effeminate *anima* or soul, which is merely capable of reason, with the virile *animus* or spirit, which has already attained it.[110] In contrast, Julian conspicuously refuses to assign gender to the two aspects of the soul, although they remain hierarchically ranked. Instead she assigns both genders to God *without* hierarchical difference. Moreover, Julian is unique in asserting that these two dimensions of human *kind* or nature, which she calls substance and sensuality, are linked not directly to one another, but only through their mutual coinherence in Christ, which she imagines as a sort of reciprocal pregnancy. Our unfallen substance lives eternally in the mind of God (otherwise known as Eternal Wisdom or the Logos), while the incarnate Christ lives within our sensuality, which he assumed from Mary and so reunited with our substance.

For our kind which is the heyer part is knitt to God in the makyng, and God is knitt
to our kinde, which is the lower partie in our flesh takyng, and thus in Crist our two
kinds are onyd. . . . For in that ilk tyme that God knitted Him to our body in the
Maydens womb, He toke our sensual soule; in which takyng, He us al haveyng
beclosid in Him, He onyd it to our substance, in which onyng He was perfect man.
For Criste, havyng knitt in Him ilk man that shall be savid, is perfit man. (ch. 57)

For the higher part of our nature [the substance] is knit to God in creation, and God
is knit to the lower part of our nature [the sensuality] in the taking of our flesh;
and thus in Christ our two natures are united. . . . For at the same time that God
knit himself to our body in the Virgin's womb, he assumed our sensual soul, and in
taking it, having all of us enclosed within himself, he united it to our substance. In
this union he was perfect man. For Christ, having knit in himself every person that
shall be saved, is the totality of humankind.

In view of these assertions, both substance and sensuality take on somewhat broader meanings. Our "substance" is not merely a dormant capacity
for union with God, waiting to be actualized in contemplative prayer or after
death. Rather, it is actual union, already given by the fact of creation. This
"substance" can be defined most broadly as the eternal being of humankind
and each member of it—before creation as an idea in the mind of God, in
the course of history as a real (though not consciously realized) unity with
God, and hereafter as the fulfillment of the blessed in the city of God. The
"sensuality," on the other hand, stands most broadly for humanity's empirical being in time—embodied, limited in perception, fallen, yet still united
with the human nature of Christ through the Incarnation, as figured by the
servant in the parable. Both of these unions—our substance "knit" to God
and God to our sensuality—presuppose the absolute unity of Christ and
Adam, which is to say, of the whole human race. That is why I have translated Julian's "perfect man" as "the totality of humankind": she means not
simply that Christ is a perfect or complete human being, but that he is the
perfection and completion of humanity as such, uniting in himself both of
its "kinds" and all of its members. "Al the soules that shall be savid in Hevyn
without end ar knitt [in this knot] and onyd in this onyng, and made holy
in this holyhede" (ch. 53).[111]
     Such Christian Platonist ontologies of exemplarism, emanation, and
return have often been stamped with the mark of the feminine, as we saw
in our examination of Bernard Silvestris and his twelfth-century peers. By
conflating the biblical Sapientia with the pagan Minerva, Bernard memorably personified the divine mind as womb of creation in his goddess Noys—
"image of living life, God's first-born, ground of all truth, substance of the

eternal plan."[112] But the general concept was common currency among theologians, by no means limited to poets or imaginative writers. Ritamary
Bradley has conveniently culled some representative examples from patristic
and scholastic authors, who developed this theme in expounding the many
biblical passages where God is compared to a mother.[113] Ambrose of Milan,
the mediator of Philo's platonizing exegesis to the West, referred to the
Father's mind as "the spiritual womb of an inner sanctuary" from which the
Son proceeded,[114] and allegorized Christ himself as a virgin who married,
gave birth, and suckles his children with breasts that never run dry.[115] Among
the scholastics, Albertus Magnus characterized Christ as "more than mother"
because he "formed us in the womb of foreknowledge, carried us in providing for our life, and suffered the pangs of childbirth in his passion."[116] In the
same vein, Bonaventure wrote that "all the exemplary reasons are conceived
from eternity in the womb of Eternal Wisdom" and brought forth in time.
Because she is our eternal mother, divine Wisdom cannot fail to love us.[117]

Thus Julian stands in a long tradition when she affirms that "God alwis-
dam is our kindly Moder," and again, "the Second Person of the Trinite is our
Moder in kynde in our substantiall makeyng, in whome we arn groundid
and rotid" (ch. 58). By the very fact of writing in English, however, she gives
the teaching a new flavor.[118] Middle English *kinde* ("nature") is etymologi-
cally linked to *kin*: like the Latin *natura* (from the verb "to be born"), the
word itself suggests a connection with motherhood. As an adjective, *kind* or
kindly means both "natural" and "kind, loving, cherishing." Julian takes full
advantage of this semantic range. When she writes that "God is kynde in His
being; that is to sey, that goodnes that is kind, it is God" (ch. 62), she is thus
making a statement richer than any single translation can convey. "God is
kynde in His being" might be rendered as "God by nature is Natura," or
alternatively, "Deus caritas est." It follows that the "goodnes that is kind"—
natural goodness, kindliness, Nature itself—is divine, and accordingly God
"is very fader and very Moder of kinde."

The metaphor of the divine mind as womb is just one of many that theologians have coined for the idea of creation's eternal, exemplary being in
the wisdom of God—what Julian calls our "kindly substance" (ch. 56). Christian mystics have based diverse spiritual practices on the doctrine of exemplarity and return, drawing from it a wide variety of inferences. Hadewijch,
for instance, looked forward to the reunion of her empirical self with her
exemplary self in the context of *mystique courtoise*: when she had become
"full-grown" in her love-quest under the auspices of Minne, she would at last
be at one with her eternal self, who already enjoyed union and parity with

the heavenly Bridegroom.[119] Marguerite Porete, on the other hand, viewed creation as essentially an exile, a fall from being into nothingness, that the loving soul was called by God (or "Dame Amour") to reverse. By the absolute surrender of her will the creature could annihilate her individual selfhood and become one with God without difference, returning to the place where she was before she was created. In this dissolution of the ego no room remains for the body: even the physical humanity of Christ is no longer cherished by the free soul.[120]

Julian differs in some interesting and instructive ways from these beguine mystics. First, her tendency is always to universalize: it is not her personal salvation that interests her, but "ours." For this reason, perhaps, she avoids the language of erotic yearning which claims and demands exclusivity. In this respect she stands as far from Hadewijch as she does from Henry Suso, who protested to Eternal Wisdom that "an intense love cannot bear a companion." Only once does Julian point to "the spouse, Gods Son, in peace with His lowvid wife which is the fair mayden of endles joye" (ch. 51)—yet this fair maiden is no privileged *minnende Seele* but an unusually inclusive version of Ecclesia. Second, the problem that concerns Julian is not the fate of our "substance," which being eternally one with God requires no salvation, but the redemption of our sensuality, very much including the body. It is to accomplish that end, Julian sees, that "the Second Person, which is our Moder substantial, . . . is become our Moder sensual" by taking our flesh (ch. 58). At this point Julian links her sapiential theology of creation with a devotional theology of redemption: the Second Person of the Trinity, who as divine Wisdom is already the womb of creation, becomes incarnate as Jesus, mother of mercy, giving his creatures new birth in hard labor on the cross and feeding his children sacramentally from the breast/wound of his side.[121] "The Moder may geven hir child soken her mylke, but our pretious Moder Jesus, He may fedyn us with Himselfe, and doith full curtesly and full tenderly with the blissid sacrament that is pretious fode of very lif" (ch. 60). Christ's divine and human natures are *both* maternal:

Thus in very Moder Jesus our life is groundid in the forseing wisdam of Himselfe from without begynnyng, with the hey myte of the Fader and the hey, sovereyn goodnes of the Holy Gost. And in the takyng of our kinde, He quicknid us; in his blissid deying upon the Cross, He bare us to endless life; and fro that time and now, and ever shall onto domysday, He fedith us and fordreth us, and ryte as that hey sovereign kindness of Moderhede and as kindly nede of childhede askith. (ch. 63)

Thus in the true Mother, Jesus, our life is grounded in his own prescient Wisdom from without beginning, with the high might of the Father and the high, sovereign goodness of the Holy Spirit. And in the taking of our nature he quickened us; in his blessed dying on the Cross, he bore us to endless life; and now, from that time even to Judgment Day, he feeds us and fosters us, just as the high sovereign kindness of motherhood and the natural need of childhood require.

Julian here distinguishes between the Second Person (or "depe wisdam") of the Trinity as our "Moder of kinde" and the crucified Jesus as our "Moder of mercy." We are eternally and substantially born of God's "prescient Wisdom from without beginning," but reborn in sensuality and time from the Mother who gives birth by dying and milk by bleeding. This distinction-in-unity is roughly parallel to the duality Suso constructs between female and male instantiations of Eternal Wisdom—the Bride to be desired and the Bridegroom to be imitated—but only roughly. For, unlike Suso, Julian does not locate the reciprocity between God and humankind in an exchange of pain. What we owe Christ in return for his passion is not ascetic toil or voluntary suffering, since in her view earthly life is penance enough,[122] but love, trust, and *pleasure* ("likyng").[123] In other words, God as Mother desires the same reward for her labors as a good human mother, namely to see her children happy and confident. Here again Julian distances herself from the Continental tradition of divine eros which, as we have seen, measures the depth of love by the intensity of violence. Yet Julian's maternal theology does call for a kind of reciprocity, and it is here that she is most paradoxical.

Although a theology grounded in divine motherhood seems to leave less room for reciprocation than one centered on God as lover, Julian confounds expectations by positing a *mutual* pregnancy between God and the soul. One of her favorite verbs is *closyd* with its variant *beclosyd*—not surprising since, as Maud McInerney points out, an English anchoress would almost certainly have read the *Ancrene Wisse* and other writings on enclosure.[124] But Julian says not a word about her cell, for the enclosure that interests her most is the maternal body, an image so pervasive in the *Revelation of Love* that it appears as a metaphor for God even when motherhood is not expressly mentioned. Consider this passage from the first showing, in which Julian explains how the goodness of God "comes down to us in the lowest part of our need."

[God's goodness] is nerest in kynde and redyest in grace, for it is the same grace that the soule sekyth and ever schalle, tylle we knowe oure god verely, that hath vs all in hym selfe beclosyde. A man goyth vppe ryght, and the soule of his body is sparyde as a purse fulle feyer. And whan it is tyme of his nescessery, it is openyde and sparyde ayen fulle honestly. And that it is he that doyth this, it is schewed ther wher he seyth he comyth downe to vs to the lowest parte of oure nede. For he hath no dispite of that he made, ne he hath no disdeyne to serue vs at the sympylest office that to oure body longyth in kynde, for loue of the soule that he made to his awne lycknesse. For as the body is cladd in the cloth, and the flessch in the skynne, and the bonys in the flessch, and the harte in the bowke, so ar we, soule and body, cladde and enclosydde in the goodnes of god.[125]

God's goodness is nearest in nature and readiest in grace, for it is the same grace that the soul seeks and always will until we truly know our God, who has enclosed us all in himself. A man walks upright, and the food[126] is locked in his body as in a well-made purse. And when the time of his need comes, the purse is opened and shut again in a most fitting way. And it is God who does this, as it is showed in the passage where he says he comes down to us in the lowest part of our need. For he has no contempt for what he made, nor does he disdain to serve us in the simplest natural function that belongs to our body, for love of the soul that he made to his own likeness. For as the body is clad in its clothes, and the flesh in the skin, and the bones in the flesh, and the heart in the trunk, so are we, soul and body, clad and enclosed in the goodness of God.

Julian has not yet formally introduced the theme of motherhood, but she already evokes it in the allusions to pregnancy that bracket this passage. No human being is ever "beclosyde" in another, in the way that all are said to be "clad and enclosed in the goodness of God," except for a fetus in its mother's womb. When Julian much later describes the mother's service to the child as "nerest, redyest, and sekirest" (ch. 60), she will echo the language she uses here of God's goodness. Between these two images of enclosure comes the remarkable passage—preserved in only one manuscript—where Julian cites the fact of defecation as an example of God's humble ministry to his creatures. She does not merely observe that the human body is cunningly fashioned, as Bernard Silvestris had shown in depicting the handiwork of Physis; she maintains rather that "it is God who does this." What is so extraordinary is not just the lack of bodily shame—although that in itself is rare enough—but Julian's assertion that God personally "hath no disdeyne to serue vs at the sympylest office that to oure body longyth in kynde." There is nothing remotely comparable to this in all theology, for the good reason that few other theologians before our generation have ever changed a diaper.

Julian harks back to this showing later when she is explicitly discussing God's motherhood. After the passage in which she presents Christ as perfect man, "havyng knitt in Him ilk man that shall be savid," she continues with a reference to Mary:

Thus our Lady is our Moder in whome we are all beclosid and of hir borne in Christe, for she that is moder of our Savior, is moder of all that shall be savid in our Savior. And our Savior is our very moder in whom we be endlesly borne and *never*

shall come out of Him. . . . And it is spoke of in the first [showing] wher he seith we
arn all in Him beclosid *and He is beclosid in us*, and that is spoken of in the sixteenth
shewing wher it seith He sittith in our soule. (ch. 57, emphasis added)

Thus our Lady is our Mother in whom we are all enclosed, and of her we are born
in Christ; for she who is mother of our Savior is mother of all that shall be saved in
our Savior. And our Savior is our true mother in whom we are endlessly born/e, and
out of whom we shall never come. . . . And this is mentioned in the first showing, where
he says we are all enclosed in him *and he is enclosed in us*; and that is spoken of in the
sixteenth showing where it says he is enthroned in our soul.

Once again Julian fashions theology from a semantic ambiguity: the divine
womb bears yet does not bear, for the Savior in whom we are "endlessly
born" (given birth) is also the one in whom we are "endlessly borne" (carried or sheltered, that is, *not* given birth). This is partly because the womb
signifies the divine mind from which there is no egress, but partly too
because Julian imagines heaven as absolute security—a state in which the
adult's conscious selfhood, or "perfect knowing," can exist without separation from the maternal body of God.[127] Thus in the tenth showing, she
sees within Christ's wounded side—metaphorically, the womb from which
his "dereworthy blode and pretious water" flow—a "fair and delectable
place, large enough for all mankind that shall be saved" (ch. 24). But in the
final showing, this enclosure is reversed:

I saw the soule so large as it were an endles world and as it were a blisfull kyngdom;
and be the conditions I saw therein, I understode that it is a worshipful syte. In the
midds of that syte sitts our Lord Jesus, God and man, a faire person and of large
stature, heyest bishopp, solemnest kinge, worshipfulliest Lord. And I saw Him clad
solemnly, and worshiply He sitteth in the soule even ryte in peace and rest. . . . For
in us is His homliest home and His endles wonyng. (ch. 67)

I saw the soul as large as if it were an infinite world and a blessed kingdom; and by
the properties I saw in it, I understood that it is an honorable city. In the midst of
that city sits our Lord Jesus, God and man, a fair person and tall, highest bishop,
most solemn king, most honorable Lord. And I saw him splendidly clothed, and
he is enthroned in the soul with great honor, in peace and rest. . . . For in us is his
homeliest home and his endless dwelling.

In one of several hermeneutic instructions to the reader, Julian actually
directs us to consider these two showings side by side so that we can see
how the enclosure is mutual: God in the soul, the soul in the body, and soul
and body alike "clad and enclosed in the goodness of God." In McInerney's
striking image, Julian constructs a Russian nesting doll according to the
aesthetics of M. C. Escher, such that "the body of the last, smallest, and most

interior doll opens to reveal the first and the largest."[128] Yet Julian does not describe the soul itself as maternal or pregnant. Rather, she returns full circle to the image of lordship: the lord's "homeliest home" lies within his redeemed and recovered servant. Thus the City of God where Christ reigns in the soul becomes the mirror image of that "fair and delectable place" where redeemed humanity dwells in Christ's cloven heart. Like Dante's idiom of coinherence, in which the elect souls in Paradise reciprocally in-dwell one another and God, Julian's convergent metaphors of motherhood and lordship affirm reciprocity between God and humans in body and soul alike. In this incarnational vision resides the "deep wisdom" that brought Julian in the twentieth century all the devoted readership that she never found in the fifteenth.

Esoteric Wisdom: The Alchemical Virgin

Henry Suso and Julian of Norwich, in their disparate ways, both sought universality: Suso in his broad international readership, Julian in her theology and rhetoric of inclusion. The writers to whom we turn in this last section mined the same biblical vein, but with another purpose and an utterly different sense of their audience, "fit though few." Cultivating a deliberate esotericism, which would survive both Reformation and Counter-Reformation, they self-consciously placed religion at the service of science. In the *Aurora consurgens*, the *Buch der heiligen Dreifaltigkeit*, and the remarkable illustrations inspired by these alchemical texts, we find all the resources of mystical allegory mobilized to deify not only the Virgin, but matter itself.

Contrary to popular belief, not all alchemists were charlatans or mystics. Many were empirical scientists, but the theory underlying their experiments was unfortunately false. In the course of their laboratory work, alchemists had many occasions to observe that sulfur and mercury (quicksilver) are not in fact the building blocks of all metals. No matter how many times one "mortifies," sublimates, distils, dissolves, or coagulates these elements, no gold will materialize; the result will be nothing nobler than mercuric sulfide. One might expect that repeated experimental failures would eventually have led practitioners to question their working hypotheses, but for centuries no such challenge occurred. The reason, as Barbara Obrist has masterfully shown, is that alchemists ascribed a sacred, revealed status to their foundational texts, especially the cryptic *Tabula smaragdina* (*Emerald Tablet*) attributed to Hermes Trismegistos. Hence, when experiments failed to produce the desired results, adepts did not discard their theories but reinterpreted their scriptures, subjecting "Hermes," Aristotle, and the rest to an endless spiral of allegorical exegesis and elaboration. By rendering theory and practice alike ever more difficult to understand, this interpretive process yielded not scientific advances but a new literary genre. Indeed, medieval alchemical writings represent a unique historical instance of literary criticism fueled by laboratory science. The alchemist Petrus Bonus, writing around 1330, admitted as much when he observed that "this art, alone among all the arts of the world, employs in its teaching foreign and unusual proper names, allegories, enigmas, metaphors, equivocations, figurative language, prosopopoeia, hyperbole, and irony."[129] In the most extravagant texts, which we might characterize as symbolic or mystical alchemy, pragmatic recipes are few and far between, occluded by layer upon layer of mystery, sacrality, and obscurity.[130]

It is in this context that we can view the anonymous treatise, perhaps from the late thirteenth century, known as *Aurora consurgens* (*Rising Dawn*).[131] The work takes its title from a beloved Marian antiphon: "Who is this that ascends like the rising dawn, fair as the moon, elect as the sun, terrible as an army with banners?" (Cant. 6.9).[132] It consists of two sections: an introduction in which a sage, playing Solomon's part, exalts Wisdom in a cascade of quotations from the sapiential books and the Song of Songs, followed by seven "parables" in which Sapientia herself speaks, using the idiom of biblical and mystical theology to veil the secrets of transmutation. Each parable ends with a solemn admonition—"He who has ears to hear, let him hear what the spirit of doctrine says to the sons of discipline"—followed by an alchemical maxim from the tenth-century Arabic writer Muhammad ibn Umail (known to the West as "Senior").[133] The biblical rhetoric is dense enough to foil the uninitiated, who might think they are reading an unusually difficult mystical tract, while the adept will recognize cryptic allusions to the philosopher's stone, the elixir, and alchemical operations. Typical is a chapter entitled "On the provocation of fools" (*De irritatione insipientum*), which justifies the use of parable and enigma to conceal secrets from the unworthy and spur the wise to greater efforts:

Does not Wisdom cry aloud in the streets and Prudence utter her voice in the books of the wise, saying: O men, to you I call, and my voice is for the sons of understanding (Prov. 8.1–4). Understand, you fools, and pay heed to the parable and its interpretation, the words and enigmas of the wise (Prov. 1.6); for the wise have used diverse figures of speech in making comparisons with everything that exists on the earth, and beneath the moon they have multiplied parables in this science. Hearing [these things], the wise will grow wiser and understand (Prov. 1.5), and he who understands this Wisdom will possess her. This is Wisdom, the Queen of the South, who is said to have come from the East (1 Kings 10) like the rising dawn (Cant. 6.9), in order to hear and understand and see the wisdom of Solomon (Matt. 12.42); and there was given into her hand power, honor, strength, and dominion (Apoc. 4.11), and she bears upon her head the crown of the kingdom shining with the rays of twelve stars (Apoc. 12.1), like a bride adorned for her husband (Apoc. 21.2); and on her garments is written (Apoc. 19.16) in golden letters in Greek, Arabic, and Latin: Reigning I will reign, and my reign will have no end (Luke 1.33) for all who find me and who subtly, ingeniously, and constantly seek me.[134]

The Wisdom extolled here is neither Christ nor Mary, but personified Alchemy. When she is said to be more precious than jewels and more priceless than gold or silver, in a passage cited verbatim from Scripture (Wisd. 7.9),[135] the initiate understands that the referent is not insight into the mysteries of divine providence, but the *lapis*, from which gold and silver can be produced at will. Speaking in her own voice, Sapientia may sound at first like Mechthild of Magdeburg or Henry Suso in a rapture, invoking the divine beloved:

the one for whose love I languish, in whose ardor I melt, in whose fragrance I live, by whose taste I regain my health, by whose milk I am nourished, in whose embrace I grow young, in whose kiss I receive the breath of life, in sleeping with whom my whole body is emptied of life; yet I will be to him a father and he will be to me a son.[136]

Who is this androgynous speaker who is at once bride and father, babe at the breast and rejuvenated crone? While the voice echoes the Church extolling her Bridegroom and God making love to the soul, the speaker is probably the elemental "moon," quicksilver, yearning for the embrace of her chemical "sun." The *lapis* was thought to contain within itself both male and female principles—sulfur and mercury, fire and water, spirit and matter—and hence was portrayed as bisexual.[137] One of its symbols was the hermaphrodite, though the two principles might also be characterized as sister and brother, bride and bridegroom, king and queen, or parent and child.

The biblical rhetoric that pervades the *Aurora consurgens* from beginning to end might sound like no more than a particularly breathless variant on the mystical dialogues we have encountered elsewhere. But in fact, it is precisely the opposite, for here the procedures of medieval sacred allegory are turned on their head: The supernatural becomes a *figura* of the natural. As Wisdom unfolds her seven parables, all the events of sacred history—creation, the flood, the fall of Adam and Eve, the incarnation, passion and resurrection of Christ, the threefold baptism of the Holy Spirit, and the eschatological union of Bride and Bridegroom—are pressed into service to signify chemical processes. It was for this reason that the sixteenth-century editor Conrad Waldkirch, though sympathetic to alchemy, considered the *Aurora consurgens* a blasphemy and refused to print it in his compendium: "the author has allegorically twisted almost all of sacred Scripture toward alchemy in spite of itself, especially Solomon, the Psalms, and above all the Song of Songs, so that they might all seem to have been written, if we believe him, for no end other than the praise and honor of Alchemy."[138] This indeed seems to have been the author's intention. Sapientia's final peroration is a biblical mosaic of which St. Bernard might have been proud, except for the few words reminding us that she is indeed the alchemical goddess:

I give and do not take back, I nourish and never fail, I safeguard and am not afraid: what more shall I say to my beloved? I am the mediatrix of the elements, making one accord with another: that which is warm I make cold, and the reverse; that which is dry I moisten, and the reverse; that which is hard I soften, and the reverse. I am the end and my beloved is the beginning; I am the whole work, and all knowledge is concealed in me; I am law in the priest, the word in the prophet, and counsel in the wise (Jer. 18.18). I will slay and I will quicken, and there is none that can deliver out of my hand (Deut. 32.39).[139]

Sometime in the fourteenth century the *Aurora consurgens* acquired a commentary, which came to be copied with the original treatise as Part II, and around 1420 this composite work inspired a startling and weirdly beautiful iconographic cycle. These paintings, which were copied in at least seven manuscripts, seem to have originated in the region of Vienna or Salzburg.[140] German and Bohemian princes around the turn of the fifteenth century took a deep interest in alchemy in the hope of improving their cash flow, so an enterprising adept could easily find patronage in that region. Several of the illustrations show how the brilliantly inventive painter, like the author, bent familiar Christian symbols to the service of esotericism. One miniature depicts Sapientia as a crowned Mother of Mercy, sheltering philosophers or alchemists beneath her cloak as the Virgin Mary shelters sinners (cf. Figure 6.8);[141] another portrays her as nursing mother, embracing two greybeard philosophers who press their lips to her naked breasts (Figure 5.10). Especially notable is the scarlet face of Wisdom, the color of dawn (*aurora consurgens*)—a symbolism more often linked with Caritas or the Holy Spirit, as in the famous illuminations of Hildegard's *Liber divinorum operum*.[142] Both Caritas and Ecclesia might be shown suckling infants (cf. Figure 1.3), but the image of two old men at the breast is rare.[143] Such grotesque and sexually titillating imagery, which is characteristic of alchemical manuscripts, doubtless enhanced their material value as well as their esoteric appeal.

Figure 5.10. Sapientia nursing two philosophers. *Aurora consurgens*, ca. 1420. Zürich, Zentralbibliothek, Codex Rhenoviensis 172, f. 13v. By permission, Zentralbibliothek, Zürich.

Stranger still is the representation of Sapientia/Maria as Black Bride (Figure 5.11). Against a vivid red background stands a young black woman with a pair of green wings, clothed in a form-fitting white tunic, which she parts to reveal the mandorla-shaped opening of her womb. Three different iconographic types of the Virgin, all significantly altered, have been superimposed here to create an image that combines striking visual appeal with the dense layering typical of esotericism. By 1420 it was a commonplace in biblical scholarship to identify Mary with Solomon's bride, who calls herself *nigra sed formosa* (Cant. 1.4). But in visual art, the Black Madonna remained an exclusively sculptural type, found especially at great miracle-working shrines such as Chartres, Rocamadour, and Montserrat. No medieval painting, to my knowledge, ever depicts a Black Madonna—except for the *Aurora consurgens*. The Black Bride also recalls the emergent type of the Immaculate Conception, based on the apocalyptic "woman clothed with the sun, with the moon beneath her feet" (Apoc. 12.1). According to the Apocalypse, a favorite text of the *Aurora* author, the *mulier amicta sole* is with child and

Figure 5.11. Alchemical hermaphrodite as *mulier amicta sole* and black bride. *Aurora consurgens*, ca. 1420. Zürich, Zentralbibliothek, Codex Rhenoviensis 172, f. 29v. By permission, Zentralbibliothek, Zürich.

cries out in her pangs as a great dragon menaces her infant. After giving birth, she "is given the two wings of a great eagle" to flee from the serpent into the wilderness (Apoc. 12.14). Artists did not usually depict the apocalyptic woman with wings, but the *Aurora* painter did; and, not coincidentally, eagles and dragons figure prominently elsewhere in this cycle. Finally, our winged Black Madonna draws on a fourteenth-century iconic type, the Virgin of the Visitation, whose transparent womb enables the viewer to see and adore Christ within her (cf. Figure 5.2). The womb of this alchemical virgin, however, reveals not Christ but a caduceus, the symbol of Mercury. To the adept, this detail identifies her as another version of the alchemical hermaphrodite, or more precisely, Aphrodite pregnant with Hermes, here representing the *lapis*.

Alchemical treatises commonly designated quicksilver as "virgin" because it was supposed to carry within its own metaphorical womb the sulfur that fertilized it. In Senior's *Tabula chemica*, the chief non-biblical source of the *Aurora*, the moon writes a letter to the sun explaining that she has received his soul within her womb: so the sun that clothes this lunar virgin is also the sun she carries. Further, insofar as the pregnant virgin signifies Mercury, the green of her wings suggests Venus. In the elaborate color symbolism of alchemy, green is the hue of oxidized copper (*cyprum*) and therefore sacred to Venus, the Cyprian goddess.[144] The remaining colors of the painting evoke the four elements required for transmutation: black for earth, blue for air, white for water, and red for fire. Thus the image can be "read" against two frames of reference, Christian and alchemical, each multiply and intricately coded. Obrist finds the artist's Marian pictorial models to be "so far deformed that they are barely recognizable."[145] Yet it is hard to believe that anyone learned enough to own such an arcane manuscript would have failed to recognize the strange transmutations worked upon this Black Madonna who is, but is not, the Virgin Mary.

A second work of symbolic alchemy, the *Buch der heiligen Dreifaltigkeit* (*Book of the Holy Trinity*), is contemporary with the *Aurora* illustrations and stems from the same south German milieu.[146] Although it too is anonymous, we know considerably more about its author and his historical circumstances.[147] The writer, almost certainly a Spiritual Franciscan, composed his treatise in the vernacular during a decade of restless travels through southern Germany. Since he dated many of his chapters, we know that he began writing in 1410 and finished his book in 1419. During the Council of Constance (1414–18)—which, like a modern academic convention, became a mecca for esoteric booksellers—he managed to present a portion of his work to the Emperor Sigismund, although he subsequently dedicated it to his new patron Friedrich, margrave of Brandenburg. Sigismund's brother, Wenceslas of Prague, was known for his excellent library in natural science, magic, and astrology, while Friedrich took such a keen interest in alchemy that he employed two noblemen to teach it to his son, who at one point engaged an adept to fabricate 100,000 gulden a year for his fiscal needs.[148] The favor of such prominent patrons explains how our impecunious author was able to supervise a lavish program of illustrations for his book almost as soon as he completed it. More successful than the *Aurora*, the *Buch* survives in about twenty manuscripts, many of them illustrated.[149] It is if anything even less intelligible, being a loosely structured yet elaborately coded jumble of political prophecies, mystical theology, and practical alchemy. Few scholars have studied the text, which has never been critically edited; among those who have, more than one has questioned the author's sanity.[150]

Fortunately, we do not need to present a full and coherent account of the *Book of the Holy Trinity*, since our concern lies only with its author's sapiential Mariology. In that sphere he seems to have been remarkably influential. He begins from the premise that Mary is the true speaker of all the biblical aretalogies of Wisdom: thus she is coeternal with God, born before the ages, fully united with her Son in all the works of creation and redemption. As a Franciscan, the author vigorously defends the Immaculate Conception, a doctrine which his order at that time championed in the face of staunch opposition from the Dominicans. Thus Jesus and Mary together, in our author's view, constitute an eternally pure humanity or "outer human body of God." This is the absolute beginning of the human race—standing over against the fallen Adam and Eve at the beginning of historical time and the Antichrist, with his corrupt mother, at its end. Because Mary is inseparable from Jesus, she is inseparable from the whole Trinity. Hence the author calls her a "mirror of the Holy Trinity" while making her in effect its fourth member—or more plausibly its third, since the Holy Spirit plays a less prominent role. Clarity is not the strong point of the text, but our Franciscan says something like this:

We perceive what the inner divine body is, that is, the inner divine being: one essence, four elements, three persons. So likewise we perceive what the outer human body is, that is, the outer human being: one essence, four elements, three persons. . . . So we confess that the outward humanity of God—Jesus-Mary, one fiery angelic body—has become one in God, his own, for Jesus Christ himself [who is] one over all. In him Mary was eternally united to his humanity, one and the same substance, together with his divine substance. . . . Thus she has been wholly and eternally like his person, divine and human, one within one, a being that no one could ever sunder. So truly, through the luminous, pure, clear and radiant essence, the noble humanity of God, Jesus-Mary was one being. . . .[151]

O what a pure love gave birth to humanity! Jesus-Mary is eternally one, and their divinity has become eternally one. Jesus Christ from eternity cannot and could not be [apart] from their outward humanity, Jesus-Mary. So it is altogether true: He is and was one and the same substance, Jesus-Mary, three persons, dual Godhead. . . . We know that no one can see his divinity; we must see his humanity along with it, intermingled as one. So too we cannot and could never have seen his humanity [alone]. We have always had to see his divinity along with it, hidden, intermingled as one. Divinity eternally was and is the being of humanity; there is no separation in him between his divinity and his humanity, which are as one. So too we cannot see God; we must see his Mother along with him, intermingled as one. Even so we cannot and could never have seen God's Mother [alone]; we must eternally see God along with her, hidden, intermingled as one. God eternally was and is his own Mother. The Father himself—who is human, both maidenly and manly—wishes to be forever hidden in the one that leads to him.[152]

To paraphrase, the *Book of the Holy Trinity* represents divinity and humanity as the two aspects, inner and outer, of one sole, eternal being. This being is composed of three persons, Father, Mother, and Son. In the Incarnation, however, the Three are visibly manifest as Two, for the divine Father cannot be seen but is only intuited through the revelation of his twofold humanity, "Jesus-Mary." In their inseparable unity, Mother and Son suggest the alchemical hermaphrodite. Their roles seem to be interchangeable, as in an endless cycle of transmutations, for if "God eternally was and is his own Mother," it can also be said that "Jesus Christ is his own Son,"[153] "the Father is Mother of the Son," and "the Son is Mother of the Father."[154] These permutations of the Trinity constitute only the most visible, exoteric layer of the text. On a different plane, the divine persons can signify gold, silver, and mercury; surrounded by symbols of the four evangelists representing other metals (lead, copper, iron, and tin), they make up the full complement of seven. Once this shifting code has been cracked, an adept could in principle translate the text's theological statements into chemical recipes. Yet another set of correspondences links the sacred company with a constellation of political figures around the emperor. Figure 6.2 features four heraldic shields surrounding an imperial coat of arms, with the crucifix and the Virgin superimposed on a double-headed imperial eagle.[155]

It may be objected that all this is heresy. Strangely, however, that objection does not seem to have occurred to anyone in the fifteenth century. The *Buch* author came and went as he pleased at the Council of Constance, where the assembled fathers had recently approved the burning of John Hus, and we do not read that he was either accused of heresy or placed under house arrest as a harmless lunatic. Instead, he gained entrée to the emperor and secured noble patronage, while manuscripts of his *Buch* were freely copied and illuminated—far more freely than those of Julian of Norwich's near-contemporary *Revelation*. With a mind-boggling irony, our peripatetic Franciscan promoted his book as an *anti*-heretical treatise: "this book shall openly proclaim to Jews, pagans, Christians, and heretics the one, true, all-encompassing Christian faith, [namely] that Mary is the mirror of the Holy Trinity, as great [as Jesus], high in the Godhead. She herself bears witness to this in the book where she says, 'I was created from the beginning and before the ages'" (Ecclus. 24.14).[156] The anonymous monk who first chose that sapiential lesson for the feast of Mary's Assumption would have been astonished, had he but known where his liturgical choice would lead.

Given the obscurity and heterodox views of the *Book of the Holy Trinity*, it might have been triumph enough for its author to have escaped prosecution and exercised some modest influence on the history of alchemy. But he seems to have achieved even more. Whoever he was, our Franciscan either invented or effectively promoted a new iconography of the Virgin, hitherto unknown or very rare, that well conveys his understanding of Mary as a member of the triune Godhead.[157] This iconic type is the Coronation of the Virgin by the Trinity (Figure 6.2), an image we will explore further in Chapter 6. Suffice it here to note that the oldest manuscripts of the *Book of the Holy Trinity*, which date from 1419, are among the very first to feature this composition, which places the Virgin squarely in the center of the Trinity on a level with the Father and Son.[158] At the time our Franciscan alchemist was writing, the Coronation of Mary by the entire Trinity (rather than Christ alone) was novel enough to require extensive justification, and the *Book of the Holy Trinity* provides it. We are fortunate enough to possess an autograph of the work, which clearly shows that the author himself planned his iconographic program. This manuscript devotes two full pages to describing the Coronation in detail, while another provides the illuminator with a rough sketch, complete with color indications and the names *filius maria pater* in the center of the page.[159] This iconography did not become widespread until after 1450. By 1500 it was normative and had acquired fully orthodox connotations, as we shall see. Nevertheless, if we can imagine an anthropologist from Mars being told that Christians worship one God in three persons, as represented in the Coronation icon, she would in all likelihood assume those three persons to be the old man, the young man, and the woman in the center, rather than the inconspicuous bird above her head. Considering the origins of the image, she would not be far wrong.

To conclude, Sophia's path through the centuries is neither straightforward nor simple. Because the biblical figure is what she is—a canonical goddess in a tradition that officially acknowledges only one God—Lady Wisdom could neither be readily explained away nor safely ignored. Medieval exegetes, liturgists, mystics and poets discovered, in effect, three solutions to the problem she posed. One—by far the earliest and the most widely championed by theologians—was to give Sophia a sex change and identify her with Christ *tout court*, as the New Testament writers had already done. Nevertheless, the pervasive goddess-imagery associated with the biblical Wisdom remained indelibly present, spurring the feminization of Jesus in forms as diverse as those of Henry Suso and Julian of Norwich. A second solution was to read Sapientia as an allegorical figure—a personification of philosophy, learning in general, or even revealed theology. Appropriations of Sophia in this vein animate a long series of texts ranging from Boethius's *Consolation of Philoso-phy* to Alan of Lille's *Anticlaudianus* (chapter 2) to the allegories of Christine de Pizan (chapter 1). In works of this type, Lady Wisdom's gender is no longer a problem; she takes her place as one personification among many, yet bestows on intellectual pursuits a numinous aura they might not other-wise have enjoyed. The *Aurora consurgens* represents the extreme case of this tendency. Here Sapientia, in the full panoply of her goddess-like grandeur, personifies the esoteric science of alchemy whose goal—the creation of the philosopher's stone—was to confer virtual divinity and godlike wealth on its possessor.

A third solution, grounded in liturgical practice, seemed at once obvi-ous and intensely problematic. This was the interpretation of Wisdom as the Virgin Mary, which proceeded by slow, halting steps from the anonymous choice of lectionary readings for Marian feasts, to the production of tentative commentaries in the Carolingian and Ottonian eras, to the twelfth-century celebration of the Virgin's eternal preexistence, to the high sapiential Mariol-ogies of the fifteenth century, such as we find in Bernardino of Siena and the *Book of the Holy Trinity*. Endowed with eternity, divine causality, celestial queenship, and the most intimate possible union with her Son, it is little wonder that Sophia/Maria emerged for all practical purposes as a goddess, not only through the familiar cultic routes (shrines, relics, pilgrimage, mira-cles), but also through theoretical elaboration of what the Scriptures them-selves now seemed to assert about her. In the sixteenth century, this brand of Marian devotion would evoke fiercer repudiations and more ardent defenses than any other aspect of Catholicism. But the late medieval deification of the Virgin went far beyond the sapiential themes we have investigated here. It is to a more popular aspect of Marian piety—her integration into the "divine family" of the Holy Trinity, which we have already seen adumbrated by an obscure Franciscan alchemist—that we turn our attention in Chapter 6.

6

Maria: Holy Trinity as Holy Family

Mary Immaculate,
Merely a woman, yet
Whose presence, power is
Great as no goddess's
Was deemèd, dreamèd . . .

—G. M. HOPKINS, "THE BLESSED VIRGIN COMPARED
TO THE AIR WE BREATHE"

WHAT IF FREUD HAD BEEN A MEDIEVALIST?
Anyone who has browsed in the great museums of Europe might ponder that question, for they devote gallery after gallery to paintings of Christ and his mother but give short shrift to Oedipus and Jocasta. The Greek tragedy, while known in the Middle Ages, enjoyed no great cultural prestige until Freud himself privileged it.[1] But what if, instead of the doomed royalty of Thebes, he had taken the king and queen of heaven as his primal incestuous pair? How does this family romance compare with Freud's paradigm?

In the Greek myth, an oracle predicts the fatal destiny of Oedipus at birth, and the events unfold as prophesied. The Christian story, too, is pre-destined "from before the foundation of the world" and foretold by a long series of prophets. Oedipus, the archetypal tragic hero, unwittingly kills his father, marries his mother, and usurps his father's throne. When he learns the truth about his identity, he blinds himself in remorse, eliciting the pity and terror named by Aristotle as the hallmarks of tragedy. The Christian family romance also involves a royal father and son, but their roles are reversed. Here it is the father who sends his son to death, but the son accepts his fate willingly and with full knowledge of his identity. In a dramatic reversal, he then rises from the dead and marries his mother, again knowingly and will-ingly. The incest taboo is not so much transgressed as transvalued, upheld in one sense even as it is overturned in another. Mother and son are joined in an intimate union characterized as "bridal," yet both remain eternal virgins. At the same time, the son inherits his father's crown not through murder, but through *being* murdered and *then* marrying the queen. In the Oedipus myth, Jocasta's discovery of the incest leads to her suicide, but the tragedians (like Freud) focus their principal attention on her son. In the Christian myth, Mary's dual role as mother and bride is glorified, and by the fifteenth century she shares the limelight equally with her son. Finally, although the myth retains its tragic element, its outcome is ultimately comic, evoking pity and terror but also desire and wonder.[2]

The story of Oedipus, as interpreted by Freud, punishes the violation of taboos in order to reinforce them. To achieve adult competence and mature sexuality, Freud believed, the son must renounce his jealous rage against the father and his sexual desire for the mother. But the price of these instinctual renunciations is tragic, as he somberly admitted in *Civilization and Its Discontents*.[3] The Christian myth, however, expresses a radically different attitude toward both taboos. It features not a competitive son who slays his father, but an omnipotent father who sacrifices his son—for the death of Christ, in medieval theology, is never merely a judicial murder carried out by an oppressive government. Rather, it is emphatically willed by the Father *and* the Son, and religious lyrics elicit the Virgin Mother's reluctant consent as well.[4] Thus a paradigm of parental child sacrifice replaces the Freudian paradigm of filial rebellion, and this sacrifice is vindicated by the resurrection with its universal redemptive power. At the same time, the quasi-incestuous love of Mother and Son is also valorized—on the sole and all-important condition that it be chaste. The myth, then, calls for renunciation not of the mother's love but of physical sexuality, and insofar as Christ and Mary serve as models for believers to imitate, the appropriate response is not exogamy but celibacy.

To interpret the Christian myth as a family romance is not to ask, yet again, how Freudian theory might explain the cult of the Virgin.[5] Nor is it necessarily to use a religious paradigm as a model for understanding the history of the family—although social historians have in fact quarried rich material from changing representations of Christ, his Mother, and the Holy Family.[6] My purpose is instead to explore one of several avenues through which Mary in the late Middle Ages came to function, for all practical purposes, as a goddess—despite the near-silence of the New Testament and the strict limitations ostensibly placed on her role by Christian dogma.[7] Mary after all was not an allegorical figure like Natura, Philosophia, or Ecclesia; nor was she a female manifestation of the one God like Frau Minne or Eternal Wisdom. As Hopkins writes, she was "merely a woman," however exceptional. Yet we have seen how by the twelfth century the liturgical identification of Mary with Sapientia had conferred eternal preexistence on her, while belief in her bodily assumption (universally accepted in the Middle Ages, though not formally defined until 1950) made her queenship everlasting. Others have investigated the nearly unlimited powers ascribed to Mary as intercessor, miracle-worker, patroness, and queen.[8] I will look in this chapter at an equally conspicuous, yet rarely discussed phenomenon: the late medieval tendency to represent the Trinity itself as a family, with Mary its honorary female member. Through the ever-shifting roles she occupied within this divine family, the Virgin provided a wide variety of models not only for devotion, but also for identification.

The Trinity as a Family

Prior to the fifteenth century, the two most important images in Christian art had always been the Crucifixion and the Madonna and Child. The Trinity, when represented at all, tended to have a doctrinal rather than devotional character. Depictions of the triune God typically emphasized the unity and equality of the three Persons, as in a celebrated twelfth-century example from the *Hortus deliciarum* where three identical "christomorphic" men sit side by side on a bench, holding a scroll that reads "Faciamus hominem ad imaginem et similitudinem nostram" ("Let us make man to our image and likeness," Gen. 1.26).[9] Another common type was the *Gnadenstuhl* or "Throne of Grace" Trinity, in which God the Father holds a crucifix bearing his Son's body, while the Spirit hovers overhead in the form of a dove. In late Gothic art, however, any lingering resistance to anthropomorphism was overcome as the Trinity icon developed into a family portrait, accentuating not likeness but difference. The Father came to be portrayed as an old man, the Son as a younger man, and Mary as their Mother/Daughter/Bride, together with the traditional dove representing the Spirit. Late medieval images of the triune God *without* the Virgin are in fact quite rare. As Alfred Hackel notes, "almost all anthropomorphic images of the Trinity are in a sense transformed into quaternities."[10] Mary's insistent presence in the divine family portrait, like Wisdom's presence in the Bible, tugged the believer in two complementary directions. Just as the sapiential liturgy could serve both to feminize Christ and to divinize the Virgin, the integration of Marian with Trinitarian piety both feminized the Godhead and divinized the family. At the same time, Mary's inclusion in representations of the triune God blurred the boundaries between heaven and earth, divine and human, history and myth.

Interestingly, the Marian Trinity of late medieval art and devotion was not a wholly new development but the return of a long-repressed motif from antiquity.[11] A few early Greek fathers, such as Theophilus of Antioch and Irenaeus of Lyon, had linked Wisdom with the Holy Spirit rather than Christ, following an ancient Syriac tradition in which the Spirit was seen as Mother (the noun for "spirit," *ruha*, is grammatically feminine).[12] For the same reason several ancient authors, especially but not exclusively Syriac speakers, had envisaged a Trinity of Father, Mother, and Son, placing the feminine Spirit in the maternal role as a celestial counterpart of Mary.[13] By the fourth century, however, all such traditions had dwindled to insignificance, relegated to the status of obscure heresies or, at best, esoteric countertraditions. Their disappearance can be ascribed in part to the eclipse of Semitic Christianity, since the word for "spirit" is neuter in Greek (*pneuma*) and masculine in Latin (*spiritus*). But other factors were instrumental as well—Greek philosophical disdain for the feminine, the ascendancy of a limited number of creedal formulas, a desire to avoid "mythological" language that might awaken gnostic or pagan echoes. Yet another factor may have been the unwelcome use of a feminine Holy Spirit to legitimize women's ordination, for Syrian church orders likened the bishop to God the Father, the deacon to the Son, and the deaconess to the Spirit.[14]

In Latin Christendom, Augustine sealed the doom of the familial metaphor for nearly a thousand years in his *De Trinitate*. While developing his famous similitude of memory, understanding, and will, the bishop bluntly rejected an analogue proposed by unnamed Christians who had observed a likeness of the Trinity in Adam, Eve, and Abel, saying that the woman "proceeded" from the first man just as the Holy Spirit proceeds from the Father. In rejecting this similitude, Augustine called it "absurd . . . to regard the Holy Spirit as the mother of the Son of God and the spouse of the Father," for such analogies could only summon impure and carnal thoughts.[15] Such was the master's perduring authority that no later theologian dared reinstate the rejected image. Even Richard of St.-Victor, the twelfth-century Latin writer who went furthest in comparing the Trinitarian relations to the love shared by humans, would not cross Augustine on this point. Arguing that perfect charity and happiness cannot exist without a plurality of persons, Richard was careful to use the egalitarian model of friendship rather than the hierarchical love within the family.[16] Only the vernacular writers of the late Middle Ages at times revisited the tempting, but forcefully resisted, familial metaphor, reincorporating the maternal into an explicit model of the Trinity. The similitude rejected by Augustine surfaces a millennium later in *Piers Plowman,* a significant work of English vernacular theology:

That [God] is thre persones departable y preue hit by mankynde,
And o god almyhty, if alle men ben of Adam.
Eue of Adam was and out of hym ydrawe
And Abel of hem bothe and alle thre o kynde . . .
Now go we to godhede: in god, fader of heuene,
Was the sone in hymsulue in a *simile* as Eue
Was, when god wolde out of the wey ydrawe.
And as Abel of Adam and of his wyf Eue
Sprang forth and spak, a spyer of hem tweyne,
So out of the syre and the sone the seynt spirit of hem bothe
Is and ay was and worth withouten ende.[17]

That God is three distinct persons and one almighty God, I prove by humankind, if all men are from Adam. Eve was from Adam and drawn out of him, and Abel was from them both, and all three were of one nature. . . . Now let us turn to the Godhead. The Son existed in God, the Father of heaven, in a likeness, just as Eve was drawn out of the man when God willed. And as Abel sprang from Adam and his wife Eve, a scion of them both, and spoke, so the Holy Spirit is from both the Father and the Son, and always was, and will be without end.

The scholastic consensus that excluded female language and imagery for the Spirit had the probably unintended consequence of marginalizing the Third Person entirely, since it denied to the Spirit in Christian art the same rich array of visual and affective connotations that swirled around the Father and the Son, rendering them lively presences in the believer's imagination.[18] The emotionally neutral (and neuter) symbol of the dove functioned more as an iconic signifier of divinity, or a reminder of God's triunity, than it did as a focus of awe, devotion, or identification.[19] Indeed, perhaps this marginality *was* on some level intended, since a vague, depersonalized notion of the Holy Spirit was less likely to inspire the emergence of charismatic movements that might threaten the centralized, hierarchical Church favored by the post-Gregorian papacy. To reclaim the personality of the Spirit meant, in at least some cases, to reclaim the fluidity of leadership, including the participation of women, thought to have characterized the primitive Church. One such charismatic movement, the Guglielmites of the late thirteenth century, went far beyond the proclamation of a utopian Age of the Spirit as prophesied by Joachim of Fiore. They not only reinstated the Holy Spirit as a female personage, but announced her incarnation and imminent Second Coming in a particular saint, Guglielma of Milan, who would return to found a new church under the leadership of a woman pope.[20]

For most believers, however, there was no need to join an ephemeral, persecuted fringe group in order to commune with female divinity, since the void left by the suppression of Our Mother the Spirit had been effectively

filled by the Virgin Mary. Among the innumerable themes of Marian hymnody, her familial relations with the Trinity had occupied a modest but persis-
tent place from the eleventh century onward. Enamored of paradox, hymnographers dwelt with a delighted glee on what Guy Philippart has called the
Virgin's "double circular relationship" with God—"mother of her father and
daughter of her son."[21] Dante's famous prayer to the *Vergine Madre, figlia del
tuo figlio* is anticipated in countless sequences of which I can provide only a
sampling, cited here in rough chronological order:

Gloriosa Dei mater,
Cuius natus est et pater,
    Patris unigenitus.[22]

Glorious Mother of God,
whose son is also your father,
    the Father's only-begotten Son.
* * * * *
Verbum patris sine matre
Facta mater sine patre
    Genuit in tempore.

O Maria, redemptoris
Creatura, creatoris
    Genetrix magnifica.[23]

She who became mother without a father
gave birth in time to the Word
    born of his Father without a mother.

O Mary, creature of your Redeemer,
magnificent mother
    of your Creator.
* * * * *
Tui patris tu, Maria,
Mater es et filia.[24]

You, Mary, are your father's
mother, and his daughter.
* * * * *
Te Deus pater,
Ut Dei mater
Fieres et ipse frater,
    Cuius eras filia,
Sanctificavit . . .[25]

God the Father sanctified you
that you might become the Mother of God
and he whose daughter you were
might be himself your brother.

* * * * *

Lactas patrem,
Qui se fratrem
   Teque matrem contulit.[26]

You nurse the father
who made himself your brother
   and you his mother.

* * * * *

Parit natum nati nata
Virgo manens illibata.[27]

The child of her Child
gives birth to a child
and still is virgin undefiled.

These riddling stanzas read almost like epigrams, elegant in their aphoristic style yet pulsing with the incestuous themes of folksong. For Mary is
also bride of the God who is at once her father, son, and brother. Theologians
applied the title *sponsa Dei* with reference to any or all of the three Persons.
Among the church fathers, Ephrem of Syria called Mary the bride of Christ,
Prudentius named her bride of the Spirit, and John of Damascus, bride of
the Father.[28] In the twelfth century, Rupert of Deutz did not shrink from
the implication of divine incest when he wrote that "the blessed Virgin, the
best part of the first church [Israel], merited to be the bride of God the
Father in order to be also the exemplar of the younger [Gentile] church—
the bride of God's and her own Son."[29] As Philippart notes, "she who is the
Virgin *par excellence* became, in the register of allegory, the figure of every incestuous transgression."[30] Of course the gods and heroes of pagan myth were
often incestuous, and medieval poets schooled from boyhood on Ovid would
have remembered many a salacious tale—Myrrha afire with love for her
father, Phaedra besotted with her chaste stepson Hippolytus, the sisterly lust
of Byblis for Caunus, not to mention the long litany of maidens raped by
gods.[31] It will hardly do to maintain that medieval hymnographers remained
somehow unconscious of everything their verses about Mary implied.[32] At
least one poet, the author of the early fourteenth-century *Ovide moralisé*,
explicitly allegorized Myrrha as "nostre mere, sainte Marie," who loved her
divine Father so perfectly that "onques si fine amour ne fu" (never was there

such courtly love). The same poet reads Byblis as divine Wisdom, who so loved her brother, the human race, that she wished to unite herself with him carnally both "par fraresche et par mariage" (in kinship and in marriage).[33]

In the late Middle Ages, the use of such paradoxical and incestuous tropes to glorify the Virgin became both more frequent and more self-consciously shocking. The German poet Heinrich von Meissen, better known as Frauenlob (d. 1318), carried this tendency to extremes in his *Marienleich*, a summa of mystical and esoteric Mariology. In one section, Maria-Sapientia speaks of her eternal relationship with God:

ich binz ein spiegel der vil klaren reinekeit,
da got von erst sich inne ersach.
ich was mit im, do er entwarf gar alle schepfenunge,
er sach mich stetes an in siner ewiclichen ger. . . .
ich binz der tron, dem nie entweich
die gotheit, sit got in mich sleich.
min schar gar clar var:
ich got, sie got, er got, das ich vor nieman spar.
ich vatermuter, er min mutervater zwar.[34]

I am a mirror of radiant purity,
in which God saw himself from the beginning.
I was with him when he fashioned all creation,
he gazed at me constantly in his eternal desire. . . .
I am the throne the Godhead never left
since God slipped into me.
My throng is altogether noble:[35]
I am God, she is God, he is God, this I withhold from none:
I am the Father-Mother, he is truly my Mother-Father.

Here Mary becomes explicitly divine: she is God's partner and parent, and he hers; both alike are Father and Mother. We are not far here from the dizzying alchemical transmutations of *The Book of the Holy Trinity*.[36]

Merely to observe the presence of these incest motifs in the Virgin's cult does not resolve the question of their meaning. My comparison of her family romance with the Oedipus tale indicates that the two myths fill different if not antithetical functions. Where the Greek drama harshly punishes incest and thereby upholds the taboo, the romance of the Virgin suggests that, on the level of fantasy, incestuous desires need not be renounced or even repressed. Yet, on the level of physical expression, the Virgin's most ardent disciples were required like her to renounce *all* sexual desires. It has often been noted that the meteoric rise of Marian devotion in the twelfth century coincided with a dramatic increase in the number of clergy and monastics, along with an intensified campaign for clerical celibacy. For this reason, Philippart plausibly argues, we can see the incestuous Virgin as offering psychic compensations for enforced celibacy, since she embodied transgression and chastity at once—not to mention maternal tenderness and idealized eroticism.[37]

Yet, while Marian piety enjoyed its first great efflorescence among twelfth-century monks, nuns, and canons, it did not remain a monopoly of the celibate and cloistered. Diffused through preaching, sacred art, and vernacular texts, devotions that originated among religious elites had by the end of the Middle Ages suffused and transformed the lay imagination as well. When the wealthy burgher, his nubile daughter, or his pregnant wife encountered the Marian Trinity, how did *they* respond to this exceptional family? We cannot forget the widely varying experiences that women and men, the celibate and the married, the old and the young, would have brought to their contemplation of a common symbol. If Mary offered herself to celibate priests as an object of sublimated desire, she might have appealed to women at various stages of life as an expectant mother, a grieving matron, a secluded contemplative, or a respected widow who wielded authority.[38] Yet insofar as the Virgin succeeded in being "all things to all people," she did so in part because the pious attitudes and behaviors ascribed to her transcended any of these specific roles. So it is unwise to project onto the Middle Ages our own cultural demand that role models should mimic their audience's age, gender, ethnicity, and status as closely as possible. One did not have to be a virgin, or even a woman, to emulate and identify with Mary's closeness to God. Her universality was best expressed by Julian of Norwich, who perceived "the hey, mervelous, singular love" of God for his Mother as a token of his singular love for every soul. In showing her a vision of Mary, as Julian understands, "our Lord God spekyth to al mankynde that shal be save, as it were al to one person, as if He seyd, 'Wilt tho seen in hir how thou art lovid?'"[39]

As art historians have demonstrated, the Virgin and the saints were not represented in late medieval paintings simply for their own sake, but as models of exemplary *pietas* to inspire imitation, as well as empathy and devotion.[40] Their actions and attitudes taught the viewer how to feel, how to behave, what to dread, and what to desire. In the case of the Marian Trinity, the Virgin's multiple and labile roles within the celestial family expressed a whole panoply of relationships to the divine and offered each in turn as a paradigm for imitation. To the *homme moyen sensuel*, such images may have conveyed little more than a sense of Mary's personal glorification. But to those who aimed at exceptional devotion, the incestuous complexity of Mary's relations with God made her the emblem not of transgression, but of a total intimacy that could not be symbolized save by the compression and fusion of all earthly ties.

Divinizing the Virgin: The Marian Trinity in Art

In late medieval art, Mary and her Son came to be integrated into a variety of family groups, including the matriarchal triad with St. Anne, the Holy Family with St. Joseph, and the Holy Kinship or extended matrilineal family. But the most significant of Mary's several "families" was the Trinity itself. By the mid-fifteenth century, the crescendo of Marian piety had swelled so high that Christians all over Europe could see before their eyes what Peter of Celle had prophesied three hundred years earlier. Mary, he had written, "approach[ed] the Trinity itself in a unique and quite ineffable, almost direct manner, so if the Trinity admitted in any way an external quaternity, [she] alone would complete" it. Since it does not, however, she remains the unique pendant to the triple Godhead, "the Mother of him whose Father is God."[41] In the thirteenth century, Stephen of Tournai expressed the same thought in a hymn:

Hoc audemus de te fari,
Quod, si sancte maiorari
Posset sancta trinitas,
Quarta tibi pars daretur,
Quod idcirco prohibetur
Ne fiat quaternitas.[42]

We dare say this of you,
That if the Holy Trinity
Could be reverently augmented,
The fourth part would be given to you—
But this is prohibited
Lest it become a quaternity.

When Pope Pius XII belatedly defined Mary's Assumption as dogma in 1950, the psychoanalyst C. G. Jung gave Rome his unsolicited, if not downright unwelcome, endorsement, for he understood the quaternity rather than the triad to symbolize psychic wholeness. Two years before the doctrinal decree, Jung had shrewdly remarked that "medieval iconology, embroidering on the old speculations about the Theotokos [Mother of God], evolved a quaternity symbol in its representations of the coronation of the Virgin and surreptitiously put it in place of the Trinity." In Jung's view, the Church's official proclamation of the Assumption thus "pave[d] the way not only for the divinity of the Theotokos (i.e., her ultimate recognition as a goddess), but also for the quaternity."[43] Theologically speaking, of course, the pope intended no such thing. Much less would he have accepted Jung's psychological inference that, along with the feminine, the principles of matter and evil were likewise being drawn into the Godhead.[44] Nevertheless, Jung— who unlike Freud really was a medievalist of sorts—had put his finger on an aspect of Catholic art and devotion that has yet to be fully explored by historians of spirituality.

Jean Fouquet, the most eminent French painter of his generation, portrayed this quasi-quaternity in his famous *Hours of Étienne Chevalier* (ca. 1452–60). In the Enthronement miniature, three identical white-robed men share the throne of deity, but just below and to the left, in the same white robe, sits the Virgin on a throne by herself.[45] The composition of the painting is modelled on a Gothic church interior, with the nave peopled by laymen, the choir by saints, and the vault aglow with bright cherubim. If the throne of the Trinity corresponds to the high altar, the Virgin's seat occupies the place of the bishop's throne. Her exalted rank was acknowledged by the contemporaries of Jean Fouquet and Étienne Chevalier in their prayers:

Ave, sedens solio, quod equale deo,
per eterna secula nos commenda eo.[46]

Hail, you who sit on the throne that is equal to God's:
commend us to him throughout eternal ages.

Nor were such lofty conceptions of the Virgin's stature confined to the ultrapious. In fact, an accused witch in 1479 acknowledged the full extent of his apostasy by confessing that he had "denied God, the glorious Virgin Mary, and the whole Trinity," in that order.[47]

While the Enthronement represents Mary's supreme exaltation as queen, her familial intimacy with God emerges in several other subjects: the Coronation of the Virgin by the Trinity, the Double Intercession, the Compassion of the Father, and the sculpted *Vierge ouvrante* or Shrine Madonna. Each of these four images crystallizes a different moment in the Virgin's myth and represents her in a different familial role, as if illustrating the petitions of the fifteenth-century litany:

Mater Dei, te rogamus audi nos.
Soror Dei, te rogamus audi nos.
Filia Dei, te rogamus audi nos. . . .

Amica Dei, impetra nobis pacem.[48]
* * * * *
Mother of God, we beseech you to hear us.
Sister of God, we beseech you to hear us.
Daughter of God, we beseech you to hear us. . . .

Beloved of God, grant us peace.

The best-known and longest-lived of the Marian Trinities was, as Jung observed, the Coronation of the Virgin. When Mary's enthronement first became a favorite theme in the twelfth century, artists' portrayals of Christ and the Virgin were congruent with the contemporary vogue for the Song of Songs.[49] For instance, in the gorgeous Roman mosaic of Santa Maria in Trastevere, the Virgin is already crowned and seated beside Christ on the throne of heaven (Figure 6.1). Both display texts alluding to the sacred Song, while the image illustrates the royal wedding psalm: "the Queen took her place at your right in golden vesture" (Vulg. Ps. 44.10).[50] Strictly speaking, this is not a "coronation," but a celebration of Mary's queenship as accomplished fact. In a similar mosaic at Santa Maria Maggiore, Christ displays the same liturgical text as his right hand sets the crown on Mary's head. This gesture is typical of other twelfth- and thirteenth-century examples. Appearing no older than her Son, Mary is imagined less as Queen Mother than as Queen Consort—the sister-bride of the Song.

Over the course of centuries, this iconography underwent several changes, among them a humbler pose for the Virgin and the inclusion of God the Father along with Christ. As we saw in Chapter 5, one of the oldest examples of Mary's Coronation by the entire Trinity appears in the heterodox *Buch der heiligen Dreifaltigkeit* of 1419 (Figure 6.2), where the text emphatically endorses the unity and equality of "Jesus-Mary." By 1450, however, this new iconography was no longer esoteric and could be seen all over Europe, and by 1500, it was the normative model for the Virgin's exaltation.[51] Allowing for regional variants, the iconography of the new subject depicts Mary in the foreground, kneeling, her hands folded in prayer (Figures 6.2, 6.4) or crossed devoutly over her breast (Figure 6.3). Unveiled, she wears the long, unbound hair of a maiden, often cascading down her shoulders in luxurious curls. In fact, her posture is strikingly reminiscent of the Annunciation. The crown does not yet rest on her brow, for, just as the

Figure 6.1. Enthronement of Christ and Mary. Apse mosaic, Santa Maria in Trastevere, Rome, ca. 1148. Photo: Alinari/Art Resource, New York.

Virgin Annunciate stands on the threshold of motherhood, this Virgin kneels on the brink of queenship. The Father to our right and the Son to our left suspend the emblem of royalty over Mary's head. Above the crown hovers the Spirit-dove, gripping it with one claw to signal his participation. The scene may be set either in heaven, against a backdrop of clouds and jubilating angels, or in a churchlike interior. Father and Son are usually distinct in age, for it was only in the fifteenth century that the much-parodied "old man with a long white beard" became standard in Christian art.[52]

Between the crowned Virgin circa 1200 and her descendant circa 1500 lies a gulf in religious sensibility. Mary as the royal sister-bride is her Son's equal in dignity: her throne is secure and she makes no gesture of submission. Mary as the kneeling suppliant humbles herself in order to be exalted. Even the Virgin's queenship—the ostensible subject of the painting—is dwarfed by its implicit subject: her induction into the celestial Family. In an orthodox reading, Mary's placement beneath the divine figures, her kneeling posture and downcast eyes, and her girlish coiffure suggest that she is being

Figure 6.2. Coronation of the Virgin by the Trinity. *Buch der heiligen Dreifaltigkeit*, 1410–19. Kupferstichkabinett, Staatliche Museen zu Berlin—Preussischer Kulturbesitz, Ms. 78 A 11, f. 31v. By permission, Bildarchiv Preussischer Kulturbesitz. Photo: Jörg Anders.

Figure 6.3. Coronation of the Virgin by the Trinity. Master of the Rohrdorf Altar (Martin Schwarz?), ca. 1480–85. Karlsruhe, Kunsthalle, inv. nr. 36. Photo: Staatliche Kunsthalle.

received not as sister, still less as mother, but as daughter of the Trinity. Since the Christian soul was also represented in didactic and mystical texts as "God's daughter," the celestial welcome accorded to this most favored child could be read as a promise of the glory awaiting all elect souls.[53] As an exemplar of human beatitude, the Virgin kneels to face not the Trinity but the viewer. In a Book of Hours from Besançon (Figure 6.4), her prayerful, semi-profile figure echoes the posture assigned to donors and patrons, inviting the viewer's direct participation in the scene.

Unlike the twelfth-century *sponsa*, the fifteenth-century Virgin crowned by the Trinity no longer functions as a type of the Church in majesty. Rather,

Figure 6.4. Coronation of the Virgin by the Trinity. Book of Hours, usage of Besançon, early sixteenth century. Besançon, Bibl. mun. ms. 136, fol. 46r. By permission, Bibliothèque Municipale de Besançon. Photo: J.-Paul Tupin.

she represents humankind's point of entry into an intimate, familial union with the Divine. The late emergence of this iconography shows an increasing complexity in the Virgin's position: like Christ, she too could model both "divinity" and "humanity" in her own way. Late medieval piety did not so much replace older motifs as supplement them with new ones, so the twelfth-century image of throne-partnership did not disappear. Even while Mary remained the Queen of Heaven, with power to bestow crowns on her worshippers, she now doubled as the meek worshipper who had first earned her own crown.[54] Both motifs at once are suggested in a liturgical manuscript from the Dominican convent of St. Katharinenthal (1312), where—in the initial that begins the office for the Assumption—it is a kneeling female soul who receives a crown from Christ and Mary (Figure 6.5). The image is a century older than the earliest Coronation of the Virgin by the Trinity.[55]

Another beloved fifteenth-century subject, the Double Intercession, highlights the dialectic of justice and mercy (Figures 6.6, 6.7). God the Father, enthroned in majesty as Judge, bears the signs of his regal authority—crown, orb, and scepter.[56] Two suppliant figures kneel beside his throne. Jesus as Man of Sorrows points to the wound in his side: he is humble and naked, dressed in nothing more than a loincloth and perhaps an open mantle. If he wears any crown, it is of thorns. Beside or opposite him kneels the Virgin, exposing her naked breast. As Caroline Bynum has observed, there is a close parallel between these two gestures of self-display: not only is the dripping wound positioned where a breast would be, but Christ's blood and Mary's milk represent twin signs of atonement proffered to appease the Father's wrath.[57] Inscriptions sometimes clarify the intended meaning: the Son offers his wounds as a sacrifice for sinners, while the Mother offers her breast.[58] Her action echoes a tradition of filial piety as old as the *Iliad*, in which a mother pleads with her adult son by exposing the breast that nursed him in infancy.

Like the Coronation, this subject evolved from an earlier version that portrayed only Mary and Christ to a later, Trinitarian version. In the earliest visual representation of the motif, from the *Speculum humanae salvationis* (*Mirror of Human Salvation*, 1324), the Virgin shows Christ her breast in one miniature while, in a later one, the Man of Sorrows shows the Father his wounds. A Florentine painting at the Cloisters in New York (1402) offers a complex synthesis: as *Mater misericordiae*, the Virgin faces Christ, exposing her breast in her left hand and presenting a crowd of petitioners with her right (Figure 6.8). Christ in turn looks up to the Father, forwarding Mary's plea to God with his left hand and displaying the wound with his right. Finally the Father signals his assent by releasing the Spirit-dove. In contrast

Figure 6.5. Coronation of the soul by Christ and the Virgin. Gradual of St. Katharinenthal, 1312. Zürich, Schweizerisches Landesmuseum, inv. nr. 49261, f. 188r. Photo: Schweizerisches Landesmuseum.

to this hierarchical image, Netherlandish painters of the mid-fifteenth century introduced a simpler composition in which the disparity of rank disappears (Figure 6.6).[59] Both Christ and Mary now address their appeal directly to the Judge. The Virgin no longer exerts maternal sway over her Son, but seconds him as an equal partner—a sister—in their joint petition to the Father. In the Coronation, Father and Son are enthroned as equals, welcoming the meek virgin daughter to their home. But in the Double Intercession the Father reigns supreme, while the Virgin and her Son (in his humanity) share a filial role as advocates for sinners.

Figure 6.6. Double Intercession. Master of the Lower Rhine, 1506. Karlsruhe, Kunsthalle, inv. nr. 133. Photo: Staatliche Kunsthalle.

What place does this iconography leave for the viewer? If the Coronation conveys an image of glory, the Double Intercession evokes the more somber thought of judgment. But what we see is not the final Doom, since Christ is not yet glorified. The image alludes instead to the particular judgment of each soul at death, inviting spectators to place themselves among the sinners sheltered by the merciful Virgin (Figure 6.7). But for the saintly elite, already assured of their favor with God, the pictorial rhetoric of the image offered not only the comfort of Mary's protection but an invitation to join in her altruistic prayer. All sinners could plead for their own salvation, but those who aspired to holiness must go beyond such self-centered petitions to emulate the Virgin's universal intercession. If the Savior offered his blood and the Mother her milk, a third bodily fluid remained as the aspirant saint's gift. To women who watered heaven with their tears, the heavenly Father promised the same sisterhood with Christ that Mary models in the Double Intercession.[60]

Figure 6.7. Double Intercession. School of Konrad Witz, ca. 1450. Basel,
Öffentliche Kunstsammlung, Kunstmuseum, inv. nr. 1590. By permission,
Öffentliche Kunstsammlung. Photo: Martin Bühler.

Figure 6.8. Intercession of Christ and the Virgin. Florentine, attributed to Lorenzo Monaco, ca. 1402. New York, Metropolitan Museum of Art, Cloisters Collection 1953 (53.37). Photo: Metropolitan Museum of Art.

One of the most popular themes of late medieval art was the Pietà or "Image of Pity": the lamenting Virgin with her Son's body slumped across her lap. Less familiar is the haunting parallel in which Christ's Father replaces his Mother as chief mourner.[61] Called *Pitié-de-Nostre-Seigneur* in French inventories and *Nood Gods* (*Not Gottes*) in Flemish ones, this subject has been variously designated Compassion of the Father, Suffering Trinity, and Pietà of the Father.[62] In many examples it forms half of a diptych: one panel shows the Madonna and Child while the other represents the Father holding Christ's body with the Dove between their heads. In others, Mary appears in the same composition with the divine figures. The iconography evolved from a convergence of the Pietà with the *Gnadenstuhl* Trinity, in which the enthroned Father displays a crucifix to recall the gift and sacrifice of his Son. But the Throne of Grace is a hieratic image, while the Pietà of the Father is an affective one. Most notably, the divine Father is cast in the image and likeness of the Mother, for the viewer cannot help but recall the grieving Virgin so often seen in the same pose.[63] The parallel between the Savior's two parents is most striking in the diptychs, where the same Christ displayed as a fetching infant in his Mother's lap appears as a naked corpse in his Father's.

An early and stunningly effective version of the Suffering Trinity is the round panel by Jean Malouel, a Netherlandish painter active at the Burgundian court circa 1400 (Figure 6.9).[64] Against a gold-tooled background, the serenely sorrowful Father and the somber Virgin, clad in the black robes of mourners, support the holy corpse. The blood dripping from Christ's wound is still fresh, his head still crowned with thorns. As in a Crucifixion or Deposition from the Cross, the composition is completed by the weeping figure of St. John, Mary's adoptive son, and a troupe of lamenting angels. Defying the boundaries of time and space, the archetypal lament is set neither in heaven nor on earth, but in the collective mind of believers. No sign or gesture marks a distinction between God and Mary: they are two parents united in a common grief. It is not hard to imagine the spectator's response when God himself doubles the role of Mary, *Mater dolorosa*, as a model of compassion:

> "So my Son is bobbed,
> And of His lif robbed."
> Forsooth then I sobbed,
> Verifying the wordes she said to me:
> "Who cannot weepe may lern at me."[65]

Similar in its dynamics is a small alabaster statue ascribed to Hans Multscher, a south German sculptor, ca. 1430–35 (Figure 6.10). Mary does

Figure 6.9. Pietà with God the Father. Jean Malouel, "La Grande Pietà ronde,"
ca. 1400–1415. Paris, Louvre, MI 692. Photo: Réunion des Musées Nationaux,
Agence photographique.

not appear in this Pietà, but her place is taken by a blond, blue-eyed, and
decidedly feminine angel, who upholds the slumped body of Jesus as the
Father lifts a hand in blessing. The angel's wings balance those of the Spirit-
dove as it nestles beneath the Father's beard and rests its beak in Christ's
hair. This configuration of the divine family summons up the Virgin as an
absent presence, not only to our eyes, but apparently to those of its medieval
owner as well. According to Henk Van Os, scuff marks on the bottom of the
statue indicate that the little Trinity was removed from its niche for private

Figure 6.10. Pietà of the Father. Hans Multscher, ca. 1430–35. Alabaster. Frankfurt, Liebieghaus-Museum alter Plastik, inv. no. St.P. 401; from Schloss Sandizell near Ingolstadt. By permission, Liebieghaus-Museum alter Plastik. Photo: Ursula Edelmann.

devotions. On its back are inscribed three prayers that evoke a different Marian Trinity: "maria hilff mir . . . hergot las mich nit . . . hilf mir anna sant dritt" ("Mary, help me . . . Lord God, do not forsake me . . . Help me, Anne, the holy third").[66] So the worshipper who venerated this Pietà prayed at the same time to another triad, the Virgin and Child with St. Anne—a matrilineal image in which Mary's own mother as the "holy third" completes the family unit.

The works we have examined so far all present the Trinity in familial terms, but differ in the roles assigned to Mary. In the Coronation she appears as God's daughter; in the Double Intercession, as Christ's sister and partner; in the Suffering Trinity, as mother of Christ and spouse of the Father. From a formal standpoint, too, the three subjects represent every possible configuration of the familial triad. The Coronation pairs the enthroned Father and Son opposite the kneeling Virgin; the Intercession poses the suppliant Christ and Mary over against the regal Father; and the Pietà sets the grieving Father and Mother beside their murdered Son. Mary's position within this family, then, is not static but intensely dynamic and labile.

There remains one additional type of Marian Trinity, called the *Vierge ouvrante* or "Shrine Madonna" because the small wooden statue of the Virgin opens up to display a complete Throne of Grace Trinity within (Figure 6.11). In diptychs, as we have seen, Mary and her Child sometimes appear on one panel and the suffering Trinity on the other. But in the *Vierge ouvrante* these two groups are related as outside to inside, with the whole Godhead literally contained in the Virgin's womb (or symbolically in her heart).[67] By 1500 Shrine Madonnas could be found in churches and convents from Portugal to Poland, and as far north as England and Sweden. French kings owned priceless golden *Vierges* inlaid with jewels, with interior carvings of ivory. The Teutonic Knights commissioned polychrome wooden specimens to use as portable altars on campaign,[68] while other statues belonged to confraternities or to highborn nuns who used them in their personal devotions. Some were later converted to eucharistic tabernacles, with the actual Body of Christ in the Host substituted for his representation on the Cross. In many examples the *Vierge ouvrante* was simultaneously represented as a Mother of Mercy, with the open wings of the statue painted to show petitioners taking refuge under Mary's mantle (Figure 6.11), as they also do in the Double Intercession.

It is difficult to know how many *Vierges ouvrantes* there actually were in the late Middle Ages, since the Tridentine church reacted strongly against the statues and many were destroyed.[69] Lately, however, the image has become

Figure 6.11. Shrine Madonna. Prussian, fifteenth century. Wood polychrome. Paris, Musée national du Moyen Age, Thermes et hôtel de Cluny, inv. nr. Cl. 12060. Photo: Réunion des Musées Nationaux, Agence photographique.

a favorite with Goddess feminists, who like to characterize it as "heretical." This fashion seems to have begun with Erich Neumann's 1955 monograph on the Great Mother archetype. The Jungian analyst described the closed *Vierge ouvrante* as "familiar and unassuming," but noted that "when opened she reveals the heretical secret within her. God the Father and God the Son, usually represented as heavenly lords who in an act of pure grace raise up the humble, earth-bound mother to abide with them, prove to be contained in her; prove to be 'contents' of her all-sheltering body."[70] In short, the Virgin stands revealed as the Great Goddess she actually was in popular devotion, *pace* orthodox dogma. But with the significant exception of Jean Gerson, as we shall see later, no medieval text suggests that the people who carved and venerated Shrine Madonnas had any heterodox intentions. In fact, a widely used Marian sequence by Adam of St.-Victor had long since proclaimed in song what the sculpture represented in wood, calling Mary "totius Trinitatis / Nobile triclinium" ("noble banqueting-hall of the whole Trinity").[71]

Recent feminist critiques of Mariology have taken it as axiomatic that the Virgin Mother, in her unique and paradoxical glory, stood beyond imitation. In Marina Warner's influential view, "the twin ideal the Virgin represents is of course unobtainable" and therefore oppressive.[72] But such critiques may hold truer for the post-Tridentine Church (or more specifically the 1950s) than they do for the medieval Church. Evidence from the late Middle Ages indicates that, even as preachers and theologians heaped ever more extravagant privileges on the Virgin, many women saw her not as standing "alone of all her sex," but as supremely imitable. Authors of medieval profeminine tracts, including Christine de Pizan, regularly cited Mary as an exemplum of female virtue without being much troubled by her singularity.[73] In a different context, Bonaventure described devout meditation as a form of spiritual childbearing, and Meister Eckhart preached that every pure and detached person could become a "virgin wife" like Mary, continually giving birth to Christ in the soul.[74] Several recent studies have illustrated the ways that nuns and visionaries modelled their imaginative experience as well as their external performance on the *imitatio Mariae*, as they followed the Virgin's life cycle from "mystical pregnancy" through experiences of bathing, rocking, and nursing the Christ Child to participation in Mary's anguish at the Crucifixion.[75] Marian Trinities, I have argued, illustrated the Virgin's familial relationship to the Godhead not primarily to exalt her uniqueness, but to furnish models for other kinds of devout imitation. To mourn Christ's death with his tearful mother, to plead beside him as his prayerful sister, to be crowned in heaven as his humble daughter, constituted three dimensions of an *imitatio Mariae* that promised deification through an intimate, multiform union with God.[76]

This union culminated in the total incorporation of the Divine, at once maternal and erotic, embodied by the *Vierge ouvrante*. In the later Middle Ages it was commonplace to call Mary the bride or chamber of the Trinity so as to celebrate the fullness of the Godhead dwelling in her soul. As a fifteenth-century Frenchwoman prayed, "it was for sinners that the Father, Son, and Holy Spirit wished to lodge themselves in you. For this reason, sweet lady, it befits you to be the advocate of poor sinners, and for this you are the chamber of the whole Trinity."[77] German poets were especially enamored of the Trinitarian theme, developing the conceit of Mary as a maiden wooed by three lovers:

die drey kamen in eine
zu diser iuncfraw reine,
also enpfieng sie got.[78]

The Three came as one
to this pure maid:
thus she conceived God.
* * * * *
si hat dri vriedel minniklich:
so gar mit eime ein ander magt benueget;
sus hat ir lip so saelden rich
mit listen alle vrouwen über klueget.
vater, sun, heileger geist taten dich,
  schoene, swanger.[79]

She has three paramours in love:
every other maid is content with one;
thus her body, so rarely rich,
has surpassed all women in wiles.
Father, Son, and Holy Ghost
  made you pregnant, lovely one.

It was Frauenlob who employed the most audacious metaphors for Mary's relations with the Trinity, using an image that recalls the pagan Thor as well as the hammer and anvil of Alan of Lille's Natura:

Der smid von oberlande
warf sinen hamer in mine schoz.
ich worchte siben heiligheit.
ich trug in, der den himel und die erden treit,
und bin doch meit.

er lag in mir und liez mich sunder arebeit.
mit sicherheit
ich slief bi drin.[80]

The smith from the high country
hurled his hammer in my womb:
I forged seven sacraments.
I carried him who carries heaven and earth
and yet am still a maid.
He lay in me and left me without labor.
Most certainly
I slept with Three.

Though unique and even shocking in its physicality, the Virgin's fullness of grace was at the same time exemplary. An *imitatio Mariae*, cast in familial terms, had already been urged on the faithful by St. Francis in his influential "Exhortation to the Brothers and Sisters of Penance":

All those who love the Lord with their whole heart . . . are children of the heavenly Father whose works they do, and they are spouses (*sponsi*), brothers, and mothers of our Lord Jesus Christ (cf. Matt. 12.50). We are spouses when the faithful soul is joined to our Lord Jesus Christ by the Holy Spirit. We are brothers to him when we do the will of the Father who is in heaven. We are mothers when we carry him in our heart and body through divine love and a pure and sincere conscience and when we give birth to him through holy action.[81]

Later homilists would elaborate on these themes, making their Marian dimensions more explicit. To the dismay of churchmen like Jean Gerson, however, female visionaries not only aspired to these graces, but frequently claimed to have received them. Unlike Francis, who often crossed the gender line by representing himself as a mother, the majority of women did not engage in such spiritual gender-bending[82] but reveled in the same familial endearments—daughter, sister, mother, bride—that belonged par excellence to Mary. As the congruence between a woman's bodily sex and her spiritual roles made her *imitatio Mariae* less transparently metaphorical, such role-playing could only heighten the intense feelings of identification with the Virgin that were available, in theory, to all devout Christians.

Enacting the Virgin: The Lability of Female Roles

Pamela Sheingorn has argued in a thought-provoking essay that the "fantasy romance" of God the Father and the Virgin may have appealed in a special way to ordinary girls—"women who were not mystics, not especially adept at or interested in spiritual exercises." Nubile girls, Sheingorn proposes, could see in Mary's life a reassuring image of their own situation, given as brides to much older men who, they hoped, would treat them as kindly as the heavenly Father treated his own spouse. If such a husband proved less than ideal, a young wife could resign herself to her plight as Mary did to the aged Joseph, often portrayed in medieval art and drama as a comic figure. A girl's earthly mate might prove to be an inept, bumbling spouse, a January to her May—but God as "fantasy husband" could provide an outlet for tender feelings, just as modern romance heroes do for the women who comprise that genre's devoted readership. In this way Marian piety could socialize girls into accepting the unequal and often undesired marriages their parents imposed on them.[83]

Tempting as it is to speculate about the way "women who were not mystics" responded to the ubiquitous image of Mary, most of our evidence comes from women who were. Although countless nuns practiced forms of *imitatio Mariae*, I have chosen to focus on three lay women who specialized, so to speak, in union with God through integration into a divine family. Mechthild of Magdeburg was among the first to elaborate her Marian devotion along these lines. Two late medieval mothers, the aristocratic Birgitta of Sweden and her English admirer Margery Kempe, carried this form of piety to its logical conclusion. Of course we cannot know the inner lives of lay men and women who have left us no testimony. Women such as Mechthild, Birgitta, and Margery were extraordinary in their public apostolate. Yet in their forms of devotion they provide our best clues to spiritual and affective responses that were probably cultivated with less urgency by a far broader public. Given the easy progression from visual images, through the visualizations taught by spiritual authors, to visions per se,[84] it would not be surprising if other women's imaginative experiences likewise introduced them into the same celestial family they so often saw portrayed in their churches.

For Mechthild, who wrote her *Flowing Light of the Godhead* in the mid-thirteenth century, Mary was the special bride of the Trinity but also the exemplar of every soul, for every soul potentially shared her privileged relationship with God.[85] To my knowledge, Mechthild is the only medieval theological writer who actually called the Virgin "goddess." In a vision of heaven, she gazes on Mary's throne and proclaims that "her Son is God and she a goddess (*göttinne*). No one can be compared to her."[86] Yet only a few pages later, when Mechthild describes the Trinity creating the soul, she imagines a solemn wedding at which "the heavenly Father bestowed his divine love on the soul and said: 'I am the God of gods; you are the goddess of all creatures, and . . . I shall never reject you.'"[87] Tragically, though, this human Psyche chose to reject her divine Eros. As Mary herself explains to Mechthild, the Father was grieved by Adam's fall because it meant the death of "his darling bride, the noble soul." But the Virgin, in her eternal pre-existence, "intercepted" God's anger and relieved his divine loneliness. So, she says, "the Father chose me for his bride—that he might have something to love. . . . The Son chose me to be his mother, and the Holy Spirit received me as his beloved. Then I alone was bride of the Holy Trinity."[88]

Mechthild's images of the Virgin both recall and anticipate the iconographic themes we have examined. The Virgin she sees as "celestial empress"[89] sharing Christ's throne is the same Queen of Heaven who made her visual debut in the twelfth century (Figure 6.1). But the visionary anticipates the pictorial image of the Double Intercession by about two hundred years. One of her visions reveals the Virgin with dripping breasts standing to the left of the Father's throne, while Jesus with bleeding wounds stands to his right (cf. Figure 6.6). Both blood and milk will continue to flow until Judgment Day for the sake of sinners, Mechthild writes; only then will the Savior's wounds be healed and the Mother's breasts become dry.[90] Even more striking is the way Mechthild imagines the Incarnation. Much like the sculptors of the *Vierges ouvrantes* (Figure 6.11), she sees the Virgin as mother of the entire Trinity.

Then the whole Holy Trinity, with the power of the Godhead, the good will of the humanity, and the noble delicacy of the Holy Spirit, passed through her whole virginal body into the fiery soul of her good will, placed itself in the open heart of her most pure flesh, and united itself with all that it found in her, so that her flesh became his flesh in such a manner that he grew into a perfect child in her body. . . . The longer she carried him, the more radiant, beautiful, and wise she became.[91]

No matter how much Mechthild glorifies the Virgin, however, Mary remains prima inter pares, the first of innumerable brides who are all, in a sense, one bride—"the noble soul."[92] In one of Mechthild's courtly dialogues, Lady Soul tells Lady Contemplation that "the least soul is a daughter of the Father and a sister of the Son and a friend of the Holy Spirit and, indeed, a bride of the Holy Trinity."[93] Interestingly, the one role omitted is that of mother. Mechthild did not share the maternal mysticism characteristic of many later visionaries, who identified with that role most of all. But in her self-designation as "the least soul," she did see herself as God's daughter, sister, and bride. Just as in the visual dynamics of the Marian Trinity, the three divine Persons stand in relation to a single feminine partner who occupies ever-shifting roles.

Mechthild's identity vis-à-vis her divine Other emerges most clearly and poignantly in a prayer she wrote near the end of her life, a petition for a holy death. Structured around the seven penitential psalms, her prayer asks that at the hour of death God may come to her in seven ways—or rather, six plus one:

> May you then come to me as a trustworthy physician . . . come to me as my very dearest friend . . . come as a trustworthy father confessor . . . come to me as a faithful brother to his dear sister . . . come to me as a trusted father to his dear child . . . *send me your virgin mother*. I cannot do without her . . . come as my dearest bridegroom.[94]

Arranging her petitions in ascending order of intimacy, Mechthild appeals to the closeness of brother and sister, father and child, mother (without a partner), and finally bridegroom and bride. The penultimate prayer to "send me your virgin mother" does not match the rest, yet Mary's presence is indispensable to complete the divine family. Although Mechthild cannot quite ask God to "come to her as a trusted mother," she does the next best thing: she calls on the Bride of the Trinity to serve as her bridesmaid. In this way the girl who had left home in her twenties to escape marriage and kindred looks forward, in her sixties, to a reunion with the only family that matters.

Far different was the life of St. Birgitta (ca. 1303–1373), cousin to the king of Sweden and mother of eight. It was not until her widowhood in 1344 that she received the call to prophesy, first to the Swedish court and later to the papal court. Leaving her native land in 1349, just as the Black Death was reaching Sweden, she followed the wake of the pestilence in reverse until she arrived at Rome, where she remained as a public figure from 1350 until her death. Her voluminous *Revelations* offer, along with much didactic and prophetic material, a compendium of Marian piety.[95] Birgitta was famed in her lifetime for an intimately detailed vision of the Nativity, which served to popularize the image of Mary kneeling in the stable before her newborn Son,[96] and for her *Sermo angelicus* (1352–53), a devotional treatise on the life, merits, and mercies of the Virgin.[97] More interesting for our purpose, however, is the way this matriarch and prophet interwove her own family life with that of the celestial family. One Christmas Eve, she experienced a "marvelous and great exultation of her heart" which turned out to be a mystical pregnancy: the Christ Child was quickening in her heart just as he had done in Mary's womb, and just as eight biological children had done in Birgitta's. Mary herself explained the meaning of this experience, which involved a shift in her own relationship to the seer:

Daughter, you are amazed about the movement that you feel in your heart. . . . do not be afraid of an illusion, but rejoice because that movement which you feel is a sign of the arrival of my son into your heart. Therefore, as my son placed on you the name of his new bride, so now I call you daughter-in-law. For as a father and mother, growing old and resting, place the burden upon the daughter-in-law and tell her what things are to be done in the house, so God and I, who are old in the hearts of people and cold apart from their love, want to proclaim our will to our friends and the world through you.[98]

Deeply identified with the Virgin, Birgitta understands herself as both mother and bride of Christ, assimilating her voice to Mary's body as an entrée for God's Word into a desperate world. Because she remained a controversial figure long after her canonization in 1391, her defenders seized on this analogy as a powerful way to authorize her prophetic speech. Such an exceptional form of validation might have seemed especially fitting for a holy woman who had herself borne children and lacked the normative credential of virginity.[99] Mary and Birgitta were, in effect, *comadres,* sharing the kind of sisterly bond that is still potent in some Latin American cultures. Each looked out for the other's interests, for while Birgitta devoted herself to Mary's son, Mary stood as midwife and godmother to Birgitta's children and allayed her anxieties about neglecting them to pursue her career as a prophet.[100] Despite this co-motherhood, the Virgin normally addressed Birgitta as "daughter"; but with the Christmas revelation, a new quaternity takes shape as the divine family confronts the problems of aging. "God and I," says the Virgin—with the casual familiarity of the long-married—are growing old, so it is time for the next generation to carry the torch. Such domestication of the sacred has annoyed male scholars from Gerson to Huizinga,[101] and the metaphor still startles today, though perhaps for new reasons. Here we see Birgitta wresting empowerment from domesticity itself, while assuming what is ordinarily the most subservient of roles.

In a no less extraordinary revelation, Birgitta reunited her divine and human families in what Clarissa Atkinson has called "a scene unique in the annals of maternal power."[102] Birgitta's prodigal son Karl had recently died, causing her immense anguish because, at the time of his death, the knight had been conducting a love affair with Queen Joanna of Naples. Fearing Karl's damnation, his mother was consoled by Mary in a vision that ushered her into the celestial curia, where she witnessed her son's naked soul trembling before Christ's tribunal while a demon accused and an angel defended him.[103] In a variant of the Double Intercession motif, two special advocates—Mary and Birgitta herself—are present to strengthen the defendant's case. Yet both the visionary and her son remain silent as the anxious courtroom drama unfolds. Mary first reveals how, once again, she has assisted at the spiritual birth of Birgitta's child: just as a midwife keeps an infant from drowning in the flow of blood or suffocating in the birth canal, so she has protected the knight's spirit in its narrow passage out of his body and kept the demons at bay. It was Karl's own love of the Virgin, she asserts, that procured him the grace of final contrition. But when she and the angel respond in turn to the demon's charges, they explain that Birgitta's prayers, tears, and almsdeeds alone have blotted out Karl's countless venial sins and unfulfilled penances. Defeated by this conspiracy of mothers, the devil cries out in fury that his sack of sins has been stolen, his text erased, and even its parchment consumed in fire; nay, his accusing tongue has been torn out at the roots, and at last he forgets the sinner's very name. Karl's new name, announces the angel—echoing St. Augustine and his mother Monica—is "son of tears."[104] Whereupon the devil departs with one final blasphemy: "How accursed is that mother of his, that she-pig, who had such a fruitful womb! For so much water was poured into her that all the cells of her womb were filled with tears."[105] It is, of course, a backhanded compliment. What self-praise could be humbler than to imagine oneself as a Mother of Mercy cursed by a demon?

But even Birgitta could scarcely have shed more tears with the Virgin than did Margery Kempe. Born in the year Birgitta died, Margery would emulate her in more ways than one.[106] The daughter of John Burnham, mayor of Lynn in East Anglia, she made what contemporaries would have considered a good but not brilliant marriage at twenty.[107] Between 1393 and 1413 she bore no fewer than fourteen children to her husband, John Kempe, despite an inauspicious first pregnancy that ended in a postpartum psychotic episode. By the time she reached forty, Margery had had enough of childbearing and decided upon a radical change in her life. Although she had been increasingly pious for several years, she now resolved to become a lay penitent and end her sexual relationship with her husband.[108] John Kempe was hardly eager for this change of status, but John Burnham's timely death had placed Margery in a good bargaining position. With money from her inheritance, she agreed to pay her husband's business debts in exchange for release from her marriage debt. Thereupon she began the extraordinary career of visions, pilgrimages, and saintly aspirations recounted so vividly in her autohagiography, *The Book of Margery Kempe*.[109] One of the most insistent themes of that book is family—not Margery's own prolific brood, whom she scarcely mentions, but the divine family consisting of the Trinity, the Virgin, and herself.

Like Birgitta, the most important of her many role models, Margery enjoyed a mother-daughter relationship with the Virgin, imagining herself as

Mary's companion at the Nativity, the flight into Egypt, and the Crucifixion.[110] But more often she envisioned herself taking the Virgin's place in the bosom of the Trinity, reveling just as the hymnographers did at the conflation of incompatible roles. We can scarcely miss the echoes of Marian (and Franciscan) piety in the reassurance Christ offers his lover:

I prove that you are a daughter indeed to me, and a mother also, a sister, a wife and a spouse. . . . When you strive to please me, then you are a true daughter; when you weep and mourn for my pain and my Passion, then you are a true mother having compassion on her child; when you weep for other people's sins and adversities, then you are a true sister; and when you sorrow because you are kept so long from the bliss of heaven, then you are a true spouse and wife.[111]

In this conversation, Margery plays all the roles opposite Jesus alone, and they all involve variations on her greatest talent—weeping. Devotional images of the *mater dolorosa*, the Pietà, and the Double Intercession surely informed Margery's visions and elicited some of her comfortable tears.

As she matures in the spiritual life, the apprentice saint is initiated into the "higher" practice of meditation on the Trinity through a mystical marriage to God the Father. This narrative, one of the strangest in Margery's book, has disconcerted readers because of its overtly incestuous character, which seems to motivate her puzzling rejection of the match proposed to her. The heavenly Father has offered to reward Margery with a union which she undoubtedly knew, from the lives of Birgitta, Catherine of Siena, and others, to be the ne plus ultra of mystical experience. Nonetheless she "kept silence in her soul . . . because she was very much afraid of the Godhead," until Jesus—the lover who had until now attracted all her desire—excuses her bad manners on account of youth (she was 41) before giving his bride to his own father. Margery "wept amazingly" at this apparent betrayal by her lover, even as the wedding continued to unfold in her vision:

And then the Father took her by the hand in her soul, before the Son and the Holy Ghost, and the Mother of Jesus, and all the twelve apostles, and St Katherine and St Margaret and many other saints and holy virgins, with a great multitude of angels, saying to her soul, "I take you, Margery, for my wedded wife, for fairer, for fouler, for richer, for poorer, provided that you are humble (*buxom*) and meek in doing what I command you to do. For, daughter, there was never a child so kind (*buxom*) to its mother as I shall be to you."[112]

A number of Margery's experiences reproduce familiar devotional formulas, but this one reverses convention. While artists sometimes painted God the Father as a priest solemnizing his Son's marriage to the human soul (cf. Figure 5.9), I know of no other case in which the Son arranges the

Father's marriage, in defiance of all social norms. Noting Margery's atypical resistance to her own fantasy, Nancy Partner reads the incident as expressing a "terrible conflict of incestuous desire" triggered by the recent death of her father, which could have awakened long-repressed oedipal wishes.[113] Others have speculated that Margery was a victim of actual father-daughter incest—the secret sin she had been too ashamed to confess when she feared death in childbed, but now projected safely into the divine realm. On this reading, Jesus behaves like a kind but complicit mother who constantly reassures the daughter that she is loved, yet does nothing to prevent the incestuous act.[114] It is telling that immediately after the marriage, the Father proposes yet another role reversal, letting himself be the child and his new wife his mother. Only a chapter later, he has disappeared and Jesus is again permitting Margery to embrace him "as your wedded husband, as your dear darling, and as your sweet son."[115]

Whatever her private history may have been, Margery's narrative shows an exceptional awareness of the incestuous themes lurking within fifteenth-century representations of the Trinity. But despite her reservations, she eventually reconciled herself to Trinitarian mysticism. Near the end of her book, she has a dream in which an angel shows her a great book with "the Trinity all in gold"—a deluxe image perhaps not unlike the ones Jean Fouquet and his compères painted for her more literate sisters. To Margery's comfort, the angel points out her own name "written at the Trinity's foot," where the Virgin might otherwise appear.[116] In the next chapter, Christ delivers a lengthy monologue that summarizes her favorite meditations—a convention that allowed Margery to instruct her audience in devotion while seeming to avoid self-praise. In one such meditation she imagines herself as a living *Vierge ouvrante*, harboring the Trinity in the guest room of her soul:

You sometimes imagine, daughter, that you have a cushion of gold, another of red velvet, the third of white silk, in your soul. And you think that my Father sits on the cushion of gold, for with him lies might and power. And you think that I, the Second Person of the Trinity, your love and your joy, sit on the red cushion of velvet . . . in remembrance of the red blood that I shed for you. Moreover, you think that the Holy Ghost sits on a white cushion, for you think that he is full of love and purity.[117]

Mary is not present because, at this advanced level, Margery *is* Mary. And if her vision of holy domesticity sounds like a commission for a book of hours, we are now fortunate to have a medieval nun's actual drawings of such intimate scenes. Jeffrey Hamburger has recently published an image of "the heart as a house" (Figure 6.12), made for private use by a nun of

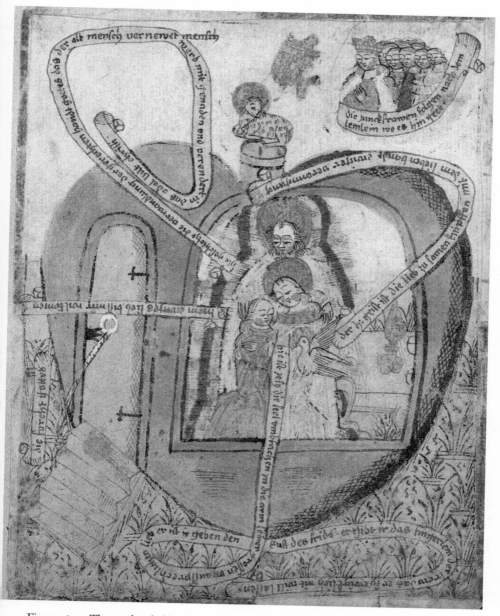

Figure 6.12. The soul as bride of the Trinity; the heart as a house. Convent of
St. Walburg, Eichstätt, ca. 1500. Berlin, Staatsbibliothek, Preussischer Kulturbesitz,
Handschriftenabteilung 417. Photo: Bildarchiv Preussischer Kulturbesitz.

St. Walburg, Eichstätt, on the eve of the Reformation.[118] Here we see what looks at first like a new kind of Marian Trinity: Christ and the Virgin in close embrace, sitting on the knees of a benign Father-God who places his arms around them both. The Spirit-dove perches opposite the maiden's heart, and an altar prepared for the eucharist is visible at right. The mystical union takes place within the locked yet transparent confines of a loving heart, here turned into a hospice for the Trinity just as Margery imagines. When this drawing was sold at Sotheby's, the catalogue identified it as "God the Father with the Virgin and Child with the Holy Ghost."[119] But in fact, as the inscriptions indicate, the virgin here is not Mary but the soul—or, put differently, the visionary artist herself. Such representations of union with the Trinity are rare, as Hamburger notes, and the few that we have occur only in manuscripts made both for and by women.[120] But, like the Dominican nuns' image of the soul crowned by Christ and the Virgin (Figure 6.5), "the heart as a house" presupposes an intimate link between mystical piety and the Marian Trinity.

To return to our original question: if Freud *had* been a medievalist—or better, if a medievalist had invented psychoanalysis—how might these materials have been interpreted? When medieval artists and visionaries reintroduced the motif of the Trinity as family, did they prove that Augustine had been right all along to resist that metaphor? Did Mary's "circular relationships" as mother of her father, daughter of her son, bride of her brother, encourage "carnal thoughts," just as the bishop had feared that a feminine Holy Spirit would? If Augustine could have read *The Book of Margery Kempe*, he might well have said yes. From a psychological standpoint, one of the most remarkable features of this intimate piety is its *unrepressed* character: the incestuous themes are right there in the open, unashamed, exultant. Divine incest is neither hemmed in by punishment and taboo, nor is it relegated to the primeval origin of the world, as in many mythic cosmogonies. Rather, it is linked to the hope of eschatological fulfillment. Mary's multiform union with the Trinity prefigures the bliss that every elect soul might hope to attain, and that contemplatives such as Mechthild, Birgitta, Margery, and the anonymous nun of Eichstätt anticipated in their visions. In short, incestuous familial love symbolizes not the primal sin but the final reward. Jocasta takes her life, Oedipus plucks out his eyes; but Christ reigns in eternal joy with the Mother who is his own and his Father's bride.

In psychoanalytic theory, we should recall, the child initially gives up oedipal desires not because they are evil but because they are impossible. Social prohibition intervenes early: when the little boy comes to realize that he *cannot* marry his mother, or the little girl her father, the forbidden wishes are repressed in favor of desires that can actually be fulfilled.[121] Moral justification comes later. Although virtually all cultures have some form of prohibition against incest, medieval society was harsher than most in this regard. Canon law not only banned marriage within seven degrees of blood relationship, but extended the stricture to relationships established by marriage and even by spiritual affinity through baptism. In fact, consanguinity was so abhorred by churchmen that, if discovered after a marriage had been consummated, it supplied one of the few canonical grounds for divorce.[122] Yet in the realm of intimate piety, where the Virgin's union with the Trinity taught the soul how to love, this most elemental transgression became the symbol of utmost purity and perfect bliss.

Some might see in this paradox merely a familiar form of compensation or splitting: what is repressed on one level is retained and idealized on another. But Freud was a pessimist, and medieval mystics were transcendental optimists who believed that "with God all things are possible." Jesus, when questioned about his ascetic teachings, famously promised that "everyone who has left houses or brothers or sisters or father or mother or children or lands, for my name's sake, will receive a hundredfold" (Matt. 19.26, 29). All renunciations, including even the primal renunciation of incestuous desire, were to be compensated beyond what is humanly possible or conceivable in the bosom of the divine family—where the Virgin Mother reigns with that God who is the source of life, the end of desire.

Domesticating the Virgin: The Invention of the Holy Family

In a Christmas sermon of 1402, Jean Gerson, the powerful chancellor of the University of Paris (d. 1429), expressed a vehement objection to the popular Shrine Madonnas that portrayed Mary as *Mater totius Trinitatis*. These statues, he complained, possessed neither beauty nor devotion, and worse, they could lead the faithful into error, for they falsely suggested that "the whole Trinity took human flesh in the Virgin Mary."[123] Johannes Molanus (d. 1722) and other Catholic reformers ritually echoed Gerson's censure until, in 1745, Pope Benedict XIV finally banned the image, which was by that time a rarity anyhow.[124] But the sculptural type seems not to have been controversial before Gerson, and, as we have seen, orthodox devotional texts often represented Mary as bride or dwelling-place of the triune God. So in this case, it looks as if Erich Neumann was right: what bothered Gerson and his successors was less a doctrinal error than the sheer, goddess-like grandeur and autonomy of the *Vierge ouvrante*—not to mention the female mystics who emulated her and aspired in their turn to become the Trinity's brides.

Gerson's objection to the Shrine Madonna may seem a trivial incident in the history of art, but it takes on new meaning in light of two endeavors to which the reformer devoted far more of his attention and energy. One was his campaign to discredit false prophets, especially visionary women, whom he perceived as a grave danger to the Church and criticized in three influential treatises on the discernment of spirits. The other was his tireless promotion of a new saint cult. The object of Gerson's devotion was none other than Joseph, the husband of Mary, whose image he aimed to rehabil-itate in the face of widespread indifference. Traditionally an abject, even ludicrous old man who figured as "God's cuckold" in legends and plays, St. Joseph became in Gerson's eyes both the legal father of Jesus and the Virgin's tender companion, whom she obeyed as a model of wifely meekness. With a young, virile Joseph at Mary's side in place of the greybeard peasant, the stage was set for the introduction of that "Holy Family" that appears in Christmas crèches to this day.[125]

The chancellor's writings on behalf of the new saint included a French treatise in two parts, *Considérations sur Saint Joseph* (1413–14);[126] a series of letters to secular and ecclesiastical patrons (1413–16) urging the establishment of a feast to celebrate the nuptials of Joseph and Mary;[127] three Latin sermons preached at the Council of Constance (1416–18);[128] a seventy-page epic poem in hexameters, the *Josephina* (1414–18);[129] and an array of sequences and epi-thalamia honoring the saint's marriage.[130] Despite the variety of media he used to address different audiences, the main lines of Gerson's hagiography remain constant. With astonishing novelty, he argued that Joseph held the number-two seat among all the saints in heaven: no one surpassed him in grace or glory save the Virgin herself.[131] In fact, Gerson adopted the cele-brated Marian principle of St. Anselm—*potuit, decuit, ergo fecit*—to discover or rather invent the prerogatives of Joseph, and he did so explicitly in the name of the patriarchal family: "Joseph was the husband of Mary and there-fore her head, for the head of woman is man, according to the Apostle (Eph. 5.23). . . . [Therefore] it was fitting for Joseph to shine with a privilege great enough to express the likeness and suitability of such a bridegroom to such a bride. . . . Hence, just as Mary's praise is the praise of Christ, her son, so the praise of Joseph redounds to the glory of both Jesus and Mary."[132]

Presenting his novel theses as "pious conjecture," Gerson proceeds to create a new Joseph modelled expressly on the Virgin's likeness.[133] Joseph, like Mary, is exalted above the choirs of angels. Like her, he was sanctified in his mother's womb and thus born (though not conceived) without stain of original sin; he therefore experienced no spark of concupiscence and remained a perpetual virgin. Mary's chastity was safeguarded by her husband's perfect continence, not his impotent old age, enabling Gerson to represent Joseph as a strong, loyal helpmate in the prime of life. If he wished to divorce Mary after discovering her pregnancy, as Matthew admits (1.19), his motive must have been profound humility rather than base suspicion. Like Mary, Joseph exulted in caring for the holy Child, kissing him, and carrying him on the flight into Egypt. But Christ's dying commendation of Mary to St. John implies that Joseph died before the Passion, so Gerson invents a pious deathbed scene in which Jesus weeps for his earthly father and Mary for her husband:

> . . . etenim sic credere fas est
> Quod patrem Jesus et sponsum flevit morientem
>   Virgo benigna suum. Fidi custodis amato
> Procumbit lecto, complexans membra, pudicis
>   Oscula dat labiis; mi vir, conclamat, abisne?
> Deseris et viduam passuram dira relinquis.
>   Velle tamen Domini fiat; dilecte vale. Nil,
> Ecce Jesus, timeas; placida te sede locabit.
>   Protinus ipse Joseph pretiosa morte quievit.[134]

> . . . And so it is right to believe
> That Jesus wept for his dying father, and the kind Virgin
>   For her spouse. She falls on the beloved bed
> Of her faithful guardian, embraces his body, kisses
>   His chaste lips. "My husband," she cries, "will you leave me?
> You abandon me, a widow, to endure harsh pain!
>   But the Lord's will be done. Beloved, farewell! Fear nothing:
> Here is Jesus; he will set you on a pleasant throne."
>   Then Joseph gave up his spirit in precious death.

Joseph, continues Gerson, may have been among those saints who rose from the dead and "appeared to many" after the Passion—in which case he surely appeared to Mary to comfort her. He now sits at the right hand of Christ in glory, and Gerson even speculates about his bodily assumption—a privilege hitherto reserved for Christ and Mary alone.

However impressive Joseph's virtues, the chancellor insists even more strongly on his parental rights. Striving to close the gap between legal and biological fatherhood, he argues that "because Mary's body was Joseph's own by right of marriage, which effects a mutual transfer of the husband's body to the wife and vice versa, let us see if we are permitted to assert with sober reason that Jesus Christ was born *of the body and flesh of Joseph*. Even this, perhaps, could be said—if we feared no offense to pious ears."[135] Whether or not pious ears were offended, pious minds remained unconvinced, for neither popular nor official piety in the fifteenth century would carry Joseph's cult to the lengths proposed by Gerson. His claim posed far too great a threat to Mary's virginal motherhood. Nevertheless, if Joseph could not win full acceptance as the father of Jesus, he did win fuller marital rights over the Virgin—and, as Dyan Elliott remarks, "there is little question that the cult of Joseph stimulated the development of a meeker, humbler, and more submissive Mary."[136] In a fervent peroration at Constance, Gerson self-consciously adapted one of St. Bernard's most famous Marian homilies to proclaim the glories of Joseph:

O how marvelous, Joseph, is your sublimity! O incomparable dignity that the Mother of God—Queen of heaven, Lady of the world—thought it not unfitting to call you "lord." I know not, orthodox fathers, which to consider more marvelous, the humility of Mary or the sublimity of Joseph—although both are incomparably surpassed by the child Jesus, who is God blessed forever, of whom it is written and stated that he was subject to them. He who fashioned the dawn and the sun was subject to a craftsman; he to whom every knee bows in heaven, on earth, and in hell was subject to a weaver-woman. How I wish that words might suffice me to explain so high a mystery, hidden from the ages, as the marvelous and venerable trinity of Jesus, Joseph and Mary.[137]

In this earthly trinity, Mary once again has two "lords," with her husband emphatically replacing the heavenly Father. As if to make sure no one missed his point, Gerson leaned heavily on the bonds of "natural authority," insisting that Joseph possessed "a certain authority, primacy, dominion and command over Mary," just as she had over Jesus "by right of natural motherhood."[138] This new family configuration had direct implications for the *imitatio Mariae*. Gerson did not contest this long-established mystical practice: for him, as for Francis of Assisi, Mechthild of Magdeburg, Meister Eckhart, and countless others, every devout soul is God's daughter by faith and has the power to become his virgin mother by grace, giving birth to the Word in the purified womb of the soul. But this mystic nativity does not occur without Joseph, who in Gerson's allegory signifies holy meditation, while Mary represents the *mens illuminata*. In his sequences on the wedding of Joseph and Mary, Gerson ceaselessly reiterates the symbolism he assigned to that union: it stands for the eschatological marriage of Jesus, "bridegroom of virgins," to the elect soul.[139] In short, the signified remains constant but the signifier has altered: Mary's chaste union with Joseph is to replace her fruitful (if incestuous) union with the Trinity as the mystic paradigm. Although the Marian Trinity would hold its own for another century, Gerson's allegory made slow but significant inroads. By 1436, Margery Kempe was familiar with it, recording that "when she saw weddings . . . at once she had in meditation how our Lady was joined to Joseph, and of the spiritual joining of man's soul to Jesus Christ."[140]

Gerson did not stand alone in promoting the sainthood of Joseph: other powerful churchmen, including his friend Pierre d'Ailly (d. 1430), Bernardino of Siena (d. 1444), Bernardino of Feltre (d. 1494), and Johann Geiler von Kaysersberg (d. 1510), supported the cause. Even so, devotion to St. Joseph and the Holy Family took root slowly. No feast was added to the calendar until 1479, fifty years after Gerson's death, and even then the solemnity on March 19 honored Joseph alone, not his marriage to the Virgin.[141] Unlike the popular cult of St. Anne, which it rivaled and eventually surpassed, the Josephine cult was decidedly imposed from the top down, as befitting a devotion intended to replace the matrilineage celebrated by the St. Anne Trinity with the patriarchal nuclear family.[142] Not only did Joseph provide an attractive model of lay masculinity and fatherhood (hitherto missing from the canon of saints), but insofar as Mary continued to personify the Church, her loyal husband could symbolize the strong papal authority so desperately needed during the Great Schism.[143] No single factor can explain the gradual rise of Joseph's cult, so deeply at odds with earlier medieval piety. From the perspective adopted here, though, Pamela Sheingorn's thesis is compelling: Gerson and his allies sought to mobilize St. Joseph as "the figure who pronounces the Father's NO," erasing the potential for both father-daughter and mother-son incest that we have seen in the Marian Trinity.[144] With her virginal husband at her side, the Queen of heaven could no longer defy patriarchal norms with even metaphorical transgression.

Gerson's Josephology, in conjunction with his resistance to the *Vierge ouvrante,* suggests an implicit critique of dominant trends in Mariology, although he in no way opposed the Virgin's cult itself.[145] But his campaign to replace the Marian Trinity with the Holy Family—to bring the Virgin safely back to earth, where she could be tamed and domesticated by her husband—struck at the heart of the piety I have been delineating. Gerson knew precisely what he was doing: to undermine the authority of female visions, he needed to discredit not only the mystics themselves, but the particular brand of Mariology that authorized them.

From this point of view, the changing roles ascribed to Mary and other holy women in the chancellor's three treatises on discernment are of particular interest. Gerson was certainly no crude misogynist: early in his career he wrote a treatise on contemplation for his virgin sisters, and in 1402 he joined his friend, Christine de Pizan, in attacking the broad antifeminist slurs of the *Roman de la Rose*.[146] Only a few months before his engagement in that celebrated *querelle*, Gerson penned his first treatise on the discernment of spirits, *On distinguishing true revelations from false* (1401). This tract is even-handed with respect to gender. The chancellor presents Mary herself as a model of discernment in her response to the angel, which demonstrated all five marks of the "true spiritual coin"—humility, discretion, patience, truth, and charity.[147] Other positive models include her cousin Elizabeth, St. Monica, and an unnamed *devota mulier* who wrote (wisely and *non muliebriter*) that she held not even the devil so suspect as feelings of love.[148] Conversely, both men and women are cited as examples of false prophecy and delusion.[149] None of Gerson's warnings in this treatise are specifically misogynistic, and even his denunciation of Marguerite Porete (under the name of "Maria de Valenciennes") is mingled with grudging praise.[150]

The chancellor published his second treatise, *On the testing of spirits* (August 1415), at Constance as the council prepared to examine St. Birgitta's revelations. These still inspired intense controversy even though her canonization, first proclaimed in 1391, had recently been reaffirmed (February 1415). At the end of this treatise Gerson again cites Mary as a model of discernment, but he is uneasy about the role she played in Birgitta's prophetic spirituality. Cautiously but skeptically, he notes that the Swedish seer was accustomed to receive visions "not only from angels, but from Christ and Mary . . . with constant familiarity, just as a bridegroom speaks to a bride."[151] The very frequency of such revelations is suspect, as is the popular vogue for them: "neglecting the study of divine Scriptures, a great number of Christians are turning their prurient eyes and ears to these visions, more pleasing because they are more recent."[152] As a backhanded comment on such visionaries' gender, Gerson introduces several antifeminist themes, including a notorious statement about "women whose ardor is excessive, greedy, changeable, unbridled, and therefore suspect," and another denouncing loquacious females who, like Margery Kempe, waste their confessors' time with over-scrupulosity and prolix narratives of their visions.[153] He also names the authority of hierarchical office (not mentioned in his earlier text) as a key aspect of discernment. Significantly, Gerson wrote this treatise at the height of his efforts to promulgate the cult of St. Joseph as Mary's rightful "head."

Finally, in his treatise *On the examination of doctrines* (1423), Gerson launches a full-scale polemic against female visionaries, claiming that they mistake mental illness for divine revelation and, in their audacity, presume to call priests of God their sons and to teach them their own profession. One such woman claims to have been mystically "annihilated," while another boasts of her intimate union with God. But these *mulierculae* are, like Eve, both deceivers and deceived, which is why "the female sex is banned by apostolic authority from teaching in public," whether in speech or in writing.[154] Gerson obliquely denounces Catherine of Siena and Birgitta of Sweden, as well as unnamed men, for leading Pope Gregory XI astray with their counsel, which had resulted in his return to Rome and thus in the current schism.[155] He further warns churchmen not to bestow the compliment of exegesis on obscure, ambiguous texts by "these new-fangled women who prophesy out of their own hearts," while the only women he cites with approval are St. Jerome's friends, Paula and Eustochium, because—in spite of their learning—they did *not* presume to write.[156] The Virgin's gift of discernment is no longer mentioned. Instead, Gerson devotes almost half his treatise to the Church's hierarchical structure, insisting that no purported revelations can be approved without passing through all five or six layers of authority.

Although the panegyrics of St. Joseph and the treatises on discernment belong to separate strands of Gerson's oeuvre, they are linked by a shared revision of the *imitatio Mariae*. The discreet, discerning Mary of *On distinguishing true revelations* and *On the testing of spirits* is the same meek woman who "rendered herself as much, or more, subject to her loyal spouse Joseph as other women should and can be to their spouses."[157] Mary's obedience to an earthly husband provides a model not only for wives, but also for visionary women, who should render themselves no less subject to the earthly Church instead of presuming to call their confessors their sons. Even in heaven, Gerson's Virgin shares her throne with St. Joseph, not the Trinity— leaving no excuse for visionaries who would use their mystical marriage to the Godhead as an authorization to teach the pope his duty.

I have argued that, for women and men who cultivated intimate pieties of the sort I have described, the Virgin's complete, multiform, and thus incestuous union with the Trinity functioned as a finite image of the infinite. Mary knew God as a daughter knows her father, a mother her child, a sister her brother, a bride her beloved. But the fusion of these incompatible relations in one stood for an imagined totality greater than the sum of its parts. Since only the impossible can represent the absolute, the Virgin at the heart of the divine family became the fifteenth century's privileged symbol of mystic union. In such a total relation, boundaries are infinitely fluid, to the extent that inside and outside become interchangeable terms. While the Coronation exalts Mary to the throne of Godhead, the *Vierge ouvrante* reverses the perspective and enthrones the Godhead in Mary's womb. Likewise, a believer who imagined her heart as a house for the Trinity might just as well envision her soul as a child carried forever in God's womb. "Our Savior," in the words of Julian of Norwich, "is our very moder in whom we be endlesly borne and never shall come out of Him."[158] If incestuous desire, as psychoanalysts speculate, represents a longing to return to the total immersion of the infant *in utero*, the symbol of the Virgin united with the Trinity stands for a no less total immersion, with the advantage of consciousness. The fervor of this desire—and more, the belief in its possible or even inevitable fulfillment—accounts for the defiantly unrepressed character of medieval mystics' intimate piety.

Jean Gerson appears to have been the first in a long train of clerics (including many modern scholars) to find such piety embarrassing, scandalous, or even blasphemous. In his own day, however, his position was exceptional, for the Marian Trinity appears so often in the art and devotional writing of the late Middle Ages that it can hardly be considered transgressive. Gerson's dissent from this form of spirituality is instructive because he was among the first to perceive a connection between widespread, culturally sanctioned themes of Mariology and a phenomenon that could be genuinely transgressive—the religious and political authority claimed by visionary women. The mystical *imitatio Mariae* afforded emotional satisfactions as well as a public voice that gave a few women the confidence to represent themselves as authors, prophets, and critics of the institutional Church in an increasingly hostile age, as we see most clearly with Birgitta. But the acceptance of women's public leadership demanded boundaries that were at least porous, if not infinitely fluid. Gerson's enterprise, on the other hand, aimed to seal the loopholes and straighten the lines of authority: "Joseph was Mary's head" just as the pope was, or ought to be, the head of the Church. Where the divine family or Marian Trinity offered mystics a utopia of metaphorical free play, the Holy Family offered churchmen a normative model of hierarchy, supporting institutional with psychological repressions. If Freud had been a medievalist, he would have spoken with the voice of Jean Gerson.

7

Goddesses and the One God

Shema Yisrael, Adonai elohenu, Adonai ehod.
Hear, O Israel: the Lord our God, the Lord is One.

Credo in unum Deum, Patrem omnipotentem.
I believe in one God, the Father Almighty.

Lā illāh illa Allāh wa-Muhammad rasūl Allāh.
There is no god but God, and Muhammad is God's prophet.

NEVER IN RECORDED HISTORY HAS A monotheistic religion worshipped a goddess. Where goddesses reign, gods hold sway also, and where God is One, that One is male. Yet in medieval imaginative theology, the one God was surrounded by—and manifested through—any number of goddesses. Since I have argued that medieval goddess theologies cannot be understood apart from their roots in Christian Platonism, it seems fitting that our explorations have themselves followed a characteristically Platonic arc of emanation and return. As St. Bonaventure wrote, "this is the whole of our metaphysics—emanation, exemplarity, and consummation; that is, to be illumined by spiritual rays and led back to the ultimate source."[1]

Natura, the first goddess we examined, "descends." From her origins in the ethereal philosophical allegories of Bernard Silvestris and Alan of Lille, she sets a steadily earthward course. Her literary career moves from Latin into the vernacular as she engages the boisterous politics of sex and gender within her own sphere of secondary divinity, shaping a discourse whose tone becomes increasingly secular without quite forgetting its theological roots. Lady Love, on the other hand, "ascends." In texts governed by this goddess, sacred and secular rhetorics converge, elevating the themes and tropes of courtly eroticism to a high sacrality, until the figures of Caritas, Dame Amour, Frau Minne become not just personifications of human loving, but also names or emanations of the One God. Latin and vernacular converge as well within this cult of sacred eros, as the monastic exegetical tradition founded on the Song of Songs fuses with the poetic traditions of troubadour lyric, Minnesang, and romance. With Sapientia and Maria, we begin anew in the realm of the sacred, taking our point of departure from the liturgy; but here too, we find that we have traced a parabolic arc from heaven to earth and back again. For Sapientia as Christ "descends," assuming human flesh and masculine gender, becoming visible, making herself available to mortals as mother, bridegroom and bride; while Sapientia as Mary "ascends," assuming divine prerogatives, taking her seat on the throne of glory as daughter, mother, and bride of the triune God.

These patterns are to some degree artificial, for a different choice of goddesses or texts might have revealed a different set of contours. Nevertheless, it is worth pausing once more to emphasize the diverse trajectories of these medieval goddesses, as well as their complex and interlocking histories. Each one is distinct, and they are no more interchangeable than Artemis and Athena; yet to follow the career of one is sooner or later to encounter them all. Hildegard of Bingen's Caritas bears a strong likeness to Alan of Lille's Natura; Christine de Pizan's Lady Reason is close kin to Boethius's Lady Philosophy; Hadewijch's Minne displays a resemblance to Suso's Eternal Wisdom; and the high Mariology of the late Middle Ages is incomprehensible without an awareness of Sophia and the sapiential liturgy. I hope I have shown, at the very least, that medieval "goddess piety" was a significant phenomenon which readily crossed linguistic and generic boundaries (not to mention gender lines), occupying a much larger place in theological, devotional, and speculative writing than had previously been observed. The case histories I have investigated do not exhaust the phenomenon and will, I hope, provide a springboard to further work by others.

In this concluding chapter, I would like to probe three larger theoretical questions posed by this material: one literary, one historical, and one theological. My first question concerns the genre of the texts we have examined—texts as diverse as the *Roman de la Rose* and the *Commedia, Piers Plowman* and *The Flowing Light of the Godhead, Anticlaudianus* and *A Revelation of Love*. A skeptical reader might have wondered at the outset whether such a collection of texts constituted anything more than a grab bag bound together by the author's personal taste. In case anyone still harbors such dark suspicions, I propose to gather these texts under the rubric of a new category of medieval writing, "imaginative theology," which crosses traditional genre lines because it is defined not by language, audience, or literary form so much as by method. Imaginative theology is the pursuit of serious religious and theological thought through the techniques of imaginative literature, especially vision, dialogue, and personification; and it is this common enterprise that links the disparate texts I have discussed. In the first part of this chapter,

I will define imaginative theology vis-à-vis other familiar categories, such as vernacular theology, allegory, and visionary literature. This analysis will enable us to revisit and refine the tenuous boundary between "authentic" and "fictional" visions.

My second question is a historical one. In teaching the texts here analyzed, especially those written by women, I have often met with an incredulous response from students: "But surely all this female God-talk was heretical?" As my students are well aware, medieval Christendom was hardly a bastion of tolerance, and many writers of imaginative theology were in fact hounded—but seldom for heresy. Mechthild of Magdeburg got in trouble for her sharp critiques of the clergy, Dante for his politics, Margery Kempe for creating a public nuisance. Indeed, Kempe was semiformally tried as a heretic, but acquitted—despite her abrasive demeanor—at the very height of persecution against the Lollards. To my knowledge only one work of high medieval imaginative theology, Marguerite Porete's *Mirror of Simple Souls*, was actually condemned as heretical and its author burned at the stake, but the reasons for Marguerite's execution had nothing to do with the feminine gender of Dame Amour. Likewise, if Julian of Norwich felt it necessary to maintain a discreet silence about her book, this was not because she had shockingly dared to imagine Jesus as Mother, but rather because her bold assurance that "all shall be well" might so easily be taken to mean that "all shall be saved." A frank profession of universalism (such as Julian carefully avoids) might indeed have constituted heresy; a feminized account of the Trinity did not.

In Chapter 1, I suggested that goddess-language, far from being condemned as heretical in itself, could at times provide a refuge *against* hostile scrutiny. In the pages that follow I will pursue this argument further, investigating the scope permitted to imaginative theology in the high Middle Ages and its relation to the two major categories of heresy—heterodox academic theology and anticlerical or anti-authoritarian mass movements. While many fine studies have probed the limits of ecclesiastical tolerance, I will chart the limits of the medieval Church's *in*tolerance, which emerge all the more clearly by contrast with the post-Tridentine suppression of many of the motifs, texts, and images I have discussed. This demonstration raises two further questions which prove yet more intriguing: Why did the medieval Church, patriarchal as it was, evince such openness to feminine God-talk, and what happened to the vestiges of this medieval goddess piety after Trent, when the reformed Church began to require a much greater uniformity not only in doctrine and observance, but also in mystical piety, iconography, and symbolism?

The third and most speculative inquiry suggested by the medieval goddesses is theological. What are the implications for Christianity, as a monotheistic faith, of addressing the Divine not only by the familiar trinitarian
titles of Father, Son, and Holy Spirit, but also by such feminine names as
Noys, Frau Minne, Sapientia Aeterna, Mother Jesus, and Lady Philosophy?:
What are the implications of giving God a bride such as Lady Poverty or a
daughter such as Natura? What indeed are the implications of making the
Trinity into a Divine Family, a quaternity in all but name, with two male
members plus one female and one neuter? Protestant polemicists of the
sixteenth century would reject such talk (especially the Marian Trinities) as
the sheerest idolatry, thereby showing how seriously they took it; while
some today might not take such questions seriously at all, seeing in them a
mere overreading of metaphors. But from the perspective I have adopted
here, metaphors in theology are no less significant than principles, and acts
of religious imagination no less important than the cultic practices they may
inspire. Indeed, from the standpoint of comparative religions, the God or
gods worshipped within any tradition are not only those that its doctrinal
formulas proclaim, but those that its devotees address in prayer, its artists
paint or sculpt, its poets celebrate in hymns, and its mystics encounter in
ecstasy. In the last section of this chapter, I will take account of the goddesses
so as to reassess the distinctive character of medieval Christianity vis-à-vis
other monotheistic systems, inclusive and exclusive, known to religionists.

Imaginative Theology

Ask any layman or woman what comes to mind at the mention of "medieval
theology," and the answer is bound to be some form of scholasticism, if only
the caricature version in which angels dance on the head of a pin. From
the mid-twelfth century onward, scholastic theology was what professional
theologians did: they taught, they debated, and they wrote their sentence
commentaries, quodlibets, and the great summas that have been likened to
Gothic cathedrals in prose. But scholastic thought, vast and impressive as
that edifice might be, was never the whole of medieval theology. As Jean
Leclercq reminded us half a century ago, the "new" learning of the schools
eclipsed but did not supersede the "old" learning of the cloister. Monastic
theology, dominant through the mid-twelfth century, continued its course
unabated through the fifteenth. Monks wrote their theological works in a
more literary vein than secular clerics or professors; their writings tend to
be exegetical rather than systematic, rhetorical rather than dialectical, and

symbolic rather than scientific, taking their inspiration from the Divine Office and the practice of *lectio divina*.[2] If Thomas Aquinas represents the epitome of scholasticism, Bernard of Clairvaux fills that role for monastic theology.

Different as they are, these two modes do not exhaust the varieties of medieval theological writing. A third great stream, taking its impetus from the Fourth Lateran Council (1215) with its ambitious program to educate the Christian rank and file, was pastoral theology. Under this umbrella we can gather the mass of sermons, catechetical treatises, confessors' manuals, ethical tracts, saints' lives, and other works written by clergy for the instruction of literate laity or parish priests. Finally, alongside the three modes of scholastic, monastic, and pastoral theology, we must consider the mystical brand. Without stirring up a hornets' nest by trying to define mysticism, we can conceive of this category as including, at the very least, those texts intended either to teach contemplative prayer or to recount their authors' experience of it. If Thomas of Cantimpré and Thomas of Chobham were pastoral theologians par excellence, Meister Eckhart and Angela of Foligno were classic mystical theologians.

These four modes of theological writing are not mutually exclusive. It is easy enough to think of theologians who were both scholastic and mystical (Bonaventure), or scholastic and pastoral (Alan of Lille), or monastic and mystical (William of St.-Thierry), or mystical and pastoral (John Tauler)— and so forth, until our mix-and-match categories begin to sound like those of the rude mechanicals in *A Midsummer Night's Dream*. But the point of these categories is not so much to classify individual figures as to differentiate the modes of theology according to their characteristic methods and goals. Scholastic theology is scientific, aiming to extend the scope of Christian knowledge and organize it into a comprehensive system by means of rational argument. Monastic theology is formative, aiming to purify Christian souls by helping them internalize the meanings of Scripture and liturgy ever more deeply. Pastoral theology is didactic, aiming to teach Christian faith and practice to ordinary believers by formulating simple, accessible versions of what C. S. Lewis would call "mere Christianity." Mystical theology, the hardest to characterize, is by turns speculative, unitive, ascetic, and erotic, aiming to midwife the soul's direct encounter with God and celebrate that event when it occurs.

In recent years a fifth category, "vernacular theology," has made its appearance in the literature. Bernard McGinn, the great historian of mysticism, first proposed this term to designate a third theological strand emerging in the thirteenth century, after the monastic and scholastic modes. Although McGinn does not formally define vernacular theology, he lists as its chief characteristics the prominence of women among both authors and audience; the choice of vernacular languages ("mother tongues" as opposed to Latin, the father tongue); a wide array of literary genres including saints' lives, vision collections, spiritual diaries, courtly dialogues, lyric poems, letters, and homilies; authorization through personal experience rather than official credentials; and a particular understanding of mystical union based on the Neoplatonic paradigm of exemplarity, emanation, and return.[3] While highlighting the importance of language itself in shaping what might be said and how, McGinn also notes that the boundaries between vernacular and Latin theology remained porous, especially in the sphere of mystical writing. Some vernacular mystics, such as Mechthild of Magdeburg and Beatrice of Nazareth, had their written texts translated into Latin; others, such as Angela of Foligno and Birgitta of Sweden, dictated vernacular revelations which their secretaries recorded in Latin; and learned men such as Eckhart and Suso often supplied both Latin and vernacular versions of the same teaching, as in the case of the *Horologium Sapientiae*. In view of such exchanges the value of the new category seems, for McGinn, to be twofold. First, the idea of vernacular theology calls attention to the medium as a determinant of the message, as well as its audience; second, it allows women writers to be given their intellectual due as theologians instead of being patronized as mere "affective mystics."

Nicholas Watson also writes about vernacular theology, but within the more historically focused context of late medieval England, where the term has a significantly different valence. In fourteenth- and early fifteenth-century England, vernacularity was associated not so much with a particular type of mystical teaching or even with women as it was with a broader debate about the intellectual and spiritual capacities of the laity. One corollary of this debate concerned the expressive powers and potential dangers of the mother tongue itself. According to Watson, the very act of writing in English could become an implicit theological statement, linked with such democratizing tendencies as a relatively nonhierarchical view of the Church, a strong view of Christian solidarity, a radical understanding of the Incarnation as the self-emptying of God, and the hope of universal salvation.[4] Beginning in the 1380s, the Lollard threat greatly intensified the debate over vernacularity and raised its political stakes, culminating as we have seen in the draconian Constitutions of Arundel (1409), with their near-total ban on biblical translation and new theological writing in English. Within this historical framework, Watson's list of English vernacular theologies looks rather different from McGinn's Continental examples. Although it includes several well-known mystical texts such as *A Revelation of Love*, *The Cloud of Unknowing*, and the English works of Richard Rolle, it also includes literary texts (*The Castle of Love*, *Piers Plowman*, *Pearl*), and a great deal of pastoral theology (*Handlyng Synne*, *The Lay Folks' Mass Book*, *The Chastizing of God's Children*, and many comparable works).[5]

In proposing to augment these categories with yet another, imaginative theology, I am not disputing the worth of existing terms so much as highlighting a different variable in the ways theology could be performed. Discussions of vernacularity call attention to the problem of *who* could write theology and who could read it. What roles, if any, were available to laymen and women? What credentials did the theologian require? Could the mere love of God suffice, or were Latin literacy and priestly ordination de rigueur? How much religious knowledge should the laity be required, or even permitted, to obtain? Imaginative theology, on the other hand, focuses on *how* theology might be performed; it draws attention to theological method and epistemology. A comparison with alternative modes will again be helpful. Scholasticism presupposes an immense faith in the power of reason, particularly dialectic: for the schoolmen, "grace perfects nature" in the sense that revelation crowns, but in no way abrogates, the achievements of enlightened philosophical thought. Monastic theology relies on personal and communal prayer as the key to the Scriptures; it is built on a belief in the infinite richness of the biblical text, which the Holy Spirit willingly opens to all who read and meditate with devotion. Mystical theology assumes that, by virtue of the *imago Dei*, some faculty of the human spirit—love or intellect or the ineffable "spark of the soul"—is capable of going forth to meet God or returning home to greet him. Imaginative theology may be compatible with any or all of these, but its methods are different. For the imaginative theologian, like the poet, works with images and believes, with Christine de Pizan, that "the road of the imagination . . . reveals the face of God to whoever follows it to the end."[6]

To be sure, the term is not itself a medieval one. Many of the texts I have designated as imaginative theology would not have been deemed "theological" by their authors, insofar as theology was viewed as a formal, professional enterprise; and the faculty of imagination had a more limited, technical meaning in medieval psychology than it has today. Yet one of the most creative figures of the early Middle Ages, John Scotus Eriugena, anticipated just such a category in his own description of the theologian's task: "Just as the poetic art presents moral or scientific teaching, using fictional stories and allegorical images to exercise human minds, . . . so the art of theology, like a kind of poetry, uses imaginative fictions to shape holy Scripture for our mind's consideration."[7] Eriugena's observation could have supplied the manifesto for such works of imaginative theology as the *Cosmographia* of his fellow Platonist, Bernard Silvestris. But in any case, the existence of a historical phenomenon does not depend on the availability of contemporary nomenclature for it. It is now commonplace, for example, to characterize all manner of works as "political" even if they do not explicitly recount power struggles, develop a theory of government, or proffer advice to the prince. By the same token, it seems fair to describe texts as "theological," regardless of their form, if they engage deeply and seriously with such issues as the nature and knowledge of God, salvation, sin and grace, creation, incarnation, and so forth. But the hallmark of imaginative theology is that it "thinks with" images, rather than propositions or scriptural texts or rarefied inner experiences—although none of these need be excluded. The devices of literature—metaphor, symbolism, prosopopoeia, allegory, dialogue, and narrative—are its working tools. A list of imaginative theological writings would overlap with the monuments of vernacular theology discussed by McGinn and Watson, but it would also include significant works in Latin (such as the *Cosmographia*, *Sacrum commercium*, and *Horologium Sapientiae*), and it would exclude many vernacular works of a pastoral or catechetical bent. Further, it would include works of visionary spirituality, such as those of Hildegard, Hadewijch, and Birgitta, while excluding some important mystical texts of a more abstract or apophatic type, such as Angela of Foligno's *Memorial* and *The Cloud of Unknowing*.

Imaginative theology also embraces many canonical poetic works, among them Dante's *Commedia*, *Piers Plowman*, and arguably Chaucer's *Parlement of Fowles*. The *Roman de la Rose* is a loose baggy monster that straddles at least half a dozen genres, but one of them is imaginative theology, for the poem takes a polemical stand on a hotly debated religious question. If my reading is correct, Jean de Meun uses the goddesses Reason and Nature to argue a position of strict supernaturalism. Like Alan of Lille but more forcefully, he demonstrates, through the devices of dream vision and allegorical dialogue, that Nature (and, by implication, natural law and natural theology) are inferior to reason, impotent to understand the grace and purpose of God, and therefore wholly unreliable as moral guides. In this connection it is worth recalling that the theological faculty of Paris saw fit to censure, not the *Rose* as a whole, but certain libertine propositions plucked out of it—on my reading, the very propositions that Jean himself wished to discredit and satirize.[8]

Imaginative theology is characterized by certain rhetorical devices that double as exploratory techniques, enabling both writer and reader to visualize, conceptualize, and interact with emissaries of the Divine. This kind of exploration is something quite different from the occasional use of metaphor and analogy that can be found in even the most rigorous scholastic thinkers. In *Cur Deus Homo*, for example, Anselm begins his account of the Atonement by praising a certain "indescribable beauty" in the symmetries of redemption: as sin took its origin from a woman, so also salvation; as the devil conquered man through a tree, he would in turn be conquered through a tree; and so forth. But his interlocutor points out that these harmonious pictures, however beautiful, will not convert an infidel who takes the whole story for a fiction; from the infidel's point of view, they are no more than paintings on a cloud.[9] In response, Anselm sets out to show by necessary reasons why God had to become man. Yet another "picture" underlies his new arguments—the analogy of a serf who has insulted the honor of his lord. But this analogy remains submerged beneath Anselm's forensic arguments about divine justice and human obligation; it is never brought clearly to the surface. In contrast, Robert Grosseteste in *Le Château d'Amour*, and later William Langland in *Piers Plowman*, would rethink the redemption by dramatizing Anselm's analogy in vividly imagined scenarios. As the serf languishes in prison, they represent the lord's four daughters arguing vehemently about his fate. Thus an abstract conflict between God's justice and mercy is personified, ostensibly for the benefit of simple believers (rather than infidels). But in the process, the theology itself subtly alters, and Anselm's severe lord is humanized in more ways than one.

Central to the enterprise of imaginative theology is the technique of the dream or waking vision. In Chapter 1, I argued that fictional visionary poems, such as *Piers Plowman* and the *Rose*, might be fruitfully compared with vision narratives that claim to report their authors' personal religious experience, such as those of Mechthild of Magdeburg or Julian of Norwich—or indeed Dante. There too I showed how devout exercises such as prayerful meditation and visualization (as practiced by Henry Suso) could procure results not unlike those of self-conscious literary scene-painting or rhetorical *inventio* (as practiced by Christine de Pizan). In other words, imaginative theology might take its point of departure from either end, from the quest for God or the drive to create. If visions could inspire a devout soul to write, the desire to write could also inspire a poet to construct visions; and the outcomes of these two procedures might not be so dissimilar as scholars tend to assume. After examining a wide range of writings of both types, we are in a better position to see how visions, so ubiquitous in medieval literature, could function as both rhetorical device and theological method.

As we saw earlier, the German medievalist Peter Dinzelbacher set forth various criteria for distinguishing between "literary" and "experiential" (or fictional and authentic) visions.[10] But once we grant that all medieval visions are by definition "literary," since they have come down to us as texts, it may be more useful to distinguish between the vision as epiphany and the vision as heuristic device. An epiphanic vision can be defined as a spiritual or imaginative experience, often mysterious and unexpected, whose meaning can be teased out by meditation, theological reflection, and exegetical practices such as allegoresis. A heuristic vision, on the other hand, is a rhetorical means to explore the implications of an idea and express it more vividly. The epiphanic vision is the mainstay of the sole medieval genre dominated by women—the visionary recital or book of revelations. Heuristic visions, frequently cast in the form of dreams, are the mainstay of allegorical and theological fiction.

Medieval authorities on the discernment of spirits, like visionaries themselves, believed epiphanic visions (if authentic) to be sent by God, although they also believed such visions could be simulated by diabolical deception, self-delusion, mental illness, or deliberate fraud. For this reason the stakes vested in visionary claims were very high, especially in the fourteenth and fifteenth centuries, as an increasing fear of false visionaries subjected all claimants to exacting and perilous scrutiny, and in the most extreme cases, to torture, imprisonment, or death.[11] Yet even inquisitors recognized that poets and other imaginative writers could construct highly convincing visions—in which they might claim to have seen Christ and his mother, saints, angels, and devils, as well as allegorical figures—without making the same truth-claims that subjected prophets and mystics to such anxious interrogation. The supreme example is of course Dante. Though exiled from Florence by his political opponents, he was never hauled before an inquisitorial court to explain why he had consigned a canonized pope to hell,[12] admitted several pagans and a condemned heretic to heaven,[13] made his Beatrice a doctor of the Church, and even claimed to experience the beatific vision while still alive.[14]

Recent interpreters of visionary writing have tended to acknowledge some such distinction in principle, while in practice treating all visions as fictional in order to evade the embarrassing question of truth-claims. By bracketing such claims, especially those made by women, as part of a culturally mandated strategy of empowerment, scholars who are not necessarily believers can avoid dismissing any number of imaginatively and intellectually powerful texts as the products of religious delusion. Such bracketing is certainly an improvement over the sort of confessional polemic that used to divide Catholic apologists from Protestant and Freudian assailants of visionary writing. Nevertheless, it tends to occlude some of the most interesting questions raised by these texts, such as how the religious imagination works in them and how medieval culture, despite its often deadly outbursts of anti-heretical and antifeminist paranoia, managed to allow a space for imaginative theology.

Few if any contemporary interpreters of this literature share the "all-or-nothing" view of divine inspiration characteristic of medieval theorists. Today, even a critic who accepts the possibility of revelation is likely to hold a more ambiguous and historicized view of it, to see divine self-disclosure in any form as more deeply enmeshed with human anxieties, fantasies, and desires, not to mention cultural conditioning, than medieval theories of biblical and prophetic inspiration would allow. In short, the category of revelation, where it survives at all, is much fuzzier than it used to be. While fuzzy doctrines of revelation create thorny problems for ecclesiastical authority, they have certain advantages for the interpreter of visionary writings. In challenging a distinction that medieval theologians preferred to sharpen, I aim not to foist my own truth-claims on resistant authors, but to demonstrate just how thin and porous the boundary between epiphanic and heuristic visions could sometimes be.

A good starting point for this demonstration is Julian of Norwich, since she was exceptionally candid and conscientious in distinguishing among the modalities of her own "vision"—bodily showings, ghostly showings, ghostly showings in bodily likeness, words formed in her understanding, interior teaching, and so forth.[15] In her crucial fourteenth revelation, we have seen that her teaching hinges on two parables of divine-human relationship: lord and servant, mother and child. The first parable originates in a vision *sensu stricto*: Julian sees "two persons in bodily likeness," a lord and a servant, and realizes in her "ghostly understanding" that these represent God and Adam. But after two decades of bewilderment, the meaning of this vision still remains "misty" to the seer until God instructs her by "teaching inwardly" that she should treat it just as an exegete would treat a difficult prophecy in Scripture—that is, attend to its minute particulars, interpret each detail allegorically, and seek for the unity among these particulars until the ensemble begins to make sense. By faithfully carrying out this directive "as far as my wit and understanding would serve," Julian at last understands that the servant in her vision represents Christ as well as Adam, and thus achieves her theological breakthrough.[16]

The showing of the lord and servant is an epiphanic vision that yields its meaning not in an immediate flash of insight, as with Julian's earlier Passion visions, but only through a slow process of exegetical labor. Conversely, her representation of Christ as Mother, which complements the parable of the servant, is not rooted in any "showing" at all. Julian never "sees" the divine maternity in the same way that she sees the bleeding head of Jesus, the hazel-nut, the enthronement of Christ within her soul, or even the lord and his servant. God's motherhood is rather an idea that she develops heuristically. The closest Julian ever comes to a visual presentation of this idea—and it is still not very close—is when she imagines a mother lovingly watching her child learn to walk: she may allow the child to stumble and fall, even at the price of tears, but she will never let it suffer "any manner of peril," wander-ing perchance into the hearth fire or the well. Significantly, this metaphori-cal vision of a kind mother parallels her earlier bodily vision of the lord, who permits his over-eager servant to fall into a ravine for his own ultimate good. In this image Mother and Lord momentarily converge, and we glimpse the inner unity of the whole complex showing.

Julian is most unusual among visionary theologians in letting the reader see how her doubts, questions, and perplexities led her to deeper under-standing. The dialectic between God's generous yet forever-incomplete revela-tion and her own continuing struggle for truth becomes in itself an exemplum of incarnational theology. But few visionaries had the courage—or perhaps we should say the luxury—to acknowledge the human element in their writ-ing at a time when even a woman's admission of literacy might disempower her as a vessel of the divine. At the opposite end of the spectrum from Julian stands Hildegard of Bingen, whose truth-claims depend on a highly literal-istic account of her own inspiration. She presents not only her visions per se, but every word of her vast trilogy as divine dictation, even when her brief vision narratives fairly stagger beneath the learned weight of allegorical, scriptural, theological, and scientific exegesis she heaps upon them. Whether Hildegard herself believed her own "fundamentalist" claims is not a question we can answer. But her twenty-first-century interpreter, no longer at risk of being dismissed as a weak-minded woman or a plaything of demons, need not choose between taking such accounts at face value and dismissing them as lies (or, to speak more politely, "conventions"). We might hypothesize instead that, in reality, Hildegard and other visionary authors experienced a creative process not unlike the one Julian describes. In between "showings" a great deal of thought, prayer, conversation, reading, and revision most likely intervened, so that even a vision initially granted as epiphany might eventually be presented as heuristic device for the benefit of readers. This process could not be acknowledged, however, lest it weaken the writer's fragile claim to inspiration and authority.

Some visionary writers experimented more or less self-consciously with different literary genres grounded in different kinds of imaginative experience. Mechthild of Magdeburg mingled visions, prophecies, lyrics, prayers, dialogues, and didactic teaching in a single, unclassifiable book, remarkable alike for its sustained literariness and its occasionally strident truth-claims. Hadewijch, on the other hand, preferred to keep her genres separate. Her book of visions, though exquisitely artful, bears all the hallmarks of authenticity to be expected in that genre: she scrupulously records the liturgical date of each vision, the time of day, her own mental and physical state, sometimes even her age. The autobiographical "I" of this text is individualized by being firmly anchored in time and the body—from which she is repeatedly raptured by her visions. Conversely, the putative male voice of the *Stanzaic Poems* is the lyric "I" of the minnesingers, the subject of an intense yet generic and readily universalized love experience. If by chance only one of these collections had survived, we could not have deduced the existence of the *Poems* from the *Visions* nor the *Visions* from the *Poems*—nor of Hadewijch's *Letters* from either of these. Yet all three collections were addressed to the same audience with the same intention: to present advanced instruction in Minne for the benefit of young beguines. The *Visions* do this by interpreting intimate personal experience (vision as epiphany); the *Stanzaic Poems* by creating a new imaginative world in response to the question: What would it be like if the beguine were a knight-errant on a quest? (vision as heuristic device).

Since the authentic visionary recital could be regarded as more prestigious (if also more dangerous) than the allegorical fiction, it is not surprising that imaginative writers imitated mystics when they wished to advance deeply serious truth-claims for their work. One way to do this was to eschew the convention of the dream vision, a surefire sign of fiction. The *Roman de la Rose* and the *Parlement of Fowles* present themselves as dream visions; the *Consolation of Philosophy* and the *Commedia* do not. Dante establishes his credentials as prophet no less audaciously than he claims the title of Poet. While any sinner might be vouchsafed a vision of hell as a spur to amendment, only the saints were privileged to contemplate heaven, and no one before or since has claimed as detailed a knowledge of it as Dante. During his tour, moreover, he is not only assured of his own final beatitude, but commissioned with a prophetic message for the Church. Dante's Franco-Italian admirer, Christine de Pizan, learned from him and used the distinction between heuristic and epiphanic visions with considerable skill. Her autobiographical narrative in *The Book of the Mutation of Fortune* is allegorical, culminating in her transformation from woman to man at the hands of the pseudo-goddess Fortune. This event takes place in a dream, since the imagined sex change is only a heuristic device to account for Christine's adoption of a new gender role, and her claim to maleness will eventually be revoked. But she begins *The Book of the City of Ladies* with a carefully literal account, devoid of allegorical details and persuasively grounded in real time and space, so that when Lady Reason and her sisters finally break in through closed doors, they shatter the confined mental universe of misogynist writers with the force of epiphany.

While imaginative theology clearly overlaps with such genres as the vision and the allegorical dialogue (which are themselves closely intertwined), it is worth emphasizing that this mode of writing served not only to *express* a religious meaning or truth already possessed, but also to *discover* meaning, no less than the exegetical query or the scholastic debate. It is this genuine exploratory function that justifies the title of "theology," for—to paraphrase Lévi-Strauss—goddesses were good to think with. If medieval authors did not expressly claim to be theologizing through such techniques as personification, visualization, and dialogue, they had good reasons for reticence on that point. For it was the unofficial, "fabulous" character of imaginative theology that accounted in large part for its toleration, so long as its practitioners did not flaunt their claims, as the unfortunate Marguerite Porete did, or presume to preach, as Margery Kempe was accused of doing, or attract suspicious saint cults during their lifetimes. If we accept imaginative theology as a real, albeit unacknowledged mode of theological thinking, our overall picture of medieval religious thought will become considerably more variegated (and more interesting) than a chronicle of purely professional theologians would allow.

The Gender of God and the Limits of Intolerance

Even though literature as such was rarely censored by medieval churchmen, the prevalence of goddesses in imaginative theology may continue to raise eyebrows. As I have noticed with amusement, the title of this book, *God and the Goddesses*, has more often than not been misquoted by the libraries and museums that have graciously supplied photographs for it. These glitches imply that there is something deeply surprising about the subject, for no one expects "goddesses" to turn up in a book about God, especially the God of the medieval Church. Their sudden eruption may suggest that someone has pulled a suspect feminist rabbit out of a tattered medieval hat. Yet the texts in which goddesses appear are numerous and varied, and although some are unfamiliar, others are quite well known. What is new is my terminology. In arguing for the category of "goddesses" rather than "female personifications," and "imaginative theology" rather than "literature," I have insisted that the religious thought expressed in such texts deserves the attention of religious historians, and further, that writers' frequent representations of the feminine Divine must be taken as integral rather than ornamental to their thought. Much is at stake here, for the traditional academic boundaries between literature and theology, along with conventional interpretations of allegory, have served to occlude the goddesses, rendering them invisible to any serious understanding of medieval religion.

But the fault, if it is one, does not begin with the analytical categories of medievalists. Goddesses have been invisible to medieval scholarship because they have been largely absent from post-medieval Christianity, with the exception of a self-consciously esoteric tradition that goes back to such texts as the *Aurora consurgens*. There are manifold reasons for this disappearing act, as we shall soon discover. But first I wish to emphasize that the textual and pictorial representation of these Christian goddesses—the female manifestations, daughters, and brides of the one God—did not constitute heresy or subversion by any valid historical standard. Nor did the goddess-language favored by so many imaginative theologians shake the foundations of medieval patriarchy, for the simple reason that the ideological bedrock of that patriarchy was not (or not yet) the masculinity of God.

The term "heresy" tends to be used more freely by literary critics than by historians. We often see texts, ideas, or even metaphors designated "heretical" because they impress a modern reader as subversive or in violation of some preconceived theological norm, a norm that may actually be patristic or modern rather than medieval. To avoid such anachronistic usage, it is helpful to recall that medieval heresy was a juridical concept. Books or beliefs could not be heretical in the abstract; they became heretical only when authoritative churchmen—popes, synods, individual bishops, or inquisitors—pronounced them so. A potentially heretical book that never drew the wrath (or the attention) of such authorities would be like the proverbial tree that falls in a deserted forest: any noise it made would be for the ears of God alone. As for the human beings who wrote the books and adhered to the beliefs, they could be executed for the crime of heresy only if they proved "obdurate" or "relapsed," that is, if they either refused to abjure their heretical views or did so under pressure but later recanted or resumed their prior activities. Marguerite Porete earned her martyrdom not merely by writing *The Mirror of Simple Souls*, but by continuing to distribute copies to prominent theologians after an express prohibition from her bishop, and then refusing to testify at her trial despite eighteen months of imprisonment. It was presumably the bishop's previous condemnation that earned her the epithet of "relapsed," for there is no evidence that she had ever abjured.

Medieval bishops were busy men, if not always godly ones, and did not have much time to spend in libraries browsing for suspicious texts. Potential heretics generally came to their attention only if their activities were sufficiently public and widespread to cause anxiety, or else if they were denounced by their enemies. The great majority of condemned heretics were men and women affiliated with movements that challenged the power, authority, and wealth of the clerical hierarchy, either directly or through attacks on the sacramental system that supplied their *raison d'être*.[17] There were many ways to do this: through rejection of the eucharist, attacks on the validity or necessity of baptism, denial of any distinction between clergy and laity, calls to boycott the sacraments of fornicating and simoniac priests, demands for clerical disendowment or radical poverty, apocalyptic prophecies identifying the pope with the Antichrist, promises of an imminent Age of the Spirit in which the present Church would be superseded, and so forth. All the well-known heretical movements (Cathars, Waldensians, Patarenes, Spiritual Franciscans, Lollards, Hussites) fell under one or more of these heads. Radical mysticism was less overtly threatening, though it could become so if the mystic laid claim to such a perfect union with God that he or she no longer required the ministrations of the Church. This is the position for which Marguerite Porete gave her life. But the inquisitors who condemned her were so accustomed to thinking in terms of organized movements that they invented one—"the heresy of the Free Spirit"—on the basis of her book alone.[18] Porete was the only medieval woman, and possibly the only author of either sex, who died solely for a written text. Other heretics brought to the stake, including Hus, may have been writers but were also, and primarily, preachers.[19]

If a heresiarch wished to spread dissident views and win converts, the most effective way to do so was through inflammatory sermons rather than books, given the comparatively low rate of literacy even in the late Middle

Ages. Thus heretical preachers and their adherents were considerably more vulnerable to prosecution, and especially to the death penalty, than were writers. Significantly, the four theologians whose writings arguably made the greatest impact on later heretics (Joachim of Fiore, Peter John Olivi, Meister Eckhart, and John Wycliffe) were all permitted to die in peace, even though works by Olivi and Wycliffe had already been condemned during their lifetimes, and propositions from all four were posthumously condemned. Other academic theologians came under suspicion of heresy because their ideas or methods threatened powerful enemies, though they neither wished to promulgate dissent nor effectively did so. We have already considered the group of twelfth-century philosophical theologians—Peter Abelard, William of Conches, and Gilbert Porreta—who fell afoul of Bernard of Clairvaux and his ally, William of St.-Thierry. Abelard's case is particularly striking because it illustrates the decisive role of personality. Although guilty of no doctrinal error, he lacked the talent for ingratiating himself with authority and wound up being condemned by two synods because Bernard, with greater political clout, had so thoroughly outmaneuvered him.

This simplified sketch indicates why imaginative theologians were in little danger of prosecution for heresy, no matter what they might say. In the first place, imaginative writers rarely preached or led mass movements. One exceptional case is telling. When *Piers Plowman* and its hero unexpectedly became a rallying cry for the rebels of 1381, Langland seems to have been so dismayed that he undertook a thorough revision of his poem in order to distance it from its most radical interpreters.[20] Although the revolt was ruthlessly suppressed by Richard II, we read of no reprisals against the poet. In the second place, the ecclesiastical method of pronouncing judgments of orthodoxy on discrete propositions, rather than books, worked in favor of imaginative writers. As a case in point, let us recall Bernard Silvestris's *Cosmographia*, an epic that asserts many heterodox ideas of Platonic origin. Among these are astral determinism, the preexistence of souls, and a view of man as *imago mundi* rather than *imago Dei*: the human being in Bernard's poem is created not directly by God or even by Noys, but by a trinity of subordinate goddesses (Urania, Natura, and Physis). By the standards of twelfth-century Catholic doctrine, all these positions are further from orthodoxy than anything in Abelard's oeuvre. Yet Pope Eugene III himself was entertained by a reading from the *Cosmographia* en route to Gilbert Porreta's heresy trial, and a manuscript witness tells us that the poem "captured his goodwill."[21] In an even more striking example, a wandering Franciscan alchemist presented his *Book of the Holy Trinity* to Emperor Sigismund at the Council of Constance,

where the leading churchmen of the day had gathered for pressing business that included the burning of Jan Hus. Although the Franciscan's book
presents Mary in no uncertain terms as a member of the Trinity, it escaped
censure and even found influential patrons, who were apparently more interested in its anti-Hussite propaganda (and the promise of alchemical gold)
than in prosecuting Trinitarian heresy.

These two cases, involving the reception of the earliest and latest texts
discussed in this book, show how a nonscholastic literary form might protect even the most audacious theological writings. The *Cosmographia* and the
Book of the Holy Trinity are hardly similar: Bernard's Latin poem is an elegant
product of twelfth-century humanism, while the Franciscan's German tract is
a wildly inelegant mélange of alchemical, political, and theological teaching.
Yet both texts make difficult reading; both are in different ways esoteric;
both stand far removed from the scholastic ideal of *claritas*. It is not easy to
pluck doctrinal propositions from either work. While the traits that modern
critics tend to value in literature—complexity, ambiguity, indeterminacy, and
the like—are not the same as those lauded by medieval rhetoricians, their
presence nonetheless inhibited the kind of fishing for suspect propositions to
which the books of Marguerite Porete and her unacknowledged disciple,
Meister Eckhart, were subjected.[22] Of course one could argue that the master
and Marguerite were harmed by their *lack* of clarity, but it would be truer to
say that they shared a dangerous flair for couching their views in the most
extreme and flamboyant language at their command. If Porete had deigned to
defend herself by submitting to "Holy Church the Little" and proving that
her ideas lay open to an orthodox interpretation, as Eckhart would do when
accused of heresy in his last months, even she might have escaped the stake.

One extraordinary case of prosecution may seem to challenge my claim
that the repressors of heresy took no interest in feminine God-language. The
Guglielmites of Milan, a small, close-knit sect extirpated by inquisitors in
1300, were devotees of "St. Guglielma" (d. 1282), a Cistercian oblate buried
at the monastery of Chiaravalle, where she was venerated liturgically by the
monks and other townsfolk.[23] For the sectarians, however, Guglielma was no
mere saint but the incarnation of the Holy Spirit, whose life and ministry
paralleled those of Jesus in all respects, and they looked forward to her imminent resurrection and Second Coming, when she would usher in the millennium by establishing a new, all-inclusive Church with a female pope. One of
their leaders, a Humiliati nun named Maifreda da Pirovano, had already
been chosen for the role of *papessa* and fulfilled it in an escalating series of
cultic activities that culminated in a solemn Mass celebrated on Easter 1300.

A thorough inquisition resulted in Guglielma's posthumous condemnation and the burning of her relics, as well as the execution of Maifreda and several others as relapsed heretics because they had abjured in a prior interrogation. In addition, all the sect's original writings (which included gospels, epistles, litanies, and hymns) were destroyed; only inquisitorial records survive.[24] The Guglielmites' spiritual feminist beliefs, which make their heresy so uniquely fascinating today, lent a new twist to Joachite apocalypticism. Yet, in the eyes of their inquisitors, the sectarians would have been no less heretical if they had designated some male saint as their incarnate Spirit and chosen to follow a male pope of their own choosing in lieu of Boniface VIII. Subversives they undoubtedly were, in a city with a long history of dissent and religious unrest. But at the time, the feminist dimension of their heresy probably made them look not more dangerous but more ridiculous. H. C. Lea, the first modern scholar to investigate the Guglielmites, could still remark in 1888 that their beliefs would seem a ludicrous jest were it not for their tragic destiny.[25]

Medieval heresy-hunters concerned themselves primarily with threats to ecclesiastical power, secondarily with speculative ideas—and not at all with poetic or devotional imagery. Even if they had been literary critics, however, it is unlikely that representations of Nature, Divine Love, or Wisdom as goddesses, or of Jesus as mother, would have disturbed them. I take the risk of belaboring this point because it flies in the face of so much recent writing about medieval patriarchy. I do not deny that the Church ruthlessly persecuted some groups of women (clerical wives, accused witches), that it subjected others (nuns, visionaries, beguines) to increasingly repressive controls, or that it excluded all without exception from the priesthood. But these persecutions and exclusions did not rest on Mary Daly's famous formula that "if God is male, then the male is God."[26] They rested instead on a firm, deeprooted, and universal belief in female inferiority. When scholastic theologians rehearsed the reasons women could not be ordained, they pointed to the natural subordination of their sex (which had preceded the more punitive subordination due to Eve's fall), along with the impurity of menstruation, the weakness of the female body, its ineradicable propensity to awaken lust, the frailty of women's minds, and the general lack of authority, stability, and constancy ascribed to the sex.[27] These beliefs could be buttressed at need with biblical proof-texts, but they did not fundamentally rest on Scripture, for Aristotle and Galen, Theophrastus and Seneca, Ovid and Juvenal could support them far better. Male supremacy and superiority were not proclaimed as doctrines of faith revealed by the Holy Spirit; they were self-evident truths perceived by man's natural reason. In fact, each time the schoolmen set about demolishing the straw woman of female equality, Scripture provided them mainly with counter-arguments and examples that had to be explained away.[28] The scholastics did lean heavily on the argument that God in Christ took the male rather than the female sex; therefore only the male body of a priest could appropriately signify Christ's body. When explaining *why* the Word became incarnate as a man, however, they did not declare that God was intrinsically male, but relied instead on the circular argument that the masculine sex was "more honorable" than the feminine (Peter Lombard), or "nobler" (Aquinas), or "of greater dignity" (Bonaventure).[29]

At this point readers may be asking impatiently, "So what? Doesn't it all come down to the same thing in the end?" With regard to the status of women, the answer is unfortunately yes. But with regard to representations of God, it is emphatically no. For goddesses were not women: they did not have bodies, and although they were symbolically virgins, lovers, mothers, and brides, they bore no taint of mortal frailty. Lady Philosophy suffers from no weakness of mind; Lady Poverty, though beautiful and nude, arouses no lust in St. Francis; Mater Ecclesia does not lack authority, nor is Frau Minne periodically unclean. When female frailty is in fact ascribed to goddess-figures, it is always a tipoff that they are something other than they appear to be. Fortuna, a pseudo-goddess, is fickle and capricious because she is an illusion born of philosophical error, not a genuine manifestation of the Divine. When Jean de Meun makes his Dame Nature speak like a loquacious, self-promoting beguine, he signals that he is satirizing rather than encouraging devotion to this goddess. Dame Raison, whose position is closer to the poet's own, is not subjected to this satirical treatment. The one goddess-figure who does have a body is of course the Virgin Mary. But here she is the exception that proves the rule, for her unique body—conceived free of original sin, fertile without seed of man, perpetually virgin, exempt from the pangs of labor, raised from the dead, assumed into heaven—is not at all like other women's. It is in her rich spiritual and affective life, not her physicality, that Mary provides a model for emulation.

By a curious paradox, the very depth of the medieval Church's anti-feminism was among the enabling conditions for its tolerance of goddess-language. Apparently no one, other than the heretical Guglielmites and the orthodox Christine de Pizan, ever suspected that a feminizing of deity in heaven might justify changes in the gender system on earth. Consider, by way of contrast, the contemporary situation. The Roman Catholic Church still does not ordain women, but the most thorough of the recent encyclicals restating this ban—issued by the conservative Pope John Paul II in 1988–is significantly entitled *Mulieris Dignitatem* (*Woman's Dignity*). True to its title, the encyclical presents itself insofar as possible as a celebration of the equality, human worth, and spiritual gifts of women. It repudiates every hint of female inferiority, describes subjection in marriage as mutual, heaps lavish praise on the Virgin Mary and women saints, and represents Christ's words and actions as "a consistent protest against whatever offends the dignity of women."[30] Yet the traditional position barring women priests must be re-affirmed, although most of the traditional arguments that sustained it can no longer be used. Thus one of the position's few remaining supports—natural likeness to Christ—now looms much larger. The encyclical's core argument for an all-male priesthood is a symbolic one: "It is the Eucharist above all that expresses the redemptive act of Christ the Bridegroom towards the Church the Bride. This is clear and unambiguous when the sacramental ministry of the Eucharist, in which the priest acts *'in persona Christi,'* is performed by a man."[31] Since even the magisterium no longer teaches the inferiority of women, yet remains committed to their exclusion from the priesthood, the maleness of Christ is compelled to bear much greater symbolic weight.

Vatican documents are too theologically sophisticated to assert the masculinity of God as such. Like the medieval sentence commentaries, they dwell only on the male humanity of Jesus. But for lay believers, God's gender has become a flashpoint for all manner of struggles related to the women's movement and the status of biblical or ecclesiastical authority. Nor is this concern confined to the Catholic church. During the 1970s and '80s, one denomination after another erupted in bitter conflict over the introduction of inclusive language lectionaries, new hymnals, prayers to "Our Father-Mother God," and so forth. Goddess-language is once again rife in contemporary religion, but it is now used almost exclusively by those who identify themselves as committed feminists, whether inside or (more often) outside the churches.[32] In a word, it is self-consciously politicized in a way that its medieval counterparts were not. Resistance to such language is no less politicized: those who object to it are also likely to oppose other feminist goals, such as the tolerance of abortion and homosexuality, as well as religious syncretism, "paganism," and the dilution of scriptural authority. An instructive case in point is the mainstream reaction to the celebrated "Re-Imagining Conference" of 1993.[33] About two thousand progressive and radical women, mainly Protestants, had gathered in Minneapolis in November 1993 to "re-imagine" God, Christ, and community in conjunction with the World Council of Churches Ecumenical Decade of Churches in Solidarity with Women.

The conference entailed a series of feminist theological talks and liturgical rites, among them the veneration of Sophia in a sacramental communion of milk and honey. Media coverage was widespread and largely hostile. In a backlash that caught participants by surprise, more conservative Christians responded by withdrawing millions of dollars in pledges, and the Presbyterians fired a high-ranking churchwoman who had been instrumental in planning the event.

The political situation of contemporary God-language is of great interest, but I mention it here to emphasize the distance between these power struggles and those that exercised the medieval Church, which confronted no mass movement for female ordination and no "womenChurch" community on the margins of Christendom. The pressures that now bear so heavily on such symbols as "Goddess" and "God our Mother" are specific to the present historical moment and should not be projected retroactively onto the Middle Ages. This is not to say that medieval religious symbolism was somehow innocent of political meaning, but rather that the meanings it bore were very different from those we now ascribe to gendered images of God. Henry Suso's Hours of Eternal Wisdom, for example, were clearly not "subversive" in the way that both proponents and foes of Re-Imagining perceived the conferees' worship of Sophia as subversive. With the exception of Christine, the medieval writers analyzed here did not deploy their goddess-language in pursuit of any conscious feminist agenda, and conversely, those who eschewed such language did not seem to find it heretical, threatening, subversive, or worth their while to repress. Medieval goddesses served a wide variety of theological and spiritual functions, but these did not include the overthrow of patriarchy.

Yet if the prevalence and tolerance of goddess-language does not allow us to qualify it as subversive, neither should we leap to the opposite conclusion. In Chapter 1 we considered the possibility that women writers in particular found goddess figures spiritually and psychologically empowering, and close readings tend to bear this out. Whether we look at Hildegard's re-envisioning of the Creator as Creatrix in the figure of Caritas, or Hadewijch's mystical heroics in the quest of Frau Minne, or Julian's filial immersion in "the deep wisdom of the Trinity, our Mother," or Birgitta's maternal bond with Mary in whose name she prophesied, or Lady Reason's annunciation to Christine, it is hard to escape the sense that such symbols carried a special resonance for women qua women, above and beyond whatever intrinsic meanings they possessed, because of the female writer's perennial need for authorization. This added valence seems to have gone largely unremarked by male writers, however, and goddesses were not perceived as uniquely or exclusively suited to women's piety. At times the reverse could be true: Suso paid only perfunctory attention to Eternal Wisdom's feminine gender in his *Büchlein der Ewigen Weisheit*, written chiefly for women, but expanded and heightened her role when he translated the text into Latin for male readers.

In sum, we may posit that the high medieval centuries constituted a golden age of goddesses, without in any way implying that the era was a golden age for women, feminist theology, or the genial toleration of dissent. But during the great religious upheavals of the sixteenth century this tolerance for goddesses came to an end. Torn apart by religious warfare, heresy, and schism as never before, a beleaguered Church could no longer sustain the freewheeling play of imagery that had been such a characteristic feature of late medieval religious culture and began to enforce a new mandate for uniformity, not only in doctrine but also in devotional literature, spirituality, and art. Responding to the vigorous Protestant attack on images, the prelates at the Council of Trent reaffirmed the propriety of venerating them, but did their best to banish superstition and idolatry. According to a decree of 3 December 1563,

In case any abuses have crept into these holy and salutary observances, the Holy Council vehemently desires to abolish them; hence no images may be exhibited that support false doctrine and give occasion of dangerous error to the uneducated. If at times the stories and narratives of Holy Scripture are represented, as expedient for the unlearned, let the people be taught that the Godhead itself is not depicted as if it could be seen with bodily eyes or expressed in color and form. Let all superstition be purged henceforth from the invocation of saints, the veneration of relics, and the sacred use of images, all base profiteering eliminated, and all lasciviousness shunned. . . . So that these decrees may be more faithfully observed, the Holy Council forbids anyone to display or cause to be displayed in any place . . . any unusual image, unless it has been approved by the bishop. In addition, no new miracles are to be admitted, nor are new relics to be accepted, unless . . . approved by the bishop.[34]

This decree stifled artistic innovation generally, as it was meant to do, but its impact on the now-contested cult of the Virgin was especially strong. The Tridentine Church downplayed the countless legendary and symbolic images of Mary, promoting only those that had strong biblical or dogmatic warrant, such as the Immaculate Conception and Assumption. Among the popular late medieval images to fall by the wayside were the St. Anne Trinity (*Anna Selbdritt*), the kiss of Joachim and Anna, the Holy Kinship, the apocryphal life of Mary, the Shrine Madonna, the Double Intercession, the Coronation by the Trinity, and the mystical hunt of the unicorn.

Needless to say, the Counter-Reformation had no interest in suppressing the Virgin's cult, and in some ways Marian piety was polemically heightened as a badge of Catholic identity and orthodoxy. Some of the iconographic types popular in Renaissance and Baroque art, especially the Immaculate Conception, could even be seen as making the Virgin *more* goddess-like insofar as they depict her alone in eternal glory, without the Child. But these images omitted Mary's intimate union with the Trinity, which had provided medieval mystics with such a focal point for identification, and at last succeeded in rendering her "alone of all her sex." In fact, all varieties of the Marian Trinity began to fall from favor, while the theme of the Immaculate Conception gradually supplanted the Coronation in sacred art. Apocryphal elements in the Marian liturgy were also suppressed, to the best of the Church's admittedly limited power in this regard. In 1568, when the breviary was revised in the wake of Trent, pseudo-Jerome's influential sermon on the Assumption (actually by Paschasius Radbertus) was deleted. At the same time Pope Pius V (1566–72) abolished the ancient Roman liturgical procession from the Lateran to Santa Maria Maggiore, which had included a ceremony commemorating Mary's reception into heaven through the solemn "meeting" of her miraculous icon with Christ's.[35]

In this context Jean Gerson, the chancellor of Paris, emerges as something of a prophetic figure. As we have seen, Gerson's concern to exert tighter ecclesiastical control over visionaries, especially women, was matched by his resistance to devotional trends that seemed to make the Virgin too autonomous. His most significant intervention in the realm of popular piety lay in his tireless efforts to promote a cult of St. Joseph and the Holy Family, which met with only limited success in his lifetime. But the activities of Gerson and other powerful churchmen did stir a rising interest in Mary's newly sainted husband. Around 1479, Pope Sixtus IV first introduced a feast of St. Joseph at Rome; in 1522, Isidore of Isolanis published the first scholastic treatise on the new saint, a *Summa de donis S. Josephi*; and by the time of Trent, at least seventy cities were observing the Josephine festival on March 19.[36] Teresa of Avila, the most important and canonical woman mystic of the sixteenth century, also promoted the cult of St. Joseph and took him as patron saint of her reformed Carmelites, because "the Lord wants us to understand that just as He was subject to St. Joseph on earth . . . so in heaven God does whatever he commands."[37] Teresa's veneration of the man who was Mary's lord symbolically parallels her own, often difficult submission to ecclesiastical authorities, who subjected her life's work to a perpetual (as well as posthumous) scrutiny beyond what even Birgitta or Catherine of Siena had to endure.

Real as well as symbolic women were suppressed in the Tridentine re-
forms. For instance, one of the last acts of the bishops at Trent was to demand
more stringent enforcement of *Periculoso*, a 1298 bull of Boniface VIII requir-
ing the strict enclosure of all nuns and tertiaries.[38] On a different front, the
ascendancy of printing served, by default, to marginalize the thin ranks of
medieval women writers even further by excluding them from literary history,
since their works were among the least likely to find publishers. Hadewijch,
Mechthild of Magdeburg, Marguerite Porete, Julian of Norwich, and most
recently "Heldris of Cornwall" were all rediscovered and printed only in
modern times. The same is true of *The Book of Margery Kempe*, although
brief, unrepresentative excerpts from it were printed in a 1521 edition that
characterized its author as a "devout anchoress."[39] Many of Christine de
Pizan's works were popular enough to attract early modern printers, yet in
England at least their authorship was frequently—if incredibly—ascribed to
their male translators.[40]

Literary, intellectual, and devotional fashions were changing rapidly. In
1570 Alcuin's *Missa de sancta Sapientia*, which had inspired Suso, was purged
from the revised missal after nearly eight centuries.[41] And in 1575 Suso himself was placed by the general of the Jesuits on a cautionary list of pious
authors not conforming to the spirit of the Society.[42] In 1576 the censored
editio princeps of Dante's *Vita Nuova* appeared, omitting the analogy between
Beatrice and Christ and the romantic theology that represents her as the
poet's "beatitude."[43] With the waning of Christian Platonism, the literary
genre I have called Platonic or Realistic allegory also waned. Although the
allegorical mode itself survived, the genre of *The Faerie Queene* or *The Pilgrim's Progress* is something quite different from the *Cosmographia* or the
Commedia: one would be hard pressed to identify "goddesses" in these later
works.[44] The prominence of imaginative theology in vernacular letters generally declined after the fifteenth century, even if such monuments as *Paradise Lost* (whose only female personification is Sin) lay still in the future.[45]
Meanwhile, in both the Reformed and Tridentine churches, theology itself
became an increasingly formalized and exclusively clerical discipline. Even
(or especially) Catholic mystics of the Counter-Reformation were expected
to conform their writings to a set pattern of mystical theology based on
approved authors, with little room for the kind of imaginative free play
characteristic of a Hadewijch or a Mechthild.

Of all the medieval goddesses, it was Frau Minne who faded most quickly
and thoroughly. Not only did the long-lasting vogue for *fin' amors* finally
exhaust itself, but the impassioned eroticism of much medieval piety came
to impress later spiritual writers (and historians) as carnal and embarrassing,

characteristic at best of women who lacked the intellectual capacity for purer forms of contemplation. In fact, the association of "love mysticism" with female inferiority and sentimentality became such a pervasive scholarly cliché that it not only distorted the evaluation of women mystics, but also obscured the extent to which male writers, such as the neglected Gérard of Liège and Lamprecht of Regensburg, cultivated and promoted this form of piety. The goddess Natura, on the other hand, retained more vitality than any of her medieval sisters. It was probably her greater secularity, her distancing from the concerns of dogmatic theology and affective devotion, that enabled this goddess to survive both Reformation and Counter-Reformation, and even to flourish with renewed vigor in the age of enlightenment. Interestingly, the early modern goddess Nature would retreat somewhat from her late medieval obsession with sexuality and gender to regain the "scientific" terrain that Bernard Silvestris had originally mapped out for her, as a personification of the cosmos and a warrant for its careful observation and study. Natura's feminine gender would also take on new and darker meanings with the rise of scientific narratives about exploration and conquest of the natural world, which included the sometimes violent baring of Nature's virginal "secrets."[46]

The most unpredictable destiny awaited Sophia, the goddess of the Bible. While the devotion to Eternal Wisdom diminished in the sixteenth century and never regained the popularity it had enjoyed in the fifteenth, Suso's *Horologium* had circulated too widely to be altogether forgotten. The Breton preacher St. Louis-Marie Grignion de Montfort (1673–1716) promoted a very similar brand of spirituality in his treatise, *The Love of Eternal Wisdom*, and even founded a women's religious order known as Les Filles de la Sagesse, the Daughters of Wisdom.[47] But the French saint, who was intensely devoted to Mary, did not preserve the dual gender of Eternal Wisdom, although he did remark on it as a notable feature of Suso's vision.[48] Instead, devotion to the feminine Sophia flourished chiefly on Protestant soil, in theosophical and esoteric circles inspired by the work of Jacob Boehme (1575–1624). The immensely influential "cobbler of Görlitz," though condemned and silenced for a time by his orthodox Lutheran pastor, wrote prolifically in his later years and gathered a circle of disciples by whom his thought was disseminated throughout Europe. Both German pietism and virtually all modern schools of theosophy have deep roots in his work.

Heir to the Rhineland mysticism of Eckhart, Suso, and Tauler, Boehme was also conversant with Neoplatonism, Renaissance kabbalah, and alchemy. He may have known the *Aurora consurgens*, for his first seminal work was

titled simply *Aurora* (1612), and he was fond of couching his difficult theosophical ideas in alchemical metaphors. As in the *Horologium Sapientiae*, the
goal of Christian life for Boehme was spiritual marriage with the Virgin
Sophia, a protean figure whom he described at one point as "the body of
the Holy Trinity," although she is also queen of heaven, bride of the soul,
virginal divine Mother, mirror of the Godhead, and much else.[49] She is
identified in distinct ways with all three Persons of the Trinity, as well as
the Virgin Mary. Moreover, it was Boehme who, for the first time, explicitly
characterized Sophia as the medium or vessel of divine imagination, and
accordingly named the imagination as the faculty through which fallen man
could best achieve reunion with her.[50] Among the disciples of Boehme's
sophianic mysticism were Johann Gichtel, Gottfried Arnold, and Franz von
Baader in Germany; John Pordage, Jane Leade, and William Law in England;
Louis-Claude de Saint-Martin in France; and Johann Conrad Beissel, who
founded the eighteenth-century pietist community of Ephrata in Pennsylvania. Boehme also exerted a decisive influence on the poets Angelus Silesius
and William Blake, and later still, on the Russian school of sophiologists—
Vladimir Solovyov, Pavel Florensky, and Sergei Bulgakov. A few recent studies have begun to address the continuities between late medieval piety and
early modern theosophy.[51] But these latter-day devotees of Sophia, whether
or not they considered themselves to be loyal Protestants, Catholics, or
Orthodox Christians, were aware of following an esoteric or alternative path
in a way that distinguishes them from most of their medieval precursors. The
goddess piety of modern Christian theosophists is necessarily more self-
conscious, because further from the mainstream, than it was in the golden
age of goddesses.

Medieval Christianity as an Inclusive Monotheism

So profound is the link between monotheism and maleness that, in the traditional symbolisms of the West, even the abstract principles of unity and
plurality are gendered male and female.[52] The great creedal assertions of
Judaism, Christianity, and Islam strenuously uphold the oneness of God,
while his maleness is simply assumed. In the more impersonal forms of
monotheism, like those developed by Plotinus in the West and Sankara in
the East, the One is elevated above all distinctions of person and gender—
but never in any instance is it female. For this reason, feminist consciousness
has contributed an ample share to the critiques of monotheism which have

arisen in recent decades from such diverse quarters as resurgent paganism, archetypal psychology, and postcolonial theory.[53] These critiques, however, sometimes flatter their object by attacking a purer, more austere form of monotheism than the more or less mitigated brands that history often presents to us.

Champions of monotheism have shared this concern for purity. Until quite recently, most scholars of comparative religion accepted a theological and developmental hierarchy that ranks monotheistic religions as "higher" or "more advanced" than polytheistic ones. In the three Abrahamic traditions, monotheism has been a point of special pride and enters into a number of polemical discourses. Judaism, for example, is often represented by its adherents as purer than Christianity because the latter admits a Trinity, thus jeopardizing the divine oneness. For Tikva Frymer-Kensky, the Christian idea of God is a "mystification of monotheism"; for Lenn Evan Goodman, it is a "compromise with pagan archetypalism."[54] In Islam, associating any partner with God (*shirk*) is the greatest of sins, and the Trinitarian doctrine is the ultimate heresy: "Say: 'He is God, One, . . . who begets not and is not begotten, and no one is His equal'" (Qur'an, Sura 112). Protestant polemicists have often condemned the Catholic cult of saints for the same reason Jews and Muslims have condemned the Trinity: it is idolatrous, an offense against the honor of God. Even today, biblical scholarship suggesting that the religion of ancient Israel was anything other than fully monotheistic is resisted by many orthodox Jews and conservative Christians.

The question of what is at stake in monotheism has been visited many times.[55] Most simply, if God is one then the universe is one. This insight is expressed both metaphysically and ethically. Only monotheism posits a single source and ultimate unity of all being; only monotheism enables the integration of all truths and values in one rational, aesthetic, and moral whole. Conversely, in a polytheistic world-view, the universe is "understood as a balance of interactive forces."[56] Gods and goddesses clash, compete, collaborate, and intercede with each other. Insofar as they represent elemental human drives or forces within nature, each acts autonomously in his or her own sphere, yet functions in complex interdependence with all the rest. Humans can work the system by playing the deities off against one another, cultivating their own special patrons, seeking help from the more propitious gods against the more threatening. Victory or slaughter, fair winds or shipwreck, fertility or barrenness, may hang in the balance. But if a single God rules over all, there can be no such division of labor, no Olympian system of checks and balances. The all-sufficient God "who made heaven and earth" must meet all human needs and command all human loyalty: "I am the Lord, and there is no other" (Isa. 45.5). Religion, like cosmology and ethics, now coheres around a single center of value. From this unique and stable center may devolve infinite gradations of being, hierarchies of perfection, chains of angelic and human command; yet all remain subordinate to the One.

While all monotheistic faiths share a conception of the divine as unified, not all have the same philosophical structure. Historically, monotheism seems never to be a primitive or indigenous faith, but can emerge from an older polytheistic matrix under varying circumstances.[57] Since classical Christian theism represents a convergence of two monotheistic systems, the Jewish and the Hellenistic, it may be instructive to look at their differences.[58] In the Hebrew Bible we see an *exclusive* monotheism that emerged as a radical reform movement, championed by prophets and occasional kings, among a people who had originally worshipped several deities in addition to their chief god, YHWH.[59] The biblical God is famously jealous, brooking no rival to his sovereignty. In Greek religion, on the other hand, Stoic and especially Platonic philosophers, culminating in Plotinus, developed versions of *inclusive* monotheism that combined belief in a supreme deity—conceived as a transcendent, unknowable One—with tolerance for the traditional cultic polytheism. Since the One was not a personal being, the potential for jealousy did not arise. The singularity of this God lay not in its numerical uniqueness, but in its ultimacy as the source of all being, both intelligible and material. Broadly speaking, in an exclusive monotheism other deities— "false gods" or demons—are *enemies* of the true God, while in an inclusive monotheism, subordinate deities are *emanations* or *emissaries* of the One God. Inclusive monotheisms seek to reconcile a belief in ultimate Oneness with a diversity of divine manifestations and mediators, while exclusive monotheisms insist radically on the adoration of one and only one God.[60]

The polemical and devotional thrust of the Hebrew Bible is strongly monotheistic. But in its histories as well as its prophetic exhortations, it reveals numerous traces of an earlier Israelite religion that was not. Biblical references to divine beings other than YHWH include several overlapping categories: (a) the inimical "gods of the nations," over whom YHWH triumphs in war; (b) indigenous deities worshipped in Israel, much to the prophets' disgust (chiefly Baal, but also El, Asherah, Chemosh, and the "Queen of heaven"); (c) idols and "graven images" denounced as false gods; (d) the council of gods, or "sons of the Most High," over whom YHWH presides in state (notably in the prologue of Job); (e) angels or "watchers," often understood as messengers or armies serving the Lord of hosts; and

(f) God's daughter, Sophia. In the prophetic crusade for exclusive monotheism, the foreign and rival gods in the first three groups were declared to be utter nonentities or else demoted to the status of demons, a form in which they continued to play a role in Jewish popular belief and folklore. As for the angels and "sons of the Most High," who constituted God's heavenly court, these might still be accommodated once they had been duly subordinated. Thus Psalm 82, according to Frymer-Kensky, stages "a mythical rendering of the advent of monotheism."[61] The true, universal God there takes "his place in the divine council: in the midst of the gods he holds judgment," dethroning the "sons of the Most High" because "they have neither knowledge nor understanding" and "judge unjustly." Those who had once been worshipped as deities are cut down to mere human stature: "I say, 'You are gods, . . . nevertheless, you shall die like men, and fall like any prince.'" Yet these angelic beings retained a role in the mystical Judaism that eventually developed into kabbalah, a more inclusive brand of monotheism; and Sophia too would have an illustrious future in Judaism as the feminized Torah, Shekinah, or Sabbath-bride.[62]

Hellenistic monotheism developed rather differently, by rationalizing and allegorizing rather than demonizing or abolishing the old pagan gods. Taking Plato's metaphysics as their starting point, the Middle and Neoplatonic philosophers, along with some Neopythagoreans and Stoics, made the fundamental innovation of positing the Forms, which in Plato's thought had been eternal, freestanding entities, as ideas within the Mind of God.[63] By thus collapsing Plato's Demiurge and his Forms into a single divine reality, these philosophers took the momentous step to a theology of inclusive monotheism. Since all beings derive from the One in a long sequence of emanations or theophanies, the existence of multiple deities at intermediate levels of reality does not compromise or threaten the ultimate unity of the Divine. Auxiliary gods need not be denied so long as they are seen to be ontologically grounded in the One. For the Alexandrian Judaism of Philo, and for the church fathers influenced by him, the most important element of this mystical monotheism was the idea of the Divine Mind itself—variously termed the "Second God" or Monad in Neoplatonism, the Logos in Stoicism, and Sophia in Jewish Platonism. Early Christians, beginning with Paul and the evangelists Matthew and John, found this dual-gendered Logos-Sophia to be exactly the mediator they required to account for the divinity and ontological status of their Messiah.

In the rise of Christianity, unlike Judaism or Islam, monotheism did not have to struggle for dominance against an older polytheism. Rather, early

Christians fought to preserve their prized heritage of Jewish monotheism against a "polytheistic" threat from within—their own overwhelming conviction of the Savior's divinity. In their determination to compromise neither the unity of God nor the divinity of Jesus, the fathers of the Church arrived after centuries of debate at their classic paradox of "one God in three divine Persons." Most analyses of the ancient Trinitarian controversies place the emphasis where it fell historically, on the orthodox refusal to accept the Arian or any other subordinationist christology that would have made the Redeemer less than perfectly divine. But the other stake in the argument, though no less significant, is usually taken for granted. Even while agreeing to speak of three divine and coequal persons, the fathers rejected the formula of "three gods" and vehemently insisted, despite Jewish objections, that they were still monotheists. Yet it would have been easy enough to speak of Christ as a "second God" beneath or beside God the Father. Such terminology had strong precedents in Neoplatonic and Gnostic theologies, and even in Philo;[64] the importance of Father-Son language in Christianity would almost have seemed to demand this solution. By analogy, one could argue that Apollo is no less divine than Zeus, yet he is *not* Zeus. Christians, however, could not accept the idea of two or three *equal* gods (as opposed to the hierarchically ordered emanations of pagan monotheism) because they would logically have limited one another: though they might be equal, they would be equally finite. An infinite God must of necessity be the sole God. It was thus the very insistence on Christ's equality with the Father that "safeguarded monotheism," though at the price of extreme paradox. As the fifth-century 'Athanasian' Creed put it, "we are compelled by Christian truth to confess that each person is individually God and Lord, as we are forbidden by the Catholic religion to say that there are three Gods or three Lords."[65] Christianity is, by any standard, a very special sort of monotheism, carrying the logic of identity-within-difference to its furthest point.

Aside from its unique Trinitarian doctrine, the early Church demonstrated tendencies toward both exclusive and inclusive monotheism in its missionary expansion. Patristic literature from Tertullian to Augustine is filled with diatribes against the pagan gods as uncompromising as any in the Hebrew prophets, and some Christian missionaries acted on this conviction by destroying pagan statues and chopping down sacred groves as if they were the haunts of bloodthirsty demons. Others were more tolerant, however. The history of early medieval conversion includes not a few pagan deities transmogrified into Christian saints (the most famous is St. Brigit of Ireland) and a great many ancient goddess temples reborn as shrines of the Virgin,

from the Parthenon to "Santa Maria sopra Minerva" in Rome to the cathedral of Chartres.[66] If a classical temple to the goddess of wisdom could be
cultically rededicated to Sapientia-Maria, the same transfer was carried out
on an intellectual plane by the mythographers. From Remigius of Auxerre
to John Ridewall and the poet of the *Ovide moralisé*, these medieval literary
critics toiled diligently at a project already commenced by the pagan Fulgentius in antiquity. The gods and goddesses of ancient Rome, cleansed of
their cultic taint by the magic wand of allegoresis, retained dominion over
their planetary spheres and at the same time gained new life as virtues, natural forces, or even figures of Christian sacrality, as when Bernard Silvestris
discovered a likeness of the Trinity in Jove, Pallas Athene, and Juno.[67]

But syncretism in the interest of converting pagans and a desire to rehabilitate classical culture were not the only motives of medieval inclusive
monotheism. Theology also responds to felt religious needs, and one such
need that almost inevitably emerges in monotheistic systems is a yearning
for mediation with the Almighty. In medieval Christianity, this demand was
met on several levels, which I will call the political or ethical, the cosmological, and the mystical.

In a polytheistic world-view, no single god is omnipotent and thus no
problem of theodicy arises. Evil, when it is not the clear responsibility of
humans, can be blamed on hostile cosmic forces, or on the defeat of one's
personal and national gods by potent rivals, as in the *Iliad*. In monotheism,
however, there is no such escape. Even if allegiance to the One God is tem-
pered by a belief in the devil or demons, these are in the last analysis God's
creatures, and the Almighty must either permit or actively will their part
in the cosmic drama. If demons are rejected, humans themselves bear the
sole responsibility for evil: even the natural world has been "subjected to
futility" and "groans in travail" on account of human sin (Rom. 8.19–22). No
longer do the gods and goddesses mediate between humankind and the
capricious forces of nature; rather, humans alone have the awesome responsibility of mediating between nature and God. The Hebrew prophets, as
Frymer-Kensky notes, rejected the utility of even ritual mediation through
sacrifice: only pure ethical behavior could secure divine favor and forestall
cosmic catastrophe. Herein lies "the dramatic inner core of monotheism: the
awesome solo mastery of God brings humans into direct unadulterated con-
tact with supreme power. All of humankind's actions stand in sharp relief,
and human destiny is irrevocably in human hands. . . . There are no intermediaries, no buffers, no intercessors. There is only us and God."[68]

For Christians, the starkness of this position was mitigated in theory by the "one mediator between God and humans, the man Christ Jesus" (1 Tim. 2.5). But in practice, since Christ was not only Savior but also Judge, the faithful quickly perceived a need for mediation with the Mediator himself. Not daring in their mortal frailty to approach the Sinless One, they cast about for supernatural helpers pure enough to win Christ's favor, yet tender-hearted enough to overlook their faults. The God-Man, too remote and majestic for direct access, was envisioned as a mighty emperor who could be petitioned most safely through his trusted intimates and courtiers. Thus medieval preachers often exhorted the faithful to act as a humble petitioner would if he needed to beg a favor from the king. While it might seem presumptuous to request an audience with His Majesty in person, the lowly servant would make the best of any connections he had at court, and above all, he would seek the favor of the queen, who was famous for her compassion and could always gain the royal ear. These roles, of course, belonged to the saints and the Virgin. Mary held her dignity as Queen of Heaven by a twofold title, for she was both queen consort and (even more powerfully) queen mother. With the royal family firmly established and a throng of dignitaries arriving daily at court, the Kingdom of God proclaimed by Jesus as an apocalyptic goal came to be seen as a quasi-political realm already flourishing in heaven.

This political or court-of-heaven model belonged to the common culture of medieval Christendom. It is a truism, but nonetheless true, to say that kings and paupers, women and men, priests and layfolk were united in prayer to the saints; and the Virgin, in her role as supreme intercessor, doubtless attracted even more supplications than she did in the roles of intimate piety we explored in Chapter 6. The favors sought from the saints were eminently practical—healing for oneself or one's child, a successful harvest, a good death, a safe delivery, strength to resist temptation. As mediators and intercessors, the saints were only human, yet received cultic honors that might well have been deemed worthy of lesser gods in a polytheistic system. But this well-known model of mediation was not the only one available in the medieval Church; the less familiar cosmological and mystical models coexisted with it. While the first model was universal and popular, the others had a more elite status, appealing to the learned or the exceptionally devout. It is here that we encounter the goddesses once again.

In ancient philosophical constructions of monotheism, the need for mediation is not so much ethical or practical as cosmological. Between the One and the many, between absolute and contingent being, deity and cosmos, spirit and matter, stretches a gulf that is bridged not by a creative *fiat* as in biblical cosmology, but by a series of divine processions or emanations that culminate in the visible world. Twelfth-century theologians, as we saw, briefly experimented with adapting the Neoplatonic triad of the One, the Nous, and the world soul to account for the creative roles of Father, Son, and Holy Spirit. But this experiment lay open to two major objections (aside from the usual charge of "novelty"): first, that the Neoplatonic trinity introduced subordination within the Godhead, which the Christian Trinity could not admit; and second, that the Holy Spirit as world soul would be *too* intimately united with the cosmos, eliding the absolute otherness that divides Creator from creature. Setting Natura in the role of mediatrix, however, resolved both philosophical problems. As a fourth "person," God's daughter rather his Son, she could be properly subordinate to the Trinity (for daughters are never equal); and she would not be the soul of the cosmos but rather its artisan, responsible for maintaining life on earth through procreation. Ancient Neoplatonists had developed their system of emanations, in part, because they believed that the One was too pure to be soiled with matter, even in the role of its Creator; hence the need to set intermediaries between God and the world. Christian Platonists could not share this view, believing as they did in the Incarnation; yet the medieval Church did resist the idea of any direct link between God and sexuality. Here too, Natura solved a cosmological problem, creating a buffer zone between the asexual author of life and the endless sexual acts required to preserve it.

Although Natura was a philosophical rather than a cultic mediator, her emergence as a goddess profoundly altered the way that at least some medieval Christians—and their heirs— perceived the world. Subjected to her secondary divinity, the natural world (including the realm of sexuality) could be re-imagined as neither wholly sacred nor wholly profane. If the cosmos had been wholly sacred, it would be ruled not by natural law but by miracle: every thunderstorm would be an act of God, every earthquake a divine intervention—as indeed they are in many a monastic chronicle. If it were wholly profane, on the other hand, the heavens could no longer tell the glory of God, nor the firmament proclaim his handiwork, and mortals could learn nothing about the Creator from the fallen estate of his creatures. Viewing the physical world as Nature's domain opened a middle way between these options. In the sexual realm, her dominion served on the one hand to liberate sexual ethics from the deep pessimism bequeathed by Augustine, while on the other, it promoted the stigmatization of homosexuality as a "sin against nature." But no univocal system of value or meaning was ever attached to the goddess. Perhaps the most striking trait shared by the texts featuring Natura is their very contentiousness, their deep ambiguity. *De planctu Naturae*, the *Roman de la Rose*, the *Roman de Silence*, and the *Parlement of Fowles* all lie open to multiple interpretations; the ones I have given are by no means definitive. In the long run, Natura's most important role in imaginative theology may have been to open precisely this space for questioning and ethical debate—in a realm beyond the bastions of scholastic thought, where laymen and at times even women could have their say.

Like the saints, the goddess Natura is a mediator who stands *between* God and the world. In our third or mystical model, the divine mediatrix is more precisely a manifestation of God *in* the world, a theophany of God's presence and saving action. This model can be applied to a great variety of medieval goddess figures, including Mater Ecclesia (or Lady Holy Church) and the Franciscans' Lady Poverty. But it is preeminently true of the two goddesses who have scriptural warrant: Lady Love ("Deus caritas est," 1 John 4.8) and Sapientia or Eternal Wisdom ("Christum . . . Dei sapientiam," 1 Cor. 1.24). The poets and mystics who cultivated relationships with these figures had discovered ways to express and experience God as a goddess, though never exclusively so, and never with the defiant edge that inescapably attends my claim. Goddesses as mystical mediators offered intimacy with the Divine, spiritual marriage, and participation in the various aspects or energies of God's being. Sometimes this participation is sacramental: Jesus as Mother both shelters the faithful in his womb/mind/wounded side and nurses them with the breast milk that is his blood. "Mother Church" does the same, giving birth through the womb/font of baptism and suckling her "babes" with the sweet milk of doctrine. Sometimes the participation is erotic: Frau Minne is a divine dominatrix and Eternal Wisdom an alluring seductress, while Lady Poverty converts the hard life of penury and homelessness into celestial romance. Sometimes the participation is revelatory: Lady Philosophy, Lady Reason, and their sisters manifest their love for mortals by revealing heavenly secrets that unlock the mystery of life on earth.

Given the overwhelming predominance of masculine God-language in Christianity, as well as the physical maleness of Jesus and his priests, a degree of androgyny almost inevitably attends these goddess figures. An imagination anchored in the concrete would never forget that, although the Church might be symbolically a mother, the priests who actually baptized, preached, taught, and administered the eucharist were all men. Suso's male Disciple sought the hand of the radiant Sapientia, while his female disciples married Jesus in their religious vows—yet the bride/groom of them all was one and the same. Dante alone reversed the positions of the abstract and the concrete term in this symbolic economy: for him a specific woman became the theophany, agent, and embodiment of the abstractly masculine Amor. Now skeptics might object that none of these medieval goddesses qualify as "real" goddesses because, in the end, they are all personifications or masks of the One God, who is "really" male. But such a view seriously underestimates the sophistication of the writers in question, who were sound enough theologians to be aware that the infinite God, free of all biological limitations, is "really" neither male nor female. More important, the skeptical view fails to explain why imaginative theology and literature were so preoccupied with goddesses in the first place. One explanation, which I have already suggested in Chapter 1, is so simple and obvious as to have been overlooked by almost everyone—namely that human beings, who come in two sexes, will always find ways to imagine personal divinity in both sexes, no matter how many barriers a formal religious system may set in their way.

Another explanation is more speculative, anchored in the particular history and structure of Christianity as an inclusive monotheism. From a very early date Christians, accustomed to thinking of God as three-yet-one, of Christ as God-yet-man, and of Mary as virgin-yet-mother, came to regard paradox itself as a touchstone of revealed truth. This love of the paradoxical is witnessed by countless formulas ranging from the famous *credo quia absurdum* ("I believe because it is absurd"), ascribed to Tertullian,[69] to the mind-bending formulations of the Athanasian Creed. The same kind of non-Euclidean logic could support a kindred paradox: this unique God might also be conceived as male-yet-female, Logos-and-Sophia, bridegroom-and-bride. Yet the androgyny of God—unlike the Trinity, the divine humanity, or the virgin birth—never became a matter of dogma. Quite the contrary: because of the prevailing climate of misogyny, reinforced by the Church's open rivalry with cultic polytheism and Gnostic speculative mythologies, this theme could be handled only at a metaphorical depth that lay well beneath the ken of doctrinal pronouncements. Neither officially affirmed nor categorically denied, the feminine Divine remained in the dark penumbra of the monotheistic sun. There it languished until the twelfth century, when the burgeoning intellectual energies of the age found expression in a new wave of imaginative theology that launched the golden age of goddesses.

When we take into consideration *all* the pantheons of medieval Christendom—the Virgin and the saints, the nine orders of angels, the allegorized pagan deities of astrology and poetry, the goddesses of imaginative theology—the religion of the *litterati* appears to have been a very inclusive monotheism indeed. Once again, "inclusive" here implies not tolerance of dissent or celebration of human diversity, but a recognition that the glory of the One God is mediated; that God can be, and is, manifest in immeasurably varied ways. Like the pagan Neoplatonism of antiquity, or kabbalistic Judaism, or certain Hindu theologies that combine philosophical monism with cultic worship of many gods, the monotheism of the medieval Church can be usefully contrasted with more exclusive monotheistic faiths, such as rabbinic Judaism, Islam, and most forms of Protestantism. The medieval Church, though notably intent on enforcing orthodox belief in a way that is not characteristic of Neoplatonism or Hinduism, could accept surprisingly bold and original forms of religious expression so long as they were conveyed through the media of poetry, sacred art, visionary experience, and devotional practice. With the Reformation, however, the clarion call of H. R. Niebuhr's "radical monotheism" rang out once more: "I am the Lord, and there is no other; besides me there is no God." Banished by the reformers and subdued by Rome—though sheltered in a secret conventicle here and a mystic brotherhood there—the goddesses dwindled until they faded from common sight; and with them, a remarkable era in the history of Christianity came to an end.

Abbreviations

CCCM	*Corpus christianorum: continuatio mediaevalis* (Turnhout: Brepols, 1966–)
CCSL	*Corpus christianorum: series latina* (Turnhout: Brepols, 1953–)
CSEL	*Corpus scriptorum ecclesiasticorum latinorum* (Vienna: C. Gerold, 1866–1974)
EETS	Early English Text Society
MGH	*Monumenta Germaniae historica*
PG	J.-P. Migne, *Patrologiae cursus completus: series graeca*, 162 vols. (Paris: Migne, 1857–66)
PL	J.-P. Migne, *Patrologiae cursus completus: series latina*, 221 vols. (Paris: Migne, 1861–64)
SC	*Sources chrétiennes* (Paris: Éditions du Cerf, 1941–)

Notes

Preface

1. Ennodius, *Carmina* I.4.84–85, in *Opera Omnia*, ed. William Hartel, CSEL 6 (Vienna: C. Gerold, 1882), 515.

2. C. S. Lewis, *The Allegory of Love: A Study in Medieval Tradition* (London: Oxford University Press, 1936), 78.

Chapter 1. God and the Goddesses

1. C. S. Lewis, *The Allegory of Love: A Study in Medieval Tradition* (London: Oxford University Press, 1936), 83.

2. Alain de Lille, *Anticlaudianus*, ed. Robert Bossuat (Paris: J. Vrin, 1955); trans. James Sheridan as *Anticlaudianus, or The Good and Perfect Man* (Toronto: Pontifical Institute of Mediaeval Studies, 1973).

3. Robert Grosseteste, *Le Château d'Amour*, ed. J. Murray (Paris: Champion, 1918); a Middle English translation was edited by Carl Horstmann in *The Minor Poems of the Vernon Manuscript*, Part I, EETS o.s. 98 (London, 1892; rpt. Millwood, N.Y.: Kraus, 1987), 355–406. The description is Murray's, p. 67.

4. "Quest' è colei ch'è tanto posta in croce / pur da color che le dovrien dar lode, / dandole biasmo a torto e mala voce; // ma ella s'è beata e ciò non ode: / con l'altre prime creature lieta / volve sua spera e beata si gode." *Inferno* VII.91–96. "This is she who is so crucified / by the very ones who ought to give her praise: / wrongly they give her blame and ill repute. // But she is blessed and does not hear them; / glad with the other primal creatures, / she turns her sphere and in bliss rejoices." Dante does not say exactly where in the heavens Fortuna resides. Perhaps he meant her to be understood as the intelligence of the first sphere, the moon—home of blessed spirits whose constancy was dimmed by adverse fortune.

5. Erich Neumann, *The Great Mother: An Analysis of the Archetype*, trans. Ralph Manheim (Princeton, N.J.: Princeton University Press, 1955); Marija Gimbutas, *The Language of the Goddess* (San Francisco: Harper, 1989).

6. *Sacrum commercium* [SC], in *Fontes Franciscani*, ed. Enrico Menestò and Stefano Brufani (Assisi: Edizioni Porziuncola, 1995): 1693–1732. The translations below are my own, but there is a published one by Placid Hermann in *St. Francis of Assisi: Writings and Early Biographies*, ed. Marion Habig (Chicago: Franciscan Herald Press, 1973), 1533–96.

7. "Ecce, iam venio, fratres et filii mei, vobiscum," says Lady Poverty, "sciens me de vobis lucraturam quamplures." SC c. 29, 728. Brufani proposes the title *Sacra alleanza* or *Sacred Alliance*, 695.

8. Barbara Rosenwein and Lester K. Little, "Social Meaning in the Monastic and Mendicant Spiritualities," *Past & Present* 63 (1974): 4–32.

9. "Adducentes eam in quodam colle ostenderunt ei totum orbem quem respicere poterant, dicentes: 'Hoc est claustrum nostrum, domina.'" SC c. 30, 1730.

10. "Actum mense iulii post obitum beati Francisci anno 1227." According to Brufani, all six mss. that include this colophon belong to the same branch of the stemma, which has no more or less authority than the branch that lacks it. Introduzione, 1696.

11. Brufani, Introduzione, 1697, 1702. According to Hermann, two late sources name the author as Friar John of Parma, who was minister general of the order from 1247 to 1257. Introduction to English translation, 1534.

12. The *Sacrum commercium* is a likely source for Dante's account of the mystical marriage of St. Francis, narrated by Thomas Aquinas in *Paradiso* XI.

13. "Cepit sedule velut curiosus explorator circuire vicos et plateas civitatis, diligenter querens quam diligebat anima sua. Interrogabat stantes, percunctabatur advenientes, sic dicens: 'Num quam diligit anima mea vidistis?' Sed erat verbum istud absconditum ab eis, et velut barbarum. Non intelligentes eum, dicebant ei: 'O homo, nescimus quid loquaris. Loquere nobis in lingua nostra et respondebimus tibi.'" SC 1, 1706. All biblical citations refer to the Vulgate.

14. "Sicque in solio nuditatis sue domina Paupertas se reclinans . . ." SC 4, 1710.

15. Guillaume de Lorris, *Le Roman de la Rose*, ll. 441–55, ed. Daniel Poirion (Paris: Garnier-Flammarion, 1974), 54.

16. "Ad te venimus, domina nostra; obsecramus, suscipe nos in pace. Servi effici cupimus Domini virtutum, quia ipse est Rex glorie. Audivimus te reginam fore virtutum et utcumque experimento didicimus. Propterea, tuis pedibus provoluti, supplicamus humiliter ut digneris esse nobiscum et sis nobis via perveniendi ad Regem glorie . . . Scimus enim quod tua est potentia, tuum regnum, tu es super omnes virtutes a Rege regum regina et domina constituta. . . . Nam ipse Rex regum et Dominus dominantium, Creator celi et terre, concupivit speciem et decorem tuum." The text plays on the double meaning of *virtus* to create a parallel between the "Lord of hosts" and the "Queen of virtues." SC 5, 1710.

17. "Non sum rudis, sicut multi putant, sed antiqua satis et dierum numero plena, sciens rerum dispositiones, creaturarum varietates, temporum mutabilitates." SC 7, 1713; cf. Wisd. 7.17–20.

18. SC 6, 1712.

19. "Verus est sermo quem audivimus in terra nostra super sermonibus tuis et super sapientia tua; et multo maior est sapientia tua quam rumor quem audivimus. Beati viri tui et beati servi tui, ii qui sunt coram te semper et audiunt sapientiam tuam." SC 28, 1727.

20. "Sicque supra nudam humum nudam se proiecit." SC 30, 1730.

21. "Petiit aliquas saltem herbas odoriferas crudas sibi preberi. Sed hortulanum non habentes et hortum nescientes, collegerunt in silva herbas agrestes et posuerunt

coram ea. Que ait: 'Parum salis afferte ut saliam herbas, quoniam amare sunt.' 'Exspecta—inquiunt—domina, quousque civitatem intremus et afferamus tibi, si fuerit qui prebeat nobis.' 'Prebete—inquit—mihi cultellum ut emundem superflua et incidam panem, quia valde durus et siccus est.' Dicunt ei: 'Domina, non habemus fabrum ferrarium, qui nobis faciat gladios; nunc autem dentibus cultelli vice utere et postea providebimus.' 'Et vinum apud vos est aliquantulum?' dixit. Responderunt illi dicentes: 'Domina nostra, vinum non habemus, quia initium vite hominis panis et aqua, et tibi bibere vinum non est bonum, quoniam sponsa Christi vinum debet fugere pro veneno.'" SC 30, 1729–30.

22. "Vere Dominus est vobiscum, et ego nesciebam. Ecce quod concupivi iam video, quod desideravi iam teneo, quoniam illis sum coniuncta in terris, qui mihi imaginem representant eius cui sum desponsata in celis." SC 31, 1730.

23. "Lady Holy Poverty" is greeted in Francis's "Salutation of the Virtues" along with her numerous "sisters," but she is not called the queen of virtues; that title is given to Wisdom in accord with tradition. On his deathbed, Francis is said to have exhorted his brothers to "always love and be faithful to our Lady Holy Poverty." See *Francis and Clare: The Complete Works*, trans. Regis Armstrong and Ignatius Brady (New York: Paulist Press, 1982), 151, 164.

24. "In eternum et in seculum seculi iuramus et statuimus custodire iudicia iustitie tue." SC 28, 1728.

25. Good treatments of Mechthild in English include Amy Hollywood, *The Soul as Virgin Wife: Mechthild of Magdeburg, Marguerite Porete, and Meister Eckhart* (Notre Dame, Ind.: University of Notre Dame Press, 1995), 57–86; Ulrike Wiethaus, *Ecstatic Transformation: Transpersonal Psychology in the Work of Mechthild von Magdeburg* (Syracuse, N.Y.: Syracuse University Press, 1996); and Bernard McGinn, *The Flowering of Mysticism: Men and Women in the New Mysticism, 1200–1350* (New York: Crossroad, 1998), 222–44. For the history of scholarship see Frank Tobin, *Mechthild von Magdeburg: A Medieval Mystic in Modern Eyes* (Columbia, S.C.: Camden House, 1995).

26. Die sele kam zuo der minne und gruoste si mit tieffen sinnen und sprach: "Got grüsse úch, vro minne." "Got lone úch, [liebú] vro kúneginne." "Vro minne, ir sint sere vollekomen." "Vro kúneginne, des bin ich allen dingen oben." "Vro minne, ir hant manig jar gerungen, e ir habint die hohen drivaltekeit dar zuo betwungen, das sú sich alzemale hat gegossen in Marien demütigen magetuom." "Frovwe kúneginne, das ist úwer ere und vrome." "Frov minne, *nu sint ir har zuo mir komen und* ir hant mir alles benomen, das ich in ertrich ie gewan." "Frovwe kúnegin, ir hant einen seligen wehsel getan." "Frovwe minne, ir hant mir benomen mine kintheit." "Frovwe kúneginne, da wider han ich úch gegeben himelsche vriheit." "Frovwe minne, ir hant mir benomen alle mine jugent." "Frovwe kúnegin, da wider han ich úch gegeben manig helige tugent." "Frovwe minne, ir hant mir benomen guot, frúnde und mage." "Eya frovwe kúnegin, das ist ein snödú klage." "Frovwe minne, ir hant mir benomen die welt, weltlich ere und allen weltlichen richtuom." "Frovwe kúnegin, das wil ich úch in einer stunde mit dem heiligen geiste nach allem úwerm willen in ertrich gelten." "Frovwe minne, ir hant mich also sere betwungen, das min licham ist komen in sunderlich *krankheit*." "Frovwe kúnegin, da wider han ich úch gegeben manig hohe bekantheit." "Frovwe minne, ir hant verzert min fleisch und min bluot." "Frovwe

kúnegin, da mitte sint ir gelútert und gezogen in got." "Frovwe minne, ir sint ein rovberinne, dennoch sont ir mir gelten." "Frovwe kúnegin, so nement reht mich selben." "Frovwe minne, nu hant ir mir vergolten hundertvalt in ertriche." "Frov kúnegin, noch hant ir ze vordernde got und *alles sin* riche." Mechthild von Magdeburg, *Das fliessende Licht der Gottheit* I.1, ed. Hans Neumann (Munich: Artemis, 1990), 5–7. I have used the translation by Frank Tobin, *The Flowing Light of the Godhead* (New York: Paulist Press, 1998): 39–40, slightly altered. Tobin translates "Frouwe kúnegin" as "Mistress and Queen" to indicate the Soul's superiority in rank, but I have used "Lady Queen" to preserve the parallelism of Mechthild's language.

27. For Minne's role in beguine spirituality see Barbara Newman, *From Virile Woman to WomanChrist: Studies in Medieval Religion and Literature* (Philadelphia: University of Pennsylvania Press, 1995), 148–58.

28. Cf. Tobin's notes to *Flowing Light*, 339.

29. My account of its authorship draws on Frank Tobin, "Henry Suso and Elsbeth Stagel: Was the *Vita* a Cooperative Effort?" in Catherine Mooney, ed., *Gendered Voices: Medieval Saints and Their Interpreters* (Philadelphia: University of Pennsylvania Press, 1999), 118–35.

30. "Der minne von altem recht höret zú liden. Nu ist doch enkein werber, er sie ein lider, noch kein minner, er si ein martrer." *Seuses Leben* I.3, in *Deutsche Schriften*, ed. Karl Bihlmeyer (Stuttgart, 1907; repr. Frankfurt: Minerva, 1961), 13. The translation is from Frank Tobin, *Henry Suso: The Exemplar* (New York: Paulist Press, 1989), 68.

31. "Und sprach frilich in im selb: 'gewerlich, ez muos recht sin, si muos reht min liep sin, ich wil ir diener sin.' Und gedahte: 'ach got, wan möhti ich die lieben núwan einest gesehen, wan möhti ich núwan einest zuo ir red komen! Ach wie ist das liep gestalt, daz so vil lustlicher dingen in im hat verborgen? Weder ist es got ald mensch, frow oder man, kunst ald list, oder waz mag ez sin?' Und als verr er si in den usgeleiten bischaften der schrift mit den inren ogen gesehen mohte, do zogte si sich ime also: si swepte hoh ob ime in einem gewúlkten throne, si luhte als der morgensterne und schein als dú spilndú sunne; irú krone waz ewikeit, ire wat waz selikeit, irú wort süzzekeit, ire umbfang alles lustes gnuhsamkeit. Si waz verr und nahe, hoh und nider, si waz gegenwúrtig und doch verborgen . . . si zerspreite sich von ende ze ende gewalteklich und richte ellú ding us süsseklich." *Leben* I.3, ed. Bihlmeyer, 14; trans. Tobin, 68–69. This chapter of the *Vita* is largely borrowed from Suso's earlier Latin work, the *Horologium Sapientiae* (I.6), ed. Pius Künzle (Freiburg: Universitätsverlag, 1977).

32. There are some parallels for this lability of gender in romance. In the *Roman de la Rose*, the beloved never appears as "herself" but is often present to her lover in the guise of a young man, Fair Welcome. The romance heroine Silence and others are also disguised as men (see Chapter 3). But a man disguised as a woman would belong in a fabliau, not a romance: crossing the gender line in the "wrong" direction would be considered dishonorable or comic.

33. "So er iez wande haben ein schön jungfrowen, geswind vand er einen stolzen jungherren. Si gebaret etwen als ein wisú meisterin, etwen hielt si sich als ein vil weidenlichú minnerin." *Leben* I.3, ed. Bihlmeyer, 14; trans. Tobin, 69.

34. Barbara Newman, "Some Mediaeval Theologians and the Sophia Tradition," *Downside Review* 108 (1990): 111–30.

35. The most important texts are Proverbs 1–9, Ecclesiasticus (Sirach) 24, and Wisdom of Solomon 7–8. While the latter two books are now considered apocryphal, the medieval liturgy drew on them extensively. See Chapter 5 below, pp. 190–92.

36. Langland's poem exists in three principal versions known as the A, B, and C texts, taken by most critics to be successive revisions by the same author. The A-text was composed sometime after 1362; the much longer B-text, cited here, can be dated circa 1377–79 on the basis of allusions to events early in the reign of Richard II. The C-text was revised after the rebellion of 1381, in part to distance the poem from the use that rebel leaders had made of it. There is little external evidence about the poet, but an early 15th-century ms. (Dublin, Trinity College ms. 212, fol. 89v) identifies him as William de Langlond, son of Stacy de Rokayle, a gentleman tenant of the Despensers in Oxfordshire.

37. If we credit the famous "autobiographical" passage in the C-text, passus 5, Langland was a minor cleric who made his living by intercessory prayer, but was debarred from the priesthood by his marriage. For recent views on his vocation, see Steven Justice and Kathryn Kerby-Fulton, eds., *Written Work: Langland, Labor, and Authorship* (Philadelphia: University of Pennsylvania Press, 1997).

38. On Will's persona see especially John Bowers, *The Crisis of Will in Piers Plowman* (Washington, D.C.: Catholic University Press, 1986); Pamela Raabe, *Imitating God: The Allegory of Faith in* Piers Plowman B (Athens: University of Georgia Press, 1990), 64–100.

39. All quotations are taken from A. V. C. Schmidt, ed., *The Vision of Piers Plowman: A Complete Edition of the B-Text* (London: Dent, 1978).

40. E. Talbot Donaldson, *Piers Plowman: An Alliterative Verse Translation* (New York: Norton, 1990), 254, 258.

41. John Yunck, *The Lineage of Lady Meed: The Development of Mediaeval Venality Satire* (Notre Dame, Ind.: University of Notre Dame Press, 1963).

42. For Langland's complex views on religious poverty see Lawrence Clopper, *"Songes of Rechelesnesse": Langland and the Franciscans* (Ann Arbor: University of Michigan Press, 1997).

43. The standard biography is Charity Cannon Willard, *Christine de Pizan: Her Life and Works* (New York: Persea Books, 1984). Useful essays can be found in E. Jeffrey Richards et al., eds., *Reinterpreting Christine de Pizan* (Athens: University of Georgia Press, 1992), and Margarete Zimmermann and Dina De Rentiis, eds., *The City of Scholars: New Approaches to Christine de Pizan* (Berlin and New York: W. de Gruyter, 1994).

44. Renate Blumenfeld-Kosinski, "Saintly Scenarios in Christine de Pizan's *Livre des Trois Vertus,*" *Mediaeval Studies* 62 (2000): 255–92; E. Jeffrey Richards, "Christine de Pizan and Jean Gerson: An Intellectual Friendship," in John Campbell and Nadia Margolis, eds., *Christine de Pizan 2000: Studies on Christine de Pizan in Honour of Angus J. Kennedy* (Amsterdam: Rodopi, 2000), 197–208.

45. Maureen Quilligan, *The Allegory of Female Authority: Christine de Pizan's* Cité des Dames (Ithaca, N.Y.: Cornell University Press, 1991): 26.

46. "Adoncques si comme se je fusse resveillee de somme et dreçant la teste pour regarder dont tel lueur venoit, vi devant moy, tout en estant, iij dames couronnees de tres souveraine reverence, desquelles la resplandeur de leurs cleres faces enluminoit moy mesmes et toute la place. Lors se je fus esmerveillee, nul nel demand, considerant

sur moy l'uys clos et elles la venues. Doubtant que ce feust aucune fantasie pour me tempter, fis en mon front le signe de la croix, remplie de tres grant paour." Christine de Pizan, *Le Livre de la Cité des Dames* I.2.1, ed. E. Jeffrey Richards in *La Città delle Dame* (Milan: Luni Editrice, 1998), 46; trans. E. J. Richards, *The Book of the City of Ladies* (New York: Persea Books, 1982), 6.

47. V. A. Kolve, "The Annunciation to Christine: Authorial Empowerment in *The Book of the City of Ladies*," in Brendan Cassidy, ed., *Iconography at the Crossroads* (Princeton,N.J.: Index of Christian Art, 1993), 171–96. Kolve's fine essay also links *The City of Ladies* with Trinitarian iconography.

48. "Si loe Dieu de toute ma puissance et vous, mes dames, qui tant honorees m'avez qu'establie suis a si noble commission, laquelle reçoy par tres grant leece. Et voycy vostre chamberiere preste d'obeir: or commandez, je obeiray, et soit fait de moy selon voz paroles." *Cité des Dames* I.7.1, ed. Richards, 64; trans. Richards, 15–16.

49. Alcuin Blamires notes that in the context of earlier medieval profeminine works, Christine's monument "should have been epoch-making," yet it had little impact at the time. "It is a major irony of literary history that the text has taken agonizingly long to regain a place in 'the field of letters.'" *The Case for Women in Medieval Culture* (Oxford: Clarendon Press, 1997), 219, 229–30.

50. *La Querelle de la Rose: Letters and Documents*, ed. Joseph Baird and John Kane (Chapel Hill: University of North Carolina Press, 1978), 48–49. Christine is especially annoyed that Jean's Reason, though called the daughter of God, "denied her heavenly father" by defending obscenity.

51. Quilligan, *Allegory*, 22. Richards translates *Droitture* as Rectitude, but that term connotes a self-righteous stuffiness in American English, so I have used simply Right.

52. "Chiere fille, saches que la providence de Dieu qui riens ne laisse vague ne vuit, nous a establies, quoyque nous soyons choses celestielles, estre et frequenter entre les gens de ce bas monde affin de mettre en ordre et tenir en equité les establissemens fais par nous mesmes selon le vouloir de Dieu en divers offices, auquel Dieu toutes iij sommes filles et de lui nees." *Cité des Dames* I.3.2, ed. Richards, 52; trans. Richards, 9.

53. "Cristine amie, je suis Justice la tres singuliere fille de Dieu, et mon essence procede de sa personne purement. . . . Je suis en Dieu et Dieu est en moy et sommes comme une mesme chose. Qui me suit ne peut faillir et ma uoye est seure. . . . et entre nous iij dames que tu uois cy sommes comme une mesmes chose ne ne pourrions l'une sans l'autre. Et ce que la premiere dispose, la ije ordene et met a oeuvre et puis moy la iije parcheve la chose et la termine." *Cité des Dames* I.6, ed. Richards, 60–62; trans. Richards, 13–14.

54. *Piers Plowman* B.XVIII.

55. Earl Jeffrey Richards, "Where Are the Men in Christine de Pizan's City of Ladies? Architectural and Allegorical Structures in Christine de Pizan's *Livre de la Cité des Dames*," in Renate Blumenfeld-Kosinski et al., eds., *Translatio Studii: Essays by His Students in Honor of Karl D. Uitti* (Amsterdam: Rodopi, 1999), 225.

56. Christine's idea of a female Trinity may have been inspired at some distance by Dante, who ascribed his own salvation to three blessed ladies: Mary, Beatrice,

and Lucia. See *Inferno* II, *Paradiso* XXXII, and Joan Ferrante, *Woman as Image in Medieval Literature from the Twelfth Century to Dante* (New York: Columbia University Press, 1975), 140–41.

57. Minerva, Ceres, and Isis appear in *Cité des Dames* I.34–38. Euhemerism, an ancient theory proposed to rationalize the corpus of mythology, was popular in the Middle Ages. Christine states in the prologue to her *Epistre d'Othéa* (1399) that "because the ancients had the custom of adoring everything that seemed blessed beyond the common level of things, they called several wise women who existed in their time goddesses." Trans. in *The Selected Writings of Christine de Pizan*, ed. Renate Blumenfeld-Kosinski (New York: Norton, 1997), 32.

58. Among the criminals are Semiramis, Medea, and Circe, whom Christine attempts to rehabilitate. Her principal source for women's history, Boccaccio's *De mulieribus claris*, did not include biblical women, saints, or contemporary figures.

59. "Justice, la tres amee de mon Filz, tres voulentiers je abiteray et demoureray entre mes seurs et amies, les femmes, et avecques elles, car Raison, Droitture, toy, et aussi Nature m'i encline. Elles me servent, loent et honneurent sanz cesser. Si suis et seray a tousjours chief du sexe femenin, car ceste chose fu dés oncques en la pensee de Dieu le Pere preparlee et ordenee ou conseil de la Trinité." *Cité des Dames* III.1.3, ed. Richards, 432; trans. Richards, 218.

60. The complete passage reads: "Dar nah gewan er mengen liechten influz götlicher warheit, dero sú im ein ursach waren, unt stuont in im uf ein kosen mit der Ewigen Wisheit; und daz geschah nit mit einem liplichen kosenne noh mit bildricher entwúrt, es geschah allein mit betrahtunge in dem lieht der heiligen schrift, der entwúrt bi núti getriegen mag, also daz die entwúrt genomen sint eintweder von der Ewigen Wisheit munde, die si selber sprach an dem evangelio, oder aber von dien höhsten lerern; und begrifent eintweder dú selben wort oder den selben sin oder aber sogtan warheit, dú nah dem sinne der heiligen scrift geriht ist, usser der mund dú Ewig Wisheit hat geredet." Henry Suso, *Büchlein der Ewigen Weisheit*, prologue, in *Deutsche Schriften*, ed. Bihlmeyer, 197.

61. "Die gesihte, die hie nach stent, die geschahen ovch nút in liplicher wise, sú sint allein ein usgeleitú bischaft. . . . Er nimt an sich, als ein lerer tuon sol, aller menschen person . . . Die sinne, die hie stant, sint einvaltig; so sint dú wort noh einveltiger, wan sú gant uzzer einer einvaltigen sele und gehörent zuo einvaltigen menschen." *Büchlein*, ed. Bihlmeyer, 197–98.

62. "Visiones . . . in sequentibus contentae non sunt omnes accipiendae secundum litteram, licet multae ad litteram contingerint, sed est figurata locutio." *Horologium Sapientiae*, prologue, 366.

63. "Le chemin que tu vois plus drois, / Plus estroit et plus verdoiant, / La face de Dieu est voiant / Cil qui le suit jusqu'a la fin." Christine de Pizan, *Le Livre du chemin de long estude*, lines 902–5, ed. Robert Püschel (Berlin, 1887; rpt. Geneva: Slatkine, 1974), 39; trans. Kevin Brownlee in *Selected Writings*, ed. Blumenfeld-Kosinski, 71.

64. Peter Dinzelbacher, *Vision und Visionsliteratur im Mittelalter* (Stuttgart: Hiersemann, 1981), 65–77. See also idem, "Zur Interpretation erlebnismystischer Texte des Mittelalters," *Zeitschrift für deutsches Altertum und deutsche Literatur* 117 (1988): 1–23. Dinzelbacher's phenomenological approach builds on that of Ernst Benz in *Die Vision: Erfahrungsformen und Bilderwelt* (Stuttgart: Klett, 1969).

65. For an interesting attempt to apply Dinzelbacher's criteria to selected authors, see Kathryn Kerby-Fulton, *Reformist Apocalypticism and Piers Plowman* (Cambridge: Cambridge University Press, 1990), 117–20. Kerby-Fulton finds that the criteria work well for most medieval visions, but yield ambiguous results when applied to apocalyptic texts or to "literary religious visions" like those of Dante and Langland.

66. Siegfried Ringler, "Die Rezeption mittelalterlicher Frauenmystik als wissenschaftliches Problem, dargestellt am Werk der Christine Ebner," in *Frauenmystik im Mittelalter*, ed. Peter Dinzelbacher and Dieter Bauer (Ostfildern: Schwabenverlag, 1985), 178–200; Ursula Peters, *Religiöse Erfahrung als literarisches Faktum: Zur Vorgeschichte und Genese frauenmystischer Texte des 13. und 14. Jahrhunderts* (Tübingen: Niemeyer, 1988). For a useful summary of the debate see Tobin, *Mechthild von Magdeburg*, 115–32.

67. Jeffrey Hamburger, *The Visual and the Visionary: Art and Female Spirituality in Late Medieval Germany* (New York: Zone, 1998); David Freedberg, *The Power of Images: Studies in the History and Theory of Response* (Chicago: University of Chicago Press, 1989), 283–316; Gertrud Jaron Lewis, *By Women, For Women, About Women: The Sister-Books of Fourteenth-Century Germany* (Toronto: Pontifical Institute of Mediaeval Studies, 1996), 89–127; Denise Despres, *Ghostly Sights: Visual Meditation in Late-Medieval Literature* (Norman, Okla.: Pilgrim Press, 1989), 19–54.

68. McGinn, *Flowering of Mysticism*, 19–24; Nicholas Watson, "Visions of Inclusion: Universal Salvation and Vernacular Theology in Pre-Reformation England," *Journal of Medieval and Early Modern Studies* 27 (1997): 145–87. See also Erich Auerbach, *Literary Language and Its Public in Late Latin Antiquity and in the Middle Ages*, trans. Ralph Manheim (Princeton, N.J.: Princeton University Press, 1965), 281–86. For a fuller discussion see Chapter 7 below, pp. 295–97.

69. See for example Shakti Gawain, *Creative Visualization: Use the Power of Your Imagination to Create What You Want in Your Life* (Novato, Calif.: New World Library, 1983); T. M. Luhrmann, *Persuasions of the Witch's Craft: Ritual Magic in Contemporary England* (Cambridge, Mass.: Harvard University Press, 1989), 180–202.

70. "Short-story writers enter fictional skins in brief bursts, but . . . some novel writers might find descriptions of their writing process under the diagnostic criteria for multiple-personality disorder. . . . Often over the past eight years I picked up the telephone with the desperate urge to speak to someone, only to realize that the person I wanted to talk to didn't exist outside my mind and pages." Gina Frangello, "Influential Characters," *Chicago Tribune*, Sunday, June 25, 2000, Section 14,3.

71. Owen Barfield, *Saving the Appearances: A Study in Idolatry* (London: Faber & Faber, 1957), 86.

72. Carolynn Van Dyke, *The Fiction of Truth: Structures of Meaning in Narrative and Dramatic Allegory* (Ithaca, N.Y.: Cornell University Press, 1985), 40, 63. The capital R indicates philosophical as opposed to narrative Realism. See also Stephen Barney, *Allegories of History, Allegories of Love* (Hamden, Conn.: Archon Books, 1979), 22–23.

73. Paul Piehler, *The Visionary Landscape: A Study in Medieval Allegory* (London: Edward Arnold, 1971), 16.

74. "Et que de ces choses dis voir dieu qui proprement est toy et toy qui proprement es lui le savez." *Lavision-Christine* III.14, ed. Sister Mary Louis Towner

(Washington, D.C.: Catholic University Press, 1932), 169. Dante refers to Philosophy as God's daughter in *Convivio* II.xii.9.

75. "Car ainsi comme ceulz qui ont droitture sont droitturiers / Et ceulz qui ont sapience sont sages / ainsi ceulz qui ont divinite sont dieux et cil qui a felicite est dieu Donc tous beneurez sont dieux / mais par nature il nest que un dieu / et par participacion il en est moult/" *Lavision-Christine* III.26, 189. Cf. Boethius, *De consolatione Philosophiae* III, prose 10: "Omnis igitur beatus deus, sed natura quidem unus; participatione vero nihil prohibet esse quam plurimos." Loeb Classical Library (Cambridge, Mass.: Harvard University Press, 1973), 280.

76. "Si dis que toy saintte theologie et divinite es une tres grasse viande qui contiens en toy toutes delices ainsi comme la manne qui aux Juifs plovoit du ciel qui assavouroit en la bouche de chascun selon sa voulente." *Lavision-Christine* III.27, 192; trans. Blumenfeld-Kosinski in *Selected Writings*, 201.

77. A well-known versicle for the feast of Corpus Christi was based on Wisd. 16.20: "Panem de caelo praestitisti eis, / omne delectamentum in se habentem."

78. Hildegard of Bingen, *Liber divinorum operum* III.5.10–15, ed. Albert Derolez and Peter Dronke, CCCM 92 (Turnhout: Brepols, 1996): 426–33. Justitia's prophetic discourse is a denunciation of the contemporary Church.

79. Lewis, *Allegory of Love*, 86–87.

80. James Paxson, *The Poetics of Personification* (Cambridge: Cambridge University Press, 1994), 7.

81. See Chapter 4 below, pp. 159–66, for the visual allegory of "Christ crucified by the Virtues."

82. Peter Dronke, "Bernard Silvestris, Natura, and Personification," *Journal of the Warburg and Courtauld Institutes* 43 (1980): 16–31; rpt. in Dronke, *Intellectuals and Poets in Medieval Europe* (Rome: Edizioni di storia e letteratura, 1992), 41–61 (quotation 41).

83. Ibid., 56, 45.

84. Mechthild, *Fliessende Licht* IV.12, ed. Neumann, 123–27; trans. Tobin, *Flowing Light*, 152–56.

85. James Paxson describes "personification in *Piers* . . . as a direct expression of nominalist principles in practical poetic terms" and thus "a parody of or *satire* on the kind of philosophical Realism described by Barfield." *Poetics of Personification*, 137–38. While I see elements of both forms of personification in Langland, I would agree that the non-Realistic type predominates.

86. In *Vita Nuova* xxv, Dante admits to personifying Amore as if he were "not only an intellectual substance, but also a bodily substance." He then apologizes for the poetic license: "This is patently false, for Love does not exist in itself as a substance, but is an accident in a substance." *Dante's Vita Nuova*, trans. Mark Musa (Bloomington: Indiana University Press, 1973), 54. Despite this piece of Aristotelian criticism, Dante had changed his mind by the time he wrote the *Commedia*. Cf. Chapter 4 below, pp. 181–88; Lewis, *Allegory of Love*, 47–48; Ferrante, *Woman as Image*, 136–37.

87. A valuable early study is that of Howard Patch, *The Goddess Fortuna in Mediaeval Literature* (Cambridge, Mass.: Harvard University Press, 1927).

88. Lady Philosophy personifies Fortune and puts a speech in her mouth in

Consolation II, prose 2. Fortune is "deconstructed" in Book IV, prose 6, where Boethius deliberately replaces the personified feminine noun with the abstract neuter *fatum*: "Nam providentia est ipsa illa divina ratio in summo omnium principe constituta quae cuncta disponit; fatum vero inhaerens rebus mobilibus dispositio per quam providentia suis quaeque nectit ordinibus." Loeb Classical Library, 358.

89. Dante, as usual, is an exception; see note 4 above.

90. Piehler, *Visionary Landscape*, 15.

91. Joseph Addison, "Dialogues upon the Usefulness of Ancient Medals," in *Miscellaneous Works*, ed. A. C. Guthkelch (London: Bell, 1914), 2: 300. See also Morton Bloomfield, "A Grammatical Approach to Personification Allegory," *Modern Philology* 60 (1963): 161–71.

92. Paxson, *Poetics of Personification*, 173.

93. A rare exception is William of St.-Thierry, who described spiritual growth as the carnal, effeminate *anima*'s gradual transformation into the virile, rational *animus*. *Epistola ad fratres de Monte Dei* 198, ed. Jean Déchanet, *Lettre aux frères du Mont-Dieu*, SC 223 (Paris: Éditions du Cerf, 1975), 306–8. The normal preference for *anima* is no doubt indebted to the Vulgate, especially the Psalter, where the feminine term is consistently used.

94. Bernard may have assumed that *nous* was feminine by analogy with the Latin *mens*. Joan Ferrante remarks that Noys has to be female "not only because the noun is feminine in Greek [*sic*], . . . but because creation begins with a kind of sexual act between God and Noys." *Woman as Image*, 42.

95. "his [divinis personis] subiectas fore rationabiles animas legi obsequentes, ministras uero potestates naturam fortunam casum et daemones inspectatores speculatoresque meritorum." Calcidius, *Commentarius in Timaeum Platonis*, c. 188, ed. J. H. Waszink (London: Warburg Institute, 1962), 213.

96. "Hec ergo nomina trinitatis—pater, nois, anima mundi—ponit in aperto sermone philosophica pagina; in mistico autem Iovis est nomen divine potentie, Pallas divine sapientie, Iuno divine voluntatis." *The Commentary on Martianus Capella's* De nuptiis Philologiae et Mercurii *Attributed to Bernardus Silvestris*, ed. Haijo Jan Westra, c. 11 (Toronto: Pontifical Institute of Mediaeval Studies, 1986): 246.

97. Ferrante, *Woman as Image*, 63–64.

98. Paxson, *Poetics of Personification*, 173–74; Rita Copeland, "The Pardoner's Body and the Disciplining of Rhetoric," in *Framing Medieval Bodies*, ed. Sarah Kay and Miri Rubin (Manchester: Manchester University Press, 1994), 146–47.

99. Gordon Teskey, *Allegory and Violence* (Ithaca, N.Y.: Cornell University Press, 1996), 22–24.

100. H. Richard Niebuhr, *Radical Monotheism and Western Culture* (New York: Harper, 1960): 31.

101. Some early Christian writers avoided this impasse by positing a feminine Holy Spirit as divine Mother; see pp. 248–49 below. More common in the late Middle Ages was the tendency to expand the Trinity into a quaternity, with the Virgin as its honorary fourth member—an option I explore in Chapter 6.

102. Marina Benedetti, *Io non sono Dio: Guglielma di Milano e i Figli dello Spirito santo* (Milan: Edizioni Biblioteca Francescana, 1998); Luisa Muraro, *Guglielma e Maifreda: Storia di un'eresia femminista* (Milan: La Tartaruga, 1985); Newman, "WomanSpirit, Woman Pope," in *From Virile Woman*, 182–223.

103. C. S. Lewis described the "religion of love" as "a temporary escape, a truancy from the ardours of a religion that was believed into the delights of a religion that was merely imagined." *Allegory of Love*, 21.

104. Van Dyke, *Fiction of Truth*, 61.

105. See also the illuminations of visions II.3 and II.4 in *Scivias*, ed. Adelgundis Führkötter and Angela Carlevaris, CCCM 43–43a (Turnhout: Brepols, 1978), or Barbara Newman, *Sister of Wisdom: St. Hildegard's Theology of the Feminine* (Berkeley: University of California Press, 1987), Figs. 8 and 11.

106. The precise philosophical underpinnings of this theology vary from case to case, and in most allegorical and visionary texts they remain implicit. For the theology of participation as developed by a leading Greek Platonist, see David Balas, *Metousia Theou: Man's Participation in God's Perfections According to St. Gregory of Nyssa* (Rome: Herder, 1966). The fully developed Platonisms of Bernard Silvestris and Alan of Lille will be treated in Chapter 2. The best general treatment is still M.-D. Chenu, "The Platonisms of the Twelfth Century," in *Nature, Man, and Society in the Twelfth Century*, trans. Jerome Taylor and Lester K. Little (Chicago: University of Chicago Press, 1968), 49–98.

107. *Scivias* III.3.3, ed. Führkötter, 375.

108. See Hope Traver, *The Four Daughters of God: A Study of the Versions of This Allegory* (Philadelphia: John Winston, 1907), and Samuel Chew, *The Virtues Reconciled: An Iconographic Study* (Toronto: University of Toronto Press, 1947). Prior Latin versions include those of Hugh of St.-Victor, *Adnotationes elucidatoriae in quosdam Psalmos David*, c. 63 (PL 177: 623–25), and Bernard of Clairvaux, *Sermo 1 in Annuntiatione Dominica*, in *Sancti Bernardi Opera*, ed. Jean Leclercq, Henri Rochais, and C. H. Talbot, 5 vols. (Rome: Editiones Cistercienses, 1957–77), 5: 13–29.

109. "Quatre filles out icest rei; / A chescune dona par sei / Sun afferant de sa sustance, / De sun sen e de sa puissance / A chescune diversement, / Solom ceo ke a li apent. / De sa sustance out chescune, / E trestut est sustance une / Ke a lur pere aveneit; / Ne sanz iceo il ne poeit / Sun regne en pès governer, / Ne od dreiture justiser" (lines 217–28). *Château d'Amour*, ed. Murray, 95.

110. "Et quamvis lingua romana coram clericis saporem suavitatis non habeat, tamen pro laicis qui minus intelligunt, opusculem [*sic*] istud aptum est, quia prudens qui norit suggerere mel de petra oleumque de saxo durissimo scriptum inveniet plenum dulcedine coelesti in quo continentur omnes articuli fidei tam divinitatis quam humanitatis." Ibid., 87.

111. Quilligan, *Allegory of Female Authority*; Newman, *Sister of Wisdom*; eadem, "*La mystique courtoise*: Thirteenth-Century Beguines and the Art of Love," in *From Virile Woman*, 137–67.

112. The argument for divine androgyny *was* made by certain Renaissance occultists, inspired by their interest in ancient hermeticism. See my essay, "Renaissance Feminism and Esoteric Theology: The Case of Cornelius Agrippa," in *From Virile Woman*, 224–43.

113. "Sed nec hoc negligendum existimo, an patris et filii, an matris et filiae magis illis apta sit appellatio, cum in eis nulla sit sexus discretio." Anselm of Canterbury, *Monologium* 42, in *Opera Omnia*, vol. 1, ed. F. S. Schmitt (Edinburgh: Thomas Nelson, 1938), 58.

114. "Queretur forsitan quare deus Pater et non mater esse dicatur, quare Filius

et non filia cum nullus sexus in deo inueniatur. Dico ideo quia sexus masculinus dignior est. . . . Uel ideo potius Pater non mater dicitur Filius non filia appellatur quia inpar numerus masculus esse dicitur in arithmetica, par uero femina. . . . Cum uero masculus sit inpar numerus qui deo ascribitur oportet reducatur ad memoriam quoniam masculus agit et non patitur: femina uero non agit sed patitur." Thierry of Chartres, *Commentum super Boethii Librum "De Trinitate"* IV.4, ed. Nikolaus M. Häring, *Commentaries on Boethius by Thierry of Chartres and His School* (Toronto: Pontifical Institute of Mediaeval Studies, 1971), 96.

115. "Designantur uero in masculino genere he persone cum possent designari his nominibus mater filia atque donatio ut res quas innuunt scilicet omnipotentia sapientia benignitas." Thierry, *Glosa super Boethii Librum "De Trinitate"* V.22, ed. Häring, *Commentaries*, 297. Cf. Peter Dronke, "Thierry of Chartres," in *A History of Twelfth-Century Western Philosophy* (Cambridge: Cambridge University Press, 1988), 365.

116. "Forte dicitis, o Judaei: si Christus Dei Sapientia est, quare vocatur Filius, et non filia? Ad quod nos respondemus, quod duabus ex causis Filius vocatur et non filia. Prima videlicet, quia honorabilius est nomen Filii, quam filiae. Secunda, quia non in persona filiae, sed in persona Filii dignatus est nasci de Virgine." Martin of Léon, *Sermo IV in Natale Domini*, PL 208:137d.

117. Joan Gibson, "Could Christ Have Been Born a Woman? A Medieval Debate," *Journal of Feminist Studies in Religion* 8, 1 (Spring 1992): 65–82.

Chapter 2. Natura (I): Nature and Nature's God

1. For three very different versions of "the big picture," see R. G. Collingwood, *The Idea of Nature* (Oxford: Clarendon Press, 1945); Susan Griffin, *Woman and Nature: The Roaring Inside Her* (New York: Harper and Row, 1978); and Carolyn Merchant, *The Death of Nature: Women, Ecology, and the Scientific Revolution* (San Francisco: Harper 1980).

2. There are now at least two full-length treatments of this tradition: George Economou, *The Goddess Natura in Medieval Literature* (Cambridge, Mass.: Harvard University Press, 1972), and Hugh White, *Nature, Sex, and Goodness in a Medieval Literary Tradition* (Oxford: Oxford University Press, 2000). I did not obtain White's fine study until after this manuscript was completed.

3. F. J. E. Raby, "*Nuda Natura* and Twelfth-Century Cosmology," *Speculum* 43 (1968): 72–77.

4. A generation ago these writers would have been designated as the "school of Chartres"—a term I avoid because the contested question of which masters actually taught or studied at Chartres is not germane to my purpose. The best general study of the movement in English remains Winthrop Wetherbee, *Platonism and Poetry in the Twelfth Century: The Literary Influence of the School of Chartres* (Princeton, N.J.: Princeton University Press, 1972).

5. Claudian, *De raptu Proserpinae* III.33–36, 41–45, ed. Claire Gruzelier (Oxford: Clarendon, 1993): 52.

6. Henri d'Andeli in *La bataille des VII Arts*, c. 1242. Cited in Bernardus Silvestris, *Cosmographia*, ed. Peter Dronke (Leiden: Brill, 1978), introduction, p. 1.

7. A prosimetrum (or "Menippean satire") is a work composed in alternating sections of verse and prose; the verse forms themselves may vary. Bernard adopted the genre from two of his chief sources, Boethius's *De consolatione Philosophiae* and Martianus Capella's *De nuptiis Philologiae et Mercurii*. Alan of Lille used the same form in *De planctu Naturae*.

8. Metrically "Noys" should be pronounced as two syllables, with the second normally stressed.

9. *Tractatus de sex dierum operibus* 2–3, in N. M. Häring, ed., *Commentaries on Boethius by Thierry of Chartres and His School* (Toronto: Pontifical Institute of Mediaeval Studies, 1971), 555–57. On the illustration of Honorius see Peter Dronke, "Bernard Silvestris, Natura, and Personification," in *Intellectuals and Poets in Medieval Europe* (Rome: Edizioni di Storia e Letteratura, 1992), 53–55, and Marie-Thérèse d'Alverny, "Le Cosmos symbolique du XIIe siècle," repr. in *Études sur le symbolisme de la Sagesse et sur l'iconographie* (Aldershot: Variorum, 1993).

10. Theodore Silverstein, "The Fabulous Cosmogony of Bernardus Silvestris," *Modern Philology* 46 (1948–49): 92–116; see esp. 110–12.

11. Wetherbee, *Platonism and Poetry*, 163; Economou, *Goddess Natura*, 70.

12. All *Cosmographia* citations are taken from the Dronke edition. For this and the following passage I have used Dronke's irresistible translations: introduction, 55–56. The remaining translations are my own unless otherwise noted.

13. "Erat Yle [Silva] Nature vultus antiquissimus": *Meg.* 2.4. "'Vere', inquit [Noys], 'et tu, Natura, uteri mei beata fecunditas, nec degeneras, nec desciscis origine . . . filia Providentie'": *Meg.* 2.1.

14. Claire Fanger, "The Formative Feminine and the Immobility of God: Gender and Cosmogony in Bernard Silvestris's *Cosmographia*," in David Townsend and Andrew Taylor, eds., *The Tongue of the Fathers: Gender and Ideology in Twelfth-Century Latin* (Philadelphia: University of Pennsylvania Press, 1998), 90.

15. "As Silva obliquely aspires to [Noys], she obliquely inclines to it. The other side of a Matter that speaks is a Mind that listens." Jon Whitman, "From the *Cosmographia* to the *Divine Comedy*: An Allegorical Dilemma," in Morton Bloomfield, ed., *Allegory, Myth, and Symbol* (Cambridge, Mass.: Harvard University Press, 1981), 70.

16. "Substantiam animis Endelichia subministrat; habitaculum anime, corpus, artifex Natura de initiorum materiis et qualitate conponit." *Meg.* 4.14; trans. Winthrop Wetherbee, *The* Cosmographia *of Bernardus Silvestris* (New York: Columbia University Press, 1973), 90.

17. Brian Stock, *Myth and Science in the Twelfth Century: A Study of Bernard Silvester* (Princeton, N.J.: Princeton University Press, 1972), 66, 117.

18. Winthrop Wetherbee offers a significantly darker reading than Dronke or Stock: "Like the life of the universe at large, human experience is an interplay of rational and irrational forces, and the tension between them as man seeks to maintain right relations with the cosmic order becomes at times a heroic, almost tragic theme." "Philosophy, Cosmology, and the Twelfth-Century Renaissance," in Peter Dronke, ed., *A History of Twelfth-Century Western Philosophy* (Cambridge: Cambridge University Press, 1988), 46–47.

19. "Quippe de splendore ad tenebras, de celo Ditis ad imperium, de eternitate ad corpora per Cancri domicilium que fuerant descensure, sicut pure, sicut simplices,

obtusum cecumque corporis quod apparari prospitiunt habitaculum exhorrebant." *Micr.* 3.8.

20. "Tanta igitur naturarum multitudine, labore Physis plurimo speciem deprehendit humanam, sublustrem, tenuem, et pagine terminantis extremam." *Micr.* 11.11, trans. Wetherbee, *Cosmographia*, 117.

21. Whitman, "From the *Cosmographia*," 72.

22. Dronke, *Cosmographia*, 48–49. Dronke renders line 178 as "he exudes life in this and annihilates the days." Wetherbee reads "he exhausts his life, and a day reduces him to nothing": *Cosmographia*, 127.

23. E. R. Curtius, *European Literature and the Latin Middle Ages*, trans. Willard Trask (Princeton, N.J.: Princeton University Press, 1953), 112.

24. Jean Jolivet, "Les principes féminins dans la 'Cosmographia' de Bernard Silvestre," in Christian Wenin, ed., *L'Homme et son univers au moyen âge* (Louvain: Éditions de l'Institut Supérieur de Philosophie, 1986), 300.

25. Peter Dronke demonstrates that Bernard's Natura is also indebted to the pagan earth-goddess known as Tellus or Terra Mater: "Bernard Silvestris, Natura, and Personification," in *Intellectuals and Poets*, 47–52.

26. Fanger, "Formative Feminine," 92–93, 96.

27. Étienne Gilson, taking Noys to be a masculine figure, presented a thoroughly orthodox reading in "La cosmogonie de Bernardus Silvestris," *Archives d'histoire doctrinale et littéraire du Moyen Age* 3 (1928): 5–24. According to Theodore Silverstein, Bernard, with Thierry of Chartres and William of Conches, taught that matter was "eternal" in some sense yet not fully coeternal with God. "Fabulous Cosmogony," 98–103.

28. "Liber iste fuit recitatus in Gallia, et capta[vi]t eius benivolentiam." Oxford, Bodleian, Laud misc. 515, fol. 188v, glossing *Meg.* 3.55–56: "Munificens deitas Eugenium comodat orbi, / Donat et in solo munere cuncta semel." Cited in Dronke, *Cosmographia*, 2.

29. Silverstein, "Fabulous Cosmogony," 116.

30. Dronke, *Cosmographia*, 3, 10–15. Bernard Silvestris's reception in Germany has not been thoroughly investigated, but he was known at least indirectly through Alan of Lille. Nicholas of Cusa owned a manuscript of the *Cosmographia* in the 15th century.

31. Alan's tombstone at Cîteaux bears the epitaph: "Alanum brevis hora brevi tumulo sepelivit, / Qui duo, qui septem, qui totum scibile scivit." The "two" are philosophy and theology; the "seven" are the liberal arts of the trivium and quadrivium. *Anticlaudianus*, ed. R. Bossuat (Paris: J. Vrin, 1955), 10.

32. For an overview of Alan's life and work see Gillian R. Evans, *Alan of Lille: The Frontiers of Theology in the Later Twelfth Century* (Cambridge: Cambridge University Press, 1983).

33. "Labra, modico tumore surgentia, Veneris tirones inuitabant ad oscula. . . . Brachia, ad graciam inspectoris perspicua, postulare uidebantur amplexus." Alan of Lille, *De planctu Naturae* 2, ed. Nikolaus M. Häring, *Studi Medievali* ser. 3, v. 19, pt. 2 (1978), 797–879, at 809. Trans. James J. Sheridan, *The Plaint of Nature* (Toronto: Pontifical Institute of Mediaeval Studies, 1980): 75.

34. *De planctu* 8, p. 833.

35. "Plerique homines in suam matrem uiciorum armentur iniuriis, . . . in me uiolentas manus uiolenter iniciunt et mea sibi particulatim uestimenta diripiunt et . . . me uestibus orphanatam, quantum in ipsis est, cogunt meretricaliter lupanare." *De planctu* 8, p. 838; trans. Sheridan, 142.

36. ". . . non materie preiacentis auxilio, non indigentie stimulante flagitio, sed solius arbitrarie uoluntatis imperio, mundialis regie ammirabilem speciem fabricauit." *De planctu* 8, p. 840; trans. Sheridan, 145. In his early summa *Quoniam homines*, Alan had condemned Plato for teaching the eternity of matter and the Ideas. *Summa Quoniam homines* I.5, ed. Palémon Glorieux, *Archives d'histoire doctrinale et littéraire du Moyen Age* 20 (1953), 126.

37. "Certissime Summi Magistri me humilem profiteor esse discipulam. . . . Eius enim operatio simplex, mea operatio multiplex. Eius opus sufficiens, meum opus deficiens. Eius opus mirabile, meum opus mutabile. . . . Ille faciens, ego facta. . . . Ille operatur ex nichilo, ego mendico opus ex aliquo. . . . Et respectu diuine potentie meam potentiam impotentiam esse cognoscas. Meum effectum scias esse defectum, meum uigorem uilitatem esse perpendas." *De planctu* 6, p. 829; my translation.

38. "Nec talis natiuitas tali indiget obstetrice sed potius ego Natura huius natiuitatis naturam ignoro." *De planctu* 6, p. 829; trans. Sheridan, 125.

39. "Ego quasi bestialiter in terra deambulo, illa celi militat in secreto." *De planctu* 6, p. 830; trans. Sheridan, 125.

40. "Auctoritatem theologice consule facultatis cuius fidelitati potius quam mearum rationum firmitati dare debes assensum." *De planctu* 6, p. 829; my translation.

41. *Summa Quoniam homines* I.2, ed. Glorieux, 121; "De clericis ad theologiam non accedentibus," ed. Marie-Thérèse d'Alverny in *Alain de Lille: Textes inédits* (Paris: J. Vrin, 1965): 275; Maurice de Gandillac, "La Nature chez Alain de Lille," in H. Roussel and F. Suard, eds., *Alain de Lille, Gautier de Châtillon, Jakemart Giélée, et leur temps* (Lille: Presses Universitaires de Lille, 1980), 61–75.

42. *De planctu* 4, p. 821. Wetherbee takes the *homo* (not *vir*) who assists Natura to be a figure of divine reason: *Platonism and Poetry*, 191. Antifeminism is evident throughout *De planctu* in the charge that homosexuals have "degenerated" from men into women. When Hymen appears in *De planctu* 16, p. 865, the narrator tells us twice that his face and hairstyle reveal no trace of *feminea mollicies*, but only *uirilis dignitas*.

43. I disagree here with Wetherbee's more optimistic reading: he takes Genius to be "ideally the lord of Nature, . . . a type of the divine Wisdom." But the character has complex philosophical dimensions that lie beyond the scope of my argument. See Wetherbee's full discussion in *Platonism and Poetry*, 202–10 (quote p. 207); for the figure's literary history see Jane Chance Nitzsche, *The Genius Figure in Antiquity and the Middle Ages* (New York: Columbia University Press, 1975).

44. "N(atura), dei gracia mundane ciuitatis uicaria procuratrix, G(enio), sibi alteri, salutem." *De planctu* 16, p. 871. In medieval epistolary form, the salutation names the higher-ranking party first, whether this is the sender or the recipient.

45. "Veritas, tamquam patris filia uerecunda, ancillatione obsequens assistebat. Que non ex pruritu Affrodites promiscuo propagata sed ex solo Nature natique geniali osculo fuerat deriuata, cum Ylem formarum speculum mendicantem eternalis salutauit Ydea." *De planctu* 18, pp. 876–77; trans. Sheridan, 217–18.

46. "In latericiis uero tabulis arundinei stili ministerio uirgo uarias rerum pic-turaliter suscitabat imagines. Pictura tamen, subiacenti materie familiariter non coherens, uelociter euanescendo moriens, nulla imaginum post se relinquebat uesti-gia." *De planctu* 4, p. 821; trans. Sheridan, 108.

47. "In quibus [vestibus] rerum ymagines momentanee uiuentes tociens expi-rabant, ut a nostre cognitionis laberentur indagine." *De planctu* 18, p. 875; trans. Sheri-dan, 215.

48. "Ille uero calamum . . . manu gerebat in dextera: in sinistra uero morticini pellem nouacule demorsione pilorum cesarie denudatam." *De planctu* 18, pp. 875–76; my translation.

49. "abhominationis filios a sacramentali ecclesie nostre communione seiungens cum debita officii sollempnitate seuera excommunicationis uirga percutias": *De planctu* 16, p. 872; my translation.

50. "Auctoritate superessentialis Vsye eiusque Notionis eterne, assensu celestis milicie, . . . a Nature gracia degradetur, a naturalium rerum uniformi concilio seg-regetur omnis qui aut legitimum Veneris obliquat incessum aut [vitiis aliis utitur]." *De planctu* 18, p. 878; my translation.

51. "Que ab orthographie semita falsigraphie claudicatione recedens, rerum figuras . . . creabat." *De planctu* 18, p. 876; my translation.

52. *De planctu* 10, p. 846.

53. Cf. Mark Jordan: "The work of Genius is shown as necessarily doubled, as producing representation and misrepresentation. . . . This reminds us of that other fruitful miscoupling—the adulterous dalliance of Antigamus ('Anti-Marriage') with Venus that produces Jocus." *The Invention of Sodomy in Christian Theology* (Chicago: University of Chicago Press, 1997), 78.

54. Thomas Hyde, *The Poetic Theology of Love: Cupid in Renaissance Literature* (London: Associated University Presses, 1986), 39.

55. Some manuscripts have "Antigenius," the reading given by both Häring and Sheridan. But Economou, Wetherbee, and Jordan all prefer "Antigamus," which I have chosen to use because Venus seems to be rejecting fidelity rather than fertility (her adulterous union is fruitful). The lover's name is not explained in the text, and the two forms could easily be interchanged by scribes.

56. De Gandillac, "La Nature chez Alain de Lille," in Roussel and Suard, eds., *Alain de Lille*, 68; Daniel Poirion, "Alain de Lille et Jean de Meun," in ibid., 136. The notion that Amor had a brother named Jocus may have been suggested by Pruden-tius, *Psychomachia*, lines 433–38.

57. Cf. James Sheridan: "We have here a fatal flaw from an artistic point of view. Alan's heroine, Nature, decides to abandon the work that God had given her to do. No sufficient reason is given. Nature simply wished to live in more pleasant sur-roundings. . . . Thus far she has been a noble and tragic figure. We can no longer look on her in this way." *Plaint of Nature*, 147 n. 44.

58. Economou, *Goddess Natura*, 82; Wetherbee, "Philosophy, Cosmology," 50–51.

59. "[Natura est] potentia rebus naturalibus indita, ex similibus procreans similia." *Distinctiones*, PL 210: 871d. Cf. *De fide catholica* 1.40 (note 67 below).

60. Jan Ziolkowski argues that Alan was propounding a "theory of verbal mod-eration," neither overly ornate nor "bald of all decoration," just as he urged a sexual

via media between abstinence and excess: *Alan of Lille's Grammar of Sex: The Meaning of Grammar to a Twelfth-Century Intellectual* (Cambridge, Mass.: Medieval Academy of America, 1985), 47. On my own reading, the only "verbal moderation" to be found in *De planctu* is the road not taken, midway between the sternness of Alan's precepts and the extravagance of his practice.

61. "Sic methonomicas rethorum positiones . . . Cypridis artificiis interdixi, ne si nimis dure translationis excursu a suo reclamante subiecto predicatum alienet in aliud, in facinus facetia, in rusticitatem urbanitas, tropus in uicium, in decolorationem color nimius conuertatur." *De planctu* 10, p. 848; my translation.

62. Maureen Quilligan, "Allegory, Allegoresis, and the Deallegorization of Language: The *Roman de la rose*, the *De planctu naturae*, and the *Parlement of Foules*," in Bloomfield, ed., *Allegory, Myth, and Symbol*, 172.

63. C. S. Lewis, *The Allegory of Love: A Study in Medieval Tradition* (London: Oxford University Press, 1936), 105–6. Lewis follows these remarks with a translation of *De planctu* 4 in the manner of sixteenth-century euphuism, a tour de force in its own right.

64. "Nolo ut prius plana uerborum planicie explanare proposita uel prophanis uerborum nouitatibus prophanare prophana, uerum pudenda aureis pudicorum uerborum faleris inaurare uariisque uenustorum dictorum coloribus inuestire." *De planctu* 8, p. 839; my translation.

65. Jordan, *Invention of Sodomy*, 68.

66. Paul Piehler, *The Visionary Landscape: A Study in Medieval Allegory* (London: Edward Arnold, 1971), 56; Economou, *Goddess Natura*, 88.

67. In his *De fide catholica contra haereticos* 1.40, Alan defended the goodness of natural law even in a fallen world: "Deus a prima mundi creatione naturam creauit, secundum quam, similia ex similibus produxit. Cum ergo Deus, mediante natura, res procreaturus esset, propter peccatum Adae noluit mutare legem naturae. Haec enim fuit lex naturae ab origine, ut ex similibus similia procrearentur, ut de homine homo, de rationali rationalis" (PL 210: 345c).

68. An *integumentum* or *involucrum* ("covering"), in twelfth-century literary theory, is the shimmering surface that intentionally hides the deeper meaning of an allegory in order to protect it from the vulgar. Alan's Natura expressly subscribes to this theory: "Sed tamen plerisque mee potestatis faciem palliare decreui figuris, defendens a uilitate secretum, ne si eis de me familiarem impartirem scientiam, que apud eos primitus ignota uigerent, postmodum iam nota uilescerent." *De planctu* 6, p. 828. For detailed accounts of twelfth-century views on myth and *fabula*, see Stock, *Myth and Science*, 31–62, and Peter Dronke, *Fabula: Explorations into the Uses of Myth in Medieval Platonism* (Leiden: Brill, 1974), 13–67.

69. Jordan, *Invention of Sodomy*, 87.

70. Häring, introduction to *De planctu*, 797–802.

71. The speech on love is *De planctu* 9, a poem beginning "Pax odio fraudique fides, spes iuncta timori / Est amor." This would soon become the best-known portion of Alan's text. Jean de Meun was also responsible for popularizing the letters of Abelard and Heloise, which remained virtually unknown until he translated them into French and retold their story in the *Rose*.

72. "In terris humanus erit, diuinus in astris." *Anticlaudianus* I, 239, ed. Bossuat,

64. All translations are my own, though I have consulted the prose version of James J. Sheridan, *Anticlaudianus, or the Good and Perfect Man* (Toronto: Pontifical Institute of Mediaeval Studies, 1973).

73. William of Auxerre comments, "Hec puella est alma Noys que sapit que sursum sunt, cui patent cause et principia rerum." Bossuat, introduction to *Anticlaudianus*, 44–45 n. 6. Two later commentaries edited by Christel Meier identify the maiden as Theologia: "Die Rezeption des *Anticlaudianus* Alans von Lille in Textkommentierung und Illustration," in Christel Meier and Uwe Ruberg, eds., *Text und Bild: Aspekte des Zusammenwirkens zweier Künste in Mittelalter und früher Neuzeit* (Wiesbaden: Reichert Verlag, 1980), 521–26.

74. Although she has supposedly left sight behind, Prudentia continues to gaze with awe on the mysteries of heaven.

75. Peter Dronke, "Boethius, Alanus and Dante," in *The Medieval Poet and His World* (Rome: Edizioni di Storia e Letteratura, 1984): 431–38. As Dronke notes, both supernatural journeys involve different guides suited to different stages: "Phronesis is guided by Ratio, and then, when Ratio must be left behind, by the unnamed *puella poli*, finally by Fides—as Dante is guided first by Virgil, then by Beatrice, and finally by Saint Bernard" (432 n. 4).

76. *Anticlaudianus* VI, 439. Here I follow Sheridan, who corrects Bossuat's readings of "Ytide" for "Iudith" and "potencia" for "patiencia." Alan is adapting the classical legend of the painter Zeuxis, who fashions a perfect woman by combining the eyes of one model, the breasts of another, and so forth. In this poem filled with wisdom goddesses, Judith (for *sensus*) is the one human female exemplar of a virtue.

77. Fides appears among these virtues, but with the meaning of "fidelity" rather than the supernatural Fides that is Theology's sister.

78. "nostroque senatu / Plebescat Natura minor" (VIII, 181–82). An anonymous commentary from ca. 1366 notes that "pauperies et senectus non possunt dici vicia, sed pocius sunt defectus; tamen auctor ponit eas inter vicia, quia eis frequenter vicia comitantur. Nam et senes sepe sunt cupidi aut auari, et pauperes plerumque inuidi. . . . Ignobilitas uix valet dici vicium. Et nobilitas cum sit fortuita et casualis, vix potest virtus appellari." Meier, "Die Rezeption des *Anticlaudianus*," 523.

79. This is a structural flaw intrinsic to Prudentian allegory, as critics have long noted: "Courage can fight, and perhaps we can make a shift with Faith. But how is Patience to rage in battle? How is Mercy to strike down her foes, or Humility to triumph over them when fallen?" Lewis, *Allegory of Love*, 69.

80. Meier, "Die Rezeption," 494.

81. I have emended Bossuat, who capitalizes *Deus*. For reasons explained below, I do not believe Alan was writing about the Incarnate Word.

82. Michael Wilks, "Alan of Lille and the New Man," in Derek Baker, ed., *Renaissance and Renewal in Christian History* (Oxford: Blackwell, 1977), 137–57; Linda Marshall, "The Identity of the 'New Man' in the *Anticlaudianus* of Alan of Lille," *Viator* 10 (1979): 77–94. Against this thesis see Evans, *Alan of Lille*, 170.

83. Evans, *Alan of Lille*, 164.

84. Adam de la Bassée, *Ludus super Anticlaudianum*, ed. Paul Bayart (Lille: Giard, 1930). The manuscript is Oxford, Corpus Christi College ms. 59.

85. "Explicit *Antirufinus* sive *Anticlaudianus* venerabilis Alani de Christi incarnatione." Prague, Universitätsbibl. Cod. 1635, cited in Meier, "Die Rezeption," 508. William of Auxerre's unpublished *Commentum in Anticlaudianum Alani* is extant in Paris, Bibl. nat. ms. lat. 8299.

86. "Si volumus huius novi hominis plasmacionem intelligere, formetur hystoria sic: omnes igitur Virtutes beatissimam virginem Mariam intraverunt et corpus eius et animam spiritu sancto cooperante ad novi et sanctissimi hominis concepcionem habilitaverunt." Peter Ochsenbein, ed., "Das *Compendium Anticlaudiani,*" *Zeitschrift für deutsches Altertum und deutsche Literatur* 98 (1969): 81–109, at 107.

87. ". . . ubi nulla potestas / Illius [Naturae], sed cuncta silent decreta, pauescunt / Leges, iura stupent, ubi regnat sola uoluntas / Artificis summi."

88. "Every rule is overruled / by this coupling of the Word." Grammar finds pure Act translated into the passive voice, Arithmetic discovers that unity and alterity coincide, Geometry sees the circle squared, and so forth. Alan of Lille, "Rithmus de Incarnatione Domini," ed. Marie-Thérèse d'Alverny in *L'Homme devant Dieu: Mélanges offerts au Père Henri de Lubac* (Paris: Aubier, 1964), 2: 126–28.

89. "Ego summa et ignea uis, que omnes uiuentes scintillas accendi et nulla mortalia efflaui, sed illa diiudico ut sunt; circueuntem circulum cum superioribus pennis meis, id est cum sapientia, circumuolans recte ipsum ordinaui. Sed et ego ignea uita substantie diuinitatis super pulcritudinem agrorum flammo et in aquis luceo atque in sole, luna et stellis ardeo; et cum aereo uento quadam inuisibili uita, que cuncta sustinet, uitaliter omnia suscito. Aer enim in uiriditate et in floribus uiuit, aque fluunt quasi uiuant, sol etiam in lumine suo uiuit; et cum luna ad defectum uenerit, a lumine solis accenditur ut quasi denuo uiuat; stelle quoque in lumine suo uelut uiuendo clarescunt. . . . Hec omnia in essentia sua uiuunt nec in morte inuenta sunt, quoniam ego uita sum. Racionalitas etiam sum, uentum sonantis uerbi habens, per quod omnis creatura facta est; et in omnia hec sufflaui, ita ut nullum eorum in genere suo mortale sit, quia ego uita sum. Integra namque uita sum, que de lapidibus abscisa non est et de ramis non fronduit et de uirili ui non radicauit; sed omne uitale de me radicatum est." Hildegard of Bingen, *Liber diuinorum operum* I.1.2, ed. Albert Derolez and Peter Dronke, CCCM 92 (Turnhout: Brepols, 1996), 47–49.

90. Barbara Newman, *Sister of Wisdom: St. Hildegard's Theology of the Feminine* (Berkeley: University of California Press, 1987), 64–71.

91. The term *supernaturalis* did not become common until the thirteenth century. In the twelfth, it appears mainly in commentaries on pseudo-Dionysius as a synonym for *superessentialis*. See Henri de Lubac, *Le Surnaturel: Études historiques* (Paris: Aubier, 1946).

Chapter 3. Natura (II): Goddess of the Normative

1. "'Altercatio Ganimedis et Helene': Kritische Edition mit Kommentar," ed. Rolf Lenzen, *Mittellateinisches Jahrbuch* 7 (1972): 161–86. There is an English translation by John Boswell in *Christianity, Social Tolerance, and Homosexuality: Gay People in Western Europe from the Beginning of the Christian Era to the Fourteenth Century* (Chicago: University of Chicago Press, 1980), 381–89. For another edition and translation

see Thomas Stehling, *Medieval Latin Poems of Male Love and Friendship* (New York: Garland, 1984), 104–21. All citations here are from the Lenzen edition; translations are my own.

2. "Erubescant Sodome, fleant Gomorei, / Convertatur, quisquis est reus huius rei! / Deus, hoc si fecero, sis oblitus mei!" One manuscript of the poem, which may be the autograph (Harvard, Houghton Library ms. Lat. 198), gives two versions of the last line in the same hand. The first, unique reading is "Deus, hoc si fecero, miserere mei." The second version, which appears in other mss. and in both editions, is "sis oblitus mei." See Boswell, *Christianity*, 260 n. 62, 389 n. 71. "Sis oblitus mei" is itself ambiguous: it could mean "overlook my transgression" (cf. Psalm 9.32 Vg), but in the Vulgate to be "forgotten by God" more often signifies divine displeasure (cf. Isaiah 49.14). In other words, it is not clear whether the poet meant to confess a personal weakness for Ganymede's sin or to profess his utter abhorrence of it—or both at once.

3. Lenzen notes eight manuscripts, widely scattered (Basel, both Cambridges, Berlin, Oxford, Paris, Rome), along with several literary citations. "Altercatio," 161–67.

4. Jan Ziolkowski, *Alan of Lille's Grammar of Sex: The Meaning of Grammar to a Twelfth-Century Intellectual* (Cambridge, Mass.: Medieval Academy of America, 1985), 36, 70; Boswell, *Christianity*, 259 n. 60; Bernard Silvestris, *Cosmographia*, ed. Peter Dronke (Leiden: Brill, 1978): 11–12. While there is no manuscript evidence for Dronke's suggestion, Alan did write "Vix nodosum valeo," a debate poem in the same form as "Ganymede," which pits the love of girls against that of married women. Ziolkowski remains agnostic on the question of priority.

5. E. R. Curtius, *European Literature and the Latin Middle Ages*, trans. Willard Trask (Princeton, N.J.: Princeton University Press, 1973), 116 n. 26.

6. "Qui sedet hac sede ganimedior est Ganimede; / cur uxoratos a clero separat omnes, / audiat: uxoris non amat officium." Poem 86, "De sodomita prelato," in Stehling, *Medieval Latin Poems*, 88. Epigrams 91–93, from the late twelfth or early thirteenth century, cite the academic centers of Chartres, Sens, Paris, and Orléans as especially notable for sodomy.

7. Boswell, *Christianity*, 305–9.

8. *De planctu Naturae* 2. This is standard bestiary lore. The bat's "hermaphrodite" status may be a metaphor for its hybrid nature, since it was believed to be part bird and part mouse. The beaver was thought to castrate itself in order to save its life when pursued by hunters, who sought the valuable medicine extracted from its testicles. See *The Plaint of Nature*, trans. J. J. Sheridan (Toronto: Pontifical Institute of Mediaeval Studies, 1980), 94 n. 79, 103 n. 129.

9. "Multi etiam alii iuuenes, mei gracia pulcritudinis honore uestiti, siti debriati pecunie, suos Veneris malleos in incudum transtulerunt officia." *De planctu Naturae* 8, ed. N. M. Häring, *Studi Medievali* ser. 3, v. 19, pt. 2 (1978): 835. "Sed male Nature munus pro munere donat / Cum sexum lucri uendit amore suum." *De planctu* 1, p. 808. On Venus's "hammers and anvils" see below.

10. For translations of these anonymous pamphlets see Katherine Henderson and Barbara McManus, eds., *Half Humankind: Contexts and Texts of the Controversy About Women in England, 1540–1640* (Urbana: University of Illinois Press, 1985), 264–89.

11. Ziolkowski, *Alan of Lille's Grammar*, 51–76.

12. I have emended Häring's text here: by placing the comma after "Nature" he distorts the sense, misleading several critics.

13. "[Venerem] uelut discipulam instruendam docui, quas artis gramatice regulas in suarum constructionum unionibus artificiosis admitteret, quas uelut extraordinarias nullius figure excusatione redemptas excluderet. Cum enim, attestante gramatica, duo genera specialiter, masculinum uidelicet et femininum, ratio nature cognouerit, quamuis et quidam homines, sexus depauperati signaculo, iuxta meam oppinionem possint neutri generis designatione censeri, tamen Cypridi sub intimis ammonitionibus minarumque immensis iniunxi tonitruis, ut in suis coniunctionibus ratione exigentie naturalem constructionem solummodo masculini femininique generis celebraret. . . . Si enim genus masculinum genus consimile quadam irrationabilis rationis deposcat iniuria nulla figure honestate illa constructionis iunctura uicium poterit excusare sed inexcusabili soloecismi monstruositate turpabitur. Preterea Cipridi mea indixit preceptio, ut ipsa in suis constructionibus, suppositiones appositionesque ordinarias obseruando, rem feminini sexus caractere presignitam suppositionis destinaret officio, rem uero specificatam masculini generis intersignis sede collocaret appositi, ut nec appositum in uicem suppositi ualeat declinare nec suppositum possit in regionem appositi transmigrare. Et cum utrumque exigatur ab altero, appositum sub adiectiua proprietate, supposito substantiue proprietatis proprium retinenti, exigentie legibus inuitatur. Preter hoc adiunxi, ne Dionea coniunctio intransitiue constructionis habitum uniformem uel reciprocationis circulum uel retransitionis anfractum reciperet, solius transitionis recta directione contenta." *De planctu Naturae* 10, pp. 846–47.

14. Ziolkowski notes in passing that "Alan did not pause to emphasize the differences between regular grammar and Nature's grammar": *Alan of Lille's Grammar*, 35. Mark Jordan points out that according to the rules of ordinary Latin, "whorish solecism would seem to be precisely the mixture of male with female." *The Invention of Sodomy in Christian Theology* (Chicago: University of Chicago Press, 1997), 88.

15. Gautier de Coincy, "Seinte Léocade," lines 1233–43; Étienne de Barbazan, ed., *Fabliaux et contes des poètes françois des XI, XII, XIII, XIV, et XVe siècles* (Paris: Crapelet, 1808), 1: 310–11.

16. Aristotle, *On Interpretation* 1.1 16a4–9; Augustine, *De doctrina christiana* II.19, 37; Jordan, *Invention of Sodomy*, 79.

17. This constellation of "virtues" and "vices" may owe something to the *Anticlaudianus*, where moral traits are similarly conflated with socially attractive ones, but there is no conclusive evidence of Guillaume's familiarity with Alan's poem.

18. For Jean de Meun as a partisan of Nature, see the massive work of Alan Gunn, *The Mirror of Love: A Reinterpretation of* The Romance of the Rose (Lubbock: Texas Tech Press, 1952). For the partisans of Reason see D. W. Robertson, Jr., *A Preface to Chaucer: Studies in Medieval Perspectives* (Princeton, N.J.: Princeton University Press, 1962), 196–203 et passim; John Fleming, *The* Roman de la Rose: *A Study in Allegory and Iconography* (Princeton, N.J.: Princeton University Press, 1969); and idem, *Reason and the Lover* (Princeton, N.J.: Princeton University Press, 1984). My own reading is in substantial agreement with Fleming's.

19. Joan Ferrante, *Woman as Image in Medieval Literature from the Twelfth Century to Dante* (New York: Columbia University Press, 1975), 117.

20. On the range of mythographic meanings these deities could evoke, see Theresa Tinkle, *Medieval Venuses and Cupids: Sexuality, Hermeneutics, and English Poetry* (Stanford, Calif.: Stanford University Press, 1996).

21. Daniel Poirion, "Alain de Lille et Jean de Meun," in H. Roussel and F. Suard, eds., *Alain de Lille, Gautier de Châtillon, Jakemart Giélée, et leur temps* (Lille: Presses Universitaires de Lille, 1980): 142. Cf. George Economou, *The Goddess Natura in Medieval Literature* (Cambridge, Mass.: Harvard University Press, 1972), 118–20.

22. "Amors, ce est paiz haïneuse, / Amors est haine amoreuse; / C'est loiautés la desloiaus, / C'est desloiauté loiaus; / C'est paor toute asseüree, / Esperance desesperee . . ." *Roman de la Rose*, 4293–98. Cf. *De planctu* 9, p. 842: "Pax odio fraudique fides, spes iuncta timori / Est amor et mixtus cum ratione furor."

23. Hugh White, *Nature, Sex, and Goodness in a Medieval Literary Tradition* (Oxford: Oxford University Press, 2000), 133.

24. "Et ut instrumentorum fidelitas praue operationis fermentum excluderet, ei duos legitimos malleos assignaui, quibus et Parcharum inaniret insidias resque multimodas essentie presentaret. Incudum etiam nobiles officinas eiusdem artificio deputaui precipiens, ut eisdem eosdem malleos adaptando rerum effigiationi fideliter indulgeret, ne ab incudibus malleos aliqua exorbitatione peregrinare permitteret." *De planctu* 10, p. 845.

25. "Cudit in incude que semina nulla monetat. / Horret et incudem malleus ipse suam." *De planctu* 1, p. 807.

26. One manuscript in fact shows Christ rather than Nature creating the animals at this point. See Lori Walters, "Illuminating the *Rose*: Gui de Mori and the Illustrations of MS 101 of the Municipal Library, Tournai," in Kevin Brownlee and Sylvia Huot, eds., *Rethinking the* Romance of the Rose: *Text, Image, Reception* (Philadelphia: University of Pennsylvania Press, 1992), 183–84.

27. Rosemond Tuve, *Allegorical Imagery: Some Mediaeval Books and Their Posterity* (Princeton, N.J.: Princeton University Press, 1966), 324.

28. Nature and Genius later discuss the situation of Mars, Venus, and Vulcan, so some readers would surely have remarked the connection. I thank Anne Sullivan for this observation.

29. "Biau seignor, gardés vous des fames, / Se vos cors amés et vos ames, / . . . Fuiés, fuiés, fuiés, fuiés / Fuiés, enfant, fuiés tel beste." *Roman de la Rose*, 16,577–83.

30. "Car riens ne jure ne ne ment / De fame plus hardiement."—"Certes, sire prestres, bien dites / Comme preus et cortois et sages. / Trop ont fames en lor corage / Et soutillités et malices." *Roman de la Rose*, 18,127–33.

31. On this tradition see Renate Blumenfeld-Kosinski, "Satirical Views of the Beguines in Northern French Literature," in Juliette Dor, Lesley Johnson, and Jocelyn Wogan-Browne, eds., *New Trends in Feminine Spirituality: The Holy Women of Liège and Their Impact* (Turnhout: Brepols, 1999), 237–49.

32. Cf. Mechthild of Magdeburg, *The Flowing Light of the Godhead* I.4, trans. Frank Tobin (New York: Paulist Press, 1998), 43. Of course Jean de Meun could not have known Mechthild's German text, but such imagery was a commonplace of beguine spirituality.

33. "Ou qui, par grant devocion / En trop grant contemplacion, / Font aparoir en lor pensees / Les choses qu'il ont porpensees, / Et les cuident tout proprement / Veoir defors apertement; / Et ce n'est fors trufle et mençonge, / Ausinc cum de

l'omme qui songe, / Qui voit, ce cuide, en lor presences / Les espirituex sustances / Si cum fist Scipion jadis; / Et voit enfer et paradis . . ." *Roman de la Rose*, 18,357–68.

34. "Genius, li bien emparlers, / En l'ost au dieu d'Amors alés, / Qui mout de moi servir se pene / . . . Dites li que salus li mant, / Et a dame Venus, m'amie, / Puis a toute la baronnie." *Roman de la Rose*, 19,335–44.

35. "Si tost cum ot esté confesse / Dame Nature, la deesse, / Si cum la loy vuet et li us, / Li vaillans prestres Genius / Tantost l'assot et si li donne / Penitance avenant et bonne." *Roman de la Rose*, 19,411–16. On the inadequacies of Genius as a confessor see Tuve, *Allegorical Imagery*, 268–69, and Fleming, *Roman de la Rose*, 207.

36. "Tantost li diex d'Amors afuble / A Genius une chesuble; / Anel li baille et croce et mitre / Plus clere que cristal de vitre. / . . . Venus . . . ne cessoit de rire." *Roman de la Rose*, 19,477–84. Cf. Economou, *Goddess Natura*, 122–23.

37. Jerome, *Adversus Iovinianum* I.36. Trans. W. H. Fremantle in *The Principal Works of St. Jerome*, Library of Nicene and Post-Nicene Fathers (New York: Christian Literature Co., 1893), 6: 373.

38. *Roman de la Rose*, 19,583–628.

39. White, *Nature, Sex, and Goodness*, 223 (a propos of Chaucer's *Parson's Tale*).

40. Larry Benson, "The Occasion of *The Parliament of Fowls*," in Larry Benson and Siegfried Wenzel, eds., *The Wisdom of Poetry: Essays in Early English Literature in Honor of Morton W. Bloomfield* (Kalamazoo, Mich.: Medieval Institute, 1982), 123–44. This nineteenth-century hypothesis has passed in and out of critical favor, but is once again widely accepted.

41. All citations are from Larry Benson, ed., *The Riverside Chaucer*, 3rd ed. (Boston: Houghton Mifflin, 1987).

42. Chaucer seems to have observed St. Valentine's Day on May 3 and, as it happens, Richard II and Anne of Bohemia were betrothed on May 3, 1381. See the fascinating study by Henry Ansgar Kelly, *Chaucer and the Cult of Saint Valentine* (Leiden: Brill, 1986).

43. D. S. Brewer, "The Genre of *The Parliament of Fowls*," in *Chaucer: The Poet as Storyteller* (London: Macmillan, 1984); Jack B. Oruch, "Nature's Limitations and the *Demande d'Amour* of Chaucer's *Parlement*," *Chaucer Review* 18 (1983): 23–37.

44. The description of this temple is adapted from Boccaccio's *Teseida*; a very similar one appears in the *Knight's Tale*.

45. Charles McDonald, "An Interpretation of Chaucer's *Parlement of Foules*," *Speculum* 30 (1955): 444–57.

46. Cf. Hugh White: "It is the function of the reason to argue the will, if necessary, into the right course of action, but Nature, at any rate in the sphere of love, respects the will's unreasonableness." *Nature, Sex, and Goodness*, 239.

47. Elaine Tuttle Hansen, *Chaucer and the Fictions of Gender* (Berkeley: University of California Press, 1992), 128.

48. As the narrator of Chaucer's *Troilus* says of Criseyde: "lik a thing inmortal semed she, / As doth an hevenyssh perfit creature, / That down were sent in scornynge of nature" (*Troilus* I, 103–5).

49. Eric Hicks, ed., *Le Débat sur le Roman de la Rose* (Paris: Champion, 1977); Joseph Baird and John Kane, ed. and trans., *La Querelle de la Rose: Letters and Documents* (Chapel Hill: University of North Carolina Press, 1978). See also Kevin Brownlee, "Discourses of the Self: Christine de Pizan and the *Romance of the Rose*," in Kevin

Brownlee and Sylvia Huot, eds., *Rethinking the* Romance of the Rose: *Text, Image, Reception* (Philadelphia: University of Pennsylvania Press, 1992), 234–61.

50. "Ma mere, qui fu grant et lee / Et plus preux que Panthasellee / (Dieu proprement la compassa!), / En tous cas, mon pere passa / De sens, de puissance et de pris, / Non obstant eust il moult appris, / Et fu royne couronnee, / Tres adoncques qu'elle fut nee. / De sa vertu, de sa puissance / Chacun a assez cognoissance. / Il appert qu'elle n'est oyseuse / Nul temps et, sanz estre noiseuse, / Chacun endroit soy embesongne / De mainte diverse besongne, / Et bien pevent estre prouvees / Ses oeuvres, partout sont trouvees; / Moult en fait tous les jours de belles; / Qui vouldroit toutes compter celles / Qu'elle a faites et tous jours fait, / Il n'aroit jamais nul jour fait. / Ancienne est, sanz enviellir, / Et ne peut sa vie faillir / Jusques au jour du jugement. / Dieu lui donna le regiment / Du monde accroistre et maintenir, / Tresqu'il l'ot fait, pour soustenir / En vie humaine creature / On l'appelle dame Nature. / Mere est celle a toute personne: / Dieu freres et seurs tous nous sonne." Christine de Pisan, *Le Livre de la mutacion de Fortune* 1.5, lines 339–68, ed. Suzanne Solente (Paris: Picard, 1959), 1, 18–19. Trans. Kevin Brownlee in *Selected Writings of Christine de Pizan*, ed. Renate Blumenfeld-Kosinski (New York: Norton, 1997), 93–94.

51. "Christine's changing of these maternal figures, the impression of restlessness she gives in seeking to represent the mother, in short, the mutability of this role in her work, bespeaks a certain uneasiness as regards the mother's purpose. There is no question that Christine accords the mother central importance; yet the character of the center is not fixed. Christine is of several minds about the mother; the father provokes no hesitation." Andrea Tarnowski, "Maternity and Paternity in 'La Mutacion de Fortune,'" in Margarete Zimmermann and Dina De Rentiis, eds., *The City of Scholars: New Approaches to Christine de Pizan* (Berlin: Walter de Gruyter, 1994), 118.

52. "Mais il failli a son entente, / Car ma mere, qui ot pouoir / Trop plus que lui, si voult avoir / Femelle a elle ressemblable, / Si fus nee fille, sanz fable; / Mais y tant fist pour lui ma mere / Que de toutes choses mon pere / Bien ressemblay et proprement, / Fors du sexe tant seulement. . . . Mais, pour ce que fille fu nee, / Ce n'estoit pas chose ordenee / Que en riens deusse amander / Des biens mon pere, et succeder / Ne poz a l'avoir qui est pris / En la fonteine de grant pris, / Plus par coustume que par droit." *Mutacion de Fortune* 1.6, lines 388–96, 413–19, ed. Solente, 1, 20–21; trans. Brownlee, *Selected Writings*, 94.

53. "Sanz faille, de l'entendement / Connois je bien que voirement / Celi ne li donnai je mie. / La ne s'estent pas ma baillie, / Ne sui pas sage ne poissant / De faire riens si connoissant. / Je ne fis onc riens pardurables; / Quant que je fais est corrumpable." *Roman de la Rose*, 19,055–62.

54. "Si ay bien ma cause prouvee / Que Nature octroye ou nous vee / Les biens de l'ame ouvrer ou corps, / Selon que les divers accors / De l'instrument si les avoye, / Combien que Dieu ou corps l'envoye." *Mutacion de Fortune* 1.9, lines 703–8, ed. Solente, I, 31; trans. Brownlee, *Selected Writings*, 98.

55. "Ma mere Nature la belle / . . . me volt mettre servir / Une dame de hault parage, / Qui. I. poy lui tient de lignage, / Mais ne s'entre ressemblent pas, / Ne sont pas faites d'un compas." *Mutacion de Fortune* 1.7, lines 469, 476–80, ed. Solente, 1, 23; trans. Brownlee, *Selected Writings*, 95.

56. "Par force de lonc plour lassee, / Une foiz toute recassee / Demouray, com chose transsie / M'endormi a une ressie; / Adont vers moy vint ma maistresse, / Qui a plusieurs la joye estrece, / Si me toucha par tout le corps; / Chacun membre, bien m'en recors, / Manÿa et tint a ses mains, / Puis s'en ala et je remains, / . . . Je m'esveillay et fu le cas / Tel qu'incontinent et sanz doubte / Transmuee me senti toute. / Mes membres senti trop plus fors / Qu'ainçois et cil grant desconfors / Et le plour, ou adés estoie, / Auques remis; si me tastoie / Moy meismes com toute esbahie. / Ne m'ot pas Fortune enhaÿe / Adont, qui si me tresmua, / Car tout soubdainement mua / Celle grant paour et la doubte, / Ou je me confondoie toute. / Si me senti trop plus legiere / Que ne souloye et que ma chiere / Estoit muee et enforcie / Et ma voix forment engrossie / Et corps plus dur et plus isnel, / Mais choit de mon doy fu l'anel / Qu'Ymeneüs donné m'avoit, / Dont me pesa, et bien devoit, / Car je l'amoie chierement." *Mutacion de Fortune* 1.12, lines 1321–55, ed. Solente, 1, 51–52; trans. Brownlee, *Selected Writings*, 106.

57. "Car Fortune a bien la puissance / Sur ceulx de son obeissance / Faire miracles trop greigneurs, / Et souvent bestes en seigneurs / Fait transmuer, quant il lui gree, / Si grans que chacun les agree, / Et chevaliers en bestes peut / Faire tourner, quant elle veult." *Mutacion de Fortune* 1.11, lines 1035–42, ed. Solente, 1, 42. The transformation of "beasts into lords" reverses the Circe tale in a disillusioned comment on contemporary politics.

58. Ovid, *Metamorphoses* 14.248–307 (Circe), 3.322–31 (Tiresias), 9.666–797 (Iphis). Christine would also have known these tales through the medieval *Ovide moralisé*.

59. *Book of the City of Ladies* 3.12–13. Perpetua is not mentioned in *The City of Ladies*, but Christine may have been familiar with her story. See Lori Walters, "Fortune's Double Face: Gender and the Transformations of Christine de Pizan, Augustine, and Perpetua," *Fifteenth-Century Studies* 25 (1999): 97–114; and Kerstin Aspegren, *The Male Woman: A Feminine Ideal in the Early Church* (Uppsala: Almqvist & Wiksell, 1990).

60. For an alternative, theological answer to this question, see E. J. Richards, "Virile Woman *and* WomanChrist: The Meaning of Gender Metamorphosis in Christine," in Jean-Claude Mühlethaler and Denis Billotte, eds., *"Riens ne m'est seur que la chose incertaine": Études sur l'art d'écrire au Moyen Âge offertes à Eric Hicks* (Geneva: Slatkine, 2001), 239–52.

61. "Com vous ouëz, encor suis homme / Et ay esté ja bien la somme / De plus de .XIII. ans tous entiers, / Mais mieulx me plairoit plus du tiers / Estre femme, com je souloie, / Quant a Ymeneüs parloie, / Mais puisque Fortune estrangiee / M'en a, si jamais plus logiee / N'y seray, homme remaindray / Et o ma dame me tendray." *Mutacion de Fortune* 1.12, lines 1395–1404, ed. Solente, 1, 53; trans. Brownlee, *Selected Writings*, 107. Christine completed *La Mutacion* in November 1403; her husband had died in 1390.

62. Sylvia Huot, "Seduction and Sublimation: Christine de Pizan, Jean de Meun, and Dante," *Romance Notes* 25 (1985): 372–73.

63. "Tout ce qui entroit par le conduit hault par ou repeus estoit convenoit que corps materiel et corruptible eust. Mais par lautre conduit ne passoit riens fraisle ne palpable." Christine de Pizan, *Lavision-Christine* 1.1, ed. Mary Louis Towner

(Washington, D.C.: Catholic University of America Press, 1932), 73. A new edition by Christine Reno and Liliane Dulac is in preparation.

64. "Delez le dit ymage avoit assistant une grant ombre coronnee de fourme femmenine comme se fust la semblance dune tres poissant royne naturelment fourmee sanz corps visible ne palpable." *Lavision* 1.2, ed. Towner, 74.

65. "Mais comme le voulsist ainsi celle qui la destrempe avoit faitte a la quel cause ce tient et non au moulle iaportay sexe femenin." *Lavision* 1.3, ed. Towner, 75.

66. "Tout ne soye mie nabugodonozor scipion ne joseph ne sont point veez les secrez du treshault aux bien simples." *Lavision* 1.1, ed. Towner, 73. On the implications of this topos see Benjamin Semple, "The Critique of Knowledge as Power: The Limits of Philosophy and Theology in Christine de Pizan," in Marilynn Desmond, ed., *Christine de Pizan and the Categories of Difference* (Minneapolis: University of Minnesota Press, 1998), 116–19.

67. Huot, "Seduction and Sublimation," 367.

68. *Book of the City of Ladies* 1.9.2; Richards, "Virile Woman *and* WomanChrist."

69. "Adonc present vint la chamberiere de la ditte dame qui buretes tenoit pleines dune liqueur doulce et tres souefve de laquelle a abruver doulcement me pris par quel vertu et continuacion mon corps de plus en plus prenoit croissance force et vigueur. Et ycelle sage croissoit et engroissoit la pasture au feur de ma force . . ." *Lavision* 1.3, ed. Towner, 75.

70. "Pour laquelle science de poesie nature en moy resiouye, me dist, fille solace toy quant tu as attaint en effait le desir que ie te donne, ainsi continuant et vacant tous iours a lestude, comprenant les sentences de mieulx en mieulx. Ne souffist pas atant a mon sentement et engin; ains volt que par lengendrement destude et des choses veues nasquissent de moy nouvelles lettures. Adonc me dist, prens les outilz et fiers sur lenclume la matiere que ie te bailleray, si durable que fer, ne feu ne autre chose ne la pourra despecer; si forge choses delictable. Ou temps que tu portoies les enfans en ton ventre, grant douleur a lenfanter sentoies. Or vueil que de toy naiscent nouveaulx volumes, lesquieulx le temps avenir et perpetuelment au monde presenteront ta memoire devant les princes et par lumiers en toutes places, lesquieulx en ioye et delit tu enfanteras de ta memoire, non obstant le labour et travail lequel tout ainsi comme la femme qui a enfante. Si tost que ot le cry de lenfant oublie son mal, oubliera le travail du labour oyant la voix de tes volumes." *Lavision* 3.10, ed. Towner, 163–64 (punctuation altered); trans. Blumenfeld-Kosinski, *Selected Writings*, 193–94.

71. *Silence: A Thirteenth-Century French Romance*, ed. and trans. Sarah Roche-Mahdi (East Lansing, Mich.: Colleagues Press, 1992). Translations designated "RM" are Roche-Mahdi's; the rest are my own.

72. On the manuscript (University of Nottingham, MS. Mi.LM.6), see Lewis Thorpe, ed., *Le Roman de Silence* (Cambridge: Heffer, 1972), 1–12.

73. Kathleen Brahney, "When *Silence* Was Golden: Female Personae in the *Roman de Silence*," in Glyn Burgess and Robert Taylor, eds., *The Spirit of the Court* (Cambridge: D.S. Brewer, 1985), 61; Roche-Mahdi, *Silence*, xi; Suzanne Akbari, "Nature's Forge Recast in the *Roman de Silence*," in Donald Maddox and Sara Sturm-Maddox, eds., *Literary Aspects of Courtly Culture* (Cambridge: D.S. Brewer, 1994), 46; Lorraine Stock, "The Importance of Being Gender 'Stable': Masculinity and Feminine Empowerment in *Le Roman de Silence*," *Arthuriana* 7 (1997): 28–29. Akbari notes

that "the misogyny undoubtedly present in the work is no evidence against female authorship, for misogyny was and is not unique to men."

74. Heldris's consistent use of masculine pronouns for the cross-dressed Silence makes her more radical than even the most Butlerian critics, who undercut their insistence on the performative quality of gender by referring to the hero/ine as "she." See Roberta Krueger, "Women Readers and the Politics of Gender in *Le Roman de Silence*," in *Women Readers and the Ideology of Gender in Old French Verse Romance* (Cambridge: Cambridge University Press, 1993), 101–27; Peggy McCracken, "'The Boy Who Was a Girl': Reading Gender in the *Roman de Silence*," *Romanic Review* 85 (1994): 517–36.

75. Simon Gaunt, "The Significance of *Silence*," *Paragraph* 13 (1990): 203–4; Roche-Mahdi, *Silence*, xviii–xix; Akbari, "Nature's Forge Recast," 41; Adolf Tobler and Erhard Lommatzsch, *Altfranzösisches Wörterbuch* (rpt. Wiesbaden: Franz Steiner Verlag, 1965), 6: 808.

76. Roche-Mahdi interprets the name as "Alas! Woman!" or *heu! femme* (xx). In this most punning of romances, multiple meanings are not only possible but likely.

77. On the centrality of inheritance law to *Silence* see Sharon Kinoshita, "Heldris de Cornuälle's *Roman de Silence* and the Feudal Politics of Lineage," *PMLA* 110 (1995): 397–409, and Craig Berry, "Heldris's Material Girl: The Romance of Property Rights in the *Roman de Silence*," paper delivered at American Comparative Literature Association, Montreal, April 1999.

78. This episode is one of several borrowed from the matter of *Tristan*. Cador's name derives from Geoffrey of Monmouth's *Historia regum Britanniae*, where he is Duke of Cornwall and foster-father of Guenevere; his son succeeds King Arthur. Cador defeats and kills one Cheldricus, the probable source of Heldris's own pen name.

79. This motif echoes the Ovidian tale of Iphis and Ianthe (*Metamorphoses* 9.666–797), also cited in Christine's *Livre de la mutacion de Fortune*.

80. On this theme see Kathleen Blumreich, "Lesbian Desire in the Old French *Roman de Silence*," *Arthuriana* 7 (1997): 47–62.

81. For *Silence* as a protofeminist romance see Brahney, "When *Silence* Was Golden"; Regina Psaki, trans., *Le Roman de Silence* (New York: Garland, 1991), introduction; Stock, "The Importance of Being Gender 'Stable.'" For Heldris as a misogynist see Gaunt, "The Significance of *Silence*"; Krueger, "Women Readers"; Blumreich, "Lesbian Desire." Deconstructive readings stressing the indeterminacy of the text include Kate Mason Cooper, "Elle and *L*: Sexualized Textuality in *Le Roman de Silence*," *Romance Notes* 25 (1985): 341–60; R. Howard Bloch, "Silence and Holes: The *Roman de Silence* and the Art of the Trouvère," *Yale French Studies* 70 (1986): 81–99; and Peter Allen, "The Ambiguity of Silence: Gender, Writing, and *Le Roman de Silence*," in Julian Wasserman and Lois Roney, eds., *Sign, Sentence, Discourse: Language in Medieval Thought and Literature* (Syracuse, N.Y.: Syracuse University Press, 1989), 98–112.

82. These rhymes occur at lines 1027–28, 2075–76, 2089–90, 2247–48, 2253–54, 2571–72, 5607–8, and 6605–6.

83. Christine nowhere alludes to *Silence*, although she would have been keenly interested in the romance's themes. One or both authors could have adapted their

image of Nature from an oral tradition; to this day, a pregnant woman is said to "have a bun in the oven."

84. Silence's ironic, self-critical stage name recalls an episode in the *Prose Lancelot* where the hero styles himself "le chevalier mal fet"—which can mean either "the knight that hath trespassed" (Malory, *Le Morte d'Arthur* XII.6) or "the ill-made knight" (T. H. White, *The Once and Future King*). If Silence is "malduit" or transgressive from one point of view, she is "bien duit" or well-bred from another.

85. Erin Labbie, "The Specular Image of the Gender-Neutral Name: Naming Silence in *Le Roman de Silence*," *Arthuriana* 7 (1997): 65.

86. For more elaborate readings of this passage see Cooper, "Elle and *L*," 341–42; E. Jane Burns, *Bodytalk: When Women Speak in Old French Literature* (Philadelphia: University of Pennsylvania Press, 1993), 243.

87. "Bad man" is Psaki's translation; "defective male" is Roche-Mahdi's. The latter recalls the Aristotelian and Thomist definition of woman as *mas occasionatus*, a defective or misbegotten male.

88. Cf. Stock, "The Importance of Being Gender 'Stable,'" 24–27. The old man who advises Silence is never expressly named as Merlin. But in Heldris's most important source, the "Grisandole" episode from the *Estoire Merlin*, a magic stag teaches the transvestite heroine how to capture a wild man of the woods, who subsequently unmasks her. At the end of the romance, it is revealed that both the wild man and the stag were Merlin in disguise.

89. Merlin's role as wild man of the woods overlaps with another tradition that makes him half human, half demonic. Eufeme describes Merlin to Ebain as "fil al diäble" (5792); Geoffrey of Monmouth, who invented the character, makes him the son of an incubus and a royal nun.

90. "Not only does cooking mark the transition from nature to culture, but through it and by means of it, the human state can be defined with all its attributes, even those that, like mortality, might seem to be the most unquestionably natural." Claude Lévi-Strauss, *The Raw and the Cooked*, trans. John and Doreen Weightman (New York: Harper and Row, 1969), 164. See also Elisabeth Moltmann-Wendel, *A Land Flowing with Milk and Honey: Perspectives on Feminist Theology*, trans. John Bowden (New York: Crossroad, 1986), 1–4.

91. William Shakespeare, *The Winter's Tale*, IV.iv.92–97.

92. Psaki, *Roman de Silence*, xxv–xxxii.

93. On the analogues see Michèle Perret, "Travesties et transsexuelles: Yde, Silence, Grisandole, Blanchandine," *Romance Notes* 25 (1985): 328–40; Valerie Hotchkiss, *Clothes Make the Man: Female Cross Dressing in Medieval Europe* (New York: Garland, 1996), 105–24; Kerstin Losert, "Weibliches Cross-Dressing in mittelalterlicher Hagiographie: Zur Legende der heiligen Euphrosyna von Alexandrien," in Andreas Bihrer and Sven Limbeck, eds., *Exil, Fremdheit und Ausgrenzung in Mittelalter und früher Neuzeit* (Würzburg: Ergon, 2000), 75–89.

94. Brahney, "When *Silence* Was Golden," 60.

95. The editions of Thorpe and Roche-Mahdi both have a comma after v. 6690 and a period at the end of 6691. I have adopted the valuable emendation of Simon Gaunt, "Significance of Silence," 211. This reading makes good sense of a passage that is garbled in both the Psaki and Roche-Mahdi translations.

96. M. Le Roux de Lincy, ed., *Le Livre des proverbes français*, 2nd ed. (Paris: Delahays, 1859), 2: 352; cited in Akbari, "Nature's Forge Recast," 41.

97. I thank Monica Green for this information and many corroborating examples. In the *De genitalibus membris* of Constantine the African, for example, the following description occurs: "Et uesicae collum nature femineae est iunctum. Natura autem feminea est spatiolum quod utraque penis ossa mediat super anum locata." Monica Green, "The *De genecia* Attributed to Constantine the African," *Speculum* 62 (1987): 313.

98. See the classic anthropological study by Sherry Ortner, "Is Female to Male as Nature Is to Culture?" in Michelle Rosaldo and Louise Lamphere, eds., *Woman, Culture, and Society* (Stanford, Calif.: Stanford University Press, 1974), 67–87, and Carol MacCormack, "Nature, Culture and Gender: A Critique," in Carol MacCormack and Marilyn Strathern, eds., *Nature, Culture and Gender* (Cambridge: Cambridge University Press, 1980), 1–24.

Chapter 4. Love Divine, All Loves Excelling

1. Ives, *Épître à Séverin sur la charité* II.14, ed. Gervais Dumeige (Paris: J. Vrin, 1955), 61. The twelfth-century author, "frater Yvo," has not been further identified.

2. "Cum aereo uento quadam inuisibili uita, que cuncta sustinet, uitaliter omnia suscito." Hildegard of Bingen, *Liber diuinorum operum* I.1.2, ed. Albert Derolez and Peter Dronke, CCCM 92 (Turnhout: Brepols, 1996), 48. For a fuller citation see Chapter 2 above, p. 88.

3. Rosalynn Voaden, *God's Words, Women's Voices: The Discernment of Spirits in the Writing of Late-Medieval Women Visionaries* (Woodbridge: York Medieval Press, 1999); Nancy Caciola, "Discerning Spirits: Sanctity and Possession in the Later Middle Ages," PhD dissertation, University of Michigan, 1994; D. Catherine Brown, *Pastor and Laity in the Theology of Jean Gerson* (Cambridge: Cambridge University Press, 1987).

4. Among these were the Cistercian poet Hélinand of Froidmont (d. ca. 1229); the crusading anti-Cathar bishop of Toulouse, Folc of Marseille (d. 1231); the early *stilnovist* Guittone d'Arezzo, later a monk (d. ca. 1294); and the missionary theologian and mystic Ramon Llull (d. 1316).

5. This chapter will deal primarily with eroticized divine love. On the complementary movement, divinized erotic love, the best study remains that of Peter Dronke, *Medieval Latin and the Rise of European Love-Lyric*, 2 vols. (Oxford: Clarendon Press, 1966).

6. "Omnia vincit amor: et nos cedamus amori." Virgil, *Eclogue* 10.69. Chaucer's Prioress carries a rosary bearing this famously ambiguous motto: *Canterbury Tales*, General Prologue, 162.

7. C. Stephen Jaeger, *The Origins of Courtliness: Civilizing Trends and the Formation of Courtly Ideals, 939–1210* (Philadelphia: University of Pennsylvania Press, 1985); idem, *The Envy of Angels: Cathedral Schools and Social Ideals in Medieval Europe, 950–1200* (Philadelphia: University of Pennsylvania Press, 1994); Gerald Bond, *The Loving Subject: Desire, Eloquence, and Power in Romanesque France* (Philadelphia: University of Pennsylvania Press, 1995).

8. C. Stephen Jaeger, *Ennobling Love: In Search of a Lost Sensibility* (Philadelphia: University of Pennsylvania Press, 1999).

9. Bond, *Loving Subject*, 163, citing Richard Lanham, *Motives of Eloquence* (New Haven, Conn.: Yale University Press, 1976), 36. Lanham opposes Ovid to Plato rather than Augustine.

10. In addition to the established correspondence, see now Constant Mews, *The Lost Love Letters of Heloise and Abelard: Perceptions of Dialogue in Twelfth-Century France* (New York: St. Martin's Press, 1999), and Jaeger, *Ennobling Love*, 160–73.

11. In his *Distinctiones dictionum theologicalium*, Alan of Lille gives five meanings for *amor*: (1) *cupiditas*; (2) *charitas*; (3) *Spiritus sanctus*; (4) *Christus*; and (5) *naturalis affectus*. PL 210: 699a.

12. "Caritatem uoco motum animi ad fruendum deo propter ipsum et se atque proximo propter deum; cupiditatem autem motum animi ad fruendum se et proximo et quolibet corpore non propter deum." Augustine, *De doctrina christiana* III.16, CCSL 32 (Turnhout: Brepols, 1962), 87.

13. "Fecerunt itaque ciuitates duas amores duo, terrenam scilicet amor sui usque ad contemptum Dei, caelestem uero amor Dei usque ad contemptum sui." Augustine, *De civitate Dei* XIV.28, CCSL 48 (Turnhout: Brepols, 1955), 451. In XIV.7 Augustine discusses *caritas*, *amor*, and *dilectio*, noting that the Bible uses all three terms interchangeably; the last two are morally neutral.

14. Augustine, *De Trinitate* VI.5.7.

15. D. W. Robertson, Jr., *A Preface to Chaucer: Studies in Medieval Perspectives* (Princeton, N.J.: Princeton University Press, 1962). For a nuanced review of the "two loves" problem and its critical history, see Theresa Tinkle, "Beyond Binary Thinking: The Two, Three, or Ten Loves," in *Medieval Venuses and Cupids: Sexuality, Hermeneutics, and English Poetry* (Stanford, Calif.: Stanford University Press, 1996), 9–41.

16. Jean Leclercq, *Monks and Love in Twelfth-Century France* (Oxford: Clarendon Press, 1979), covers some of this ground, but is marred by the author's defensive attitude toward his subject.

17. William's anonymous biographer also refers to *De natura et dignitate amoris* as the "Anti-Naso." David Bell, ed., "The *Vita Antiqua* of William of St. Thierry," *Cistercian Studies* 11 (1976): 252.

18. "Nam et fedus amor carnalis feditatis sue olim habuit magistros, in eo quo corrupti erant et corrumpebant tam perspicaces, tam efficaces, ut ab ipsis feditatis amatoribus et sociis, doctor artis amatorie recantare cogeretur, quod intemperantius cantauerat; et de amoris scribere remedio, qui de amoris carnalis scripserat incendio." William of St.-Thierry, *De natura et dignitate amoris* 3, ed. M.-M. Davy in *Deux traités de l'amour de Dieu* (Paris: J. Vrin, 1953), 72.

19. "Ars est artium ars amoris, cujus magisterium ipsa sibi retinuit natura, et Deus auctor nature. Ipse enim amor a Creatore nature inditus, nisi naturalis ejus ingenuitas adulterinis aliquibus affectibus prepedita fuerit, ipse, inquam, se docet sed docibiles sui, docibiles Dei." Ibid. 1, p. 70.

20. "Librum etiam 'De amore', sive 'De Deo amoris', qui sic incipit: *Cogit me multum*, etc., et sic terminatur: *Cave igitur, Galtere . . .* per eandem sententiam nostram condempnamus." *Chartularium Universitatis Parisiensis*, vol. 1, no. 473, ad 1277, ed. Henri Denifle (Paris: Delalain, 1889), 543.

21. "Cum enim in tragoediis uanisue carminibus quisquam iniuriatus fingitur, uel oppressus, cuius amabilis pulchritudo, fortitudo mirabilis, gratiosus praedicetur affectus; si quis haec uel cum canuntur audiens, uel cernens si recitentur, usque ad expressionem lacrymarum quodam moueatur affectu, nonne perabsurdum est, ex hac uanissima pietate de amoris eius qualitate capere coniecturam, ut hinc fabulosum illum nescio quem affirmetur amare, pro cuius ereptione, etiamsi haec omnia uere prae oculis gererentur, ne modicam quidam substantiae suae portionem pateretur expendi?" Aelred of Rievaulx, *De speculo caritatis* II.17.50, in *Opera omnia*, ed. A. Hoste and C. H. Talbot, CCCM 1 (Turnhout: Brepols, 1971), 90.

22. "Nam et in fabulis, quae uulgo de nescio quo finguntur Arthuro, memini me nonnunquam usque ad effusionem lacrimarum fuisse permotum. Vnde non modicum pudet propriae uanitatis, qui si forte ad ea quae de Domino pie leguntur, uel cantantur, uel certe publico sermone dicuntur, aliquam mihi lacrimam ualuero extorquere, ita mihi statim de sanctitate applaudo, ac si magnum aliquid ac inusitatum mihi miraculum contigisset." Ibid.

23. "Nam utique meliores, quia certiores, erant primae illae litterae . . . quam illae, quibus tenere cogebar Aeneae nescio cuius errores oblitus errorum meorum et plorare Didonem mortuam, quia se occidit ab amore, cum interea me ipsum in his a te morientem, deus, uita mea, siccis oculis ferrem miserrimus." Augustine, *Confessiones* I.13.20, CCSL 27 (Turnhout: Brepols, 1981), 11. Augustine's disparaging "nescio cuius," echoed twice by Aelred, is the stylistic marker of his debt; but this literary echo is no reason to doubt that Aelred had a similar experience.

24. On Aelred's early life see Marsha Dutton, "The Conversion and Vocation of Aelred of Rievaulx: A Historical Hypothesis," in Daniel Williams, ed., *England in the Twelfth Century* (Woodbridge, Suffolk: Boydell, 1990), 31–49.

25. Bernard of Clairvaux, *De diligendo Deo* VIII–X, in *Sancti Bernardi Opera*, vol. 3, ed. Jean Leclercq and Henri Rochais (Rome: Editiones Cistercienses, 1963), 119–54. For an incisive account of gender and psychology in this text see Ann Astell, "Telling Tales of Love: Julia Kristeva and Bernard of Clairvaux," *Christianity and Literature* 50 (2000): 125–48.

26. "Saepe in tragoediis et aliis carminibus poetarum, in joculatorum cantilenis describitur aliquis vir prudens, decorus, fortis, amabilis et per omnia gratiosus. Recitantur etiam pressurae vel injuriae eidem crudeliter irrogatae, sicut de Arturo et Gangano et Tristanno, fabulosa quaedam referunt histriones, quorum auditu concutiuntur ad compassionem audientium corda, et usque ad lacrymas compunguntur. Qui ergo de fabulae recitatione ad misericordiam commoveris, si de Domino aliquid pium legi audias, quod extorqueat tibi lacrymas, nunquid propter hoc de Dei dilectione potes dictare sententiam? Qui compateris Deo, compateris et Arturo. Ideoque utrasque lacrymas pariter perdis, si non diligis Deum, si de fontibus Salvatoris, spe scilicet fide et charitate, devotionis et poenitentiae lacrymas non effundis." Peter of Blois, *Liber de confessione sacramentali*, PL 207: 1088–89.

27. "Sed quid est amor, Deus meus? Mira, ni fallor, animi delectatio, eo dulcior quo castior, eo suauior quo sincerior, eo iucundior quo latior: et est palatum cordis cui sapis, quia dulcis es; oculus quo uideris, quia bonus es; et est hic locus capax tui, qui summus es. Qui enim amat te, capit te; et tantum capit, quantum amat, quia ipse amor es, quia caritas es." *De speculo caritatis* I.1.2, p. 13.

28. Ibid., I.4.13, p. 17.

29. "Ipsa sola incommutabilis et aeterna requies eius, aeterna et incommutabilis tranquillitas eius, aeternum et incommutabile Sabbatum eius. Ipsa sola causa cur creauit creanda, regit regenda, administrat administranda, mouet mouenda, promouet promouenda, perficit perficienda. . . . Caritas enim eius, ipsa est uoluntas eius, ipsa est et bonitas eius: nec hoc totum aliud quam esse eius." *De speculo caritatis* I.19.56, p. 35. Trans. Elizabeth Connor, *The Mirror of Charity*, Cistercian Fathers Series 17 (Kalamazoo, Mich.: Cistercian Publications, 1990), 119.

30. Still valuable on this theme is C. S. Lewis, *The Allegory of Love: A Study in Medieval Tradition* (London: Oxford University Press, 1936), 18–23.

31. Tinkle, *Medieval Venuses*, 33.

32. Thomas Hyde, *The Poetic Theology of Love: Cupid in Renaissance Literature* (London: Associated University Presses, 1986), 18.

33. R. Freyhan has shown that in virtue-vice iconography, *caritas* under the aspect of *misericordia* was opposed to *avaritia*; under the aspect of *amor Dei*, she was opposed to *invidia*. "The Evolution of the Caritas Figure in the Thirteenth and Fourteenth Centuries," *Journal of the Warburg and Courtauld Institutes* 11 (1948): 68–86.

34. "O bona mater caritas, quae sive foveat infirmos, sive exerceat provectos, sive arguat inquietos, diversis diversa exhibens, sicut filios diligit universos! Cum te arguit, mitis est; cum blanditur, simplex est. Pie solet saevire, sine dolo mulcere; patienter novit irasci, humiliter indignari. Ipsa est quae hominum mater et angelorum, non solum quae in terris, sed etiam quae in caelo sunt pacificavit. Ipsa est quae Deum homini placans, hominem Deo reconciliavit. . . . Haec talis tamque honorabilis mater a te se queritur offensam, expostulat laesam. . . . Licet laesa, licet offensa, si conversus fueris ad illam, obviavit tibi quasi mater honorificata. Contemptus oblita sui, ruet in amplexum tui, gaudens quem perdiderat esse inventum, qui mortuus fuerat vivum." Bernard of Clairvaux, *Epistola* 2.1, in *Sancti Bernardi Opera* 7, ed. Jean Leclercq and Henri Rochais (Rome: Editiones Cistercienses, 1974), 12–13.

35. Cited without attribution by Christopher Holdsworth, Foreword to the new edition of *The Letters of St. Bernard of Clairvaux*, trans. Bruno Scott James (Kalamazoo, Mich.: Cistercian Publications, 1998), vi.

36. "Ego enim, ut verum fatear, propter te, mi Ogeri, ipsis meis curis compellor irasci, quamquam in his, teste conscientia, soli caritati cupiam deservire. . . . Quid ergo? Caritas tibi denegat quod tu petis ex caritate? Petisti, quaesisti, pulsasti, et caritas te frustrata est. Quid mihi indignaris? Si vis, si audes, irascere caritati. . . . Vides quam invitus avellor a longiore epistola, dum, ductus delectatione tibi colloquendi et desiderio satisfaciendi, dominae caritati molestus fio, qua iamdudum imperante finem fieri, necdum taceo. O quam lata in tuis litteris patet materia respondendi. . . . Sed quae aliud praecipit, domina est, immo Dominus est. Deus enim caritas est, et satis agit pro imperio, quatenus debeam potius obtemperare sibi quam vel mihi, vel tibi." Bernard, *Epistola* 88.2, in *Opera* 7, pp. 232–33.

37. Hugh of St.-Victor, "De substantia dilectionis," in *Six opuscules spirituels*, ed. Roger Baron, SC 155 (Paris: Éditions du Cerf, 1969), 82–93.

38. "Tu es plenitudo justitiae, perfectio legis, consummatio virtutis, agnitio veritatis. Via igitur es, o charitas. . . . Tu Deum ad hominem deducis, tu hominem ad Deum dirigis. Ille descendit quando ad nos venit; nos ascendimus, quando ad illum

imus. Nec ille tamen nec nos nisi per te ad alterutrum transire possumus. Tu mediatrix es, adversos concilians, disjunctos socians, et tantum dispares, quodammodo
coaequans, Deum humilians, nos sublimans, illum ad ima trahens, nos ad summa eri-
gens. Sic tamen ut nec abjecta, sed pia sit ejus descensio, nec superba, sed gloriosa
sit nostri exaltatio; magnam ergo vim habes, charitas, tu sola Deum trahere potuisti
de coelo ad terras. O quam forte est vinculum tuum, quo et Deus ligari potuit, et
homo ligatus vincula iniquitatis disrupit! . . . O charitas! quantum potes? si tantum
invaluisti erga Deum, quanto magis erga homines! Si Deus propter hominem tanta
pertulit, quid homo propter Deum tolerare recusabit? Sed fortassis facilius vincis
Deum quam hominem, magis praevalere potes Deo quam homini, quia quo magis
beatum, eo magis Deo est debitum a te superari. . . . adhuc nos rebelles habuisti,
quando illum tibi obedientem de sede paternae majestatis usque ad infirma nostrae
mortalitatis suscipienda descendere coegisti. Adduxisti illum vinculis tuis alligatum,
adduxisti illum sagittis tuis vulneratum. Amplius ut puderet hominem tibi resistere,
cum te videret etiam in Deum triumphasse. Vulnerasti impassibilem, ligasti insuper-
abilem, traxisti incommutabilem, aeternum fecisti mortalem." Hugh of St.-Victor, *De
laude charitatis*, PL 176, 974a-975a.

39. "Multi jam in suis praecordiis sagittas tuas infixas portant, et altius adhuc
eas infigi desiderant. Delectabiliter enim et suaviter vulnerati sunt, et plagas tuas se
percepisse nec dolent, nec erubescunt. O charitas! quanta est victoria tua!" Ibid.,
975a.

40. "Talia in me utinam multiplicet vulnera a planta pedis usque ad verticem, ut
non sit in me sanitas. Mala enim sanitas, ubi vulnera vacant quae Christi pius infligit
aspectus." Gilbert of Hoyland, *Sermones in Canticum Salomonis* 30.2, PL 184, 156b.

41. "O charitas! . . . Nescio enim an forte majus sit te Deum dicere an Deum te
superasse. Quod si majus est, etiam hoc libenter et fiducialiter de te dicam: 'Deus
charitas est, et qui manet in charitate in Deo manet, et Deus in eo.' Audi, homo, et
ne amplius parum reputes si charitatem habes, audi quod Deus charitas est. Nunquid
parum est Deum in se manentem habere? tantum est charitatem possidere, Deus
enim charitas est. Hoc privilegium sola charitas habet ut Deus dicatur et sit, ita ut
nulli alteri hoc convenire possit. Non enim dicitur: Deus humilitas est, aut: Deus
patientia est, sicut dicitur: Deus charitas est." Hugh, *De laude charitatis*, PL 176, 975b.

42. On Hildegard see Chapter 2 above, pp. 88–89, and Barbara Newman, *Sister
of Wisdom: St. Hildegard's Theology of the Feminine* (Berkeley: University of California
Press, 1987), chap. 2. On Hadewijch see below, pp. 169–81.

43. The name "Pan," Ridewall explains, means *deus totius*. Just as this god was
conquered by a beautiful girl, "sicud et nos dicimus dei filium victum amore nature
humane in virginis uterum corporaliter descendisse." The prooftext for this assertion
is the passage from *De laude charitatis*. John Ridewall, *Fulgentius metaforalis*, ed. Hans
Liebeschütz (Leipzig: Teubner, 1926), 81.

44. This is Cant. 2.5 in the Old Latin version, based on the Septuagint; the Vulgate reads "quia amore langueo." Both versions deeply influenced the development of
mystical writing.

45. "Caritas vulnerat, caritas ligat, caritas languidum facit, caritas defectum
adducit. Quid horum non validum? Quid horum non violentum?" Richard of St.-
Victor, *De IV gradibus violentae caritatis* 4, ed. Gervais Dumeige, in *Ives, Epître à*

Séverin sur la charité, 129. The word *defectus* may denote either terminal illness or the swoon of ecstasy.

46. "Hic est ille gradus, ut diximus, qui defectum adducit et de remedio jam desperare facit." *De IV gradibus* 15, p. 141.

47. For discussions of Richard's treatise see Gervais Dumeige, *Richard de Saint-Victor et l'idée chrétienne de l'amour* (Paris: Presses Universitaires de France, 1952), 133–53; Bernard McGinn, *The Growth of Mysticism: Gregory the Great Through the Twelfth Century* (New York: Crossroad, 1994), 415–18. Dumeige notes that more than 30 manuscripts of the treatise are extant in libraries throughout Europe, from Oxford to Prague.

48. Andreas's *De amore* has a dramatic date of 1174, but was probably composed in the mid-1180s at the court of Marie de Champagne. The early works of Chrétien (ca. 1135–after 1190), another of Marie's protégés, included a French adaptation of Ovid's *Ars amatoria* and a version of the *Tristan* romance, which do not survive. His extant romances (*Erec et Énide*, *Cligés*, *Yvain*, and the unfinished *Lancelot* and *Perceval*) date from the 1160s through the 1180s.

49. "Hec tibi anime vulnerate certa sint signa, gemitus atque suspiria, vultus pallens atque tabescens." Richard, *De IV gradibus* 6, p. 131.

50. "Sepe itaque [amor] recedens semperque seipso major rediens paulatim animum emollit, viresque effringit atque exhaurit, donec plene animum sibi subigat atque substernat, jugique sui memoria totum occupet, totum implicet, totum obliget, ita ut hoc ei excidere aut aliud cogitare non possit." Ibid.

51. "Omnis consuevit amans in coamantis aspectu pallescere"; "Verus amans assidua sine intermissione coamantis imaginatione detinetur." Andreas Capellanus, *De amore* II.8 ("Regulae amoris" 15 and 30), ed. P. G. Walsh (London: Duckworth, 1982), 282–84.

52. "Nonne tibi corde percussus videtur, quando igneus ille amoris aculeus mentem hominis medullitus penetrat . . . ?" Richard, *De IV gradibus* 6, p. 131.

53. "[Amors] si dolcemant le requiert / que par les ialz el cuer le fiert; / et cist cos a plus grant duree / que cos de lance ne d'espee: / cos d'espee garist et sainne / molt tost, des que mires i painne; / et la plaie d'Amors anpire / quant ele est plus pres de son mire." Chrétien de Troyes, *Yvain, ou Le Chevalier au Lion*, vv. 1369–76, ed. Jan Nelson and Carleton W. Carroll (New York: Appleton-Century-Crofts, 1968), 80–81. Trans. Ruth Harwood Cline, *Yvain* (Athens: University of Georgia Press, 1984), 38. Although *Yvain* was composed a few years after Richard's death in 1173, the motif of Love as archer was already ubiquitous.

54. Chrétien de Troyes, *Erec and Énide*, vv. 2396–2430, ed. and trans. Carleton W. Carroll (New York: Garland, 1987), 106–9.

55. "In hoc autem gradu amoris nimietas ad languoris similitudinem, manus ac pedes enervat, ut deinceps mens nichil penitus pro arbitrio agat." Richard, *De IV gradibus* 11, p. 137.

56. Chrétien de Troyes, *Lancelot* (*Le Chevalier de la charrete*), vv. 711–71, ed. and trans. William Kibler (New York: Garland, 1981), 32–35.

57. Numerous oral versions of the *Tristan* romance were circulating in Richard's lifetime. Of the written texts, he might have known either the lost version of Chrétien or that by Thomas of Brittany (ca. 1160), the basis of Gottfried von

Strassburg's classic *Tristan*. Cf. Barbara Newman, *From Virile Woman to Woman-Christ* (Philadelphia: University of Pennsylvania Press, 1995), 159–61.

58. "Les traités de Gérard de Liège sur l'amour illicite et sur l'amour de Dieu," ed. André Wilmart, *Analecta reginensia: Extraits des manuscrits latins de la reine Christine conservés au Vatican*, Studi e testi 59 (Rome: Vatican, 1933, rpt. 1966), 181–247. The text of the *Incitamenta* appears on pp. 205–47. The following discussion of Gérard is adapted from my article, "The Mirror and the Rose: Marguerite Porete's Encounter with the *Dieu d'Amours*," in *The Vernacular Spirit*, ed. Renate Blumenfeld-Kosinski, Duncan Robertson, and Nancy Warren (New York: Palgrave, 2002), 105–23.

59. The prologue to its companion piece, *Septem remedia contra amorem illicitum valde utilia*, is addressed to lovers of both sexes, *amatores et amatrices*. Wilmart, *Les traités*, 184.

60. Nico van den Boogaard demonstrates that Gérard took many of his French lyrics from preexisting motets—a polyphonic genre that similarly yokes sacred texts in Latin with secular ones in the vernacular. "Les insertions en français dans un traité de Gérard de Liège," in *Marche romane: Mélanges de philologie et de littératures romanes offerts à Jeanne Wathelet-Willem* (Liège: Cahiers de l'Association des romanistes de l'Université de Liège, 1978), 679–97.

61. *Quinque incitamenta* I.5, p. 209. I have printed Gérard's French quotations as verse, though they appear in Wilmart's edition as prose.

62. Ibid. III.4, p. 228.

63. Ibid. III.4.3, p. 232.

64. Ibid., p. 233.

65. Jean Seznec, *The Survival of the Pagan Gods: The Mythological Tradition and Its Place in Renaissance Humanism and Art*, trans. Barbara Sessions (New York: Bollingen Foundation, 1953), 105.

66. Renaut de Bâgé [or Beaujeu], *Le Bel Inconnu (Li Biaus Descouneüs; The Fair Unknown)*, ed. Karen Fresco, trans. Colleen Donagher (New York: Garland, 1992). This romance, indebted to Chrétien de Troyes, is dated ca. 1191–1230.

67. *Quinque incitamenta* IV.1, p. 240. The lines quoted by Gérard do not appear in Renaut's text, but there were numerous versions of the Fair Unknown romance, and the lyric here cited might have been sung independently of the full narrative.

68. Ibid. III.3.3, p. 224.

69. "Certe ille qui diutius et magis continue tenet galeam in capite et amplius patitur et diutius in conflictu moratur. Talis laudatur et appretiatur, et de iure, quantumcumque pauper sit, pretium et gloriam torneamenti debet habere." Ibid. III.4.3.1, p. 234.

70. Henry Suso, *The Life of the Servant*, ch. 44, in *The Exemplar*, trans. Frank Tobin (New York: Paulist Press, 1989), 171–73. As in Gérard's text, the winner is not the knight who defeats the most rivals (as in many romance tournaments), but the one who endures the most blows.

71. "Sic sine dubio amor siue caritas passio est fortissima, quam nullus sentire et degustare potest quin de necessitate oporteat eum omnes sensus et motus corporeos amittere et etiam motus anime, scilicet scire suum, posse suum et uelle suum, captiuare in obsequium amoris. Hoc enim bene senserat et cognouerat Augustinus,

li anguisseus damours, qui dicebat: O potens et prepotens passio caritatis. Iure enim potens, quia animum quem possederit sui ipsius efficit impotentem." *Quinque incitamenta* III.3.1, p. 223.

72. "Elle a perdu l'usage de ses sens . . . car Amour l'a ravie du lieu ou elles estoit." Marguerite Porete, *Le Mirouer des simples ames*, ch. 110, ed. Romana Guarnieri, CCCM 69 (Turnhout: Brepols, 1986), 300.

73. *Quinque incitamenta* III.2.2, p. 219.

74. "Si autem uiolentiam requirit amor noster, *cest con li face force*, nullus maiorem uiolentiam pro eo faciet quam ipse. Petit enim eum quasi gladio euaginato. Aut enim eum amabis aut eterna morte morieris. Unde Dauid: Nisi conversi fueritis, ab amore mundi scilicet ad amorem dei, gladium suum vibrabit. Unde hic potest dici quoddam carmen quod uulgo canitur: *Tout a force maugre uostre uorsai uostre amour auoir*." *Quinque incitamenta* II, p. 211.

75. Kathryn Gravdal, *Ravishing Maidens: Writing Rape in Medieval French Literature and Law* (Philadelphia: University of Pennsylvania Press, 1991). On sexual violence in the pastourelle, which occasionally features the rape of a shepherdess by a knight, see pp. 104–21.

76. "On est tenté de croire que ce fut là plutôt chez Gérard une sorte de manie qui n'a fait que grandir, un désir instinctif et bizarre de se distinguer et, tout ensemble, de se distraire au moyen de cet artifice un peu puéril." André Wilmart, "Gérard de Liège: Un traité inédit de l'amour de Dieu," *Revue d'ascétique et de mystique* 12 (1931): 373.

77. Dronke, *Medieval Latin and the Rise of European Love-Lyric*, I: 62.

78. *Quinque incitamenta* IV.4, p. 246.

79. Karl Christ, ed., "*La Règle des Fins Amans*: Eine Beginenregel aus dem Ende des XIII. Jahrhunderts," in B. Schädel and W. Mulertt, eds., *Philologische Studien aus dem romanisch-germanischen Kulturkreise: Festschrift Karl Voretzsch* (Halle: Max Niemeyer, 1927), 173–213; Newman, *From Virile Woman*, 139–43.

80. "Das Liebesconcil," ed. Georg Waitz, *Zeitschrift für deutsches Alterthum* 7 (1849): 160–67; "Das Kloster der Minne," ed. E. Schaus, *Zeitschrift für deutsches Altertum und deutsche Literatur* 38 (1894): 361–68; Ingeborg Glier, "Kloster der Minne," *Die deutsche Literatur des Mittelalters: Verfasserlexikon* IV: 1235–38.

81. Exceptions include Anselm of Bec and John of Fécamp, among the earliest medieval authors of "affective prayer." See Jean Leclercq, *The Love of Learning and the Desire for God: A Study of Monastic Culture*, trans. Catharine Misrahi (New York: Fordham University Press, 1961); Rachel Fulton, *From Judgment to Passion: Devotion to Christ and the Virgin Mary, 800–1200* (New York: Columbia University Press, 2002), chapter 3.

82. See Denys Turner, *Eros and Allegory: Medieval Exegesis of the Song of Songs* (Kalamazoo, Mich.: Cistercian Publications, 1995), which includes an anthology of texts in English; E. Ann Matter, *The Voice of My Beloved: The Songs of Songs in Western Medieval Christianity* (Philadelphia: University of Pennsylvania Press, 1990); Ann Astell, *The Song of Songs in the Middle Ages* (Ithaca, N.Y.: Cornell University Press, 1990); Friedrich Ohly, *Hohelied-Studien: Grundzüge einer Geschichte der Hohelied-Auslegung des Abendlandes bis um ca. 1200* (Wiesbaden: F. Steiner, 1958).

83. Paris, Bibliothèque nationale f. fr. 14,966, fol. IV; cited in Joris Reynaert,

"Hadewijch: Mystic Poetry and Courtly Love," in *Medieval Dutch Literature in Its European Context*, ed. Erik Kooper (Cambridge: Cambridge University Press, 1994), 219. For Marguerite Porete's response to the influence of the *Rose*, see my essay "The Mirror and the Rose."

84. "Duplex est motus in caritate, videlicet motus amicitiae et motus concupiscentiae. Motus amicitiae est ille quo quis desiderat Deo placere et servire; motus concupiscentiae est quo desiderat Deum habere et videre." Bonaventura, III *Sent.* dist. 27, a. 2, q. 2, t. 2, in *Opera omnia* III (Quaracchi: Collegium S. Bonaventurae, 1887), 607. Conversely, Thomas Aquinas denied that *concupiscentia* could have any part in *caritas*: "Amor qui est in concupiscibili est amor sensitivi boni. Ad bonum autem divinum, quod est intelligibile, concupiscibilis se extendere non potest, sed sola voluntas. Et ideo concupiscibilis subjectum caritatis esse non potest." *Summa theologiae* II–II, q. 24, a. 1.

85. "Du hast mich gejagt, gevangen, gebunden und so tief gewundet, das ich niemer wirde gesunt. Du hast mir manigen kúlenschlag geben, sage mir, sol ich ze jungest vor dir genesen? . . . Die minne: Das ich dich jagete, des luste mich; das ich dich vieng, des gerte ich; das ich dich bant, des fröwete ich mich; do ich dich wundote, do wurde du mit mir vereinet; so ich dir kúlinschlege gibe, so wirde ich din gewaltig. Ich han den almehtigen got von dem himelrich getriben und han ime benomen sin mönschlich leben und han in mit eren sinem vatter wider gegeben, wie wenest du snöder wurm mögen vor mir genesen?" Mechthild von Magdeburg, *Das fliessende Licht der Gottheit* I.3, ed. Hans Neumann (Munich: Artemis, 1990), 9–10; trans. Frank Tobin, *The Flowing Light of the Godhead* (New York: Paulist Press, 1998), 42.

86. "Wer von minnen stirbet, den sol man in gotte begraben." Mechthild, ed. Neumann, p. 10.

87. Hildegard E. Keller, *My Secret Is Mine: Studies on Religion and Eros in the German Middle Ages* (Leuven: Peeters, 2000), 232.

88. Ibid., 153.

89. Lamprecht von Regensburg, *Tochter Syon*, lines 3190–3200, in *Sanct Francisken Leben und Tochter Syon*, ed. Karl Weinhold (Paderborn: F. Schöningh, 1880), 445.

90. Ibid., lines 4188–95, p. 489.

91. Heike Kraft, *Die Bildallegorie der Kreuzigung Christi durch die Tugenden* (dissertation, Freie Universität Berlin, Frankfurt, 1976), with a catalogue of 25 examples; Gertrud Schiller, *Iconography of Christian Art* (London: Lund Humphries, 1972), 2: 137–40 and Figs. 446–54; Jeffrey Hamburger, *The Rothschild Canticles: Art and Mysticism in Flanders and the Rhineland circa 1300* (New Haven, Conn.: Yale University Press, 1990), 72–77; Keller, *My Secret Is Mine*, 248–52.

92. Cf. Caesarius of Heisterbach, *Dialogus miraculorum* VIII.19: "Qui autem sunt Christi, qui cum Apostolo dicere possunt: 'Christo confixi sumus cruci.' . . . Tres clavi quibus corpus monachi cruci debet esse affixum, tres sunt virtutes, per quas teste Hieronimo martyres efficiuntur, scilicet obedientia, patientia, humilitas. . . . Crux monachorum rigor ordinis est." Ed. Joseph Strange (Cologne: J. M. Heberle, 1851), 2: 97. Cf. Hamburger, *Rothschild Canticles*, 76.

93. Oscar Wilde, "The Ballad of Reading Gaol."

94. Hamburger, *Rothschild Canticles*, 75.

95. Hellmut Rosenfeld, "Der mittelalterliche Bilderbogen," *Zeitschrift für deutsches Altertum und deutsche Literatur* 85 (1954): 66–75.

96. P. Romuald Banz, ed., *Christus und die minnende Seele: Zwei spätmittel-hochdeutsche mystische Gedichte* (Breslau: Marcus, 1908); Hellmut Rosenfeld, "Christus und die minnende Seele," in *Die deutsche Literatur des Mittelalters: Verfasserlexikon* I: 1235–37; Jeffrey Hamburger, *The Visual and the Visionary: Art and Female Spirituality in Late Medieval Germany* (New York: Zone, 1998), 124–27; Keller, *My Secret Is Mine*, 185–229. The poem edited by Banz (pp. 259–63) is an elaboration based on the fourteenth-century broadsheet, which has been reconstructed from later woodcuts such as Figure 4.6.

97. Annemarie Klecker, "Das Büchlein von der geistleichen Gemahelschaft in Cod. 295 des Wiener Schottenstiftes," *Festschrift für Dietrich Kralik* (Horn, Austria: Ferdinand Berger, 1954), 193–203, at 197. In this poem seven drops of blood—the seven gifts of the Holy Spirit—fall from the Bridegroom's wounded heart.

98. Ulrich von Liechtenstein, *Frauendienst*, ed. Reinhold Bechstein, 2 vols. (Leipzig: Brockhaus, 1888); trans. J. W. Thomas, *Ulrich von Liechtenstein's* Service of Ladies (Chapel Hill: University of North Carolina Press, 1969).

99. For the invitation and challenge issued by "Queen Venus" in a letter to "all of the knights who reside in Lombardy, Friuli, Carinthia, Styria, Austria, and Bohemia," see Thomas, *Service of Ladies*, 100.

100. Yet nineteenth-century scholars (cousins to those who read Andreas's *De amore* as a solemn "bible of courtly love") took the *Frauendienst* at face value as a realistic account of love-service. On its critical history see Thomas, 12–14.

101. Matter, *Voice of My Beloved*, 56–58; Fulton, *From Judgment to Passion*, chap. 5; Sylvia Huot, *From Song to Book: The Poetics of Writing in Old French Lyric and Lyrical Narrative Poetry* (Ithaca, N.Y.: Cornell University Press, 1987).

102. Ursula Peters questions even this datum in *Religiöse Erfahrung als literarisches Faktum: Zur Vorgeschichte und Genese frauenmystischer Texte des 13. und 14. Jahrhunderts* (Tübingen: Niemeyer, 1988), but her extreme skepticism has not been generally accepted.

103. There are now two complete English translations of the *Stanzaic Poems*: the received version by Columba Hart in *Hadewijch: The Complete Works* (New York: Paulist Press, 1980), and a parallel Dutch/English edition by Marieke van Baest, *Poetry of Hadewijch* (Leuven: Peeters, 1998). I have cited Hart's translations.

104. On the *Visions* and their audience see Frank Willaert, "Hadewijch und ihr Kreis in den 'Visionen,'" in Kurt Ruh, ed., *Abendländische Mystik im Mittelalter* (Stuttgart: Metzler, 1986): 368–87.

105. Discussions of Hadewijch's theology can be found in Bernard McGinn, *The Flowering of Mysticism: Men and Women in the New Mysticism, 1200–1350* (New York: Crossroad, 1998): 200–22; John Giles Milhaven, *Hadewijch and Her Sisters: Other Ways of Loving and Knowing* (Albany, N.Y.: SUNY Press, 1993); Louis Bouyer, *Figures mystiques féminines* (Paris: Éditions du Cerf, 1989), 13–47; Paul Mommaers, "Hadewijch: A Feminist in Conflict," *Louvain Studies* 13 (1988): 58–81; Kurt Ruh, "Beginenmystik: Hadewijch, Mechthild von Magdeburg, Marguerite Porete," *Zeitschrift für deutsches Altertum* 106 (1977): 265–77; J.-B. Porion, introduction to Hadewijch, *Lettres spirituelles* (Geneva: Martingay, 1972), 7–58. See also Newman, "*La*

mystique courtoise: Thirteenth-Century Beguines and the Art of Love," in *From Virile Woman*, 137–67.

106. For literary treatments see Joris Reynaert, "Hadewijch: Mystic Poetry and Courtly Love," in Kooper, ed., *Medieval Dutch Literature*, 208–25; Elizabeth Petroff, "Gender, Knowledge, and Power in Hadewijch's *Strophische Gedichten*," in *Body and Soul: Essays on Medieval Women and Mysticism* (New York: Oxford University Press, 1994), 182–203; Wilhelm Breuer, "Philologische Zugänge zur Mystik Hadewijchs: Zu Form und Funktion religiöser Sprache bei Hadewijch," in Margot Schmidt and Dieter Bauer, eds., *Grundfragen christlicher Mystik* (Stuttgart: Frommann-Holzboog, 1987), 103–21; Elizabeth Wainwright-deKadt, "Courtly Literature and Mysticism: Some Aspects of Their Interaction," *Acta Germanica* 12 (1980): 41–60; Tanis Guest, *Some Aspects of Hadewijch's Poetic Form in the "Strofische Gedichten"* (The Hague: Martinus Nijhoff, 1975); and Theodoor Weevers, *Poetry of the Netherlands in Its European Context, 1170–1930* (London: Athlone, 1960), 26–39.

107. For a discussion of the gender and divinity of Hadewijch's Minne, see Newman, "*La mystique courtoise*: Thirteenth-Century Beguines and the Art of Love," in *From Virile Woman*, 137–67; cf. Petroff, "Gender, Knowledge, and Power."

108. *Orewoet* is according to Kurt Ruh "a Dutch technical term for ecstasy": "Beginenmystik," 244. This keyword, which appears only in mystical and hagiographic texts, has been variously translated as "love's fierce fury" (van Baest), "madness of love" (Hart), "primal fury" (Mommaers), "stormy longing" (Petroff). Hart takes it as a translation of *insania amoris*, a term used by William of St.-Thierry in *De natura et dignitate amoris* 3.2. Hart, *Complete Works* 375, n. 19.

109. Van Baest, *Poetry*, 26–30.

110. This is Letter 22. On Hadewijch and Abelard see Newman, *From Virile Woman*, 168–71.

111. Cited in *Moriz von Craun*, a Middle High German poem. See Weevers, *Poetry of the Netherlands*, 16, and Reynaert, "Hadewijch," 216.

112. For Romance features of Hadewijch's versification see Weevers, *Poetry of the Netherlands*, 34–38. These features may have been introduced by the poet herself, but they may also have entered the Dutch lyrical repertoire through some of her precursors whose work does not survive. See also Guest, *Some Aspects*, 48–50.

113. Weevers, *Poetry of the Netherlands*, 36. On Folc (also known as Fulk, Folco, or Folquet), see Nicole Schulman, *Where Troubadours Were Bishops: The Occitania of Folc of Marseille (1150–1231)* (New York: Routledge, 2001).

114. Ria Vanderauwera, "The Brabant Mystic Hadewijch," in Katharina Wilson, ed., *Medieval Women Writers* (Athens: University of Georgia Press, 1984), 191–92.

115. Beguines in Hadewijch's day were still loosely organized and attended Mass with other laymen and women at their parish churches. See Walter Simons, "The Beguine Movement in the Southern Low Countries: A Reassessment," *Bulletin de l'Institut historique belge de Rome* 59 (1989): 63–105.

116. "Be good toward those who have need of you, devoted toward the sick, generous with the poor, and recollected in spirit": Letter 2 in Hart, p. 49. Cf. Letters 16 (p. 81) and 24 (p. 103) as well as Poem 8, stanza 4: "He who wishes to become Love performs excellent works, / . . . Whether he serves the sick or the well, / The blind, the crippled or the wounded— / He will accept this as his debt to Love"

(p. 148). Sara, Emma, and Margriet are mentioned in Letter 25 (pp. 105–6), which is addressed to another unnamed disciple.

117. "Maer die met waerheiden minne ghestaen / Si selen met minnen in minne doregaen / Al dat rike daer minne es vrouwe / Ende al dat heerscap een met hare ontfaen / Ende doresmaken hare edele trouwe." Van Baest, 232; trans. Hart, 225.

118. Guest, *Some Aspects*, 84–87, summarizing earlier discussions.

119. Mary Suydam, "Beguine Textuality: Sacred Performances," in Mary Suydam and Joanna Ziegler, eds., *Performance and Transformation: New Approaches to Late Medieval Spirituality* (New York: St. Martin's Press, 1999), 169–210. Suydam imagines Hadewijch's *visions* as ecstatic performances, but does not consider the likelier possibility that she might have performed her lyrics.

120. A later German mystic, Henry Suso, also defined his identity in part through the role of *Minneritter*. See Julius Schwietering, "Zur Autorschaft von Seuses Vita," in Kurt Ruh, ed., *Altdeutsche und altniederländische Mystik* (Darmstadt: Wissenschaftliche Buchgesellschaft, 1964), 309–23.

121. Frank Willaert, *De poëtica van Hadewijch in de Strofische Gedichten* (Utrecht: HES, 1984), 347; Breuer, "Philologische Zugänge," 114; van Baest, *Poetry*, 35.

122. Hendrik van Veldeke, "Sô wê der minnen is sô vrût," lines 1–7, in Olive Sayce, ed., *Poets of the Minnesang* (Oxford: Clarendon Press, 1967), 27. Translations of Minnesang are my own.

123. Cf. 28, 51–2: "In high Love's school / Is learned the madness of Love." Trans. Hart, 207.

124. "Alle schuole sint gar ein wint / wan diu schuole al eine, dâ der Minne junger sint: / diu ist sô künsterîche, daz man ir muoz der meisterschefte jehen. / ir besem zamt sô wilden man, / daz er nie gehôrte noch gesach, daz er daz kan: / wâ hât ieman mêre sô hôher schuole gehoeret oder gesehen?" Reinmar von Zweter, "Alle schuole," 1–6, in Sayce, *Poets,* 148.

125. Walther von der Vogelweide, "Ich hân ir sô wol gesprochen," 2,6–8 and 4,1–2, in Ingrid Kasten, ed., *Deutsche Lyrik des frühen und hohen Mittelalters* (Frankfurt: Deutscher Klassiker Verlag, 1995), 398–400.

126. "Minne, ich diene dir: du solt / solt mir geben minneclîchen. / rîchen maht du mich an fröiden, des ist zît. / ob mir daz dîn helfe erholt, / holt bin ich dir inneclîchen; / wîchen muoz von mir leit daz mir nâhe lît. / minneclîchiu Minne, ich was gebunden / dir von kinde ie. wiltu mich nu wunden, / was tougt danne staetiu triuwe? Minne, daz verbir." Gottfried von Neifen, "Sumer, nû wil dîn gewalt," lines 37–45, in Sayce, *Poets,* 170.

127. "Sint ic al minnen soude / Wan gave si mi al minne / . . . Ic en weet wies mi gheneren / Si weet wel wat ic meene / Want ic hebbe so dat mine verlevet / Ic en hebbe el niet sine ghevet." Van Baest, p. 70; trans. Hart, p. 143.

128. "Ay minne weder spaerdi mi / So sparic u dies manic di / Mi wondert bi wat saken dat si / Dat ghi mi dus vremde sijt / Ghi sijt mi verre ende ic u bi / Dies lidic altoes droeven tijt." Van Baest, p. 286; trans. Hart, p. 256.

129. Vision 13 in Hart, p. 300; cf. Letter 8, p. 65.

130. *Poems in Couplets*, 10, lines 93–97, in Hart, p. 337.

131. "Ez ist unnôt daz ieman mîner verte vrâge: / ich sage wol für wâr die reise mîn. / mich vienc diu Minne und lie mich varn ûf mîne sicherheit. / nu hât si mir

enboten bî ir liebe daz ich var. / ez ist unwendic: ich muoz endelîchen dar: / wie kûme ich braeche mîne triuwe und mînen eit! // Sich rüemet maniger waz er dur die Minne taete: / wâ sint die werc? die rede hoere ich wol. / doch saehe ich gern daz si ir etes-lîchen baete / daz er ir diente als ich ir dienen sol. / ez ist geminnet, der sich dur die Minne ellenden muoz. // ich wil mich rüemen, ich mac wol von minnen singen, / sît mich diu Minne hât und ich si hân. / daz ich dâ wil, seht daz wil alse gerne haben mich." Hartmann von Aue, "Ich var mit iuwern hulden," lines 3–13, 19–21, in Sayce, *Poets*, 70–71.

132. Ulrich von Winterstetten, "Sumer ouget sîne wunne," lines 37–45, in Sayce, *Poets*, 175.

133. Exceptions to this rule are Hadewijch's poems on biblical subjects, such as Poems 26 (Solomon and the Queen of Sheba) and 29 (Mary and the prophets). She also makes use of allegorical figures, including Reason, Pleasure, and Fidelity.

134. "Oec moet hi trecken Sere die minne sal voltijen / Hare wide wijt hare hogheste hoghe Hare diepste afgront / Hi sal in alle storme die weghe doresien / Hem wert haers wonders wonder cont / Dat es die weelde wide te gane / Te dorel-openne ende niet te stane / Die hoghede dore vlieghen ende dore clemmen / Ende dien afgront dore swimmen / Daer minne al minne te ontfane." Van Baest, 152; trans. Hart, 183–84.

135. "Waer henen es minne in vinder niet / Minne heeft mi al minne ontseghet / Waer mi dat ye bi minnen ghesciet / Dat ic een ure hadde ghelevet / In hare hulde hoe soet mi staet / So sochtic ane hare trouwe aflaet / Nu moetic swighen doghen ende dueren / Scarp ordel met nuwen uren // Minne heeft mi recht loes ghedaen / Ane wiene salic nu soeken raet / Dats ane trouwe . . . " Van Baest, 238–40; trans. Hart, 228–29.

136. Van Baest, *Poetry*, 39–41.

137. Letter 4 in Hart, 54.

138. We can catch a faint echo of Hadewijch's passion in *Der Schürebrand* (*The Firebrand*), a late-medieval treatise of spiritual guidance, which addresses its teenage female reader by the title of *liebe junge Gottes ritterin*—"dear young woman-knight of God." Keller, *My Secret Is Mine*, 240.

139. Poem 12, lines 66–70: " sine leven so vri / Alse ic al minnen ende minne al mi / Wat mach hen dan meer werren / Want in hare ghenaden staen si / Die sonne die mane die sterren." Van Baest, 106; trans. Hart, 159. The pronoun *hare* is ambigu-ous; Van Baest translates "in hare ghenaden" as "at *their* mercy." Hart's translation may be influenced by the verses of Dante cited below.

140. I cite the *Commedia* from the edition of John Sinclair, *The Divine Comedy of Dante Alighieri*, 3 vols. (New York: Oxford University Press, 1961).

141. I am nevertheless indebted to the following works: Charles Williams, *The Figure of Beatrice: A Study in Dante* (London: Faber and Faber, 1943); Charles Single-ton, *An Essay on the* Vita Nuova (Cambridge, Mass.: Harvard University Press, 1949); Mark Musa, "An Essay on the *Vita Nuova*," in *Dante's* Vita Nuova: *A Translation and an Essay* (Bloomington: Indiana University Press, 1973); Joan Ferrante, *Woman as Image in Medieval Literature from the Twelfth Century to Dante* (New York: Columbia University Press, 1975), 129–52; eadem, *Dante's Beatrice: Priest of an Androgynous God*, Occasional Papers 2, Center for Medieval and Early Renaissance Studies (Binghamton,

N.Y.: Medieval and Renaissance Texts and Studies, 1992); Thomas Hyde, *The Poetic Theology of Love*, 45–58; Robert P. Harrison, *The Body of Beatrice* (Baltimore: Johns Hopkins University Press, 1988); Jaroslav Pelikan, *Eternal Feminines: Three Theological Allegories in Dante's* Paradiso (New Brunswick, N.J.: Rutgers University Press, 1990).

142. "Ella non parea figliuola d'uomo mortale, ma di Dio." *Vita Nuova* ch. 2, citing "Homer." I have used the annotated edition of Guglielmo Gorni, *Vita Nova* (Turin: Giulio Einaudi, 1996), while retaining the traditional chapter divisions.

143. *Vita Nuova* ch. 2, ch. 3, ch. 24 (Giovanna and Beatrice), ch. 29 (the number nine); *Purgatorio* XXIX-XXX (the pageant of revelation).

144. "Dico che quando ella apparia de parte alcuna, per la speranza della mirabile salute nullo nemico mi rimanea, anzi mi giugnea una fiamma di caritade, la quale mi facea perdonare a chiunque m'avesse offeso. . . . Sì che appare manifestamente che nelle sue salute abitava la mia beatitudine, la quale molte volte passava e redundava la mia capacitade." *Vita Nuova* ch. 11; Gorni, pp. 51–53.

145. In the *canzone* "Donne ch'avete intelletto d'amore," *Vita Nuova* ch. 19.

146. "Ita n'è Beatrice in alto cielo, / . . .ché luce della sua umilitate / passò li cieli con tanta virtute, / che fé maravigliar l'eterno Sire, / sì che dolce disire / lo giunse di chiamar tanta salute." *Vita Nuova* ch. 31; trans. Musa, *Dante's* Vita Nuova, 64.

147. *Vita Nuova* ch. 3, 12; trans. Musa, p. 18.

148. "God is an intelligible sphere whose center is everywhere, whose circumference is nowhere." Alan of Lille, *Theologicae regulae* 7, PL 210: 627a. The figure was also used by Aquinas and Bonaventure.

149. "Potrebbe qui dubitare persona degna da dichiararle ogne dubitatione, e dubitare potrebbe di ciò che io dico d'Amore come se fosse una cosa per sé, e non solamente sustantia intelligentia, ma sì come fosse sustantia corporale: la quale cosa, secondo la verità, è falsa, ché Amore non è per sé sì come sustantia, ma è uno accidente in sustantia." *Vita Nuova* ch. 25; Gorni, pp. 146–47.

150. *Vita Nuova* ch. 9, trans. Musa, 15.

151. "E chi volesse sottilmente considerare, quella Beatrice chiamerebbe Amore per molte simiglianze che à meco." *Vita Nuova* ch. 24, trans. Musa, 52.

152. Sir Philip Sidney, *Astrophil and Stella*, sonnet 1, in *Poems*, ed. William Ringler, Jr. (Oxford: Clarendon Press, 1962), 165.

153. Jean Leclercq, "Riccardo di San Vittore," in *Enciclopedia Dantesca* (Rome, 1973), 4: 904–5. Yvo's treatise was formerly ascribed to Richard of St.-Victor and bears a strong likeness to *De IV gradibus*.

154. "Quomodo enim de amore loquitur homo qui non amat, qui vim non sentit amoris? De aliis nempe copiosa in libris occurrit materia; hujus vero aut tota intus est, aut nusquam est, quia non ab exterioribus ad interiora suavitatis sue secreta transponit, sed ab interioribus ad exteriora transmittit. Solus proinde de ea digne loquitur qui secundum quod cor dictat interius exterius verba componit. Ne mireris igitur si alium audire de hac mallem quam loqui ipse. Illum, inquam, audire vellem, qui calamum lingue tingeret in sanguine cordis, quia tunc vera et veneranda doctrina est . . ." *Epistola ad Severinum* 1, ed. Dumeige, 45.

155. Williams, *Figure of Beatrice*, 204. See also Karl Morrison, *I Am You: The Hermeneutics of Empathy in Western Literature, Theology, and Art* (Princeton, N.J.: Princeton University Press, 1988).

156. Ferrante, *Dante's Beatrice*, 26.

157. The figure of Caritas in the illuminated Lucca ms. of Hildegard's *Liber divinorum operum* is also winged; but that figure represents the Trinity and otherwise has little in common with Lorenzetti's.

158. Freyhan, "Evolution of the Caritas Figure," 81.

159. *Vita Nuova* ch. 3.

160. Williams, *Figure of Beatrice*, 21–22; Singleton, *An Essay*, 4–5.

Chapter 5. Sapientia: The Goddess Incarnate

1. There is a vast bibliography on Hebrew wisdom literature. I have consulted Gerhard von Rad, *Wisdom in Israel*, trans. James Marton (Nashville, Tenn.: Abingdon Press, 1972); Bernhard Lang, *Frau Weisheit: Deutung einer biblischen Gestalt* (Düsseldorf: Patmos, 1975); Robert Wilken, ed., *Aspects of Wisdom in Judaism and Early Christianity* (Notre Dame, Ind.: University of Notre Dame Press, 1975); James Crenshaw, ed., *Studies in Ancient Israelite Wisdom* (New York: Ktav, 1976); Roland Murphy, *The Wisdom Literature* (Grand Rapids, Mich.: Eerdmans, 1981); Claudia Camp, *Wisdom and the Feminine in the Book of Proverbs* (Decatur, Ga.: Almond Press, 1985); Maurice Gilbert, ed., *La Sagesse de l'Ancien Testament*, 2nd ed. (Leuven: Leuven University Press, 1990).

2. James Reese, *Hellenistic Influence on the Book of Wisdom and Its Consequences* (Rome: Biblical Institute Press, 1970), 42–49; Hans Conzelmann, "The Mother of Wisdom," in James Robinson, ed., *The Future of Our Religious Past*, trans. Charles Carlston and Robert Scharlemann (New York: Harper and Row, 1971), 230–43.

3. Richard Horsley, "Spiritual Marriage with Sophia," *Vigiliae Christianae* 33 (1979): 30–54; Paul Beauchamp, "Épouser la Sagesse—ou n'épouser qu'elle? Une énigme du Livre de la Sagesse," in Gilbert, *La Sagesse*, 347–69.

4. For Christ as Sophia in the New Testament, see C. H. Dodd, *The Interpretation of the Fourth Gospel* (Cambridge: Cambridge University Press, 1953), 263–78; Felix Christ, *Jesus Sophia: Die Sophia-Christologie bei den Synoptikern* (Zurich: Zwingli Verlag, 1970); M. Jack Suggs, *Wisdom, Christology, and Law in Matthew's Gospel* (Cambridge, Mass.: Harvard University Press, 1970); R. G. Hamerton-Kelly, *Pre-Existence, Wisdom, and the Son of Man* (Cambridge: Cambridge University Press, 1973); Wilken, *Aspects of Wisdom*; James Dunn, *Christology in the Making* (Philadelphia: Westminster Press, 1980): 163–212; John Balchin, "Paul, Wisdom and Christ," in Harold Rowdon, ed., *Christ the Lord* (Leicester: Inter-Varsity, 1982), 204–19; William Gray, "Wisdom Christology in the New Testament: Its Scope and Relevance," *Theology* 89 (1986): 448–59; Ronald Piper, *Wisdom in the Q-Tradition: The Aphoristic Teaching of Jesus* (Cambridge: Cambridge University Press, 1989); Elisabeth Schüssler Fiorenza, *Jesus, Miriam's Child, Sophia's Prophet: Critical Issues in Feminist Christology* (New York: Continuum, 1994).

5. Fairy von Lilienfeld, "'Frau Weisheit' in byzantinischen und karolingischen Quellen des 9. Jahrhunderts—Allegorische Personifikation, Hypostase oder Typos?" in Margot Schmidt and C. F. Geyer, eds., *Typus, Symbol, Allegorie bei den östlichen Vätern und ihren Parallelen im Mittelalter*, Internationales Kolloquium, Eichstätt 1981

(Regensburg: Pustet, 1982), 146–86; Marie-Thérèse d'Alverny, *Études sur le symbolisme de la Sagesse et sur l'iconographie*, ed. Charles Burnett (Aldershot, Hampshire: Ashgate/Variorum, 1993).

6. See Chapter 1 above, pp. 31–33.

7. On this movement see John Van Engen, ed. and trans., *Devotio Moderna: Basic Writings* (New York: Paulist Press, 1988); Hans Janowski, ed., *Geert Groote, Thomas von Kempen und die Devotio Moderna* (Olten, Switzerland: Walter, 1978); R. R. Post, *The Modern Devotion: Confrontation with Reformation and Humanism* (Leiden: Brill, 1968).

8. There is actually some warrant for Jerome's translation. *Qanah* most commonly means "to acquire," or more broadly, to possess through purchase, creation, or some other means. The meaning "create" occurs only in poetic contexts, generally those with Canaanite parallels. I thank my colleague Benjamin Sommer for this information.

9. M. Van Parys, "Exégèse et théologie trinitaire: Prov. 8,22 chez les Pères cappadociens," *Irénikon* 43 (1970): 362–79; Jaroslav Pelikan, *The Emergence of the Catholic Tradition (100–600)* (Chicago: University of Chicago Press, 1971), 186–93.

10. See for example Alcuin, *Grammatica*, PL 101, 853bc.

11. Georges Florovsky, "The Hagia Sophia Churches," in *Aspects of Church History* (Belmont, Mass.: Nordland, 1975), 131–35; John Meyendorff, "Wisdom—Sophia: Contrasting Approaches to a Complex Theme," *Dumbarton Oaks Papers* 41 (1987): 391–401. The Parthenon of Athens, once christianized, seems to have moved in the reverse direction: as of 1019 it was consecrated to the All-Holy Virgin, but Western accounts of 1669 and 1672 refer to it as dedicated to St. Sophia or Eternal Wisdom. Martin Luther D'Ooge, *The Acropolis of Athens* (New York: Macmillan, 1908), 306, 341 n. 208.

12. Marvin Kantor and Richard White, trans., *The Vita of Constantine and The Vita of Methodius* (Ann Arbor: Michigan Slavic Publications, 1976), 5–7.

13. *Commentarii in parabolas Salomonis et in Ecclesiasten*, ed. Carmelo Curti (Catania: Centro di Studi sull'antico cristianesimo, 1964). This commentary was formerly attributed to Salonius, bishop of Geneva.

14. Étienne Catta, "*Sedes Sapientiae*," in Hubert du Manoir, ed., *Maria: Études sur la sainte Vierge*, 8 vols. (Paris: Beauchesne, 1949–71), 6: 689–866, at 741–42.

15. Rachel Fulton, *From Judgment to Passion: Devotion to Christ and the Virgin Mary, 800–1200* (New York: Columbia University Press, 2002), 269.

16. My information on the Marian sapiential liturgy is drawn from Bernard Capelle, "La liturgie mariale en occident," in du Manoir, *Maria*, 1: 215–45; Georges Frénaud, "Le culte de Notre Dame dans l'ancienne liturgie latine," in ibid., 6: 157–211; Catta, "*Sedes Sapientiae*"; and Paula Seethaler, "Die Weisheitstexte in der Marienliturgie," *Benediktinische Monatschrift* 34 (1958): 111–20.

17. Capelle, "La liturgie," 236–37; Catta, "*Sedes Sapientiae*," 693–94.

18. Frénaud, "Le culte," 175, 181.

19. I have translated these liturgical texts directly from the Vulgate, since no modern version comes very close.

20. Frénaud, "Le Culte," 188–90; Catta, "*Sedes Sapientiae*," 695–96.

21. "Sabbato missa de sancta Maria," PL 101, 455c.

22. Frénaud, "Le culte," 175.

23. This lesson is attested in two German mss. of the eleventh century (for the Vigil of the Assumption) and also in the Mozarabic liturgy. See PL 85, 844b (Nativity of Mary) and 933bc (Conception of Mary); Frénaud, "Le culte," 189–90; Seethaler, "Die Weisheitstexte," 111.

24. Rachel Fulton, "'Quae est ista quae ascendit sicut aurora consurgens?' The Song of Songs as the *Historia* for the Office of the Assumption," *Mediaeval Studies* 60 (1998): 55–122, at 61. See also eadem, "Mimetic Devotion, Marian Exegesis, and the Historical Sense of the Song of Songs," *Viator* 27 (1996): 85–116.

25. Seethaler, "Die Weisheitstexte," 118–20.

26. "Sed haec particula a catholicis et eruditis Patribus in solemnitate perpetuae virginis Mariae, de qua eadem Dei sapientia carnem assumpsit, ad legendum ordinata est. Potest pars quaedam illius non incongrue eidem Dei genitrici aptari, quae ab ipsa Dei sapientia talis creata est, ut per illam ad redimendam humanam naturam Dei Filius sine humana concupiscentia crearetur." "Homilia 5 in solemnitate perpetuae virginis Mariae," PL 118, 765cd. Migne ascribes this homily to Haimo of Halberstadt, but it is more likely the work of his contemporary Haimo of Auxerre, if not a tenth-century interpolation in the homiliary of Auxerre. Henri Barré, *Les homéliaires carolingiens de l'École d'Auxerre: authenticité, inventaire, tableaux comparatifs, initia* (Vatican City: Biblioteca apostolica vaticana, 1962), 50–58. I thank E. Ann Matter and Burton Van Name Edwards for advice on this point.

27. "Haec sapientia itaque aedificavit sibi domum, vel matrem de qua sumpsit carnem, vel corpus in Virgine." Remigius of Auxerre, Homilia 4 in Matthaeum, PL 131, 888b.

28. "Et reuera priusquam nascerer, illi praesens aderam, antequam fierem, bene illi cognita fueram . . . quia elegit me ante mundi constitutionem, ut essem sancta et immaculata in conspectu eius." Rupert of Deutz, *In Canticum canticorum* 2.10, ed. Hraban Haacke, CCCM 26 (Turnhout: Brepols, 1974), 47. Further references in Barbara Newman, *Sister of Wisdom: St. Hildegard's Theology of the Feminine* (Berkeley: University of California Press, 1987), 160–62.

29. "Prouidentia dei, in qua omnis sapientie et scientie thesauri sunt absconditi, continens, complens, ambiens, regens comprehendit omnia simul. . . . Cum igitur in sapientia uerbi dei essent omnia, que, quomodo, quando natura, modo, ordine, specificis differentiis explicanda, quomodo mater non erat cum filio, . . . in qua fundamentum quoddam eterne structure, id est celestis Ierosolime eterna dispositione parabatur? . . . Quomodo igitur ab eterno ordinata et ex antiquis in sacramenti unitate non erat mater cum filio, in quibus omnium diuinorum operum latuit inuisibiliter principalis origo et eterne uoluntatis summeque benignitatis tempore prefinito explicande perfecta plenitudo?" *Speculum virginum* 5, ed. Jutta Seyfarth, CCCM 5 (Turnhout: Brepols, 1990), 118–19. I have translated portions of the text in Constant Mews, ed., *Listen, Daughter: The* Speculum Virginum *and the Formation of Religious Women in the Middle Ages* (New York: Palgrave, 2001), 269–96.

30. Donald Fiene notes that "the entire visual dynamic of the icon equates the Virgin with Sophia," yet this iconic type was not formally designated as an image of Wisdom until the eighteenth century. "What Is the Appearance of Divine Sophia?" *Slavic Review* 48 (1989): 449–76, at 472–73.

31. Thomas Schipflinger, *Sophia—Maria: A Holistic Vision of Creation*, trans. James Morgante (York Beach, Me.: Samuel Weiser, 1998), 101.

32. Alcuin, "Missa de sancta sapientia," in F. E. Warren, ed., *The Leofric Missal* (Oxford: Clarendon Press, 1883): 176 (also in *Liber sacramentorum*, PL 101, 450–51); Gerald Ellard, "Alcuin and Some Favored Votive Masses," *Theological Studies* 1 (1940): 37–61.

33. Alcuin, *Officia per ferias, litania, quarta feria*, PL 101, 596.

34. Paschasius Radbertus, *Carmina* 4, "Ad Karolum Regem de corpore et sanguine Domini," in MGH *Poetae Latini medii aevi* (Berlin: Weidmann, 1896), 3: 52–53.

35. "Ex diversis mundi partibus amatores illius [sapientiae] vestrae bonae voluntati adiutores convocare studuistis. Inter quos me etiam, infimum eiusdem sanctae sapientiae vernaculum, de ultimis Brittaniae finibus adsciscere curastis." Alcuin to Charlemagne, *Epistolae* 229, ed. Ernst Dümmler, in MGH *Epistolae* (Berlin: Weidmann, 1895), 4: 373.

36. Wolfgang Edelstein, *Eruditio und sapientia: Weltbild und Erziehung in der Karolingerzeit: Untersuchungen zu Alcuins Briefen* (Freiburg im Breisgau: Rombach, 1965).

37. "Nam philosophi non fuerunt conditores harum artium, sed inventores. Nam creator omnium rerum condidit eas in naturis, sicut voluit." Alcuin, *Epistolae* 148, p. 239. On the seven arts as the pillars of Wisdom's house see *Grammatica*, PL 101, 853c.

38. Pierre Courcelle, "Étude critique sur les commentaires de la *Consolation* de Boèce (IXe-XVe siècles)," *Archives d'histoire doctrinale et littéraire du Moyen Age* 12 (1939): 5–140.

39. "Et dextera quidem eius libellos, sceptrum vero sinistra gestabat." Boethius, *De consolatione Philosophiae* I, prose 1. Cf. Marie-Thérèse d'Alverny, "La Sagesse et ses sept filles," *Mélanges dédiés à la mémoire de Félix Grat* (Paris, 1946), I: 245–78, and eadem, "Le symbolisme de la Sagesse et le Christ de Saint Dunstan," *Bodleian Library Record* 5 (1956): 232–44, both reprinted in *Études sur le symbolisme de la Sagesse*.

40. Henri Rochais, "Ipsa Philosophia Christus," *Mediaeval Studies* 13 (1951): 244–47.

41. Odo of Battle Abbey, sermon for the Assumption, ed. Jean Leclercq in "Maria Christianorum philosophia," *Mélanges de sciences religieuses* 13 (1956): 103–6.

42. Rupert of Deutz, *In Canticum canticorum* I.6, CCCM 26, p. 24.

43. John of Morigny, *Liber Visionum*; dream vision in prologue, ch. 8 (ca. 1304–1311). Introduction, text, and translation by Claire Fanger and Nicholas Watson, in the on-line journal *Esoterica* 3 (1999): 108–217, at <www.esoteric.msu.edu/VolumeIII/Morigny.html>. For more on this text see the essays in Claire Fanger, ed., *Conjuring Spirits: Texts and Traditions of Medieval Ritual Magic* (University Park: Pennsylvania State University Press, 1998), Part II.

44. "Meglio cognosceva tutto, che nessuno filosofo del mondo"; "La maggiore teologa, che fusse nel mondo, fu la Vergine Maria"; "La mente sua, che tanto amava Iddio, si trasformava in Dio, intanto che stando nel ventre della madre era in contemplazione continua." Bernardino of Siena, Sermon 51 on the Incarnation (preached at Florence, 1425), in Dionisio Pacetti, ed., *Le Prediche volgari inedite* (Siena: Cantagalli, 1935), 321, 333, 331.

45. See my *Sister of Wisdom*, especially ch. 2.

46. Caroline Walker Bynum, *Holy Feast and Holy Fast: The Religious Significance of Food to Medieval Women* (Berkeley: University of California Press, 1987). See also "'... And Woman His Humanity': Female Imagery in the Religious Writing of the Later Middle Ages," in *Fragmentation and Redemption: Essays on Gender and the Human Body in Medieval Religion* (New York: Zone, 1991), 151–79.

47. Heinrich Seuse, *Büchlein der Ewigen Weisheit*, ch. 7, ed. Karl Bihlmeyer in *Deutsche Schriften* (Stuttgart, 1907; repr. Frankfurt am Main: Minerva, 1961), 223. For an English version see *The Exemplar*, trans. Frank Tobin (New York: Paulist Press, 1989), 205–304.

48. See Jeffrey Hamburger, "Medieval Self-Fashioning: Authorship, Authority, and Autobiography in Suso's *Exemplar*," in *The Visual and the Visionary: Art and Female Spirituality in Late Medieval Germany* (New York: Zone, 1998), 233–78.

49. On the dilemma of the male mystic in love with a God who is also perceived as male, see Howard Eilberg-Schwartz, *God's Phallus and Other Problems for Men and Monotheism* (Boston: Beacon, 1994). Stephen Moore, in "The Song of Songs in the History of Sexuality," *Church History* 69 (2000): 328–49, argues that the whole history of exegesis constitutes a "queering" of the Song by male monastic exegetes, who threw themselves with such performative gusto into the role of Bride.

50. Heinrich Seuse, *Horologium Sapientiae*, ed. Pius Künzle (Freiburg, Switzerland: Universitätsverlag, 1977), B1. Henry Suso, *Wisdom's Watch upon the Hours*, trans. Edmund Colledge (Washington, D.C.: Catholic University of America Press, 1994). Translations cited here are my own. Suso's title alludes to the 24 hours of the day (corresponding to the book's 24 chapters), as well as the seven canonical hours. This theme was traditional; as early as the mid-thirteenth century, Hadewijch devoted her Letter 20 to the "Twelve Nameless Hours of Minne."

51. "Et sic diversimode stilum vertit secundum quod tunc materiae congruit. Nunc etiam Dei Filium ut devotae animae sponsum inducit; postea eundem tamquam aeternam sapientiam viro iusto desponsatam introducit." Prologue to *Horologium*, ed. Künzle, 366.

52. "Ecce e regione in summis excelsisque verticibus apparuit quasi flos campi conspicuus et ad videndum delectabilis, omnibusque quos antea videram floribus incomparabiliter pulchrior apparebat. Ad quem videndum cum festinassem, ecce subito immutatus non comparuit, sed quasi dea totius pulchritudinis ante me stetit, quae velut rosa rubens et candore niveo refulgens, sole clarius rutilabat, et eloquia pulchritudinis dabat. Haec cunctorum in se summam optabilium perferebat, odoreque suavissimo ad modum pantherae longe lateque diffuso circumquaque, ad amorem suum cunctos trahebat, voceque dulcissima sic dicebat: 'Transite ad me omnes qui concupiscitis me, et a generationibus meis adimplemini. Ego mater pulchrae dilectionis et timoris et agnitionis et sanctae spei.'" *Horologium* I.6, pp. 418–19.

53. "Sic, sic sapientia aeterna, sol iustitiae, quinimmo ipsa, cuius pulchritudinem sol et luna mirantur, lucem habitans inaccessibilem, in splendoribus sanctorum, ex utero ante luciferum genitus." *Horologium* I.6, p. 423. This passage is dense with liturgical echoes: "sol iustitiae" (Mal. 4.2) comes from one of the great O antiphons of Advent, "ex utero ante luciferum" (Ps. 109.3) from the Christmas liturgy, and "cuius pulchritudinem . . . mirantur" from the feast of St. Agnes.

54. "Simplicissimae essentiae meae iucundissima visio, supersubstantialissimae divinitatis meae peroptata fruitio, interminabilis vitae tota simul et perfecta possessio." *Horologium* I.6, p. 424, citing Boethius, *De consolatione Philosophiae* 5, prose 6.

55. "Respice, quaeso, mentis nunc in iubilo, quam habilis sim ad amandum, quam affabilis ad amplexandum et ad perosculandum animae sincerae, quam summe delectabilis. O dulce et pretiosissimum osculum, labiis mellifluis affectuose impressum. O quam beata anima, cui vel in tota vita sua saltem unica vice fuerit hoc concessum. Quod si propter hoc etiam mori contingerit, grave non erit." *Horologium* I.6, p. 425.

56. Colledge, introduction to *Wisdom's Watch*, 23.

57. On Suso's debt to the literature of secular love, see J.-A. Bizet, *Suso et le Minnesang, ou la morale de l'amour courtois* (Paris: Aubier, 1947).

58. According to a letter he sent to Margaretha (21 Sept. 1339), Heinrich of Nördlingen had borrowed a copy of the *Horologium* from Tauler and was sending it to her via the prior of Kaisheim. Jeanne Ancelet-Hustache, "Quelques indications sur les manuscrits de l'*Horloge de Sapience*," in Ephrem Filthaut, ed., *Heinrich Seuse: Studien zum 600. Todestag, 1366–1966* (Cologne: Albertus Magnus Verlag, 1966), 161–70, at 161. For Heinrich's role in the diffusion of Mechthild's book see Frank Tobin, introduction to Mechthild of Magdeburg, *The Flowing Light of the Godhead* (New York: Paulist Press, 1998), 7–8. Künzle mentions the Latin version of Mechthild's text, *Lux divinitatis*, as an influence on Suso: *Horologium*, 83.

59. As Abelard wrote to Heloise in the 1130s, "you became my superior from the day when you began to be my lady on becoming the bride of my Lord." Letter 4 in Betty Radice, trans., *The Letters of Abelard and Heloise* (Harmondsworth: Penguin, 1974), 137. For later men's envy of visionary brides of Christ, see John Coakley, "Gender and the Authority of Friars: The Significance of Holy Women for Thirteenth-Century Franciscans and Dominicans," *Church History* 60 (1991): 445–60, and idem, "A Marriage and Its Observer: Christine of Stommeln, the Heavenly Bridegroom, and Friar Peter of Dacia," in Catherine Mooney, ed., *Gendered Voices: Medieval Saints and Their Interpreters* (Philadelphia: University of Pennsylvania Press, 1999): 99–117.

60. Suso's unconventional but straightforward assertion that God's daughter has become his bride apparently baffled Colledge, whose otherwise elegant and accurate translation falters here: "that great King and divine emperor has joined me to him, me, Eternal Wisdom, his only beloved, as his spouse." *Wisdom's Watch*, 315; see below for the Latin.

61. "De regalibus nuptiis venio, ex vino caeli potatus madeo, nuptiali thalamo potitus gaudeo. Insuper bonum nuntium porto, cunctisque nova gaudia fero. Et ideo me ipsum prae iubilo non capio, sed totus iucunditate infusus exulto in domino. Quaeris, unde tam rara tamque insolita gaudiorum materia sit in terra nostra suborta. Nimirum ex hoc, quod in his paschalibus gaudiis, videlicet regalibus ac spiritualibus nuptiis, ipse rex summus ac imperator divinus suam mihi unicam ac dilectam, aeternam scilicet sapientiam in sponsam copulavit, sponsalia contraxit et me quodam modo suum generum fecit. O quis ego, qui sim gener regis? Quis ad tantam dignitatem audeat aspirare? O quam magnum est hoc, quod tam pauper et modicus,

tam vilis et indignus, nullis meritis praecedentibus, ad tantam dignitatem debuit sublimari. . . . Sed neque his contentus rex magnificus adauxit munera. . . . Nam humilis ille huius sapientiae discipulus in ea visionis gratia quodam novo et mystico nomine ab ipsa vocatus Frater Amandus, dum in cordis cubiculo, nuptiali thalamo, cum divinissima sponsa sua secreta silentia petisset et inter ipsius amoris brachia dulciter soporatus obdormisset, cordis tamen fervido affectu admodum perfecte vigilaret, atque de aliorum pariter salute secum tractaret, praedicta sponsa huiuscemodi verba nimium dulcia intellectualiter ac supernaturaliter omniumque mortalium vocum condicionibus dissimiliter depromebat dicens: 'Ex te namque egredietur, in quo omnes gentes benedicentur.'" *Horologium* II.7, pp. 590–91.

62. "Die Vermählung des hl. Franziskus mit Frau Armut, der damit Christus gewinnt, und Seuses Gemahlschaft mit der ewigen Weisheit, . . . kommen sich im Endeffekt gleich. Aber literarisch liegen zwei Ausgestaltungen der Brautmystik vor, die sich voneinander unterscheiden wie die beiden Orden in ihrer Grundidee." Künzle, *Horologium*, 94. On Lady Poverty see Chapter 1, pp. 3–9 above.

63. "Tu scis, expertissimum etenim alloquor in arte amandi, quia amor intensus socium non patitur, non sustinet pluralitatem." *Horologium* I.6, p. 426, alluding to Ovid, *De arte amatoria* III, 564: "Non bene cum sociis regna Venusque manent."

64. Hugh of St.-Victor, *Soliloquium de arrha animae*, ed. M. K. Müller, *Kleine Texte für Vorlesungen und Übungen*, no. 123 (Bonn: Markus und Weber, 1913); also in PL 176, 951–70; trans. Kevin Herbert, *Soliloquy on the Earnest Money of the Soul* (Milwaukee: Marquette University Press, 1956).

65. "The bridegroom . . . is essentially polygamous, but seems to expect total commitment from each individual bride." Hildegard Keller, *My Secret Is Mine: Studies on Religion and Eros in the German Middle Ages* (Leuven: Peeters, 2000), 58.

66. "Liber devotissimus et vere devotissimus, imo devotis mentibus et bone voluntatis religiosis utriusque sexus saluberrimus." From Basel, Universitätsbibliothek C.III.2 (1490), cited in Künzle, *Horologium*, 283. For male and female images of Eternal Wisdom in the *Exemplar* see Hamburger, "Medieval Self-fashioning."

67. This is the title of chapter I.15: "Quomodo verus Christi discipulus debet se configurare passionibus ipsius."

68. Bizet notes that the pronounced penitential character of Suso's Marian piety "excludes the fiction of courtly gallantries," which he reserves for Eternal Wisdom. *Suso et le Minnesang*, 33.

69. Richard Kieckhefer, *Unquiet Souls: Fourteenth-Century Saints and Their Religious Milieu* (Chicago: University of Chicago Press, 1984), 89–121; Ellen Ross, *The Grief of God: Images of the Suffering Jesus in Late Medieval England* (New York: Oxford University Press, 1997).

70. "Et uir divinitatem, femina uero humanitatem filii Dei significat." Hildegard of Bingen, *Liber divinorum operum* I.4.100, ed. Albert Derolez and Peter Dronke, CCCM 92 (Turnhout: Brepols, 1996), 243; see also Bynum, "'. . . And Woman His Humanity.'"

71. This paragraph summarizes the information in Künzle, *Horologium*, 215–28 and 250–89.

72. On other English adaptations of the text see Rebecca Selman, "Spirituality and Sex Change: *Horologium sapientiae* and *Speculum devotorum*," in Denis Renevey

and Christiania Whitehead, eds., *Writing Religious Women: Female Spiritual and Textual Practices in Late Medieval England* (Toronto: University of Toronto Press, 2000), 63–79.

73. Bihlmeyer, *Deutsche Schriften*, 11*.

74. Peter Rolfe Monks, *The Brussels Horloge de Sapience: Iconography and Text of Brussels, Bibliothèque Royale, MS. IV 111* (Leiden: Brill, 1990), includes black and white reproductions of all the paintings, an edition and translation of the *Déclaration*, and commentary. There is no edition of the *Horloge* itself; for the French translator's preface see Ancelet-Hustache, "Quelques indications," 167–69.

75. "Premierement au commencement du livre est dame Sapience en forme et figure de femme signifient Jhesus Nostre Sauveur qui est dit et appellé vertus et sapience de Dieu le pere, laquelle est assise en throne de magesté comme vray Dieu. Et tient ung livre a sa main dextre, et a la senestre, le monde, signifiant que par elle et d'elle est ysseue toute science et sapience par laquelle est le monde gouverné et reparé. A la dextre de ycelle dame Sapience est le disciple aucteur et composeur de ce livre estant en chaire comme preschant a divers estas du monde que ilz sentent et gouttent de Dieu en bonté, et le quierent en simplesse de cuer." *Déclaration*, ed. Monks, 134.

76. Ibid., 190.

77. "Et est en l'ystoire dame Sapience en une arbre appellee therebintus qui est moult vertueuse et souef fleurent, et tient dame Sapience a la main dextre une bouette plaine de ongnement souef fleurent, et ung brain de baulme, et a la senestre ung livre, signifient que sa doctrine est doulce, souef fleurent, plaine de grace et d'onneur." Ibid., 146.

78. "Eum salutavit dicens: Praebe fili cor tuum mihi. Quo audito, prae nimia amoris dulcedine liquefactus et quasi in exstasi positus ad pedes eius procidit, gratias agens, eius praesentia magnifice delectatus." *Horologium* I.1, p. 380.

79. "Verum licet quaelibet persona per se accepta sit sapientia, et omnes personae simul una aeterna sapientia, tamen quia sapientia attribuitur Filio, et quia ratione suae generationis sibi convenit, ideo dilectum Patris Filium sub eodem significato consuetudinaliter accepit nunc quidem ut Deum, deinde ut hominem, ut in utroque pariter devotionis exercitia et amoris solatia inveniret." *Horologium* I.1, p. 381.

80. Monks, *Brussels Horloge*, 99. For the martyrs' legend see Jacobus de Voragine, *The Golden Legend*, trans. William Granger Ryan, vol. 1 (Princeton, N.J.: Princeton University Press, 1993), 185–86.

81. "En cest estat est l'ame devote en grant consolation, en grant joye et devocion. Mais n'en puet pas demourer longuement en ceste presente vie pour la corrupcion du corps qui aggreve et appesantit l'ame qu'elle ne puet penser a ce que elle ayme, mais se descent a penser les choses terriennes avecques lesquelles elle et son corps habitent." *Déclaration*, ed. Monks, 174.

82. "Quomodo ergo tu dicis amabilem, quem evidentia facti ostendit miserabilem?" *Horologium* I.2, p. 385.

83. "At contra animae tuae sponsa, aeterna sapientia, exterius quidem secundum faciem humilis, abiecta ac despicabilis putatur, interius autem vivae lucis triclinio decoratur." *Horologium* I.2, p. 386.

84. "Et c'est ce qui est figuré en ceste hystoire, ou est Dieu le pere comme souverain prestre conjoingnent le disciple amant a la Divine Sapience qui est vray filz de Dieu." *Déclaration*, ed. Monks, 198.

85. François Boespflug, "Dieu en pape: Une singularité de l'art religieux de la fin du moyen âge," *Revue Mabillon* n.s. 2 (1991): 167–205.

86. In one manuscript from 1461 (Hamilton, Canada, McMaster University Library MS 107), the *Cursus de eterna Dei sapientia* is appended to John of Morigny's *Liber visionum* (see p. 205 above). Nicholas Watson, "John the Monk's *Book of Visions of the Blessed and Undefiled Virgin Mary, Mother of God*," in Fanger, ed., *Conjuring Spirits*, 187.

87. "Quicumque desiderat Sapientiam aeternam familiarem sibi sponsam habere, debet ei has horas cotidie devote legere." "Cursus de Aeterna Sapientia," in Künzle, *Horologium*, 606–18. The Hours are not included in Colledge's translation.

88. "O Sapientia aeterna, splendor gloriae et figura substantiae Patris, qui universa de nihilo creasti et, ut hominem ad paradisi gaudia reduceres, in hanc vallem miseriae descendisti eique viam redeundi per tuam dulcissimam conversationem demonstrasti et pro satisfactione cunctorum tamquam agnus innocens Patri in cruce immolari voluisti! Aperi per tuam pretiosam mortem cor meum, ut te Regem regum et Dominum dominantium oculis integrae fidei semper aspiciam. Pone meam in tuis vulneribus philosophiam, in tuis stigmatibus sapientiam, ut ulterius in te, solo caritatis libro, et morte tua proficiam, et omnibus mutabilibus deficiam ita, ut ego iam non ego, sed tu in me et ego in te indissolubili vinculo amoris aeternaliter maneamus." "Cursus," 607–8.

89. Künzle, *Horologium*, 273–74.

90. Ibid., 262–63; Anton Weiler, ed., *Getijden van de Eeuwige Wijsheid naar de Vertaling van Geert Grote* (Baarn, Netherlands: Ambo, 1984); Nicolaas van Wijk, ed., *Het Getijdenboek van Geert Groote* (Leiden: Brill, 1940).

91. For Christ blessing see London, BL Harley 1662, fol. 89v; London, BL Add. 15267, fol. 109v; for the Christ Child among the doctors see Oxford, Bodleian Buchanan f. 1, fol. 39v; The Hague, Koninklijke Bibliotheek 76 F31, fol. 51v; for the Pietà with God the Father, see London, BL Add. 29887, fol. 94v. In London, BL Harley 2943, the Hours of Eternal Wisdom begin with a scene of Pentecost, with the Virgin Mary as its central figure (fol. 49v).

92. "Sapientia clamitat in plateis. Si quis diligit Sapientiam, ad me declinet, et eam inveniet, et eam cum invenerit, beatus erit, si tenuerit eam." Antiphon for Lauds, "Cursus," 609.

93. Julian of Norwich, *Shewings* (Long Text), ch. 21, ed. Georgia Ronan Crampton (Kalamazoo, Mich.: Medieval Institute Publications, 1993), 66.

94. *Shewings*, ch. 27, p. 72. The passage occurs in ch. 13 of Julian's original Short Text.

95. Ward also points out that, if Julian had belonged to any religious community, it would have been extraordinary for the nuns to preserve no record of such a remarkable member's burial place or even her date of death, let alone her writings. "Julian the Solitary," in Kenneth Leech and Sister Benedicta, *Julian Reconsidered* (Fairacres, Oxford: Sisters of the Love of God, 1988): 11–35.

96. *Book of Margery Kempe*, ch. 18, ed. Lynn Staley (Kalamazoo, Mich.: Medieval

Institute Publications, 1996): 53–54. Julian would have been about 70 at the time of their meeting and Margery about 40.

97. Felicity Riddy, in a speculative account of the relationships among existing manuscripts, argues that "before 1500 there must have been, at an absolute minimum, at least two or three copies of the short version and five or six of the long, . . . in order to account for the ones we have today." But if these were owned by laypersons rather than religious communities, they would have been less likely to survive. "Julian of Norwich and Self-Textualization," in Ann Hutchison, ed., *Editing Women* (Cardiff: University of Wales Press, 1998), 122.

98. The work has no uniformly accepted title. Editions prior to Crampton's include the *editio princeps* of Serenus Cressy, *Sixteen Revelations of Divine Love* (London, 1670); Marion Glasscoe, ed., *A Revelation of Love* (Exeter: University of Exeter Press, 1976); and Edmund Colledge and James Walsh, eds., *A Book of Showings to the Anchoress Julian of Norwich*, 2 vols. (Toronto: Pontifical Institute of Mediaeval Studies, 1978). *A Revelation of Love* is the closest thing we have to an authorial title, as it appears in both the incipit of BL ms. Sloane 2499 ("This is a Revelation of love that Jesus Christ, our endless blisse, made in sixteen Sheweings") and the explicit ("Thus endith the Revelation of love of the blissid Trinite shewid by our Savior, Christ Jesu").

99. Nicholas Watson, "The Composition of Julian of Norwich's *Revelation of Love*," *Speculum* 68 (1993): 637–83; idem, "Censorship and Cultural Change in Late-Medieval England: Vernacular Theology, the Oxford Translation Debate, and Arundel's Constitutions of 1409," *Speculum* 70 (1995): 822–64.

100. "Statuimus igitur et ordinamus, ut nemo deinceps aliquem textum sacrae scripturae auctoritate sua in linguam Anglicanam, vel aliam transferat, per viam libri, libelli, aut tractatus, nec legatur aliquis hujusmodi liber, libellus, aut tractatus jam noviter tempore dicti Johannis Wycliff, sive citra, compositus, aut inposterum componendus, in parte vel in toto, publice, vel occulte, sub majoris excommunicationis poena, quousque per loci dioecesanum, seu, si res exegerit, per concilium provinciale ipsa translatio fuerit approbata: qui contra fecerit, ut fautor haeresis et erroris similiter puniatur." *Constitutio* 7, in David Wilkins, ed., *Concilia Magnae Britanniae et Hiberniae*, 4 vols. (London: R. Gosling, 1737), 3: 317. The sixteenth-century translation is by John Foxe, *Acts and Monuments*, 8 vols. (New York: AMS Press, 1965), 3: 245, cited in Watson, "Censorship," 829.

101. Crampton, ed., *Shewings*, 155.

102. The unique ms. of Julian's Short Text (London, BL Add. 37790), a mid-fifteenth-century Carthusian anthology, also contains an excerpt from the English version of Suso's *Horologium*, in addition to works of Richard Rolle, William of St.-Thierry, Jan van Ruusbroec, Birgitta of Sweden, and Marguerite Porete's *Mirror of Simple Souls*.

103. There is no scholarly consensus on the extent of Julian's learning. Colledge and Walsh claim "beyond any doubt" that she "had received an exceptionally good grounding in Latin, in Scripture and in the liberal arts, and that thereafter she was able and permitted to read widely in Latin and vernacular spiritual classics" (I, 44). Glasscoe on the other hand finds marks of oral composition even in the Long Text, which she thinks it "very probable" that Julian "dictated to an amanuensis" (xviii).

Crampton's summary seems just: she finds the evidence for Julian's Latin literacy to be "weighty and plausible" but "not conclusive" (5).

104. Nicholas Watson, "'Yf wommen be double naturelly': Remaking 'Woman' in Julian of Norwich's *Revelation of Love*," *Exemplaria* 8 (1996): 1–34, at 26.

105. Caroline Walker Bynum, "Jesus as Mother and Abbot as Mother: Some Themes in Twelfth-Century Cistercian Writing," in *Jesus as Mother: Studies in the Spirituality of the High Middle Ages* (Berkeley: University of California Press, 1982), 110–69.

106. Neither theme is mentioned in the table of contents (ch. 1), and if we skip from the end of ch. 43 to the beginning of ch. 64 in the Sloane ms., the transition is very smooth, as if these chapters had originally belonged together. The Paris ms. (edited by Colledge and Walsh) and the Cressy edition of 1670 (based on a lost ms.) begin ch. 64 at different points, as if earlier exemplars had left some uncertainty as to where the greatly-expanded fourteenth showing ended and the fifteenth began.

107. "For oure lord god dooth lyke a lovynge modir; a louynge modir that is wys and weel taught, sche wole that here childern be vertuouse and weel norischid, and if sche may knowe ony of hem with a defaughte, sche wole yeve hem a knocke on the heed, and if thei don a great defaute, sche wol yeve hem a buffet vndir the cheke, and if thei have don a grettere trespas, sche wole bylasche hem scharpely." William Flete, *Remedies Against Temptations*, c. 9, ed. Edmund Colledge and Noel Chadwick, Archivio italiano per la storia della pietà 5 (Rome: Edizioni di storia e letteratura, 1968), 201–40, at 235. Cf. Valerie Lagorio, "Variations on the Theme of God's Motherhood in Medieval English Mystical and Devotional Writings," *Studia mystica* 8, 2 (1985): 15–37.

108. This paragraph is indebted to Denise Baker's fine study, *Julian of Norwich's Showings: From Vision to Book* (Princeton, N.J.: Princeton University Press, 1994), 107–34. On "sensuality" and "substance" see also Joan Nuth, *Wisdom's Daughter: The Theology of Julian of Norwich* (New York: Crossroad, 1991), 104–16.

109. Augustine, *De Trinitate*, Book 12; the marital analogy begins in 12.3.3. *The Trinity*, trans. Stephen McKenna (Washington, D.C.: Catholic University of America Press, 1962), 345.

110. "Ubi [anima] perfectae rationis incipit esse, non tantum capax, sed et particeps, continuo abdicat a se notam generis feminei, et efficitur animus. . . . Quamdiu enim anima est, cito in id quod carnale est effeminatur; animus vero, vel spiritus, non nisi quod virile est et spirituale meditatur." William of St.-Thierry, *Epistola ad fratres de Monte Dei* 198, ed. Jean Déchanet, *Lettre aux frères du Mont-Dieu*, SC 223 (Paris: Cerf, 1975), 306–8.

111. The words "in this knot," omitted by the Sloane scribe, are supplied from Colledge and Walsh's edition (II, 560) of the slightly earlier Paris ms. (Bibl. nat., Fonds anglais 40)

112. See Chapter 2 above, p. 59.

113. Ritamary Bradley, "Patristic Background of the Motherhood Similitude in Julian of Norwich," *Christian Scholar's Review* 8 (1978): 101–13; eadem, "Mysticism in the Motherhood Similitude of Julian of Norwich," *Studia mystica* 8, 2 (1985): 4–14.

114. Ambrose, *De patriarchis* 11.51, in *Seven Exegetical Works*, trans. Michael McHugh (Washington, D.C.: Catholic University of America Press, 1972), 269.

115. "Virgo est ergo quae nupsit, virgo quae nos suo utero portavit, virgo quae genuit, virgo quae proprio lacte nutrivit . . . Qualis est haec virgo quae Trinitatis fontibus irrigatur: cui de petra fluunt aquae, non deficiunt ubera, mella funduntur?" Ambrose, *De virginibus* I.5.22 (PL 16, 195ab).

116. "Sum plus quam mater, qui vos ab aeterno in luce praescientiae meae formavi et portavi. . . . Formavit enim dominus nos in utero praescientiae, gestavit in procuratione vitae, angustias parturitionis adhibuit in redemptionis passione." Albertus Magnus, *Postilla super Isaiam* 49.15, ed. Ferdinand Siepmann in *Opera omnia*, vol. 19 (Aschendorff: Monasterii Westfalorum, 1952): 491.

117. "Omnes enim rationes exemplares concipiuntur ab aeterno in vulva aeternae sapientiae seu utero, et maxime praedestinationis. Unde quia ab aeterno rationes praedestinationis concepit, non potest nos non diligere; et sicut ab aeterno concepit, sic in tempore produxit sive peperit, et postea in carne patiendo parturivit." Bonaventure, *Collationes in Hexaemeron* 20.5, in *Opera omnia*, vol. 5 (Quaracchi: Collegium S. Bonaventurae, 1891), 426.

118. For a range of theological meanings associated with the vernacular itself, see Nicholas Watson, "Conceptions of the Word: The Mother Tongue and the Incarnation of God," *New Medieval Literatures* 1 (1997): 85–124.

119. Hadewijch, Vision 4, in *Complete Works*, ed. Columba Hart (New York: Paulist Press, 1980), 273–75. For analysis of this vision see Barbara Newman, *From Virile Woman to WomanChrist: Studies in Medieval Religion and Literature* (Philadelphia: University of Pennsylvania Press, 1995), 146–47.

120. Marguerite Porete, *Le Mirouer des simples ames*, ch. 79, ed. Romana Guarnieri, CCCM 69 (Turnhout: Brepols, 1986). On Marguerite's indifference to the body see Amy Hollywood, *The Soul as Virgin Wife: Mechthild of Magdeburg, Marguerite Porete, and Meister Eckhart* (Notre Dame, Ind.: University of Notre Dame Press, 1995), 109–12, 185–86.

121. For more on this theme see Kari Børresen, "Christ notre mère, la théologie de Julienne de Norwich," *Mitteilungen und Forschungsbeiträge der Cusanus-Gesellschaft* 13 (1978): 320–29; Paula Barker, "The Motherhood of God in Julian of Norwich's Theology," *Downside Review* 100 (1982): 290–304; Rachel Jacoff, "God as Mother: Julian of Norwich's Theology of Love," *Denver Quarterly* 18 (1984): 134–39; Sarah McNamer, "The Exploratory Image: God as Mother in Julian of Norwich's *Revelations of Divine Love*," *Mystics Quarterly* 15 (1989): 21–28.

122. "I will that thou wisely know thi penance and shalt then sothly seene that all thi living is penance profitable. This place is prison, and this life is penance; and in the remedy He will we enjoyen. The remedy is that our Lord is with us, kepand and ledand into the fulhede of joye." Ch. 77, Crampton p. 146.

123. God's will that we take pleasure in his love for us is a leitmotif of the Long Text. Cf. ch. 22, where Christ asks Julian, "Art thou wele payd [pleased] that I suffrid for thee?" and she responds, "ya, good Lord, gramercy." Crampton, p. 66.

124. Maud Burnett McInerney, "*In the Meydens Womb*: Julian of Norwich and the Poetics of Enclosure," in John Carmi Parsons and Bonnie Wheeler, eds., *Medieval Mothering* (New York: Garland, 1996), 157–82.

125. Long Text, ch. 6, cited from Colledge and Walsh, II, 306–7. The passage "A man goyth vppe ryght . . . to the lowest parte of oure nede" is omitted in the Sloane ms., probably because it embarrassed the scribe.

126. Colledge and Walsh derive *soule* at this point in the ms. from OE *sufol*, "cooked or digested food" (II, 306, n. 35). The word was obsolescent in Julian's day, but makes better sense than the alternative reading "soul."

127. For a strong psychoanalytic reading based on the theories of D. W. Winnicott, see Andrew Sprung, "The Inverted Metaphor: Earthly Mothering as *Figura* of Divine Love in Julian of Norwich's *Book of Showings*," in Parsons and Wheeler, eds., *Medieval Mothering*, 183–99.

128. McInerney, "*In the Meydens Womb*," 164. Cf. the literalization of this image in the late medieval sculpture of Mary as *vierge ouvrante*, housing the whole Trinity within her womb (Fig. 6.11).

129. "Et est sciendum, quod ars ista quasi sola inter omnes mundi, in sui doctrina utitur nominibus propriis, et extraneis, et inusitatis, et allegoriis, et aenigmatibus, et metaphoris, et aequivocationibus, et transsumptionibus, et involucris, et prosopopoeis, et hyperbolis, et ironiis." Petrus Bonus, *Margarita pretiosa novella correctissima*, in *Theatrum chemicum* (Strasbourg: Eberhard Zetzner, 1659–61), 4: 516.

130. Barbara Obrist, *Les débuts de l'imagerie alchimique (XIVe–XVe siècles)* (Paris: Le Sycomore, 1982), 48–54; Richard Kieckhefer, *Magic in the Middle Ages* (Cambridge: Cambridge University Press, 1990), 133–44.

131. *Aurora consurgens*, ed. Marie-Louise von Franz, trans. R. F. C. Hull and A. S. B. Glover (New York: Bollingen Foundation, 1966). The text was discovered by C. G. Jung and edited by his disciple von Franz at his request, as a companion piece to Jung's own *Mysterium conjunctionis*. Von Franz's commentary is of limited use to historians, as she defends the ms. ascription to Thomas Aquinas with the dubious argument that the text represents a "breakthrough of the unconscious" experienced by the saint in a deathbed ecstasy (xi). But she demonstrates that none of the alchemical authorities quoted by the author are later than the mid-thirteenth century, so a date around the time of Thomas's death (1274) might be correct. The independent treatise that passed as "Part II" of the *Aurora* is considerably later.

132. On the liturgical use of this verse see Fulton, "'Quae est ista,'" *Mediaeval Studies* 60 (1998): 55–122.

133. Obrist, *Les débuts*, 186–87.

134. "Numquid sapientia non clamitat in plateis et prudentia dat vocem in libris sapientum dicens: O viri, ad vos clamito et vox mea ad filios intelligentiae: Intelligite insipientes et animadvertite parabolam et interpretationem verba sapientum et aenigmata eorum; sapientes enim usi sunt diversis locutionibus in assimilatione de omni re, quae est supra terram, et sub globo lunari multiplicaverunt parabolas in hac scientia. Audiens autem sapiens sapientior erit et intelliget, intelligens sapientiam hanc possidebit illam. Haec est sapientia, regina scilicet austri, quae ab Oriente dicitur venisse, ut *aurora consurgens*, audire intelligere nec non videre sapientiam Salomonis et data est in manu eius potestas honor virtus et imperium, ferens regni coronam in capite suo radiis duodecim stellarum rutilantem, tamquam sponsa ornata viro suo habensque in vestimentis suis scriptum litteris aureis graecis, barbaris et latinis: Regnans regnabo et regnum meum non habebit finem omnibus invenientibus me et perquirentibus subtiliter ingeniose et constanter." *Aurora consurgens* 5, ed. von Franz, 52–54.

135. "Hanc Salomon pro luce habere proposuit et super omnem pulchritudinem et salutem; in comparatione illius lapidis pretiosi virtutem illi non comparavit.

Quoniam omne aurum tamquam arena exigua et velut lutum aestimabitur argentum in conspectu illius." *Aurora* 1, p. 34.

136. ". . . cuius amore langueo, ardore liquesco, odore vivo, sapore convalesco, cuius lacte nutrimentum suscipio, amplexu iuvenesco, osculo spiraculum vitae recipio, cuius condormitione totum corpus meum exinanitur, illi vero ero in patrem et ipse mihi in filium." *Aurora* 6, p. 58.

137. Obrist, *Les débuts*, 155–57.

138. "Totam fere sacrosanctam Scripturam, Salomonis praesertim, et Psaltes ipsius scripta, maxime vero Cantica canticorum, allegorice, ad Alchimiam etiam invita[m] detraxit auctor, ita ut nulla alia de causa, illa omnia scripta esse videantur (si huic credimus) quam in honorem et laudem Alchimiae: imo (quod nefandum est) ipsum sacratissimum mysterium Incarnationis et mortis Christi Domini nostri, ad mysterium lapidis prophanissime contorsit." Conrad Waldkirch, *Artis auriferae quam chemiam vocant* (Basel: Waldkirch, 1593), 1: 183–84; cited in Obrist, 184.

139. "Ego do et non resumo, ego pasco et non deficio, ego securo et non paveo, quid plus referam dilecto meo? Ego sum mediatrix elementorum, concordans unum alteri: illud, quod calidum est frigesco et viceversa, et illud, quod siccum est humecto et viceversa, et illud, quod est durum mollifico et viceversa. Ego finis et dilectus meus principium, ego totum opus et tota scientia in me occultatur, ego lex in sacerdote et sermo in propheta et consilium in sapiente. Ego occidam et vivere faciam et non est, qui de manu mea possit eruere." *Aurora* 12, p. 142.

140. Obrist, *Les débuts*, 275–84; von Franz, *Aurora*, 25–27. Obrist reproduces the entire iconographic cycle from two mss.: Zürich, Zentralbibliothek, Rhenoviensis 172, and Prague, University Library, ms. VI Fd. 26. Adam McLean describes an illuminated ms. unknown to Obrist and von Franz (Glasgow, University Library, ms. Ferguson 6) on his web site: www.levity.com/alchemy/aurorafi.html.

141. Obrist, Fig. 39.

142. The portrayal of Wisdom or the Holy Spirit with a scarlet face is itself an esoteric motif. For the Hildegard illustrations see her *Liber divinorum operum*, ed. Albert Derolez and Peter Dronke, CCCM 92 (Turnhout: Brepols, 1996), plates I,1, I,2. A thirteenth-century portrait of Guglielma of Milan, whom devotees venerated as the incarnation of the Holy Spirit, depicted her with a crimson face. The motif also appears, from the sixteenth century, in Russian esoteric icons of Sophia as "angel of great counsel." Newman, *From Virile Woman to WomanChrist*, 191; Fiene, "What Is the Appearance of Divine Sophia?" 458–59.

143. At least one other instance of Sapientia nursing the philosophers can be found in an illuminated mythography contemporary with the *Aurora consurgens* illustrations (Rome, Vat. pal. lat. 1066, fol. 235; also London, Wellcome Library, ms. 49, fol. 58v). The image is reproduced in Erich Neumann, *The Great Mother*, trans. Ralph Manheim (Princeton, N.J.: Princeton University Press, 1963), plate 174.

144. Obrist, *Les débuts*, 238–40.

145. Ibid., 241.

146. *Das "Buch der Heiligen Dreifaltigkeit" in seiner zweiten, alchemistischen Fassung (Kadolzburg 1433)*, ed. Uwe Junker (Cologne: F. Hansen, 1986). This edition, the only one available, is far from satisfactory. It is an unpunctuated, diplomatic transcription of one late manuscript (Wolfenbüttel, Herzog August Bibliothek, cod.

guelf. 188 Blankenburg), which is itself a copy of a lost 1433 revision of the author's original text.

147. The name "Ulmannus" later ascribed to him is not attested in contemporary sources.

148. Obrist, *Les débuts*, 122–26. The Kadolzburg recension of 1433 was made for Friedrich's son, Johannes von Brandenburg, who abdicated in order to devote more time to alchemical studies.

149. On the manuscripts see Junker, *Das Buch*, 368; Obrist, *Les débuts*, 261–75; Herwig Buntz, "Das *Buch der heiligen Dreifaltigkeit*, sein Autor und seine Überlieferung," *Zeitschrift für deutsches Altertum* 101 (1972): 150–60.

150. Obrist, pp. 117–18, cites the Russian librarian R. Minzloff, who wrote in 1874 that "in meditating too deeply on this book, one can go mad; that is no doubt what happened to [the author.]" Junker, a psychologist, notes several possibly "schizophrenic" features of the text (pp. 72–76), such as its general strangeness, conceptual slippage, inaccessibility, and confused and stammering language, as well as delusional beliefs about the *lapis* (its possessor can fly, become invisible at will, and so forth).

151. "So vornemen wir das der jnn wendige gotlicher leichnam ist das ist der jnnwendig gotlicher syn ein syn vier elemente drej personen So das eyn gleich vornemen wir das der vswendig menschliche leichnam ist das ist der vswendig menschliche syn / Eyn syn vier elemente drej personen . . . So bekennen wir das die vswendig menschheit gotes ihesus maria ein feurisch engelissch leichnam / ist gewesen ein jn got sein eigen ihesu cristo selber aller oberst ein jnne ym maria was ewig sein menscheit voreyniget ein gleich substancien mit ein jn seiner gotlichen substancien. . . . So was sie es gancz ewig seine persone gleich gotliche menschliche eyne inne eyne / Do nye kein scheiden kunde an sein / Also recht durch leuchtig reyne lauter clar seyn was die edele menssscheit gotes ihesu maria syn eine." Junker, pp. 93–94.

152. "O welche eyne reine liebe erbar menscheit ihesus maria ist ewig eyne / vnd ist gewesen ewig eyne jr gotheit ihesus cristus kan ewig nicht / vnd konde ewig nicht von / irer vsswendiger menssscheit ihesus. maria / Also gancz fur war ist vnd was er ein gleich substancie ihesus maria ist drey personen czwifalt gotheit / . . . Also wissen wir das man seine gotheit nicht kan sehen man muss seine menssscheit mit sehen / durch menget gleich eine so kan man nicht, vnd konde nye nicht sein menssscheit sehen Man musste / vnd man muss sein gotheit mit sehen also verborgen durchmenget gleich eine ewig was / vnd ist gotheit menssscheit sein vnder seiner gotheit vnd under seiner menssscheit gleich eine welche nye Jren teil er mere jn ym. — Also kan man auch nicht got sehen man muss seine muter mitsehen durch menget gleich eine / So konde man ewig nye nicht / vnd man kan ewig nymer nicht gotes muter sehen man muste ewig vnd man muss ewig got mit sehen also verborgen durchmenget gleich eine ewig was vnd ist got seine eigen muter / Vater selber mensschlich magtlich manlich er mere jn ym verborgen wil das leyt an ym." Junker, 94–95.

153. "Also ist got ihesus cristus selber sein eigen son. Jung alt Also ist got ihesus cristus selber sein eigen heiliger geist Jung alt." Junker, 116.

154. "Vater son ist muter / Son vater ist muter. . . . *Omnia sunt vnum esse.*" Junker, 117.

155. Obrist, *Les débuts*, 165–77.

156. "Also offenbar sal man diss buch juden heiden cristen keczern kundigen

einen waren cristenglauben uber alle empfahende / das maria / also gros hoch jn der gotheit spigel / der heyligen driualdikeit ist das beczeuget sie selber jndem buche do sie sprichet *Ab inicio et ante secula creata sum*." Junker, 95.

157. Junker, 19, claims that the 1419 Berlin ms. of the *Buch* (Stiftung Preussischer Kulturbesitz, Kupferstichkabinett, Ms. 78 A 11) contains the earliest Coronation by the Trinity. Marielene Putscher says more cautiously that this is "among the earliest representations of this type": "the peculiar theological speculation of the Franciscan monk Ulmannus, understanding the 'Trinity' as Father, Son, and virgin Mother, finds its expression in the image." "Das *Buch der heiligen Dreifaltigkeit* und seine Bilder in Handschriften des 15. Jahrhunderts," in Christoph Meinel, ed., *Die Alchemie in der europäischen Kultur- und Wissenschaftsgeschichte*, Wolfenbüttel Symposium (Wiesbaden: Harrassowitz, 1986), 154–55.

158. Another very early example is the "Coronation of the Virgin" at the Cleveland Museum of Art, part of an altarpiece by a Spanish painter known as the "Rubielos Master." The precise date of this early fifteenth-century painting is not certain. See Cleveland Museum of Art, *European Paintings Before 1500* (Cleveland: Cleveland Museum of Art, 1974), 166–68 and plate 28. I thank Stanton Thomas, curatorial assistant of the Cleveland Museum, for information on this work.

159. Obrist, *Les débuts*, 263–64. The autograph is London, Wellcome Library, ms. 164; the Coronation is described on fols. 45v–46r and roughly sketched on fol. 208r.

Chapter 6. Maria: Holy Trinity as Holy Family

1. The principal Latin source for the tragedy of Oedipus was Seneca; neither Ovid nor Virgil told his tale. For a good overview of this theme in medieval literature, see now Elizabeth Archibald, *Incest and the Medieval Imagination* (Oxford: Clarendon Press, 2001). The best-known medieval narrative of incest is Hartmann von Aue's romance *Gregorius* (ca. 1195), a tale retold in Thomas Mann's novel *Der Erwählte* (*The Holy Sinner*).

2. I use the term "myth" here in a sense commonly adopted by religionists: a sacred narrative encapsulating core beliefs and values of the society that creates and retells it. My usage is not pejorative and has no bearing on truth-claims.

3. Sigmund Freud, *Civilization and Its Discontents* (1929), in Peter Gay, ed., *The Freud Reader* (New York: W.W. Norton, 1989), 722–72; see also *The Ego and the Id*, part III, in ibid., 637–45.

4. Barbara Newman, *From Virile Woman to WomanChrist: Studies in Medieval Religion and Literature* (Philadelphia: University of Pennsylvania Press, 1995), 82–83.

5. For recent work in that vein see Michael P. Carroll, *The Cult of the Virgin Mary: Psychological Origins* (Princeton, N.J.: Princeton University Press, 1986). For feminist psychoanalytic approaches to Marian piety, see Julia Kristeva, "Stabat Mater" (1976), in *Tales of Love*, trans. Leon Roudiez (New York: Columbia University Press, 1987), 234–63, and the work of Luce Irigaray, especially her *Speculum de l'autre femme* (Paris: Éditions du Minuit, 1974) and the edited volume, *Le souffle des femmes* (Paris: ACGF, 1996).

6. David Herlihy, "The Making of the Medieval Family: Symmetry, Structure,

Sentiment," *Journal of Family History* 8 (1983): 116–30, reprinted in Herlihy, *Women, Family and Society in Medieval Europe: Historical Essays, 1978–1991,* ed. Anthony Molho (Providence, R.I.: Berghahn, 1995), 135–53; Christiane Klapisch-Zuber, *Women, Family, and Ritual in Renaissance Italy,* trans. Lydia Cochrane (Chicago: University of Chicago Press, 1985), 326–29; John Bossy, *Christianity in the West, 1400–1700* (Oxford: Oxford University Press, 1985), 8–11, 95–97.

7. Several anthologies devoted to the cross-cultural study of goddesses include chapters on Mary. See E. Ann Matter, "The Virgin Mary: A Goddess?" in Carl Olson, ed., *The Book of the Goddess, Past and Present* (New York: Crossroad, 1983): 80–96; David Kinsley, "Mary: Virgin, Mother, and Queen," in *The Goddesses' Mirror: Visions of the Divine from East and West* (Albany, N.Y.: SUNY Press, 1989), 215–60; Elinor Gadon, *The Once and Future Goddess: A Symbol for Our Time* (San Francisco: Harper and Row, 1989); Andrew Harvey and Anne Baring, "Queen of Heaven," in *The Divine Feminine: Exploring the Feminine Face of God Around the World* (Berkeley, Calif.: Conari Press, 1996), 102–19.

8. There is a voluminous literature tracing the rise and development of Mariology. Hilda Graef, *Mary: A History of Doctrine and Devotion,* 2 vols. (New York: Sheed and Ward, 1963, 1965), remains indispensable for the Mariology of individual theologians. Among the best general histories are Marina Warner, *Alone of All Her Sex: The Myth and the Cult of the Virgin Mary* (New York: Knopf, 1976); Sally Cunneen, *In Search of Mary: The Woman and the Symbol* (New York: Ballantine, 1996); and Jaroslav Pelikan, *Mary Through the Centuries: Her Place in the History of Culture* (New Haven, Conn.: Yale University Press, 1996)—the works respectively of a lapsed Catholic, a Catholic feminist, and an Orthodox church historian.

9. Herrad of Hohenbourg, *Hortus deliciarum* (ca. 1170), as reconstructed by Rosalie Green, Michael Evans, et al. (London: Warburg Institute, 1979), fol. 8r.

10. Alfred Hackel, *Die Trinität in der Kunst: Eine ikonographische Untersuchung* (Berlin: Reuther und Reichard, 1931), 79.

11. Joan Chamberlain Engelsman, *The Feminine Dimension of the Divine: A Study of Sophia and Feminine Images in Religion* (Philadelphia: Westminster Press, 1979), offers a Jungian account of medieval Mariology as embodying "the return of the repressed."

12. Irenaeus of Lyon, *Contra haereses* III.24.2, IV.7.4 (PG 7, 967 and 993); Theophilus of Antioch, *Ad Autolycum* II.10, ed. and trans. Robert M. Grant (Oxford: Clarendon Press, 1970): 38–41; *Clementine Homilies* 16.12 (PG 2, 373–76). For the Syriac tradition see the Jewish-Christian *Odes of Solomon,* ed. and trans. J. H. Charlesworth (Missoula, Mont.: Scholars Press, 1977).

13. For a fuller review of this tradition, see Newman, "The Alternative Trinity," in *From Virile Woman,* 198–209 and the works there cited; also Jane Richardson Jensen, "Father, Son, and Holy Spirit as Mothers in Early Syrian Literature," *Continuum* 2 (1993): 27–49. Some of the pertinent primary texts have been translated in Rosemary Radford Ruether, *Womanguides: Readings Toward a Feminist Theology* (Boston: Beacon Press, 1985), 27–32.

14. *Didascalia apostolorum* 9, ed. Arthur Vööbus, *Corpus Scriptorum Christianorum Orientalium* 176 (Leuven: Peeters, 1979), 100; *Les Constitutions apostoliques* II.26, ed. Marcel Metzger, SC 320 (Paris: Éditions du Cerf, 1985), 238–41.

15. Augustine, *De Trinitate* XII.5; trans. Stephen McKenna, *The Trinity* (Washington, D.C.: Catholic University of America Press, 1968), 346–47. Augustine goes on to state that the woman is only partially and derivatively made in God's image: XII.7, p. 352.

16. Richard of St.-Victor, *De Trinitate*, Book III; trans. Grover Zinn in Richard of St. Victor, *The Twelve Patriarchs* (New York: Paulist Press, 1979), 373–97.

17. William Langland, *Piers Plowman* (C-text), XVIII.215–39, ed. Derek Pearsall (Berkeley: University of California Press, 1979), 303. On the importance of this theme see M. Teresa Tavormina, *Kindly Similitude: Marriage and Family in "Piers Plowman"* (Woodbridge, Suffolk: Boydell, 1995), chap. 3. Langland's version of the analogy diverges from the ancient form because, following the Western "Filioque" doctrine, he must liken Eve to the Son and Abel to the Spirit "proceeding from both."

18. The marginality of the Holy Spirit in scholastic theology has often been noted by twentieth-century theologians. Among the many who have tried to correct it are Yves Congar, *The Word and the Spirit*, trans. David Smith (San Francisco: Harper and Row, 1986); Hans Urs von Balthasar, *Creator Spirit*, trans. Brian McNeil (San Francisco: Ignatius, 1993); Karl Barth, *The Holy Spirit and the Christian Life*, trans. R. Birch Hoyle (Louisville, Ky.: Westminster/John Knox Press, 1993); and Jürgen Moltmann, *The Spirit of Life: A Universal Affirmation*, trans. Margaret Kohl (Minneapolis: Fortress Press, 1992). Donald Gelpi revived the ancient maternal theme with a feminist slant in *The Divine Mother: A Trinitarian Theology of the Holy Spirit* (Lanham, Md.: University Press of America, 1984). See also Elizabeth Johnson, *Women, Earth, and Creator Spirit* (New York: Paulist Press, 1993), and, for a wry comment on the Spirit's gender, Frederick Dale Bruner and William Hordern, *The Holy Spirit—Shy Member of the Trinity* (Minneapolis: Augsburg, 1984): "The Holy Spirit does not mind being Cinderella outside the ballroom if the Prince is honored inside his Kingdom" (16).

19. The weak valence of this symbol is suggested by an apocryphal story once current in ecumenical circles. A Japanese proselyte is supposed to have responded to a Western missionary's preaching with baffled courtesy: "Honorable Father—very good! Honorable Son—very good! But Honorable Bird, I do not understand at all."

20. Luisa Muraro, *Guglielma e Maifreda: Storia di un'eresia femminista* (Milan: La Tartaruga, 1985); Marina Benedetti, *Io non sono Dio: Guglielma di Milano e i Figli dello Spirito santo* (Milan: Edizioni Biblioteca Francescana, 1998); Newman, "Woman-Spirit, Woman Pope," in *From Virile Woman*, 182–223.

21. Guy Philippart, "Le récit miraculaire marial dans l'Occident médiéval," in *Marie: Le Culte de la Vierge dans la société médiévale*, ed. Dominique Iogna-Prat, Éric Palazzo, and Daniel Russo (Paris: Beauchesne, 1996), 563–90, at 582. For early and vernacular examples, see Anton Mayer, "Mater et Filia: ein Versuch zur stilgeschichtlichen Entwicklung eines Gebetsausdrucks," *Jahrbuch für Liturgiewissenschaft* 7 (1927): 60–82, and Andrew Breeze, "The Virgin Mary, Daughter of Her Son," *Études celtiques* 27 (1990): 267–83.

22. Sequence to Christ and the Virgin from St. Gall (11th c.). *Analecta hymnica Medii Aevi*, ed. Clemens Blume et al., 55 vols. (Leipzig, 1866–1922; rpt. New York: Johnson Reprint Corp., 1961), 54: 336, no. 215.

23. Victorine sequence for Saturday in the octave of the Assumption (twelfth century). *Analecta* 54: 326–28; no. 206, stanzas 10 and 23.

24. Thirteenth-century hymn. G. G. Meersseman, *Der Hymnos Akathistos im Abendland*, 2 vols. (Freiburg: Universitätsverlag, 1958, 1960), 1: 188; no. 36, stanza 16.

25. Northern French sequence to the Virgin (thirteenth century). *Analecta* 54: 396; no. 252.

26. French or English sequence to the Virgin (thirteenth century) *Analecta* 54: 401–2; no. 256, stanza 15.

27. Sequence to the Virgin from Missal of Uppsala, printed 1513. *Analecta* 54: 417; no. 276, stanza 2.

28. Michael O'Carroll, "Spouse of God (Bride of God), Mary as," in his *Theotokos: A Theological Encyclopedia of the Blessed Virgin Mary* (Wilmington, Del.: Michael Glazier, 1982), 333–34. In medieval hymnody *sponsa Christi* is the most common title. For *sponsa dei patris* see Meersseman, *Hymnos Akathistos*, II: 145, 241, 247; for *sponsa spiritus sancti*, II: 172, 206, 248.

29. "Sic autem beata Virgo, prioris ecclesiae pars optima, Dei Patris sponsa esse meruit, ut exemplar quoque fuerit iunioris ecclesiae sponsae Filii Dei, filii sui." Rupert of Deutz, *De operibus Spiritus sancti* I.8, ed. Hraban Haacke, CCCM 24 (Turnhout: Brepols, 1972), 1829.

30. Philippart, "Le récit miraculaire," 584.

31. Ovid, *Metamorphoses* Bk. 9 (Byblis and Caunus), Bk. 10 (Myrrha and Cinyras); *Heroides* 4 (Phaedra and Hippolytus).

32. I disagree here with Philippart ("Le récit," 584) and others who assume that medieval writers must have been unconscious of the incest motifs in Marian piety, or more generally, of the eroticism that colors so much devotional and mystical writing. To be sure, they may or may not have been aware of psychological motives for their *interest* in such material, but the themes themselves are explicit and unmistakable. Then as now, degrees of psychological sophistication varied widely across the population; we cannot assume universal naïveté simply because psychoanalysis had not yet been invented.

33. *Ovide moralisé*, Bk. 10, line 3764 (Myrrha); for the complete allegory see lines 3750–3800. Ed. C. de Boer, Verhandelingen der Koninklijke Akademie van Wetenschappen te Amsterdam, Afdeeling Letterkunde, 5 vols. (Amsterdam: J. Müller, 1915–38), 4: 100–101. For Byblis see Bk. 9, line 2604; vol. 3: 284–85. Cf. Archibald, *Incest*, 86–88.

34. Frauenlob, *Marienleich* I, 12, in *Frauenlob: Leichs, Sangsprüche, Lieder*, ed. Karl Stackmann and Karl Bertau (Göttingen: Vandenhoeck and Ruprecht, 1981), 1: 260–61.

35. This line is obscure. Another possibility is "my plowshare plows utterly straight."

36. Frauenlob himself seems to have been acquainted with alchemical imagery. In strophe 14 of the *Marienleich*, Mary calls herself the "mirror-vessel" (*spiegelvaz*) in which the divine Master reveals his mastery. In strophe 17 she is the *forma formarum*, neighbor to the *prima materia*, which underlies and outlasts all mixtures.

37. Philippart, "Le récit miraculaire," 584–85. See also Dyan Elliott, *Fallen Bodies: Pollution, Sexuality, and Demonology in the Middle Ages* (Philadelphia: University

of Pennsylvania Press, 1999), 107–15. For an alternative account of the Marian incest motif see Archibald, *Incest*, 238–44.

38. On the range of laywomen's responses to Mary see Newman, *From Virile Woman*, 95–96; Clarissa Atkinson, *The Oldest Vocation: Christian Motherhood in the Middle Ages* (Ithaca, N.Y.: Cornell University Press, 1991), 161–62; Pamela Sheingorn, "The Maternal Behavior of God: Divine Father as Fantasy Husband," in John Carmi Parsons and Bonnie Wheeler, eds., *Medieval Mothering* (New York: Garland, 1996), 77–99.

39. Julian of Norwich, *Shewings*, Long Text ch. 25; ed. Georgia Ronan Crampton (Kalamazoo, Mich.: Medieval Institute Publications, 1993), 70.

40. F. O. Büttner, *Imitatio pietatis: Motive der christlichen Ikonographie als Modelle zur Verähnlichung* (Berlin: Mann, 1983); James Marrow, "Symbol and Meaning in Northern European Art of the Late Middle Ages and the Early Renaissance," *Simiolus* 16 (1986): 150–69; Hans Belting, *The Image and Its Public in the Middle Ages: Form and Function of Early Paintings of the Passion*, trans. Mark Bartusis and Raymond Meyer (New Rochelle, N.Y.: Caratzas, 1990); Jeffrey Hamburger, *The Visual and the Visionary: Art and Female Spirituality in Late Medieval Germany* (New York: Zone, 1998).

41. "Singulari et quodam modo inaestimabili pene immediate accedis ipsi Trinitati, ut si ullo modo Trinitas illa quaternitatem externam admitteret, tu sola quaternitatem compleres; sed est Trinitas, nec aliquatenus ibi fieri potuit aut poterit quaternitas." Peter of Celle, Sermon 13, PL 202: 675d; trans. Hilda Graef in *Mary*, I: 253.

42. Meersseman, *Hymnos Akathistos,* I: 213; no. 69, stanza 12.

43. C. G. Jung, "A Psychological Approach to the Dogma of the Trinity" (1948), in *Psychology and Religion: West and East*, trans. R. F. C. Hull, *Collected Works*, vol. 11 (Princeton, N.J.: Princeton University Press, 1969), 170–71. The frontispiece to this volume is Jean Fouquet's "Enthronement of the Virgin," discussed below.

44. Ibid., 171–80. See also *Answer to Job*, in ibid., 453–70, and *Mysterium Coniunctionis*, *Collected Works*, vol. 14 (New York: Bollingen Foundation, 1963), 186–88.

45. For a color reproduction of this painting, see the cover of *Religion and Literature* 31, 1 (Spring 1999), which contains an abridged version of this chapter.

46. Meersseman, *Hymnos Akathistos*, I: 228, no. 74, stanza 60.

47. "Ipse negabat Deum, gloriosam Virginem Mariam et totam Trinitatem." Claude Bochet, cited in Eva Maier, *Trente ans avec le diable: Une nouvelle chasse aux sorciers sur la Riviera lémanique (1477–1484)* (Lausanne: Université de Lausanne, 1996), 188.

48. Meersseman, *Hymnos Akathistos*, II: 251.

49. Philippe Verdier, *Le Couronnement de la Vierge: Les origines et les premiers développements d'un thème iconographique* (Paris: Vrin, 1980).

50. Christ holds an open book with the liturgical text, "Veni electa mea et ponam in te thronum meum." This is an antiphon for the Common of Virgins, no. 5322 in R.-J. Hesbert, ed., *Corpus antiphonalium officii* (Rome: Herder, 1963–79), 3: 527. The text on Mary's scroll, "Leva eius sub capite meo et dextera illius amplexabitur me" (Cant. 2.6), is used in the same office, suggesting her role as *Virgo virginum*. She is also *Sedes Sapientiae*, the one who "enthrones" Christ in her body before he enthrones her in heaven. Cf. Warner, *Alone of All Her Sex*, 121–22.

51. Hackel, *Die Trinität*, 79–85; Louis Réau, *Iconographie de l'art chrétien*, vol. 2,

pt. 2 (Paris: Presses universitaires de France, 1957), 621–26; Gertrud Schiller, *Ikonographie der christlichen Kunst*, vol. 4, pt. 2 (Gütersloh: Gerd Mohn, 1980), plates 735, 741–50 (Renaissance and Baroque examples); Ines Dresel, Dietmar Lüdke, and Horst Vey, *Christus und Maria: Auslegungen christlicher Gemälde der Spätgotik und Frührenaissance aus der Karlsruher Kunsthalle* (Karlsruhe: Staatliche Kunsthalle, 1992), 153–57 and figs. 177, 179, 181, 182.

52. François Boespflug, "Dieu en pape: Une singularité de l'art religieux de la fin du moyen âge," *Revue Mabillon* n.s. 2 (1991): 167–205, at 169. Once God the Father emerged as an artistic figure in his own right, he could be depicted as king, emperor, bishop, or pope; the long white beard was common though not de rigueur. In certain French examples, like the famous Coronation by Enguerrand Charonton at Villeneuve-lès-Avignon (1453), Father and Son are identical.

53. Verdier, *Couronnement*, 110; Büttner, *Imitatio pietatis*, 124–31. Visionaries such as Catherine of Siena, Margery Kempe, and even Henry Suso were addressed in their revelations as "daughter." In *Le Ménagier de Paris*, a conduct book written by an elderly French burgher for his young wife c. 1393, we find the following: "our soul . . . is [God's] daughter that he loaned to us clean and healthy without stain or blemish, but which we have poisoned with the drafts of mortal sin. If he accuses us of murder saying that we have slain his daughter that he put in our care, what defense shall we have?" Trans. W. P. Barret, revised by John Shinners in his *Medieval Popular Religion, 1000–1500: A Reader* (Peterborough, Ont.: Broadview Press, 1997), 254.

54. Richard Kieckhefer, "Major Currents in Late Medieval Devotion," in Jill Raitt, ed., *Christian Spirituality: High Middle Ages and Reformation* (New York: Crossroad, 1987), 100.

55. Jeffrey Hamburger, *Nuns as Artists: The Visual Culture of a Medieval Convent* (Berkeley: University of California Press, 1997), 139; Büttner, *Imitatio pietatis*, 129–31.

56. In some early sixteenth-century examples the motif of God's wrath comes to the fore: the Father brandishes a sword or a sheaf of arrows, ready to take vengeance on a sinful world. See Dresel et al., *Christus und Maria*, figs. 53–55.

57. Bynum, *Fragmentation and Redemption*, 106–8.

58. Dresel et al., *Christus und Maria*, 49–50. The scrolls in fig. 7 read as follows. Son: "O Vater las dir die wund myn / eyn opper vor alle sunder syn." ("O Father, let my wounds be to you a sacrifice for all sinners.") Virgin: "O Vater diz ist die brust dyn sun gesoge haet / verzieh den sunder . . . missethaet." ("O Father, this is the breast that nursed your Son. Forgive sinners their misdeeds.") Father: "Viel lieber sun und maria reine meit / kein mogelich bede ist uch verseit." ("Dearest Son and Mary, pure maid, no possible prayer is denied you.")

59. Dresel et al., *Christus und Maria*, 53–54. This iconography first appears ca. 1450 in the Turin-Milan Book of Hours, a Netherlandish production despite its title. For a reproduction see Caroline Walker Bynum, *Holy Feast and Holy Fast: The Religious Significance of Food to Medieval Women* (Berkeley: University of California Press, 1987), plate 28.

60. On prayerful weeping as a charism of holy women, see Newman, *From Virile Woman*, 108–36; Ellen Ross, "'She Wept and Cried Right Loud for Sorrow and for Pain': Suffering, the Spiritual Journey, and Women's Experience in Late Medieval Mysticism," in Ulrike Wiethaus, ed., *Maps of Flesh and Light: The Religious Experience*

of Medieval Women Mystics (Syracuse, N.Y.: Syracuse University Press, 1993), 45–59; Jo Ann McNamara, "The Need to Give: Suffering and Female Sanctity in the Middle Ages," in Renate Blumenfeld-Kosinski and Timea Szell, eds., *Images of Sainthood in Medieval Europe* (Ithaca, N.Y.: Cornell University Press, 1991), 199–221.

61. Hans Belting has shown that the terms *Pietà* and *imago pietatis* in medieval documents could refer to any image of the dead Christ, whether depicted alone, upheld by angels, lying in the Virgin's lap, or displayed by the Father, as in the examples discussed below. *The Image and Its Public*, 84–85, 191–96.

62. Georg Troescher, "Die 'Pitié-de-Nostre-Seigneur' oder 'Notgottes,'" *Wallraf-Richartz-Jahrbuch* 9 (1936), 148–68; François Boespflug, "La compassion de Dieu le Père dans l'art occidental (XIIIe–XVIIe siècles)," *Supplément* 172 (March 1990): 123–59. According to Boespflug, more than 200 examples of the subject are extant, although it is rarely discussed. "La compassion," 124.

63. Boespflug, "La compassion," 140, 144.

64. Troescher, "'Pitié-de-Nostre-Seigneur,'" 156–58; Dresel et al., *Christus und Maria*, 120; James Snyder, *Northern Renaissance Art: Painting, Sculpture, the Graphic Arts from 1350 to 1575* (New York: Harry Abrams, 1985), 69–70.

65. "A Woman Sat Weeping," anonymous poem (c. 1475–1500), ed. Celia and Kenneth Sisam in *The Oxford Book of Medieval English Verse* (Oxford: Clarendon Press, 1970), 486–87.

66. Henk Van Os, with Eugène Honée, Hans Nieuwdorp, and Bernhard Ridderbos, *The Art of Devotion in the Late Middle Ages in Europe, 1300–1500*, trans. Michael Hoyle (Princeton, N.J.: Princeton University Press, 1994), 124.

67. In less common variants, the interior of the Madonna holds a Crucifixion or scenes from the life of Mary, rather than the Trinity. The most exhaustive study is that of Christoph Baumer, "Die Schreinmadonna," *Marian Library Studies* 9 (1977): 239–72, with 54 plates. See also François Boespflug, *Dieu dans l'art: Sollicitudini Nostrae de Benoît XIV (1745) et l'affaire Crescence de Kaufbeuren* (Paris: Éditions du Cerf, 1984), 280–85; Wolfgang Braunfels, "Maria, Marienbild," in *Lexikon der christlichen Ikonographie* (Rome: Herder, 1968–76), 3: 194.

68. The sculpture now at Cluny (Figure 6.11) belonged to this group: among the kneeling figures in the first row of suppliants is a Teutonic Knight in the insignia of his order (white mantle with black cross). Baumer, "Die Schreinmadonna," 264.

69. Baumer catalogues only 27 extant specimens and mentions half a dozen lost ones, including one possible forgery, while Braunfels estimates that "about 40" remain. No Shrine Madonna made of precious metal survives.

70. Erich Neumann, *The Great Mother: An Analysis of the Archetype*, trans. Ralph Manheim (Princeton, N.J.: Princeton University Press, 1955), 331. Warner describes the *Vierge ouvrante* as a "fetish-like Madonna" and "parthenogenetic goddess": *Alone of All Her Sex*, 47. Elinor Gadon claims the sculpture "illustrates a popular but heterodox view that without [Mary], redemption would not have taken place." *Once and Future Goddess*, 208.

71. From the sequence "Salve mater salvatoris," *Analecta* 54: 383–84. Henk Van Os cites a German translation from Salzburg: "Salve, mueter gueter rete / der gedreiten trinitete / edels, schöns, gedreits geslos." *Art of Devotion*, 57. For the epithet "Trinitatis triclinium" see the fifteenth-century hymns in Meersseman, *Hymnos*

Akathistos, I: 201, 211; II: 146; and Peter Kern, *Trinität, Maria, Inkarnation: Studien zur Thematik der deutschen Dichtung des späteren Mittelalters* (Berlin: Erich Schmidt Verlag, 1971), 133–35.

72. Warner, *Alone of All Her Sex*, 337. For critiques of Warner's position see Pelikan, *Mary Through the Centuries*, 215–23; Rachel Fulton, *From Judgment to Passion: Devotion to Christ and the Virgin Mary, 800–1200* (New York: Columbia University Press, 2002), 242.

73. Alcuin Blamires, *The Case for Women in Medieval Culture* (Oxford: Clarendon Press, 1997), 120–24.

74. Bonaventure, *Bringing Forth Christ: Five Feasts of the Child Jesus*, trans. Eric Doyle (Oxford: SLG Press, 1984). On Eckhart see Rosemary Hale, "*Imitatio Mariae*: Motherhood Motifs in Late Medieval German Spirituality," PhD dissertation, Harvard University, 1992, 121–30; Amy Hollywood, *The Soul as Virgin Wife: Mechthild of Magdeburg, Marguerite Porete, and Meister Eckhart* (Notre Dame, Ind.: University of Notre Dame Press, 1995), 150–55.

75. The theme has been most fully explored in Hale, "*Imitatio Mariae*," but see also Büttner, *Imitatio pietatis*; Christiane Klapisch-Zuber, "Holy Dolls: Play and Piety in Florence in the Quattrocento," in *Women, Family, and Ritual*, 310–29; Sandro Sticca, *The Planctus Mariae in the Dramatic Tradition of the Middle Ages*, trans. Joseph Berrigan (Athens: University of Georgia Press, 1988); Elisabeth Vavra, "Bildmotiv und Frauenmystik: Funktion und Rezeption," in Peter Dinzelbacher and Dieter Bauer, eds., *Frauenmystik im Mittelalter* (Ostfildern: Schwabenverlag, 1985), 201–30.

76. Stanley Weed explores a similar appeal in convent-owned paintings that depicted the Virgin among female saints: "My Sister, Bride, and Mother: Aspects of Female Piety in Some Images of the *Virgo inter Virgines*," *Magistra* 4 (1998): 3–26.

77. "Vueiliez ouvrir les oreilles de vostre très-grant doulceur à escouter les prières de moy povre pécheresse, quant pour les pécheurs se voust en vous hebergier le Père, le Filz et le Seint-Esperit. Pour quoy, doulce dame, à vous appartient estre advocate aux povres pécheurs, et par quoy vous estes la chambre de toute la Trinité." Baumer, "Die Schreinmadonna," 251.

78. Philipp Wackernagel, *Das deutsche Kirchenlied von der ältesten Zeit bis zu Anfang des XVII. Jahrhunderts*, 5 vols. (Leipzig: Teubner, 1864–77), 2: 871. On this literary theme see Kern, *Trinität, Maria, Inkarnation*, 92–138.

79. Friedrich Heinrich von der Hagen, ed., *Minnesinger: Deutsche Liederdichter des zwölften, dreizehnten und vierzehnten Jahrhunderts*, 5 vols. (Leipzig: Teubner, 1838), 3: no. 138.

80. Frauenlob, *Marienleich* I,11, ed. Stackmann and Bertau, 1: 256.

81. *Francis and Clare: The Complete Works*, trans. Regis Armstrong and Ignatius Brady (New York: Paulist Press, 1982), 63, slightly modified.

82. One notable exception is Hadewijch: see Chapter 4 above, pp. 169–81.

83. Sheingorn, "The Maternal Behavior of God," 89.

84. Vavra, "Bildmotiv und Frauenmystik"; Hamburger, *The Visual and the Visionary*, 111–48; David Freedberg, *The Power of Images: Studies in the History and Theory of Response* (Chicago: University of Chicago Press, 1989), 301–12; Bernard McGinn, *The Flowering of Mysticism: Men and Women in the New Mysticism, 1200–1350* (New York: Crossroad, 1998), 30, 302.

85. For insights on Mechthild's Mariology I am indebted to an unpublished paper by Maeve Callan, "'Hail, Celestial Empress': The Virgin Mary in the Mystical Theology of Mechthild of Magdeburg." See also Newman, "*La mystique courtoise*: Thirteenth-Century Beguines and the Art of Love," in *From Virile Woman*, 137–67.

86. "Ir sun ist got und sie göttinne, es mag ir nieman gliche gewinnen." Mechthild von Magdeburg, *Das fliessende Licht der Gottheit* III.1, ed. Hans Neumann (Munich: Artemis, 1990), 75; trans. Frank Tobin, *The Flowing Light of the Godhead* (New York: Paulist Press, 1998): 103. Cf. III.4, where Mary is called "noble Goddess above all pure humans" (Neumann 82; Tobin 110). Latin hymnody avoids the titles *dea* and *diva*, though often implying their substance.

87. "Der himmelsche vatter teilte mit der sele sin götlich minne und sprach: 'Ich bin got aller götten, du bist aller creaturen göttinne und ich gibe dir mine hanttrúwe, das ich dich niemer verkiese.'" *Flowing Light* III.9; Neumann 87–88, Tobin 115.

88. "Do erwelte mich der vatter zü einer brut, das er etwas ze minnende hette, wand sin liebú brut was tot, die edel sele; und do kos mich der sun zü einer müter und do enpfieng mich der helig geist ze einer trútinne. Do was ich alleine brut der heligen drivaltekeit." *Flowing Light* I.22; Neumann 18, Tobin 50.

89. "Gegrüsset siestu, himmelschú keyserinne, gottes müter und herzeliebú vrowe min." *Flowing Light* VII.20; Neumann 273, Tobin 292.

90. *Flowing Light* II.3; Neumann 40, Tobin 71–72. See also I.22; Neumann 19, Tobin 51–52. This vision is discussed by Ulrike Wiethaus in *Ecstatic Transformation: Transpersonal Psychology in the Work of Mechthild of Magdeburg* (Syracuse, N.Y.: Syracuse University Press, 1996), 132–33.

91. "Do trat dú ganze helige drivaltekeit mit der gewalt der gotheit und mit dem güten willen der menscheit und mit der edelen gevügheit des heligen geistes dur den ganzen lichamen ires magtümes in der vürigen sele irs güten willen und saste sich in das offen herze ires allerreinosten vleisches und vereinete sich mit allem dem, das er an ir vant, also das ir vleisch sin vleisch wart, also das er ein vollekomen kint wüchs in irme libe. . . . Also ei si in langer trüg, ie lihtor, schönor und wisor si wart." *Flowing Light* V.23; Neumann 175, Tobin 198 (slightly modified).

92. The simultaneous unity and plurality of the Bride is also expressed through Mary's, and the Soul's, identification with the collective female personification of Christendom or the Church (*helige cristanheit*). In I.22 Mary "suckles" the Church beneath the Cross (Neumann 19, Tobin 51); in IV.3 Mary, the Church, and Mechthild herself are assimilated as three "playmates" (*gespile*) who all "have the same Bridegroom" (Neumann 114–16, Tobin 144–46).

93. "Dú minste sele ist ein tohter des vatters und ein swester des sunes und ein vrúndinne des heligen geistes und werliche ein brut der heligen drivaltekeit." *Flowing Light* II.22; Neumann 55, Tobin 87. In V.27 the Father tells the Son that his own human soul is "the most intimate (*allernehstú*) bride of our Three Persons," suggesting a virtual equivalence between Mary and the humanity of Christ (Neumann 186, Tobin 208).

94. "Vil lieber, ich bitte dich, . . . das du denne komen wellest zü mir als ein getrúwer arzat . . . das du denne komen wellest als min allerliebster vrúnt . . . als ein getrúwer bichter . . . als ein getrúwer brüder zü siner lieben swester . . . als ein getrúwer vatter zü sinem lieben kinde . . . das du mir denne wellist senden dine

mägetliche müter, der mag ich nit enbern . . . das du denne wellest komen als min allerliebster brútgom." *Flowing Light* VII.35; Neumann 282–83, Tobin 303–04.

95. Claire Sahlin, "'His Heart Was My Heart': Birgitta of Sweden's Devotion to the Heart of Mary," in *Heliga Birgitta—budskapet och förebilden*, ed. Alf Härdelin and Mereth Lindgren (Stockholm: Almqvist & Wiksell, 1993), 213–27; eadem, "The Virgin Mary and Birgitta of Sweden's Prophetic Vocation," in *Maria i Sverige under Tusen År*, ed. Sven-Erik Brodd and Alf Härdelin (Skellefteå, Sweden: Artos, 1996), 227–54.

96. Henrik Cornell, "The Iconography of the Nativity of Christ," *Uppsala Universitets Årsskrift* 1 (1924): 1–101. The Nativity vision is in St. Birgitta, *Revelaciones* VII.21–25, ed. Birger Bergh (Uppsala: Almqvist & Wiksell, 1967), 187–94, and Birgitta of Sweden, *Life and Selected Revelations*, ed. Marguerite Tjader Harris, trans. Albert Kezel (New York: Paulist Press, 1990): 202–6.

97. Birgitta of Sweden, *Opera minora II, Sermo angelicus*, ed. Sten Eklund (Uppsala: Almqvist & Wiksell, 1972); *The Word of the Angel*, trans. John Halborg (Toronto: Peregrina, 1996).

98. "Filia, miraris de motu, quem sentis in corde tuo. . . . non timeas illusionem sed gratulare, quia motus iste, quem tu sentis, signum aduentus filii mei est in cor tuum. Ideo, sicut filius meus imposuit tibi nomen noue sponse sue, sic ego voco te nunc nurum filii mei. Nam sicut pater et mater senescentes et quiescentes imponunt nurui onus et dicunt ei ea, que sunt facienda in domo, sic Deus et ego in cordibus hominum senes et frigidi a caritate eorum indicare volumus amicis nostris et mundo per te voluntatem nostram." *Revelaciones* VI.88, ed. Birger Bergh (Stockholm: Almqvist & Wiksell, 1991), 247–48, trans. Sahlin in "The Virgin Mary," 234.

99. Sahlin, "The Virgin Mary," 228–32, and Claire Waters, "Doctrine Embodied: Gender, Authority, and Performance in Late-Medieval Preaching," PhD dissertation, Northwestern University, 1998, chap. 5.

100. See Atkinson, *Oldest Vocation*, 170–84, for Birgitta's deep ambivalence about motherhood. Obviously devoted to her children, she nonetheless understood familial love as a temptation opposed to the disinterested love of God. On the extent of this cultural attitude see Newman, "'Crueel Corage,'" in *From Virile Woman*, 76–107.

101. Johan Huizinga, *The Waning of the Middle Ages: A Study of the Forms of Life, Thought and Art in France and the Netherlands in the Dawn of the Renaissance*, trans. Frederick Hopman (1924; rpt. New York: Doubleday Anchor, 1954). See especially chap. 12, "Religious Thought Crystallizing into Images."

102. Atkinson, *Oldest Vocation*, 178.

103. *Revelaciones* VII.13, pp. 152–62; trans. Kezel, *Life and Selected Revelations*, 181–87.

104. Augustine, *Confessions* 3.12. St. Ambrose had reassured Monica, mother of the still-unconverted Augustine, that "the son of such tears could not be lost."

105. "O, quam maledicta est illa scrofa seu porca mater eius, que tam prolixum habuit ventrem, quod tanta aqua in ipsam infusa fuit, quod omnia ventris eius spacia impleta fuerunt humoribus lacrimarum!" *Revelaciones* VII.13, p. 161.

106. For Birgitta's influence on Margery see Julia Bolton Holloway, "Bride, Margery, Julian, and Alice: Bridget of Sweden's Textual Community in Medieval

England," in Sandra McEntire, ed., *Margery Kempe: A Book of Essays* (New York: Garland, 1992), 203–21; Janette Dillon, "Holy Women and Their Confessors or Confessors and Their Holy Women? Margery Kempe and Continental Tradition," in Rosalynn Voaden, ed., *Prophets Abroad: The Reception of Continental Holy Women in Late-Medieval England* (Cambridge: D.S. Brewer, 1996), 115–40. For Margery's attempt to emulate Birgitta's "motherhood of tears" on behalf of her own son, see Newman, *From Virile Woman*, 92.

107. On Margery's social, religious, and literary contexts, see Anthony Goodman, "The Piety of John Brunham's Daughter, of Lynn," in *Medieval Women*, ed. Derek Baker (Oxford: Blackwell, 1978), 347–58; Clarissa Atkinson, *Mystic and Pilgrim: The Book and the World of Margery Kempe* (Ithaca, N.Y.: Cornell University Press, 1983); Susan Dickman, "Margery Kempe and the Continental Tradition of the Pious Woman," in Marion Glasscoe, ed., *The Medieval Mystical Tradition in England* (Cambridge: D.S. Brewer, 1984), 150–68; David Wallace, "Mystics and Followers in Siena and East Anglia: A Study in Taxonomy, Class, and Cultural Mediation," in ibid., 169–91; and Lynn Staley, *Margery Kempe's Dissenting Fictions* (University Park: Pennsylvania State University Press, 1994).

108. On relationships of this kind see Dyan Elliott, *Spiritual Marriage: Sexual Abstinence in Medieval Wedlock* (Princeton, N.J.: Princeton University Press, 1993), esp. 224–45.

109. *The Book of Margery Kempe*, ed. Lynn Staley (Kalamazoo, Mich.: Medieval Institute Publications, 1996). For convenience I cite the familiar translation by B. A. Windeatt (Harmondsworth: Penguin, 1985).

110. *Book* ch. 6 (Nativity), 7 (flight into Egypt), 73 (death of the Virgin), 79 (Crucifixion).

111. *Book* ch. 14, ed. Staley 44; Windeatt 66–67.

112. *Book* ch. 35, ed. Staley 91–92; Windeatt 122–23.

113. Nancy Partner, "Reading *The Book of Margery Kempe*," *Exemplaria* 3 (1991): 29–66, at 58–60, 64.

114. Diana Black, "The Sin of Incest: *The Book of Margery Kempe* as Healing the Wound," unpublished paper (Northwestern University, 1992). Several of my students have proposed similar readings, but I have not seen this speculation in print.

115. *Book* ch. 36, ed. Staley 94; Windeatt 126.

116. *Book* ch. 85, ed. Staley 195; Windeatt 247–48.

117. *Book* ch. 86, ed. Staley 198–99; Windeatt 251–52.

118. Hamburger, *Nuns as Artists*, plate 12. On the complex meaning of this image see ch. 4, pp. 137–75.

119. Ibid., 149.

120. Ibid., 139.

121. "No doubt the simplest course for the child would be to choose as his sexual objects the same persons whom, since his childhood, he has loved with what may be described as damped-down libido. But, by the postponing of sexual maturation, time has been gained in which the child can erect, among other restraints on sexuality, the barrier against incest. . . . Respect for this barrier is essentially a cultural demand made by society." Sigmund Freud, *Three Essays on the Theory of Sexuality*, in Gay, *Freud Reader*, 290.

122. David Herlihy, *Medieval Households* (Cambridge, Mass.: Harvard University Press, 1985), 61; Christopher Brooke, *The Medieval Idea of Marriage* (Oxford: Oxford University Press, 1991), 134–36. After the Fourth Lateran Council (1215) the strict ban on consanguinity was modified somewhat, reducing the domain of "incestuous" relationships from seven degrees to four.

123. "Et pour tant on se doit bien garder de poindre faulsement une hystoire comme de l'escrire faulsement tant que bonnement se puet faire. Je le dy en partie pour une ymaige qui est aux Carmes et semblables qui ont dedans leur ventre une Trinité comme se toute la Trinité eus prins cher humainne en la Vierge Marie. Et qui plus merveille est, il y a enfer dedans paint. Et ne vois pas pour quelle chose on le mire ainsy, car a mon petit jugement il n'y a beauté ne devocion en telle ouverture, et puet estre cause d'erreur et d'indevocion." Jean Gerson, Sermon 385, "Puer natus est nobis," in *Oeuvres complètes*, ed. Palémon Glorieux, 10 vols. (Paris: Desclée, 1961–73), 7: 963.

124. The bull *Sollicitudini Nostrae* reads: "Inter reprobatas Imagines Sanctissimae Trinitatis ea procul dubio recensenda est, quam pluribus insectatur Ioannes Gerson, . . . ubi nimirum repraesentabatur Deipara Virgo Trinitatem ipsam in utero gerens, quasi vero tota Trinitas humanam carnem ex Virgine assumpsisset." The pope explicitly approved the *Gnadenstuhl* Trinity and the *Not Gottes*. Boespflug, *Dieu dans l'art*, 42 (text) and 280–85 (discussion).

125. On the origins of Joseph's cult see Francis L. Filas, "Joseph, St., Devotion to," in *New Catholic Encyclopedia* (Washington, D.C.: Catholic University of America Press, 1967), 7: 1108–13; Palémon Glorieux, "Saint Joseph dans l'oeuvre de Gerson," *Cahiers de Josephologie* 19 (1971): 414–28; D. Catherine Brown, *Pastor and Laity in the Theology of Jean Gerson* (Cambridge: Cambridge University Press, 1987), chap. 7; Rosemary Drage Hale, "Joseph as Mother: Adaptation and Appropriation in the Construction of Male Virtue," in Parsons and Wheeler, eds., *Medieval Mothering*, 101–16.

126. "Considérations sur saint Joseph," *Oeuvres* 7: 63–94; "Autres considérations sur saint Joseph," 7: 94–99.

127. "Ecclesiis universis" (17 Aug. 1413), *Oeuvres* 8: 61–66; "Exhortation générale pour la fête de la desponsation Notre Dame" (26 Sept. 1413), *Oeuvres* 7: 11–15; "En considerant moult" (23 Nov. 1413, to the Duke of Berry), *Oeuvres* 2: 155–57; "Reverendo patri, domino ac magistro" (7 Sept. 1416, to Dominique Petit, cantor of Chartres), *Oeuvres* 2: 167–69.

128. Sermon 232, "Jacob autem genuit" (8 Sept. 1416), *Oeuvres* 5: 344–62; Sermon 234, "Nuptiae factae sunt" (17 Jan. 1417), *Oeuvres* 5: 376–98; Sermon 248, "Suscepimus Deus" (2 Feb. 1418), *Oeuvres* 5: 538–46.

129. *Oeuvres* 4, no. 138, pp. 31–100.

130. *Oeuvres* 4, nos. 107, 125, 135, 137, 148, 156, 202.

131. Few if any medieval writers before Gerson would have endorsed this claim, which did not receive official sanction until Leo XIII's encyclical of 1889, *Quamquam pluries*. In 1870 Pope Pius IX had named St. Joseph patron of the universal Church.

132. "Joseph fuit vir Mariae, et ita caput ejus quia caput mulieris vir, secundum Apostolum. . . . decuit ut Joseph tanta praerogativa polleret quae similitudinem et

convenientiam exprimeret talis sponsi ad talem sponsam Mariam. . . . Unde sicut laus Mariae est laus Christi filii sui, ita laus Joseph in praeconium redundat utriusque, Jesu et Mariae." Sermon 232, *Oeuvres* 5: 344–45.

133. Rosemary Hale shows how Joseph's iconography was likewise modeled on that of Mary: he came to be depicted in the "Madonna pose" holding the Christ Child, and appropriated such Marian emblems as the lily and the crown. "Joseph as Mother," 102.

134. Sermon 232, *Oeuvres* 5: 356; modified from *Josephina*, distich 12, in *Oeuvres* 4: 95.

135. "At vero quia corpus Mariae fuit ipsius Joseph jure matrimoniali quo fit mutua translatio corporum viri ad mulierem et e contra, videamus si cum intelligentiae sobrietate dicere fas nobis sit quod *ex corpore et carne Joseph* natus est Jesus Christus. Et hoc dici forsitan posset nisi piarum aurium timeretur offensio." Sermon 232, *Oeuvres* 5: 357; emphasis added.

136. Elliott, *Spiritual Marriage*, 180. See also Herlihy, *Medieval Households,* 127–30; Warner, *Alone of All Her Sex*, 188–90.

137. "O miranda prorsus, Joseph, sublimitas tua. O dignitas incomparabilis ut mater Dei, regina coeli, domina mundi, appellare te dominum non indignum putaverit. Nescio sane, patres orthodoxi, quid hic amplius habeat mirabilis vel humilitas in Maria vel in Joseph sublimitas, quamvis incomparabiliter exsuperet utrumque puer Jesus Deus benedictus in saecula, de quo scriptum et jam dictum est quod erat subditus eis; subditus fabro is qui fabricavit auroram et solem; subditus feminae textrinae cui flectitur omne genu, coelestium, terrestrium et infernorum. Cuperem mihi verba suppeterent ad explicandum tam altum et absconditum a saeculis mysterium, tam admirandam venerandamque trinitatem Jesu, Joseph et Mariae." Sermon 232, *Oeuvres* 5: 358. Cf. Bernard's first homily in praise of the Virgin Mother (I.7), trans. Marie-Bernard Saïd and Grace Perigo in *Magnificat: Homilies in Praise of the Blessed Virgin Mary* (Kalamazoo: Cistercian Publications, 1979), 10–11.

138. "Joseph . . . fuit caput Mariae, habens inde auctoritatem aliquam, principatum, dominationem vel imperium in Mariam sicut et Maria suo modo in filium suum Jesum jure naturalis maternitatis." Sermon 232, *Oeuvres* 5: 358.

139. This theme appears in many places, but see especially the "Prosa super epithalamium Joseph," no. 148, *Oeuvres* 4: 111–12. The sequence addresses Joseph as both *virgo* and *parens*, ending with the strophe: "Joseph et Virgo beati / Ope vestra majestati / Conjungamur vestri nati / Qui sponsus est virginum." "Blessed Joseph and Virgin, by your aid may we be joined to the majesty of your [plural] Son, who is the bridegroom of virgins." Compare the "Exhortation générale," *Oeuvres* 7: 14–15.

140. *Book* ch. 82, Staley 189; Windeatt 239–40.

141. A second feast of "St. Joseph the Worker" was established by Pius XII on May 1, 1955, to compete with the Communist celebration of May Day.

142. On St. Anne, see Kathleen Ashley and Pamela Sheingorn, eds., *Interpreting Cultural Symbols: Saint Anne in Late Medieval Society* (Athens: University of Georgia Press, 1990). On the Holy Family, see Cynthia Hahn, "'Joseph will perfect, Mary enlighten and Jesus save thee': The Holy Family as Marriage in the Merode Triptych," *Art Bulletin* 68 (1986): 54–66; Joseph Chorpenning, ed., *The Holy Family in Art and Devotion* (Philadelphia: St. Joseph's University Press, 1996).

143. Gerson makes this patronage explicit at the end of Sermon 232: "meritis et intercessione tanti tamque potentis et imperiosi quodammodo patroni apud sponsam suam, de qua natus est Jesus qui vocatur Christus, reddatur Ecclesia unico viro vero et certo, Summo Pontifici sponso suo vice Christi." *Oeuvres* 5: 362.

144. Pamela Sheingorn, "The Holy Family and Pollution in Late Medieval Visual Culture," paper presented at the Newberry Library, Chicago, March 1998.

145. For Gerson's Mariology, see his treatise of 1426, *De susceptione humanitatis Christi* (*Oeuvres* 2: 263–74), and the lengthy *Collectorium super Magnificat* of 1427–28 (*Oeuvres* 8: 163–534). Gerson accepted the still-controversial doctrine of the Immaculate Conception, but criticized Marian "excesses" like those of Bernardino of Siena, who claimed that the Virgin possessed not only sinless purity but omniscience from the moment of her conception.

146. Jean Gerson, "Le Traité de Gerson contre le *Roman de la Rose*," ed. Ernest Langlois, *Romania* 45 (1919): 23–48; trans. in Joseph Baird and John Kane, eds., *La Querelle de la Rose: Letters and Documents* (Chapel Hill: University of North Carolina Press, 1978), 70–91. For a summary of Gerson's views on women and marriage see Brown, *Pastor and Laity*, 209–51.

147. "Humilitas dat pondus; discretio flexibilitatem; patientia durabilitatem; veritas configurationem; caritas dat colorem. Has quinque virtutes legimus Mariam habuisse in angelica revelatione sibi facta." *De distinctione verarum revelationum a falsis* (*Oeuvres* 3: 36–56), at 39.

148. "Quocirca scripsit quaedam devota mulier, nihil ita se habere suspectum sicut dilectionem, et plus quam diabolum, etiam dum circa divina et personas probatae sanctitatis versatur. Hoc non muliebriter traditum est." Ibid., 51.

149. Among the delusional characters Gerson cites are a man persuaded by "revelation" that he was destined to become first pope, then Antichrist, and a woman who feigned sanctity through immoderate fasting. Curiously, Gerson would state more than twenty years later that he wrote *De distinctione* after being nearly seduced by the revelations of one Hermina of Rheims; but he does not mention her in the present treatise. See his *De examinatione doctrinarum* (*Oeuvres* 9: 458–75), at 474.

150. "Argumentum hujus rei est in quodam libello incredibili pene subtilitate ab una foemina composito, quae Maria de Valenciennes dicebatur; haec agit de praerogativa et eminentia dilectionis divinae, ad quam si quis devenerit fit secundum eam ab omni lege praeceptorum solutus, adducens pro se illud ab Apostolo [*sic*] sumptum: Caritatem habe, et fac quod vis." Gerson says that, had the author been speaking of the blessed in heaven rather than pilgrims on earth, "vix altius quicquam de divina fruitione, quoad aliqua, dici potuerat; sed fallebat eam sua tumiditas animi tantae passioni dilectionis immixta." *De distinctione*, 51–52.

151. ". . . in hoc sacro Concilio, quaeritur tractari de canonizatione sanctorum, et examinatione doctrinarum suarum, praesertim unius quae Brigitta nominatur, assueta visionibus quas nedum ab angelis, sed a Christo et Maria et Agnete et caeteris sanctis, familiaritate jugi, sicut sponsus ad sponsam loquitur, se asserit divinitus suscepisse." *De probatione spirituum* (*Oeuvres* 9: 177–85), at 179.

152. ". . . omisso divinarum Scripturarum studio magna christianorum pars ad has visiones, ideo placentiores quia recentiores, converterent oculos et aures prurientes." Ibid., 181.

153. "Quaeritur ergo si persona sit novitia in zelo Dei, quia novitius fervor cito fallitur si regente caruerit; praesertim in adolescentibus et foeminis, quarum est ardor nimius, avidus, varius, effrenis, ideoque suspectus." Ibid., 180. On p. 184 Gerson adds, "Hoc praecipue considerare necesse est, si sit mulier, qualiter cum suis confessoribus conversatur et instructoribus, si collocutionibus intendit continuis, sub obtentu nunc crebrae confessionis, nunc prolixae narrationis visionum suarum, nunc alterius cujuslibet confabulationis. Expertis credite: . . . vix est altera pestis vel efficacior ad nocendum, vel insanabilior."

154. "Postremo sexus muliebris ab apostolica prohibetur auctoritate ne palam doceat; doctrinam intellige, seu verbo seu scripto, nomine suo publicatam, maxime si fuerit ad viros . . . Quid si talis sexus apposuerit ambulare in magnis et mirabilibus super se, visiones quotidie super visiones addere, laesiones quoque cerebri per epilepsiam vel congelationem, aut aliam melancholiae speciem ad miraculum referre, . . . appellare sacerdotes Dei filios suos; docere eos professionem suam in qua nutriuntur assidue." *De examinatione doctrinarum, Oeuvres* 9: 467.

155. According to Gerson, Gregory XI confessed on his deathbed—"habens in manibus sacrum Christi corpus"—that he had dismissed the rational advice of his own counsellors and brought the Church to schism because he had been "seductus . . . ab hominibus, tam viris quam mulieribus, sub specie religionis visiones loquentibus sui capitis." Ibid., 469.

156. "Ubi sunt scripta tot eruditissimarum ac devotissimarum foeminarum: Paulae, Eustochium similiumque? Certe nulla supersunt, quia nulla praesumpserunt. . . . Notetur ad extremum quod sancti prophetae et doctores jam universaliter approbati recipiunt in suis verbis obscuris vel ambiguis interpretationem, qualis non debetur novellis de corde suo prophetantibus." *De examinatione*, 468.

157. "Et n'est point a doubter que l'umilité Nostre Dame estoit si grande qu'elle se rendit autant ou plus subgette a son loyal espous Joseph comme autre femme doit et peut faire a son espous," *Considérations sur St. Joseph, Oeuvres* 7: 66. Cf. the sermon "Poenitemini: de la chasteté," *Oeuvres* 7: 843, and the "Exhortation générale," *Oeuvres* 7: 14.

158. Julian, *Shewings*, Long Text ch. 57; ed. Crampton, 120.

Chapter 7. Goddesses and the One God

1. "Haec est tota nostra metaphysica: de emanatione, de exemplaritate, de consummatione, scilicet illuminari per radios spirituales et reduci ad summum." Bonaventure, *Collationes in Hexaemeron* 1.17, in *Opera Omnia* 5 (Quaracchi: Collegium S. Bonaventurae, 1891), 332.

2. Jean Leclercq, *The Love of Learning and the Desire for God: A Study of Monastic Culture*, trans. Catharine Misrahi (New York: Fordham University Press, 1961).

3. Bernard McGinn, "Meister Eckhart and the Beguines in the Context of Vernacular Theology," in McGinn, ed., *Meister Eckhart and the Beguine Mystics: Hadewijch of Brabant, Mechthild of Magdeburg, and Marguerite Porete* (New York: Continuum, 1994), 1–14; idem, *The Flowering of Mysticism: Men and Women in the New Mysticism, 1200–1350* (New York: Crossroad, 1998), 19–24.

4. Nicholas Watson, "Visions of Inclusion: Universal Salvation and Vernacular Theology in Pre-Reformation England," *Journal of Medieval and Early Modern Studies* 27 (1997): 145–87; idem, "Conceptions of the Word: The Mother Tongue and the Incarnation of God," *New Medieval Literatures* 1 (1997): 85–124.

5. Nicholas Watson, "Censorship and Cultural Change in Late-Medieval England: Vernacular Theology, the Oxford Translation Debate, and Arundel's Constitutions of 1409," *Speculum* 70 (1995): 822–64.

6. "Mais celle autre [voie] est ymaginee . . . / La face de Dieu est voiant / Cil qui le suit jusqu'a la fin." Christine de Pizan, *Le livre du chemin de long estude*, ed. Robert Püschel (Berlin, 1887; rpt. Geneva: Slatkine, 1974), lines 916, 904–5, p. 39; trans. Kevin Brownlee in Renate Blumenfeld-Kosinski, ed., *The Selected Writings of Christine de Pizan* (New York: W.W. Norton, 1997), 71.

7. "Quemadmodum ars poetica per fictas fabulas allegoricasque similitudines moralem doctrinam seu physicam componit ad humanorum animorum exercitationem . . . ita theologica veluti quaedam poetria sanctam Scripturam fictis imaginationibus ad consultum nostri animi . . . conformat." Eriugena, *Expositiones super Ierarchiam caelestem S. Dionysii* 2.1; PL 122: 146bc.

8. *Chartularium Universitatis Parisiensis*, vol. 1, no. 473, ad 1277, ed. Henri Denifle (Paris: Delalain, 1889), 553. Censured propositions that echo the views of Genius in the *Rose* are no. 168 ("Quod continentia non est essentialiter virtus"), 169 ("Quod perfecta abstinentia ab actu carnis corrumpit virtutem et speciem"), and 183 ("Quod simplex fornicatio, utpote soluti cum soluta, non est peccatum").

9. Anselm of Canterbury, *Cur Deus Homo* I.3–4, ed. René Roques, SC 91 (Paris: Éditions du Cerf, 1963), 218–24.

10. Peter Dinzelbacher, *Vision und Visionsliteratur im Mittelalter* (Stuttgart: Hiersemann, 1981), 65–77.

11. Peter Dinzelbacher, *Heilige oder Hexen? Schicksale auffälliger Frauen in Mittelalter und Frühneuzeit* (Zurich: Artemis and Winkler, 1995); Dyan Elliott, "Women and Confession: From Empowerment to Pathology," in Mary Erler and Maryanne Kowaleski, eds., *Gendering the Master Narrative: Medieval Women and Power* (Ithaca, N.Y.: Cornell University Press, 2003).

12. Pope Celestine V, an elderly hermit who reigned for a few months in 1294 before becoming the only pope in history to abdicate, was canonized in 1313. Dante placed him in hell (*Inferno* III.60), though without naming him, because his *gran rifiuto* paved the way for the hated Boniface VIII.

13. The pagans are Ripheus, whom Virgil in the *Aeneid* commends as the most just among the Trojans; the emperor Trajan, resurrected by the prayers of Pope Gregory I just long enough to convert (both in *Par.* XX); and Statius (*Purg.* XXI–XXII), whom Dante imagines to have been converted by the study of Virgil's Fourth Eclogue. The heretic is Joachim of Fiore (*Par.* XII.140); Dante puts his praise in the mouth of Bonaventure, who in life had condemned his teaching.

14. A controversy over the beatific vision broke out in 1331, a decade after Dante's death, when Pope John XXII began to preach that the full beatific vision would be delayed until the soul's reunion with the body after the Last Judgment—a position that was ultimately rejected in Benedict XII's bull of 1336, "Benedictus Deus." See Caroline Walker Bynum, *The Resurrection of the Body in Western Christianity, 200–1336* (New York: Columbia University Press, 1995), 283–91. The position

that the soul might achieve perfect beatitude in its present life ("quod homo potest ita finalem beatitudinem secundum omnem gradum perfectionis in praesenti assequi") was among the "errors of the beghards and beguines" condemned in a bull of 1312, "Ad nostrum qui." Henricus Denzinger, ed., *Enchiridion symbolorum, definitionum et declarationum de rebus fidei et morum*, 33rd ed. (Barcelona: Herder, 1965), 282.

15. Nicholas Watson, "The Trinitarian Hermeneutic in Julian of Norwich's *Revelation of Love*," in Marion Glasscoe, ed., *The Medieval Mystical Tradition in England: Exeter Symposium V* (Cambridge: D.S. Brewer, 1992), 79–100.

16. Julian of Norwich, Long Text ch. 51, in *Shewings*, ed. Georgia Ronan Crampton (Kalamazoo, Mich.: Medieval Institute Publications, 1993), 101–4.

17. Good general studies include R. I. Moore, *The Origins of European Dissent* (Oxford: Blackwell, 1977); Malcolm Lambert, *Medieval Heresy: Popular Movements from the Gregorian Reform to the Reformation*, 2nd ed. (Oxford: Blackwell, 1992); Jeffrey Burton Russell, *Dissent and Order in the Middle Ages: The Search for Legitimate Authority* (New York: Twayne/ Macmillan, 1992).

18. Robert Lerner, *The Heresy of the Free Spirit in the Later Middle Ages* (Berkeley: University of California Press, 1972).

19. One possible exception is Nicholas of Buldesdorf, a Joachite burned by the rump Council of Basel in 1446; his books perished with him. It is not clear whether he also preached. See Robert Lerner, *The Feast of Saint Abraham: Medieval Millenarians and the Jews* (Philadelphia: University of Pennsylvania Press, 2001), 111–17.

20. Steven Justice, *Writing and Rebellion: England in 1381* (Berkeley: University of California Press, 1994), 231–51.

21. Bernard Silvestris, *Cosmographia*, ed. Peter Dronke (Leiden: Brill, 1978), 2.

22. For Porete's influence on Eckhart, see Edmund Colledge and J. C. Marler, "'Poverty of the Will': Ruusbroec, Eckhart and *The Mirror of Simple Souls*," in Paul Mommaers and Norbert de Paepe, eds., *Jan van Ruusbroec: The Sources, Content, and Sequels of His Mysticism* (Leuven: Leuven University Press, 1984), 14–47; and the essays by Maria Lichtmann, Amy Hollywood, and Michael Sells in McGinn, ed., *Meister Eckhart and the Beguine Mystics*.

23. On the Guglielmites see Barbara Newman, "WomanSpirit, Woman Pope," in *From Virile Woman to WomanChrist: Studies in Medieval Religion and Literature* (Philadelphia: University of Pennsylvania Press, 1995), 182–223; Luisa Muraro, *Guglielma e Maifreda: Storia di un'eresia femminista* (Milan: La Tartaruga, 1985); and now Marina Benedetti, *Io non sono Dio: Guglielma di Milano e i Figli dello Spirito santo* (Milan: Edizioni Biblioteca Francescana, 1998).

24. Marina Benedetti, ed., *Milano 1300: I processi inquisitoriali contro le devote e i devoti di santa Guglielma* (Milan: Scheiwiller, 1999).

25. H. C. Lea, *A History of the Inquisition of the Middle Ages* (New York: Harper, 1888), 3: 95.

26. Mary Daly, *Beyond God the Father: Toward a Philosophy of Women's Liberation* (Boston: Beacon Press, 1973), 19.

27. A. J. Minnis, "*De impedimento sexus*: Women's Bodies and Medieval Impediments to Female Ordination," in Peter Biller and A. J. Minnis, eds., *Medieval Theology and the Natural Body* (Woodbridge, Suffolk: York Medieval Press, 1997), 109–39.

28. Minnis, "*De impedimento sexus*"; Alcuin Blamires et al., eds., *Woman Defamed and Woman Defended: An Anthology of Medieval Texts* (Oxford: Clarendon Press, 1992), 250–60; Blamires, *The Case for Women in Medieval Culture* (Oxford: Clarendon Press, 1997).

29. Minnis, "*De impedimento sexus*," 118; Joan Gibson, "Could Christ Have Been Born a Woman? A Medieval Debate," *Journal of Feminist Studies in Religion* 8, 1 (Spring 1992): 69.

30. Pope John Paul II, *Mulieris Dignitatem* (*On the Dignity and Vocation of Women*) V.15 (Washington, D.C.: U. S. Catholic Conference, 1988), 57. The encyclical was issued on 15 August (the feast of the Assumption) in an official Marian Year.

31. *Mulieris Dignitatem* VII.26, p. 98, restating a similar argument in *Inter Insigniores*, par. 31. The earlier declaration was published under the auspices of Pope Paul VI on 15 Oct. 1976 (the feast of St. Teresa of Avila). John Paul II's apostolic letter of 22 May 1994, *Ordinatio Sacerdotalis*, attempts to close off the debate with an infallible declaration: "I declare that the Church has no authority whatsoever to confer priestly ordination on women and that this judgment is to be definitively held by all the Church's faithful."

32. On the revival of pagan goddess religion see Cynthia Eller, *Living in the Lap of the Goddess: The Feminist Spirituality Movement in America* (Boston: Beacon Press, 1993).

33. See the periodical *Re-Imagining: Quarterly Newsletter of the Re-Imagining Community* (Minneapolis, 1994–), and Laurel Schneider, *Re-Imagining the Divine: Confronting the Backlash Against Feminist Theology* (Cleveland: Pilgrim Press, 1998).

34. "In has autem sanctas et salutares observationes si qui abusus irrepserint: eos prorsus aboleri sancta Synodus vehementer cupit, ita ut nullae falsi dogmatis imagines et rudibus periculosi erroris occasionem praebentes statuantur. Quod si aliquando historias et narrationes sacrae Scripturae, cum id indoctae plebi expediet, exprimi et figurari contigerit: doceatur populus, non propterea divinitatem figurari, quasi corporeis oculis conspici, vel coloribus aut figuris exprimi possit. Omnis porro superstitio in Sanctorum invocatione, reliquiarum veneratione et imaginum sacro usu tollatur, omnis turpis quaestus eliminetur, omnis denique lascivia vitetur . . . Haec ut fidelius observentur, statuit sancta Synodus, nemini licere, ullo in loco . . . ullam insolitam ponere vel ponendam curare imaginem, nisi ab episcopo approbata fuerit. Nulla etiam admittenda esse nova miracula, nec novas reliquias recipiendas nisi . . . approbante episcopo." "Decretum de invocatione, veneratione et reliquiis Sanctorum, et sacris imaginibus," Council of Trent (3 December 1563), in Denzinger, *Enchiridion*, 420.

35. Marina Warner, *Alone of All Her Sex: The Myth and the Cult of the Virgin Mary* (New York: Knopf, 1976), 106.

36. F. L. Filas, "Joseph, St., Devotion to," *New Catholic Encyclopedia* (Washington, D.C.: Catholic University of America Press, 1967), 7, 1108–13; Michael O'Carroll, "Joseph, St.," in *Theotokos: A Theological Encyclopedia of the Blessed Virgin Mary* (Wilmington, Del.: Michael Glazier, 1982), 206–9.

37. *Life*, ch. 6, in *The Collected Works of St. Teresa of Avila*, trans. Kieran Kavanaugh and Otilio Rodriguez (Washington, D.C.: Institute of Carmelite Studies, 1976), 1: 53.

38. Jo Ann McNamara, *Sisters in Arms: Catholic Nuns through Two Millennia* (Cambridge, Mass: Harvard University Press, 1996), 317, 461.

39. This was a Catholic anthology printed by Henry Pepwell in the context of an anti-Lutheran campaign. See Jennifer Summit, *Lost Property: The Woman Writer and English Literary History, 1380–1589* (Chicago: University of Chicago Press, 2000), 126–38.

40. Summit, *Lost Property*, 61–71.

41. Gerald Ellard, "Alcuin and Some Favored Votive Masses," *Theological Studies* 1 (1940): 61.

42. Pius Künzle, introduction to Henry Suso, *Horologium Sapientiae* (Freiburg: Universitätsverlag, 1977), 218.

43. Charles Williams, *The Figure of Beatrice: A Study in Dante* (London: Faber and Faber, 1943), 21–22; Charles Singleton, *An Essay on the* Vita Nuova (Cambridge, Mass.: Harvard University Press, 1949), 4–5.

44. Yet Spenser's fairy queen, Gloriana, is one of several idealized representations of Elizabeth I, who deliberately incorporated elements of the Catholic Marian cult into her persona as Virgin Queen. See Helen Hackett, *Virgin Mother, Maiden Queen: Elizabeth I and the Cult of the Virgin Mary* (New York: St. Martin's Press, 1995).

45. Sin in *Paradise Lost* is actually called a goddess in diabolical parody of Minerva. Speaking to her sire and lover, Satan, she asserts: "All on a sudden miserable pain / Surpris'd thee, dim thine eyes, and dizzy swum / In darkness, while thy head flames thick and fast / Threw forth, till on the left side op'ning wide, / Likest to thee in shape and count'nance bright, / Then shining heav'nly fair, a Goddess arm'd / Out of thy head I sprung." *Paradise Lost* II.752–58.

46. Carolyn Merchant, *The Death of Nature: Women, Ecology, and the Scientific Revolution* (San Francisco: Harper and Row, 1980), 164–91.

47. English translations of the treatise and the women's rule can be found in *God Alone: The Collected Writings of St. Louis Marie de Montfort* (Bay Shore, N.Y.: Montfort Publications, 1987).

48. *The Love of Eternal Wisdom*, ch. 11, in ibid., 86.

49. Peter Erb, introduction to Jacob Boehme, *The Way to Christ* (New York: Paulist Press, 1978), 9–10. See pp. 56–62 of *The Way* for a love dialogue, reminiscent of Suso, between the masculine soul and his bride, the Noble Virgin Sophia.

50. Antoine Faivre, *Theosophy, Imagination, Tradition: Studies in Western Esotericism*, trans. Christine Rhone (Albany, N.Y.: SUNY Press, 2000): 138–43.

51. See, for example, Peter Erb, *Pietists, Protestants, and Mysticism: The Use of Late Medieval Spiritual Texts in the Work of Gottfried Arnold (1666–1714)* (Metuchen, N.J.: Scarecrow Press, 1989); Arthur Versluis, *Theosophia: Hidden Dimensions of Christianity* (Hudson, N.Y.: Lindisfarne, 1994).

52. Such symbolism, common to ancient and medieval thought and still prevalent in modern esotericism, dates back to the Pythagorean correlation of such binary pairs as odd/even, unity/plurality, male/female, spirit/matter, good/evil.

53. David Miller, *The New Polytheism: Rebirth of the Gods and Goddesses* (New York: Harper and Row, 1974); Naomi Goldenberg, *Changing of the Gods: Feminism and the End of Traditional Religions* (Boston: Beacon Press, 1979); James Hillman,

ed., *Facing the Gods* (Irving, Tex.: Spring, 1980); Jean Shinoda Bolen, *Goddesses in Everywoman: A New Psychology of Women* (San Francisco: Harper and Row, 1984); Carol Christ, *Laughter of Aphrodite: Reflections on a Journey to the Goddess* (San Francisco: Harper and Row, 1987); Regina Schwartz, *The Curse of Cain: The Violent Legacy of Monotheism* (Chicago: University of Chicago Press, 1997).

54. Tikva Frymer-Kensky, *In the Wake of the Goddesses: Women, Culture, and the Biblical Transformation of Pagan Myth* (New York: Free Press/Macmillan, 1992), 218; Lenn Evan Goodman, *Monotheism: A Philosophic Inquiry into the Foundations of Theology and Ethics* (Totowa, N.J.: Allanheld, Osmun, 1981), 27.

55. For a succinct summary of the arguments see Goodman, *Monotheism*, 1–34. See also Stanislas Breton, *Unicité et monothéisme* (Paris: Éditions du Cerf, 1981), and André Manaranche, *Le monothéisme chrétien* (Paris: Éditions du Cerf, 1985).

56. Frymer-Kensky, *In the Wake of the Goddesses*, 86.

57. This consensus is shared by most scholars; for the contrary view see Wilhelm Schmidt, *The Origin and Growth of Religion: Facts and Theories*, trans. H. J. Rose (New York: Dial Press, 1931).

58. The conception of Christian theology as a fusion of Judaism and Hellenism goes back to Adolf Harnack, *Outlines of the History of Dogma*, trans. E. K. Mitchell (London: Hodder and Stoughton, 1893), prolegomena.

59. Baruch Halpern, "'Brisker Pipes Than Poetry': The Development of Israelite Monotheism," in Jacob Neusner et al., eds., *Judaic Perspectives on Ancient Israel* (Philadelphia: Fortress Press, 1987), 77–115; Saul Olyan, *Asherah and the Cult of Yahweh in Israel* (Atlanta: Scholars Press, 1988); Mark Smith, *The Early History of God: Yahweh and the Other Deities in Ancient Israel* (San Francisco: Harper and Row, 1990); Christian Frevel, *Aschera und der Ausschliesslichkeitsanspruch YHWHs* (Weinheim: Beltz Athenäum, 1995).

60. For the contrast of inclusive and exclusive monotheisms I am indebted to John Kenney, *Mystical Monotheism: A Study in Ancient Platonic Theology* (Hanover, N.H.: University Press of New England, 1991), 150–56. The concept of inclusive monotheism is akin to what feminist theologian Laurel Schneider describes as "monistic polytheism": *Re-Imagining*, 198–99. See also Eller, *Living in the Lap*, 134–35.

61. Frymer-Kensky, *In the Wake of the Goddesses*, 85.

62. Gershom Scholem, *Major Trends in Jewish Mysticism*, 3rd ed. (New York: Schocken, 1961); Moshe Idel, *Kabbalah: New Perspectives* (New Haven, Conn.: Yale University Press, 1988); Margaret Barker, *The Great Angel: A Study of Israel's Second God* (London: SPCK, 1992).

63. For versions of this Christian Platonist teaching (exemplarism) in the Middle Ages, see pp. 56–60 on Bernard Silvestris and 228–29 on Julian of Norwich.

64. Alan Segal, *Two Powers in Heaven: Early Rabbinic Reports About Christianity and Gnosticism* (Leiden: Brill, 1977); Barker, *The Great Angel*, 162–89.

65. "Quia, sicut singillatim unamquamque personam Deum ac Dominum confiteri christiana veritate compellimur, ita tres Deos aut Dominos dicere catholica religione prohibemur." From the so-called Athanasian creed (actually a Western document), also known as "Quicunque vult." Denzinger, *Enchiridion*, 41.

66. A less famous "Santa Maria sopra Minerva," in Assisi, still has its classical façade. On the Parthenon see Chapter 5, note 11 above.

67. Haijo Jan Westra, ed., *The Commentary on Martianus Capella's* De nuptiis Philologiae et Mercurii *attributed to Bernardus Silvestris*, c. 11 (Toronto: Pontifical Institute of Mediaeval Studies, 1986), 246.

68. Frymer-Kensky, *In the Wake of the Goddesses*, 152.

69. What Tertullian actually wrote is "credibile est, quia ineptum est . . . certum est, quia impossibile." *De carne Christi* 5, ed. and trans. Ernest Evans, *Tertullian's Treatise on the Incarnation* (London: SPCK, 1956), 18. For the history of the famous misquotation see Robert Sider, "Credo Quia Absurdum?" *Classical World* 73 (1980): 417–19.

Works Cited

PRIMARY SOURCES

Abelard, Peter, and Heloise. *The Letters of Abelard and Heloise*. Trans. Betty Radice. Harmondsworth: Penguin, 1974.

Adam de la Bassée. *Ludus super Anticlaudianum*, ed. Paul Bayart. Lille: Giard, 1930.

Aelred of Rievaulx. *De speculo caritatis*. In *Opera omnia*, ed. A. Hoste and C. H. Talbot, CCCM 1. Turnhout: Brepols, 1971. Trans. Elizabeth Connor, *The Mirror of Charity*. Kalamazoo, Mich.: Cistercian Publications, 1990.

Alan of Lille. *Anticlaudianus*, ed. Robert Bossuat. Paris: J. Vrin, 1955. Trans. James J. Sheridan, *Anticlaudianus, or The Good and Perfect Man*. Toronto: Pontifical Institute of Mediaeval Studies, 1973.

———. *De fide catholica contra haereticos libri quatuor*. PL 210: 305–430.

———. *Distinctiones dictionum theologicalium*. PL 210: 685–1012.

———. *Liber de planctu Naturae*, ed. Nikolaus Häring. *Studi Medievali*, terza serie, 19.2 (1978): 797–879. Trans. James J. Sheridan, *The Plaint of Nature*. Toronto: Pontifical Institute of Mediaeval Studies, 1980.

———. "Rithmus de Incarnatione Domini," ed. Marie-Thérèse d'Alverny. In *L'Homme devant Dieu: Mélanges offerts au Père Henri de Lubac*. Paris: Aubier, 1964. 2: 126–28.

———. *Summa Quoniam homines*, ed. Palémon Glorieux. *Archives d'histoire doctrinale et littéraire du Moyen Age* 20 (1953): 113–364.

———. *Textes inédits*, ed. Marie-Thérèse d'Alverny. Paris: J. Vrin, 1965.

———. *Theologicae regulae*. PL 210: 617–84.

Albertus Magnus. *Postilla super Isaiam*, ed. Ferdinand Sipemann, in *Opera omnia* 19. Aschendorff: Monasterii Westfalorum, 1952.

Alcuin of York. *Epistolae*, ed. Ernst Dümmler, in *MGH Epistolae* 4. Berlin: Weidmann, 1895.

———. *Grammatica*. PL 101: 849–902. *Liber sacramentorum*. PL 101: 445–66.

———. *Officia per ferias*. PL 101: 509–612.

"'Altercatio Ganimedis et Helene': Kritische Edition mit Kommentar," ed. Rolf Lenzen. *Mittellateinisches Jahrbuch* 7 (1972): 161–86.

Ambrose of Milan. *De virginibus*. PL 16: 187–232.

———. *Seven Exegetical Works*, trans. Michael McHugh. Washington, D.C.: Catholic University of America Press, 1972.

Analecta hymnica Medii Aevi, ed. Clemens Blume et al. 55 vols. Leipzig, 1866–1922; reprint New York: Johnson Reprint Corp., 1961.

Andreas Capellanus. *De amore et amoris remedio*, ed. and trans. P. G. Walsh. London: Duckworth, 1982.

Anselm of Canterbury. *Cur Deus Homo*, ed. René Roques. SC 91. Paris: Éditions du Cerf, 1963.

———. *Monologium*, in *Opera Omnia*, vol. 1, ed. F. S. Schmitt. Edinburgh: Thomas Nelson, 1938.

Aristotle. *On Interpretation*, trans. Harold P. Cooke. Loeb Classical Library 325. Cambridge, Mass.: Harvard University Press, 1983.

Augustine of Hippo. *Confessiones*. CCSL 27. Turnhout: Brepols, 1981.

———. *De civitate Dei*. CCSL 48. Turnhout: Brepols, 1955.

———. *De doctrina christiana*. CCSL 32. Turnhout: Brepols, 1962.

———. *De Trinitate*. Trans. Stephen McKenna, *The Trinity*. Washington: Catholic University of America Press, 1968.

Aurora consurgens, ed. Marie-Louise von Franz, trans. R. F. C. Hull and A. S. B. Glover. New York: Bollingen Foundation, 1966.

Baird, Joseph, and John Kane, ed. and trans. *La Querelle de la Rose: Letters and Documents*. Chapel Hill: University of North Carolina Press, 1978.

Banz, P. Romuald, ed. *Christus und die minnende Seele: Zwei spätmittelhochdeutsche mystische Gedichte*. Breslau: Marcus, 1908.

Bell, David, ed. "The *Vita Antiqua* of William of St Thierry." *Cistercian Studies* 11 (1976): 246–55.

Benedetti, Marina, ed. *Milano 1300: I processi inquisitoriali contro le devote e i devoti di santa Guglielma*. Milan: Scheiwiller, 1999.

Bernard of Clairvaux. *The Letters of St. Bernard of Clairvaux*, rev. ed., trans. Bruno Scott James, foreword by Christopher Holdsworth. Kalamazoo, Mich.: Cistercian Publications, 1998.

———. *Sancti Bernardi Opera*, ed. Jean Leclercq, Henri Rochais, and C. H. Talbot. 5 vols. Rome: Editiones Cistercienses, 1957–77.

Bernard Silvestris. *The Commentary on Martianus Capella's* De nuptiis Philologiae et Mercurii *Attributed to Bernardus Silvestris*, ed. Haijo Jan Westra. Toronto: Pontifical Institute of Mediaeval Studies, 1986.

———. *Cosmographia*, ed. Peter Dronke. Leiden: Brill, 1978. Trans. Winthrop Wetherbee, *The "Cosmographia" of Bernard Silvestris*. New York: Columbia University Press, 1973.

Bernardino of Siena. *Le Prediche volgari inedite*, ed. Dionisio Pacetti. Siena: Cantagalli, 1935.

Birgitta of Sweden. *Life and Selected Revelations*, ed. Marguerite Tjader Harris, trans. Albert Kezel. New York: Paulist, 1990.

———. *Opera minora* II, *Sermo angelicus*, ed. Sten Eklund. Uppsala: Almqvist & Wiksell, 1972. Trans. John Halborg, *The Word of the Angel*. Toronto: Peregrina, 1996.

———. *Revelaciones* VI, ed. Birger Bergh. Stockholm: Almqvist & Wiksell, 1991.

———. *Revelaciones* VII, ed. Birger Bergh. Uppsala: Almqvist & Wiksell, 1967.

Boehme, Jacob. *The Way to Christ*, trans. Peter Erb. New York: Paulist, 1978.

Boethius. *De consolatione Philosophiae*, ed. and trans. S. J. Tester. Loeb Classical Library. Cambridge, Mass.: Harvard University Press, 1973.

Bonaventure. *Bringing Forth Christ: Five Feasts of the Child Jesus*, trans. Eric Doyle. Oxford: SLG Press, 1984.

————. *Opera omnia.* 10 vols. Quaracchi: Collegium S. Bonaventurae, 1882–1901.

Bonus, Petrus. *Margarita pretiosa novella correctissima.* In *Theatrum chemicum.* 6 vols. Strasbourg: Eberhard Zetzner, 1659–61. 4: 507–713.

Buch der heiligen Dreifaltigkeit in seiner zweiten, alchemistischen Fassung (Kadolzburg, 1433). Ed. Uwe Junker. Cologne: F. Hansen, 1986.

Caesarius of Heisterbach. *Dialogus miraculorum,* ed. Joseph Strange. 2 vols. Cologne: J. M. Heberle, 1851. Trans. H. von E. Scott and C. C. Swinton Bland, *The Dialogue on Miracles.* 2 vols. London: Routledge, 1929.

Calcidius. *Commentarius in Timaeum Platonis,* ed. J. H. Waszink. London: Warburg Institute, 1962.

Chartularium Universitatis Parisiensis, ed. Henri Denifle. Vol. 1. Paris: Delalain, 1889.

Chaucer, Geoffrey. *The Riverside Chaucer,* ed. Larry Benson et al. Boston: Houghton Mifflin, 1987.

Chrétien de Troyes. *Erec and Énide,* ed. and trans. Carleton W. Carroll. New York: Garland, 1987.

————. *Lancelot (Le Chevalier de la charrete),* ed. and trans. William Kibler. New York: Garland, 1981.

————. *Yvain, or The Knight with the Lion,* trans. Ruth Harwood Cline. Athens: University of Georgia Press, 1984.

————. *Yvain, ou Le Chevalier au Lion,* ed. Jan Nelson and Carleton W. Carroll. New York: Appleton-Century-Crofts, 1968.

Christ, Karl, ed. "*La Règle des Fins Amans*: Eine Beginenregel aus dem Ende des XIII. Jahrhunderts." In Bernhard Schädel and Werner Mulertt, eds., *Philologische Studien aus dem romanisch-germanischen Kulturkreise: Festschrift Karl Voretzsch.* Halle: Max Niemeyer, 1927. 173–213.

Christine de Pizan. *Lavision-Christine,* ed. Sister Mary Louis Towner. Washington, D.C.: Catholic University of America Press, 1932.

————. *Le Livre de la Cité des Dames,* ed. E. Jeffrey Richards. In *La Città delle Dame.* Milan: Luni Editrice, 1998. Trans. E. Jeffrey Richards, *The Book of the City of Ladies.* New York: Persea Books, 1982.

————. *Le Livre de la mutacion de Fortune,* ed. Suzanne Solente. 4 vols. Paris: Picard, 1959–1966.

————. *Le Livre du chemin de long estude,* ed. Robert Püschel. 2nd ed. Berlin: Hettler, 1887; reprint Geneva: Slatkine, 1974.

————. *The Selected Writings of Christine de Pizan: A Norton Critical Edition,* ed. Renate Blumenfeld-Kosinski, trans. Renate Blumenfeld-Kosinski and Kevin Brownlee. New York: Norton, 1997.

Claudian. *De raptu Proserpinae,* ed. Claire Gruzelier. Oxford: Clarendon Press, 1993.

Clementine Homilies. PG 2: 57–468.

Constitutions apostoliques, ed. Marcel Metzger. SC 320. Paris: Éditions du Cerf, 1985.

Corpus antiphonalium officii, ed. R.-J. Hesbert. 6 vols. Rome: Herder, 1963–1979.

Curti, Carmelo, ed. *Commentarii in parabolas Salomonis et in Ecclesiasten.* Catania: Centro di Studi sull'antico cristianesimo, 1964.

Dante Alighieri. *Commedia,* ed. and trans. John Sinclair. 3 vols. New York: Oxford University Press, 1961.

————. *Vita Nova,* ed. Guglielmo Gorni. Turin: Giulio Einaudi, 1996. Trans. Mark

Musa, *Dante's* Vita Nuova: *A Translation and an Essay*. Bloomington: Indiana University Press, 1973.

De Barbazan, Étienne. *Fabliaux et contes des poètes françois des XI, XII, XIII, XIV, et XVe siècles*. Paris: Crapelet, 1808.

Denzinger, Henricus, ed. *Enchiridion symbolorum, definitionum et declarationum de rebus fidei et morum*. 33rd ed. Barcelona: Herder, 1965.

Didascalia apostolorum, ed. Arthur Vööbus. *Corpus scriptorum christianorum orientalium* 176. Leuven: Peeters, 1979.

Eriugena, John Scotus. *Expositiones super Ierarchiam caelestem S. Dionysii*. PL 122: 125–266.

Flete, William. *Remedies Against Temptations*, ed. Edmund Colledge and Noel Chadwick. *Archivio italiano per la storia della pietà*, vol. 5. Rome: Edizioni di storia e letteratura, 1968. 201–40.

Foxe, John. *Acts and Monuments*. 8 vols. New York: AMS Press, 1965.

Francis of Assisi and Clare of Assisi. *Francis and Clare: The Complete Works*, ed. and trans. Regis Armstrong and Ignatius Brady. New York: Paulist Press, 1982.

Frauenlob (Heinrich von Meissen). *Leichs, Sangsprüche, Lieder*, ed. Karl Stackmann and Karl Bertau. 2 vols. Göttingen: Vandenhoeck and Ruprecht, 1981.

Geoffrey of Monmouth. *Historia regum britanniae*, ed. Jacob Hammer. Cambridge, Mass.: Medieval Academy of America, 1951. Trans. Lewis Thorpe, *The History of the Kings of Britain*. Harmondsworth: Penguin, 1966.

Gérard de Liège. "Les traités de Gérard de Liège sur l'amour illicite et sur l'amour de Dieu," ed. André Wilmart. In *Analecta Reginensia: Extraits des manuscrits latins de la reine Christine conservés au Vatican*, Studi e testi 59. Rome: Vatican, 1933, reprint 1966, 181–247.

Gerson, Jean. *Oeuvres complètes*, ed. Palémon Glorieux. 10 vols. Paris: Desclée, 1961–73.

———. "Le Traité de Gerson contre le *Roman de la Rose*," ed. Ernest Langlois. *Romania* 45 (1919): 23–48.

Gilbert of Hoyland. *Sermones in Canticum Salomonis*. PL 184: 11–252.

Grignion de Montfort, Louis-Marie. *God Alone: The Collected Writings of St. Louis Marie de Montfort*. Bay Shore, N.Y.: Montfort Publications, 1987.

Grosseteste, Robert. *Le Château d'Amour*, ed. J. Murray. Paris: Champion, 1918. Middle English version ed. Carl Horstmann, *The Minor Poems of the Vernon Manuscript*, Part I. EETS o.s. 98, pp. 355–406. London, 1892; reprint Millwood, N.Y.: Kraus, 1987.

Guillaume de Lorris and Jean de Meun. *Le Roman de la Rose*, ed. Daniel Poirion. Paris: Garnier-Flammarion, 1974.

Hadewijch of Brabant. *The Complete Works*, trans. Columba Hart. New York: Paulist Press, 1980.

———. *Lettres spirituelles*, trans. J.-B. Porion. Geneva: Martingay, 1972.

———. *Poetry of Hadewijch*, ed. and trans. Marieke van Baest. Leuven: Peeters, 1998.

Häring, Nikolaus M., ed. *Commentaries on Boethius by Thierry of Chartres and His School*. Toronto: Pontifical Institute of Mediaeval Studies, 1971.

Haimo of Auxerre (misattributed to Haimo of Halberstadt). *Homiliae*. PL 118: 9–816.

Heinrich von Meissen. *See* Frauenlob.

Heldris of Cornwall. See *Silence*.

Henderson, Katherine, and Barbara McManus, eds. *Half Humankind: Contexts and*

Texts of the Controversy About Women in England, 1540–1640. Urbana: University of Illinois Press, 1985.

Herrad of Hohenbourg. *Hortus deliciarum.* Reconstructed by Rosalie Green, Michael Evans, et al. 2 vols. London: Warburg Institute, 1979.

Hicks, Eric, ed. *Le Débat sur le Roman de la Rose.* Paris: Champion, 1977.

Hildegard of Bingen. *Liber divinorum operum,* ed. Albert Derolez and Peter Dronke, CCCM 92. Turnhout: Brepols, 1996.

——. *Scivias,* ed. Adelgundis Führkötter and Angela Carlevaris, CCCM 43–43a. Turnhout: Brepols, 1978. Trans. Columba Hart and Jane Bishop. New York: Paulist, 1990.

Hugh of St.-Victor. *Adnotationes elucidatoriae in quosdam Psalmos David.* PL 177: 589–634.

——. *De laude charitatis.* PL 176: 969–76.

——. *Six opuscules spirituels,* ed. Roger Baron. SC 155. Paris: Éditions du Cerf, 1969.

——. *Soliloquium de arrha animae,* ed. M. K. Müller. Kleine Texte für Vorlesungen und Übungen 123. Bonn: Markus und Weber, 1913. Trans. Kevin Herbert, *Soliloquy on the Earnest Money of the Soul.* Milwaukee: Marquette University Press, 1956.

Irenaeus of Lyon. *Contra haereses libri quinque.* PG 7: 433–1118.

Ives [Yvo]. *Épître à Séverin sur la charité,* ed. Gervais Dumeige. Paris: J. Vrin, 1955.

Jacobus de Voragine. *The Golden Legend: Readings on the Saints,* trans. William Granger Ryan. 2 vols. Princeton, N.J.: Princeton University Press, 1993.

Jean de Meun. *Roman de la Rose. See* Guillaume de Lorris.

Jerome. *Adversus Iovinianum.* Trans. W. H. Fremantle. *The Principal Works of St. Jerome,* Vol. 6. Library of Nicene and Post-Nicene Fathers. New York: Christian Literature Co., 1893.

John of Morigny. Prologue to *Liber Visionum,* ed. and trans. Claire Fanger and Nicholas Watson. *Esoterica* 3 (1999): 108–217; <www.esoteric.msu.edu/VolumeIII/Morigny.html>.

John Paul II. *Mulieris dignitatem (On the Dignity and Vocation of Women).* Washington, D.C.: United States Catholic Conference, 1988.

Julian of Norwich. *A Book of Showings to the Anchoress Julian of Norwich,* ed. Edmund Colledge and James Walsh. 2 vols. Toronto: Pontifical Institute of Mediaeval Studies, 1978. Trans. Edmund Colledge and James Walsh, *Showings.* New York: Paulist Press, 1978.

——. *A Revelation of Love,* ed. Marion Glasscoe. Exeter: University of Exeter Press, 1976.

——. *Shewings,* Long Text, ed. Georgia Ronan Crampton. Kalamazoo, Mich.: Medieval Institute Publications, 1993.

Kantor, Marvin, and Richard White, eds. and trans. *The Vita of Constantine and the Vita of Methodius.* Ann Arbor: Department of Slavic Languages and Literature, University of Michigan.

Kasten, Ingrid, ed. *Deutsche Lyrik des frühen und hohen Mittelalters.* Frankfurt: Deutscher Klassiker Verlag, 1995.

Kempe, Margery. *The Book of Margery Kempe,* ed. Lynn Staley. Kalamazoo, Mich.: Medieval Institute Publications, 1996. Trans. B. A. Windeatt. Harmondsworth: Penguin, 1985.

Lamprecht von Regensburg. *Sanct Francisken Leben und Tochter Syon*, ed. Karl Wein-hold. Paderborn: F. Schöningh, 1880.

Langland, William. *Piers Plowman: An Edition of the C-Text*, ed. Derek Pearsall. Berkeley: University of California Press, 1979.

———. *The Vision of Piers Plowman: A Complete Edition of the B-Text*, ed. A. V. C. Schmidt. London: Dent, 1978. Trans. E. Talbot Donaldson, *Piers Plowman: An Alliterative Verse Translation*. New York: Norton, 1990.

Malory, Sir Thomas. *Le Morte D'Arthur*, ed. Janet Cowen. 2 vols. Harmondsworth: Penguin, 1969.

Martin of Léon. *Sermo IV in Natale Domini*. PL 208: 83–550.

Mechthild of Magdeburg. *Das fliessende Licht der Gottheit*, ed. Hans Neumann. Munich: Artemis, 1990. Trans. Frank Tobin, *The Flowing Light of the Godhead*. New York: Paulist Press, 1998.

Meersseman, G. G. *Der Hymnos Akathistos im Abendland*. 2 vols. Freiburg: Univer-sitätsverlag, 1958, 1960.

Milton, John. *Paradise Lost*, ed. Christopher Ricks. New York: New American Library, 1968.

Ochsenbein, Peter, ed. "Das *Compendium Anticlaudiani*." *Zeitschrift für deutsches Alter-tum und deutsche Literatur* 98 (1969): 80–109.

Odes of Solomon, ed. and trans. J. H. Charlesworth. Missoula, Mont.: Scholars Press, 1977.

Ovid. *Ars amatoria*, ed. Henri Bornecque. Paris: Les belles lettres, 1960.

———. *Metamorphoses*, ed. William Anderson. 7th ed. Stuttgart: Teubner, 1996.

Ovide moralisé: poème du commencement du XIVe siècle, ed. C. de Boer. Verhandelingen der Koninklijke Akademie van Wetenschappen te Amsterdam, Afdeeling Letter-kunde, n.s. 15, 21, 30, 37, 43. Amsterdam: Johannes Müller, 1915–38.

Paschasius Radbertus. *Carmina*. In *MGH Poetae Latini medii aevi* 3. Berlin: Weid-mann, 1896.

Peter of Blois. *De confessione sacramentali*. PL 207: 1077–92.

Porete, Marguerite. *Le Mirouer des simples ames*, ed. Romana Guarnieri, CCCM 69. Turnhout: Brepols, 1986. Trans. Edmund Colledge, J. C. Marler, and Judith Grant, *The Mirror of Simple Souls*. Notre Dame, Ind.: University of Notre Dame Press, 1999.

Prudentius. *Psychomachia*, ed. and trans. H. J. Thomson. Loeb Classical Library. Cambridge, Mass.: Harvard University Press, 1949.

Psaki, Regina, trans. *Le Roman de Silence*. New York: Garland, 1991.

Remigius of Auxerre. *Commentum in Martianum Capellam*, ed. Cora Lutz. 2 vols. Leiden: Brill, 1962.

———. *Homiliae*. PL 131: 865–932.

Renaut de Bâgé. *Le Bel inconnu (Li Biaus descouneüs; The Fair Unknown)*, ed. Karen Fresco, trans. Colleen Donagher. New York: Garland, 1992.

Richard of St.-Victor. *De IV gradibus violentae caritatis*, ed. Gervais Dumeige. In *Ives: Épître à Séverin sur la charité*. Paris: J. Vrin, 1955. Trans. Clare Kirchberger, "Of the Four Degrees of Passionate Charity." In *Richard of Saint-Victor: Selected Writings on Contemplation*. New York: Harper, 1957.

———. *De Trinitate*. Trans. Grover Zinn in *The Twelve Patriarchs*. New York: Paulist Press, 1979.

Ridewall, John. *Fulgentius metaforalis*, ed. Hans Liebeschütz. Leipzig: Teubner, 1926.

Rupert of Deutz. *De operibus Spiritus sancti*, ed. Hraban Haacke. CCCM 24. Turnhout: Brepols, 1972.

———. *In Canticum canticorum*, ed. Hraban Haacke. CCCM 26. Turnhout: Brepols, 1974.

Sacrum commercium. In *Fontes Franciscani*, ed. Enrico Menestò and Stefano Brufani. Assisi: Edizioni Porziuncola, 1995, pp. 1693–1732. Trans. Placid Hermann in Marion Habig, ed., *St. Francis of Assisi: Writings and Early Biographies*. Chicago: Franciscan Herald Press, 1973, pp. 1533–96.

Saïd, Marie-Bernard, and Grace Perigo, trans. *Magnificat: Homilies in Praise of the Blessed Virgin Mary*. Kalamazoo, Mich.: Cistercian Publications, 1979.

Sayce, Olive, ed. *Poets of the Minnesang*. Oxford: Clarendon Press, 1967.

Schaus, E., ed. "Das Kloster der Minne." *Zeitschrift für deutsches Altertum und deutsche Literatur* 38 (1894): 361–68.

Shakespeare, William. *The Winter's Tale*, ed. Stephen Orgel. New York: Oxford University Press, 1996.

Sidney, Sir Philip. *Poems*, ed. Wlliam Ringler, Jr. Oxford: Clarendon Press, 1962.

Silence: A Thirteenth-Century French Romance, ed. and trans. Sarah Roche-Mahdi. East Lansing, Mich.: Colleagues Press, 1992.

Sisam, Celia, and Kenneth Sisam, eds. *The Oxford Book of Medieval English Verse*. Oxford: Clarendon Press, 1970.

Speculum virginum, ed. Jutta Seyfarth. CCCM 5. Turnhout: Brepols, 1990.

Spenser, Edmund. *The Faerie Queene*, ed. Thomas Roche, Jr. New Haven, Conn.: Yale University Press, 1981.

Stehling, Thomas, ed. and trans. *Medieval Latin Poems of Male Love and Friendship*. New York: Garland, 1984.

Suso, Henry. *Deutsche Schriften*, ed. Karl Bihlmeyer. Stuttgart, 1907; reprint Frankfurt: Minerva, 1961. Trans. Frank Tobin, *Henry Suso: The Exemplar*. New York: Paulist Press, 1989.

———. *Horologium Sapientiae*, ed. Pius Künzle. Freiburg: Universitätsverlag, 1977. Trans. Edmund Colledge, *Wisdom's Watch upon the Hours*. Washington, D.C.: Catholic University of America Press, 1994.

Teresa of Avila. *The Collected Works of St. Teresa of Avila*, trans. Kieran Kavanaugh and Otilio Rodriguez. Vol. 1, *The Book of Her Life. Spiritual Testimonies. Soliloquies*. Washington, D.C.: Institute of Carmelite Studies, 1976.

Tertullian. *De carne christi*, ed. and trans. Ernest Evans, *Tertullian's Treatise on the Incarnation*. London: SPCK, 1956.

Theophilus of Antioch. *Ad Autolycum*, ed. and trans. Robert M. Grant. Oxford: Clarendon Press, 1970.

Thierry of Chartres. *Tractatus de sex dierum operibus*. See Häring, Nikolaus M.

Thomas Aquinas. *Summa theologiae*, Latin and English. 61 vols. Cambridge: Blackfriars, 1964–1981.

Thorpe, Lewis, ed. *Le Roman de Silence*. Cambridge: Heffer, 1972.

Ulrich von Liechtenstein. *Frauendienst*, ed. Reinhold Bechstein. 2 vols. Leipzig: Brockhaus, 1888. Trans. J. W. Thomas, *Ulrich von Liechtenstein's Service of Ladies*. Chapel Hill: University of North Carolina Press, 1969.

Van Engen, John, ed. and trans. *Devotio Moderna: Basic Writings*. New York: Paulist Press, 1988.

Van Wijk, Nicolaas, ed. *Het Getijdenboek van Geert Groote*. Leiden: Brill, 1940.

Von der Hagen, Friedrich Heinrich, ed. *Minnesinger: Deutsche Liederdichter des zwölften, dreizehnten und vierzehnten Jahrhunderts*. 5 vols. Leipzig: Teubner, 1838.

Wackernagel, Philipp, ed. *Das deutsche Kirchenlied von der ältesten Zeit bis zu Anfang des XVII. Jahrhunderts*. 5 vols. Leipzig: Teubner, 1864–77.

Waitz, Georg, ed. "Das Liebesconcil." *Zeitschrift für deutsches Alterthum* 7 (1849): 160–67.

Waldkirch, Conrad, ed. *Artis auriferae quam chemiam vocant*. 2 vols. Basel: Waldkirch, 1593.

Warren, F. E., ed. *The Leofric Missal*. Oxford: Clarendon Press, 1883.

Weiler, Anton, ed. *Getijden van de Eeuwige Wijsheid naar de Vertaling van Geert Grote*. Baarn, Netherlands: Ambo, 1984.

Wilkins, David, ed. *Concilia Magnae Britanniae et Hiberniae*. 4 vols. London: R. Gosling, 1737.

William of St.-Thierry. *De natura et dignitate amoris*, ed. M. M.-Davy. In *Deux traités de l'amour de Dieu*. Paris: J. Vrin, 1953.

———. *Epistola ad Fratres de Monte Dei*, ed. Jean Déchanet, *Lettre aux frères du Mont-Dieu*. SC 223. Paris: Cerf, 1975. Trans. Theodore Berkeley, *The Golden Epistle: A Letter to the Brethren at Mont Dieu*. Kalamazoo, Mich.: Cistercian Publications, 1976.

Wilmart, André, ed. "Gérard de Liège: Un traité inédit de l'amour de Dieu." *Revue d'ascétique et de mystique* 12 (1931): 349–430.

Secondary Sources

Addison, Joseph. *Miscellaneous Works*, ed. A. C. Guthkelch. London: Bell, 1914.

Akbari, Suzanne. "Nature's Forge Recast in the *Roman de Silence*." In Donald Maddox and Sara Sturm-Maddox, eds., *Literary Aspects of Courtly Culture*. Cambridge: D.S. Brewer, 1994. 39–46.

Allen, Peter. "The Ambiguity of Silence: Gender, Writing, and *Le Roman de Silence*." In Julian Wasserman and Lois Roney, eds., *Sign, Sentence, Discourse: Language in Medieval Thought and Literature*. Syracuse, N.Y.: Syracuse University Press, 1989. 98–112.

Ancelet-Hustache, Jeanne. "Quelques indications sur les manuscrits de l'*Horloge de Sapience*." In Ephrem Filthaut, ed., *Heinrich Seuse: Studien zum 600. Todestag, 1366–1966*. Cologne: Albertus Magnus Verlag, 1966. 161–70.

Archibald, Elizabeth. *Incest and the Medieval Imagination*. Oxford: Clarendon Press, 2001.

Ashley, Kathleen, and Pamela Sheingorn, eds. *Interpreting Cultural Symbols: Saint Anne in Late Medieval Society*. Athens: University of Georgia Press, 1990.

Aspegren, Kerstin. *The Male Woman: A Feminine Ideal in the Early Church*. Uppsala: Almqvist & Wiksell, 1990.

Astell, Ann. *The Song of Songs in the Middle Ages*. Ithaca, N.Y.: Cornell University Press, 1990.

———. "Telling Tales of Love: Julia Kristeva and Bernard of Clairvaux." *Christianity and Literature* 50 (2000): 125–48.

Atkinson, Clarissa. *Mystic and Pilgrim: The Book and the World of Margery Kempe*. Ithaca, N.Y.: Cornell University Press, 1983.

———. *The Oldest Vocation: Christian Motherhood in the Middle Ages*. Ithaca, N.Y.: Cornell University Press, 1991.

Auerbach, Erich. *Literary Language and Its Public in Late Latin Antiquity and in the Middle Ages*, trans. Ralph Manheim. Princeton, N.J.: Princeton University Press, 1965.

Baker, Denise. *Julian of Norwich's Showings: From Vision to Book*. Princeton, N.J.: Princeton University Press, 1994.

Balas, David. *Metousia Theou: Man's Participation in God's Perfections According to St. Gregory of Nyssa*. Rome: Herder, 1966.

Balchin, John. "Paul, Wisdom and Christ." In Harold Rowdon, ed., *Christ the Lord*. Leicester: Inter-Varsity, 1982. 204–19.

Barfield, Owen. *Saving the Appearances: A Study in Idolatry*. London: Faber and Faber, 1957.

Barker, Margaret. *The Great Angel: A Study of Israel's Second God*. London: SPCK, 1992.

Barker, Paula. "The Motherhood of God in Julian of Norwich's Theology." *Downside Review* 100 (1982): 290–304.

Barney, Stephen. *Allegories of History, Allegories of Love*. Hamden, Conn.: Archon Books, 1979.

Barré, Henri. *Les Homéliaires carolingiens de l'École d'Auxerre: Authenticité, inventaire, tableaux comparatifs, initia*. Vatican City: Bibiblioteca apostolica vaticana, 1962.

Barth, Karl. *The Holy Spirit and the Christian Life*, trans. R. Birch Hoyle. Louisville, Ky.: Westminster/John Knox, 1993.

Baumer, Christoph. "Die Schreinmadonna." *Marian Library Studies* 9 (1977): 239–72.

Beauchamp, Paul. "Épouser la Sagesse—ou n'épouser qu'elle? Une énigme du Livre de la Sagesse." In Gilbert, ed., *La Sagesse de l'Ancien Testament*, 347–69.

Belting, Hans. *The Image and Its Public in the Middle Ages: Form and Function of Early Paintings of the Passion*, trans. Mark Bartusis and Raymond Meyer. New Rochelle, N.Y.: Caratzas, 1990.

Benedetti, Marina. *Io non sono Dio: Guglielma di Milano e i Figli dello Spirito santo*. Milan: Edizioni Biblioteca Francescana, 1998.

Bennett, J. A. W. *The Parlement of Fowles: An Interpretation*. Oxford: Clarendon Press, 1957.

Benson, Larry. "The Occasion of the *Parliament of Fowls*." In Larry Benson and Siegfried Wenzel, eds., *The Wisdom of Poetry: Essays in Early English Literature in Honor of Morton W. Bloomfield*. Kalamazoo, Mich.: Medieval Institute, 1982. 123–44.

Benz, Ernst. *Die Vision: Erfahrungsformen und Bilderwelt*. Stuttgart: Klett, 1969.

Berry, Craig. "Heldris's Material Girl: The Romance of Property Rights in the *Roman de Silence*." Paper delivered at American Comparative Literature Association, Montreal, April 1999.

Bizet, J.-A. *Suso et le Minnesang, ou la morale de l'amour courtois.* Paris: Aubier, 1947.

Black, Diana. "The Sin of Incest: *The Book of Margery Kempe* as Healing the Wound." Unpublished paper, Northwestern University, 1992.

Blamires, Alcuin. *The Case for Women in Medieval Culture.* Oxford: Clarendon Press, 1997.

Blamires, Alcuin, Karen Pratt, and C. William Marx, eds. *Woman Defamed and Woman Defended: An Anthology of Medieval Texts.* Oxford: Clarendon Press, 1992.

Bloch, R. Howard. "Silence and Holes: The *Roman de Silence* and the Art of the Trouvère." *Yale French Studies* 70 (1986): 81–99.

Bloomfield, Morton. "A Grammatical Approach to Personification Allegory." *Modern Philology* 60 (1963): 161–71.

———, ed. *Allegory, Myth, and Symbol.* Cambridge, Mass.: Harvard University Press, 1981.

Blumenfeld-Kosinski, Renate. "Saintly Scenarios in Christine de Pizan's *Livre des Trois Vertus.*" *Mediaeval Studies* 62 (2000): 255–92.

———. "Satirical Views of the Beguines in Northern French Literature." In Juliette Dor, Lesley Johnson, and Jocelyn Wogan-Browne, eds., *New Trends in Feminine Spirituality: The Holy Women of Liège and Their Impact.* Turnhout: Brepols, 1999. 237–49.

Blumreich, Kathleen. "Lesbian Desire in the Old French *Roman de Silence.*" *Arthuriana* 7 (1997): 47–62.

Boespflug, François. "La Compassion de Dieu le Père dans l'art occidental (XIIIe–XVIIe siècles)." *Supplément* 172 (March 1990): 123–59.

———. *Dieu dans l'art:* Sollicitudini Nostrae *de Benoît XIV (1745) et l'affaire Crescence de Kaufbeuren.* Paris: Éditions du Cerf, 1984.

———. "Dieu en pape: Une singularité de l'art religieux de la fin du moyen âge." *Revue Mabillon* n.s. 2 (1991): 167–205.

Bolen, Jean Shinoda. *Goddesses in Everywoman: A New Psychology of Women.* San Francisco: Harper and Row, 1984.

Bond, Gerald. *The Loving Subject: Desire, Eloquence, and Power in Romanesque France.* Philadelphia: University of Pennsylvania Press, 1995.

Børresen, Kari. "Christ notre mère, la théologie de Julienne de Norwich." *Mitteilungen und Forschungsbeiträge der Cusanus-Gesellschaft* 13 (1978): 320–29.

Bossy, John. *Christianity in the West, 1400–1700.* Oxford: Oxford University Press, 1985.

Boswell, John. *Christianity, Social Tolerance, and Homosexuality: Gay People in Western Europe from the Beginning of the Christian Era to the Fourteenth Century.* Chicago: University of Chicago Press, 1980.

Bouyer, Louis. *Figures mystiques féminines.* Paris: Éditions du Cerf, 1989.

Bowers, John. *The Crisis of Will in Piers Plowman.* Washington, D.C.: Catholic University of America Press, 1986.

Bradley, Ritamary. "Mysticism in the Motherhood Similitude of Julian of Norwich." *Studia mystica* 8, 2 (1985): 4–14.

———. "Patristic Background of the Motherhood Similitude in Julian of Norwich." *Christian Scholar's Review* 8 (1978): 101–13.

Brahney, Kathleen. "When *Silence* Was Golden: Female Personae in the *Roman de Silence.*" In Glyn Burgess and Robert Taylor, eds., *The Spirit of the Court.* Cambridge: D.S. Brewer, 1985. 52–61.

Breeze, Andrew. "The Virgin Mary, Daughter of Her Son." *Études celtiques* 27 (1990): 267–83.

Breton, Stanislas. *Unicité et monothéisme*. Paris: Éditions du Cerf, 1981.

Breuer, Wilhelm. "Philologische Zugänge zur Mystik Hadewijchs: Zu Form und Funktion religiöser Sprache bei Hadewijch." In Margot Schmidt and Dieter Bauer, eds., *Grundfragen christlicher Mystik*. Stuttgart: Frommann-Holzboog, 1987. 103–21.

Brewer, Derek S. *Chaucer: The Poet as Storyteller*. London: Macmillan, 1984.

Brooke, Christopher. *The Medieval Idea of Marriage*. Oxford: Oxford University Press, 1991.

Brown, D. Catherine. *Pastor and Laity in the Theology of Jean Gerson*. Cambridge: Cambridge University Press, 1987.

Brownlee, Kevin. "Discourses of the Self: Christine de Pizan and the *Romance of the Rose*." In Kevin Brownlee and Sylvia Huot, eds., *Rethinking the* Romance of the Rose*: Text, Image, Reception*. Philadelphia: University of Pennsylvania Press, 1992. 234–61.

Bruner, Frederick Dale, and William Hordern. *The Holy Spirit—Shy Member of the Trinity*. Minneapolis: Augsburg, 1984.

Buntz, Herwig. "Das *Buch der heiligen Dreifaltigkeit*, sein Autor und seine Überlieferung." *Zeitschrift für deutsches Altertum* 101 (1972): 150–60.

Burns, E. Jane. *Bodytalk: When Women Speak in Old French Literature*. Philadelphia: University of Pennsylvania Press, 1993.

Büttner, F. O. *Imitatio pietatis: Motive der christlichen Ikonographie als Modelle zur Verähnlichung*. Berlin: Mann, 1983.

Bynum, Caroline Walker. *Fragmentation and Redemption: Essays on Gender and the Human Body in Medieval Religion*. New York: Zone, 1991.

——. *Holy Feast and Holy Fast: The Religious Significance of Food to Medieval Women*. Berkeley: University of California Press, 1987.

——. *Jesus as Mother: Studies in the Spirituality of the High Middle Ages*. Berkeley: University of California Press, 1982.

——. *The Resurrection of the Body in Western Christianity, 200–1336*. New York: Columbia University Press, 1995.

Caciola, Nancy. "Discerning Spirits: Sanctity and Possession in the Later Middle Ages." Dissertation, University of Michigan, 1994.

Callan, Maeve. "'Hail, Celestial Empress': The Virgin Mary in the Mystical Theology of Mechthild of Magdeburg." Unpublished paper, Northwestern University, 1998.

Camp, Claudia. *Wisdom and the Feminine in the Book of Proverbs*. Decatur, Ga.: Almond Press, 1985.

Capelle, Bernard. "La liturgie mariale en occident." In du Manoir, ed., *Maria*, 1: 215–45.

Carroll, Michael P. *The Cult of the Virgin Mary: Psychological Origins*. Princeton, N.J.: Princeton University Press, 1986.

Catta, Étienne. "*Sedes Sapientiae*." In du Manoir, ed., *Maria*, 6: 689–866.

Chenu, M.-D. *Nature, Man, and Society in the Twelfth Century*, ed. and trans. Jerome Taylor and Lester K. Little. Chicago: University of Chicago Press, 1968.

Chew, Samuel. *The Virtues Reconciled: An Iconographic Study*. Toronto: University of Toronto Press, 1947.

Chorpenning, Joseph, ed. *The Holy Family in Art and Devotion*. Philadelphia: St. Joseph's University Press, 1996.

Christ, Carol. *Laughter of Aphrodite: Reflections on a Journey to the Goddess*. San Francisco: Harper and Row, 1987.

Christ, Felix. *Jesus Sophia: Die Sophia-Christologie bei den Synoptikern*. Zurich: Zwingli Verlag, 1970.

Cleveland Museum of Art. *European Paintings Before 1500*. Cleveland: Cleveland Museum of Art, 1974.

Clopper, Lawrence. *"Songes of Rechelesnesse": Langland and the Franciscans*. Ann Arbor, Mich.: University of Michigan Press, 1997.

Coakley, John. "Gender and the Authority of Friars: The Significance of Holy Women for Thirteenth-Century Franciscans and Dominicans." *Church History* 60 (1991): 445–60.

——. "A Marriage and Its Observer: Christine of Stommeln, the Heavenly Bridegroom, and Friar Peter of Dacia." In Mooney, ed., *Gendered Voices*, 99–117.

Colledge, Edmund, and J. C. Marler. "'Poverty of the Will': Ruusbroec, Eckhart and *The Mirror of Simple Souls*." In Paul Mommaers and Norbert de Paepe, eds., *Jan van Ruusbroec: The Sources, Content, and Sequels of His Mysticism*. Leuven: Leuven University Press, 1984. 14–47.

Collingwood, R. G. *The Idea of Nature*. Oxford: Clarendon Press, 1945.

Congar, Yves. *The Word and the Spirit*, trans. David Smith. San Francisco: Harper and Row, 1986.

Conzelmann, Hans. "The Mother of Wisdom." In James Robinson, ed., *The Future of Our Religious Past*, trans. Charles Carlston and Robert Scharlemann. New York: Harper and Row, 1971. 230–43.

Cooper, Kate Mason. "Elle and L: Sexualized Textuality in *Le Romance de Silence*." *Romance Notes* 25 (1985): 341–60.

Copeland, Rita. "The Pardoner's Body and the Disciplining of Rhetoric." In Sarah Kay and Miri Rubin, eds., *Framing Medieval Bodies*. Manchester: Manchester University Press, 1994, 138–59.

Cornell, Henrik. "The Iconography of the Nativity of Christ." *Uppsala Universitets Årsskrift* 1 (1924): 1–101.

Courcelle, Pierre. "Étude critique sur les commentaires de la *Consolation* de Boèce (IXe–XVe siècles)." *Archives d'histoire doctrinale et littéraire du Moyen Age* 12 (1939): 5–140.

Crenshaw, James, ed. *Studies in Ancient Israelite Wisdom*. New York: Ktav, 1976.

Cunneen, Sally. *In Search of Mary: The Woman and the Symbol*. New York: Ballantine, 1996.

Curtius, Ernst R. *European Literature and the Latin Middle Ages*, trans. Willard Trask. Princeton, N.J.: Princeton University Press, 1973.

d'Alverny, Marie-Thérèse. *Études sur le symbolisme de la Sagesse et sur l'iconographie*, ed. Charles Burnett. Aldershot, Hampshire: Ashgate Variorum, 1993.

D'Ooge, Martin Luther. *The Acropolis of Athens*. New York: Macmillan, 1908.

Daly, Mary. *Beyond God the Father: Toward a Philosophy of Women's Liberation*. Boston: Beacon Press, 1973.

De Gandillac, Maurice. "La Nature chez Alain de Lille." In Roussel and Suard, eds., *Alain de Lille*, 61–75.

De Lubac, Henri. *Le Surnaturel: Études historiques*. Paris: Aubier, 1946.

De Rougemont, Denis. *Love in the Western World*, trans. Montgomery Belgion. Rev. ed. New York: Pantheon, 1956.

Desmond, Marilynn, ed. *Christine de Pizan and the Categories of Difference*. Minneapolis: University of Minnesota Press, 1998.

Despres, Denise. *Ghostly Sights: Visual Meditation in Late-Medieval Literature*. Norman, Okla.: Pilgrim Press, 1989.

Deutsche Literatur des Mittelalters: Verfasserlexikon. 2nd ed., 11 vols. Berlin: de Gruyter, 1978–.

Dickman, Susan. "Margery Kempe and the Continental Tradition of the Pious Woman." In Glasscoe, ed., *Medieval Mystical Tradition in England*, 150–68.

Dillon, Janette. "Holy Women and Their Confessors or Confessors and Their Holy Women? Margery Kempe and Continental Tradition." In Rosalynn Voaden, ed., *Prophets Abroad: The Reception of Continental Holy Women in Late-Medieval England*. Cambridge: D.S. Brewer, 1996. 115–40.

Dinshaw, Carolyn. *Chaucer's Sexual Poetics*. Madison: University of Wisconsin Press, 1989.

Dinzelbacher, Peter. *Heilige oder Hexen? Schicksale auffälliger Frauen in Mittelalter und Frühneuzeit*. Zurich: Artemis & Winkler, 1995.

———. *Vision und Visionsliteratur im Mittelalter*. Stuttgart: Hiersemann, 1981.

———. "Zur Interpretation erlebnismystischer Texte des Mittelalters." *Zeitschrift für deutsches Altertum und deutsche Literatur* 117 (1988): 1–23.

Dinzelbacher, Peter, and Dieter Bauer, eds. *Frauenmystik im Mittelalter*. Ostfildern: Schwabenverlag, 1985.

Dodd, C. H. *The Interpretation of the Fourth Gospel*. Cambridge: Cambridge University Press, 1953.

Dresel, Ines, Dietmar Lüdke, and Horst Vey. *Christus und Maria: Auslegungen christlicher Gemälde der Spätgotik und Frührenaissance aus der Karlsruher Kunsthalle*. Karlsruhe: Staatliche Kunsthalle, 1992.

Dronke, Peter. *Fabula: Explorations into the Uses of Myth in Medieval Platonism*. Leiden: Brill, 1974.

———, ed. *A History of Twelfth-Century Western Philosophy*. Cambridge: Cambridge University Press, 1988.

———. *Intellectuals and Poets in Medieval Europe*. Rome: Edizioni di storia e letteratura, 1992.

———. *Medieval Latin and the Rise of European Love-Lyric*. 2 vols. Oxford: Clarendon Press, 1966.

———. *The Medieval Poet and His World*. Rome: Edizioni di storia e letteratura, 1984.

Du Manoir, Hubert, ed. *Maria: Études sur la sainte Vierge*. 8 vols. Paris: Beauchesne, 1949–71.

Dumeige, Gervais. *Richard de Saint-Victor et l'idée chrétienne de l'amour*. Paris: Presses universitaires de France, 1952.

Dunn, James. *Christology in the Making*. Philadelphia: Westminster, 1980.

Dutton, Marsha. "The Conversion and Vocation of Aelred of Rievaulx: A Historical Hypothesis." In Daniel Williams, ed., *England in the Twelfth Century*. Woodbridge: Boydell, 1990. 31–49.

Economou, George. *The Goddess Natura in Medieval Literature*. Cambridge, Mass.: Harvard University Press, 1972.

Edelstein, Wolfgang. *Eruditio und sapientia, Weltbild und Erziehung in der Karolingerzeit: Untersuchungen zu Alcuins Briefen*. Freiburg im Breisgau: Rombach, 1965.

Eilberg-Schwartz, Howard. *God's Phallus and Other Problems for Men and Monotheism*. Boston: Beacon Press, 1994.

Ellard, Gerald. "Alcuin and Some Favored Votive Masses." *Theological Studies* 1 (1940): 37–61.

Eller, Cynthia. *Living in the Lap of the Goddess: The Feminist Spirituality Movement in America*. Boston: Beacon Press, 1993.

Elliott, Dyan. *Fallen Bodies: Pollution, Sexuality, and Demonology in the Middle Ages*. Philadelphia: University of Pennsylvania Press, 1999.

——. *Spiritual Marriage: Sexual Abstinence in Medieval Wedlock*. Princeton, N.J.: Princeton University Press, 1993.

——. "Women and Confession: From Empowerment to Pathology." In Mary Erler and Maryanne Kowaleski, eds., *Gendering the Master Narrative: Medieval Women and Power*. Ithaca, N.Y.: Cornell University Press, 2003.

Engelsman, Joan Chamberlain. *The Feminine Dimension of the Divine: A Study of Sophia and Feminine Images in Religion*. Philadelphia: Westminster, 1979.

Erb, Peter. *Pietists, Protestants, and Mysticism: The Use of Late Medieval Spiritual Texts in the Work of Gottfried Arnold (1666–1714)*. Metuchen, N.J.: Scarecrow, 1989.

Evans, Gillian R. *Alan of Lille: The Frontiers of Theology in the Later Twelfth Century*. Cambridge: Cambridge University Press, 1983.

Faivre, Antoine. *Theosophy, Imagination, Tradition: Studies in Western Esotericism*, trans. Christine Rhone. Albany, N.Y.: SUNY Press, 2000.

Fanger, Claire, ed. *Conjuring Spirits: Texts and Traditions of Medieval Ritual Magic*. University Park: Pennsylvania State University Press, 1998.

——. "The Formative Feminine and the Immobility of God: Gender and Cosmogony in Bernard Silvestris's *Cosmographia*." In David Townsend and Andrew Taylor, eds., *The Tongue of the Fathers: Gender and Ideology in Twelfth-Century Latin*. Philadelphia: University of Pennsylvania Press, 1998. 80–101.

Ferrante, Joan. *Dante's Beatrice: Priest of an Androgynous God*. Occasional Papers 2, Center for Medieval and Early Renaissance Studies. Binghamton, N.Y.: Medieval and Renaissance Texts and Studies, 1992.

——. *Woman as Image in Medieval Literature from the Twelfth Century to Dante*. New York: Columbia University Press, 1975.

Fiene, Donald. "What Is the Appearance of Divine Sophia?" *Slavic Review* 48 (1989): 449–76.

Filas, F. L. "Joseph, St., Devotion to." *New Catholic Encyclopedia*. Washington, D.C.: Catholic University of America Press, 1967. 7: 1108–13.

Fleming, John. *Reason and the Lover*. Princeton, N.J.: Princeton University Press, 1984.

——. *The Roman de la Rose: A Study in Allegory and Iconography*. Princeton, N.J.: Princeton University Press, 1969.

Florovsky, Georges. *Aspects of Church History*. Belmont, Mass.: Norland, 1975.

Frangello, Gina. "Influential Characters." *Chicago Tribune*, Sunday, June 25, 2000, sec. 14, p. 3.

Freedberg, David. *The Power of Images: Studies in the History and Theory of Response*. Chicago: University of Chicago Press, 1989.

Frénaud, Georges. "Le Culte de Notre Dame dans l'ancienne liturgie latine." In du Manoir, ed., *Maria*, 6: 157–211.

Freud, Sigmund. *Civilization and Its Discontents*. In *The Freud Reader*, ed. Gay. 722–72.

——. *The Freud Reader*, ed. Peter Gay. New York: Norton, 1989.

Frevel, Christian. *Aschera und der Ausschliesslichkeitsanspruch YHWHs*. Weinheim: Beltz Athenäum, 1995.

Freyhan, R. "The Evolution of the Caritas Figure in the Thirteenth and Fourteenth Centuries." *Journal of the Warburg and Courtauld Institutes* 11 (1948): 68–86.

Frymer-Kensky, Tikva. *In the Wake of the Goddesses: Women, Culture, and the Biblical Transformation of Pagan Myth*. New York: Free Press/Macmillan, 1992.

Fulton, Rachel. *From Judgment to Passion: Devotion to Christ and the Virgin Mary, 800–1200*. New York: Columbia University Press, 2002.

——. "Mimetic Devotion, Marian Exegesis, and the Historical Sense of the Song of Songs." *Viator* 27 (1996): 85–116.

——. "'Quae est ista quae ascendit sicut aurora consurgens?' The Song of Songs as the *Historia* for the Office of the Assumption." *Mediaeval Studies* 60 (1998): 55–122.

Gadon, Elinor. *The Once and Future Goddess: A Symbol for Our Time*. San Francisco: Harper and Row, 1989.

Gaunt, Simon. "The Significance of Silence." *Paragraph* 13 (1990): 202–16.

Gawain, Shakti. *Creative Visualization: Use the Power of Your Imagination to Create What You Want in Your Life*. Novato, Calif.: New World Library, 1983.

Gelpi, Donald. *The Divine Mother: A Trinitarian Theology of the Holy Spirit*. Lanham, Md.: University Press of America, 1984.

Gibson, Joan. "Could Christ Have Been Born a Woman? A Medieval Debate." *Journal of Feminist Studies in Religion* 8, 1 (Spring 1992): 65–82.

Gilbert, Maurice, ed. *La Sagesse de l'Ancien Testament*. 2nd ed. Leuven: Leuven University Press, 1990.

Gilson, Étienne. "La cosmogonie de Bernardus Silvestris." *Archives d'histoire doctrinale et littéraire du Moyen Age* 3 (1928): 5–24.

Gimbutas, Marija. *The Language of the Goddess*. San Francisco: Harper, 1989.

Glasscoe, Marion, ed. *The Medieval Mystical Tradition in England: Papers Read at Dartington Hall, July 1984*. Cambridge: D.S. Brewer, 1984.

Glier, Ingeborg. "Kloster der Minne." *Die deutsche Literatur des Mittelalters: Verfasserlexikon*, 4: 1235–38.

Glorieux, Palémon. "Saint Joseph dans l'oeuvre de Gerson." *Cahiers de Josephologie* 19 (1971): 414–28.

Goldenberg, Naomi. *Changing of the Gods: Feminism and the End of Traditional Religions*. Boston: Beacon Press, 1979.

Goodman, Anthony. "The Piety of John Brunham's Daughter, of Lynn." In Derek Baker, ed., *Medieval Women*. Oxford: Blackwell, 1978. 347–58.

Goodman, Lenn Evan. *Monotheism: A Philosophic Inquiry into the Foundations of Theology and Ethics*. Totowa, N.J.: Allanheld, Osmun, 1981.

Graef, Hilda. *Mary: A History of Doctrine and Devotion.* 2 vols. New York: Sheed & Ward, 1963–65.

Gravdal, Kathryn. *Ravishing Maidens: Writing Rape in Medieval French Literature and Law.* Philadelphia: University of Pennsylvania Press, 1991.

Gray, William. "Wisdom Christology in the New Testament: Its Scope and Relevance." *Theology* 89 (1986): 448–59.

Green, Monica. "The *De genecia* Attributed to Constantine the African." *Speculum* 62 (1987): 299–323.

Griffin, Susan. *Woman and Nature: The Roaring Inside Her.* New York: Harper and Row, 1978.

Guest, Tanis. *Some Aspects of Hadewijch's Poetic Form in the "Strofische Gedichten."* The Hague: Martinus Nijhoff, 1975.

Gunn, Alan. *The Mirror of Love: A Reinterpretation of* The Romance of the Rose. Lubbock: Texas Tech Press, 1952.

Hackel, Alfred. *Die Trinität in der Kunst: Eine ikonographische Untersuchung.* Berlin: Reuther und Reichard, 1931.

Hackett, Helen. *Virgin Mother, Maiden Queen: Elizabeth I and the Cult of the Virgin Mary.* New York: St. Martin's Press, 1995.

Hahn, Cynthia. "'Joseph will perfect, Mary enlighten and Jesus save thee': The Holy Family as Marriage in the Merode Triptych." *Art Bulletin* 68 (1986): 54–66.

Hale, Rosemary Drage. "*Imitatio Mariae*: Motherhood Motifs in Late Medieval German Spirituality." PhD dissertation, Harvard University, 1992.

——. "Joseph as Mother: Adaptation and Appropriation in the Construction of Male Virtue." In Parsons and Wheeler, eds., *Medieval Mothering*, 101–16.

Halpern, Baruch. "'Brisker Pipes Than Poetry': The Development of Israelite Monotheism." In Jacob Neusner, Baruch A. Levine, Ernest S. Frerichs, and Caroline McCracken-Flesher, eds., *Judaic Perspectives on Ancient Israel*. Philadelphia: Fortress Press, 1987. 77–115.

Hamburger, Jeffrey. *Nuns as Artists: The Visual Culture of a Medieval Convent.* Berkeley: University of California Press, 1997.

——. *The Rothschild Canticles: Art and Mysticism in Flanders and the Rhineland circa 1300.* New Haven, Conn.: Yale University Press, 1990.

——. *The Visual and the Visionary: Art and Female Spirituality in Late Medieval Germany.* New York: Zone, 1998.

Hamerton-Kelly, R. G. *Pre-Existence, Wisdom and the Son of Man.* Cambridge: Cambridge University Press, 1973.

Hansen, Elaine Tuttle. *Chaucer and the Fictions of Gender.* Berkeley: University of California Press, 1992.

Harnack, Adolf. *Outlines of the History of Dogma*, trans. E. K. Mitchell. London: Hodder and Stoughton, 1893.

Harrison, Robert. *The Body of Beatrice.* Baltimore: Johns Hopkins University Press, 1988.

Harvey, Andrew, and Anne Baring. *The Divine Feminine: Exploring the Feminine Face of God around the World.* Berkeley, Calif.: Conari Press, 1996.

Herlihy, David. "The Making of the Medieval Family: Symmetry, Structure, Sentiment." *Journal of Family History* 8 (1983): 116–30.

———. *Medieval Households*. Cambridge, Mass.: Harvard University Press, 1985.

———.*Women, Family, and Society in Medieval Europe: Historical Essays, 1978–1991*, ed. Anthony Molho. Providence, R.I.: Berghahn, 1995.

Hillman, James, ed. *Facing the Gods*. Irving, Tex.: Spring, 1980.

Holloway, Julia Bolton. "Bride, Margery, Julian, and Alice: Bridget of Sweden's Textual Community in Medieval England." In Sandra McEntire, ed., *Margery Kempe: A Book of Essays*. New York: Garland, 1992. 203–21.

Hollywood, Amy. *The Soul as Virgin Wife: Mechthild of Magdeburg, Marguerite Porete, and Meister Eckhart*. Notre Dame, Ind.: University of Notre Dame Press, 1995.

Horsley, Richard. "Spiritual Marriage with Sophia." *Vigiliae Christianae* 33 (1979): 30–54.

Hotchkiss, Valerie. *Clothes Make the Man: Female Cross Dressing in Medieval Europe*. New York: Garland, 1996.

Huber, Christoph. *Aufnahme und Verarbeitung des Alanus ab Insulis in mittelhochdeutschen Dichtungen*. Munich: Artemis, 1988.

Huizinga, Johan. *The Waning of the Middle Ages: A Study of the Forms of Life, Thought and Art in France and the Netherlands in the Dawn of the Renaissance*, trans. Frederick Hopman. New York: Doubleday Anchor, 1954.

Huot, Sylvia. *From Song to Book: The Poetics of Writing in Old French Lyric and Lyrical Narrative Poetry*. Ithaca, N.Y.: Cornell University Press, 1987.

———. "Seduction and Sublimation: Christine de Pizan, Jean de Meun, and Dante." *Romance Notes* 25 (1985): 361–73.

Hyde, Thomas. *The Poetic Theology of Love: Cupid in Renaissance Literature*. London: Associated University Presses, 1986.

Idel, Moshe. *Kabbalah: New Perspectives*. New Haven, Conn.: Yale University Press, 1988.

Irigaray Luce, ed. *Le Souffle des femmes*. Paris: ACGF, 1996.

———. *Speculum de l'autre femme*. Paris: Minuit, 1974.

Jacoff, Rachel. "God as Mother: Julian of Norwich's Theology of Love." *Denver Quarterly* 18 (1984): 134–39.

Jaeger, C. Stephen. *Ennobling Love: In Search of a Lost Sensibility*. Philadelphia: University of Pennsylvania Press, 1999.

———. *The Envy of Angels: Cathedral Schools and Social Ideals in Medieval Europe, 950–1200*. Philadelphia: University of Pennsylvania Press, 1994.

———. *The Origins of Courtliness: Civilizing Trends and the Formation of Courtly Ideals, 939–1210*. Philadelphia: University of Pennsylvania Press, 1985.

Janowski, Hans, ed. *Geert Groote, Thomas von Kempen und die Devotio Moderna*. Olten, Switzerland: Walter, 1978.

Jensen, Jane Richardson. "Father, Son, and Holy Spirit as Mothers in Early Syrian Literature." *Continuum* 2 (1993): 27–49.

Johnson, Elizabeth. *Women, Earth, and Creator Spirit*. New York: Paulist Press, 1993.

Jolivet, Jean. "Les Principes féminins dans la *Cosmographia* de Bernard Silvestre." In Christian Wenin, ed., *L'homme et son univers au moyen âge*. Leuven: Éditions de l'Institut Supérieur de Philosophie, 1986. 296–305.

Jordan, Mark. *The Invention of Sodomy in Christian Theology*. Chicago: University of Chicago Press, 1997.

Jung, Carl Gustav. *Mysterium Coniunctionis*, trans. R. F. C. Hull. *Collected Works*, vol. 14. New York: Bollingen Foundation, 1963.

——. *Psychology and Religion: West and East*, trans. R. F. C. Hull. *Collected Works*, vol. 11. Princeton, N.J.: Princeton University Press, 1969.

Justice, Steven. *Writing and Rebellion: England in 1381*. Berkeley: University of California Press, 1994.

Justice, Steven, and Kathryn Kerby-Fulton, eds. *Written Work: Langland, Labor, and Authorship*. Philadelphia: University of Pennsylvania Press, 1997.

Keller, Hildegard E. *My Secret Is Mine: Studies on Religion and Eros in the German Middle Ages*. Leuven: Peeters, 2000.

Kelly, Henry Ansgar. *Chaucer and the Cult of Saint Valentine*. Leiden: Brill, 1986.

Kenney, John. *Mystical Monotheism: A Study in Ancient Platonic Theology*. Hanover, N.H.: University Press of New England, 1991.

Kerby-Fulton, Kathryn. *Reformist Apocalypticism and Piers Plowman*. Cambridge: Cambridge University Press, 1990.

Kern, Peter. *Trinität, Maria, Inkarnation: Studien zur Thematik der deutschen Dichtung des späteren Mittelalters*. Berlin: Erich Schmidt Verlag, 1971.

Kieckhefer, Richard. *Magic in the Middle Ages*. Cambridge: Cambridge University Press, 1990.

——. "Major Currents in Late Medieval Devotion." In Jill Raitt, ed., *Christian Spirituality: High Middle Ages and Reformation*. New York: Crossroad, 1987. 75–108.

——. *Unquiet Souls: Fourteenth-Century Saints and Their Religious Milieu*. Chicago: University of Chicago Press, 1984.

Kinoshita, Sharon. "Heldris de Cornuälle's *Roman de Silence* and the Feudal Politics of Lineage." *PMLA* 110 (1995): 397–409.

Kinsley, David. *The Goddesses' Mirror: Visions of the Divine from East and West*. Albany, N.Y.: SUNY Press, 1989.

Klapisch-Zuber, Christiane. *Women, Family, and Ritual in Renaissance Italy*, trans. Lydia Cochrane. Chicago: University of Chicago Press, 1985.

Klecker, Annemarie. "Das Büchlein von der geistleichen Gemahelschaft in Cod. 295 des Wiener Schottenstiftes." In *Festschrift für Dietrich Kralik*. Horn, Austria: Ferdinand Berger, 1954. 193–203.

Kolve, V. A. "The Annunciation to Christine: Authorial Empowerment in *The Book of the City of Ladies*." In Brendan Cassidy, ed., *Iconography at the Crossroads: Papers from the Colloquium Sponsored by the Index of Christian Art, Princeton University, 23–24 March 1990*. Princeton, N.J.: Index of Christian Art, 1993. 171–96.

Kraft, Heike. *Die Bildallegorie der Kreuzigung Christi durch die Tugenden*. Dissertation, Freie Universität Berlin; Frankfurt, 1976.

Kristeva, Julia. "Stabat Mater." In *Tales of Love*, trans. Leon Roudiez. New York: Columbia University Press, 1987. 234–63.

Krueger, Roberta. *Women Readers and the Ideology of Gender in Old French Verse Romance*. Cambridge: Cambridge University Press, 1993.

Labbie, Erin. "The Specular Image of the Gender-Neutral Name: Naming Silence in *Le Roman de Silence*." *Arthuriana* 7 (1997): 63–77.

Lagorio, Valerie. "Variations on the Theme of God's Motherhood in Medieval English Mystical and Devotional Writings." *Studia mystica* 8, 2 (1985): 15–37.

Lambert, Malcolm. *Medieval Heresy: Popular Movements from the Gregorian Reform to the Reformation*. 2nd ed. Oxford: Blackwell, 1992.

Lang, Bernhard. *Frau Weisheit: Deutung einer biblischen Gestalt*. Düsseldorf: Patmos, 1975.

Lanham, Richard. *Motives of Eloquence*. New Haven, Conn.: Yale University Press, 1976.

Le Roux de Lincy, M. *Le Livre des Proverbes Français*. 2nd ed. Paris: Delahays, 1859.

Lea, H. C. *A History of the Inquisition of the Middle Ages*. 3 vols. New York: Harper, 1888.

Leclercq, Jean. *The Love of Learning and the Desire for God: A Study of Monastic Culture*, trans. Catharine Misrahi. New York: Fordham University Press, 1961.

——. "Maria Christianorum philosophia." *Mélanges de sciences religieuses* 13 (1956): 103–6.

——. *Monks and Love in Twelfth-Century France*. Oxford: Clarendon Press, 1979.

——. "Riccardo di San Vittore." In *Enciclopedia Dantesca* (Rome: Istituto della Enciclopedia Italiana, 1973): 4, 904–5.

Lerner, Robert. *The Feast of Saint Abraham: Medieval Millenarians and the Jews*. Philadelphia: University of Pennsylvania Press, 2001.

——. *The Heresy of the Free Spirit in the Later Middle Ages*. Berkeley: University of California Press, 1972.

Lévi-Strauss, Claude. *The Raw and the Cooked*, trans. John Weightman and Doreen Weightman. New York: Harper and Row, 1969.

Lewis, C. S. *The Allegory of Love: A Study in Medieval Tradition*. London: Oxford University Press, 1936.

Lewis, Gertrud Jaron. *By Women, For Women, About Women: The Sister-Books of Fourteenth-Century Germany*. Toronto: Pontifical Institute of Mediaeval Studies, 1996.

Lexikon der christlichen Ikonographie. 8 vols. Rome: Herder, 1968–76.

Lomperis, Linda. "From God's Book to the Play of the Text in *Cosmographia*." *Medievalia et Humanistica* n.s. 16 (1988): 51–71.

Losert, Kerstin. "Weibliches Cross-Dressing in mittelalterlicher Hagiographie: Zur Legende der heiligen Euphrosyna von Alexandrien." In Andreas Bihrer and Sven Limbeck, eds., *Exil, Fremdheit und Ausgrenzung in Mittelalter und früher Neuzeit*. Würzburg: Ergon, 2000. 75–89.

Luhrmann, T. M. *Persuasions of the Witch's Craft: Ritual Magic in Contemporary England*. Cambridge, Mass.: Harvard University Press, 1989.

MacCormack, Carol. "Nature, Culture and Gender: a Critique." In Carol MacCormack and Marilyn Strathern, eds., *Nature, Culture and Gender*. Cambridge: Cambridge University Press, 1980. 1–24.

Maier, Eva. *Trente ans avec le diable: Une nouvelle chasse aux sorciers sur la Riviera lémanique (1477–1484)*. Lausanne: Université de Lausanne, 1996.

Manaranche, André. *Le Monothéisme chrétien*. Paris: Cerf, 1985.

Marrow, James. "Symbol and Meaning in Northern European Art of the Late Middle Ages and the Early Renaissance." *Simiolus* 16 (1986): 150–69.

Marshall, Linda. "The Identity of the 'New Man' in the *Anticlaudianus* of Alan of Lille." *Viator* 10 (1979): 77–94.

Matter, E. Ann. "The Virgin Mary: A Goddess?" In Carl Olson, ed., *The Book of the Goddess, Past and Present*. New York: Crossroad, 1983. 80–96.

———. *The Voice of My Beloved: The Song of Songs in Western Medieval Christianity.* Philadelphia: University of Pennsylvania Press, 1990.

Mayer, Anton. "Mater et Filia: Ein Versuch zur stilgeschichtlichen Entwicklung eines Gebetsausdrucks." *Jahrbuch für Liturgiewissenschaft* 7 (1927): 60–82.

McCracken, Peggy. "'The Boy Who Was a Girl': Reading Gender in the *Roman de Silence*." *Romanic Review* 85 (1994): 517–36.

McDonald, Charles. "An Interpretation of Chaucer's *Parlement of Foules*." *Speculum* 30 (1955): 444–57.

McGinn, Bernard. *The Flowering of Mysticism: Men and Women in the New Mysticism, 1200–1350.* New York: Crossroad, 1998.

———. *The Growth of Mysticism: Gregory the Great Through the Twelfth Century.* New York: Crossroad, 1994.

———, ed. *Meister Eckhart and the Beguine Mystics: Hadewijch of Brabant, Mechthild of Magdeburg, and Marguerite Porete.* New York: Continuum, 1994.

McInerney, Maud Burnett. "*In the Meydens Womb*: Julian of Norwich and the Poetics of Enclosure." In Parsons andWheeler, eds., *Medieval Mothering*, 157–82.

McNamara, Jo Ann. "The Need to Give: Suffering and Female Sanctity in the Middle Ages." In Renate Blumenfeld-Kosinski and Timea Szell, eds., *Images of Sainthood in Medieval Europe*. Ithaca, N.Y.: Cornell University Press, 1991, 199–221.

———. *Sisters in Arms: Catholic Nuns Through Two Millennia.* Cambridge, Mass.: Harvard University Press, 1996.

McNamer, Sarah. "The Exploratory Image: God as Mother in Julian of Norwich's *Revelations of Divine Love*." *Mystics Quarterly* 15 (1989): 21–28.

Meier, Christel. "Die Rezeption des *Anticlaudianus* Alans von Lille in Textkommentierung und Illustration." In Christel Meier and Uwe Ruberg, eds., *Text und Bild: Aspekte des Zusammenwirkens zweier Künste in Mittelalter und früher Neuzeit.* Wiesbaden: Reichert Verlag, 1980. 408–549.

Merchant, Carolyn. *The Death of Nature: Women, Ecology, and the Scientific Revolution.* San Francisco: Harper and Row, 1980.

Mews, Constant. *The Lost Love Letters of Heloise and Abelard: Perceptions of Dialogue in Twelfth-Century France.* New York: St. Martin's Press, 1999.

———, ed. *Listen, Daughter: The* Speculum Virginum *and the Formation of Religious Women in the Middle Ages.* New York: Palgrave, 2001.

Meyendorff, John. "Wisdom—Sophia: Contrasting Approaches to a Complex Theme." *Dumbarton Oaks Papers* 41 (1987): 391–401.

Michel, Alain. "Rhétorique, poétique et nature chez Alain de Lille." In Roussel and Suard, eds., *Alain de Lille*, 113–24.

Milhaven, John Giles. *Hadewijch and Her Sisters: Other Ways of Loving and Knowing.* Albany, N.Y.: SUNY Press, 1993.

Miller, David. *The New Polytheism: Rebirth of the Gods and Goddesses.* New York: Harper and Row, 1974.

Minnis, A. J. "*De impedimento sexus*: Women's Bodies and Medieval Impediments to Female Ordination." In Peter Biller and A. J. Minnis, eds., *Medieval Theology and the Natural Body*. Woodbridge: York Medieval Press, 1997. 109–39.

Moltmann, Jürgen. *The Spirit of Life: A Universal Affirmation*, trans. Margaret Kohl. Minneapolis: Fortress Press, 1992.

Moltmann-Wendel, Elisabeth. *A Land Flowing with Milk and Honey: Perspectives on Feminist Theology*, trans. John Bowden. New York: Crossroad, 1986.

Mommaers, Paul. "Hadewijch: A Feminist in Conflict." *Louvain Studies* 13 (1988): 58–81.

Monks, Peter Rolfe. *The Brussels Horloge de Sapience: Iconography and Text of Brussels, Bibliothèque Royale, MS. IV III*. Leiden: Brill, 1990.

Mooney, Catherine, ed. *Gendered Voices: Medieval Saints and Their Interpreters*. Philadelphia: University of Pennsylvania Press, 1999.

Moore, R. I. *The Origins of European Dissent*. Oxford: Blackwell, 1977.

Moore, Stephen. "The Song of Songs in the History of Sexuality." *Church History* 69 (2000): 328–49.

Morrison, Karl. *I am You: The Hermeneutics of Empathy in Western Literature, Theology, and Art*. Princeton, N.J.: Princeton University Press, 1988.

Muraro, Luisa. *Guglielma e Maifreda: Storia di un'eresia femminista*. Milan: La Tartaruga, 1985.

Murphy, Roland. *The Wisdom Literature*. Grand Rapids, Mich.: Eerdmans, 1981.

Musa, Mark. *Dante's Vita Nuova: A Translation and an Essay*. Bloomington: Indiana University Press, 1973.

Neumann, Erich. *The Great Mother: An Analysis of the Archetype*, trans. Ralph Manheim. Princeton, N.J.: Princeton University Press, 1955.

Newman, Barbara. *From Virile Woman to WomanChrist: Studies in Medieval Religion and Literature*. Philadelphia: University of Pennsylvania Press, 1995.

———. "The Mirror and the Rose: Marguerite Porete's Encounter with the *Dieu d'Amours*." In Renate Blumenfeld-Kosinski, Duncan Robertson, and Nancy Warren, eds., *The Vernacular Spirit*. New York: Palgrave, 2002. 105–23.

———. *Sister of Wisdom: St. Hildegard's Theology of the Feminine*. Berkeley: University of California Press, 1987.

———. "Some Mediaeval Theologians and the Sophia Tradition." *Downside Review* 108 (1990): 111–30.

Niebuhr, H. Richard. *Radical Monotheism and Western Culture*. New York: Harper, 1960.

Nitzsche, Jane Chance. *The Genius Figure in Antiquity and the Middle Ages*. New York: Columbia University Press, 1975.

Nuth, Joan. *Wisdom's Daughter: The Theology of Julian of Norwich*. New York: Crossroad, 1991.

O'Carroll, Michael. *Theotokos: A Theological Encyclopedia of the Blessed Virgin Mary*. Wilmington, Del.: Michael Glazier, 1982.

Obrist, Barbara. *Les débuts de l'imagerie alchimique (XIVe–XVe siècles)*. Paris: Le Sycomore, 1982.

Ohly, Friedrich. *Hohelied-Studien: Grundzüge einer Geschichte der Hohelied-Auslegung des Abendlandes bis um ca. 1200*. Wiesbaden: F. Steiner, 1958.

Olyan, Saul. *Asherah and the Cult of Yahweh in Israel*. Atlanta: Scholars Press, 1988.

Ortner, Sherry. "Is Female to Male as Nature Is to Culture?" In Michelle Rosaldo and Louise Lamphere, eds., *Woman, Culture, and Society*. Stanford, Calif.: Stanford University Press, 1974. 67–87.

Oruch, Jack B. "Nature's Limitations and the *Demande d'Amour* of Chaucer's *Parlement*." *Chaucer Review* 18 (1983): 23–37.

Parsons, John Carmi, and Bonnie Wheeler, eds. *Medieval Mothering*. New York: Garland, 1996.

Partner, Nancy. "Reading *The Book of Margery Kempe*." *Exemplaria* 3 (1991): 29–66.

Patch, Howard. *The Goddess Fortuna in Mediaeval Literature*. Cambridge, Mass.: Harvard University Press, 1927.

Paxson, James. *The Poetics of Personification*. Cambridge: Cambridge University Press, 1994.

Pelikan, Jaroslav. *The Emergence of the Catholic Tradition (100–600)*. Chicago: University of Chicago Press, 1971.

———. *Eternal Feminines: Three Theological Allegories in Dante's* Paradiso. New Brunswick, N.J.: Rutgers University Press, 1990.

———. *Mary Through the Centuries: Her Place in the History of Culture*. New Haven, Conn.: Yale University Press, 1996.

Perret, Michèle. "Travesties et transsexuelles: Yde, Silence, Grisandole, Blanchandine." *Romance Notes* 25 (1985): 328–40.

Peters, Ursula. *Religiöse Erfahrung als literarisches Faktum: Zur Vorgeschichte und Genese frauenmystischer Texte des 13. und 14. Jahrhunderts*. Tübingen: Niemeyer, 1988.

Petroff, Elizabeth. *Body and Soul: Essays on Medieval Women and Mysticism*. New York: Oxford University Press, 1994.

Philippart, Guy. "Le Récit miraculaire marial dans l'Occident médiéval." In Dominique Iogna-Prat, Éric Palazzo, and Daniel Russo, eds., *Marie: Le Culte de la Vierge dans la société médiévale*. Paris: Beauchesne, 1996. 563–90.

Piehler, Paul. *The Visionary Landscape: A Study in Medieval Allegory*. London: Edward Arnold, 1971.

Piper, Ronald. *Wisdom in the Q-Tradition: The Aphoristic Teaching of Jesus*. Cambridge: Cambridge University Press, 1989.

Poirion, Daniel. "Alain de Lille et Jean de Meun." In Roussel and Suard, eds., *Alain de Lille*, 135–51.

Post, R. R. *The Modern Devotion: Confrontation with Reformation and Humanism*. Leiden: Brill, 1968.

Putscher, Marielene. "Das *Buch der heiligen Dreifaltigkeit* und seine Bilder in Handschriften des 15. Jahrhunderts." In Christoph Meinel, ed., *Die Alchemie in der europäischen Kultur- und Wissenschaftsgeschichte*, Wolfenbüttel Symposium. Wiesbaden: Harrassowitz, 1986. 151–78.

Quilligan, Maureen. "Allegory, Allegoresis, and the Deallegorization of Language: The *Roman de la Rose*, the *De planctu Naturae*, and the *Parlement of Foules*." In Bloomfield, ed., *Allegory, Myth, and Symbol*. 163–86.

———. *The Allegory of Female Authority: Reading Christine de Pizan's* Livre de la Cité des Dames. Ithaca, N.Y.: Cornell University Press, 1991.

———. *The Language of Allegory: Defining the Genre*. Ithaca, N.Y.: Cornell University Press, 1979.

Raabe, Pamela. *Imitating God: The Allegory of Faith in* Piers Plowman B. Athens: University of Georgia Press, 1990.

Raby, F. J. E. "*Nuda Natura* and Twelfth-Century Cosmology." *Speculum* 43 (1968): 72–77.

Réau, Louis. *Iconographie de l'art chrétien*, vol. 2, pt. 2. Paris: Presses Universitaires de France, 1957.

Reese, James. *Hellenistic Influence on the Book of Wisdom and Its Consequences*. Rome: Biblical Institute Press, 1970.

Re-Imagining: Quarterly Newsletter of the Re-Imagining Community. Minneapolis, 1994–.

Reynaert, Joris. "Hadewijch: Mystic Poetry and Courtly Love." In Erik Kooper, ed., *Medieval Dutch Literature in Its European Context*. Cambridge: Cambridge University Press, 1994. 208–25.

Richards, Earl Jeffrey. "Christine de Pizan and Jean Gerson: An Intellectual Friendship." In John Campbell and Nadia Margolis, eds., *Christine de Pizan 2000: Studies on Christine de Pizan in Honour of Angus J. Kennedy*. Amsterdam: Rodopi, 2000. 197–208.

——. "*Virile Woman and* WomanChrist: The Meaning of Gender Metamorphosis in Christine." In Jean-Claude Mühlethaler and Denis Billotte, eds., *"Riens ne m'est seur que la chose incertaine": Études sur l'art d'écrire au Moyen Âge offertes à Eric Hicks*. Geneva: Slatkine, 2001. 239–52.

——. "Where Are the Men in Christine de Pizan's City of Ladies? Architectural and Allegorical Structures in Christine de Pizan's *Livre de la Cité des Dames*." In Renate Blumenfeld-Kosinski, Kevin Brownlee, Mary Speer, and Lori Walters, eds., *Translatio Studii: Essays by His Students in Honor of Karl D. Uitti*. Amsterdam: Rodopi. 1999. 221–43.

——, ed., with Joan Williamson, Nadia Margolis, and Christine Reno. *Reinterpreting Christine de Pizan*. Athens: University of Georgia Press, 1992.

Riddy, Felicity. "Julian of Norwich and Self-Textualization." In Ann Hutchison, ed., *Editing Women*. Cardiff: University of Wales Press, 1998. 101–24.

Ringler, Siegfried. "Die Rezeption mittelalterlicher Frauenmystik als wissenschaftliches Problem, dargestellt am Werk der Christine Ebner." In Dinzelbacher and Bauer, eds., *Frauenmystik im Mittelalter*, 178–200.

Robertson, D. W., Jr. *A Preface to Chaucer: Studies in Medieval Perspectives*. Princeton, N.J.: Princeton University Press, 1962.

Rochais, Henri. "Ipsa Philosophia Christus." *Mediaeval Studies* 13 (1951): 244–47.

Rosenfeld, Hellmut. "Christus und die Minnende Seele." *Die deutsche Literatur des Mittelalters: Verfasserlexikon*. 1: 1235–37

——. "Der mittelalterliche Bilderbogen." *Zeitschrift für deutsches Altertum und deutsche Literatur* 85 (1954): 66–75.

Rosenwein, Barbara, and Lester K. Little. "Social Meaning in the Monastic and Mendicant Spiritualities." *Past & Present* 63 (1974): 4–32.

Ross, Ellen. *The Grief of God: Images of the Suffering Jesus in Late Medieval England*. New York: Oxford University Press, 1997.

——. "'She Wept and Cried Right Loud for Sorrow and for Pain': Suffering, the Spiritual Journey, and Women's Experience in Late Medieval Mysticism." In Ulrike Wiethaus, ed., *Maps of Flesh and Light: The Religious Experience of Medieval Women Mystics*. Syracuse, N.Y.: Syracuse University Press, 1993. 45–59.

Roussel, H., and François Suard, eds. *Alain de Lille, Gautier de Châtillon, Jakemart Giélée, et leur temps: Actes du Colloque de Lille, Octobre 1978*. Lille: Presses Universitaires de Lille, 1980.

Ruether, Rosemary Radford. *Womanguides: Readings Toward a Feminist Theology*. Boston: Beacon Press, 1985.

Ruh, Kurt. "Beginenmystik: Hadewijch, Mechthild von Magdeburg, Marguerite Porete." *Zeitschrift für deutsches Altertum* 106 (1977): 265–77.

Russell, Jeffrey Burton. *Dissent and Order in the Middle Ages: The Search for Legitimate Authority*. New York: Twayne/Macmillan, 1992.

Sahlin, Claire. "'His Heart Was My Heart': Birgitta of Sweden's Devotion to the Heart of Mary." In Alf Härdelin and Mereth Lindgren, eds., *Heliga Birgitta — budskapet och förebilden*. Stockholm: Almqvist & Wiksell, 1993. 213–27.

——. "The Virgin Mary and Birgitta of Sweden's Prophetic Vocation." In Sven-Erik Brodd and Alf Härdelin, eds., *Maria i Sverige under Tusen År*. Skellefteå, Sweden: Artos, 1996. 227–54.

Schaus, E. "Das Kloster der Minne." *Zeitschrift für deutsches Altertum und deutsche Literatur* 38 (1894): 361–68.

Schiller, Gertrud. *Iconography of Christian Art*. 2 vols. London: Lund Humphries, 1972.

——. *Ikonographie der christlichen Kunst*, vol. 4, pt. 2. Gütersloh: Gerd Mohn, 1980.

Schipflinger, Thomas. *Sophia — Maria: A Holistic Vision of Creation*, trans. James Morgante. York Beach, Me.: Samuel Weiser, 1998.

Schmidt, Wilhelm. *The Origin and Growth of Religion: Facts and Theories*, trans. H. J. Rose. New York: Dial Press, 1931.

Schneider, Laurel. *Re-Imagining the Divine: Confronting the Backlash Against Feminist Theology*. Cleveland: Pilgrim Press, 1998.

Scholem, Gershom. *Major Trends in Jewish Mysticism*. 3rd ed. New York: Schocken, 1961.

Schulman, Nicole. *Where Troubadours Were Bishops: The Occitania of Folc of Marseille (1150–1231)*. New York: Routledge, 2001.

Schüssler Fiorenza, Elisabeth. *Jesus, Miriam's Child, Sophia's Prophet: Critical Issues in Feminist Christology*. New York: Continuum, 1994.

Schwartz, Regina. *The Curse of Cain: The Violent Legacy of Monotheism*. Chicago: University of Chicago Press, 1997.

Schwietering, Julius. "Zur Autorschaft von Seuses Vita." In Kurt Ruh, ed., *Altdeutsche und altniederländische Mystik*. Darmstadt: Wissenschaftliche Buchgesellschaft, 1964. 309–23.

Seethaler, Paula. "Die Weisheitstexte in der Marienliturgie." *Benediktinische Monatschrift* 34 (1958): 111–20.

Segal, Alan. *Two Powers in Heaven: Early Rabbinic Reports about Christianity and Gnosticism*. Leiden: Brill, 1977.

Selman, Rebecca. "Spirituality and Sex Change: *Horologium sapientiae* and *Speculum devotorum*." In Denis Renevey and Christiania Whitehead, eds., *Writing Religious Women: Female Spiritual and Textual Practices in Late Medieval England*. Toronto: University of Toronto Press, 2000. 63–79.

Semple, Benjamin. "The Critique of Knowledge as Power: The Limits of Philosophy and Theology in Christine de Pizan." In Marilynn Desmond, ed., *Christine de Pizan*, 108–27.

Seznec, Jean. *The Survival of the Pagan Gods: The Mythological Tradition and Its Place in Renaissance Humanism and Art*, trans. Barbara Sessions. New York: Bollingen Foundation, 1953.

Sheingorn, Pamela. "The Holy Family and Pollution in Late Medieval Visual Culture." Paper presented at the Newberry Library, Chicago, 1998.

———. "The Maternal Behavior of God: Divine Father as Fantasy Husband." In Parsons and Wheeler, eds., *Medieval Mothering*, 77–99.

Shinners, John. *Medieval Popular Religion, 1000–1500: A Reader*. Peterborough, Ont.: Broadview Press, 1997.

Sider, Robert. "Credo Quia Absurdum?" *Classical World* 73 (1980): 417–19.

Silverstein, Theodore. "The Fabulous Cosmogony of Bernard Silvestris." *Modern Philology* 46 (1948–49): 92–116.

Simons, Walter. "The Beguine Movement in the Southern Low Countries: A Reassessment." *Bulletin de l'Institut historique belge de Rome* 59 (1989): 63–105.

Singleton, Charles. *An Essay on the* Vita Nuova. Cambridge, Mass.: Harvard University Press, 1949.

Smith, Mark. *The Early History of God: Yahweh and the Other Deities in Ancient Israel*. San Francisco: Harper and Row, 1990.

Snyder, James. *Northern Renaissance Art: Painting, Sculpture, the Graphic Arts from 1350 to 1575*. New York: Harry Abrams, 1985.

Spearing, A. C. *Medieval Dream-Poetry*. Cambridge: Cambridge University Press, 1976.

Sprung, Andrew. "The Inverted Metaphor: Earthly Mothering as *Figura* of Divine Love in Julian of Norwich's *Book of Showings*." In Parsons and Wheeler, eds., *Medieval Mothering*, 183–99.

Staley, Lynn. *Margery Kempe's Dissenting Fictions*. University Park: Pennsylvania State University Press, 1994.

Steinmetz, Ralf-Henning. *Liebe als universales Prinzip bei Frauenlob: Ein volkssprachlicher Weltentwurf in der europäischen Dichtung um 1300*. Tübingen: Max Niemeyer, 1994.

Sticca, Sandro. *The Planctus Mariae in the Dramatic Tradition of the Middle Ages*, trans. Joseph Berrigan. Athens: University of Georgia Press, 1988.

Stock, Brian. *Myth and Science in the Twelfth Century: A Study of Bernard Silvester*. Princeton, N.J.: Princeton University Press, 1972.

Stock, Lorraine. "The Importance of Being Gender 'Stable': Masculinity and Feminine Empowerment in *Le Roman de Silence*." *Arthuriana* 7 (1997): 7–34.

Suggs, M. Jack. *Wisdom, Christology, and Law in Matthew's Gospel*. Cambridge, Mass.: Harvard University Press, 1970.

Summit, Jennifer. *Lost Property: The Woman Writer and English Literary History, 1380–1589*. Chicago: University of Chicago Press, 2000.

Suydam, Mary. "Beguine Textuality: Sacred Performances." In Mary Suydam and Joanna Ziegler, eds., *Performance and Transformation: New Approaches to Late Medieval Spirituality*. New York: St. Martin's Press, 1999. 169–210.

Tarnowski, Andrea. "Maternity and Paternity in 'La Mutacion de Fortune.'" In Zimmermann and De Rentiis, eds., *City of Scholars*, 116–26.

Tavormina, M. Teresa. *Kindly Similitude: Marriage and Family in "Piers Plowman."* Woodbridge: Boydell, 1995.

Teskey, Gordon. *Allegory and Violence*. Ithaca, N.Y.: Cornell University Press, 1996.

Tinkle, Theresa. *Medieval Venuses and Cupids: Sexuality, Hermeneutics, and English Poetry*. Stanford, Calif.: Stanford University Press, 1996.

Tobin, Frank. "Henry Suso and Elsbeth Stagel: Was the *Vita* a Cooperative Effort?" In Mooney, ed., *Gendered Voices*, 118–35.

———. *Mechthild von Magdeburg: A Medieval Mystic in Modern Eyes*. Columbia, S.C.: Camden House, 1995.

Traver, Hope. *The Four Daughters of God: A Study of the Versions of This Allegory*. Philadelphia: John Winston, 1907.

Troescher, Georg. "Die 'Pitié-de-Nostre-Seigneur' oder 'Notgottes.'" *Wallraf-Richartz-Jahrbuch* 9 (1936): 148–68.

Turner, Denys. *Eros and Allegory: Medieval Exegesis of the Song of Songs*. Kalamazoo, Mich.: Cistercian Publications, 1995.

Tuve, Rosemond. *Allegorical Imagery: Some Mediaeval Books and Their Posterity*. Princeton, N.J.: Princeton University Press, 1966.

Van den Boogaard, Nico. "Les insertions en français dans un traité de Gérard de Liège." In *Marche romane: Mélanges de philologie et de littératures romanes offerts à Jeanne Wathelet-Willem*. Liège: Cahiers de l'Association des Romanistes de l'Université de Liège, 1978. 679–97.

Van Dyke, Carolynn. *The Fiction of Truth: Structure and Meaning in Narrative and Dramatic Allegory*. Ithaca, N.Y.: Cornell University Press, 1985.

Van Os, Henk, with Eugène Honée, Hans Nieuwdorp, and Bernard Ridderbos. *The Art of Devotion in the Late Middle Ages in Europe, 1300–1500*, trans. Michael Hoyle. Princeton, N.J.: Princeton University Press, 1994.

Van Parys, M. "Exégèse et théologie trinitaire: Prov. 8,22 chez les Pères cappadociens." *Irénikon* 43 (1970): 362–79.

Vanderauwera, Ria. "The Brabant Mystic Hadewijch." In Katharina Wilson, ed., *Medieval Women Writers*. Athens: University of Georgia Press, 1984, 186–93.

Vavra, Elisabeth. "Bildmotiv und Frauenmystik: Funktion und Rezeption." In Peter Dinzelbacher and Dieter Bauer, eds., *Frauenmystik im Mittelalter*, 201–30.

Verdier, Philippe. *Le Couronnement de la Vierge: les origines et les premiers développements d'un thème iconographique*. Paris: J. Vrin, 1980.

Versluis, Arthur. *Theosophia: Hidden Dimensions of Christianity*. Hudson, N.Y.: Lindisfarne, 1994.

Voaden, Rosalynn. *God's Words, Women's Voices: The Discernment of Spirits in the Writing of Late-Medieval Women Visionaries*. Woodbridge: York Medieval Press, 1999.

Von Balthasar, Hans Urs. *Creator Spirit*, trans. Brian McNeil. San Francisco: Ignatius, 1993.

Von Lilienfeld, Fairy. "'Frau Weisheit' in byzantinischen und karolingischen Quellen des 9. Jahrhunderts—Allegorische Personifikation, Hypostase oder Typos?" In Margot Schmidt and C. F. Geyer, eds., *Typus, Symbol, Allegorie bei den östlichen Vätern und ihren Parallelen im Mittelalter*. Internationales Kolloquium, Eichstätt 1981. Regensburg: Pustet, 1982. 146–86.

Von Rad, Gerhard. *Wisdom in Israel*, trans. James Marton. Nashville, Tenn.: Abingdon, 1972.

Wainright-deKadt, Elizabeth. "Courtly Literature and Mysticism: Some Aspects of Their Interaction." *Acta Germanica* 12 (1980): 41–60.

Wallace, David. "Mystics and Followers in Siena and East Anglia: A Study in Taxonomy, Class, and Cultural Mediation." In Glasscoe, ed., *Medieval Mystical Tradition in England*, 169–91.

Walters, Lori. "Fortune's Double Face: Gender and the Transformations of Christine de Pizan, Augustine, and Perpetua." *Fifteenth-Century Studies* 25 (1999): 97–114.

———. "Illuminating the *Rose*: Gui de Mori and the Illustrations of MS 101 of the Municipal Library, Tournai." In Brownlee and Huot, eds., *Rethinking the Romance of the Rose*, 167–200.

Ward, Benedicta. "Julian the Solitary." In Kenneth Leech and Sister Benedicta Ward, *Julian Reconsidered*. Fairacres, Oxford: Sisters of the Love of God, 1988. 11–35.

Warner, Marina. *Alone of All Her Sex: The Myth and the Cult of the Virgin Mary*. New York: Knopf, 1976.

Waters, Claire. "Doctrine Embodied: Gender, Authority, and Performance in Late-Medieval Preaching." Dissertation, Northwestern University, 1998.

Watson, Nicholas. "Censorship and Cultural Change in Late-Medieval England: Vernacular Theology, the Oxford Translation Debate, and Arundel's Constitutions of 1409." *Speculum* 70 (1995): 822–64.

———. "The Composition of Julian of Norwich's *Revelation of Love*." *Speculum* 68 (1993): 637–83.

———. "Conceptions of the Word: The Mother Tongue and the Incarnation of God." *New Medieval Literatures* 1 (1997): 85–124.

———. "John the Monk's *Book of Visions of the Blessed and Undefiled Virgin Mary, Mother of God*." In Fanger, ed., *Conjuring Spirits*, 163–215.

———. "The Trinitarian Hermeneutic in Julian of Norwich's *Revelation of Love*." In Glasscoe, ed., *Medieval Mystical Tradition in England*, 79–100.

———. "Visions of Inclusion: Universal Salvation and Vernacular Theology in Pre-Reformation England." *Journal of Medieval and Early Modern Studies* 27 (1997): 145–87.

———. "'Yf wommen be double naturelly': Remaking 'Woman' in Julian of Norwich's *Revelation of Love*." *Exemplaria* 8 (1996): 1–34.

Weed, Stanley. "My Sister, Bride, and Mother: Aspects of Female Piety in Some Images of the *Virgo inter Virgines*." *Magistra* 4 (1998): 3–26.

Weevers, Theodoor. *Poetry of the Netherlands in Its European Context, 1170–1930*. London: Athlone, 1960.

Wetherbee, Winthrop. "Philosophy, Cosmology, and the Twelfth-Century Renaissance." In Dronke, ed., *A History of Twelfth-Century Western Philosophy*, 21–53.

———. *Platonism and Poetry in the Twelfth Century: The Literary Influence of the School of Chartres*. Princeton, N.J.: Princeton University Press, 1972.

White, Hugh. *Nature, Sex, and Goodness in a Medieval Literary Tradition*. Oxford: Oxford University Press, 2000.

Whitman, Jon. "From the *Cosmographia* to the *Divine Comedy*: An Allegorical Dilemma." In Bloomfield, ed., *Allegory, Myth, and Symbol*, 63–86.

Wiethaus, Ulrike. *Ecstatic Transformation: Transpersonal Psychology in the Work of Mechthild of Magdeburg*. Syracuse, N.Y.: Syracuse University Press, 1996.

Wilken, Robert, ed. *Aspects of Wisdom in Judaism and Early Christianity*. Notre Dame, Ind.: University of Notre Dame Press, 1975.

Wilks, Michael. "Alan of Lille and the New Man." In Derek Baker, ed., *Renaissance and Renewal in Christian History*. Oxford: Blackwell, 1977. 137–57.

Willaert, Frank. "Hadewijch und ihr Kreis in den 'Visionen.'" In Kurt Ruh, ed.,
   Abendländische Mystik im Mittelalter. Stuttgart: Metzler, 1986. 368–87.
———. *De poëtica van Hadewijch in de Strofische Gedichten*. Utrecht: HES, 1984.
Willard, Charity Cannon. *Christine de Pizan: Her Life and Works*. New York: Persea
   Books, 1984.
Williams, Charles. *The Figure of Beatrice: A Study in Dante*. London: Faber and Faber,
   1943.
Yunck, John. *The Lineage of Lady Meed: The Development of Mediaeval Venality Satire*.
   Notre Dame, Ind.: University of Notre Dame Press, 1963.
Zimmermann, Margarete, and Dina De Rentiis, eds. *The City of Scholars: New
   Approaches to Christine de Pizan*. Berlin: de Gruyter, 1994.
Ziolkowski, Jan. *Alan of Lille's Grammar of Sex: The Meaning of Grammar to a
   Twelfth-Century Intellectual*. Cambridge, Mass.: Medieval Academy of America,
   1985.

Index

Abelard, Peter, 39, 65, 173, 307; and Heloise, 347 n.71, 378 n.59; on the world soul, 52, 88, 138

Adam, 8, 64, 83, 128, 275; and Christ, 227–28, 301–2; and Eve, 236, 241, 248–49

Adam de la Bassée, 83

Adam of St.-Victor, 271

Addison, Joseph, 36

Aelred of Rievaulx, 143–46, 225

Alan of Lille, 39, 91, 208, 295, 298; *Anticlaudianus*, 52, 73–86, 95, 193, 244, 292; and Bernard Silvestris, 65–67, 75, 87, 138, 291; career of, 1, 66; *De planctu Naturae*, 52, 66–73, 91, 94–97, 272, 325; *Distinctiones*, 360 n.11; epitaph of, 344 n.31; and hermeticism, 183, 372 n.148; illustrations of, 76–80, 84–86; influence of, 73, 100–102, 108–11; on natural law, 347 n.67

Albertus Magnus, 229

Alchemy, 194, 234–44, 307–8, 316–17, 391 n.36

Alcuin, 198, 200, 203, 220, 315

Alfred the Great, 36

Allegory, 30–50, 217, 298; in alchemical texts, 235–37; and gender, 36–38, 40; and philosophical realism, 30–31, 33–35, 40–43; and violence, 38–39; and visionary literature, 30–31, 293. *See also* Imaginative theology; Personification; Visions

"Altercatio Ganimedis et Helene," 52, 90–94, 99

Ambrose of Milan, 229

Ancrene Wisse, 231

Andreas Capellanus, 143, 149, 151–52, 364 n.48

Angela of Foligno, 295–96, 298

Angelus Silesius, 317

Anima mundi. See World soul

Animals, 91–92, 131, 313, 350 n.8

Anne, St., 254, 269, 287, 313

Anne of Bohemia, 111, 114

Annunciation, 21, 30, 84, 195; in art, 45–46, 153, 256–57

Anselm of Canterbury, 45, 225, 284, 366 n.81; *Cur Deus Homo*, 299; *Monologium*, 48

Antichrist, 241, 306, 401 n.149

Aphrodite, 11, 69, 139, 239. *See also* Venus

Apocalypse, biblical, 210, 238–39

Apollo, 1, 37, 90, 321

Aquinas, Thomas, 2, 295, 372 n.148; on gender, 121, 310; spurious alchemical work of, 194, 385 n.131

Archibald, Elizabeth, xii

Aristotle, 56, 127, 245; and alchemy, 235; on gender, 48, 121, 309; on language, 97

Arnaut Daniel, 185

Arnold, Gottfried, 317

Arthurian romance, 131, 143–44, 150, 153, 357 n.78, 358 n.88

Arundel, Thomas, 224

Assumption of the Virgin, 313; Jungian view of, 254–55; liturgy of, 195–200, 208, 242, 261, 314

Athanasian Creed, 321, 326

Atkinson, Clarissa, 277

Augustine, xi, 97, 227, 278, 282, 321, 324; as authority on love, 146, 151, 154, 173, 360 n.13; *On Christian Doctrine*, 141; *City of God*, 23, 141; *Confessions*, 143; *On the Trinity*, 248

Aurora consurgens, 194, 234–40, 244, 305, 316

Bacon, Roger, 2

Baker, Augustine, 224

Barfield, Owen, 30

Beatific vision, 300, 403 n.14

Beatrice, in Dante, 181–89, 300, 315

Beatrice of Nazareth, 149, 296

Bede, Venerable, 196

Beguines, 151, 155–56, 174, 309, 369 n.115; satire of, 107–8

Beissel, Johann Conrad, 317
Belting, Hans, 394 n.61
Benedict XII, pope, 403 n.14
Benedict XIV, pope, 283
Bernard of Clairvaux, 209, 237, 295, 307;
    influence of, 143, 152, 173, 206; *Letters*,
    145–46; on Mary, 199, 286; on the Song of
    Songs, 149
Bernard Silvestris, 72, 138, 228, 232, 291, 316;
    Cosmographia, 34, 36–39, 48, 52, 55–65, 298,
    307–8; influence of, 65, 91, 344 n.30
Bernardino of Feltre, 287
Bernardino of Siena, 205, 244, 287, 401 n.145
Berry, Craig, xii
Bible. *See* individual books
Birgitta of Sweden, 274, 282, 290, 298, 314;
    critiques of, 288–89; texts of, 296; and the
    Virgin Mary, 276–79, 312
Black, Diana, xii
Black Madonna, 238–40
Blake, William, 317
Blamires, Alcuin, 336 n.49
Blumenfeld-Kosinski, Renate, xii–xiii
Boccaccio, Giovanni, 23, 65, 337 n.58
Boehme, Jacob, 316–17
Boethius, xi, 39, 203, 208, 292; *Consolation of
    Philosophy*, 31, 35, 67, 193, 244, 303; *On the
    Trinity*, 48
Bonagiunta da Lucca, 185
Bonaventure, 196, 271, 295, 372 n.148; on
    charity, 157; on gender, 310; and Joachim
    of Fiore, 403 n.13; Platonism of, 229, 291
Bond, Gerald, 140–41
Boniface VIII, pope, 309, 315, 403 n.12
Bonus, Petrus, 235
Book of the Holy Trinity, 194, 234, 240–44,
    252, 307–8; illustrations of, 243, 256, 258
Boswell, John, 91–92
Bouyer, Louis, 172
Bradley, Ritamary, 229
Brigit of Ireland, St., 321
Brufani, Stefano, 4, 10
Bulgakov, Sergei, 317
Bunyan, John, *Pilgrim's Progress*, 36, 315
Burnham, John, 278
Bynum, Caroline Walker, 206, 226, 261

Calcidius, 37, 56
Callan, Maeve, xii, 396 n.85
Caritas, 11, 193, 291; in Aelred of Rievaulx,
    143–45; in Bernard of Clairvaux, 145–46; in
    Bonaventure, 157; compared to *amor* and

cupiditas, 139, 141–50, 169, 182, 360 nn.11,
    13; in Hildegard of Bingen, 88, 138–39, 205,
    373 n.157; in Hugh of St.-Victor, 146–48;
    iconography of, 160, 164–65, 188, 237; as
    killer of Christ, 160, 164–66; in Richard of
    St.-Victor, 148–51. *See also* Lady Love;
    Minne
Cathars, 66, 72, 306
Catherine of Siena, 279, 289, 314, 393 n.53
Cats, xiii, 55
Cavalcanti, Guido, 184
Caxton, William, 212
Celestine V, pope, 403 n.12
Ceres, 23
Chaos, as deity, 120–21
Charlemagne, 203
Charles VI, king of France, 111
Charles the Bald, 203
Charonton, Enguerrand, 393 n.52
Chartres: cathedral of, 205, 322; school of,
    342 n.4
Chastizing of God's Children, 297
Chaucer, Geoffrey, 20, 65; *Canterbury Tales*,
    7, 35, 98, 115; and Jean de Meun, 35, 108,
    113; *Legend of Good Women*, 26, 113; *Par-
    lement of Fowles*, 35, 54–55, 111–15, 298, 303,
    325; *Troilus and Criseyde*, 35, 115
Chrétien de Troyes, 149–51, 364 n.48
Christ. *See* Incarnation; Nativity; Passion;
    Trinity
Christine de Pizan, 111, 244, 271, 292, 310;
    Book of the City of Ladies, 19–27, 31, 115–16,
    119, 121, 136, 304, 312; *Book of the Mutation
    of Fortune*, 52, 116–19, 136, 304; *Book of the
    Path of Long Study*, 27–28, 116; *Christine's
    Vision*, 31, 35, 52, 116, 119–22, 136, 193; and
    Dante, 27, 121, 304, 336 n.56; early editions
    of, 315; on imagination, 27, 297, 299;
    influence of, 336 n.49; and *Romance of the
    Rose*, 22, 115, 117, 122, 288
Christus und die minnende Seele, 167–68
Churches: Chartres, 205, 322; Hagia Sophia,
    195–96; Parthenon, 322, 374 n.11; Santa
    Maria in Trastevere, 256–57; Santa Maria
    Maggiore, 197, 256, 314; Santa Maria sopra
    Minerva, 322
Cicero, 88, 141
Claudian, 55, 58, 64, 73
Cloud of Unknowing, 297–98
Coinherence, 159, 187, 227, 234
Colledge, Edmund, 207–8, 378 n.60, 382 n.103
Compendium Anticlaudiani, 83–84

Constance, Council of, 240, 242, 284, 288, 307
Constantine (Cyril), St., 196
Constantine, emperor, 195
Constantine the African, 359 n.97
Constitutions of Arundel, 224, 296
Coronation of the Virgin, 255–61, 263, 269, 290; origins of, 243, 256, 388 nn.157, 158; suppression of, 313–14
Council of Remiremont, 155
Counter-Reformation, 234, 314–16
Court of Sapience, xi
Courtly love. *See* Cupid; *Fin' amors*; Minnesingers; Troubadours
Crossover, as artistic mode, 151, 155–58, 167
Crucifixion by the Virtues, 160–65
Crusading, 178
Cupid, 36, 54; in Alan of Lille, 67; as angel, 152–53; and Caritas, 147, 151, 159, 169; in Chaucer, 112–13; as Christ, 140; in *Romance of the Rose*, 98–99, 108, 135, 145
Curtius, E. R., 64, 91

D'Ailly, Pierre, 287
D'Alverny, Marie-Thérèse, 87
Daly, Mary, 309
Damian, Peter, 199
Dante Alighieri, 234, 325; and Christine de Pizan, 27, 121, 304, 336 n.56; *Commedia*, 2, 37, 76, 181–88, 331 n.4, 403 n.13; politics of, 293, 300; truth claims of, 303; and Virgin Mary, 250; *Vita Nuova*, 171, 181–85, 187–89, 315, 339 n.86
Daughters of Wisdom, 316
David, king of Scotland, 143
Deguileville, Guillaume de, xi
Devotio Moderna, 173, 193, 212
Diana (Artemis), 53, 292
Dieu d'Amors. See Cupid
Dinzelbacher, Peter, 27–29, 300
Discernment of spirits, 139, 288–90
"Dispute Between Ganymede and Helen," 52, 90–94, 99
Dominicans, 211, 214, 241, 282
Double Intercession, 255, 261–65, 269, 275, 277, 279, 313
Dream of Scipio, 111
Dronke, Peter, xiii, 34, 63, 91, 155
Duccio, 188

Ebner, Margaretha, 208, 223, 378 n.58
Ecclesia: personified, 17, 43, 205, 230, 325; in art, 16, 41–42, 160, 164–65, 237

Ecclesiasticus (Sirach), 190–91, 196–99, 208, 214
Eckhart, Meister, 295–96, 316; as heretic, 307–8; and Marguerite Porete, 308; on spiritual childbirth, 271, 286
Edwards, Burton Van Name, xii, 375 n.26
Elisabeth of Schönau, 223
Elizabeth I, queen of England, 406 n.44
Elliott, Dyan, 286
Ennodius, xi
Ephrem of Syria, 251
Eriugena, John Scotus, 56, 79, 297–98
Escher, M. C., 233
Esotericism, 165, 252, 305, 386 n.142, 406 n.52; in alchemy, 194, 234, 237; early modern, 316–17, 327
Esther, book of, 210
Eternal Wisdom: in Henry Suso, 12–14, 48, 153, 193, 206–22; Hours of, 193, 220, 222. *See also* Sapientia; Sophia
Eugene III, pope, 39, 65, 307
Euhemerism, 23, 337 n.57
Eustochium, 289
Evans, G. R., 83
Eve, 309; and Adam, 236, 241, 248–49; and Mary, 18, 68
Exegesis, 139–40, 229, 237; of Song of Songs, 147, 171, 198–99, 291, 377 n.49; of wisdom books, 64, 192–93, 195–200, 214
Exemplarism, 227–29, 291, 296

Fair Unknown, romance of, 153
Fanger, Claire, 64
Ferrante, Joan, 37
Fiene, Donald, 375 n.30
Fin' amors, 40, 53, 139, 142, 193, 220; in beguine literature, 151–56; decline of, 315; rise of, 140–41; in *Romance of the Rose*, 99
Flaubert, Gustave, 29
Flete, William, 226
Florensky, Pavel, 317
Folc of Marseille, 173, 186, 359 n.4
Fortuna, 37, 310; in *Anticlaudianus*, 78; in Boethius, 35, 339 n.88; in Christine de Pizan, 116, 118–19, 304; in Dante, 2, 331 n.4
Fouquet, Jean, 255, 279
Four daughters of God: in art, 45–46, 160, 163–64; in Grosseteste, 2, 23, 44–47, 299; in *Piers Plowman*, 23, 34, 299
Fourth Lateran Council, 295, 399 n.122
Francesca da Rimini, 185

Francis of Assisi, 78, 210, 273, 286, 333 n.23; in *Sacrum commercium*, 3–9

Franciscans, 4, 47, 148, 211, 325; Spiritual, 9, 240, 306

Frangello, Gina, 338 n.70

Frau Minne. *See* Lady Love; Minne; Venus

Frauendienst, 169–71

Frauenlob, xi, 252, 272–73, 391 n.36

Freud, Sigmund, 43, 255, 301; on incestuous desire, 245–46, 282–83, 290, 398 n.121

Freyhan, Robert, 188

Friedrich, margrave of Brandenburg, 240, 387 n.148

Frymer-Kensky, Tikva, 318, 320, 322

Fulgentius, 322

Fulton, Rachel, xiii, 199

Gadon, Elinor, 394 n.70

Galahad, 83

Galen, 309

Ganymede, 90–97

Gaunt, Simon, 358 n.95

Gautier de Coincy, 96

Geiler von Kaysersberg, Johann, 287

Gender: in Dante, 187–88; of God, 40, 48, 64, 194; grammatical, 36, 93–97, 119, 188, 248, 357 n.74; in Hadewijch, 172, 179–80; in Hildegard of Bingen, 205–6; in Julian of Norwich, 227; natural versus socially constructed, 122–34; in Suso, 210

Genesis, 60, 66, 68, 71, 101, 209, 247

Genius: priest of Nature, 54; in *De planctu Naturae*, 37, 66, 69–70, 79, 346 n.53; in *Romance of the Rose*, 99, 105–10

Geoffrey of Monmouth, 357 n.78, 358 n.89

Gerald of Wales, 65

Gérard of Liège, 151–55, 157, 173, 316

Gerson, Jean, 212 , 273, 277; and Christine de Pizan, 20, 288; and cult of St. Joseph, 284–87, 314; on discernment of spirits, 288–90; Mariology of, 401 n.145; on the *vierge ouvrante*, 271, 284

Gertrude of Helfta, 223

Gichtel, Johann, 317

Gilbert of Hoyland, 147, 154

Gilbert Porreta, 39, 65, 307

God of Love. *See* Cupid

Goddesses, 35–50, 291–327; androgyny of, 325–26; and Christian Platonism, 40–41, 291–92; compared, 24–25, 34–35, 291–92, 310, 325; as daughters and brides of God, 1–2, 40; as mediators, 40–43, 49, 53,

324–26; named as such in medieval texts, 2, 22, 182, 207–8, 274; not heretical, 39–40, 65, 304–10; thinking with, 304; and women's empowerment, 47, 312. *See also* individual goddesses

Godfrey of Admont, 199

Goodman, Lenn Evan, 318

Gottfried von Neifen, 176

Gottfried von Strassburg, 171, 364 n.57

Grammar, metaphorical use of, 93–97, 100, 129, 136–37, 340 n.93

Green, Monica, xii, 359 n.97

Gregory I, pope, 403 n.13

Gregory XI, pope, 289

Grignion de Montfort, Louis-Marie, 316

Grosseteste, Robert, 23; *Château d'Amour*, 2, 44–47, 160, 299

Grote, Geert, 193, 212, 222

Guglielma of Milan, 249, 308–9; in art, 386 n.142

Guglielmites, 40, 249, 308–10

Guillaume de Lorris, 6, 43, 78, 97, 110, 152. See also *Romance of the Rose*

Guinizelli, Guido, 185

Guittone d'Arezzo, 359 n.4

Hackel, Alfred, 247

Hadewijch of Brabant, 148, 292, 298, 312, 315; exemplarism of, 229–30; *Letters*, 303, 377 n.50; as literary artist, 303; and Richard of St.-Victor, 149; *Stanzaic Poems*, 169–81, 303; *Visions*, 303

Haec Vir, 93

Haimo of Auxerre, 375 n.26

Hamburger, Jeffrey, xii, 280, 282

Handlyng Synne, 297

Hansen, Elaine Tuttle, 114–15

Häring, Nikolaus, 73

Hartmann von Aue, 178, 388 n.1

Hauteville, Jean de, xi

Heinrich of Nördlingen, 208, 378 n.58

Heinrich von Meissen. *See* Frauenlob

Heldris of Cornwall, 52, 315; identity of, 123; as pseudonym, 357 n.78. See also *Silence*

Hélinand of Froidmont, 359 n.4

Heloise, 141, 347 n.71, 378 n.59

Hendrik van Veldeke, 173, 175

Heresy, 305–9; Arian, 195, 321; Cathar, 66, 72, 306; clerical, 39, 65, 307; Guglielmite, 40, 249, 308–10; and imaginative theology, 65, 293, 307; Lollard, 224–25, 293, 296, 306;

major categories of, 293, 306; Trinitarian, 39–40, 242, 308; universalist, 293

Hermaphrodites, 93–94; alchemical, 236, 242

Hermas, 15

Hermes (Mercury), 239–40

Hermes Trismegistos, 234–35

Hic Mulier, 93

Hildebert of Lavardin, 91, 173

Hildegard of Bingen, xi, 47, 148, 151, 205–6, 211; on Caritas, 88–89, 138–39, 237, 292, 312, 373 n.157; *Liber divinorum operum*, 88–89, 138–39, 237; *Liber vite meritorum*, 120; Mariology of, 199; music of, 174; orthodoxy of, 39; *Scivias*, 41; visionary experience of, 33, 298, 302–3

Hinduism, 317, 327

Holy Family, 254, 283–89, 314

Holy Spirit, 195, 200; as Charity, 142, 145, 237; incarnate, 40, 249, 308; joke about, 390 n.19; marginality of, 249; in modern theology, 390 n.18; as mother, 248–49; as world soul, 52, 88, 138. *See also* Trinity

Homosexuality, 311, 324; in *De planctu Naturae*, 53, 67, 70–71, 94–97, 101; in "Ganymede and Helen," 90–94; in *Romance of the Rose*, 109; and Song of Songs, 377 n.49

Honorius Augustodunensis, 56–57, 171, 199

Hopkins, Gerard Manley, 51–52, 245–46

Horloge de Sapience, 212–22

Hortus deliciarum, 247

Hours of Eternal Wisdom, 193, 220, 312; manuscripts of, 222, 381 n.91

Hours of Étienne Chevalier, 255

Hrotsvit, 217

Hugh of Balma, 211

Hugh of St.-Victor, 146, 173; *De arrha animae*, 210; *De laude charitatis*, 147–48, 155, 160, 165

Huizinga, Johan, 277

Huot, Sylvia, 121

Hus, Jan, 242, 306, 308

Hymen, god of marriage: in Christine de Pizan, 118–19; in *De planctu Naturae*, 37, 67, 70–71, 110, 345 n.42

Iliad, 261, 322

Imaginative theology, 292–304, 315, 326

Imitation of Christ, 211

Immaculate Conception, 238, 241, 313–14, 401 n.145

Incarnation, 83, 153, 194, 200, 296, 324; in

Julian of Norwich, 227–34; in Mechthild of Magdeburg, 275

Incest, 66, 245–46, 280, 398 n.121; in Mariology, 250–54, 282–83, 287, 289–90, 391 n.32

Integumentum, 73, 347 n.68

Irenaeus of Lyon, 248

Isaiah, 195, 200, 319

Isidore of Isolanis, 314

Isis, 23, 191

Islam: and monotheism, 291, 318, 320, 327; Christian debates with, 66, 196

Jacques de Vitry, 173

Jaeger, C. Stephen, 140–41

Jakob von Lilienstein, 212

Jean de Meun, 98–111, 152, 310; and Alan of Lille, 73, 97, 100–102, 110–11, 138, 208, 298; and Christine de Pizan, 22, 115, 117, 122; influence of, 347 n.71. *See also* *Romance of the Rose*

Jerome, St., 109–10, 195, 289, 374 n.8

Joachim of Fiore, 249, 307, 403 n.13

Joanna, queen of Naples, 277

Job, 76, 172, 177, 319

John, gospel of, 13, 33, 122, 163, 165, 192

John of Damascus, 251

John of Fécamp, 366 n.81

John of Morigny, 205

John of Salisbury, 82

John XXII, pope, 403 n.14

John Paul II, pope, 311, 405 n.31

Jolivet, Jean, 64

Jordan, Mark, 72–73, 346 n.53, 351 n.14

Joseph, St., cult of, 254, 284–87, 314; modern, 399 n.131, 400 n.141

Jove (Jupiter), 37, 55, 90, 322

Judaism, 191, 318; mystical, 320, 327

Julian of Norwich, 26, 193–94, 222–34, 242–43, 315; divine motherhood in, 225–34, 290, 302, 312; learning of, 382 n.103; manuscripts of, 224, 382 nn. 97, 98, 102, 383 n.106; on Mary, 232–33, 253; and universalism, 293; visionary experience of, 223, 299, 301–2

Jung, C. G., 43, 254–56, 385 n.131

Juno, 37, 90, 322

Justinian, Emperor, 195

Juvenal, 309

Kabbalah, 316, 320, 327

Keller, Hildegard, 158

Kempe, John, 278
Kempe, Margery, 156, 224, 287–88, 293, 304,
    393 n.53; as "devout anchoress," 315; Marian
    piety of, 274, 278–82
Kieckhefer, Richard, xiii
Kloster der Minne, 155
Künzle, Pius, 211
Kynde, 17, 229. *See also* Nature

Labbie, Erin, 129
Lady Holy Church, 14–19, 41, 325, 396 n.92.
    See also Ecclesia
Lady Justice, 22–24, 33
Lady Love, 141, 148, 291; in Hadewijch,
    172–81; in Mechthild of Magdeburg, 10–12,
    157–58, 165. *See also* Caritas; Minne; Venus
Lady Meed, 17–18
Lady Philosophy: in art, 32, 203–5; in
    Boethius, 31, 35–36, 67, 75; in Christine de
    Pizan, 31–33, 116, 122, 193
Lady Poverty, 210, 325, 333 n.23; in *Sacrum
    commercium*, 3–9, 24–25
Lady Reason, 54, 90; in *Anticlaudianus*,
    75–76, 79; in Christine de Pizan, 22–24,
    115–16, 121, 136; in Hadewijch, 181; in
    Romance of the Rose, 98–100, 117; in *Silence*,
    130–31, 134
Lady Right, 22–24
Lady Theology, 31, 68, 75–76, 79
Lamentations of Mathéolus, 20
Lamprecht of Regensburg, 158–59, 316
Langland, William, 14–19, 23, 299, 307; and
    nominalism, 339 n.85; identity of, 335
    nn.36, 37. See also *Piers Plowman*
Lanham, Richard, 141
Latini, Brunetto, xi
Law, William, 317
Lay Folks' Mass Book, 297
Lea, H. C., 309
Leade, Jane, 317
Leclercq, Jean, 294
Lenzen, Rolf, 91
Leo XIII, pope, 399 n.131
Lerner, Robert, xii
Lévi-Strauss, Claude, xii, 131, 304
Lewis, C. S., xi, 33, 72, 295, 341 n.103
Liberal arts: allegories of, 69, 75, 86, 193; in
    art, 74, 79–80, 203–5, 214–15
Little Book on Spiritual Marriage, 169
Liturgy, sapiential, 194–203, 208, 220, 244,
    292. *See also* specific feasts
Llull, Ramon, 359 n.4

Lollards, 224–25, 293, 296, 306
Lombard, Peter, 2, 310
Lorenzetti, Ambrogio, 188–89
Love, Nicholas, 212
Ludolph of Saxony, 211
Ludus super Anticlaudianum, 83
Luke, gospel of, 146, 163, 192

Magic, 205
Maifreda da Pirovano, 308–9
Malouel, Jean, 266–67
Manesse Codex, 169–70
Marian Trinity, 275; in art, 254–73; defined,
    247; heretical version of, 241–43; meanings
    of, 289–90; suppressed, 294
Marie de Champagne, 364 n.48
Mark, gospel of, 117, 165
Marriage, 72, 150, 274, 399 n.122; allegorical,
    192, 227, 236; of Christ and Mary, 251–52;
    of Constantine and Sophia, 196; of God
    and the soul, 274–75, 279–80; of John and
    Margery Kempe, 278; of Mary and Joseph,
    220, 286–89; polygamous, 41, 93, 210; of
    Richard II and Anne of Bohemia, 111–14,
    353 n.42; of Suso and Eternal Wisdom, 48,
    193, 206–22
Martianus Capella, 39; *Marriage of Philology
    and Mercury*, 74, 193
Martin of Léon, 48
Martini, Simone, 188
Mass of Holy Wisdom, 200, 203, 220, 315
Maternity: in Christine de Pizan, 121–22, 354
    n.51; of God, 225–34, 302; of Julian of
    Norwich, 224–25; of St. Birgitta, 276–78,
    397 n.100; spiritual, 271, 286. *See also*
    Virgin Mary
Mathéolus, 20
Matter, E. Ann, xiii, 375 n.26
Matthew, gospel of, 179, 192, 283, 285
Matthew of Vendôme, 91
McGinn, Bernard, 30, 172, 295–96, 298
McInerney, Maud, 231, 233
Mechthild of Hackeborn, 223
Mechthild of Magdeburg, 47, 107, 169, 236,
    299, 315; and the Church, 396 n.92;
    Flowing Light of the Godhead, 10, 157, 292;
    influence of, 208; and Lady Love, 10–12,
    148, 157–59, 165; Latin translation of, 296;
    and literary genres, 303; and the Virgin
    Mary, 274–76, 282, 286
Ménagier de Paris, 393 n.53
Menippean satire, 343 n.7

Merlin, 124–25, 131–32, 358 nn.88, 89
Methodius, St., 196
Milton, John, 47; *Paradise Lost*, 315, 406 n.45
Minerva, 23, 58, 75, 140, 228, 406 n.45
Minne, 12, 155, 167, 193; in Hadewijch,
    172–81; in Lamprecht of Regensburg,
    158–59; in Mechthild of Magdeburg, 10–12,
    157–58; in Minnesang, 171, 173, 175–79. *See
    also* Lady Love; Venus
Minnesingers, 139, 158, 173–81, 291
Molanus, Johannes, 283
Monica, St., 278, 288
Monk of Farne, 225
Monotheism, 1, 38, 294; in ancient Israel,
    319–20; critiques of, 317–18; hellenistic,
    320, 323–24; inclusive versus exclusive,
    317–27, 407 n.60; and maleness, 291, 317
Moore, Stephen, 377 n.49
Motets, 365 n.60
Muhammad ibn Umail, 235
Mulieris dignitatem, 311
Multscher, Hans, 266–68
Music, 83, 174, 365 n.60
Mythography, 73, 140, 148, 251–52, 322

Nativity: of Christ, 29, 84, 276, 279; of Mary,
    195–97
Nature: in Alan of Lille, 66–86; and art,
    102–5, 135; as bakerwoman, 120, 127, 357
    n.83; in Bernard Silvestris, 55–65; in
    Chaucer, 111–15; in Christine de Pizan,
    115–22; and culture, 79, 115–22, 135–36; in
    early modern era, 316; as gynecological
    term, 135; at her forge, 101–5, 122, 160;
    and homosexuality, 53, 67, 70, 90–97, 101,
    109; in *Romance of the Rose*, 97–111; and
    Romanticism, 52, 137; and science, 52,
    61–62, 86, 316; as secondary divinity, 87,
    136–39, 192–93, 291, 324–25; in *Silence*,
    122–34; and the supernatural, 68, 71,
    79–82, 84–86, 89, 105, 110–11, 298
Neoplatonism, 139, 225, 296; causality in, 56;
    divine triad in, 88, 324; gender symbolism
    in, 64; and inclusive monotheism, 320,
    327. *See also* Platonism
Nequam, Alexander, 65
Neumann, Erich, 271, 283
Nicholas of Buldesdorf, 404 n.19
Nicholas of Cusa, 212, 344 n.30
Niebuhr, H. Richard, 38, 327
Noys: as divine mind, 56–62, 64–65, 76,
    86; gender of, 36–37, 56, 64, 340 n.94;

pronunciation of, 343 n.8; as womb of
    creation, 64, 228–29
Nurture, personified, 123–25, 128, 130–31, 134

Obrist, Barbara, 234, 240
Obscenity, 100, 116
Oedipus, myth of, 245–46, 252, 282
Olivi, Peter John, 307
Ontrouwe, 177
Orewoet, 172, 369 n.108
Origen, 196
Otto III, Emperor, 197
Ovid, 141–43, 152, 309; *Ars amatoria*, 97,
    143, 149; *Metamorphoses*, 118–19, 149, 251;
    Remedia amoris, 142–43
Ovide moralisé, 139, 251, 322, 355 n.58

Paganism. *See* Polytheism; individual deities
Pallas Athene, 37, 292, 322. *See also* Minerva
Partner, Nancy, 280
Paschasius Radbertus, 203, 314
Passion of Christ, 29, 165, 206; imitation of,
    160, 211; visions of, 218, 223, 225, 302
Paul, letters of, 149; Colossians, 192; 1
    Corinthians, 140, 152, 192, 217, 325; 2
    Corinthians, 220; Ephesians, 15, 192, 284;
    Romans, 71, 322; 1 Timothy, 141, 323
Paul VI, pope, 405 n.31
Paula, 289
Paxson, James, 33, 36, 339 n.85
Pearl, 297
Periculoso, 315
Personification, 30, 292; of Caritas, 145–51;
    and grammatical gender, 36–37, 48;
    Platonic versus Aristotelian, 33–35, 183–84,
    339 n.85; psychology of, 43. *See also*
    Allegory
Peter of Blois, 65, 91, 144
Peter of Celle, 254
Peter of Compostela, 65
Peters, Ursula, 29
Philip Augustus, king of France, 82
Philippart, Guy, 250–51, 253, 391 n.32
Philo of Alexandria, 192, 229, 320–21
Piehler, Paul, 35–36
Piers Plowman, 292, 297–98; and the four
    daughters of God, 23, 299; and Lady Holy
    Church, 14–19, 41; and Peasants' Revolt,
    307, 335 n.36; and the Trinity, 248–49;
    versions of, 335 n.36
Pietà, 266–69, 279, 394 n.61
Pius V, pope, 314

Pius IX, pope, 399 n.131
Pius XII, pope, 254, 400 n.141
Plato, 320; *Timaeus*, 56, 64, 68, 86, 120
Platonism, 72, 138, 192, 291, 319, 341 n.106;
   and allegory, 30–31, 34–35; cosmology
   of, 54, 62, 320; Jewish, 320. *See also*
   Neoplatonism
Plotinus, 317, 319
Polygamy, 41, 93, 210
Polytheism, 318–22, 326; monistic, 407 n.60
Pordage, John, 317
Porete, Marguerite, 47, 223, 230, 288, 304,
   315; *Mirror of Simple Souls*, 154, 293; trial
   and death of, 224, 306, 308
Proverbs: biblical book, 190–91, 195–200,
   208, 214; French, 123, 134
Prudentius, 39, 43, 251; *Psychomachia*, 40, 75
Psalms, 45, 149, 208, 237, 256
Psychoanalysis, 245–46, 271, 282–83, 290, 391
   n.32. *See also* Freud; Jung
Putscher, Marielene, 388 n.157
Pythagoras, 48, 406 n.52

Querelle de la Rose, 99, 115, 288
Quest of the Holy Grail, 83
Quilligan, Maureen, 20

Rabanus Maurus, 196
Re-Imagining Conference, 311–12
Reformation, 234, 316
Règle des Fins Amans, 155, 174
Reinmar von Zweter, 175
Remigius of Auxerre, 199, 322
Renaut de Bâgé, 153
Richard de Fournival, 65
Richard of St.-Victor, 157, 173, 248; *De IV
   gradibus violentae caritatis*, 148–51, 155
Richard II, king of England, 111–12, 307, 335
   n.36
Riddy, Felicity, 382 n.97
Ridewall, John, 148, 322
Ringler, Siegfried, 29
Robert of Rheims, 157
Robertson, D. W., Jr., 142
Rolle, Richard, 222, 297
Romance of the Rose, 157, 292, 303; and
   Alan of Lille, 97, 100–102, 108–11, 298;
   allegorical technique of, 43; and Chaucer,
   108, 113–14; and Christine de Pizan, 22, 115,
   117, 122, 288; ecclesiastical censure of, 298;
   Genius in, 99, 105–10; God of Love in,
   98–99, 108, 135, 145, 152; iconography of,

101–6, 160; Nature in, 97–111, 123, 298, 325;
   Poverty in, 6–7; Reason in, 98–100, 117.
   See also Guillaume de Lorris; Jean de
   Meun
Rothschild Canticles, 165–66
Rubielos Master, 388 n.158
Ruh, Kurt, 172, 369 n.108
Rupert of Deutz, 171, 199, 205, 251
Ruusbroec, Jan, 173

Sacrum commercium, 3–9, 18, 24–25, 298
Saint-Martin, Louis-Claude de, 317
Sankara, 317
Sapientia: as allegorical figure, 193, 196,
   203–5, 217, 235–40, 243–44; in Bible,
   190–92, 208; as Christ, 40, 192–95, 200,
   206–22, 226–29, 243; in iconography,
   200–205, 212–22, 237–40; as Virgin Mary,
   194–200, 205, 238–44, 292. *See also* Eternal
   Wisdom; Sophia
Schneider, Laurel, 407 n.60
Scholasticism, 39, 54, 294–95, 297, 310
Schürebrand, 371 n.138
Seneca, 309, 388 n.1
Sens, Council of, 65
Sergius I, Pope, 196
Serlo of Wilton, 91
Seuse, Heinrich. *See* Suso, Henry
Shakespeare, William, 91, 132, 295
Sheingorn, Pamela, xii, 273–74, 287
Sheridan, James, 346 n.57
Shrine Madonna. *See Vierge ouvrante*
Sibyl, 27–28, 116
Sidney, Sir Philip, 186
Sigismund, emperor, 240, 307
Silence, romance of, 52, 122–34, 325
Silva (Hyle), 69, 90; in *Cosmographia*, 55–60,
   62, 64; defined, 38
Silverstein, Theodore, 58, 344 n.27
Sixtus IV, Pope, 314
Solovyov, Vladimir, 317
Sommer, Benjamin, xii, 374 n.8
Song of Songs, 4, 17, 140, 149, 155–56,
   171–73, 208, 235, 237; in Marian liturgy,
   198–99; and the wounds of love, 147–48,
   165–67
Sophia, 75, 203, 226, 292; in Bible, 190–92,
   243, 320; churches dedicated to, 195–96,
   374 n.11; esoteric devotion to, 316–17, 320;
   in feminist theology, 312; icons of, 375
   n.30, 386 n.142. *See also* Eternal Wisdom;
   Sapientia

Sophiology, Russian, 317
Speculum humanae salvationis, 261
Speculum virginum, 199–200
Spenser, Edmund, 406 n.44; *Faerie Queene*, 315
Stagel, Elsbeth, 12, 206
Stammheim Missal, 200–201
Statius, 185, 403 n.13
Stephen of Tournai, 254
Stilnovisti, 182, 185–86, 359 n.4
Stock, Brian, 61
Suffering Trinity, 266–69
Sullivan, Anne, xii, 352 n.28
Suso, Henry, 236, 292, 299, 393 n.53; censored by Jesuits, 315; *Exemplar*, 12, 153, 206; *Horloge de Sapience*, 212–22; *Horologium Sapientiae*, 27, 193, 207–22, 296, 298; Hours of Eternal Wisdom, 193, 220, 222, 312; influence of, 316; and Julian of Norwich, 193–94, 225, 230–31, 243; *Life*, 12–14, 24–25, 206; *Little Book of Eternal Wisdom*, 13, 26, 206–7, 209, 212, 313; manuscripts of, 211–12, 222
Suydam, Mary, 174
Syncretism, 1, 322

Talmud, 2
Tarnowski, Andrea, 354 n.41
Tauler, John, 295, 316, 378 n.58
Tempier, Étienne, 143
Tennyson, Alfred, 51–52
Teresa of Avila, 314, 405 n.31
Tertullian, 321, 326, 408 n.69
Teskey, Gordon, 37–38, 47
Teutonic Knights, 269
Textual emendations: in *Anticlaudianus*, 348 nn.76, 81; in *De planctu Naturae*, 94, 346 n.55, 351 n.12; in *Silence*, 134, 358 n.95
Theophilus of Antioch, 248
Theophrastus, 309
Theosophy, 316
Thierry of Chartres, 48, 52, 56, 72
Thomas, Stanton, xii, 388 n.158
Thomas de Pizan, 116–17
Thomas of Brittany, 364 n.57
Thomas of Cantimpré, 295
Thomas of Chobham, 295
Thor, 272
Tochter Syon, 158–59
Translations: medieval, 6, 155, 173, 296; of *Romance of the Rose*, 113; of Suso, 24, 193, 212

Transvestism, 334 n.32, 358 n.88; of female saints, 119; metaphorical, 172, 209; in *Silence*, 123–24, 133
Trent, Council of, 293, 313–15
Tridentine Church, 189, 269, 271, 315
Trinity, 45–47, 159, 195, 217; in art, 243, 254–71; in Augustine, 142, 248; as creator, 56; in early Christianity, 321, 326; as family, 247–54, 294; female, 19–24, 37, 48, 225, 336 n.56; heretical doctrines of, 39, 241–42; and monotheism, 321, 326; and quaternity, 247, 254–55, 294
Tristan, 78, 144, 150, 171, 364 n.57; and *Silence*, 129, 357 n.78
Troubadours, 150, 157, 171, 173, 184–86, 291

Ulmannus, 387 n.147, 388 n.157
Ulrich von Liechtenstein, 169–72, 180
Ulrich von Winterstetten, 178–79

Valentine's Day, origin of, 112, 353 n.42
Van Baest, Marieke, 172
Van den Boogaard, Nico, 365 n.60
Van Dyke, Carolynn, 31, 40
Van Os, Henk, 267
Venus, 54, 145; in Alan of Lille, 70–72, 78, 87, 94–97, 100–101; alchemical, 240; in Chaucer, 111–13; in *Romance of the Rose*, 101, 108; in Ulrich of Liechtenstein, 169–71, 180. *See also* Aphrodite; Lady Love; Minne
Vernacular theology, 30, 224, 248, 293, 295–98
Vierge ouvrante, 255, 269–72, 394 n.70; Jungian view of, 271; and mystical piety, 272, 275, 280, 290, 385 n.128; objections to, 283–84, 313
Vincent of Beauvais, 65
Virgil, 140; *Aeneid*, 143, 403 n.13; Fourth Eclogue, 75, 82, 403 n.13
Virgin Mary, 24, 82; as black bride, 238–40; called a goddess, 274; eternal predestination of, 199–201; imitation of, 271–83, 286, 289–90; as *mater dolorosa*, 211, 266, 279; as *mater misericordiae*, 41, 237, 261; omniscience of, 205, 401 n.145; queenship of, 256–61, 275, 323; sapiential liturgy of, 194–200; and the Trinity, 241–43, 247, 254–73; as universal mother, 232–33; unlike other women, 310. *See also* specific motifs and doctrines
Virginity, 67, 109–10

Virtues and vices: personified, 33, 140; in *Anticlaudianus*, 75, 78–81, 351 n.17; in art, 145, 160–64; in Prudentius, 40, 75

Visions, 25–30, 274; epiphanic versus heuristic, 300; false, 108, 289, 300, 401 n.149; as literary genre, 26–27, 299–300, 303; psychology of, 31, 299, 302–3; techniques for inducing, 29–30, 205; truth claims of, 300–304

Von Baader, Franz, 317

Von Franz, Marie-Louise, 385 n.131

Vulcan, 101

Waldkirch, Conrad, 237

Walter of Châtillon, 91

Walther von der Vogelweide, 176

Ward, Benedicta, 223, 381 n.95

Warner, Marina, 271, 394 n.70

Waters, Claire, xii

Watson, Nicholas, xiii, 30, 224, 226, 296, 298

Wenceslas of Prague, 240

Wetherbee, Winthrop, 343 n.18, 345 n.43

White, Hugh, 353 n.46

Wilde, Oscar, 164–65

William of Auxerre, 83

William of Conches, 39, 72, 307; on the world soul, 52, 65, 88, 138

William of St.-Amour, 4

William of St.-Thierry, 65, 150, 173, 227, 295, 307; *De natura et dignitate amoris*, 142–43

Wilmart, André, 155

Wisdom, morality play, 212

Wisdom, personified. *See* Eternal Wisdom; Sapientia; Sophia

Wisdom literature. *See* Ecclesiasticus; Exegesis; Proverbs; Wisdom of Solomon

Wisdom of Solomon, 13, 190–92, 196, 203, 206, 208

Women's ordination, 310–11, 405 n.31

Worde, Wynkyn de, 222

Wordsworth, William, 51–52

World soul, 52, 65, 88, 138, 192, 324

Wycliffe, John, 224, 307

Yvo, 138, 186

Zeus, 321. *See also* Jove

Zeuxis, 348 n.76

Ziolkowski, Jan, 94, 346 n.60, 351 n.14